Chinatowne

The Screenplays of Robert Towne
1960-2000

Elaine Lennon

Contents

Illustrations

INTRODUCTION

On 27 March 1973 Francis Ford Coppola accepted the Academy Award honouring Best Adapted Screenplay for *The Godfather*. He stunned Hollywood when he thanked Robert Towne from the podium and said the Oscar also belonged to him, despite the fact that he did not receive a credit on the film, and for good reason. Towne was a legendary script doctor and consultant, best known to a discrete group of insiders whose confidence he inspired since his role on *Bonnie and Clyde* (1967), at the insistence of star/producer Warren Beatty. While Towne received a unique screen credit on that production (as "Special Consultant"), it was - and remains - understood that the highly paid job of script fixer, or doctor, is one which remains uncited, unremarked and mostly, uncredited. Which made Coppola's announcement to the world all the more astonishing.

*   *   *   *

This study was originally provoked by a desire to replace the notion of the director, with that of the screenwriter, as auteur. It was not merely the opportunity to revise the history of screenwriting but to give credit where it is due: simply put, it is based on the supposition that it is frequently the screenwriter whose vision inspires countless great films. To quote the director Michael Powell, whose collaborator, Emeric Pressburger, wrote and edited all of the duo's films, "I am the teller of the tale, not the creator of the story." [1]

What follows is an empirical examination of Robert Towne's full career, as both writer and director, engaging with some of the formative debates on authorship both in the industry and in critical writing, while acknowledging that the exigencies of cinematic collaboration suggest a more nuanced form of authorship attribution.

On the one hand this text is partially driven by what Foucault has termed 'the rediscovery of the writer'; on the other by what Richard Corliss cheekily christened '*la politique des scenaristes*', when 30 years ago, *Film Comment* took the unprecedented step of devoting an entire issue to that rare genus, the screenwriter. [2] It did indeed have a polemical aspect: it was a riposte to Andrew Sarris' bowdlerisation of '*la politique des auteurs*', which had virtually driven the writer underground more than a decade earlier. In recent years however, the centrality of the screenwriter's role has been enhanced by any number of biographies and the publication of Patrick McGilligan's *BACKSTORY* series at the University of California. [3] It therefore constitutes an addition to a body of work which, in Lee Server's terms, considers, "... a director's cinema, a producer's cinema, a screenwriter's cinema. These are some of the variables of authorship in Hollywood." [4]

---

[1] Michael Powell quoted in Kevin Macdonald. *EMERIC PRESSBURGER: The Life and Death of a Screenwriter*. London: Faber & Faber, 1994, 143.

[2] Michel Foucault. 'What is an Author?' was published in *Screen* 20/21 and can be found in *THE FOUCAULT READER* (ed. Paul Rainbow). New York: Pantheon Books, 1984. Corliss is in the Winter 1970-71 Screenwriter special issue.

[3] Patrick McGilligan (ed.). *BACKSTORY 1: Interviews with Screenwriters of Hollywood's Golden Age*. Berkeley: University of California Press, 1986; *BACKSTORY 2: Interviews with Screenwriters of the 40s and 50s*. Berkeley: University of California Press, 1991; *BACKSTORY 3: Interviews with Screenwriters of the 60s*. Berkeley: University of California Press, 1996; *BACKSTORY 4: Interviews with Screenwriters of the 70s and 80s*. Berkeley: University of California Press, 2006.

[4] Lee Server. *SCREENWRITER: Words Become Pictures*. Pittstown, New Jersey: Main Street Press,

A model for the type of discourse I intend to pursue is to be found in a BFI-published study of *The Big Heat* by Colin McArthur, in the Film Classics series. [5] This demonstrates an admirable combination of rigorous textual and extra-diegetic analysis. It manages a balance between considerations of the material itself and the context in which it was produced: it effects therefore a judicious understanding of the place of the writer (Sidney Boehm) and his contribution to a work which is invariably credited to its director (in this case, Fritz Lang). McArthur looks at the original novel as source; the intervention of Columbia Pictures when the rights are acquired and a writer attached to adapt it from its incarnation as a serial in The Saturday Evening Post; through the construction of the film's meaning via its reception and its place in an aesthetic, narrative and cultural context. This in itself is a useful objective but perhaps beyond the scope of what seems to lie at the heart of this particular study - the intention of the author, his contribution to the finished film, and his credit on the production. The project as a whole is contextualised within a necessarily synoptic theoretical and historical analysis of the American studio system since 1960 in four key phases, according to the canonical accounts: 1960-1966; 1967-1975; 1976-1989; and from 1990 onwards. [6] That Towne's work has not been the focus of a major academic study is also a boon.[7] This backwards glance employs a methodology derived from dramatic structure and also lends a paradigmatic coda to the American film industry and cultural and historical contexts.

What is proposed therefore is an intervention into what is traditionally understood as authorship and auteur study, utilising some of its more useful taxonomic components in an attempt to facilitate a better understanding of the writer and his place in the production process – specifically, in the case of Robert Towne – the Hollywood machine since 1960.

Through a systematic examination of those elements in the films which Towne has written or had an otherwise significant involvement, the notion of authorship is reclaimed, to a degree, in the name of the screenwriter. [8] The auteur theory, which has so dominated our understanding of film for the past fifty years, implies a singular controlling vision, that of the director, tracing his influence through plot elements,

---

1987, 10.

[5] Colin McArthur. *THE BIG HEAT*. London: BFI Classics, British Film Institute, 1992.

[6] We might include here David Bordwell, Janet Staiger, and Kristin Thompson. *THE CLASSICAL HOLLYWOOD CINEMA: Film Style and Mode of Production to 1960*. London: Routledge, 1994; James Monaco's *AMERICAN FILM NOW*. New York: Plume Books, 1979; and *THE NEW WAVE* . New York and Oxford: Oxford University Press, 1991; Michael Pye and Linda Myles' *THE MOVIE BRATS: How the Film Generation Took Over Hollywood*. New York: Holt Rinehart and Winston, 1979; and Robert Sklar's *MOVIE-MADE AMERICA: A Cultural History of American Movies*. New York: Vintage Books, 1994.

[7] Towne is just one of the subjects considered in a study of three contemporary screenwriters by Robert Arnett at the University of Southern Mississippi (1997). His thesis, entitled *A SEPARATE CINEMA: The Screenplays of Robert Towne, Richard Price and Quentin Tarantino*, claims that Towne's work breaks into two clear divisions – screenplays about a hero in a world other than their own; and screenplays about a hero who is a master of his own unique world. There is no other academic study or scholarly article about Towne extant.

[8] To echo David A. Gerstner and Janet Staiger, "authorship is an ennabling tool." Gerstner and Staiger (eds.). *AUTHORSHIP AND FILM: Trafficking with Hollywood*. New York: Routledge, 2003, xi.

narrative style, genre, structure, character types, conventions, themes and visual motifs. By appropriating this system, a version of auteur-structuralism, albeit from the perspective of the screenwriter and his use of the form's internal coordinates, certain assumptions are made, which, film by film, are either discarded or argued: namely, that Robert Towne is indeed the sole author of those screenplays; and suggesting that, in certain instances, he was merely doing 'hack' work, in other words, that the screenwriter's voice was moderated and modulated by the nature of his contribution, the project itself and the pragmatism of the collaboration necessitated in Hollywood filmmaking. The basis of the auteur theory is unravelled in a complex skein of contributors and influences involved in the making of the various films discussed here.[9] The overriding strategy is the examination of textual evidence in defence of the position of the screenplay. In examining the various origins and sources of Towne's work it may be concluded that he is from time to time worthy of the title, 'author.'

The concept of the film author is codified in the manual of the Writers' Guild of America, itself the site of internecine warfare, divided literally, philosophically and physically (into East and West) by the Mississippi River:

> A screenplay consists of individual scenes and full dialogue, together with such prior treatment, basic adaptation, continuity, scenario and dialogue as shall be used in, and represent substantial contributions to the final script.
> A "Screenplay by" credit is appropriate when there is source material of a story nature (with or without a "Screen Story "'credit) or when the writer(s) entitled to "Story by" credit is different than the writer(s) entitled to "Screenplay by" credit.
> The term "Written by" is used when the writer(s) is entitled to both the "Story by" credit and the "Screenplay by" credit.
> This credit shall not be granted where there is source material of a story nature.
> However, biographical, newspaper and other factual sources may not necessarily deprive the writer of such credit.
> - from the *SCREEN CREDITS MANUAL of the Writers' Guild of America*

To simplify the notion of narrative and amplify the idea of an author, we could describe narration as a representation of the world. Ken Dancyger and Jeff Rush put it this way:

> No matter how realistic the representation, we are not watching reality – the act of representing the world implies narration. The narrating may be overt or virtually invisible, but it is always present.[10]

The issue of screenplay credit is of course an inevitable element of the screenwriter's story. Towne's case is more complex than most because of his supreme

---

[9] Andrew Sarris has written, "… if I had to do it all over again, I would reformulate the auteur theory with a greater emphasis on the tantalizing mystery of style than on the romantic agony of the artists." 'The Auteur Theory Revisited,' in Virginia Wright Wexman, (ed.) *FILM AND AUTHORSHIP*. London: Rutgers University Press; and New Brunswick, New Jersey: 2003. 23. He said to Marion Wolberg Weiss, "If I had to do it over again, I would not have written so much about the director, but about genre instead, because I think that was the key." 'A Film By…,' *The Independent*, March 1998: 31. However he still makes no reference to the screenwriter.
[10] Ken Dancyger and Jeff Rush. *ALTERNATIVE SCRIPTWRITING: Writing Beyond the Rules*, Second Edition. Boston and London: Focal Press, 1995, 171

achievement as a collaborative screen artist and as script doctor. His greatest achievements are arguably those in situations of what could be described as multiple authorship – with Francis Ford Coppola on *The Godfather* (1972); adapting the novel which formed the basis for *The Last Detail* (1973); rewriting with Roman Polanski on *Chinatown* (1974); sharing (and later regretting doing so) screenplay credit with Warren Beatty on *Shampoo* (1975.)

Towne's career has been that of the Screenwriter as Superstar – he is the only example of a writer who has successfully traversed exploitation cinema (his years with Roger Corman), art cinema (the Nouvelle Vague-style *Bonnie and Clyde*), Academy Award cinema (*The Last Detail, Chinatown, Shampoo*), auteur cinema (*Personal Best, Tequila Sunrise, Without Limits*) and the Nineties Blockbuster phenomenon encapsulated in the rise and rise of Tom Cruise (*Days of Thunder*, the *Mission: Impossible* franchise). Not to mention his frequent (and obviously uncited) forays into many genres of cinema in his continuing role of script doctor. He is a unique and controversial figure in world cinema and Hollywood; his productions have been beset by crises, difficult relationships with directors and studios, and questionable professional judgement; yet his central motivational concerns are punctuated by allusions to Greek tragedy, the nature of male friendship, anti-authoritarianism, democratic ideals and references to the banal levels of corruption and the acts of casual disloyalty that dramatise the everyday. The meta-narrative that constitutes Towne's career possesses the cumulative dramatic continuity and rising action obtained in a reading of his films: it is a story of deep male friendships, collaborations, ruptured loyalties, and reversals of fortune. In Towne's case his professional career involved the ongoing patronage of a number of powerful men – Beatty, Nicholson, Cruise, Bruckheimer, rendering the idea of individual authorship from a single, controlling artistic intelligence extremely complicated if not entirely impossible. [11] These form the subtext from which many of his subjects arise yet this is not a work of hagiography or a brutal work of guardianship. As Richard Corliss said, "the creation of a Hollywood movie involves a complex weave of talents, properties, and personalities." [12] The conclusion leads to the consideration of the possibilities of multiple authorship, within the representational system preferred by Hollywood in the form of three-act structure. [13]

Towne's body of work spans perhaps the most interesting time in Hollywood – the transition from what is called Old Hollywood to New Hollywood, when the studios' traditional power structure was seemingly on the wane, through the blockbuster years,

---

[11] Jack Stillinger states that "multiple authorship has implications for almost any kind of theory postulated on the existence (and possibly, in the thinking of author-banishing critics, even the non-existence) of a unified mind, personality, or consciousness in or behind a text that is being studied, interpreted, or edited." *MULTIPLE AUTHORSHIP AND THE MYTH OF SOLITARY GENIUS*. New York: Oxford University Press, 1991, 183.

[12] Richard Corliss, 'The Hollywood Screenwriter,' *Film Comment*, Winter 1970-71: 6.

[13] The subject of much discussion during the 1970s in the pages of British magazine *Screen* and elsewhere, the classic realist style is one to which Robert Towne has declared a great affinity and in *Chinatown* the use of a strictly controlled point of view style falls neatly into the strategy employed by so many of the nineteenth century realists in order to assume an overall attitude to the action (and the accumulation of detail). As Mark Horowitz asserts, "Towne is a classicist – at least in form – not an innovator. He does not subvert or 'appropriate' old forms in the postmodern fashion; he embraces the conventions of whatever genre he happens to be working in – whether detective story, romantic melodrama, even Restoration Comedy (*Shampoo* was inspired by Wycherley's 'The Country Wife'.)" 'Fault Lines and the Career of Robert Towne,' *Film Comment*, Vol. 26, No. 6, 1990: 52-58.

and the present day. He does not suffer from the 'complex obscurity' that is the destiny of some: his name is associated with some of the biggest and most challenging films made in the last 40 years yet he is still, to some, a peripheral figure in Hollywood history. Despite the contemporary proliferation of screenwriting courses, he says that, to his knowledge,

> there wasn't a single course in screenwriting anywhere in the country when I wrote my first film. I remember, when Roman [Polanski] and I began the rewrite on *Chinatown*, he actually found a lone book on the subject and inscribed: 'To my dear colleague, with fond hope.' His inscription was the only thing either one of us read. [14]

While it seems somewhat ironic if not completely paradoxical to argue for the centrality of the screenwriter's role in the era of American auteur cinema, it is Towne's career which merits this consideration. Ultimately, authorship functions as a lens through which film history itself may be reconsidered.

As Scott Foundas points out, Towne almost single-handedly introduced the possibility of the writer as author of his films:

> Towne, though, came up through the ranks at a time when the very role of the screenwriter as the potential author of a film was in widespread debate. Through his work in the 1970s, Towne helped to make the writer as viable a force as the director in the creation and execution of a project, and through his collaborations greatly increased the profile of writers in a business that had often previously treated them like so much disposable garbage. [15]

Some of the consistencies that can be detected in his oeuvre are signature motifs – the obsession with naïveté transformed; the subcultures produced by the professional worlds occupied by his heroes and the concomitant exigencies demanded of them, leading to failure or even tragedy; the fetish objects such as shoes, cigarette lighters, flowers, landscapes, animals, all of which decorate and control his expertly constructed work. Critic Michael Sragow says of him, "He knows how to use sly indirection, canny repetition, unexpected counterpoint, *and* a unique poetic vulgarity to stretch a scene or an entire script to its utmost emotional capacity. He's also a lush visual artist with an eye for the kind of images that go to the left and right sides of the brain simultaneously." [16]

'invisible' profession." [17] While acknowledging that author criticism as an historical discourse necessarily denied many of the practicalities of screenwriting for the cinema, this particular text seeks to redress its shortcomings by contextualising some of the aspects of the screenplays by Robert Towne in terms of those relevant elements of their production histories possible to include; it attempts to partially conflate The purpose of this study is twofold: firstly, to assert that the elements of screenplay structure can be

---

[14] Robert Towne, 'Gauguin, Van Gogh, James Agee and Me,' *Los Angeles Times*, 03 November 2002: Back Story. Elsewhere, however, Towne has said he learned all there was to know about dramatic structure in acting class.
[15] Scott Foundas, 'Right Down to the Last Detail,' in *The Daily Trojan*, 10 September 1998.
[16] Michael Sragow, 'Return of the Native,' *New Time Los Angeles*, 3-9 September 1998: 14.
[17] Patrick McGilligan, 1986, 9. We could interpret this as an insinuation that screenwriters have yet to receive the recognition they deserve in terms of their contribution to a collaborative praxis which requires their creativity first and foremost.

utilised as identifying 'markers of authorship' as it applies to the screenwriter; [18] secondly, to acknowledge that even in the complex matter of cinematic authorship and the concomitant demands of the screenwriter working within the limits of Hollywood dramaturgy, it is possible to locate the signature of the screenwriter within a collaborative environment of probable multiple authorship.[19]   Therefore the significance of this study lies in its examination of a broad range of work by a screenwriter whose work nonetheless demonstrates the thematic consistency demanded of an auteur; and it demonstrates that such an analysis can offer a prism by which to view the American film industry. Towne's career is particularly interesting as a case of a screenwriter who sought more authorial control by becoming a director; and in a theoretical sense his career emerges at the same time as the debates on authorship and auteurism. It is entwined with the American film industry since 1960 and his biography straddles Exploitation Cinema, New Hollywood (the American New Wave) and Post-Classical Cinema.

In taking the baton from Richard Corliss, this study will be attempting to move slowly forward to aid in the creating of a conceptual framework for the understanding of the screenwriter's specific contribution to cinema and name (and credit) many of those complex personalities and institutions involved in the filming of Towne's work, because, as Patrick McGilligan states, "screenwriting, for all its genuine 'progress,' remains an the underlying orientations of what Wollen stated were the two principal schools of auteur criticism: the one that insists on a core of meanings; the other attending to mise-en-scène.[20]

In the chapters that follow, the markers of authorship are systematically examined as they occur in Towne's screenplays to reveal the consistencies (or otherwise) of the writing techniques and worldview conveyed in his screenplays. Dramatic structure articulates a means by which to identify the screenwriting process, the screenplay itself and the screenwriter's signature in the collaborative filmic text, proceeding from auteurism proper, although containing its more extreme formal ambitions.   In other words, the principles of auteurism are used here to create a formal methodology (specifically that which might be applied to a screenwriter) in an attempt to uncover the elements of Towne's imprint on the works he has written (Corliss' 'authorial personality'), which have been translated to the screen both by himself and by other directors.

The paradigm of this particular text is based on the structure of Towne's screenplays and their operation within classical Hollywood narrative and the studio system; while the theoretical framework or matrix (of conventional codes and markers) identifies the basic structural elements of the screenplay (derived as they are from the dramatic tenets of playwriting) as the markers of the screenwriter's authorship. A mythic tendency is identified in Towne's work but the textual analyses are not derived from structuralist writing, which forms a separate (if not entirely unconnected) area of film

---

[18] Charles Barr. *ENGLISH HITCHCOCK*. Scotland: A Movie Book, 1999, 188. Harold Love says that evidence for attribution is required and markers constitute one criterion; probability is to be proven from a band which he describes. *ATTRIBUTING AUTHORSHIP: An Introduction*. Cambridge: University Press, 2002, 209-216.

[20] Peter Wollen. *SIGNS AND MEANING IN THE CINEMA* (2nd. Ed.) London: Secker and Warburg, 1972.

studies – viz. Towne's reworking of elements of the Oedipus story in *Chinatown*; his allusion to Greek myth - the Trojan horse, Bellerophon and Chimera in *Mission: Impossible 2*; his proceeding from myth to reality and back again in screenplays as diverse as *Greystoke* and *Without Limits*; his Biblical resurrection fantasies in *Mission: Impossible 2* and *Tequila Sunrise* (whether he originated them or not); and his ironic, sometimes inconclusive and usually downbeat endings foil the generic requirements of Hollywood, that generic cinema par excellence. [21]

The methods employed here are broadly those of comparative textual analysis, contained within the taxonomic framework outlined above. In closely reading Towne's screenplays within an historical context and using a systematic theoretical structure based on the more applicable principles and assumptions traditionally attributed to auteurism, the strategies he employs in creating his screen narratives are uncovered and can be used further afield. [22] The principal sources for this study are Robert Towne's screenplays; and, from time to time, the way in which they are brought to the screen both by himself and other directors is traced, as well as the clear influence wrought by collaborators, principally actors and producers.

Robert Towne: A Brief Biographical Note

The criteria for considering the screenwriter as auteur might be said to lie in what Warren Buckland correctly identifies as internal auteurism - that personal style which is evident in a director's use of compositional norms; but also perhaps evident in the text of the screenplay, whose structural elements are mostly attributed to traditional dramatic structure but sometimes lie more significantly in those intangible aspects of the writer's personality – his outlook, his politics, his experience, his reflection of and on the culture. [23] And as Dudley Andrew reminds us, "structural methods ... offer no motive for the existence of stories in general or of any particular story." [24]

As Bywater and Sobchack remind us, auteurist criticism lies somewhere between the textual and the contextual:

> On the one hand, the auteurist critic is primarily engaged in identifying formal and rhetorical patterns in single films (individual texts), in discovering and describing cinematic structures and personal visions that are consistent from film to film in the work of a single film artist. On the other hand, auteurism is

---

[21] Maltby and Craven state: "Critics place movies into generic categories as a way of dividing up the map of Hollywood cinema into smaller, more manageable, and relatively discrete areas. Their analyses often suggest a cartographer's concern with defining the exact location of the boundary between one genre and another. Audiences and producers use generic terms much more flexibly..." Richard Maltby and Ian Craven. *HOLLYWOOD CINEMA: An Introduction*. Oxford, UK and Cambridge, USA: Blackwell Publishers 1995, *Op.cit.*, 107. The authors continue: "Genre criticism also shares with auteurism a concern to delineate Hollywood cinema by defining sub-sets within the whole..." (114.)

[22] Robert Paul Arnett, 1997, as before.

[23] Warren Buckland. *DIRECTED BY STEVEN SPIELBERG: Poetics of the Contemporary Hollywood Blockbuster*. London and New York: Continuum Books, 2006, 13. Buckland opposes this to external auteurism ie the production of the film; he also differentiates between the classical auteur (a skilled craft worker) and the Romantic auteur (a lone genius).

[24] Dudley Andrew. *CONCEPTS IN FILM THEORY*. New York: Oxford University Press, 1984, 38-39.

connected to the extratextual (contextual) considerations of film as an intersection of social and personal history, through questions of authorship, artistic influence, and biography. [25]

This leads to the ultimate ambition of this study, which is to assert the primacy of the screenplay in understanding Hollywood cinema and to cast a backwards glance on that institution since 1960 using Towne's work as a looking glass. Biography is therefore a highly significant element of auteur/author studies. [26] This is particularly the case with Towne, whose commercial *nous*, strong collaborations and endlessly quotable dialogue alone mark him out from other screenwriters of his era. Auteurist criticism is, after all, a variant on formal criticism as Bywater and Sobchack have adverted. [27]

The integrating of salient elements of biography into Towne's body of work is significant insofar as his career reflects changes in the Hollywood industry, involving powerful collaborators, studio policy and his own gravitation towards directing as a means of establishing authorial control. Towne's career as screenwriter can be divided into four distinct phases, which map onto the contours of Hollywood cinema from its transitional phase through its post-classical era. [28]

I.1960-1966, years of turmoil for the industry in which it was significantly regrouped as a modern entity and years which coincided with a new critical understanding of cinema as an artform; II. 1967-1975, which saw the emergence of a new generation of directors and which is usually termed New Hollywood or New American Cinema and which Towne participated in by virtue of his collaborations first with Warren Beatty and then Francis Ford Coppola; followed by his troika of Academy Award-winning films made with Jack Nicholson, Robert Evans, Roman Polanski; Hal Ashby; and again with Beatty; III.1976-1989, in which Towne struggled to create a new career for himself as writer-director in the years dominated by the blockbuster phenomenon and continued to work as script doctor on several major films and some lesser ones; IV. and, finally, 1990-2000, in which the industry had consolidated and Towne continued his professional relationships with Hollywood's power élite, in this case, Tom Cruise, Don Simpson and Jerry Bruckheimer. His name is still mentioned occasionally for script doctoring work, particularly for the Bruckheimer stable of blockbusting action films. [29]

---

[25] Tim Bywater and Thomas Sobchack. *AN INTRODUCTION TO FILM CRITICISM: Major Critical Approaches to Narrative Film.* New York: Longman, 1989, 51.

[26] *Ibid.*

[27] *Ibid.*

[28] Post-classical cinema sometimes refers to the post-war realignment of the industry but for the purposes of this study it is proposed to use it in the more usual context of New Hollywood and thereafter.

[29] Towne's position as one of the industry's top script doctors is in no doubt, as John Gregory Dunne pointed out in 1997, where he also explains the rationale: "The exorbitance of rewriting fees - $100,000 to $200,000 a week for the top script doctors, with everyone knowing what everyone else gets paid, because it is in one's best interests to know what the competition is getting – makes a production rewrite the most sought-after script job in the Industry... The justification for such fees is that if a studio is forced to cancel a picture because of script difficulties, it is still liable for preproduction costs that could have mounted into the millions of dollars before a frame of film was shot. In such a situation, the agents for the in-demand writers hold the hammer. While the studios complain, they also know that paying a script doctor $150,000 a week is in their terms chump change when the alternative is pulling the plug on a $50 million or $60 million film." John Gregory Dunne. *MONSTER: Living Off the Big Screen.* New

It is clear that Towne has always sought out the most powerful people in Hollywood (or, conversely, they have sought him out). He has been variously affiliated with Beatty, Nicholson and Cruise; his close friendships with producers such as Robert Evans and Jerry Bruckheimer cultivated his reputation. Towne's career is therefore interwoven with that of powerful Hollywood actors who have followed in the wake of such men as Kirk Douglas in fashioning the elements of external authorship such as financing, production and the deal-making, the organizational and economic environment which enhance their control of the filmmaking process; which remains however a collaborative undertaking.[30] He then sought out his own position as an external author in the same way, turning to directing his own work. It is not always possible to ascertain the intricacies of creative collaborations, and as Robin Wood reminds us, it is difficult to reduce an artist's work to "a single, structural pattern."[31] However it must be remembered that it is in that overall context that Towne's most significant screenplays are examined.

Robert Schwartz was born on 23 November 1934 to a Jewish emigré family in the Southern California seaport of San Pedro, south of Los Angeles. Towne's parentage was Romanian on his mother's side, Russian on his father's. One grandmother fled a pogrom, another was a Gypsy fortune-teller.[32] San Pedro is home to the Port of Los Angeles, built between 1920 and 1940 at a cost of $60 million. In the Forties and Fifties it was a traditional fishing port and the place where the nascent literature and philosophy student Robert Schwartz would learn to ply his trade as fisherman. He spent time around South Bay and Manhattan Beach and worked for Starkist Tuna during holidays from Pomona College, 35 miles east of Los Angeles in Claremont. Towne didn't do all his growing up in San Pedro however, although the place features in most of his screenplays, if only nominally. Before he moved into real estate, Robert's father, Lou Schwartz, ran a ladies clothing emporium, called the Towne Smart Shop on 6th Street and it's this that gave the family their new, anglicised surname. Lou Schwartz would become a successful property developer and allegedly the inspiration for Towne when creating the character of the other Jake (Berman) for the *Chinatown* (1974) sequel, *The Two Jakes* (1990). The family moved to a gated community called Rolling Hills, in Palos Verdes, completing the process of assimilation into Protestant culture so familiar to Jewish families in the United States at the time. Towne's first memory of cinema was the Warner Brothers theatre opposite his father's store and he recalled his mother's alarm when, as a young boy, he tried to throw himself into the action onscreen by clambering onto the stage and attempting to 'enter' the war film being shown. According to biographical material released with *The Firm* (1993), Towne wrote his first short story at the age of 6. He attended the exclusive Chadwick Prep School, followed by Redondo Union High, to which he would pay tribute in *Tequila Sunrise* (1988).

Towne studied English literature and philosophy at Pomona, where he continued to write stories, and spent his summers off the shores of San Pedro, the place he has always called home.[33] He then spent a brief time working in real estate in his father's

York: Vintage Books, 1997, 144.

[30] Buckland. *Op.cit.,* 14.

[31] Robin Wood. *PERSONAL VIEWS: Explorations in Film.* London: Gordon Fraser, 1976, 201; revised, Detroit, Michigan: Wayne State University Press, 2006, 236.

[32] See 'The Towne,' in David Thomson's *BENEATH MULHOLLAND: Thoughts on Hollywood and Its Ghosts.* London: Abacus, 1997, 100.

[33] Robert Towne, 'Growing Up in a City of Senses,' *Los Angeles,* May 1975: 49-50.

booming business: it was the mid 1950s and the suburbanisation of the country had begun in earnest. Towne was eager to find his own path, however, and after a six-month stint in Navy intelligence he began taking acting classes with Jeff Corey, the blacklisted actor and renowned pedagogue and whom he credits for teaching him everything there is to know about acting and thereby screenwriting:

> … the great thing that one took away from that was that the dialogue, in a certain sense, was completely insignificant. It really didn't matter what was said so much as what was behind it. [34]

Towne was accompanied by another aspiring actor and friend from Pomona, Richard Chamberlain. Over three or four years Towne would build up his ideas for screenplays while attending classes, as well as discovering, perhaps sadly, that his future did not lie in acting. Robert Blake, Sally Kellerman, James Coburn; screenwriters Carole Eastman (aka Adrien Joyce), John Shaner and Irvin Kershner [also a future director] were all classmates. At Corey's house Towne and Chamberlain quickly befriended New Jersey native Jack Nicholson, an aspiring actor who spent his days at the mailroom in MGM's animation studios, learning the business from the bottom up. He would prove the most important influence on Towne's writing: according to Patrick McGilligan's (unauthorised) biography of Nicholson, "Towne and Nicholson had struck up an instant rapport from the day they met. Introvert and extrovert, they were matched opposites ... Towne told Nicholson, 'Kid, you're going to be a movie star. I'm going to write scripts for you.' Jack grinned his grin of delight. And Towne smiled, the confident prophet." [35]

Auditing the classes provided independent producer and director Roger Corman with a means whereby he could spot acting talent and cultivate contacts for his low-budget stable, he was out of the country when the decision was taken to cast Nicholson in his first leading role, *The Cry Baby Killer* (1958).[36] Nicholson's most notorious role for Corman would be in *Little Shop of Horrors* (1960) as Wilbur Force, two years later, in the film famous for its supposed two-day shoot.

After learning his writing craft with Corman between 1958 and 1960, Towne would continue his screenwriting apprenticeship when he graduated to episodic TV, before Corman gave him the gift of a Poe adaptation for his acclaimed franchise (*The Tomb of Ligeia*). This brought Towne wider attention and a later Western script attracted Warren Beatty who needed a rewrite on his debut as a producer, *Bonnie and Clyde*. This would give Towne insider status in Hollywood and led to his being trusted with bigger projects, culminating most successfully in *The Last Detail*, starring Nicholson. He then turned down the opportunity to adapt *THE GREAT GATSBY* for Robert Evans in favour of finishing an original screenplay which would become *Chinatown*, the screenplay he intended to be his directing debut. Following another, somewhat troubled,

[34] Towne speaking at the AFI's Harold Lloyd Master Seminar, 1994. Accessed online at www.afi.com.

[35] McGilligan, 1995, 123. In writing about James Cagney's effect on the films he made, McGilligan discovered that Cagney was in fact creditable as author (or *auteur*) of the films in which he starred, an idea that bears fruit when applied to the very active collaborations between Nicholson and Towne, and Nicholson's own career as screenwriter and writer-director. *CAGNEY: The Actor as Auteur.* New York: A.S. Barnes & Co., 1975.

[36] Patrick McGilligan. *JACK'S LIFE A Biography of Jack Nicholson*. New York: W.W.Norton & Co., 1995, 103.

collaboration with Beatty, on *Shampoo*, he adapted *Greystoke*, possibly his best work – only to lose the property when he made his actual debut, *Personal Best*, as a result of a financing problem.

Between 1976 and 1989, Towne's career is distinguished by his directorial efforts, which are not inflected with the political or ideological concerns usually associated with the so-called New Hollywood. While both Ashby and Beatty would make films like *Coming Home* (1978) and *Reds* (1981), it could be seen that Towne's concerns were both more universal and local. If Reagan's election could be seen as ending both New Hollywood and the counter-culture, then these politics were now replaced with

> films and cycles whose primary function was 'reactionary,' defined as a cunning mixture of repression and reassurance, with story-lines that were not only politically conservative and flag-wavingly patriotic. [37]

The loss (both personal and professional) of *Greystoke* was a wound from which Towne has perhaps never recovered. Loss was no longer just a theme permeating his work, it was a metaphor for his life. In the following decade and a half he directed just two more productions from his own screenplays, *Tequila Sunrise* (1988) and *Without Limits* (1998). In this time he ceded his right to direct the screenplay *Two Jakes* (1984) aka *The Two Jakes* (1988), the sequel to *Chinatown*; and thereby severed his valuable friendships with both Robert Evans and Jack Nicholson, relationships he eulogised in disguised form in the story of *Tequila Sunrise*, proving once again that he could convert controversial aspects of his private and professional life into engaging drama. Nonetheless he continued his highly lucrative script doctoring on a wide variety of projects. Towne had embarked on a strikingly personal cinema, yet one marked by lessons learned from his collaborations with both Hal Ashby and Roman Polanski; and laced with tributes to films from Hollywood's greatest era, the 1940s, both in terms of story content and generic style.

Towne's work therefore, while not always directly autobiographical, is undoubtedly bound up in his experience. After *Tequila Sunrise* it would be another decade before he would direct again, the barely released *Without Limits*. Eight years later, he would make *Ask the Dust* from his own adaptation of the 1930s John Fante novel, which had breathed life into *Chinatown* thirty-five years earlier. Towne commented of his choice of romantic, Los Angeles-set subject matter,

> It's about a writer who feels neglected, unappreciated … What writer doesn't feel that way? How could I not identify with that? [38]

A Proposal

---

[37] Thomas Elsaesser, 'American Auteur Cinema - The Last – or First – Great Picture Show,' in Elsaesser, Horwath and King, (eds.). *THE LAST GREAT AMERICAN PICTURE SHOW: New Hollywood Cinema in the 1970s (Film Culture in Transition Series)*. Netherlands: Amsterdam University Press, 2004, 60. He argues that this periodisation is relevant because the idea of spectacle suggests technological innovation predicated on the re-emergence of genres following the counter-cultural preference for more unconventional stories with unresolved endings. *Ibid.*

[38] Linda Renaud, 'In Conversation with Robert Towne,' www.palisadespost.com, 06 April 2006.

In simple terms, the project of authorship cannot be discarded.[39] As Neil Sinyard reminds us, "the professional screenwriter in Hollywood has always been undervalued."[40] And, as screenwriting guru Frank Daniel says, "the total abandonment of the screenwriting metier in the past thirty years of unrestricted rule by the director-as-*auteur* theory has led to an unhappy result."[41] As Sidney Lumet points out in his memoir,

> …the theme (the what of the movie) is going to determine the style (the how of the movie)… What the movie is about will determine how it will be cast, how it will look, how it will be edited, how it will be musically scored, how it will be mixed, how the titles will look, and, with a good studio, how it will be released. What it's about will determine how it is to be made.[42]

The remainder of this study will necessarily deny many of the values pertaining to auteurism *per se*, particularly its supposedly self-defeating notion of personal expression which has the effect of rebutting any form of professionalism espoused by the filmmaker; but the project's recuperative strategy will continue questioning the overarching applicability of Romantic, originary, auteurism and appropriate some of its structures, meanings and applications via some of the more appropriate tenets of dramatic structure in order to prove that, despite his reputation, as 'a director's writer', Towne has a signature writing style and an overriding and repeated theme of loss (and compromise) which meet the consistency demanded of auteur study even in considering

---

[39] Peter Wollen, as before.

[40] Sinyard continues: "The professional screenwriter's situation in Hollywood has always been tinged with a sense of grievance, deriving from insufficient respect and recognition. During the 1930s and 1940s, the cavalier attitude of studios, actors and directors towards the text often drove writers into becoming directors in order to protect their own scripts… A further irritant came in the 1960s when the 'auteur' theory deified certain directors, at the expense of other collaborators, notably the writer… The writing achievements for film have been insufficiently acknowledged for a number of reasons… but one of them is undoubtedly the cinema's inferiority complex in relation to literature." Neil Sinyard, *FILMING LITERATURE: The Art of Screen Adaptation* (London: Croom Helm, 1986, viii-ix). Let me also refer to writer/producer Stirling Silliphant whom I mention later in this volume He says, in conversation with William Froug, "… I take terrible issue with the auteur theory, because auteurs really are writers who are using cameras. There is no reason why I cannot take up a camera instead of a typewriter, because I probably understand lenses and know more about cameras than most directors. Everything I see, I see only in the visual sense, not in the literary sense. I only think in terms of frames of film. Everything I see is a composition off arrangements, of elements within a photograph. It would be very simple for me to direct a film. But I choose not to." Quoted in William Froug, *THE SCREENWRITER LOOKS AT THE SCREENWRITER*. Los Angeles: Silman-James Press, 1972 and 1991, 320.

[41] Frank Daniel in his introduction to *THE TOOLS OF SCREENWRITING: A Writer's Guide to the Craft and Elements of a Screenplay* by David Howard and Edward Mabley. New York: St Martins' Griffin, 1995, xx. This book in itself offers an insight into the vagaries of authorship, dual or otherwise: as co-author David Howard explains in the Preface, the book *DRAMATIC CONSTRUCTION* by Edward Mabley had been out of print for years although it "was still the book of choice for giving a simple and clearly laid out introduction to dramatic theory to screenwriting students" (xi). Howard was given the opportunity to update it and tailor it to the needs of aspiring screenwriters by replacing essays for the stage with essays on film, utilising examples from Aristotle and more contemporary European dramatists. Howard also credits Frank Daniel, who as lecturer at Columbia University Film Division and Dean of the School of Cinema-Television at the University of Southern California, had a founding influence on hundreds, if not thousands, of screenwriters since the late 1960s.

[42] Sidney Lumet. *MAKING MOVIES*. London, Bloomsbury, 1996, 10.

collaborative authorship. [43] In other words, the Towne canon is a text which merits the kind of attention normally attributed to a film genre produced in Hollywood which is the locus of industrial production, limited in its potential for expression by dint of a representational range, which itself is, perhaps ironically, driven by the tenets of dramatic structure. [44] The significance of the nexus of Towne's intertwining professional relationships to his writing output is such that a biographical element is a necessary (if necessarily minor) part of this study.[45]

Any text of this nature should commence by declaring its limitations. This study examines most of Towne's screenplays as they were available; and appropriate references are made to the way in which they are brought to the screen both by himself and other directors as well as the clearly detectable influence wrought in some cases by other collaborators, principally powerful actors and producers.[46] David Bordwell issues this caution: "Even authorial differences, those systematic choices within the stylistic paradigm, can be translated back into production procedures; alternative schemata correspond to concrete choices available to the filmmakers, and the limits upon those schemata parallel the work options open at any specific historic juncture." [47] The ambition of the work is to privilege Robert Towne wherever possible and because of the extent of his career, it is placed outside the realm of discourse theory and intentionality and within the rubric of auteurism. [48] Given the large number of screenplays to which he contributed as 'doctor' it is not always possible to claim that his writing stands independent of his collaborators' intentions; nor is it always possible to discern that element of the screenplays which is undeniably his (non-disclosure being innate to the craft not to mention the contract.) [49]

---

[43] Jesse Kornbluth, 'Will Success Keep Bob Towne Awake?' *New York*, 21 April 1975: 73. Collaborative filmmaking practice is extensively explored by Alan Lovell and Gianluca Sergi. *MAKING FILMS IN CONTEMPORARY HOLLYWOOD*. London: Hodder Arnold, 2005.

[44] Maltby and Craven claim that "in their several guises as ideological projects Hollywood movies represent and legitimise the already dominant power. Dismissing them, whether as entertainment, ideology, or art, does not make that cultural function disappear, and its persistence and power provide, for us, an important justification for analysis of the movies." *Op.cit.*, 456.

[45] Tom Stempel provides a landmark expansive biographical and analytical account of the Hollywood screenwriter in *SCREENWRITER: The Life and Times of Nunnally Johnson*. New York: A.S. Barnes & Co., 1980.

[46] As screenwriter Mary Agnes Donoghue reminds us. "It's amazing how much a director can change a script. You don't need to alter the words for the whole thing to be destroyed." From Lizzie Francke's *SCRIPT GIRLS: Women Screenwriters in Hollywood*. London: British Film Institute, 1995, 84. As Kipen points out, "Any critic worth his salt ought to be able to tease out themes common to each of its writers in turn … Collaboration doesn't preclude analysis; it compels analysis. … By sifting the drafts and interviewing the surviving principals and recognizing their styles – in short, by doing the kind of old-fashioned spadework that requires too much patience for most film scholars, and too much time for even the most well-meaning daily reviewers – the nut could be cracked." David Kipen. *THE SCHREIBER THEORY: A Radical Rewrite of American Film History*. Hoboken, New Jersey: Melville House Publishing, 2006, 29; 30.

[47] Bordwell, in Bordwell, Staiger and Thompson. *Op.cit.*, 1994, 84.

[48] C. Paul Sellors enumerates the difficulties in authorship attribution and intention in his essay, 'Collective Authorship in Film,' *Journal of Aesthetics and Art Criticism*, 65, 3, Summer 2007: 263-27. We might also term this *the intentionalist fallacy*.

The project is thus circumscribed by the number of drafts, if any, available to this author (usually just one and occasionally none, as is unfortunately the case of some of his teleplays and the screenplays for: *Love Affair* (1994), which thus remains unexamined, along with *A Time for Killing* (1967); *Villa Rides!* (1968); and *Cisco Pike* (1972); as well as the level of relevant production information accessible in the public domain.[50]) Essentially, this project proposes an enhanced theoretical perspective on screenwriting practice with particular regard to the applicability or otherwise of the tenets of auteurism. In effect, it represents a continuing variant on auteurism and pays particular attention to screenwriting pedagogy. As Powdermaker reminds us,

> The script is the basic raw material from which a movie is made... The importance of the script to the finished movie cannot be overestimated. Therefore, how scripts are written is significant not only in understanding Hollywood, but also in answering the question of why movies are good or bad entertainment. [51]

What Henry James once described as the 'muffled majesty of authorship' is becoming a more complex component of film studies with wide-reaching implications. [52] Far from being dead or even simply repressed, as Timothy Corrigan points out, auteurism may "in fact be more alive now than at any other point in film history." [53] Towne is dismissive of the *auteur* theory and reasons that "a script can be interpreted on the screen in so many ways, it's difficult to tell... it isn't just writing style; it's really an attitude. And a certain body of work - or a close personal knowledge of the writer – is required to be able to pick out the attitudes that identify a screenwriter." [54] However, the value of auteurist study is in its origins as a form of textual interpretation and therefore the opportunity that it provides for formal analysis. If we propose that authorship presents a means by which familiar territory may be re-examined, then Towne's work as writer and writer/director makes it doubly relevant, since his career coincides with the popular emergence of authorship debates. [55]

---

[49] Stillinger basically argues against the possibility of singular authorship in *any* medium. Stillinger, 1991.

[50] David Thomson wished this author luck with the project in its early days, warning me via electronic correspondence that everything I would require could only be found in Robert Towne's desk. (Email to this author, dated 26 November 2002.)

[51] Hortense Powdermaker. *HOLLYWOOD: The Dream Factory*. Boston: Little, Brown & Co., 1950, 150.

[52] Henry James. *THE GOLDEN BOWL*. London: Penguin, 1987, Preface, 20.

[53] Timothy Corrigan. *A CINEMA WITHOUT WALLS: Movies and Culture after Vietnam*. New Brunswick, New Jersey, Rutgers University Press, 1991, 135. And as James Naremore points out, "discussion of authorship isn't incompatible with theory." 'Authorship and the Cultural Politics of Film Criticism,' *Film Quarterly* Vol. 44, No. 1, 1990: 14.

[54] Towne in John Brady. *THE CRAFT OF THE SCREENWRITER*. New York: Simon & Schuster, 1981, 428. Ironically, and perhaps unconsciously, Towne is recasting the *auteur* theory in precisely the terms that the structuralists and even *Cahiers* critics did: formulating a set of terms in which the signature of the *auteur* director can be realised, but in his case, and in the case of this study, voting firmly in favour of the screenwriter.

[55] It is pertinent to remind ourselves that "the discourse on authorship, of which auteurism *per se* is only a small part, is full of contradictions. In certain contexts it serves as a force for change, but in others it serves the economic interests of book publishers. Marginalized social groups can declare solidarity and create a collective identity by adopting authors as culture heroes – names that signify complex, coded meanings; indeed I would argue that international auteurism in its

Changes in regard for one type of critical weight over another can give rise to narratives that outfit old objects with new emphases and meanings. [56]

Towne was honoured in 1997 by the Writers Guild of America with its Screen Laurel Award, the WGA's highest honour. Brad Radnitz, then president of the WGA (West), said of Towne:

> He is the writer's writer, singular in the depth, scope and success of his work. His screenplays have resulted in powerful images indelibly etched in our cultural consciousness. He stands out as the consummate craftsman. [57]

The paradox of Towne's consistency (or otherwise) as an author is that despite his multiple collaborations with different co-writers and cinematic authors, he has not surrendered his overarching signature to a heterogeneity of voices. [58]

Narrative voice is a concept directly relevant to an understanding of literature but becomes more problematic an idea when applied to cinema. Dancyger and Rush, however, claim that

> The late 19th-century development of the narrator within the story provides an analogy for the classic film style.
> … They [the nineteenth-century novelists] saw the omniscient, judging narrator as problematic and shifted their interest from the question of what we know, to how we know it. They asked, Where did this voice of God come from? What
>
> explained the certainty with which a omniscient narrator created and claimed to know the fictive world? [59]

The authors define structure as

> … pattern. It may be made of anything that organizes our attention – a repeated line of dialogue, a recurrent situation, a musical theme, an external historical moment, a radio in the background, a return to the same location. The less structure relates to plot, the more formal it seems to be. The more external to the action, the more structure reads as the filmmaker's voice. [60]

---

early phases had roughly that use. Once these same culture heroes have been established and widely recognized, however, they can become icons or mass memory or touchstones in a 'great tradition.' Thus auteurism always had two faces. It mounted an invigorating attack on convention, but it also formed canons and fixed the names of people we should study… these tensions are inescapable, if only because writing about individual careers is necessary to any proper sociology of culture." Naremore, *op.cit.*, 21.

[56] Robert Spadoni, 'Geniuses of the Systems: Authorship and Evidence in Classical Hollywood Cinema,' *Film History*, Vol.7, 1995: 378

[57] From the Hollywood Film Festival web page re: Towne Festival 01-08 October 2002. David Denby describes Towne's work as follows: "Towne has a genius for structure; he not only joins the foreground and background of a movie, he also sets up a wide network of relations among the characters, establishing the hero not so much as the hub of a wheel but as the center of a web." 'Rear Window: Delivering His Personal Best,' in *Premiere*, December 1988: 78.

[58] See Love, 2002, as before.

[59] Dancyger and Rush. Op.cit., 173.

[60] Dancyger and Rush, *Op.cit.*, 175.

As Al Alvarez says, "… the story matters less than how it is told …; [the writer's voice] is the means by which a writer expresses his aliveness." [61]

Chapter 1 surveys the screenwriter and the screenplay in history, theory and criticism. It is a critique of the literature concerning the identification of the screenwriter and the screenplay in history, theory and criticism against a background dominated by a discourse of authorship. It explores the possibility of utilising elements of dramatic structure as a grid of determinants by which the screenwriter's signature might be construed in an auteurist fashion.

Chapter 2 (1960-1966) surveys Towne's apprenticeship as a screenwriter in which he mastered a variety of genres on film and TV. It examines his work as screenwriter from his association with Roger Corman through certain of his teleplays for series such as *The Outer Limits*. His first feature screenplay proper was produced in 1960, the year that Classical Hollywood Cinema is declared to have expired. His work in genre provided him with a grounding in economic writing, limited textual forms and exposure to the vagaries of the industry.

Chapter 3 (1967-1975) examines Towne's classical period as a collaborator extraordinaire within the rubric of New Hollywood which sees the emergence of the American auteur cinema and the so-called Movie Brats. It briefly interrogates the position of the director in an era which paradoxically proved to be a golden era of screenwriting, with Towne himself receiving two Academy Award nominations and an Oscar for his screenplay *Chinatown*, the subject of a comprehensive case study of the three drafts. This chapter also looks at the concept of multiple authorship in terms of the influential collaborations which distinguish Towne's career at the point where the reception of his work reached perhaps its critical and commercial peak.

Chapter 4 (1976-1989) charts the struggles Towne endured as he strove to direct his own screenplays. His career as a script doctor continued throughout this period. The desire to acquire more creative control over his screenplays' realisation derived from Towne's failure to direct *Greystoke*, arguably the cornerstone of his writing history. *Personal Best* offers a clear example of mythology at work in his screenwriting; while Towne's second film as director, *Tequila Sunrise*, is an example of Classical Hollywood in terms of star power, and narrative structure.

Chapter 5 (1990-2000) is a time of consolidation, both for Towne and the industry, and he engages in high-paying action film jobs as well as returning to direct a personal project. It includes his collaboration on a sequence of blockbusters, principally with Tom Cruise and Simpson/Bruckheimer, throughout the 1990s. It examines the detailed texture of his adaptations and rewrites of some of his contemporaries' ideas in that decade, as well as the film that marked his return to directing, *Without Limits*, another example of a sports film centering on the athlete/mentor relationship.

The focus of this study, however, while perhaps not aiming to make a wholly original aesthetic statement, but rather to complement that increasing body of literature extant, and proceeding *from* auteurism, remains primarily on the career of Robert Towne and is therefore concerned with what could be described in literary terms as a form of

---

[61] Al Alvarez. *THE WRITER'S VOICE*. London: Bloomsbury, 2005, 18; 21.

authorship attribution marked by changing collaborative roles. The framework, whilst not exclusively authorship but the screenplay itself, assumes a degree of partiality towards the contribution of the screenwriter in terms of the cinematic signature and an accent on story construction as the bearer of filmic meaning. As Corliss wrote in 1970,

> a screenwriter's work should, and can, be judged by considering his entire career, as is done with a director. If a writer has been associated with a number of favorite films, if we can distinguish a common style in films with different directors and actors, and if he has received sole writing credit on several films, an authorial personality begins to appear. [62]

Through the agency of the narrative tools provided by dramatic structure, this thesis aims to reframe the terms of the argument for cinematic authorship in order to reposition the screenwriter's contribution, in history, theory and criticism. [63] However, contemporary literary study is experiencing a shift; the contribution being made by this particular text might more correctly be described as an attempt to further the cause of multiple or collaborative authorship as critical discourse, the truly dimensional model for an understanding of filmmaking. Robert Towne is indeed a Hollywood author and a dominant contributory figure in those films in which he is the screenwriter. [64] For, as Patrick McGilligan reminds us, "even in Hollywood, in the beginning is the word." [65]

---

[62] Richard Corliss, 'The Hollywood Screenwriter,' as before: 6.

[63] Towne himself remarks that "the pervasive tendency to underestimate the true difficulty of the screenplay form ... started with contempt for the form itself, born and bred in those decades when novelists and playwrights would come out to a California bungalow and condescend to knock out a script in a couple of weeks for big bucks so they could go back to their daytime job and do some really serious writing. It's rare, however, that anyone has an understanding of how disciplined a good script must be, and how much work goes into achieving that discipline." He also states that 'Causing the movie to be made,' incidentally, is no small thing. From it stems, I believe, the historic hatred Hollywood has always displayed for the screenwriter. No matter what is said about how a movie gets made, one fact is inescapable: until the screenwriter does his job, nobody else *has* a job.
"The hatred on their part usually takes the form of contempt for him because he's not good enough to put them to work and fear of him because they need him to go to work." Towne, 1997, ix.
[64] As Nystrom asks, "After all, what was the motivation of prescriptive auteurism if not the hope that personal artistic expression would become the central organizing principle of an otherwise commercial form of mass culture?" Derek Nystrom, 'Hard Hats and Movie Brats: Auteurism and the Class Politics of the New Hollywood,' *Cinema Journal* 43, No. 3, Spring 2004: 36.
[65] Patrick McGilligan, 1986, 14.

Chapter 1
THE SCREENWRITER & AUTHORSHIP: A LITERATURE REVIEW

Introduction

In a 1997 issue of the international journal *Film History*, John Belton called for a revised history of screenwriting, a mere twenty-six years after Richard Corliss's ground-breaking quest had begun. [66] The theme of that particular issue was 'Screenwriters and Screenwriting,' and its editorial is a plea to reinstate the screenwriter in his proper place in film history, and popular writing about cinema, just as revisionist film historiographers have analysed filmmaking in terms of group stylistic practices. [67]

The paradox, that great screenplays are only recognised when they are filmed, thereby attracting attention to the original texts, makes the case for recognition all the more significant. This point is made by Robert Towne, when he remarks

> The only way a screenplay can be evaluated, almost by definition, is not on the page, but by viewing the movie it caused to be made. It certainly can be read and even enjoyed, but you're stuck with the inescapable fact that it was written to be seen. [68]

Prescriptive writings on film, and much film criticism, are founded on the notion of the director as author. The questions arising from this traditionally Romantic originary concept invariably centre on the role of director and his deployment of mise-en-scène and narrative stratagems. This construction has frequently ignored the true nature of the production process yet it has had far-reaching effects on the industry itself in the form of the auteur theory (and it remains the only film 'theory' to do so.) The classical Hollywood model, far from being a result of some director-led aesthetic, was in fact oriented towards a production line dictated by patterns of consumption, measured by studios, financed by Wall Street and guided by producers.

Definitions of the cinematic and the assigning of both meaning and names to the narrative models which provide our cultural self-image have ceaselessly proved their attraction in the area of film studies.   However, the naming of names is no easier now than it has ever been. Screen authorship remains keenly debated in both popular and academic criticism.   The artistic neglect of the screenwriter and the identity of the screenplay has its roots in the origins of American cinema, as Tom Stempel reminds us in his landmark book, *FRAMEWORK: A History of Screenwriting in the American Film*:

---

[66] John Belton, Introduction, *Film History,* Vol. 9, No. 3, 1997: 2-3. Belton was repeating the call made by Lee Server a decade previously: "… it would seem that the time has come to shine a bit more light in the direction of the neglected screenwriter, to revise the revisionists' view of American film history." *SCREENWRITER: Words Become Pictures*. Pittstown, New Jersey: Main Street Press, 1987, 11. And John Brady quotes Hollis Alpert in Saturday Review, 1970: "…I've yet to come across any full-fledged biographical or critical treatment of a film writer … The relationship of writer to film and, perhaps more important, of writer to director has never been sufficiently explored, one reason being that few people ever bother talking to writers." John Brady. *Op.cit,* 25.

[67] Richard Corliss, 'The Hollywood Screenwriter,' *Film Comment*, Winter 1970-71: 4-7.

[68] Towne, 'On Moving Pictures,' in *CHINATOWN/THE LAST DETAIL.* New York: Grove Press, 1997, ix.

Much film history about screenwriting is inaccurate because the sources are those who have reasons for downplaying the role of the screenwriter: actors, producers, directors, and their publicity machines, both in the industry and in film studies. [69]

The scholar Richard Fine also opens his work on American screenwriters with the reminder,

> For more than fifty years American authors have regularly accepted work in the movie industry, and for more than fifty years they have been warning that there is no territory more dangerous for a talented writer than Hollywood. [70]

While in contemporary terms the script is viewed as the template for the final product - the exhibited feature film - the writer has not gained in stature to the degree that might be expected. This has historical reasons which are documented in anecdotal form, through exposition of the screenwriting process and the team-writing practices especially in the 1930s, which meant that only the last writer would get credit. [71] Accreditation is further problematised by the events of the 1940s and 1950s when the HUAC witch hunts meant that many writers used 'fronts' and even won Academy Awards pseudonymously - these credits are only latterly being restored. In the midst of this chaos comes the formation of the Screenwriters Guild which itself is extremely problematic and fraught with internecine political difficulties. [72] Robert Carringer reminds us that

> By industry custom, authorship and screen credit were treated as separate issues. Though a screenwriter signed away all claim to authorship of his work, he could still assert a right to public acknowledgment of his authorship of it. [73]

The various critical methodologies which have evolved around film are principally to do with a film's provenance. And, as Matthew Sweet reminds us, "the history of film criticism has created its own orthodoxies." [74] Like a piece of art, a film's

---

[69] Tom Stempel. *FRAMEWORK: A History of American Film*. New York: Continuum, 1991, xi.
[70] Richard Fine. *WEST OF EDEN Writers in Hollywood, 1928-1940*. Washington and London: Smithsonian Institute Press, 1.
[71] Ben Hecht comments on the "pleasant anonymity" experienced by the screenwriter in his memoir of working with Charles MacArthur, *CHARLIE* (1957), excerpted as 'Let's Make the Hero a MacArthur,' in Christopher Sylvester (ed.) *THE PENGUIN BOOK OF HOLLYWOOD*. London: Penguin, 1999, 193.

[72] Nunnally Johnson said that the Guild was formed partly because of a producer called Barney Glazer: "Oddly enough, no matter what the picture was, Barney name was on it as one of the writers. Well, this happened so often, not just with me, for God's sake, but a dozen others, that his victims met to see how they could stop him from taking credit and the result was the Screen Writers Guild." Quoted in Michael Sragow, 'Ghostwriters: Unraveling the Enigma of Movie Authorship,' *Film Comment* 19, March-April 1983: 10. The history of the development, problems and eventual separation into two coastal divisions of the Writers' Guild until 1952 is traced by the late Nancy Lynn Schwartz in *THE HOLLYWOOD WRITERS' WARS*. New York: Knopf, 1982. In 1981 Kirk Honeycutt asserts that "credits should reflect authorship ... In an art as collaborative as filmmaking, how often does the WGA's credit process represent, as John Carpenter puts it, 'rules for the guild, not necessarily the truth?'" 'Whose Film is it Anyway?,' *American Film* Vol.6, No.7, May 1981: 36.
[73] Robert Carringer. *THE MAKING OF CITIZEN KANE*. (Revised and updated edition). Berkeley: University of California Press, 1996, 32.
[74] Matthew Sweet, 'Our Greatest Lost Film Critic,' Film & Music, *The Guardian*, 09 May 2008: 4.

value is directly attributable to the signature in the corner of the frame. However, if it is possible to accept in principle that film is a collaborative venture where does that leave the screenwriter in terms of the attributing of a single cinematic signature? Problems of authorship in the literary canon stretch back to Homeric poetry, the Bible, Shakespeare and beyond. In Hollywood, what Lee Server terms 'the variables of authorship' means that ownership – for that is essentially what the term describes - could be ascribed to directors, writers, producers, cinematographers, composers, production designers – the list is very nearly endless. [75] Theories of film authorship and genre evolved separately from, and in opposition to, each other, to address these conflicts of enquiry, in relation to the position of the director. However, they finally turn on the notion of personal expression and vision and they have been responsible for the sidelining of the screenwriter's contribution. This leads to the inevitable conclusion that a new critical framework is required.

Foucault has written that the purpose of author-centred textual analysis is

> to construct the rational entity we call an author. Undoubtedly this construction
> is to assign a 'realistic' dimension as we speak of an individual's 'profundity' or 'creative'
> power … Nevertheless, these aspects of the individual … which comprise an
> individual as author … are projections … of our way of handling texts: in the
> comparisons we make, the traits we extract as pertinent, the continuities we assign,
> or the exclusions we practise. [76]

'Handling the text' has seen many variations in the study of film. Theories range from the humanist, seemingly straightforward director-led attribution coined in the 1950s by *Cahiers du cinéma* (but in reality dating from the 1910s when directors like Griffith et al were lauded) and taken up by the influential American writer, Andrew Sarris, via director studies by Robin Wood; to the abnegation of the author in favour of the reader, or audience, as favoured by French post-structuralists and eventually the postmodernists. Directors were not universally admired however as screenwriter Anita Loos candidly admitted: "The directors were dunces, you know. [But] if you've got a good writer, the director has got the whole thing in his pocket." [77]

As the editors of *The Velvet Light Trap* remind us in their special Authorship issue,

> Almost since the earliest constructions of the moving image, notions of
> authorship have been developed and alternately contested. While such
> aspects as authors' roles, creative circumstances, and perceived autonomy
> change across cultures and across time, ideas of 'authorship' have persisted
> - even in discourse that has proclaimed the very death of the author. Perhaps
> owing its greatest historical debt to 'auteur theory,' authorship within cinematic
> traditions has, in cycles, embraced this idea, attempted to disengage itself from
> that ideal, or perhaps, even denied its relevance. [78]

---

[75] Lee Server. *Op.cit.* Jon Lewis says: "the literary-historical concept of authorship and ownership promoted by the auteur theory at once conflates and confuses issues of art and commerce that are essential when one considers studio-produced movies." *THE NEW AMERICAN CINEMA*. Durham & London: Duke University Press, 1998, Introduction, 3.

[76] Michel Foucault, 'What is an Author?' *Screen* 20/1: 21.

[77] Anita Loos, interviewed in *Women's Wear Daily*, 23 August 1974. Quoted in Marsha McCreadie, *THE WOMEN WHO WRITE THE MOVIES: From Frances Marion to Nora Ephron*. New York: Birch Lane Press, 1994, 3.

They continue that the project of authorship and the viability of a single authorship theory is rendered impossible, due to

> … the range of authorship experiences and diversity of authored products thriving in contemporary societies. [79]

This paragraph captures the essence of the conflict that dominates discussion of cinematic authorship: it notes the particularity of the circumstances of production; the culture in which the particular cinema resides; and it also suggests the precariousness of 'naming' the author; yet all the while, the very idea persists as a dominant discourse of engagement. The notion of author in cinematic terms can denote a single individual and usually it means the expressivity of the film's director; a collective partnership; and a dominant studio production mode.

The theme of authorship persists as a major component of film studies which might be said to be encapsulated in three broad and interconnected categories: history, theory and criticism. [80]

At a panel of writers and directors moderated by Frank Pierson and staged by the Writers Guild Foundation in 1997, the possessory credit and the auteur theory was discussed in some detail. Writer Patrick S. Duncan makes the point that "there are certain directors in the auteurs who only did their good work with certain writers…"; Steven Zaillian says that, "the possessory credit, the vanity credit, has no reason for being,"; while writer/director Mark Rydell states that, "there's no denying by anybody of any intelligence whatsoever that the writer is certainly the single critical element in the genesis of a film." [81] The unanimity of writers or even writer/directors on this subject is constantly undermined by their Guild's own tactics during negotiation rounds: as Pierson concludes it was the Machiavellian machinations of Lew Wasserman in the early Seventies, allegedly on behalf of Disney Studios, that changed the situation whereby

> … the use of the apostrophe, was limited only to writers…
> And the negotiating committee walked out thinking that we had a clear understanding that it was only going to be for this limited use. And then that opened the floodgates and that's how we got to where we are now. I hate to confess that it was our own

---

[78] *The Velvet Light Trap* – Authorship Issue No. 57, Spring 2006: 1. In 1921 Jean Epstein used the word 'author' in his essay, 'Le Cinéma et les lettres modernes'; while what Stephen Crofts calls 'proto-auteurism' could also be seen in Louis Delluc's analyses of films directed by D.W. Griffith, Ince, Tourneur et al. Stephen Crofts, 'Authorship and Hollywood,' in John Hill and Pamela Church Gibson, (eds.), *THE OXFORD GUIDE TO FILM STUDIES*. Oxford: Oxford University Press, 1998, 312.

[79] *Ibid*. See also Alan Lovell and Gianluca Sergi. *MAKING FILMS IN CONTEMPORARY HOLLYWOOD*. London: Hodder Arnold, 2005: "The authorship of a film always has to be established, it cannot be taken for granted. It is likely to be collective; the most likely candidates for inclusion are director, producer, star and writer. Other candidates are always possible." (116)

[80] The Screenwriter & Screenplay in Film History and Literature, are surveyed in Appendix 1.

[81] 'Whose Picture Is It Anyway? A Debate on Possessory Credit and the Auteur Theory,' *Written By (The Journal of the Writers' Guild of America, West)*, October 1997, Vol.1, No.10: 46-52. This subject is also discussed in Lovell and Sergi, 2005, 56-7.

As Patrick McGilligan notes, the joint project of the Academy of Motion Picture Arts & Sciences and the Writers Guild of America, West, *WHO WROTE THE MOVIE AND WHAT ELSE DID HE WRITE? An Index of Screen Writers and their Film Works 1936-1969*, did not refer to pre-Guild screenplays and toed the line of official accreditation thereafter. [83] According to the screenwriter Arthur Laurents, in his exacting memoirs, the consequences of not getting a credit can have serious professional and personal ramifications.[84] The ongoing opacity of the Guild's anonymous decision-making process makes investigation of arbitration proceedings impossible. [85]

Authorship and the Screenplay

Authorship could be defined as, "an explicit way of assigning responsibility and giving credit for intellectual work." [86] Eighteenth century critics were concerned with the rules of rhetoric and the creativity of the author was at the centre of discourse: at the

---

[82] *Ibid.* Wasserman's extraordinary influence in Hollywood is traced in Dennis McDougal. *THE LAST MOGUL: Lew Wasserman, MCA and the Hidden History of Hollywood.* New York: Da Capo Press, 1998, rpt. 2001. Michael Sragow comments that "although the easiest way to clear up the credits controversy would be to list every writer who ever worked on a given movie, the Guild tries to cut the number down both to bolster the dignity of the writing credit and to enhance the final rewards of the writers who do the most work." Sragow, 12. In the meantime the credits problem persists, as screenwriter Miles Millar explains: "Although the first writer on a project is almost assured credit, all the subsequent writers have to fight it out. The process effectively pits writer against writer. Because the Writers' Guild favours structure over dialogue, a writer can create all the dialogue in a movie and still not receive credit." Miles Millar, 'I Wrote That!' *The Guardian*, The Guide, 27 February 1999: 15.

[83] Published in Los Angeles, 1970. Referenced in McGilligan, 1991, 13.

[84] Referring to an (unexpectedly) uncredited rewrite he did for director Anatole Litvak as a young playwright starting out in Hollywood, he says: "Basically, I didn't understand the practical importance of the credit on *The Snake Pit*. Nor did I have a clue that someday, four decades later, despite all the movies I had written, I would not be entitled to health benefits from the Writers Guild because I didn't meet the credits requirement. *The Snake Pit* credit could have tipped the scales. The Guild's health coverage is substantial but its complicated, arcane rules have a paradoxical result: benefits become unavailable just when they are most needed. Screenwriters who haven't gotten a credit for too long and are sliding over the hill and seeing doctors too frequently are the very screenwriters who lose the health coverage paid for by their union just when they really need it. Arthur Laurents *ORIGINAL STORY BY: A Memoir of Broadway and Hollywood.* New York: Alfred A. Knopf, 2000, 116. When John Gregory Dunne underwent expensive heart surgery he contacted Philip Dunne to thank him for setting up the Guild so many years before; ironically, Dunne [Philip] was himself no longer covered by the Guild's provisions for which he had so strenuously fought. *MONSTER: Living Off the Big Screen.* New York: Vintage Books, 1997, 66.

[85] The contemporary problem facing the screenwriter is whether he delivers structure or dialogue – if the former, a credit is guaranteed; if the latter, there is a chance that he may not see his name on the screen. Attempts to gain access to records at the Writers Guild regarding past arbitration processes are fruitless: it operates an opaque system wherein a few writers are nominated to adjudicate various drafts of a script and the ruling is by majority. As David Kipen points out, somewhat harshly given the predicament in which most jobbing screenwriters find themselves, the negotiations at the Writers' Guild usually focus on healthcare, not credits, as was the case in 2004. *THE SCHREIBER THEORY: A Radical Rewrite of American Film History.* Hoboken, New Jersey: Melville House Publishing, 2006, 63.

[86] President and Fellows of Harvard College, adapted from the paper version of *Faculty Policies on Integrity in Science*, 1996, Introduction.

heart of all discussion was the making of meaning. Contradictions abound in this theoretical discourse due to the collaborative nature of the filmmaking medium, yet its convenience as a criterion of value supersedes any inherent contradictions in it as a tool of study.

As Maltby and Craven point out,

> Literary texts and paintings assert authorship as a principle of creativity. Hollywood's commercial aesthetics, on the other hand, not only advertises its products as being created by a multiplicity of personnel, but also concedes the authority to decide what a movie's content means to the individual viewer, who is provided with a host of opportunities to exercise that authority to maximize his or her pleasure from the movie. Within limits, Hollywood movies are constructed to accommodate, rather than predetermine, their audiences' reaction, and this has involved devising systems and codes of representation that permit a range of interpretations and a degree of instability of meaning. [87]

The idea of authorship as an expression of the Romantic notion of the artist has a long history, albeit in literary media. In his account of the evolution of the Romantic idea, M.H. Abrams sums up the phenomenon in terms of 'Literature as a Revelation of Personality'. [88]

Cinematically speaking, authorship seeks definition in terms of individual, personal aesthetics and vision – and, for reasons which will be outlined below, has usually been framed in terms of the careers of film directors. Essentially, its impact in terms of film criticism is to categorise film as part of an ongoing cinematic dialogue that a director is engaging in with his muse. It is true, however, that the screenwriter has not been entirely neglected. Indeed since Richard Corliss' *TALKING PICTURES* first appeared there have been biographies, oral histories (Patrick McGilligan's invaluable *BACKSTORY* series, published by the University of California) and a volume of literary biography devoted to the genus, not to mention several journals (*Creative Screenwriting*, *Scr(i)pt*, *Scenario* and *Written By*, the journal of the Writers' Guild of America (West).)

Perhaps the only screenwriter to have been contractually guaranteed not just as much money as the director, but to have his screenplays shot *exactly as written* is Paddy Chayefsky. He didn't believe in collaboration unless it was intended to enhance his writing; he didn't think that becoming a director would help the screenwriter because he

---

[87] Maltby and Craven. *Op.cit.*, 43.
[88] M.H. Abrams. *THE MIRROR AND THE LAMP: Romantic Theory and the Critical Condition.* Oxford: Oxford University Press, 1953, 226-256. In terms of a direct application of structure as a means of understanding artistic contributions to film, it is interesting to note the principles which the Rev. John Keble says characterize literary biography. Specifically in his own case, he sought to detect personality in the works of Greek and Roman Antiquity: The Canon of the Significant Theme; the Canon of Identification with the Hero; the Canon of Fervor; the Canon of Imagery and the Canon of Style (259-261). Abrams quotes Flaubert, who believed that, "The author in his work ought to be like God in the universe, present everywhere, and visible nowhere. Since art is a second nature, the creator of this nature ought to act in analogous ways, so that one may feel in all its atoms, and in every aspect, a hidden, infinite impassibleness." (262, from *Correspondence*, ed. Eugène Fasquelle, Paris: 1900, II, 155) [In the case of T.S. Eliot, he famously dismissed the significance of authorial biography when he referred to 'Shakespeare's laundry bills.']

would lose his writing perspective. His experience was perhaps tarnished by *Altered States* (1980) but his example remains the beacon for all screenwriters. [89]

.

The Screenwriter in Theory and Criticism

James Goodwin states that

> auteurism is a practice of criticism before it can even be considered to be a theory of cinema. [90]

Film studies has frequently cast its discursive eye on the industry in terms of traditional forms of criticism, particularly in the early years of cinema. [91] This had the effect of decontextualising the product from its industrial and business background, thereby shifting the focus from a critical engagement with practice to an indulgence of critical style. The director rarely had a say in the choice of originating material and was rarely privy to the editing process, when films might be said to be truly 'made.' Orders of discourse aside, cinematic authorship – or, who made the film – poses its own inimical series of problems. Dudley Andrew differentiates between theory and criticism as follows:

> While most criticism begins with some general theoretic principles, most theories begin with questions generated by individual films or techniques; but the answers must always be applicable to more films than the one which generated the question. [92]

Hence the need for academic scholarship to open up the study of the cinema as aesthetic form with criteria necessary for entry to arts, humanities and the social sciences.

As he states, "the auteur theory… is not a theory at all but a critical method." [93] He continues:

> Like all critical methods it relies on certain theoretical principles, but they are directed not so much at systematic understanding of a general phenomenon as at the evaluation of particular examples of that phenomenon… Like its blood brother 'genre criticism,' it organizes our film history for us and makes us sensitive to certain aspects of it, showing us what movies we have valued or ought to begin valuing. [94]

---

[89] Chayefsky reportedly said, "The director is an assassin in terms of story. You have to stand ceaseless guard against the director's ambushes." Quoted by Joe Eszterhas. *HOLLYWOOD ANIMAL: A Memoir of Love and Betrayal.* New York: Random House, 2004, 41. However, Chayefsky did not attract what might be described as the best directors to his work – possibly because of the nature of his power in what has always been a collaborative medium

[90] James Goodwin, 'The Author is Dead: Long Live the Author,' *Quarterly Review of Film Studies,* Spring 1984: 114.

[91] Maltby and Craven. *Op.cit.,* 31.
[92] Dudley Andrew. *THE MAJOR FILM THEORIES.* London and New York: Oxford University Press, 1976, 5.
[93] Andrew. *Op.cit,* 4.
[94] Dudley Andrew. *Op.cit.,* 4-5.

The term 'auteur' originated in French film criticism in the 1920s and was later modified in terms of a focus on post-WWII cinema in the early 1950s, principally through the work of André Bazin whose ideologically informed writings shifted the meaning towards mise-en-scène analysis. Bazin's essays were a version of Kracauer's theoretical line and his emphasis on epochal analysis defined by technology led him to an ironic privileging of realism.

The idea of auteur as metaphor underpinned much critical writing in France in the 1950s.
First popularised in the pages of *Cahiers du cinéma* in 1954, *La politique des auteurs* (or 'the policy of authors') has become ingrained in discussions of cinema, this version of formalist criticism so favoured by Kracauer in the earlier years of the industry which evolved partly via the caméra-stylo writings of Alexandre Astruc.

Cahiers critics developed a sophisticated theory of film genre. André Bazin, the editor of the journal, believed that the genius of the American cinema lay in its repository of ready-made forms: westerns, thrillers, musicals, action films, comedies, and so forth. Genre was thereby identified as an enriching rather than constricting tradition (and in fact the history of Hollywood might well be construed as a history of genre cinema). The auteurists argued that the best movies are dialectical, in which the conventions of a genre are held in creative tension with the personality of the artist.

Truffaut's article, 'Une Certaine Tendence du cinéma français,' may have been a product of Romantic idealism; but it was also a polemic by an aspiring filmmaker railing against the strictures of the contemporary French film industry. It was a new departure, doctrinal in its expression, steadfastly opposing that criticism stemming from mass culture theories which privileged the audience. His main argument focussed in particular (and rather unfairly) upon the work of screenwriting duo Jean Aurenche and Pierre Bost, whose most heinous crime was an apparently flourishing career, albeit one based almost wholly on very faithful adaptations of the classics. Technically perfect, these scenarios represented a 'tradition of quality' and provided a bulwark against personal expression in cinema. Where was the creative persona of the director in these films? Truffaut denies the possibility of these writers' talents and says, "I consider an adaptation of value only when written by a man of the cinema." Aurenche and Bost are for him, literary men, contemptuous of cinema. The 'tendency' to which Truffaut alludes is that of 'psychological realism', which has as its dominant trait 'anti-bourgeois will'. [95] However, for the purposes of this study, Truffaut's highlighting of screenwriting as a criterion of excellence and the notion of 'man of the cinema,' are of immense value. Susan Hayward (the British academic) makes the telling observation that,

> This quasi-Oedipal polemic established the primacy of the author/auteur and as such proposed a rather romantic and, therefore, conservative aesthetic… A further problem with this polemic is that by privileging the auteur it erases context (that is, history) and therefore sidesteps ideology. Equally, because film is being looked at for its formalistic, stylistic and thematic structures, unconscious structure (such as the unspoken dynamics between film-maker and actor, the economic pressures connected with the industry) is precluded. [96]

---

[95] François Truffaut, 'Une Certaine Tendence du cinéma français,' originally published by *Cahiers du Cinéma* 31, January 1954 in Paris, reprinted in Bill Nichols, ed., *MOVIES AND METHODS Volume I*. London: University of California Press, 1976, 224-237.
[96] Susan Hayward. *KEY CONCEPTS IN CINEMA STUDIES*. London: Routledge, 1997, 14.

Auteurism is often relegated as an outmoded form of Romantic criticism when in fact its origins lie in the fundaments of dramatic structure and the social and industrial nature of cinema's constituent forces. (Its apolitical nature was therefore an issue in the ideologically-driven scholarship of the Seventies and Eighties.) This conflict – between art and commerce – lies at the heart of the problem for students of Hollywood cinema in particular, for as Pam Cook comments,

> At the time of the emergence of the *politique des auteurs*, then, the idea that a
> Hollywood film could be related back to the intentions of an individual director
> in the same way as it was in the case of films which fell into the category of art cinema,
> had an important polemical impetus. It attempted to break down the barrier between
> art cinema and commercial cinema by establishing the presence of artists in the
> apparently monolithic commodity production of Hollywood. Although the idea of
> the director as artist was prevalent in writing on art cinema, it was not important to
> writing on Hollywood at that time. [97]

This critical airbrushing would of course eliminate the screenwriter and forms an important part of auteurism's unconscious rewriting of cinema history, in common with most traditional forms of film criticism, which, until relatively recently, did not contextualise filmmaking within the industrial system. DeRosa observes of the contemporary effect on American filmmaking:

> The politics of the studio system and the widening acceptance of the auteur theory
> downplayed the significance of the screenwriter's contribution to the art of
> filmmaking. [98]

While it raised crucial questions about American cinema, therefore, the 'politique' related intimately to the essentially apolitical nature of the French critics at the time. John Hess would later examine the content of Truffaut's claims for a need to express cinematically personal visions and concerns and conclude that in fact it was regressive and reactionary, a post-war decision to regress following a movement towards social and political signification in the arts by the Resistance-led cultural bodies. [99]   As Haberski states,

> The significance of French film criticism … was not so much its insight into
> movies but its ability to illustrate a shift toward the intellectualisation of mass
> culture and democratisation of criticism. [100]

Buckland's concept of internal and external authorship – and the conjoining of the two in a career such as that of Spielberg – provides ready evidence of the necessity for inclusion of a production history in the consideration of the industry's output. Buckland, *Op.cit.*

[97] Pam Cook. *THE CINEMA BOOK.* London: British Film Institute, 1990, 135.

[98] Steven DeRosa. *WRITING WITH HITCHCOCK: The Collaboration of Alfred Hitchcock and John Michael Hayes.* London & New York: Faber and Faber, 2001, x.

[99] John Hess, 'La politique des auteurs, Part One,' *Jump Cut*, 1 May-June 1974: 19-22. Andrew Sarris. *THE AMERICAN CINEMA: DIRECTORS AND DIRECTIONS, 1929-1968.* New York: Dutton, 1968; and rept., Da Capo Press, 1996.

[100] Raymond J.Haberski, Jr.   *IT'S ONLY A MOVIE! Films and Critics in American Culture.* Lexington: University Press of Kentucky, 2001, 113.

The importance of early auteur criticism was its contribution to the analysis of formal style: composition, photography, lighting, iconography, colour, ie the mise-en-scène devices innate to the form. [101] These are crucial elements in organising a structured response to the cinematic text. What must be remembered about the popularity of this approach, is that at the time of its appearance, the film industry was (not for the first or last time), in crisis. In fact the major contribution of the *Cahiers* critics may have been toward a more discriminating appreciation of mise-en-scène and many of the magazine's contributors preferred the work of metteurs en scene to that of so-called auteur directors.

Bazin's work could be broadly categorised under the heading of Authorship as Personality, along with that of Astruc, (the later) Sarris, and M.H. Abrams. In a 1957 article, Bazin warned about the aesthetic of the cult of personality but said that the politique

> has the merit of treating the cinema as an adult art, and of reacting against
> the impressionistic relativism which still prevails most often in film criticism…

His purpose in critiquing the approach was

> Not at all to deny the role of the auteur, but to restore it to the preposition without
> which the noun is only a lame concept. 'Auteur,' without doubt, but *of* what? [102]

As late as 1976 - by which time Bazin's warnings against the cult of personality had had no discernible effect on critics - Bill Nichols could state with assurance that auteurist criticism wasn't so much resolved as suppressed. [103]

Lopate argues that

> The 1960s and 1970s, whether because of the remarkable bounty of good films,
> or the rising interest in film culture, or both, spawned a golden age in American
> movie criticism.[104]

Andrew Sarris' interpretation of 'la politique des auteurs' as 'The Auteur Theory' has had a long and not entirely healthy legacy in the reading of film which persists today. Sarris's coining of the term was a mistranslation of Truffaut's article and the subsequent 'attitude' emanating from the French critics; however his transposing of their ideas of criticism into something resembling a critical methodology means that he could be said to be heir to both Bazin and Munsterberg in his attempts to fuse a theory of visual composition with a sense of hierarchical significance within the motion picture industry. And his contribution of an evaluative methodology to critical discourse in the United States cannot be discounted. Sarris did however point out that Truffaut's worst fault lay

---

[101] John Caughie, ed. *THEORIES OF AUTHORSHIP*. London: Routledge and Kegan Paul, 1981, Introduction, 13.
[102] André Bazin, 'On the Politique des Auteurs,' *Cahiers du Cinéma in English I*, January 1966:14, 18. Bazin observed that it was "the prior conception of the scenario" which allowed an elliptical narrative structure to occur in Italian neo-realist cinema. *WHAT IS CINEMA? Vol. II*, translated by Hugh Gray. Berkeley: University of California Press, 1971, 58.
[103] Nichols, ed. *Op.cit.*, 221.
[104] Lopate. *Op.cit.*, xvii.

"… in his ascribing authorship to Hollywood directors hitherto tagged with the deadly epithet of commercialism." [105]

Sarris' article, 'Notes on the Auteur Theory in 1962, ' postulates the ranking of directors as an historically respectable activity which persists in all art forms – music, painting and so on. In a special issue of *Film Culture* in 1963, Sarris modelled a reference text of American directors' careers on *Cahiers'* American Cinema editions and it became his later, highly influential, book, *THE AMERICAN CINEMA: Directors and Directions,* in which he establishes a 'Pantheon' of directors, boasting Chaplin, Ford, Griffith, Welles, et al; 'Expressive Esoterica' in which are included Tay Garnett and Arthur Penn; 'Less Than Meets the Eye' numbers John Huston (a director similarly underwhelming to Sarris' counterparts at *Cahiers*), Kazan and Wyler:

> These [the Pantheon] are the directors who have transcended their technical problems with a *personal vision* of the world. To speak any of their names is to evoke a self-contained world with its own laws and landscapes. They were also fortunate enough to find the proper conditions and collaborators for the full expression of their talent. [106]

This echoes the director-centric discussions from proto-auteurist European writings of the 1920s but it is the term 'personal vision' which persists in relevance. The term auteur, which is of course now in common usage, can serve in an evaluative sense to distinguish good filmmakers (auteurs) from mere technicians (metteurs en scène). Auteurism was in fact the first cinematic discipline to raise the significance of a film's mise-en- scène. On an historic level, then, auteurism evolved from its origins in Romanticism, and has tended to promote film as a cult of personality.

Sarris claims that the director's personality can be extrapolated as follows: "… the first premise of the auteur theory is the technical competence of a director as a criterion of value"; "the second premise of the auteur theory is the distinguishable personality of the director as a criterion of value"; and finally, "The third and ultimate premise of the auteur theory is concerned with interior meaning, the ultimate glory of the cinema as an art. Interior meaning is extrapolated from the tension between a director's personality and his material." [107]
Sarris made his claim for this as a methodology of cinematic evaluation since it

> values the personality of the director precisely because of the barriers to its expression. It is as if a few brave spirits had managed to overcome the gravitational pull of the mass of movies. [108]

---

[105] Sarris, 1968, 28.

[106] Andrew Sarris, 'The American Cinema,' *Film Culture*, No. 28, Spring 1963: Haberski says it is "archaeology masquerading as criticism." *Op.cit.*, 131; *THE AMERICAN CINEMA: DIRECTORS AND DIRECTIONS, 1929-1968*. New York: Dutton, 1968, 39.

[107] From 'Notes on the Auteur Theory in 1962,' excerpted in Caughie (ed.), *op.cit.*, 63-64. Pauline Kael dispatches this claim with the statement, "Sarris does some pretty fast shuffling with Huston and Bergman; why doesn't he just come out and admit that writer-directors are disqualified by his third premise? They can't arrive at that 'interior meaning, the ultimate glory of the cinema' because a writer-director has no tension between his personality and his material, so there's nothing for the auteur critic to extrapolate from." Pauline Kael, 'Circles and Squares: Joys and Sarris,' *Film Quarterly*, Vol. 16, No. 3, Spring 1963, reprinted in *I LOST IT AT THE MOVIES: Film Writings 1954-1965*. New York and London: Marion Boyars, 1994, 304.

This was to denigrate what Bazin (and later Thomas Schatz, whose work exemplifies the move towards more exacting industry analysis from the mid-Eighties onward) would memorably term "the genius of the system, the richness of its ever-vigorous tradition, and its fertility when it comes into contact with new elements." [109] Auteurism in their terms decries the machine, or set of corporate studio rules, which itself creates the possibility of personal expression, and it ignores the way in which the *effect* of this individuation (or the belief in the possibility of its existence) is manufactured. Sarris even went so far as to explain Truffaut's 'policy' (now a 'theory') as "a reaction against sociological criticism that enthroned the WHAT against the HOW." [110]

While Sarris would later acknowledge the shortcomings of the auteurist method, which laid an unfortunate emphasis on the director's consistency of subject and theme, he was the writer most responsible for its effect, locating the individual voices in the cogs and wheels of the Hollywood machine, the conventions of which gave directors a series of limitations or areas of transgression, and a way in which to make their name.

> The auteur theory derives its rationale from the fact that the cinema could not be a completely personal art under even the best of conditions.[111]

The writings of Robin Wood represent director-centred auteurism at its best – or most extreme, maintaining the director's personal commitment to the material as a classical artist. [112] His account of director Arthur Penn in the eponymous monograph is telling:

> Penn's films reveal a strikingly consistent personality; even when one is aware of tensions or contradictions within his work, these come across as the expression of that personality. The films also suggest a conscious artist with the developed technique to express what he needs or wants to express. When the genuineness and intensity of a director's response are as evident as they are in THE MIRACLE WORKER, the film becomes his. These are Arthur Penn's films; the lines in a very real sense belong to him even if he didn't write them. One cannot always be acknowledging collaborators, but this doesn't imply unawareness or denigration of their contributions. [113]

---

[108] Sarris, 1968,31.

[109] André Bazin, 'La Politique des auteurs,' in THE NEW WAVE, ed. Peter Graham. London, Secker & Warburg, 1968, 153-154; Thomas Schatz, THE GENIUS OF THE SYSTEM London: Faber & Faber, 1996. It should be noted however that Schatz nonetheless acknowledged the guiding sensibilities provided by producer-authors.

[110] Andrew Sarris, 'Towards a Theory of Film History,' in Nichols, ed. Op.cit., 246-247. The article by was originally published in Film Culture No.27 (Winter 1962-1963) and is also reprinted in Gerald Mast, Marshall Cohen and Leo Braudy (eds.) FILM THEORY AND CRITICISM 4th edition. New York and London: Oxford University Press, 1992, 585-588. This Romantic notion – the filmmaker as artist – was influential to an unexpected degree, its legacy being regular lists of the 'Ten Best Films Ever Made' in magazines like Sight & Sound or the American Film Institute. Thus was the rationale laid for the Pantheon, differentiating the great from the merely good.

[111] Sarris, 1968, 30; 34. Sarris always wanted it both ways; as James Naremore states, "auteurism always had two faces. It mounted an invigorating attack on convention, but it also formed canons and fixed the names of people we should study." 'Authorship and the Cultural Politics of Film Criticism,' Film Quarterly Vol. 44, No. 1, 1990: 21.

[112] Robin Wood. HOWARD HAWKS. London: Secker & Warburg/BFI, 1968.

[113] Robin Wood. ARTHUR PENN. London: Movie Magazine, 1967, 40.

This is central both to grasping the academic perception of the screenwriter and the contradiction inherent in auteur study – the obfuscation of the screenwriter in his entirety – "*the lines in a very real sense belong to him even if he didn't write them.*" Yet Robert Towne's contribution to *Bonnie and Clyde* (1967) was key – as he admitted of his rewrite, "Remember the scene with the undertaker and Velma? You know? It's a terrific scene which was really right from the original script. That was probably the one scene that was never touched at all." [114] Thus the polemicism driving much auteurist-centred writing continued, despite the availability of the facts.

Peter Wollen formalised the decipherment of the director's identity by applying the tenets of structuralist or semiotic theory (as opposed to pure narratology or even psychoanalysis, which also fall under the rubric of structuralism as a discipline). He criticised Sarris for the over-formalising of the *Cahiers* critics' views because they had not emanated from a codified system or manifesto and thus did not represent a unified position. He also denied the purely autonomous value of the director and thereby auteurism's extraordinary potential for personality cults.

Wood may have been consciously opposed to Peter Wollen's modernism; however he was regularly referring to unconscious auteurism in his writings. A classic model of auteurist methodology is exemplified by his essay, 'To Have (Written) and Have Not (Directed).' [115] He examines stage by stage the adapting of Hemingway's, *TO HAVE AND HAVE NOT*, by William Faulkner and Jules Furthman; the studio and star vehicle format; the genre of Americans in exotic locales; and finally the outcome, the characteristic 'Hawksian' film. [116]

Provenance and Contributions

The term auteur can also be interpreted as a kind of trademark as well as insurance value. In other words, the name is a promise or guarantee of value or entertainment based on the filmmaker's previous activities and credits. On this basis, an auteur's work can be recognised by recurring themes, characters, setting and imagery. A director's creative personality could be revealed through the tensions displayed between form and content.

The auteurist approach promoted a hitherto unknown seriousness and analytical method in film studies; it developed a comparative methodology in which directors could be compared and their own works understood in relation to each other. This helped sort out and distinguish films long lumped together under studio banners; and helped bring attention to the accomplishments of many neglected directors and perhaps, most significantly, supported a new direction in film making, where directors had unprecedented control over their work. Its rationale is derived, states Sarris, "from the fact that the cinema could not be a completely personal art under even the best of conditions." [117] In terms of the industry, its undoubted appeal in the troubled era of the studio system in the late Sixties, lay in its possibilities for commodification and brand identity. For a director, the opportunity to claim genius for himself on an individual basis in a highly collaborative industry, was evidenced in the title of Joseph Gelmis's

---

[114] Speaking at the American Film Institute; transcript in the Louis B. Mayer Library, 22; 24.
[115] 'To Have (Written) and Have Not (Directed),' by Robin Wood; reprinted in Nichols, (ed.), 1982, 297-305.
[116] *Op.cit.*, 298.
[117] Sarris in Nichols, *Op.cit.,* 247.

tome, *THE FILM DIRECTOR AS SUPERSTAR*. [118] Sarris would constantly revise his work and claimed in 1998:

> Film history is always in the process of revision, and some of our earliest masters are still alive. *THE AMERICAN CINEMA* was a very tentative probe designed mainly to establish the existence of a subject worthy of study. The rest is refinement and elaboration. [119]

Bordwell, Staiger and Thompson in *CLASSICAL HOLLYWOOD CINEMA* manage to classify a hundred years or so into two types of end-product: standardisation and differentiation - a paradigm that contrives to ignore the possibility of individual contributions to works great or otherwise. [120] This is arguably one of the advantages to the legacy of auteurism as critical method – it categorises an otherwise unwieldy body of otherwise unrelated works; and it also works in complementary fashion to genre study, which, however, blurs any understanding of the conditions of production in similar critical fashion to the tenets of auteurism: Thomas Schatz decried it as "stalling film history and criticism in a prolonged state of adolescent romanticism because it denies the conditions in which films are actually made." [121]

The New Wave of Criticism

Peter Kramer writes of

> The fundamental reorientation of the American film industry in the late 1960s, which was further solidified by the explicit counter-cultural concerns of popular films such as EASY RIDER [and] led to a more sustained engagement with contemporary Hollywood by auteurist critics. [122]

Pauline Kael was one of the most influential American film critics from the mid-Sixties onwards; along with Sarris, Ferguson, Farber and Agee she is acknowledged as America's greatest. [123] Her style was occasionally contradictory, sentimental but always intense to the point of hyperbole. Her polemical attack on Sarris and auteurism, 'Circles

---

[118] London: Secker and Warburg, 1971.

[119] Andrew Sarris, 'Billy Wilder Reconsidered,' reprinted in Philip Lopate, (ed.) *AMERICAN MOVIE CRITICS: An Anthology From The Silents Until Now.* New York: Library of America, 2006, 307; originally published in Sarris, *YOU AIN'T HEARD NOTHIN' YET.* New York: Oxford University Press, 1998. Lopate comments that "Pauline Kael.... claimed that she never saw a movie more than once if she could help it. Her criteria were based more on parsing in tranquility her first-time visceral responses to the viewing experience. (She was aided by a phenomenal memory.) Andrew Sarris, in this way Kael's polar opposite, never stopped mulling over, re-viewing, and changing his mind about certain movies." Lopate. *Op.cit.*, xxii.

[120] David Bordwell, Janet Staiger and Kristin Thompson, *THE CLASSICAL HOLLYWOOD CINEMA Film Style and Mode of Production to 1960.* London: Routledge, 1994.

[121] Thomas Schatz. *THE GENIUS OF THE SYSTEM: HOLLYWOOD FILMMAKING IN THE STUDIO ERA.* New York: Pantheon, 1988, 5. A theoretical construct that also complicates our understanding of who actually writes a film is the assumption that the biological individual who has conceived of it is the same as the reader's construction of him. This is not merely a postmodern dilemma, for what writer - apart from Hemingway, probably - ever truly lived up to the image they created of themselves?!

[122] Peter Kramer, 'Post-classical Hollywood,' in Hill and Church Gibson, 1998, 299.

[123] Philip Lopate. *Op.cit.*, 109. In Sarris' terms we might christen them the Critics' Pantheon.

and Squares: Joys and Sarris,' was published in the wake of his promulgating of the auteur theory in the pages of *Film Quarterly,* the West Coast journal. She stated,

> When a famous director makes a good movie, we look at the movie, we don't think about the director's personality; when he makes a stinker we notice his familiar touches because there's not much else to watch. [124]

She took issue with Sarris's criteria for recognising an auteur since 'technical competence' was beyond question; 'distinguishable personality' was pointless since it just trivialised style in favour of finding endless repetition; while 'interior meaning' was entirely vague and was a reminder of the fact that the politique was essentially rooted in a kind of mysticism that was entirely detached from reality. She criticised the insistence upon continuity and wondered if it really took the auteur theory for Sarris to notice the repetition in those films directed by Raoul Walsh. Her withering critique left no stone unturned:

> What … makes the auteur critics so incomprehensible, is … their truly astonishing inability to exercise taste and judgment *within* their area of preference. [125]

And on that most problematic of its aspects, its ahistoricism, she declares:

> May I suggest that if, in order to judge movies, the auteur critics must wrench the directors from their historical environments (which is, to put it mildly, impossible) so that they can concentrate on the detection of that 'élan,' they are reducing aesthetics to a form of idiocy. Élan as the permanent attribute Sarris posits can only be explained in terms of a cult of personality. [126]

Sarris rejoined the debate, weakly, with 'The Auteur Theory and the Perils of Pauline.' [127] A collection of Kael's writings, *I LOST IT AT THE MOVIES*, was published in 1965 and become a best seller, the first of many. Unlike Sarris, who is basically a formalist, Kael focuses on content and had an eclectic take on her subjects. Her arrival at *The New Yorker* coincided with the emergence of the American New Wave whose efforts she trumpeted at every opportunity. Her review of *The Godfather* was also instrumental in its public reception.[128] Her basic opposition to Sarris derived from her opposition to formalism as a means of understanding cinema. [129]

---

[124] Pauline Kael, 'Circles and Squares,' as before, 298.

[125] Kael, 'Circles and Squares,' 297. V.F. Perkins says that "when the auteur was produced on the basis of recurrence, an observation about authors – that their works often display striking continuities and coherent development – was transformed into a test of authorship, a qualification for author-status. The material invoked as a demonstration of authorship sidled into use as a definition of authorship." 'Film Authorship: The Premature Burial,' *CineAction*, No. 21/22, Summer/Fall 1990: 58.

[126] Kael, 'Circles and Squares,' 301.

[127] Andrew Sarris, 'The Auteur Theory and the Perils of Pauline,' *Film Quarterly* 16, Summer 1963: 26-33.

[128] Robert Towne said of *The Godfather* in a panel programme discussing Kael following her death: "Her review of it was so extraordinary. It was something that found its way into the country and allowed the country to embrace it and, and have fun with it and also take it seriously. I, I think it really-- made a tremendous difference" Speaking on WNYC Radio, 01 December 2001. www.onthemedia.org/transcripts.

[129] Philip Lopate, in Lopate, 2006, 330. David Thomson christened her 'The Godmother' and said "her affinity with movie stars is a critical strength." Thomson, *OVEREXPOSURES: The*

Her essay in support of Herman Mankiewicz, as writer and producer of 'the greatest newspaper picture of them all,' 'Raising Kane,' is instrumental in the tide turning (albeit briefly) against auteur directors, whom she (typically) supported. "Orson Welles wasn't around when *Citizen Kane* was written, early in 1940," she claimed. She also stated, "a good movie is not always the result of a single artistic intelligence. It can be the result of a fortunate collaboration, of cross-fertilizing accidents." [130]

Kael's comments on *Kane* are refuted by Robert Carringer, when he states that Kael's portrait of Herman Mankiewicz is " … a flagrant misrepresentation." He continues:

> To summarize: Mankiewicz (with assistance from [John] Houseman and with input from Welles) wrote the first two drafts. His principal contributions were the story frame, a cast of characters, various individual scenes, and a good share of the dialogue … Welles added the narrative brilliance – the visual and verbal wit, the stylistic fluidity, and such stunningly original strokes as the newspaper montages and the breakfast table sequence. He also transformed Kane from a cardboard fictionalisation of Hearst into a figure of mystery and epic magnificence. *Citizen Kane* is the only major Welles film on which the writing credit is shared. Not coincidentally, it is also the Welles film that has the strongest story, the most fully realized characters, and the most carefully sculpted dialogue. Mankiewicz made the difference. While his efforts may seem plodding next to Welles' flashy touches of genius, they are of fundamental importance nonetheless. [131]

Kael's contradictory position gave her detractors much to discuss but her dedication to film criticism in essay form pushed the boundaries for much of the 1970s, itself an era in which film studies proliferated steadily in third level institutions and film reviewing influenced the industry itself; however, Sarris' legacy was in critical methodology and remains much discussed and revised (not least by Sarris himself) today. [132]

Crisis in American Filmmaking. New York: William Morrow & Co., 1981, 269.

[130] Pauline Kael, 'Raising Kane,' reprinted in THE CITIZEN KANE BOOK. Boston: Little, Brown, 1971, 23; 62.

[131] Carringer, 1996, 34-35. Perhaps it's best to leave the last word to Corliss, who says, "You could call CITIZEN KANE either the culmination of Herman Mankiewicz's dreams or the beginning of Orson Welles' nightmares; but it would be silly to ignore either man's contribution." Richard Corliss. *TALKING PICTURES: Screenwriters in the American Cinema*, Woodstock, New York: Overlook Press, 1975, xxviii. Perhaps paradoxically, her support of European-style auteurs such as Beatty, from *Bonnie and Clyde* onwards, when Kael wrote an enthusiastic 7,000 word defence of the film (promoting Newman and Benton rather than Towne's rewrite) that had such poor support from Warners, was such that Beatty eventually hired her to work with him in Hollywood, with perhaps predictably disastrous results. Peter Biskind portrays Beatty's move as a Machiavellian stroke to keep her from giving *Reds* a bad review while she was busy working with James Toback on a film Beatty was producing for him; meanwhile, Beatty went on location. Biskind. *EASY RIDERS RAGING BULLS*. New York, Simon & Schuster, 1998, 365-367.

[132] On the eventual silence of his idol, James Wolcott wrote in *Vanity Fair* that "movie criticism has become a cultural malady, a group case of chronic depression and low self esteem." Quoted by J. Hoberman, 'The Film Critic of Tomorrow, Today,' in Lopate, 2006, 531, from *Vanity Fair*, April 1997. Hoberman continues, "Reinforcing his point is the fact that the vehicle for his screed is a journal devoting an extraordinary amount of space to movies and movie stars without apparently feeling the need for regular film criticism." "

Kael's assessment of *Shampoo* in which she concludes that Robert Towne is 'a flaky classicist,' is a pertinent comment which has further ramifications for this particular text and will be commented upon where appropriate, in particular his reliance on plot, character and nuance derived from classical Hollywood films. [133]

The debate (or duel, as it has been described) between Sarris and Kael was very much of its time and place in the wake of the publication of James Agee's reviews in 1958: both Sarris and Kael served a specific kind of audience; foreign films were now regularly screened on university campuses and in dedicated cinemas of the type that Kael herself ran; extensive retrospective screenings of Hollywood films meant the enthusiastic film buff or scholar could indulge in multiple viewings (as Sarris did); both argued passionately for the films they loved, sometimes wholly irrationally. Haberski says that

> the debate between these two critics established the parameters of American movie criticism for at least the next two decades. [134]

Bordwell and Thompson argue that the term 'author' has three meanings: firstly as that of the production worker, the director whose role is to synthesise the technicality of the film process; secondly as personality, the Romantic (and auteurist/*Cahiers*) view in which a personal directing style is proof of the artist's worth; and finally as a "system of relations among several films bearing the same signature." The last view fits in with the *auteur*-structuralist readings of 'Ford' and 'Hawks' as opposed to John Ford, or Howard Hawks, film directors typified by the work of Peter Wollen in *SIGNS AND MEANINGS IN THE CINEMA*. [135] Andrew Sarris had attempted to stake out this territory for the director in pragmatic fashion:

> The director is both the least necessary and most important component of
> film-making. He is the most modern and most decadent of all artists in his
> relative passivity toward everything that passes before him. He would not be
> worth bothering with if he were not capable now and then of a sublimity of
> expression almost miraculously extracted from his money-oriented environment. [136]

---

[133] Pauline Kael, 'Beverly Hills as a Big Bed,' 17 February 1975, reprinted in *REELING: Film Writings 1972-1975*. New York and London: Marion Boyars, 1992, 442. Despite her general air of contempt for *Tequila Sunrise* (1988), she opened her review as follows: "Michelle Pfeiffer tells Mel Gibson how sorry she is that she hurt his feelings. He replies, "C'mon, it didn't hurt that bad," pauses, and adds, "Just lookin' at you hurts more." If a moviegoer didn't already know that *Tequila Sunrise* was the work of a master romantic tantalizer, Gibson's line should cinch it. That's the kind of ritualized confession of love that gave a picture like *To Have and Have Not* its place in moviegoers' affections. What makes the line go ping is that Mel Gibson's blue eyes are wide with yearning as he says it, and Michelle Pfeiffer is so crystalline in her beauty that he seems to be speaking the simple truth... It's a line that Gary Cooper might have spoken to Marlene Dietrich...." From Louis Menand's review of *FOR KEEPS* in *New York Review of Books*, Volume 42, No. 5, March 1995. Accessed online via www.nybooks.com/article/1959. Patrick McGilligan says Hawks "was not famous for giving much credit to screenwriters where it might otherwise reflect favourably upon himself." McGilligan, (ed.), *BACKSTORY 2: Interviews with Screenwriters of the 40s and 50s*. Berkeley: University of California Press, 1991, 383.

[134] Haberski, 2001, 124.
[135] Jim Kitses' *HORIZONS WEST* (1969) and Geoffrey Nowell-Smith's *VISCONTI* (1967) also fall into this category. David Bordwell and Kristin Thompson. *FILM ART: An Introduction*. New York: McGraw-Hill, 1997, 38-39.
[136] Sarris in Nichols, ed. *Op.cit.,* 251.

A test case for auteur theory is Wollen's examination of the work of director Howard Hawks. [137] Hawks worked in almost every genre: westerns, gangster films, war movies, thrillers, science fiction, musicals, comedies, and even historical epic. Wollen finds that these films exhibit the same thematic pre-occupations, the same recurring motifs and incidents, the same visual style and tempo. Wollen achieves this by reducing all these genres to two basic types: the adventure drama and the crazy comedy expressing inverse views of the world, the positive and negative poles of the Hawksian vision, what Wollen describes as 'structural antinomies'. For Hawks the highest human emotion is the camaraderie of the exclusive, self-sufficient male group. The group is often excluded from wider society. Hawks' heroes are cattle men, fishermen, racing-drivers, pilots, big game hunters, etc. The elite group strictly preserves its exclusivity: it is necessary to pass a test of ability and courage to win admittance. The members of the group pride themselves on their professionalism; the group's internal tensions come when one member lets the others down, and they must redeem themselves through some act of exceptional bravery. The films' overarching theme is masculinity and men versus women.[138] This digression is pertinent because elements of Hawks' themes regularly resonate in the work of Robert Towne. The argument towards author-structuralism was much in evidence in *Movie*. [139] Its rigour permitted its entry to the academy; but its flaws are perhaps its overriding concern with a film's internal organisation. Maltby and Craven find that

> What most differentiated auteur-structuralism from auteurist studies was not its
> mode of analysis so much as its project of detaching the common structural features
> of a body of movies 'signed' by the same name from the cult of personality
> encouraged by auteurism… [140]

Thus, while the focus shifted from that of homage, it remained ahistorical and disengaged from the complexities of industrial production; meanwhile trade and University presses began publishing monographs centering on directors.

---

[137] Peter Wollen, 'The Auteur Theory,' 1972, 74-115. Wollen would revise his work in this edition, rendering much of his scholarship problematic: he tempers his views in the afterword, in which he debates the value of seeking a singular vision from a solo artist operating in this medium but claims the validity of the artist's name as a heading under which to investigate contesting ideas within the oeuvre, while explicitly stating that a universal model for understanding structural commonalities does not exist. His work in aligning film with the structural study of myth undoubtedly enriched scholarship in the area. Wollen's concept of structural antinomies is utilised to some extent by Robert Arnett in that part of his doctoral thesis which refers to Towne: he divides Towne's protagonists into two groups, the Hero in Their World and the Hero in Another World. *A SEPARATE CINEMA: The Screenplays of Robert Towne, Richard Price and Quentin Tarantino.* University of Southern Mississippi PhD 1997: 57-138 (Proquest Dissertation Service).

[138] Hawks is also of course a subject of an eponymous study by arch auteurist Robin Wood, in which he states, "Hawks is ultimately unanalyzable." *HOWARD HAWKS.* London: Secker and Warburg, 1968, 10. Wood's work is essential auteurism, outlining the films directed and sometimes co-written by Hawks thematically, without any attention paid to the industrial components of their production. It is an archetypal work. Wood was unimpressed by Wollen and eventually issued a rejoinder to what he saw as unnecessary and decontextualised simplifications in 'Hawks De-Wollenized.' See Wood, 2006.

[139] See Appendix 2.

[140] Maltby and Craven. *Op.cit.*, 423.

In 1971 TV producer William Froug published a collection of interviews with some of the era's outstanding writers, including such veterans as Nunnally Johnson, Stirling Silliphant and Walter Brown Newman, as well as younger writers like David Giler and Lewis John Carlino. It would pave the way for Corliss's later work, and, the interviewer, Froug himself, demonstrated that unlike his successor, he actually read the screenplays. In his introduction to the text he quotes a letter from Writers' Guild President Ranald McDougall circulated among members in 1970 in which he writes

> The highly questionable "auteur concept," whereby films are never written,
> merely directed, is an approach to the art of films that genuine authors
> have had to endure from esoteric and dilettante sources for many years.
> We are not inclined, however to support such an amateurish approach. [141]

Froug echoes the many histories and anecdotes emergent since silent cinema, arguing for the centrality not merely of the screenwriter but also that of the producer and the studio heads, whom he describes as "those ultimate American 'auteurs'." He makes the case that "the history of American cinema is diametrically opposed to the auteur concept. The director was often brought to the production long after the conceptual work had been done. His job was to interpret the work of the writer, just as the actor's job was to interpret the role, the character, that the writer had conceived." [142]

In Winter 1970-1971 Richard Corliss' essay, 'The Hollywood Screenwriter,' appeared in a special issue of *Film Comment* dedicated to the screenwriter and in it he states that "the director is almost always an interpretive artist, not a creative one, and … the Hollywood film is a corporate art, not an individual one." He cautions that "the cry 'cherchez l'auteur' can lead unwary film scholars astray – or rather, when the script is the basis for a film's success. More often than not, when a fine film is signed by a mediocre director, the film's distinctive qualities can be traced to the screenwriter." He adds that, "the size of a screenwriter's contribution to any given film is often far more difficult to ascertain." He supplies his own 'Acropolis' of screenwriters, placing Sidney Buchman on the Parthenon with Charles Bracket gracing the Pandroseion. [143]

Corliss' 1972 book, *THE HOLLYWOOD SCREENWRITERS,* repeats his call for a 'politique des collaborateurs': his argument originates in his claims for the significance of the contributions made by screenwriters to films directed by John Ford. This orchestral model is probably the most significant critical framework for an understanding of the screenwriter's role to arise in this era. [144] Corliss also points out that far from stylistic consistency being the hallmark of an auteur, "the hallmark of many fine screenwriters is versatility, not consistency. Subject matter dictates style." [145] Corliss claims that as with the study of directors' work, so it is with screenwriters:

---

[141] Ranald McDougall quoted by William Froug. *Op.cit.,* Introduction, xiii.

[142] Froug, 1970, xviii. He adds, "Screenwriters today are involved in film as they have never been before. (Perhaps in a perverse way, they have the auteur theory to thank for that.)" (xxi.)

[143] Corliss, 'The Hollywood Screenwriter,' *Film Comment*, Winter 1970-71: 4; 5; 7.

[144] Corliss. *THE HOLLYWOOD SCREENWRITER.* New York: Avon, 1972. Bruce Kawin says that, "in film terms the composer is often the writer, the conductor is often the director and the orchestra is a vast array of professionals, from actors to lab technicians." Kawin, *HOW MOVIES WORK.* Berkeley: University of California Press, 1987, 281.

[145] Corliss, 'The Hollywood Screenwriter,' as before: 6.

a screenwriter's work should and can be judged by analysing his entire career, as is done with a director. If a writer has been associated with a number of favorite films, if he has received sole writing credit on some of these films, and if we can decipher a common style in films with different directors and actors, an authorial personality begins to appear. [146]

He advises that there are also several layers of screenwriting authorship:

… the indifferent work of a mediocre writer, whether it's an original script or an adaptation (which we may call procrustean); the gem-polishing of a gifted adapter … (protean); and the creation of a superior original script, like Herman J. Mankiewicz's *Citizen Kane* or Abraham Polonsky's *Body and Soul* (promethean)… At worst, this research will exhaust and discourage the critic; at best, it will convince him that the creation of a Hollywood movie involves a complex weave of talents, properties, and personalities. [147]

These quotations reveal Corliss' own contribution to the debate not merely over the attribution of cinematic personality but screen credits and the revelation of a worldview; however Corliss doesn't seek to analyse the complex theme of the author, rather a signature personality – and, crucially, he doesn't appear to have read the screenplays.

His 1975 book, *TALKING PICTURES*, sought to replace the notion of the director as auteur and Sarris, his former lecturer, provides the Preface. [148]   In this 'revisionist enterprise of enthroning screenwriters where once not so long ago only directors reigned,' Sarris addresses the shortcomings of the 'movement' which he had unwittingly spawned and urges caution, while mooting the value of some of the preoccupations of the critics:

How can anyone say *a priori* that any director is automatically the author of the film for which he is credited as a director? [149]

The preoccupation with 'style', or mise-en-scène, is simultaneously the key and the lock in which the arguments are routed:

We seem to be fencing around with the roles of the director and screenwriter in that I would grant the screenwriter most of the dividends accruing from dialogue, and Corliss would grant the director the interpretive insights of a musical conductor. Where we grapple most desperately and most blindly is in that no man's land of narrative and dramatic structure. And here I think the balance of power between the director and the screenwriter is too variable for any generalization. [150]

---

[146] *Ibid.*

[147] *Ibid.*

[148]   Corliss, also states in that issue, "The director need not be the only dominant force in a successful film. Often the actor is the *auteur*. Keaton and Chaplin may be fine actors, but it is their screen personalities that we especially cherish. Who would trade Keaton the actor for Keaton the director? … The unique cinema personae of W.C. Fields, Mae West and Laurel and Hardy also flourished with little regard to the director of record, and can be defined without much reference to him – although, quite naturally, the combination of the comedians with different scripts and directors produced varying results. The same can be said of such incandescent performers such as Greta Garbo, Katharine Hepburn and Cary Grant. Richard Corliss, 'The Hollywood Screenwriter,' *as before*: 5.

[149] Sarris's Preface in Corliss, 1975, xii; xiii.

Corliss's own 'Introduction: Notes on a Screenwriter's Theory, 1973,' in the same volume, lucidly dispatches Sarris' derogatory vision of the 'dialogue' provider (as he assumes the screenwriter to be) but grants that, "Sarris examined films as the creations of artists rather than social forces" – and reminds us that in the silent era and even later, critics ascribed 'responsibility' for a film to the director. He credits Sarris with the beginnings of 'a systematic expansion of American film history'; but this instead gave rise to an industry in biography and memoirs – and rarely did these include screenwriters'. Sarris' core problem, in Corliss' view, is perhaps that he believes strong directors are channelling some kind of higher power when they direct – hence the mystical nuances of auteurism (perhaps a legacy of the French writings):

> One restraint on the poetic tendencies of a screenwriter-oriented critic, as opposed to that of an auteurist, is that the screenwriter *makes* words and situations occur, while the director *allows* actions to occur. Thus, the process of creating a screenplay is more formal, less mystical than the image, which is created by the director, photographer, designer, and actors. [151]

He takes issue with this kind of criticism on the grounds that

> … if auteur criticism had lived up to its early claim to be truly concerned with visual style, there would be no need for any systematic slighting of the screenwriter. Given a certain text, or pretext, the director could be said to weave the writer's design into a personal, visual subtext through the use of camera placement and movement, lighting, cutting, direction of actors, etc…
> But visual style is not the auteurist's major interest. Auteur criticism is essentially theme criticism; and themes – as expressed through plot, characterization, and dialogue – belong primarily to the writer. [152]

Perhaps the problem, then, with using Sarris as the introductory essayist is that what follows seems like cavil – the screenwriter doth protest too much: at this point, Sarris, himself much given to revisionism, appears to be the very voice of reason. Years later he would lament

> I have tried to give screenwriters their due whenever I could in good conscience, but as a tribe they still loathe me for allegedly demeaning their role in cinematic creation even more than the studio satraps had done in the past. [153]

Ultimately, Philip Lopate makes the claim for him that Corliss "provided an indispensable corrective emphasis." [154]

Maltby and Craven state:

> Debates about authorship evaporated in the 1970s, more because poststructuralist criticism bypassed them than because the idea of directorial authorship was recognized as being an historically inaccurate account of Hollywood production…
> Nevertheless, the great majority of academic criticism continues to be written as if the director could be named as the author of the text… [155]

---

[150] Sarris' Preface in Corliss. *Op. cit.*, xv.

[151] Corliss, 'Introduction: Notes on a Screenwriter's Theory, 1973,' in Corliss, 1975, xx.

[152] Corliss, 1975, xxi-xxii.

[153] Sarris, 'Notes of an Accidental Auteurist,' *Film History*, Vol. 7, 1995: 360.

[154] Lopate, 2006, 485.

[155] Maltby and Craven. *Op.cit.*, 436.

While the decentering position adopted in poststructuralist debate can offer no direct impact on this particular study, there is no doubt that it contributed to the expansion of the debate about authorship, as its consideration of the text's reader would prove.

However, the golden age of what came to be called the New Hollywood would be crowned with a number of books, amongst them the contemporary (1977) publication of Diane Jacobs' *HOLLYWOOD RENAISSANCE* whose subtitle, *The New Generation of Filmmakers and Their Works* indicates the distinctive manner in which these directors were embraced as being essentially different than their predecessors. She finds that,

> What distinguishes certain films of the Seventies is neither artistic superiority nor administrative autonomy – but a happy combination of the two, a fusion of ability, accessibility, and yes, inspiration, at a fortuitous juncture in time. [156]

Jacobs writes impressively about seven directors but mentions a number of contemporary screenwriters in her introduction, amongst whom she declares,

> I find Robert Towne most impressive, portraying an intuitive sense of character and the ability to insinuate affecting relationships into exceptionally cogent scripts… [157]

The New Hollywood

By 1975 the modern phase had produced a substantial body of work by a group of high-profile directors, which Thomas Elsaesser referred to as "the new Hollywood of Altman, Pollack, Boorman, of Rafelson, Hellman, Spielberg or Ashby". If classical Hollywood cinema had 'a fundamentally affirmative attitude to the world it depicts', key films of the Seventies expressed a 'liberal outlook' which led them to 'reject affirmation' and instead reflected 'a radical scepticism … about the American virtues of ambition, vision, drive' and personified in actors 'attempting to create an objective realism.' He says that the virtues of the Seventies cinema he writes about are 'its down-to-earth realism, its unostentatious detachment'. [158] Towne himself would characterise this

---

[156] Diane Jacobs. *HOLLYWOOD RENAISSANCE: The New Generation of Filmmakers and Their Works*. New York: Delta Books, 1977 and 1980, 6.

[157] Jacobs. *Op.cit..*, 7. Jacobs is hinting at what has become a truism – that while the Seventies may well have been a Golden Age of filmmaking, it was also a Golden Age for Screenwriters, Towne not least among an impressive list that might include Paul Schrader, Robert Getchell, Nancy Dowd, Bo Goldman, Elaine May, Alvin Sargent, Neil Simon, William Goldman and Paul Mazursky. And of course most of those mentioned directed their own material, at one time or another.

[158] Thomas Elsaesser, 'The Pathos of Failure. American Films in the 70s: Notes on the Unmotivated Hero,' *Monogram*, 6, 1975: 13-19. An alternative approach to auteurism focussing on the professional-managerial class strategy is demonstrated by Derek Nystrom in 'Hard Hats and Movie Brats: Auteurism and the Class Politics of the New Hollywood,' *Cinema Journal* 43, No. 3, Spring 2004: 18-41. Nystrom writes that "the rise of the New Hollywood auteurs was accomplished through the weakening of organized labor's power within the film industry. By forcing changes in work rules, by challenging the film unions' bargaining power by encouraging the participation of rival unions, or by avoiding unionised labor altogether, New Hollywood filmmakers tipped the industry's professional and managerial interests. Auteurism was more often than not the legitimating discourse for this class practice." (21.)

regrettable scission with the past and the contemporary difficulties posed for screenwriters as the lack of shared beliefs:

> They give us substance and structure, allow us to interpret and make sense of experience, tell us how we should and shouldn't behave, help us find significance in our lives.[159]

It was the disintegrating of shared beliefs which nourished the background to Towne writing his most acclaimed work in the Seventies in screenplays (*Chinatown*, *Shampoo*) that questioned the possibility of believing in anything in America at that time. The 'New Hollywood' was enshrined in debate as those films produced after 1967 which expressed the kind of liberal values to which Elsaesser refers.[160] Classical Hollywood became not merely the older style of production to 1960, and encompassed in the films released in the Bazinian-styled turning point year of 1939, it sometimes encompassed more recent films as the notion of a classical text became pervasive.[161] Towne's screenplays, while classic in form, rarely have a happy ending and never end in marriage.

Meanwhile, the industrial format itself appeared to have shifted with the success of blockbusters such as *Jaws* (1975) but in reality these special effects films were a component of Hollywood since *Airport* (1970) and what had actually happened was a new approach to distribution. It coincided with a change in audiences as well as a generational change in filmmakers. The authorial mode provides a means of interpreting these complex developments in a more succinct fashion than they perhaps deserve but the period 1967 through 1975 expresses a particular phase in Towne's career, which this periodic definition fits.[162] David A. Cook makes the valid point that in this era, auteurism provided (once again) not just a critical shorthand for audiences but a marketing tool exploited by studios.[163] Screenwriting manuals such as Syd Field's *SCREENPLAY* (1979) were now becoming part of the script developer's toolbox as Story Departments grew in size at the major studios; and structure, as Ken Dancyger points out, "has dominated thinking and writing about script for the past twenty years."[164]

---

[159] Towne, 'On Moving Pictures,' *CHINATOWN/THE LAST DETAIL*. New York: Grove Press, 1997, xii.

[160] John Orr describes CHINATOWN'S 'political helplessness', pointing out the screenplay's "close attention to the politics of LA corruption over that precious commodity of a desert city, the water-supply." *CONTEMPORARY CINEMA*. Edinburgh: Edinburgh University Press, 1998, 172.

[161] Bordwell, Staiger, and Thompson, acknowledge that the choice of 1960 is fairly arbitrary and that in fact classical practice did not cease there. *THE CLASSICAL HOLLYWOOD CINEMA: Film Style and Mode of Production to 1960*. London: Routledge, 1994.

[162] See Michael Pye and Lynda Myles. *THE MOVIE BRATS: How the Film Generation Took Over Hollywood*. New York: Holt, Rinehart & Winston, 1979. Also Robert Philip Kolker, *A CINEMA OF LONELINESS: Penn, Kubrick, Coppola, Scorsese, Altman*. New York: Oxford University Press, 1980.

[163] David A. Cook, 'Auteur Cinema and the "Film Generation" in 1970s Hollywood,' in Jon Lewis (ed.). *THE NEW AMERICAN CINEMA*. Durham & London: Duke University Press, 1998, 35.

[164] Syd Field. *SCREENPLAY The Foundations of Screenwriting: A Step-by-Step Guide from Concept to Finished Script* (3rd ed.). New York: Dell Publishing, 1994; Ken Dancyger. *GLOBAL SCRIPTWRITING*. Boston, Mass: Focal Press, 2001, 43. By the mid-Nineties, four story structure 'gurus' dominated the marketplace in screenwriting manuals and classes which were being exported to Europe, Africa and South America. The gurus named are Syd Field, Robert

John Caughie's 1981 collection, *THEORIES OF AUTHORSHIP,* was published when film history was going through a period of review, if not de-legitimisation. The collection summarises the evolution of the various currents in the authorship debate and reprints several of the key arguments in the three phases of auteur theory (auteurism, auteur-structuralism and fiction of the author/author of the fiction.) Caughie points out in his Introduction that,

> Auteurism was at its most productive in its contradictions, and the systematic and rigorous attempt to confront them marks a shift out of auteurism as a critical policy towards work on a theory of authorship.[165]

Maltby and Craven comment on the contemporary debate:

> By the 1980s, authorship in Hollywood had become a commercially beneficial fiction, indicated by the opening credits of movies that declared themselves to be 'a Taylor Hackford film' or 'a Robert Zemeckis film.' But the multiple logics and intentions that continue to impinge on the process of production ensure that authorship remains an inadequate explanation of how movies work. [166]

By now, David Thomson could observe, "with the breakdown of the studio system, and the need to set up every movie individually, the script becomes a far more dynamic, external instrument." [167]

In 1984 William Miller asked these questions: "What is the screenwriter's place in the authorship of the film? What can we learn about narrative from the way the screenwriter constructs it? What factors in the writer's narrative story affect audience/spectator responses? What are important narrative figures? How can we experiment with narrative?" [168] Little scholarship since then addresses these important issues but some at least has attempted to deal with the first part of his quest and the journal appeared to spawn a wave of analyses in its wake. Tom Stempel's 1988 publication, the aforementioned *FRAMEWORK,* following his 1980 study of Nunnally

---

McKee, John Truby and Linda Seger. See Todd Coleman's 'The Story Structure Gurus,' *Journal of Writers' Guild of America (West),* June 1995, Vol. 8, No.6: 14-21. Playwright Mark Ravenhill lamented the curse of Robert McKee and the cult of Story, which he claims, "…could only have come out of America, birthplace of Fordism… It was only a matter of time before the same principles were applied to Hollywood films. By the 1980s, the studios had created a blueprint for the perfect film, a tool by which any script could be analysed and 'improved'." 'Arts Comment,' *The Guardian,* Film and Music, 25 June 2007: 32.

[165] John Caughie (ed.). *THEORIES OF AUTHORSHIP: A READER.* London: Routledge & Kegan Paul and British Film Institute, 1981, 14. Caughie continues that auteurism "… has become the tradition, producing evaluations and interpretations which are frequently impressively and seductively perceptive, but which very seldom throw into question, in any rigorous way, the premises on which the cinema depends." (15.) The point about film history is made in a number of volumes, including the editors of *REINVENTING FILM STUDIES.* Christine Gledhill and Linda Williams, eds. London: Hodder Arnold, 2000, 97.

[166] Malby and Craven. *Op.cit.,* 33.

[167] Thomson, 1981, 74. Thomson is perhaps suggesting the concomitant rise in value of the screenplay which would now see itself part of a burgeoning speculation market. See Thom Taylor. *THE BIG DEAL: Hollywood's Million Dollar Spec Script Market.* New York: William Morrow and Co., Inc., 1999.

[168] William Miller (ed.), Screenwriting [special issue], *Journal of Film and Video,* Summer 1984, Vol. 36, No.3.

Johnson, echoed Froug's earlier work in the quest to replace the ahistorical nature of auteur director-driven film histories with a book which examines the process of screenwriting in American cinema to also include the role of producers. Part of what might be termed the volume's recuperative strategy is to clarify why the apparent decline in the quality of the Hollywood film coincided with the shift in power to directors. Its major contribution to film history is the author's conscientious selection, reading and interpretation of screenplays from early cinema to the present. [169]

In a round-table discussion focussing on the *auteur* theory at *Cahiers du Cinéma*, 'Twenty Years On', Jean-Louis Comolli says,

> The concept of the 'auteur' as argued by *Cahiers* was at first, I think, fairly close to that of the writer or painter: a man who controls his work in accordance with his own wishes and is himself totally immersed in it … A confusion arose between the concept of *auteur* and the concept of theme: you only had to identify certain constants, a particular obsession in a film-maker, for him to be labelled an '*auteur*' – which is fair enough – and for him to be considered great – which is in most cases not justified… To put it in a nutshell, every great *auteur* had a thematic, every film-maker you decided to call a great *auteur* had a thematic, and the slightest trace of a thematic meant that the *oeuvre* fell within the *politique des auteurs*. [170]

Comolli's statement encapsulates the dilemma that had befallen film appreciation in the previous 30 years. *Cineaction*'s Summer/Fall 1990 issue was a special double issue dedicated to 'Rethinking Authorship,' because, as its editors claimed,

> the author is not isolated from a social and political context and a work is never wholly attributable to the artist's individual genius… as obvious as this now seems, the Barthesian notion that the 'author is written' in all its manifestations is, today, untenable and in need of revision…Aside from discussions of style, the term implies that people are responsible for the works they create…
> The complexities of collaborative authorship have yet to be investigated. Clearly stars, script-writers, cinematographers etc. significantly contribute to and inform the work of art, and can, at times, subvert an intended project. [171]

On the reprinting of his 1971 publication *THE SCREENWRITER LOOKS AT THE SCREENWRITER*, William Froug stated hopefully of its original edition, "perhaps in a small way it contributed to the demise of the simple-minded auteur theory it attacked." [172] This invaluable collection, which in a sense McGilligan's 1990s interview series continues, was itself followed by a collection of interviews with contemporary screenwriters in *THE NEW SCREENWRITER LOOKS AT THE NEW SCREENWRITER*. [173]

[169] Tom Stempel, 1988; rept, 1991, xi.
[170] Jean-Louis Comolli, 'Twenty Years On,' in *CAHIERS DU CINÈMA Volume 2, 1960-1968: New Wave, New Cinema, Re-evaluating Hollywood.* Jim Hillier (ed.) London: Routledge & Kegan Paul, 1986, 197-199.
[171] Florence Jacobowitz and Richard Lippe, 'Rethinking Authorship,' editors, *Cineaction*, No. 21/22, Summer/Fall 1990: 2.

[172] William Froug, 1970; rept., 1990, x.
[173] Froug. *THE NEW SCREENWRITER LOOKS AT THE NEW SCREENWRITER.* Los Angeles: Silman-James Press, 1991.

Six years on, in another Special Issue on Screenwriting, *Journal of Film and Video* guest editors Ken Dancyger and Jeff Rush could comment on the fact that

> The proliferation of screenwriting books and courses has fully fleshed out the form and conventional structure of mainstream narrative films…something still seems to be missing. Working within commercially defined forms, writers appear to have lost the ability to bring any deviation to the screen. Polished, but uninspired, lacking anything of the writer's own self, most screenplays read the same. [174]

While postmodernism and its destabilising play on differences which dominated scholarly debate in this era has not directly offered us a practical means by which to understand the screenwriter's contribution to cinema, it has created an environment in which alternative approaches to authorship have emerged in order to understand a proliferation of texts and meanings.

We move then to the potential application of this study and what it ultimately suggests: the opening up of the concept of authorship to a form of rhetoric which might be likened to the multiple or orchestral model, as suggested by Corliss and explored by Jack Stillinger in relation to literature. Stillinger offers the proviso that "… the authorship of films is so complicated and diffuse as to be for all practical purposes, unassignable." He asks, "whether 'pure' authorship is possible under any circumstances – single authorship without any influence, intervention, alteration, or distortion whatsoever by someone other than the nominal author." [175] This is a concept considered by Philip Dunne to be an accurate description of the screenwriter's working situation in his memoir. [176] Any pragmatic approach must engage with the nature of the generic, economic and collaborative determinants that are involved in contemporary film production. Joe Eszterhas says of his work on *Betrayed* (1988),

> I didn't view the script as a collaborative process. I viewed it as my creation. The rest of the movie was a collaboration between the director and the actors and the editor and some of the technicians.
> I viewed myself as the composer. The director was the conductor. The others were part of the orchestra.[177]

Likewise, Harold Love's study on authorship attribution provides some new parameters in which the literary study might be posed. Although he concludes that "attribution studies is probably wise not to pursue it [individuality] too intently but to be content with the lesser achievement of cataloguing the derivatives that mark particular individualities." [178]

In a situation such as that readily exemplified by a cinematic auteur like Robert Towne, where a consistency of vision, theme and character might be extrapolated from a

---

[174] *Journal of Film and Video,* Vol.42, No. 3, Fall 1990: 3. The issue encompassed a range of articles mostly outside the parameters of commercial film ("going beyond the conventions of the mainstream"), examining the influence of journalism and pictorial art on films; the writing of the short film; the non-verbal; and resources for the screenwriting teacher.

[175] Jack Stillinger. *Op.cit.,* 183.
[176] Philip Dunne. *TAKE TWO: A Life in Movies and Politics.* New York: Limelight Editions, 1992.
[177] Joe Eszterhas. *Op.cit.,* 34.

[178] Harold Love. *Op.cit.,* 227.

large body of work, an approach in which a lead or principal author can be considered amongst a large number of contributors, a concept well explored elsewhere in Robert Carringer's study of *Strangers on a Train* (1951). [179]

In his essay, 'The Film Critic of Tomorrow, Today,' J. Hoberman, the former auteurist/formalist colleague of Andrew Sarris at *The Village Voice*, engages with Arnheim's statement that "the work of a critic ... must [instead] deal with everyday production, which can only be subjected to aesthetic criticism when a production falls into the realm of aesthetics in principle; that is, when it has the possibility of creating works of art." Hoberman sides with Arnheim and claims Godard as the greatest contemporary critic, sidelining the daily and weekly reviewers for a filmmaker who himself has latterly turned the agency of directing to a colleague. [180] Hoberman might be said to be a prime example of the postmodern, decentered film critic, keen to adopt current ideological positions yet ironically returning to the kind of content-based work that essentialist auteurism sought to replace, yet facing the same tangled web of authorship attribution – however acknowledging the screenwriter as originary source.

Far from being an outmoded concept, in 2003 alone two volumes on authorship were published which provided a timely update of John Caughie's seminal 1981 book and foregrounded new scholarship in the area: Virginia Wright Wexman edited *FILM AND AUTHORSHIP*; while David A. Gerstner and Janet Staiger edited *AUTHORSHIP AND FILM: Trafficking with Hollywood*. [181] Gerstner reminds us that the project of authorship (a Western, Judaeo-Christian obligation) "is always a way of looking at films, and obviously other ways exist as do other questions." [182] Gerstner and Staiger rationalise their use of the concept of authorship as an enabling tool, arguing that the author is demonstrably not dead; and they claim that the idea of authorship has functions for what they call social action (in that it allows for a focus on identity, be it of race, gender, and so forth.) In other words, authorship is now linked with ideas of identity – film, marketplace, culture, society - in order to suggest ways forward for its role within the academy. [183]

Virginia Wright Wexman's collection, a volume which recaps the theories anthologised and acknowledges its indebtedness to Caughie, offers some thoughts on the under-representation of certain areas at the time: the relationship between authors and institutions; an historical account of authorship; and the way authorship functions in both avant garde and documentary film-making. [184]

---

[179] Robert L. Carringer, 'Collaboration and Concepts of Authorship,' in *PMLA*, March 2002 (116, 2),370.

[180] J. Hoberman, 'The Film Critic of Tomorrow, Today,' in Lopate, *op.cit.*, 536-537. Originally published in Maurice Berger (ed.) *THE CRISIS IN CRITICISM*. New York: New Press, 1998.

[181] *FILM AND AUTHORSHIP*, as before; *AUTHORSHIP AND FILM*, as before.

[182] David A. Gerstner, 'Approaches to Authorship,' in Gerstner and Staiger. *Op.cit.*, 28.

[183] Staiger's own essay in the volume elaborates on authorship in terms of 7 potential critical strategies.The list provides a useful checklist by which to survey the achievements within the history of writing on authorship, bearing in mind of course that they are originally intended as measures by which to exemplify the director's contribution. *Op.cit.*

[184] Wexman's volume spans approaches including post-structuralism, feminism, queer theory, postcolonialism, and cultural studies divided into three major sections: Theoretical Statements, Historical and Institutional Contexts, and Case Studies. It should be noted that a number of cogent theories emerged during this period which demonstrate the importance of postmodernist

It is now appropriate to consider structural and conceptual issues in authorship.

The Screenwriter as Auteur

In Spring 2006 another herald for the screenwriter arrived in the form of critic David Kipen's *THE SCHREIBER THEORY: A Radical Rewrite of American Film History*, a slim volume (or manifesto, as the author has it) which seeks to dispel the pernicious tyranny of what came to be known as the auteur theory but in reality merely succinctly replays the arguments in favour of the screenwriter, albeit in compellingly quotable and untheoretical form which appealed to op-ed writers in American newspapers. However Kipen has the grace to disavow any major scholarly potential in the book, stating,

> *Schreiberism* is, among other things, an attempt to rescue reviewing and scholarship from those who would have us forget just how collaborative filmmaking truly is. If the idea of finding recurrent patterns and themes in anyone but a director's work seems heretical today, chalk it up to auteurism's fifty-year head start. [185]

So while not claiming to stake out new ground, he merely reiterates what several scholars have omitted to mention: the centrality of the screenplay to successful filmmaking in Hollywood. Preston Sturges commented on the sheer number of screenwriters assigned to any single project:

> Four writers were considered the rock-bottom minimum required. Six writers, with the sixth member to puff up the lighter parts, was considered ideal. Many, many more writers have been used on a picture, of course; several writers have even been assigned the same story unbeknownst to each other. The Screen Writers Guild of the day had even worked out some rather shameful rules governing the conduct and approach of one writer toward another when he has secretly been given the other's job: he was not in honor bound to volunteer any information, but if asked directly, he must not deny the sad truth. [186]

However as Fine surmises of Sturges' own attempt to direct as a bid for control, directors and producers resented the move to alter the status quo, while "some veteran screenwriters grouched that jobs would disappear if only one writer worked on each script." [187]

Story and Plot

Cohan and Swires say that

> … a story orders events temporally (ie in relations of succession or concurrence) and logically (ie in relations of comparability or causality). [188]

---

thought on the subject of cinematic authorship, however all are dedicated to the enshrining of the director as the centre of a film's meaning. Wright Wexman (ed.), **2003**.

[185] Kipen. *Op.cit.,* 167; 169.

[186] Preston Sturges, 'The Wrong Racket,' excerpted from *PRESTON STURGES BY PRESTON STURGES* (1990) in Sylvester, 158.

[187] Richard Fine. *WEST OF EDEN: Writers in Hollywood 1928-1940*. Washington and London: Smithsonian Institute Press, 1993. 144.

According to Monroe Beardsley, a story is "not merely a sequence of events, but a sequence that has some continuity, because each stage grows out of previous stages and leads with naturalness to the future." [189] In terms of Hollywood, Bordwell, Staiger and Thompson state that "classical films are especially likely to bare the central principle of causal linearity." [190] They define the classical Hollywood narrative in terms of

> ... grasping how a classical film unifies itself... this unity is a matter of motivation. Motivation is the process by which a narrative justifies its story material and the plot's presentation of that story material. [191]

The ordering (or reordering) of story elements amounts to a narrative syntax around certain points which Ricoeur refers to as 'emplotment.' Referring to the interaction between story, event and emplotment, Paul Ricoeur writes that

> ... an event must be more than just a singular occurrence. It gets its definition from its contribution to the development of the plot. A story, too, must be more than just an enumeration of events in serial order; it must organise them into an intelligible whole, of a sort such that we can always ask what is the 'thought' of this story. In short, emplotment is the operation that draws a configuration out of a simple succession. [192]

Emplotment is not limited to events, it is also a process through which a kind of identity is constructed.

> There is . . . not just an emplotment of actions; there is also an emplotment of characters. And an emplotted character is someone seeking his or her or its identity. [193]

David Bordwell identifies the basic story structure as:

> ... an undisturbed stage, the disturbance, the struggle, and the elimination of the disturbance. [194]

We might then suggest that the term 'structure' be applied to the narrative configuration of emplotment; and that the rhetoric of dramatic structure could be denoted as described: action (story or plot); character; dialogue; genre; location; theme; tone (point of view) and visuals. This, then, is the foundation of the identity of the screenplay.

---

[188] Steve Cohan and Linda M. Shires. *TELLING STORIES: A Theoretical Analysis of Narrative Fiction.* New York & London: Routledge, 1988. 58.

[189] Monroe C. Beardsley. *AESTHETICS: Problems in the Philosophy of Criticism.* New York: Harcourt, Brace and World, Inc., 1958, 249-250.

[190] Bordwell, Staiger and Thompson. *Op.cit.*, 22.

[191] Bordwell, Staiger and Thompson. *Op.cit.*, 18.

[192] Paul Ricoeur. *TIME AND NARRATIVE Volume 1.* Chicago: University of Chicago Press, 1990, 65.

[193] Paul Ricoeur and David Pellauer. *FIGURING THE SACRED: Religion, Narrative and the Imagination.* Minneapolis: Augsburg Fortress, 1995, 309.

[194] David Bordwell. *NARRATION IN THE FICTION FILM.* Madison: University of Wisconsin Press, 1985, 157.

According to Bordwell, linear development in classical Hollywood structure is complicated by plot being split into two lines of action, the one dominated by heterosexual romance; the other to do with work or an occupation that takes place in the public sphere. [195] Genre deploys oppositional elements (contrasts) in the narrative, which encourages analysis of a structuralist nature. [196]

Writer turned director Philip Dunne claims, perhaps rather contentiously, in his memoir,

> The director may contribute visual and technical style, but the essential style of any picture is in the delineation of character, in the building of conflict and drama, in what stimulates the viewer's mind, not his eyes, and that is the contribution of the writer. [197]

It is to the possibility of a theoretical matrix of the writer's contribution that this chapter now turns, utilising the elements of dramatic writing as a basis for understanding the screenwriter's signature.

Methodology: Screenplay Structure

To discover the bedrock of Robert Towne's identity as a screenwriting author it is necessary (where possible) to delineate his distinctive approach to each of these aspects of screenplay structure. However "structural methods ... offer no motive for the existence of stories in general or of any particular story"; therefore, we should also acknowledge Towne's own debt to classical Hollywood. [198] Not only does he employ the three act structure with its system of beginning, middle and ending (and in that order); rising action, scene sequences and various turning points; his work provides a direct link to some of classical cinema's greatest artistes, to the extent that he has paid (ironic?) homage to the works of both Howard Hawks and Jean Renoir, as well as Alfred Hitchcock. *Tequila Sunrise* (1988) has connections to both the infamously loose Hemingway adaptation, *To Have and Have Not* (1944, written by Jules Furthman and William Faulkner), as well as the later *Red Line 7000* (1965, written by George Kirgo from a story provided by Hawks, plundering his own *The Crowd Roars*, 1932, written by John Bright, Niven Busch, Kubec Glasmon, Hawks and Seton I. Miller, from an original story by Hawks) which also has links to *Days of Thunder*. (See chapters 4 & 5). *Chinatown*(1974) in its various drafts has whole scenes replicating elements of Raymond Chandler's *The Big Sleep* (1946, by Furthman, Faulkner and Leigh Brackett); as well as boasting a panoply of

---

[195] *Ibid.*

[196] See Steven Cohan, 'Case Study: Interpreting *Singin' in the Rain*,' in Gledhill and Williams. *Op.cit.*, 56-58.

[197] Philip Dunne. *Op.cit.,* 244. Dunne further describes the differences between his screenplay for HOW GREEN WAS MY VALLEY and a BBC TV version, commenting, "Perhaps their vision was truer than mine; I simply don't know. I only know that their production was almost completely different, and the difference lay not in the direction but in the writing. It is a point worth remembering the next time you see that obnoxious credit 'a film by' some director, or some critic gives sole praise to an 'Auteur' whose principal contribution to the structure of a picture my have been merely deciding where to place the camera." (244-245) He was referring to the fact that the BBC version seemed to imitate the film shot for shot. Earlier in his memoir, on the subject of the same film, he declares that "the entire premise of the [Auteur] theory is false." (98)

[198] Dudley Andrew. *CONCEPTS IN FILM THEORY.* New York: Oxford University Press, 1984, 38-9.

its fetish objects and a theme redolent of Dashiell Hammett's *The Glass Key* which was adapted for the screen by Jonathan Latimer and released in 1945. (See Chapter 3). Perhaps Towne located in Hawks what David Thomson astutely finds:

> The clue to Hawks' greatness is that this somber lining is cut against the cloth of the genre in which he is operating. Far from the meek purveyor of Hollywood forms, he always chose to turn them upside down… The ostensible comedies are shot through with exposed emotions, with the subtlest views of the sex war, and with a wry acknowledgement of the incompatibility of men and women. Men and women skirmish in Hawks' films on the understanding that an embrace is only a prelude to withdrawal and disillusion. [199]

Renoir, who is Towne's personal idol, and was an acquaintance of Towne's good friend and collaborator Warren Beatty, is paid explicit homage in the satire *Shampoo* (1975), which is a loose reworking of *La Règle du Jeu* (1939, itself an homage to Beaumarchais' *Le Mariage de Figaro*). [200] *Mission: Impossible 2* (2000) is in some respects a (somewhat controversial) reworking of *Notorious* (1946, written by Ben Hecht), however much he might dispute it, yet has some of the mythological elements favoured by Towne. And *Tequila Sunrise* also owes a major debt to everyone's favourite Hollywood classic, *Casablanca* (1942, written by Julius & Philip Epstein and Howard Koch and honoured as the WGA's best screenplay of all time, 2006). Crucially for an understanding of Towne, the Epstein twins specialised in sharp byplay and romantic triangles, an emotional shape which dominates *Tequila Sunrise*. *Tequila…* also cannibalises Towne's own screenplay for *Cisco Pike* (1972), which was allegedly rewritten by a third party (probably writer/director, B.L. Norton). In Towne's work, therefore, we can trace a line from classical cinema - however loosely - through New Hollywood and the current, blockbuster phase of, post-classical American cinema. That his most critically acclaimed work probably occurs in the New Hollywood era, the period of transition from approximately 1967-1975, hallmarked by the achievements of a new wave of American auteur directors, makes the forging of his centrality as author all the richer, in what can be read retrospectively as a great screenwriting age in Hollywood.

It might be supposed that a grammar or lexicon of screen authorship is required; the better to reveal a film's true author (or authors). The identity of the screenplay as a generic narrative form can be deducted from its structural components, which derive from the rules of dramatic playwriting. Screenwriting manuals have been in existence from the early days of cinema and generally their contemporary equivalents continue to explain the dramaturgical strategies underlying the narrative screenplay. Writing in 1913, Eustace Hale Ball issues advice on such practical matters as, "unity of place … will permit the use of the same settings for many scenes. In this way the producer feels justified in spending more money upon the settings themselves … and the result is more elaborate and artistic stage effects." [201]

---

[199] David Thomson. *A BIOGRAPHICAL DICTIONARY OF FILM*. London: Andre Deutsch, 1994, 322.

[200] See Marc Lee, 'Filmmakers on Film: Robert Towne on Jean Renoir's LA GRANDE ILLUSION (1937),'*The Daily Telegraph*, 27 May 2006: 20.

[201] Eustace Hale Ball. *THE ART OF THE PHOTOPLAY*, New York: G.W. Dillingham Company, 1913; quoted in Leonard J. Leff, 'Resources for the Screenwriting Teacher,' *Journal of Film and Video*, Vol. 36, No. 3, 1984: 8.

These books broadly take one of three approaches to their subject: the character-centred approach, the action-based approach or the sequence approach; coupled with advice on development, contract and production matters. The wide availability of instruction manuals has undoubtedly contributed to the mainstream's acceptance of pedagogy via entertainment. The rules of screenplay writing have entered the quotidian to the extent that they are a regular feature of genre fiction, which is perhaps an indication of the narrative's own cinematic potential or perhaps the underlying ambition of the writer. [202]

> Virtually all tragedians, one might say, use these formal elements; for in fact
> every drama alike has spectacle, character, plot, diction, song and reasoning.
> But the most important of them is the structure of the events. [203]

The importance of Aristotle's writings to dramatic structure for theatre and the screen cannot be underestimated. Aside from his edict on time, manner and place, and general rules about tragedy and comedy, he teased out various strands of the play's effect on the audience (pity, or *eleos*; or fear, *phobos*) which should be enumerated since they continue to dictate our understanding today of how drama works. In RHETORIC, he describes imminent fear (*phobos*) as the anticipating of anxiety which is caused by an idea (*phantasia*) or expectation (*prosdokia*) of impending danger (*mellontos*). The audience is released from the feelings of pity or fear through pleasurable relief (*katharsis*), which unfortunately was never wholly defined by Aristotle but which we presume occurs via the overall structure of the drama.[204] Robert Towne himself has commented on the problem of understanding screenwriting, that

> No one, I think, can really say what makes an effective screenplay because no one
> really knows what makes a screenplay effective.[205]

A screenplay is described by Meg Wolitzer as

> …a form that is more often about architecture and imagery and movement
> than it is about language…
> …screenplays are about giving a story momentum. [206]

---

[202] For instance, in Richard Montanari's thriller, THE SKIN GODS, we learn, "There is a moment in every film where the main character finds himself unable to return to his former life, that part of his continuum that existed before the opening of the narrative. Generally, this point of no return occurs at the midway point of the story, but not always." London, Arrow, 2007: 337. This observation is made after what might be described as the midpoint sequence of the novel.

[203] Aristotle. POETICS. Translated with an introduction and notes by Malcolm Heath. London: Penguin, 1996, 11.

[204] Ari Hiltunen. ARISTOTLE IN HOLLYWOOD. Bristol: Intellect Books, 2002. 8-12. Michael Tierno explains Aristotle's ongoing relevance as follows: "The POETICS is useful to screenwriters because Aristotle explains why we humans respond to dramatic story. Basically, we respond to dramatic story when we can relate to it." Michael Tierno. ARISTOTLE'S POETICS FOR SCREENWRITERS. New York: Hyperion Books, 2002, 63.

[205] Towne, 1997, ix. He characterises screenwriting as "a peculiar act of prophecy." (x). Joe Eszterhas comments, "I am a militant … and militantly insufferable screenwriter … who insists that the screenwriter is as important as the director … who insists that the director serves the screenwriter's vision … and whose most famous and most memorable screen moment … was created by the director, Paul Verhoeven." Eszterhas. *Op.cit.,* 35.

While three-act structure is generally accepted as the Hollywood formula (accounting for over 90% of screenplays), it is not a form stipulated as essential to drama by Aristotle: he draws attention to the ideas of complication and denouement or resolution (also known as falling action):

> By complication I mean everything from the beginning up to and including
> the section which immediately precedes the change to good fortune or bad
> fortune; by resolution I mean everything from the beginning of the change to
> the end. [207]

Dancyger interprets structure as essentially composed of four macro-elements which he says are three-act structure, plot, the character layer and genre. [208] A more literal interpretation of Aristotle encapsulates exposition, conflict, peace, transition and climax, a five-act interpretation of the form that can be seen in the screenplays of Alain Resnais and Oliver Stone. [209] However this is easily transposed onto the three-act structure, which is essentially an industrially compact version of the same concepts.

> A movie, I think, is really only four or five moments between two people;
> the rest of it exists to give those moments their impact and resonance.
> And when actors are really into it, giving you those moments – nobody
> is more remarkable than they are. [210]

While Towne's screenplays have rarely been ideological or espoused the era's New Left politics; and they mainly cleave to the traditional, classic pattern of transgression, recognition and redemption, there are some key exceptions within the oeuvre (*The Last Detail, Chinatown*). Dancyger and Rush describe this three-act pattern as 'restorative act structure,' and it might be said to demonstrate the American way of redemption. Towne has kept within the rubric of the three-act structure without consistently using all of that structure's elements (midpoints, redemptive finales) in order to express a point of view that is ultimately tragic and at times deeply cynical about the bourgeois family.

Action

Philip Dunne declares that "in movie-making drama is action." [211] The importance of plot to dramatic action can be observed in chapters 7 through 14 of *POETICS*:

---

[206] Meg Wolitzer. *FITZGERALD DID IT: The Writer's Guide to Mastering the Screenplay*. London: Penguin, 1999, 6.

[207] Aristotle. *POETICS*. Translated with an introduction and notes by Malcolm Heath. London: Penguin, 1996, 29.

[208] Dancyger, 2001, 43.

[209] See Rachid Nougmanov, 'Building a Screenplay: A Five-Act Paradigm, or, What Syd Field Didn't Tell You,' in Andrew Horton, ed., *SCREENWRITING FOR A GLOBAL MARKET: Selling Your Scripts from Hollywood to Hong Kong*. Berkeley and Los Angeles: University of California Press, 2004, 141-151. This structure is also evident in the screenplay for BONNIE AND CLYDE. See: John G. Cawelti (ed.). *FOCUS ON BONNIE AND CLYDE*. Englewood Cliffs, N.J.: Prentice-Hall, 1973, 148-150.

[210] Towne in John Brady. *Op.cit.*, 377.

[211] Dunne. *Op.cit..*, 57.

... the source and (as it were) the soul of tragedy; character is second. [212]

Malcolm Heath explains that Aristotle

... is talking about an *ordered structure*. His definitions of beginning, middle and end show that there are two aspects of the structure of a plot which he wants to bring out when he uses these terms. First, the plot consists of a *connected* series of events: one thing follows on another as a necessary consequence. Secondly, the plot consists of a *self-contained* series of events: the first thing in the series is in some sense self-explanatory – it is not a necessary consequence of something else; equally, the last event in the series brings it to a definitive end – there is no further necessary consequence in the series. Another term for this self-containment is *closure*. The series of events which constitutes a well-formed plot is therefore closed at both ends, and connected in between. [213]

Field's approach in *SCREENPLAY*, analysing the form through act structure, was not new; indeed the year prior to its first publication saw another, equally valuable text on screenwriting by Constance Nash and Virginia Oakey, published with no less to offer the aspiring screenwriter in which the authors offer a simple guide to what they call 'script divisions' along the lines of three-act structure (setup, confrontation, resolution):

Divide your script into several parts or acts, preferably three. Determine what you mean to say in each, how each will be developed, and how each will build to a crisis that will propel the story forward. The acts will provide the framework within which your script will be filled out, and will serve as your guide in writing the rough draft ... The following diagram illustrates this:

Act I	Act II	Act III
Problems Introduced	Conflict between protagonist and antagonist leading to conflict	Action providing solution to the seemingly unsolvable problem
(Approx. 30 pages)	(App. 60 pages)	(App. 30 pages – totalling 120 pages)

Keep in mind that all the action leads into and away from the time of the seemingly unsolvable problem. A screenplay is a series of crises; the first comes at the beginning, within the first few pages, to make a change of status quo in the protagonist's situation. Each crisis will become more severe than the last, finally rising to the climax which comes at or toward the end of act 3. [214]

Those crises can be called plot points, or turning points, and are

---

[212] Aristotle, 1996, 12.

[213] Heath in Aristotle, 1996, xxiii.

[214] Constance Nash and Virginia Oakey. *THE SCREENWRITER'S HANDBOOK: What to Write How to Write It Where to Sell It* . New York: Perennial Library, 1978, 2-3. This also appears in the authors' *THE TELEVISION WRITER'S HANDBOOK (Writing for the Movies)*. New York: HarperPerennial, 1993, 4-5; first published in 1978. The authors use CHINATOWN to illustrate "how the subject of the shot is correctly identified" on pages 23-4; and the screenplay is excerpted later in the book, "to illustrate how expertly a single scene is constructed through dialog and a minimum of action so that it rises to a sharp and shocking crisis."(123). Syd Field. *SCREENPLAY*, as before.

an incident, or event, that 'hooks' into the action and spins it around in another direction. It moves the story forward. The plot points at the end of Acts I and II hold the paradigm in place. They are the anchors of your story line. [215]

How those anchors are constructed and utilised by Towne will be explored in various of the screenplays to be examined.

Character

Andrew Horton offers us the following definition of the classical Hollywood narrative structure as follows:

> The classical Hollywood narrative is a very specific plot-driven, cause-and-effect-organized narrative centering on a central protagonist with a successful ('happy') resolution, a pattern that has not changed since 1917 for most Hollywood films. [216]

In making the choice about who the protagonist might be, the writer is selecting something that will determine the entire nature of their story. The protagonist can be viewed in two ways – in close-up, and in relation to the social world about them. Not only that, but the protagonist must grow over the course of the story, if only in knowledge about their own particular situation. In John Howard Lawson's *THEORY AND TECHNIQUE OF PLAYWRITING AND SCREENWRITING*, the aspiring screenwriter is advised to ask of their prospective protagonist the following questions:

1. What does the protagonist want?
2. Why does he want it?
3. What does the protagonist need emotionally or psychologically?

Lawson advises that the protagonist must be active in order to drive the plot; that he must be committed to something and forced to take action because of that commitment. [217]

A protagonist (or hero, if indeed the protagonist is heroic) is the driving force of any story. In the Aristotelian formulation, 'we are what we do.' "Character," he states, "gives us qualities, but it is in our actions – what we do – that we are happy or the reverse." [218] Whereas Aristotle prioritises plot in story construction (he calls it the soul of the tragedy), Lew Hunter reminds us that "character and plot must intertwine." [219] And, advises Lajos Egri, "If we wish to know the structure of conflict, we must first know character. But since character is influenced by environment, we must know that too. It might seem that conflict springs spontaneously from one single cause, but this is not true. A complexity of many reasons makes one solitary conflict." [220]

---

[215] Field. *Op.cit.,* 115.

[216] Andrew Horton. *WRITING THE CHARACTER-CENTRED SCREENPLAY.* Berkeley and Los Angeles: University of California Press, 1999, 117.

[217] Adapted from John Howard Lawson. *THEORY AND TECHNIQUE OF PLAYWRITING AND SCREENWRITING.* Reprinted by New York: Garland, 1985, 168. Ray Bradbury advises, "First, find out what your hero wants, then just follow him!" From *CS Weekly,* issue unknown.

[218] Aristotle. *ON THE ART OF POETRY.* Oxford: Oxford University Press, 1920, 37.

[219] Hunter. *Op.cit.,,* 81-82.

[220] Lajos Egri. *THE ART OF DRAMATIC WRITING: Its Basis in the Creative Interpretation of Human Motives.* New York, Touchstone Books, 1946, 1960, 136.

In other words it is the gap – or lack – between what the character wants and what the character needs that creates narrative motion. Whereas Aristotle's analysis of drama focuses exclusively on plot and action, it is true to say that what grips an audience is character, a fact that Lajos Egri emphasises to expose the structural tenets of dramatic writing:

> There must be something to *generate* tension, something to *create* complication, without any conscious attempt on the playwright's part to do so. There must be a force which will unify all parts, a force out of which they will grow as naturally as limbs grow from the body. We think we know what that force is: human character, in all its infinite ramifications and dialectical contradictions. [221]

He continues that

> …all that is required of a well-constructed premise: character, conflict, and conclusion. [222]

For Robert Towne, "'You must ask what it is he or she is really afraid of. It's my best way of getting into a character." Towne thinks the writer has more control over his art than the director. "When I write," he says, "the only limits are my imagination and my ability to do it'." [223] Towne's protagonists are invariably male, trapped by their occupation or situation, and forced by dint of circumstance (usually misplaced loyalty) to an unhappy compromise. Towne himself states of his protagonists,

> I've always been fascinated by people who love what they do. I don't think I've ever been able to do a movie in which somebody's profession wasn't critical to it. I've thought about everything I've done in almost every movie, whether it's *Chinatown*, or *Shampoo* or *Personal Best* or *Tequila Sunrise*. What people do, their profession, seems to me critical and central to what interests me. [224]

Critic Stephen Schiff offers a telling interpretation of Towne's characters:

> Towne's characters shrug off conventional mores in favor of a code that is somehow loftier and more stringent, an unarticulated ethic that reveals itself only in its heroes' day-to-day behavior – in their deeds. His people aren't made of the same stuff as the larger-than-life figures who now dominate the movies – they don't save the world like Schwarzenegger or Eastwood or Stallone; they aren't Supermen or James Bonds: 'I don't believe most of us have the capacity to make a change in the world,' says Towne. 'That's unrealistic. And my idea in all the screenplays was to bring a different level of reality into a movie.' [225]

---

[221] Egri. *Op.cit.,*, xvi.

[222] Egri. *Op.cit.*, 8.

[223] www.americanfilmfoundation.com/order/robert_towne.shtml

[224] Towne, 'On Directing,' in John Boorman and Walter Donahue (eds.). *PROJECTIONS 6*. London: Faber and Faber, 1996, 125-6.

[225] Stephen Schiff, 'Talk of the Towne,' *Vanity Fair*, January 1989: 41. He continues: "Towne's heroes, like their creator, are forever caught between accommodation and rage – that, in fact, is the dramatic tug-of-war that keeps his screenplays tense and humming." (42)

For Towne's characters to attain that 'different level of reality,' he frequently deprives them of dialogue: Kurt Russell, cast by Towne as Nick Frescia in *Tequila Sunrise*, describes Towne's writing,

> it was the first time that I had read a screenplay and thought I understood it, then after spending hours with Bob, realized I understood very little about the screenplay. I had to dissect, an entirely different kind of approach to writing a screenplay. Bob demanded of the actors and of the audience that they know the character so well that when they didn't speak it actually turned the plot. It demands the best of you, in all aspects of working in the film. [226]

Dialogue

As Andrew Horton rightly points out, "It may surprise you how much of most films breaks down to a series of dialogue scenes between two characters." [227]   For Aristotle, diction (or dialogue) must form part of the dramatic action. He states:

> Diction should be handled with particular care in those parts in which little is happening, and which are expressive neither of character nor of reasoning; excessively brilliant diction overshadows character and reasoning. [228]

Michael Tierno reiterates,

> Dialog is part of the action and gets its power from the plot, whose effect builds in a cumulative as well as linear way. Dialog forms story action and derives life and energy from the action it helps build. [229]

Dialogue is not, then, conversation; it affects the impact of conversation and carries character and action forward. It must differentiate characters from one another, imitate the rhythm of speech and at its best reveal subtext and deep character.

Towne acknowledges his rare ability to write great dialogue:

> If I have a gift, it's that I'm very sensitive to the sounds of different voices…
> The movement that I hear in people's voices affects me emotionally – it excites me; it drives me mad. [230]

This ear gives *Chinatown* one of its best running jokes, as virtually everyone pronounces Jake's surname differently, leading to constant inexpressible exasperation on his part at being the butt of humour. Simplicity is Towne's forte and this is demonstrated in *Chinatown*'s brilliant but apparently throwaway line, early in the screenplay:

---

[226] Speaking at a WGA event. Accessed online at www.wga.com. This explains the attraction of Towne's writing for the acting fraternity.

[227] Horton. *Op.cit.*, 145.

[228] Aristotle, 1996, 42.

[229] Tierno. *ARISTOTLE'S POETICS FOR SCREENWRITERS*. New York: Hyperion Books, 2002, 129-130. Tierno continues: "…in even the most dialog-dependent script like *My Dinner with Andre*, the dialog is intrinsic to the action – to the plot, meaning, causality of the incidents and the dramatic unity." (131.)

[230] Schiff, as before, 41. Towne's use of the vernacular (not to mention the vulgar) would cause him problems with his work – see Chapter 3 on *The Last Detail*.

What can I tell you, Kid?
You're right. When you're
right, you're right, and
you're right.

(*Chinatown*, 3rd draft: 2)

This line exemplifies Towne's use of the demotic, his pared-down eloquence, his exquisite sense of character – it is precise, personal and persuasive. The deceptive triadic structure underscores the line's meaning as well as shading the rhythm with irony and foreshadowing, because throughout the screenplay Jake is consistently proven wrong, although the clear insinuation in his confident assertion is that it is he who is right. [231]

Towne explains dialogue (and all writing for the screen) as a function of dramatic compression:

... in a good movie, every scene, even though it may seem utterly realistic and the dialogue may seem realistic, is kind of a compression of experience so that scene stands for ten scenes that are not there. Experience is sort of stacked and heightened, so much of it, because there's such a subtext to good screenwriting... it's almost as if the dialogue in a good screenplay is contrapuntal to the picture. Because why do you need to say what you see? [232]

The formal elegance of his screen dialogue is one of Towne's main attractions to actors and audiences alike. [233]

Genre

Kaminsky says that

Genre helps us see the unique properties of individual works by permitting comparison of these works with others of the same basic type. [234]

Far from being devalued, genre filmmaking is more important to the film industry than ever before. Langford writes that the area of genre study has become intensely complicated in recent years following a period of consensus throughout the 1970s and 1980s. Ideological formation and cultural hegemony underlie genre studies as

---

[231] Towne obviously realised the brilliance of the line – he gives it to Lester to say no fewer than three times in *Shampoo* the following year. Al Alvarez comments: "This ear for the inner music of a line – for the immediacy and disturbance that go to create an authentic voice - is the poetic equivalent of perfect pitch." *Op.cit.*, 49.

[232] Towne speaking at the Harold Lloyd Master Seminar, AFI, 1994. Accessed at www.afi.com.

[233] Kurt Russell said of his role in *Tequila Sunrise*: "it was the first time that I had read a screenplay and thought I understood it, then after spending hours with Bob, realized I understood very little about the screenplay. I had to dissect, an entirely different kind of approach to writing a screenplay. Bob demanded of the actors and of the audience that they know the character so well that when they didn't speak it actually turned the plot. It demands the best of you, in all aspects of working in the film." (Speaking at a WGA event.)

[234] Stuart M. Kaminsky. *AMERICAN FILM GENRES: Approaches to a Critical Theory of Popular Film*. New York: Dell Publishing Co., 1977, 12. He continues, "the roots of genre are not solely in the literary tradition, but in the fabric of existence itself."14.

a given, while the transgeneric blockbuster and industrial realignments of recent years have combined to prove an overwhelming challenge for analysts. As the author reminds us, "Hollywood films today are as intensely generic as ever, perhaps even more so." [235]

Dancyger cautions that

> when we speak of structure in genre, implicitly the question devolves to plot or
> character layer or both, or to what proportion of each is appropriate in each genre.
> In order to understand structure in a meaningful way, it's best to link the issue
> of structure to the dramatic arc of a genre. [236]

Towne's work includes sci-fi and horror (for Roger Corman and television); gangster (*Bonnie and Clyde* – which might also be called a road movie – *The Godfather, The Yakuza*); Western (*A Time for Killing, Villa Rides!*); police drama (*The New Centurions, Tequila Sunrise*); the buddy film (*The Last Detail*); satire (*Shampoo*); noir (*Chinatown, The Two Jakes*); adventure (*Greystoke*); sports (*Personal Best, Days of Thunder, Without Limits*); thriller (*The Firm*); and spy/action (*Mission: Impossible, Mission: Impossible 2*). What is significant is the linkage between them through Towne's deployment of character and theme within the parameters long established within Hollywood's representational system, which, during the Sixties, the crucial period for Towne's formation, writer/director Oliver Stone has characterised as "impersonal." [237] Underwriting Towne's screenplays always is a commitment to his version of realism, or plausibility. While this places him firmly in the tradition of the classical screenwriter, working the melodramatic model, it also enriches those genres in which he has worked. Furthermore, his innovativeness lies in his offsetting some elements of those genres against myth, as we shall see.

Location & Visuals

Towne's work is notable for its focus on Los Angeles. He also acknowledges that he was influenced by a famously unmade screenplay in the 1950s written by Chuck Eastman, claiming it

> ...affected me strongly because there was a guy who was able to use life
> around him and push as far as anybody writing a novel was going to push. [238]

---

[235] Barry Langford. *FILM GENRE: Hollywood and Beyond*. Edinburgh: Edinburgh University Press, 2005, 274.

[236] Dancyger, 2001, 65. He asks, "if a character layer is introduced to this plot-driven [police story] genre, what are the consequences? Will it enhance the film or will it slow down the advance of the plot? These are structural issues." 66.

[237] Stone interviewed by Lawrence Grobel. *ABOVE THE LINE: Conversations About the Movies. HOW TO WRITE A STORY AND SELL IT*. Garden City, New York: Doubleday & Co, 1956.

[238] Interviewed by Grobel. *Op.cit.,* 129. Towne has also admitted being influenced by critic James Agee's unproduced screenplay about Gauguin, NOA NOA: 'Robert Towne: Gauguin, Van Gogh, James Agee and Me,' *Los Angeles Times*, 03 November 2002. He says of one scene: "... I suddenly felt that I wasn't reading a scene, I was seeing it, and I realized then that a good screenplay could actually read like it's describing a movie already made. It made me realize that so much of what I wanted to say I wanted to show, or to put it another way, what I wanted to show is so much of what I had to say. I was pretty much stuck with movies as a way of saying it. And so I've given it a whirl."

Like a novelist, the totality of Towne's background, lifestyle and personal friendships and collaborations has exercised a profound influence on his career success and the somewhat nostalgic theme of loss which can be detected through a significant number of his screenplays.[239] Towne also notes that

> ...the notion of writing moving pictures is absurd. One can't write a picture. One describes a picture. And one thing can be said about a really good screenplay: it reads like it's describing a movie already made. So if you look at a movie and then read the screenplay and the movie seems fully realized in it, recognize and wonder. It's nearly as miraculous as getting struck by lightning and living to tell the tale.[240]

Towne's pictorial gifts as a screenwriter give further emphasis to his controlling contribution to a finished film. It is significant therefore that a signal influence on the writing of *Chinatown*, central to his body of work, was in fact a photo essay seen by Towne in a magazine supplement in 1969, which depicted 'Raymond Chandler's Los Angeles' in a series of photographs by John Waggaman, accompanied by text written by Laurence Dietze. Towne would revisit not merely Los Angeles, but his hometown seaport of San Pedro, on a number of occasions, even just by line mentions, in other screenplays; *Tequila Sunrise* (1988) was another nostalgic, even elegiac, return to Pedro in the form of a police thriller, complete with major Hollywood stars and a classical genre format. Towne acknowledges of this aspect of his writing, the visual, that

> The image inevitably conveys more than the word. Movies can make you, as a writer, feel very foolish. [241]

While auteurist criticism is, as Corliss asserts, usually theme criticism, in a departure here from that tradition, it is important to note the pictorial qualities of Towne's writing, as well as those visual components utilised in his forays into directing which are usually termed mise-en-scène. [242]

Theme

Perhaps the most significant element of any screenwriting signature is the overarching theme, a distinguishing feature of Robert Riskin's oeuvre and also that of Steven Spielberg. [243]

---

[239] Adela Rogers St John provides a list of notable works which she says "were written … right where the writer was." *HOW TO WRITE A STORY AND SELL IT*. Garden City, New York: Doubleday & Co, 1956, 111. The theme of loss (of integrity, of innocence, of friendship, of love, of values) is attenuated throughout the oeuvre with a significant emphasis on betrayal in certain of the major works.

[240] Robert Towne, 1997, xv.

[241] Peter Rainer, '*Chinatown's* Robert Towne,' *Mademoiselle,* November 1974: 234.

[242] Corliss, 1975, xxi-xxii.

[243] Warren Buckland, 2006, 14-15; 23; and Ian Scott. *IN CAPRA'S SHADOW: The Life & Career of Robert Riskin, Screenwriter.* Kentucky: University of Kentucky Press, 2006, 125-6, 128: in 1938 Riskin wrote an article entitled, 'The Theme's the Thing.' which, Ian Scott claims, "was [also] a rededication to his own instincts as a writer, to his abilities of forming character and narrative, and a promise of the direction of his future work. The article contended that he was foremost a writer and that themes were the heart and soul of his writing." (126)

Egri formulated the classic approach to dramatic writing in which he states premise – or theme – as the central component of the successfully written play:

> Every good play must have a well-formulated premise. There may be more than one way to phrase the premise, but, however it is phrased, the thought must be the same.

He urges the playwright:

> You must have a premise – a premise which will lead you unmistakably to the goal your play hopes to reach. [244]

A screenplay's structure is integrated fully with its controlling idea, or theme, which Linda Cowgill now defines as follows: "Theme defines what a film experience is about; it determines the choice of incidents and events which make up the plot... At the end, when they are added up in the mind of the viewer, each scene and sequence should contribute to the ultimate discovery of what the film is about." [245] Theme also "gives direction to the plot, defines the key issues for the characters and ultimately determines the depth of meaning for a work. It is the integrative force behind a great film and is essential for understanding what makes a film great." [246]

Similarly, Robert Riskin believed that theme was the most important element of the writer's armoury. In his essay, 'The Theme's the Thing,' first published in 1937-1938, he stressed the importance of this to his own screenplays and also dedicated several pages to the organisation and construction of his stories, which always adhered to the three-act structure. [247]

In their guide to aspiring screenwriters, John Emerson and Anita Loos called theme 'the chief trick of the trade.' [248] For Blacker, it is

> An intellectual abstraction; the idea that unifies the structure and is represented by the actions of the characters as a whole dramatic piece.[249]

It might also be described as

> ... the screenwriter's point of view toward the material. Since it hardly

---

[244] Egri. *Op.cit.*, 6. He also states: "In a well-constructed play or story, it is impossible to denote just where premise ends and story or character begins." (29) "Neither the premise nor any other part of a play has a separate life of its own. All must blend into an harmonious whole." (31)
[245] Cowgill. *Op.cit.*, 151.
[246] Cowgill. *Op.cit.*, 64.
[247] Ian Scott. 2006, 125-126. Scott comments, "The article placed great emphasis on a writer's knowing his or her theme and how that theme can and should work, whether the genre is comedy, melodrama, or message film." *Ibid.*
[248] John Emerson & Anita Loos. *HOW TO WRITE PHOTOPLAYS*. Philadelphia: 1920; reprinted George W. Jacobs & Co, 1923, 21.

[249] Irwin R. Blacker. *THE ELEMENTS OF SCREENWRITING: A Guide for Film and Television Writing*. New York: Collier Books, 1986, 5. He says that "the writer's basic responsibility is unity and arrangement... In a tightly unified script, every action should be related to the central conflict, the theme." 26.

seems possible to write a screenplay, even the most frivolous one, without an attitude toward the people and the situations one has created, every story must therefore have a theme of some kind. And there is one spot in the screenplay where this theme can invariably be discerned: the resolution. For here the author reveals, perhaps even unconsciously, what interpretation he or she puts on the material. [250]

Towne has never been drawn to expand on that singular theme which dominates his body of work: loss. [251] If a writer's theme can be detected in the endings to his screenplays it can be confirmed that Towne's worldview is somewhat realistic if not completely fatalistic. This is perhaps the major influence of *Bonnie and Clyde* on Towne's writing style: the hail of bullets killing the protagonists (whose story, was, after all a true one transmuted into myth) is echoed throughout the oeuvre. Consistency of structural elements including theme engenders an interpretation of Towne's work as an auteur.

The idea of loss translates as a form of nostalgia in some of Towne's work: in *Chinatown*, as one reviewer noted at the time, Gittes' inflexion as a romantic knight, "caught in a fantasy of his own making … locks him into the past and leaves him helpless against the man of the future." [252] Characteristic of the detective genre, this tension between past and present nonetheless implies itself throughout the oeuvre, less as a political force than a sentiment of pure longing.

Tone
Tone has been described as "the visual and verbal detail that directs us toward meaning." [253] Al Alvarez states that "… it is the business of writers to create as true a voice as they can." [254] In Aristotle's formulation,

> …the action is performed by certain agents. These must be people of a certain kind with respect to their character and reasoning. (It is on the basis of people's character and reasoning that we say that their actions are of a certain kind, and in respect of their actions that people enjoy success or failure.) [255]

Aristotle is stating that the 'agents' of the drama set the tone and influence the audience.
Towne himself frequently refers to the importance of tone in his work: it is perhaps the ineffable marker of any writer's work, expressing their point of view and therefore constitutes the totality of their 'voice' – or pitch. Tone can be described as a general or prevailing character, traceable across an oeuvre.

Towne expresses difficulty with the notion of tone on film:

---

[250] Howard and Mabley. *Op.cit.,* 55.
[251] Interviewed by Lawrence Grobel, Towne remarks that while working on *Tough Guys Don't Dance* for Norman Mailer he said to Mailer that "all writing was about loss. And just as quick as you can imagine he said, 'All *your* writing is about loss'." Towne's response, he admitted to Grobel, was "… I thought, okay, he's got my number. He taught me something about myself in a fucking hurry."*Op.cit.,* 130. Grobel asks Towne if Steve Prefontaine's story (in *Without Limits*) is 'ultimately about the triumph of losing'. (120)
[252] Tom Milne's review of the film appeared in *Sight & Sound*, Autumn 1974, Vol. 43, No.4, 243-244.
[253] Ken Dancyger. *GLOBAL SCRIPTWRITING* . Boston, Mass., Focal Press, 2001, 75.
[254] Alvarez. *Op. cit.*, 121.
[255] Aristotle, 1996, 11.

The most difficult thing to capture, and what finally makes a movie, is its tone. Tone is a very delicate matter. It requires a keen understanding from everyone involved, the director, producer, stars, writer; it's called the Lubitsch touch. [256]

What of Towne's 'touch'? He says specifically of *Chinatown*'s Jake Gittes that it is not Raymond Chandler's voice, but that of Jack Nicholson. [257] Yet throughout the *Chinatown* text – the story and narrative choices – Towne's voice can be located. And, indeed as we analyse Towne's career, it can be observed that he has paradoxically appeared to have found his voice on occasions when adapting other people's work to the screen – *Greystoke* being the most profound example. However, although an occasional victim of mannerism in his imitation of other writing forms, he also demonstrates an authentic writing voice, which Alvarez likens to

> perfect pitch... a natural gift, innate and distinctive, by which the best poets give new life to exhausted conventions and mold them to suit themselves. [258]

Sequence

As Cohan and Swires remind us, "story consists of events placed in a sequence to delineate a process of change, the transformation of one event into another." [259] Aristotle suggests that the connective tissue between incidents can be organised in such a way that the entire action of a drama can be united as a whole with individual sections of action which relate to the overweening arc of the drama itself:

> Just as in other imitative arts the imitation is unified if it imitates a single object, so too the plot, as the imitation of an action, should imitate a single, unified action – and one that is also a whole. So the structure of the various sections of the events must be such that the transposition or removal of any one section dislocates and changes the whole. If the presence or absence of something has no discernible effect, it is not part of the whole. [260]

Sequences are a readily identifiable structural tool, as described by Wolitzer:

> All scripts contain sequences – a series of thematically connected scenes that are powerful and memorable and direct the reader through the story...[261]

A sequence approach is utilised by Gulino, who reminds the reader that the structuring of screenplays into explicit sequences approximating 15 pages was standard practice until the 1950s (and in fact early screenplay manuals advised writers to construct stories according to reel divisions.). In this way the point of view could more easily be shifted to characters other than the protagonist in order to create more dramatic tension and sustain audience attention. [262]

---

[256] Towne, interviewed in Joel Engel. *SCREENWRITERS ON SCREENWRITING*. New York: Hyperion, 1995, 214.

[257] Engel *Op.cit.*, 216.

[258] Alvarez. *Op.cit.*, 49.

[259] Cohan and Shires. *Op.cit.*, 53.

[260] Aristotle, 1996, 15.

[261] Wolitzer. *Op.cit.*, 91.

[262] He says "the difference between a sequence and a stand-alone fifteen-minute film is that the conflicts and issues raised in a sequence are only partially resolved within the sequence, and when

According to Linda Cowgill, the midpoint sequence is a major structuring element in any screenplay. It is the 'heart' of a film, representing in any well-constructed film its emotions and concerns in microcosm. Cowgill defines it thus:

> A midpoint links the action of the plot in the first half of Act Two (and the first Half of the film) to the second half of Act Two (and the last half of the film). It is an incident or episode in the plot which culminates a line of action on one hand and, on the other hand, pushes the plot forward toward the second act climax. An effective midpoint is one that is active and dramatic, either solving a problem or crisis, or creating more of them. The midpoint often takes us to a surprise, reversal, discovery or new complication, at the same time strengthening the relationship between the first half of the second act and the last half. It does not have to come exactly at the halfway mark in a film, but it generally occurs somewhere in the middle. [263]

Towne builds long scene and midpoint sequences which deploy all the structural components in order to build plot and reveal character, examined where appropriate in forthcoming chapters. His greatest midpoint sequence is probably in *Greystoke*.

> Scene sequences are similar to action sequences but do not usually involve violent confrontation. Generally, they do not put the protagonist in direct conflict with the antagonist. But there is still a problem that must be faced. The scenes are structured in cause and effect relationships, showing the protagonist of the sequence trying to accomplish something. They are also structured around the meeting of an obstacle, complication or problem that the character has to deal with in the course of the plot. [264]

All of these manuals, derived as they are from the tenets of Aristotle, provide a utilitarian framework for an understanding of contemporary screenwriting and have in common a desire to contextualise the Hollywood style which is historically linked to Greek playwriting and its foundations in comedy and tragedy, pity, terror and catharsis. [265] This would seem to point to the conclusion that post-classical Hollywood is more clearly identifiable in approaches to the dominating economic imperatives than in narrative structures per se, albeit the cause and effect unified narrative persists in relevance. [266]

---

they are resolved, the resolution often opens ups new issues, which in turn become the subject of subsequent sequences." Paul Gulino. *SCREENWRITING: The Sequence Approach*. New York: Continuum, 2004, 2-3.

[263] Linda Cowgill. *THE SECRETS OF SCREENPLAY STRUCTURE*. California: Lone Eagle Press, 1999, 29.

[264] Cowgill. *Op.cit.*, 174.

[265] Kristin Thompson applies her scholarly analysis to a number of screenplays and disagrees that the three-act structure dominates as the narrative paradigm; according to her interpretation, film has become inured to the post-classical effect, dramatising story around computer generated special effects and the whims of overpaid stars. She instead argues towards a four-act structure of set up, complication, development and resolution. In effect, however, she is merely splitting Act 2 in half and adhering to traditional dramatic elements in order to suggest acts of approximately equal duration, thus conforming to the traditional layout of dramatic structure and perhaps highlighting the usefulness of the midpoint (sequence) as a major turning point in screenplay construction. Kristin Thompson. *STORYTELLING IN THE NEW HOLLYWOOD: Understanding Classical Narrative Technique*. New York: McGraw-Hill, 2001.

[266] Peter Kramer, 'Post-classical Hollywood,' in Hill and Church Gibson, 1998, 289-309; Thompson. *Op.cit.*, 12.

Former Hollywood creative advisor Chris Vogler's Hero's Journey as interpreted in *THE WRITER'S JOURNEY* proved a popular text in the 1990s, not least among Hollywood's development executives, but also among film and screenwriting students. It provides an accessible reading of Joseph Campbell's take on Carl Jung through direct application to screenplay analysis. Providing a paradigmatic model for the practising screenwriter, Vogler discusses the major elements of Campbell's *THE HERO WITH A THOUSAND FACES* in terms of mainstream Hollywood cinema. The twelve-point template Vogler proposes is as follows and maps onto traditional dramatic structure thus:

Act I:
1. The hero lives in the Ordinary World.
2. The hero receives a Call to Adventure.
3. The hero Refuses the Call.
4. The hero Meets his Mentor.
5. The hero Crosses the Threshold,

Act II:
6. and encounters Tests, Allies and Enemies.
7. He approaches the Inmost Cave,
8. where he endures the Supreme Ordeal.
9. The hero Seizes the Sword.

Act III:
10. and journeys on the Road Back.
11. The hero experiences Resurrection
12. and Returns with the Elixir. [267]

This structure can be easily mapped onto mainstream Hollywood storytelling, and increasingly, global, film narratives – and not merely because Vogler is a regular on the global script lecturing circuit, frequently employed by state-sponsored media bodies. [268] This breakdown of Acts and sequences into their mythic elements has relevance for understanding Towne's work, particularly as we move into the post-classical period (in every sense) of his career; the mythic structure seems to dominate *Shampoo* and *Greystoke* as well as *Personal Best*; and the circularity it implies imposes a question/answer structure to the openings and conclusions of the screenplays he directs, viz., *Personal Best, Tequila Sunrise* and *Without Limits.*

---

[267] Chris Vogler. *THE WRITER'S JOURNEY: Mythic Structure for Storytellers & Screenwriters.* Los Angeles: Michael Wiese Productions, 1992, 236. Vogler's impetus to write the book came from his experiences as a creative analyst at a major studio – Disney - when he decided to collate the lessons he had learned from world storytelling into a model for understanding screenplays. A memo to this effect, outlining his findings about the shape of popular stories, circulated in Hollywood and eventually mutated into the published book. By the time this had occurred, his tenure at Disney saw the studio return to top form with unprecedented box office grosses by creating traditionally structured fare - along the lines suggested by Vogler - such as *The Little Mermaid* and *The Lion King.*
[268] See Ken Dancyer's *GLOBAL SCRIPTWRITING* for an account of the influence Hollywood's screenwriting pedagogues are having on the commercial potential of international filmmaking in the English-speaking world and beyond. Boston, Mass: Focal Press, 2001. This is also covered in Horton, ed., 2004, as before.

The narrative paradigm (or metastructure) of Towne's authorial identity (or theme) might be stated as follows: a morally ambiguous protagonist, trapped in his chosen profession_and in conflict with authority, discovers the truth of his situation through other people's lies but unhappily yields to compromise and ultimately settles for second best. A corollary to this might be Towne's characters' inexorable path towards death, romantic, spiritual or actual, a trend exacerbated by Towne's inclination toward the mythic. The super-structural Townean paradox is that in distinct writing phases throughout his career, he has engaged in linear structures when tackling overtly mythical themes; and circular structures when tackling less obviously mythical ideas. The classic Towne text is *Chinatown*, although, it is, as we shall see, disputably so: nonetheless, it is the cornerstone of his career.

Endings should be inevitable, if not necessarily predictable: the endings of Towne's screenplays are occasionally controversial, most particularly that of *Chinatown*, whose conclusion was famously altered on the set by the director, Roman Polanski from Towne's intended ending, which had Evelyn killing her father and going to jail, to a scene that Towne describes as "too melodramatic... I was wrong and he was right." [269] The film however has a profoundly bleak tone as it contemplates the decadence of power, exacerbated by Jake's blindness and ultimate sense of loss, which accelerates the narrative towards the desperate conclusion.

The conclusion to *Tequila Sunrise* (in which Mac dies) was altered at the behest of Warners, so that he instead rises, Messiah-like, from his watery grave, to embrace Jo Ann, while Nick, the apparent architect of their union, is the true loser in the narrative's newly imposed structure. Ironically, this plays into the fatalistic thread imposed by Polanski on Towne's writing thematic which is more compelling to an audience, perhaps, but betrays Towne's overweening tendency towards authentic conclusions of bittersweet compromise. [270]

The primary influence on this form of narrative is undoubtedly Towne's work on *Bonnie and Clyde* (1967), when his famous consultancy birthed a spectacular reputation (and his Poe adaptation, *The Tomb of Ligeia*, should also be mentioned inasmuch as Towne has regularly indulged a kind of shallow phantasmal perversity, particularly in his Seventies screenplays.) What is less frequently recognised is the form of that film and its own influence on Towne's approach to his subsequent work: not just the sense of loss, but the necessity of compromise (the connective tissue in Towne's professional career). While Towne has written many fine screenplays, the inevitable focus of much of this study must turn on *Chinatown*, a seminal work and, arguably perhaps, an anomaly within his oeuvre following the intervention of director Roman Polanski, whose classical filmmaking style and black European modernist tone is usually thought to cut through Towne's more conventional American narrative style to provide a ghastly if logical ending to Hollywood noir and help inaugurate a phase of what would latterly be identified as neo-noir. Towne himself has regularly summed up the theme of *Chinatown* as 'the futility of good intentions,' a term that invariably describes the fate of many of his protagonists, before and after *Chinatown*, perhaps *the* exemplary screenplay from the

---

[269] Grobel. *Op.cit.*,127.
[270] For, as Love instructs, in constructing an author profile, it "... will extend beyond ethos to consider all aspects of the text which have any bearing on personality, including singularities of style." Love. *Op.cit.,* 87. He adds, "when looking at individual authors it is necessary to distinguish those elements that remain stable over a lifetime from those that evolve, the first kind being the valuable ones for attribution as such, and the second kind important for dating." (92.)

1970s, an era latterly recognised as a Golden Age for cinema, less exalted perhaps for the quality of the screenplays which gave rise to it in the first place than the directors who took rich advantage of the writing talent surrounding them.

Auteurism & Hollywood Today

The journalistic use of auteurism as a kind of populist shorthand is dismissed by commentator John Patterson, stating:

> It's a cult of personality. It's a marketing scheme. It's become a misleading umbrella-term falsely uniting a diverse body of collectively created work under a single name. And it just encourages the tacky, egomaniacal film-school cult of the writer-director as lone presiding genius. More and more I tend to find myself believing in what the writer Thomas Schatz called 'the genius of the system'. [271]

Patterson acknowledges that the system per se no longer exists in the same form extolled by Schatz and that "the auteurs are still out there, but most of them bore me...It's easiest to do it with actors, some of whose careers run like golden threads through the work of others, and can come to constitute entire genres unto themselves." [272]

In auteurist methodology we must conclude that it is possible to detect a film maker's 'signature' through an examination of his total output, which is characterised by an overall unity of theme and style. It is thus the stylistic treatment of a film, rather than its subject matter, which is considered to be the more important in the case of a director – but as we have seen, the subject (and theme), for a writer, is paramount. To make a claim for the centrality of a screenwriter whose heyday might be perceived as being during the accession of these new Hollywood auteurs may be paradoxical; however the contribution of a number of screenwriters to the key films of the era has been denied by the overviews of cinema published in recent years, most notably, perhaps, Peter Biskind's *EASY RIDERS, RAGING BULLS*. [273] The key element of Sarris' commentary as it might pertain to screenwriting authorship are the terms 'personal vision' and 'authorial personality'. Any screenwriter with a body of work consistent in its thematic concerns finds a way of expressing such a vision throughout a variety of production conditions, with a variety of collaborators (directors, producers, and so on.)

---

[271] John Patterson, 'On Film,' *The Guardian*, Film & Music, 20 April 2007, 2. Billy Wilder claims that in becoming a director, "'I just wanted to protect the script. It's not that I had a vision or theory I wanted to express as a director; I had no signature or style...".' Interviewed by James Linville in *The Paris Review*, 138, Spring 1996, 70.

[272] *Ibid.*

[273] Peter Biskind. *EASY RIDERS, RAGING BULLS How the Sex-Drugs-and-Rock'n'Roll Generation Saved Hollywood.* New York: Simon & Schuster, 1998.It might contrarily be argued, however, that because the writers, for the most part, were less flagrantly indulgent than the directors concerned, that Biskind is paying ironic tribute to their achievements.

In Towne's work we can trace a line from classical cinema - however loosely - through New Hollywood and the current, blockbuster phase of, post-classical American cinema utilising the tenets of dramatic structure. That his most critically acclaimed work probably occurs in the New Hollywood era, the period of transition from approximately 1967-1975, hallmarked by the achievements of a new wave of American auteur directors, makes the forging of his centrality as author all the richer, in what can be read retrospectively as a great screenwriting age in Hollywood.

Acknowledgements:

Thanks to Professor James Goodwin for kindly providing a copy of his article.

Chapter 2 1960-1966: APPRENTICESHIP

The Last Woman on Earth (1960) (screenplay)
The Chameleon (1964) (written by)
The Dove Affair (1964) (written by)
The Tomb of Ligeia (1964) (screenplay)

The Screenwriter for Hire

"Theme," states Margaret Mehring, "is the reason for telling stories. Theme is the work of the artist." [274] While Towne's early Sixties work is primarily generic we can also detect those points in the texts where his concerns depart from the narratives' direct concerns and express his personal worldview. If we accept the screenplay as a finite form with certain formal limitations, the genre work is an even more compressed and specialised (or limited) vision. While screenwriters might always be said to be 'for hire,' given their particular situation in the chain of production and the customary system of vertical integration, it is particularly the case at the commencement of any screenwriter's career that their efforts are at the behest of producers and directors and their choices are naturally limited. Thus it was that Towne's career began with the help of producer Roger Corman.

The commencement of Towne's career is deeply rooted in exploitation cinema, episodic television and the rules of cinematic genres. James Monaco says that, "movie genres are simply formulaic patterns, some stricter than others." [275] Barry Langford explains that genre films can be "understood as the systematic, routinised production of genre films for a regular mass-audience spectatorship." [276] Genre could also be said to exist in different stages of development. According to Thomas Schatz, whose *HOLLYWOOD GENRES* (1981) encapsulates many of the aspects of writings on the subject, genres evolve, from a pure, conventionalized form that becomes a purely self-conscious form. He quotes Focillon, who observes that there is an experimental stage, a classic stage and an age of refinement which could be called a baroque or self-reflexive age. [277] In terms of the dialogue that exists between an audience and the making of a genre film, Schatz refers to Leo Braudy whom he quotes as follows: " 'Change in genre occurs when the audience says, 'That's too infantile a form of what we believe. Show us something more complicated'." [278] Generic structures, then, are embedded in the audience's collective

---

[274] Margaret Mehring. *THE SCREENPLAY A Blend of Film Form and Content.* Boston & London: Focal Press, 1990, 221. Mehring continues, "A theme emerges from the combination of all of the filmic and dramatic elements – both linear and non-linear. It is none of the individual elements but the amalgamation of all. It emerges as the end result of the many threads woven in a particular manner to communicate a particular statement. It is what the completed tapestry says." (223).

[275] James Monaco. *AMERICAN FILM NOW The People, The Power, The Money, The Movies.* New York, Plume Books, New American Library, 1979: 54.

[276] Barry Langford. *FILM GENRE: Hollywood and Beyond.* Edinburgh, Edinburgh University Press, 2005: 274. He explains that, "film genre theory … acknowledges that representational and narrative conventions supply important frameworks for meaning construction." (261).

[277] Schatz, 1981, 37

[278] Schatz continues: "Thus the end of a genre's classic stage can be viewed as that point at which the genre's straightforward message has 'saturated' the audience… we no longer look through the form (or perhaps 'into the mirror') to glimpse an idealized self-image, rather we look at the form itself to examine and appreciate its structure and cultural appeal.

"A genre's progression from transparency to opacity – from straightforward storytelling to self-mind. Schatz concludes, "The genre film reaffirms what the audience believes both on individual and on communal levels. Audience demand for variation does not indicate a change in believe, but rather that the belief should be re-examined, grow more complicated formally and thematically, and display, moreover, stylistic embellishment."

Towne would come of age as a screenwriter during a period when, as McGilligan comments

> ...the studios were undergoing a process of collapse and renovation, when turmoil in the world meant extreme changes in narrative style and screen values, when events in Hollywood, as elsewhere, sometimes seemed a confusing, delirious stampede. Screenwriters were as ever part of and integral to what was happening on- and offscreen. [279]

Fraternity Hell Week (?)
Little is known about this programmer, which was Towne's very first writing job for Roger Corman. Towne said:

> When they went to revise the script, they took scissors to it to cut it up. They lost all the pieces and that was the end of my first script. [280]

The Last Woman on Earth (1960) (screenplay)
Many years later, Towne would recall the result of his first screenwriting foray as "a grim science fiction thing" that he would rather forget.[281]

> When I was about 21, Corman was making two of his cheapies back-to-back in Puerto Rico and he persuaded me to take on a package deal in which I wrote a dreadful science fiction movie (*The Last Woman on Earth*, 1960) and worked as an actor as well. It was a deeply embarrassing experience, because I didn't know what I was doing and I can't act. But it was a start. [282]

Last Woman ... was one half of a package deal offered the nascent screenwriter. This was the third production shot by Corman while on vacation in Puerto Rico, where he also made *Creature from the Haunted Sea* with the same cast and crew, including Towne in an acting role; and produced *Battle of Blood Island*, all on the same trip. *Last Woman* ... may be a slight entry in the nuclear genre but it nonetheless demonstrates Towne's facility with character and dialogue. [283]

---

conscious formalism – involves its concerted effort to explain itself, to address and evaluate its very status as a popular form." Schatz, 1981,38.

[279] McGilligan 1996, 1. He continues: "The quantity of films may have dropped in the 1960s, but thanks to screenwriters, at the same time the range of subjects widened. There were old-fashioned dramas and comedies, musicals and westerns, historical epics and thrillers, but also clever new hybrid genres, breakthroughs in form and substance, changes in filmmaking that were challenging as well as liberating." (5.)

[280] Towne speaking to Michael Dwyer, 'Call the Script Doctor,' *The Irish Times*, 22 July 2006: 7.

[281] John Brady. *Op.cit.*, 367.

[282] Towne in Pirie, 1981, 150.

[283] *Synopsis* ("They Fought for the Ultimate Prize!") A gangster named Harold (Anthony Carbone), his moll, Evelyn (Betsy Jones Moreland), and his lawyer, Martin (Edward Wain, aka Robert Towne), are scuba diving in Puerto Rico when (presumably) H-bombs wipe out the world. Since these three happened to be underwater at the time, they are the sole survivors and

Figure 1 Edward Wain aka Robert Towne as Martin in *The Last Woman on Earth*

Towne's description is very telling of the priorities he was now exercising as screenwriter: a literal obstacle which serves as metaphor; a story of male friendship and the problem of loyalty; and the motif of smoking, which would crop up time and time again in his screenplays and serves as a form of communication between captor and captive.

The film has been described as both 'largely forgettable' and 'ineffably pretentious.' [284] Towne wrote it on the set of the production, while the film was being shot, which probably didn't help matters. However it has humour and a sense of its own ridiculousness, as borne out in the slightly camp characterizations and the beat-style soundtrack, not to mention the recurring motif of The Jabberwock. (Indicative of the Beat sensibility, Martin's key line is, "All that's left for us is to live without pain.") There is a rather gaping hole in the narrative – why is the oxygen suddenly restored to the island of Puerto Rico when the threesome decide to play house in the pleasant colonial villa? That Towne (or Wain, as he is credited) is the hero of the hour is without question – and interestingly, from the point of view of social commentary, if that is appropriate within the limited confines of this genre, the whole basis of marriage (or rather, marriage as the basic unit of society) is brought into question. The striking looking Jones-Moreland would not be the last blonde to play 'Evelyn' in Towne's work.

```
                    HAROLD
     This one woman two men situation --
     I guess we'll just have to live with
     it.


                    MARTIN
     You mean I'll have to live with it.
```

---

get to wander the empty streets and engage in lots of dialogue about humankind's future. Eventually the men fight over who will mate with Mary-Belle and rebuild civilization. Martin is afraid if she spawns with the thuggish Harold, the world will be repopulated with violent people doomed to a future of more bomb building. On Harold's side is the strong-survive theory of Darwinian natural selection.

[284] John Baxter. *SCIENCE FICTION IN THE CINEMA*. New York: A.S. Barnes & Co., 1970, 162; Tony Rayns' review is in *THE TIME OUT FILM GUIDE*. (2nd edition, edited by Tom Milne). London: Penguin, 1991, 373.

Some of the best dialogue features in the film's closing moments, which take place inside a modernist church: Towne was already demonstrating his keen observational skills for the way people spoke and behaved, even in the mock-existentialist set-up of *Last Woman* … where simple dialogue could conclude the complex plot in a Gordian exchange:

```
                    HAROLD
        I killed him.  Will we never learn?


                    EVELYN
        He didn't think so.


                    HAROLD
        Let's go home.


                    EVELYN
        Where's that?


                    HAROLD
        Help me find that.
```

(*The Last Woman on Earth*)

Creature from the Haunted Sea ("What Was the Unspeakable Secret of the SEA OF LOST SHIPS?") was made after *Last Woman*… and *The Battle of Blood Island* – Corman had another week to kill and called Charles Griffith to write the script, which arrived piece by piece and concerned a gangster on the lam who tries to cover up his crime wave by creating a panic about a non-existent sea monster. Then the real thing turns up… Corman had been inspired by the sound of machine gunfire in Havana when Castro took over and this was the result. Towne was already in Puerto Rico for *Last Woman*… and so completed the trio of actors for the mildly satiric comedy, with Roger set to play Happy Jack Monahan, a role that eventually went to his boom man, Bobby Bean. *Creature*… is usually labeled 'another camp classic from Roger Corman.' Only Towne (aka Edward Wain) as Sparks Moran, secret service agent, and Betsy Jones-Moreland as Mary-Belle, survive the monster. It has little interest for students of Towne the screenwriter but is an amusing comment on Corman's reading of the political situation in Cuba (the film's setting) and yet another risible creature-feature to add to the canon. The tone is one of bemused satire, with a number of good lines and amusing exchanges. The production overall however has little to recommend it. It was an inauspicious debut for Towne – as either actor or screenwriter.

The Television Scripts [285]
My Daddy Can Lick Your Daddy (1962) (teleplay); A Personal Matter (1963) (teleplay)

Sci-fi and horror may not have been Towne's preferred genres but he wrote for several of the more acclaimed series on American television in the early Sixties, between

---

[285] The only teleplay to which I had access was *The Chameleon* (Outer Limits) (1964), which I also viewed. I also viewed *The Dove Affair'* (The *Man From U.N.C.L.E.)*

1962 and 1964, including *The Lloyd Bridges Show*, an anthology series. He contributed two episodes to Season One: Episode 18: "My Daddy Can Beat Your Daddy," aka "My Daddy Can Lick Your Daddy," which was directed by John Cassavetes and starred Bridges; and also Episode 20:"A Personal Matter," 1963.

It was around this time that Corman also asked Towne to create a script based around the embarrassing Francis Gary Powers/U-2 incident, concerning the eponymous pilot who was sent to spy on Russia and was shot down and then imprisoned by the Kremlin. The film was to be called *I Flew a Spy Plane Over Russia* but Towne couldn't write fast enough so Corman made a muscleman, Steve Reeves-type outing called *Atlas* (1960) in Puerto Rico instead. It would appear that Towne made use of the idea in any case: he wrote it as an episode for the anthology series, *The Richard Boone Show*, a series which boasted Clifford Odets as story editor and featured the same cast in different weekly stories.

This is a crucial stage in Towne's development, not least because television is perhaps the only medium which privileges the writer (and had proven its dramatic worth with the previous decade's groundbreaking teleplays by such stalwarts as Paddy Chayefsky, Rod Serling, Reginald Rose and Gore Vidal) and therefore provides us with some testing ground for an analysis of those elements of screenplay structure which could be seen to be unencumbered with the weight of feature film collaborations; albeit the teleplays were of course written within the strict generic parameters imposed by their respective series' producers.

Breaking Point 'So Many Pretty Girls, So Little Time' (1963) (teleplay) (written by)
The *Breaking Point* episode, entitled 'So Many Pretty Girls, So Little Time,' concerned a compulsive Don Juan, a subject which would form the basis of *Shampoo* a decade later, albeit in mutated fashion.

If television - society's major storyteller - is the main reflection of our contemporary fears and desires, that which defines to us the nature of reality, the Cold War era in the United States, as elsewhere, boasted several series designed to capitalize on nuclear and foreign anxiety. *The Outer Limits* series was the brainchild of Leslie Stevens and Joseph Stefano (who would write *Psycho* for Alfred Hitchcock.) Stefano had a policy of hiring the best professional mainstream writers rather than pure science fiction authors and his hunch paid off with the employing of Anthony Lawrence (*Roustabout*), David Duncan (*The Time Machine*) and Dean Riesner (*Dirty Harry* and *Rich Man, Poor Man*). They, and Towne, who wrote 'The Chameleon', produced what were probably the most acclaimed entries to the series. Stefano wrote eleven episodes in the first series, while Stevens contributed three.

The Outer Limits - 'The Chameleon' (1964) TV Episode (writer)
Towne's other episode that year, 'The Chameleon,' was for the more widely screened series *The Outer Limits* in which the protagonist was a man trapped by his occupation: this would form the thematic basis for many later screenplays by Towne.

A man's survival can take many shapes and the shape in which a man finds his humanity is not always a human one.

Here, the man in question (played by Robert Duvall) is a formerly compromised secret service agent who impersonates an alien in order to infiltrate a party of creatures on a downed aircraft. Also known as 'The Seamaness Drug,' or 'The Drug'(the original titles), it first aired on 27 April 1964 and was directed by Gerd Oswald, who had a number of feature credits to his name. The story was devised by Towne, Lou Morheim and Stefano. Duvall's character, Louis Mace, is a haunted man, now living as a virtual derelict. Hired by Chambers, his ex-boss, to participate in a special mission, he learns that he is to be transformed, albeit temporarily, into an alien in order to prevent nuclear war due to an amount of 'fissionable material' in a temporarily downed spacecraft. He has nothing to lose and knows that nobody else would do the job.

> LOUIS
> Whatever it involves no-one else would
> do it - -right?

Louis is existentially aware of the meaninglessness of his existence and the script boasts the kind of dialogue that would be labeled 'pretentious' in the Corman films but seems oddly apposite in a series so close to human fears at the height of the Cold War. Fully half of the episode, which deals with 'the bizarre problem of our identity,' is devoted to Louis' apparent fearlessness and his transformation into an alien. The contents of his life are held on a spool of genetic information:

> LOUIS
> You mean to say that's all I am --
> everything that's me -- is on that spool
> of tape?

He claims to be an expert in his chosen field and yet doesn't appear to fully comprehend the future implications of his actions:

> LOUIS
> I have one capacity, Dr. Tillyard, the
> capacity to survive.

> DR. TILLYARD
> You've survived against mortals, and
> dangerous mortals no doubt. But these
> are aliens.

> LOUIS
> The scales are balanced then. We're
> aliens to them. I'll survive, Dr.
> Tillyard.

As he is going under, counting back from one hundred, the General, Chambers and Tillyard hear him mumbling his regrets about his past, about 'doing something constructive,' and finally, he says, 'All I have is what I can do.' His transformation is described as 'Mace's life being rewritten.'

As they observe his behaviour on board the spaceship, his employers wonder why he laughs continually. 'It's as if he knew something that we could never know.' The aliens recognize that his impersonation is a good one – but not good enough to fool them.

<pre>
                      LOUIS
        I feel like I belong here -- that
        I've been here.

                      ALIEN
        You are -- if only in part -- one of us.
</pre>

Chambers is worried:

<pre>
                    CHAMBERS
        General, we may be losing our agent -
        not through death but through defection.
</pre>

'Defection' of course was another buzz word of the time, with the motif being readily applicable to any number of the political hotspots – Berlin, Cuba or Russia (including the Powers story; just as, years later, *Chinatown*, a film set in the late 1930s, could be read as a gloss on the 1970s Watergate scenario.) Louis claims there are no weapons on board the ship. After a confusing 'escape,' [confusing because all the 'aliens' are wearing identical suits and masks], he agrees to accompany the surviving alien to his planet:

<pre>
                      LOUIS
        I'm neither Mace nor one of them.
</pre>

He is going 'where *The Chameleon* no longer has to change his colour to survive.'

It is clear that as in any television episodic, this is confined by the demands not merely of the genre and the budget but also by the ambitions within the series itself. However certain tropes emerge which begin to affect Towne's personal signature: economy of expression; beautifully crafted dialogue which speaks beyond the immediacy of the given situation and which marks a development from the Beatnik-styled pretentiousness of his Corman screenplays; a certain longing for contentment and a yearning for opportunities lost, which would be explicit here yet in later work would be rather more subtle; and, of course, a deep-seated attitude of anti-authoritarianism, an ideological (and even political) preoccupation which would form the backbone of many of Towne's great Seventies screenplays. These elements are deeply connected to the protagonist's character and his occupation. All of these aspects would form part of Towne's later, more overtly characteristic screenplays; and the experience of collaborating with a production team under pressure to deliver major network television would give him a deeper understanding of the backdrop to successful production involving regular studio interference. While the teleplay boasts the customary twist ending that marks this particular series, it also seals Towne's own optimistic view of Mace's future.

The Man from U.N.C.L.E. – 'The Dove Affair' (1964) TV Episode (written by)

Sean Connery began the spy movie boom playing James Bond in *Dr. No* and *From Russia With Love*. The success of the franchise inspired every studio in Hollywood and Europe to release everything from serious knockoffs to spoofs on the genre featuring debonair men, futuristic gadgets, exotic locales. Television's answer came in the form of The Man from U.N.C.L.E. 1964 would see Towne writing '*The Dove Affair*' for the series, his last television episode and an invaluable experience that would serve him well thirty years on, when, at the behest of Tom Cruise, he undertook one of the biggest film franchises of them all: *Mission: Impossible*. Originally aired on 15 December 1964 and directed by John Peyser, the logline for the show is as follows: THRUSH have assassinated the leader of an East European country and Napoleon Solo must stop them from taking power.

> SATINE
> Are you going to kill me?

> SOLO
> Unfortunately I can't just because
> I want to -- I have to know why.

Napoleon Solo [286] plays spy vs. spy with Satine, ace intelligence agent of an Eastern European country. The nation's leader has been assassinated by THRUSH. Both Solo and Satine want to prevent THRUSH from taking power but both are on the defensive from government officials allied with Thrush. (Ilya Kuryakin doesn't feature in this episode.) As is usual in the series it's divided into four acts: I is Incident in the Balkans; II The Running Men; III Togetherness, when Solo and Satine are forced to help/threaten each other on an outward bound train, encumbered by Miss Taub and her 'juvenile delinquents'; IV is End of the Line, when, appropriately, they all get over the border and elude the army – Satine by killing the one general who can put a face to his name.

Towne's script is replete with sardonic witticisms and Ricardo Montalban excels as Satine, the saturnine double-agent from KREB who has a variety of quirks such as a fear of teenagers – which is unfortunate, since TV stalwart June Lockhart (as Sarah Taub), and her American students, are the innocents who keep getting in the middle of the murky Cold War action. Satine is a master of disguise and serves drinks at the American Embassy, where he and Solo instantly sniff each other out at the reception where the masque of diplomacy slips regularly. Satine suffers from a stomach ailment and at one striking moment on a bridge he warns Solo, "Be ready, something may explode," while clutching his abdomen. In fact he drops a box of cigarettes, eagerly grabbed by Russian soldiers – and it blows up, enabling Solo's escape. The two play an amusing game of cat and mouse (and dove), finally making good their escape from their common enemy with the aid of the sweet-natured spinster teacher who achieves a poignancy decidedly uncommon in the series. The ending is somewhat unsatisfactory since the titular dove refers to a medal with the names of THRUSH agents engraved in microscopic letters. Satine gets the dove and Solo gets a picture of the dove. How could this possibly help UNCLE?! Never mind. Although Satine and Solo are ostensibly enemies, the screenplay concludes on a note of friendship – loyal servants of their respective states who wind up sharing a point of view in a script that is distinguished by

---

[286] The name was apparently dreamed up by Ian Fleming, who met producer Norman Felton but didn't want further involvement for fear of complicating his relationship with Harry Saltzmann, the producer of the James Bond film series. Nonetheless, Felton attached Fleming's name to the outline written by Sam Rolfe which won the commission. See Tom Stempel. *STORYTELLERS TO THE NATION: A History of American Television Writing*. New York: Continuum, 1992, 102.

masquerade, double-talk and disguise. This is a trope that would appear in Towne's feature screenplays, despite his feelings about working in the medium:

> … I wrote for television for a couple of years on shows like *The Man from U.N.C.L.E.* and *The Outer Limits* and a lesser known series called *Breaking Point*, which was probably the best TV show I ever scripted. But almost everything I did was fouled by continuity or editorial interference. My experiences there were not at all happy. [287]

As noted on *The Man From U.N.C.L.E.* listserver, Towne's later script for the 1996 *Mission: Impossible* feature appears to have reworked some scenes from this episode, notably the meetings on the bridge, the Embassy party and of course the internecine double-crossing. In other words, major structural elements, including themes and scenes would be reworked by Towne almost three decades later in a blockbuster film which would also bear a co-writer's name. But there were to be many more screenplays written in the thirty years before that would happen and '*The Dove Affair*' would be Towne's last teleplay. What can also be noted here is something referenced by Charles Barr in his study of Hitchcock's English films:

> This initial linking of personal and public worlds, of character psychology and espionage plot, establishes with brilliant economy the logic of the film, and of the Hitchcock thriller. [288]

Towne was working not just from the technical and dramatic demands of the immediate plot, he was borrowing technique from those writers who honed their skills in collaboration with Alfred Hitchcock: he would in time be accused not merely of imitating their style but of stealing their plot. [289]

---

[287] Towne in Pirie, 1981, 150.
[288] Charles Barr. *ENGLISH HITCHCOCK.* Scotland: A Movie Book, 1991, 137.
[289] cf. discussion *Mission: Impossible 2* and *Notorious*, in Chapter 5 of this volume.

The Tomb of Ligeia (1964) (screenplay)

Film production was declining in response to the harsh economic reality of the early sixties. Even the Production Code would be revised and finally dumped by 1966 when it had a purely nominal advisory role. Thomas Schatz notes that even MGM was financing just ten films a year and releasing less than twice that number in this period; its huge profits derived from television production. In contrast, the fortunes of Twentieth-Century Fox had already faded, refusing to acknowledge the changing demographics of the audience. [290]

The horror film came to prominence once more in the early Sixties, a time of transition in the Hollywood system. A single film would alter everything - *Psycho*, a somewhat experimental low-budget film for Alfred Hitchcock, shot by his television crew at Universal Studios. It was released on 08 March 1960 and its ultra-realistic take on American Gothic would change horror cinema forever, with its unsympathetic characters and atmosphere, and a cruel engagement with viewer psychology culminating in the heroine's vicious murder in the shower a mere forty minutes into the film, punishing the audience for its voyeurism. Thomas Schatz calls it "perhaps the single most influential film made during Hollywood's transitional period." He continues to venture that it "probably has had more impact on the techniques, subject matter, thematics, and even the marketing strategies of subsequent moviemaking than any other film made since Hollywood's classic era." He correctly notes that "the film gave considerable impetus and a degree of legitimacy to the 'exploitation film,' proving that the kind of low-budget, sex-cum-violence thrillers churned out by the likes of Corman's AIP could attract larger audiences and considerable critical attention." [291] That would be proved true just a few months later with the release of Corman's first Gothic horror for AIP on 22 June 1960.

In 1964 Roger Corman was coming to the end of his cycle of Edgar Allan Poe adaptations. They had been a striking success for the independent producer, both in terms of their artistic achievement and in revenue. The series had commenced as a serious rival to the Hammer Horrors of the late 1950s which had made inroads at American cinemas. Corman's own literary studies and his insights into the American academic curriculum aided his decision to begin 'serious' work, as opposed to his usual exploitation fare. (His own attempt at serious filmmaking, *The Intruder* (1961), which dealt with race problems in the South, prevented him from ever tackling such difficult social issues as director again because of its commercial failure.) He hired notable writers such as Richard Matheson, R.Wright Campbell and Charles Beaumont on previous entries which had varied from the sublime (*The Pit and the Pendulum*, 1961) to the

---

[290] Thomas Schatz. *OLD HOLLYWOOD/NEW HOLLYWOOD: Ritual, Art and Industry*. Ann Arbor, Michigan: UMI Research Press, 1983, 189. He continues: "By 1970 … three-quarters of all 'frequent moviegoers' (which accounted for about 90% of all admissions) were between the ages of twelve and twenty-nine, and fully three-quarters of that group had had some college education. This was the generation born between World War II and 1960 – the so-called baby boom, that aberrant blip in America's demographic history that would, as the babies grew older, determine the general evolution of movies, TV, pop music, dress, and other aspects of our consumer culture. This generation had gleaned the grammar of screen narrative and learned film history from hours spent with television; foreign films, classic Hollywood movies, even the youth-marketed exploitation films meted out via Roger Corman's American International Pictures (AIP)." (190)

[291] See Schatz, 1983.

ridiculous (*The Raven*, 1963). [292] So it was that he hired Robert Towne to write his first serious feature screenplay, *The Tomb of Ligeia* (1965), a particularly difficult entry in the cycle.

Michael J. Collins writes of the value of Corman's horror cycle,

> Corman's Poe adaptations work well as pop-psychology character studies because they echo Poe's recurring theme of psychological breakdown. Madness burns away at the protagonists of these films, finally exploding outward in deranged, destructive climaxes. In fact, the image of the mentally unstable hero is a staple of Corman's work.

He continues, however, that

> humor has always had its place in Corman's work. His lonely, tormented heroes have never been the excessively gloomy types familiar to viewers of upscale foreign films. As American as the movies themselves, his characters usually find themselves lost within a spiralling anarchy, in which they follow a series of bad impulses that lead to their own destruction. [293]

It is clear, therefore, that not only had Towne to contend with the genre itself and the particular problems posed by Poe; he was also dealing with Corman's method of working; his preferred interpretation of Poe; and the interpretations offered by previous writers for the franchise.

A concept hitherto under-explored elsewhere and which will prove of use in further like-minded studies, is the chasm dividing external and internal authorship, according to Buckland's terms; the former having to do with the director's managerial position; the latter being the way in which auteurism is classically understood in its Romantic, artistic manner.[294] We might therefore look at the way in which Towne tried to put his own stamp on a series in which Corman was keen to be seen as a literary

---

[292] It is worth noting Corman's care in the collaborators he chose for this series: Richard Matheson was an author of some note and he adapted his own novel for the classic sci-fi film *The Incredible Shrinking Man* (1957), directed by Jack Arnold. His post-apocalyptic vampire fantasy I AM LEGEND was a mixture of Gothic myth and doomsday allegory and would be most successfully brought to the screen as *The Omega Man* (1971). He provided the screenplay for *Night of the Eagle* (1961) (an adaptation with Charles Beaumont of Fritz Leiber's 'Conjure Wife' for Anglo Amalgamated) and he would also successfully adapt the Dennis Wheatley novel *T he Devil Rides Out* (1967). He imbued his work with carefully constructed mythological and allegorical elements and was ideal for such a project as Corman's, where heightened psychological and symbolic aspects could amplify the more intriguing character situations of what were inherently problematic narratives. David Pirie considers that Matheson was probably influenced by the out of favour Freudian reading of Poe favoured by Marie Bonaparte, 'Edgar Poe, Sa Vie et Son Oeuvre.' Pirie comments: "Certainly, no medium could be more suited to render the dream-like aspect of Poe's world than the film, and this is effectively what Corman has done. At times, he adds to the purely psychological dimension, and other aspects of Poe spring to life, but, in the main, he has concentrated on capturing the surrealistic Freudian imagery, so that almost every scene carries a compelling aura of decadent Romanticism. The result is some beautiful films, that are very far from betraying the Poe spirit." Pirie, in Paul Willemen, David Pirie, David Will and Lynda Myles (eds.) *ROGER CORMAN: The Millennic Vision.* Edinburgh: Edinburgh Film Festival, 1970, 48-49.

[293] Michael J. Collins, 'Roger Corman,' in *THE FEARMAKERS The Screen's Directorial Masters of Suspense and Terror* by John McCarty, ed. London: Virgin Books, 1995, 56-57.

[294] Buckland, 2006.

tastemaker in a business where his occasionally camp productions were much seen but little admired. Unpicking the strands of authorship in this series is troublesome, particularly at the point at which Towne joined the team, for the final entry in the Poe cycle, when all the tropes and visual strategies would appear long-established. Corman can be identified as auteur through his work as producer, director, writer, company owner and distributor and therefore as someone in the business of vertical integration. [295]

Corman described his approach to the films thus: "What I generally did was to take the story as written by Poe and use that as the third act or climax of my film and try to write or invent a first and second act that would lead logically to what Poe had written and hopefully stay within the style and spirit of Poe." [296]   Towne said of their collaboration:

> Roger and I were really a classic mismatch. It was very painstaking, the screenplay
> of *The Tomb of Ligeia*. In fact, I worked harder on the horror screenplay for him
> than on anything I think I have ever done. And I still like the screenplay. I think
> it's good. [297]

Ligeia was made when Corman decided that the cycle required a shift in emphasis. He had shot *Masque* … on borrowed sets left over on sound stages after the shooting on *Beckett* and *A Man for All Seasons* had finished, and crucially opted to utilise actual English locations once again for the production of *Ligeia*. Mark Thomas McGee comments of the production: "Vincent Price had always wanted to do a picture in a ruin so he was happy. But they weren't allowed to put furniture in the monastery because it was considered a national monument so some interiors were created at Shepperton Studios." [298] Roger Corman takes up the point: "What I think that the filmmaker does now or in the past or in the future is to break through the defences of the conscious mind and to attack and expose those fears of the unconscious mind. If you do it right the audience *will* scream!" [299]

A Question of Interpretation
        The French (Freudian) critic Marie Bonaparte summarises the essential Poe

narrative:

> Time and again, we find the same manifest situation, of some ideal woman who
> sickens and dies, yet does not really die, since she lives on in unearthly radiance;
> putrescent and ethereal at one and the same time. Always and forever it is the same
> latent theme: that of Elizabeth Arnold's last agony and death-repeated in after years in
> the little Virginia's agony and death. And yet I am unable to spare him. For the very
> monotony of these tales, their endless repetitions, are themselves expressions of Poe's
> psyche. [300]

---

[295] Buckland. *Op.cit.*, 15.

[296] Corman speaking on *The Curse of Corman*, BBC2 TV, 1990.

[297] Towne in Brady. *Op.cit*, 390

[298] McGee. O*p.cit.,* 75.

[299] Corman speaking on *The Curse of Corman* as before.

[300] Marie Bonaparte. *EDGAR POE, SA VIE ET SON OEUVRE*, translated by John Rodker, reprinted in *THE EDGAR ALLAN POE READER*. Philadelphia, Pennsylvania: Courage Books, 1993, 5.

The screenplay was adapted from 'Ligeia,' which relates the tale of Poe's haunted protagonist, once again doomed to love a woman who has departed the living world:

> ... although I perceived that her loveliness was indeed 'exquisite,' and felt that
> there was much of 'strangeness' pervading it, yet I have tried in vain to
> detect the irregularity and to trace home my own perception of the 'strange.'
> - 'Ligeia,'1838 [301]

Adapting any material for the screen would appear a problematic task: transposing material from one medium to another is fraught with difficulty. Many screenwriting manuals engage with the creative aspect of screenwriting but find it wiser to avoid detailed advice on adapting materials, gauging, correctly perhaps, that it is a process dependent on the individual genre or story form. Robert Towne's attitude however, is markedly different. Interviewed by John Brady, he explains himself thus:

> I think that almost always it's easier to adapt. Your writing inhibitions are lower.
> In a sense, you might even be writing a little bit better when you're adapting
> someone else's material because vanity, fear and all the things that inhibit you
> as a writer don't come into play. You tend to be a little looser, taking shots from
> different parts of the court that you wouldn't normally attempt – and making them
> - just because you are looser. Sometimes with your own material you get constipated,
> vain and stupid. For that reason it's somewhat easier to adapt. But not always.[302]

No literary work survives translation to the screen without alteration, however minor. While somewhere between 80-90% of all film works are an adaptation of one description or another, there is no precise manner in which those films can be analysed, nor is there a proven technique by which the work can be translated for a primarily visual (albeit narrative) medium.

Dudley Andrew's description of the adaptation process is significant because he locates the crux of the issue as the transmission of meaning from one textual model to another, visual form. He states that "its distinctive feature, the matching of the cinematic sign system to prior achievement in some other system" and "can be shown to be distinctive of all representational cinema." He continues, "in a strong sense adaptation is the appropriation of a meaning from a prior text." [303]

Comparative analysis of a screen experience necessarily obviates many of the features that make the transposition from page to screen interesting in the first place. While acknowledging that this is the case, it is a problem intrinsic to examining any film put onscreen and is also a basic method to this study, which is concerned with the tendencies of bringing screenplays to the screen. Gabriel Miller sums up the differences between novels and films thus:

> Fiction achieves a greater density because of its length ... while most films are
> limited to about two hours' running time, and the film audience's experience is bound,
> to a large extent, by the speed of the projector, which allows no breaks (except for the
> rare intermission), and no opportunities to review what happened earlier. The film must
> make its point and deal with its characters and subject quickly and directly, in a basically
> linear sequence of images. Writers and directors must recognize and try to work within

---

[301] From *THE EDGAR ALLAN POE READER*, 161.
[302] Robert Towne interviewed by John H. Brady 1981, 420.
[303] Dudley Andrew. *Op.cit.,* 96-106.

these simple and seemingly obvious guidelines in order to achieve a successful transformation of the novelist's art into the language of the cinema. [304]

When considering the success or otherwise of a screen adaptation, there are several elements to be remembered: how closely the material has been followed; if only key scenes or story points have been used in simplifying or amplifying the material; if subplots have been curtailed or eliminated altogether; different forms of expression in different media, for instance, overly symbolic dialogue which doesn't work particularly well onscreen; point of view; structure; location; techniques of editing, compression or expansion; improvements; original ideas or new characters that might have been incorporated into the story; new themes; and so on.

At the purely narrative level, then, it is necessary to examine those elements of the original story 'Ligeia,' which survived, and those which Towne felt were unnecessary to maintain the narrative spine. Part of that struggle was reworking themes which had occurred in previous entries in the cycle. 'Ligeia' had in fact been used before, as padding, in Corman's portmanteau film *Tales of Terror* (1964), where it was loosely combined with 'Morella' (and part of 'Eleanora') to form that particular narrative. Poe's 'The Case of Mr Valdemar' similarly dealt with mesmerism.[305] Thus, the roots of Towne's inspiration came not only from Poe, but also from Charles Beaumont's prior interpretation of Poe for Corman and the tropes that had already been tried and proven for his valuable franchise.

> I listened – in extremity of horror. The sound came again – it was a sigh. Rushing to the corpse, I saw – distinctly saw – a tremor upon the lips. In a minute afterwards they relaxed, disclosing a bright line of the pearly teeth. Amazement now struggled in my bosom with the profound awe which had hitherto reigned there alone. I felt that my vision grew dim, that my reason wandered; and it was only by a violent effort that I at length succeeded in nerving myself to the task which duty thus once more had pointed out.
> - 'Ligeia' [306]

George Bernard Shaw observes of the story,

> The story of the Lady Ligeia is not merely one of the wonders of literature: it is unparalleled and unapproached. There is really nothing to be said about it: we others simply take off our hats and let Mr. Poe go first. [307]

In his analysis of the horror genre, author Stuart Kaminsky comments:

> The dark, isolated castles are distortions of smaller homes, exotic versions of our own domestication... Graves and crypts seem constantly to be defiled in horror films. The actors (representing the audience) frequently are called upon to exhume

---

[304] Gabriel Miller. *SCREENING THE NOVEL: Rediscovered American Fiction in Film.* New York: Frederick Ungar Publishing, 1980, xiv.

[305] See David Pirie, 'Roger Corman's Descent Into The Maelstrom,' in Paul Willemen, David Pirie, David Will, Lynda Myles. *ROGER CORMAN: The Millennic Vision.* Edinburgh Film Festival '70 in association with *CINEMA* magazine,1970, 45-67.

[306] From *THE EDGAR ALLAN POE READER.* Philadelphia, Pennsylvania: Courage Books, 1993, 171.

[307] George Bernard Shaw in *THE EDGAR ALLAN POE READER,* 310.

a corpse, to find it missing, and to deal with the meaning of the body's disappearance – to view this possible resurrection as a horror, rather than as a Christ-like miracle. [308]

What is noticeable about the entire Poe series until the filming of *Ligeia* is that external reality is avoided, save for the atmospheric introductory shots, usually of a castle, preferably situated on the edge of a cliff framed by crashing waves below: this sets up the audience for a literally cliffhanging narrative, with suitably nerve-wracking tension and a closed group of participants in the manner of an Agatha Christie murder mystery. It was in fact the first of the series to be shot on location, and in England, at that.[309] Critic David Pirie commented that the script "is probably the most *literate* ever derived from Poe's work. This is not to belittle [Richard] Matheson, for it cannot help drawing on some of his ideas, but its approach to the material is quite different. Poe's story, 'Ligeia', his own personal favourite, was essentially a prose-poem, and what *The Tomb of Ligeia* does is to incorporate, visually and orally, onto its much-extended narrative structure, some of the breadth of poetic reference in the original." [310]

Therefore we can see another aspect of Towne's emergent trademark as screenwriter: realism, or at least authenticity, to the extent that this can be expressed in a generic format whose visual strategies were virtually predetermined by the series' true auteur, Roger Corman. On a purely narrative level Towne was now mature enough as a writer to use the original text as propulsion to truly express something else in the screenplay. In other words, he was beginning to find his voice. He has commented of his approach:

> When I proceed to write the script, I find that I'm as likely to go 180 degrees in the opposite direction of my own treatment as I am to go with it; sometimes it's useful when I use it, and sometimes it provides the vehicle for me to argue with when I don't. What dictates that is, as you start the process of writing a screenplay – or probably anything – you're dreaming a dream. The job is to make a dream come true. It starts as a daydream, which is to say that you're the one who's actively pushing the fantasy. If you get lucky, at a certain point the conscious part of you goes to sleep and it becomes a night dream. It takes over.

---

[308] Stuart Kaminsky. *AMERICAN FILM GENRE: Approaches to a Critical Theory of Popular Film.* New York: Dell Publishing, 1977, 138. Such a scene occurs in the story of 'Ligeia' thus: "The greater part of the fearful night had worn away, and she who had been dead, once again stirred – and now more vigorously than hitherto, although arousing from a dissolution more appalling in its utter hopelessness than any. I had long ceased to struggle or to move, and remained sitting rigidly upon the ottoman, a helpless prey to a whirl of violent emotions, of which extreme awe was perhaps the least terrible, the least consuming. The corpse, I repeat, stirred, and now more vigorously than before. The hues of life flushed up with unwonted energy into the countenance – the limbs relaxed – and, save that the eyelids were yet pressed heavily together, and that the bandages and draperies of the grave still imparted their charnel character to the figure, I might have dreamed that Rowena had indeed shaken off, utterly, the fetters of Death. But if this idea was not, even then, altogether adopted, I could at least doubt no longer, when arising from the bed, tottering, with feeble steps, with closed eyes, and with the manner of one bewildered in a dream, the thing that was enshrouded advanced boldly and palpably into the middle of the apartment." - 'Ligeia.' *Op.cit.*, 172.

[309] Geoff Andrew comments says that the finished film is "... a subtle tale of necrophilic obsession, shot, for once, on location at a Norfolk abbey." *THE FILM HANDBOOK.* Essex: Longman, 1989, 63.

[310] Pirie, in Willemen, Pirie, Will and Myles. *Op.cit.*, 62.

You lose conscious control over it. The characters have a life of their own, and you just have to follow the logic of them and say, 'Oh, that's what they do.' [311]

Figure 2 Cover of *The Tomb of Ligeia* VHS

Towne discovered the form of writing required for a horror film to be "...the toughest kind. Really, it's a tough form." [312] He explains the basis for his important decision on the formation of Ligeia's character as follows:

'Ligeia' was a very short story. I remember reading all the body of Poe's work, and I felt the best thing to do would be to take Poe's themes and expand on them. There was a strong hint of mesmerism in the story. I decided to make it overt – with all that emphasis on Ligeia's eyes and how they held the beholder. Also in Poe there is a lot of necrophilia – implied if not expressed. So I took the combination of mesmerism, which was there, and necrophilia, which was sort of there (because the first wife was always in the background), and brought them together. It provided a natural explanation for this woman. [313]

---

[311] Towne in Engel. *Op.cit*, 203
[312] Towne in Brady. *Op.cit.*,390.
[313] Towne, in Brady. *Op.cit.*,391.

Towne comments on his use of the props of mesmerism and necrophilia in his establishing of the eponymous character:

> It provided a natural explanation for this woman. She had hypnotized the
> protagonist, and he was making love to this body under posthypnotic
> suggestion, literally being controlled by someone who was dead – which is kind
> of a gruesome notion, but perfectly consistent with Poe. I was trying to use
> a theme consistent with him, even though it wasn't in the story. [314]

This is an important point, since Towne is inputting his own view not merely of the genre but of the author – in other words, he is placing himself in Poe's position and asking, "What would Poe do [if by inference, Poe were alive and well and presumably writing in Hollywood]?" [315] Those 'endless repetitions' of death to which Bonaparte alludes create a tapestry of difficulty for the screenwriter but Towne's response – to enter into Poe's subversive mindset and extrapolate the latent theme (including an obsession with eyes and vision) – proves his dedication to the craft of adaptation, visualising the intention of the original text and translating that into its closest cinematic equivalent.

The story, then, conforms to Poe's basic template of a narrator hopelessly in love with a woman whose strength of will enables her to return from the dead. She is as strong as she is beautiful, with a vast intellect and knowledge; but Poe would later regret allowing her to transmogrify into the fair Rowena, believing the story to be ultimately flawed.

Towne was not in England when the film was being shot there on location and he disapproved of the casting of Price, which he felt undermined the story's purpose. [316]

Horror writer and critic David Pirie obviously disagrees with Towne's assessment of the project's outcome:

> There is a long early sequence involving a long monologue by Verden Fell (Price),
> juxtaposed against Rowena (Elizabeth Shepherd) climbing a Gothic tower, which
> has a syntactic originality that has rarely been equalled in horror movies. But even
> more importantly, Corman – like Michael Reeves in *Witchfinder General* – utilized the
> English landscape in a way that Hammer had often neglected. [317]

Towne's tendency towards realism (or, more accurately, plausibility) is a vision that is already having an impact on his collaborators and not only reaffirms his conceptualising of Poe's themes but radically resituates the Poe narrative within a realm of realist fiction to which it would not naturally belong. While he remained faithful to the

[314] Towne in Brady. *Ibid.*
[315] Towne continues his commentary more widely on the horror genre itself, and specifically the problems lying behind adapting the realm of American Gothic fiction to the screen: "American horror stories tend to provide natural explanations for events – like, 'Oh, well, she was hypnotized' – whereas the English tend to go for supernatural explanations. I tried to have my cake and eat it too in *Ligeia*. There was that natural explanation of posthypnotic suggestion, along with the supernatural explanation of a possession. That was also a theme in the story – this vaguely pantheistic notion of being able to come back from the dead in a blade of grass or an animal – and there was the cat and all that. Some people liked the movie quite a bit. I think it was a little dull. It think it would have been better if it had been done with a man who didn't look like a necrophiliac to begin with…" Towne in Brady. *Ibid.*
[316] Both quotes are from Towne's in Brady. *Op.cit*, 391-392.
[317] David Pirie's review appears in *THE TIME OUT FILM GUIDE* 1991, 684.

plot (or arrangement of incidents, as Aristotle would have it) he also, crucially, remained faithful to the spirit or intention of the original text. He therefore proved himself to be the most pragmatic of screenwriting collaborators.

Pirie extrapolates from the film's structure an interesting narrative system, as he explains in his essay 'Roger Corman's Descent into the Maelstrom', and argues that "what *The Tomb of Ligeia* does is to incorporate, visually and orally, onto it's [sic] much-extended narrative structure, some of the breadth of poetic reference in the original." [45] In other words, as Towne had placed himself in Poe's position, he had also immersed himself in the world of American Gothic, a very distinct form of poetic, and he had utilised the elements to create a screenplay that Edgar Allan Poe might himself have written, albeit with a more intrinsic optimism. [46]

Pirie also refers to the multiplicity of visual symbols in the film, which accumulate in significance as the story progresses, again deriving from the references to vision, Egyptology and the preceding films in the series. [47] This use of visual tropes and fetishes as thematic and story symbol is replicated throughout Towne's work.

While it received what were probably the most unanimously favourable reviews of any Corman film, *Ligeia* was not entirely without its critics and the review in the *Monthly Film Bulletin* alluded to problems that would feature in readings of Towne's later work:

---

[45] Pirie in Willemen et al, 1970, **62**.

[46] The system operates as follows: 1. Visually, using the references throughout the story to Ligeia's eyes, and the Egyptian art and concept of reincarnation, represented by the cat (This is corroborated by Towne's claims, pp. 60-61 of this text.) 2. Psychologically and emotionally, a positive aspect has been introduced to the story through the self-awareness of the protagonist, Verden Fell (a classically emblematic name) whose regard for his second wife, Rowena, he sees as means of relinquishing the dead Ligeia's grasp. 3.The enactment of Fell's inner turmoil is actualized by Corman's decision to cast the same actress (Elizabeth Shepherd) to play Ligeia and Rowena. Pirie, in Willemen, Pirie, Will and Myles. *Op.cit.*, 62. Towne commented on his involvement in adaptations: "In rewriting someone or in adapting a work, you can come to feel it's your very own, too. Or you can feel that you are in the service of somebody else's material that you love very much, and you want to work." Towne in Brady, 1981, 407. We might see in the fair Rowena a direct homage to Kim Novak's dual role in *Vertigo* (1958).

[47] From Willemen, et al. *Op.cit.*, 64-65. Corman consciously appealed to the arthouse film critics with his public proclamations of the film's lofty ambitions as Mark Thomas McGee quotes from the film's pressbook: "You don't have to be an egg head to enjoy the new Poe terror film *Tomb of Ligeia* but an understanding of psychology helps, according to its director Roger Corman. "While most movie fans are familiar with the menacing roles played by Vincent Price, Corman declares that enjoyment of the Poe films in which Price has been starring recently is greatly enhanced if you are acquainted with the philosophy of Sigmund Freud. "'I went deeply into Freud when I first began interpreting Edgar Allan Poe stories for the screen,' he says. 'Poe was a writer obsessed with symbolism and Freud was the master of symbolism. In fact, Poe's whole world of ruined sanctuaries, brooding trees, cawing birds, cats, deaths and funerals was a symbolic one. As an American obsessed with Europe's decadence, he was himself symbolic of America's long, regretful farewell to the Europe it wanted to believe was all evil.'
"As a result, Corman makes what might best be described as a quality horror picture of the kind which attracts the egg head as well as the masses. "Magnificently mounted and filmed in Color and Scope on location in a 100-year old (sic) English abbey, *Tomb of Ligeia* is a screenplay developed by Robert Towne from a Poe short story which dramatizes incidents surrounding the life after death of a woman of such powerful will that her evil spirit terrorizes her widower and the girl he later marries." McGee. *Op.cit.*, 175.

Though Corman's admirers are unlikely to be too disappointed by his new film, one may still regret the loss of narrative clarity which featured so strongly in *The Masque of the Red Death*. The crowded metamorphoses of the last ten minutes make for a confused climax. Moreover, the blinding of Fell, the destruction of the abbey, by fire, the blood-stained embraces of the doomed man and his ghostly beloved, are all too reminiscent of earlier Corman films – too much, in fact, of a formulary, melodramatic hotchpotch. [48]

A lack of clarity and a fondness for melodrama and mythic structure number among those criticisms that would also be levelled at Towne for later screenplays. However the reviewer finds that

> Luckily there are ample compensations. The earlier intimations of horror are put over casually and briskly, notably where the black cat is concerned. Much of the incident is genuinely strange – the cat climbing the bell-tower with Fell's dark glasses gripped between its teeth; the dream in which Rowena is smothered by Ligeia's black tresses. Technically, the film is less accomplished than *The Masque of the Red Death*, but it is still better – certainly more serious – than Corman's Hollywood Poe cycle. [49]

Towne's ability to believably recreate the point of view of the original work's author even when departing from the original text would be repeated in a pair of very different adaptations, many years apart: *The Last Detail* (1973) and *Ask the Dust* (2006.)

The Hollywood Reporter announced on 15 October 1965 that Towne was signing up to Twentieth-Century Fox for a Paul Monash production of *Deadfall*. Nothing came of it.

Authorship

As we have seen, the horror genre has its own internal narrative logic, as well as cinematic demands that go beyond the strictures of the purely generic, not to mention the limitations placed by Corman on his own valuable Poe franchise. Towne's admission, that *Ligeia* was by far the most difficult screenplay he had ever written, is borne out by his subsequent failure to return to the form. However it can be seen from his adaptation of 'Ligeia' that Towne was fully aware of Poe's own preoccupations and he layers imaginatively into the screenplay those concerns both subtly implied and directly expressed, bringing the Corman-Poe cycle to an aesthetically pleasing conclusion. David Pirie's claim that British writer Paul Mayersberg (Corman's assistant on the picture and later a fully fledged screenwriter and director himself) collaborated on the screenplay with Corman remains to be confirmed elsewhere. At the very least, Mayersberg can be seen standing in for Vincent Price in long shot, when Price had left the production.

Towne may not have been aware of it but he was already laying out a perfect strategy for a career as a successful screenwriter. He had now worked in low-budget, so-called exploitation cinema; graduated to writing teleplays for major networks; and excelled in what was the ultimate and most acclaimed contribution to the Roger Corman cycle of literary horror films adapted from Edgar Allan Poe's classic stories. If we can attribute a character arc to Robert Towne in the wider story of Hollywood thus far, his career was now becoming a prism by which to view the changes occurring in the

---

[48] P.F.D., '*The Tomb of Ligeia*,' in the *Monthly Film Bulletin*, Vol.31, No. 371, December 1964: 173.
[49] *Ibid*.

American film industry and the outline of his resumé would come to resemble the contours of post-1960 cinema. He commented of his learning curve:

> You keep relearning the same thing on every movie: that you need to say less than you thought you did. The image inevitably conveys more than the word. Movies can make you, as a writer, feel very foolish. You see a scene that didn't work and you say, 'Jesus, he should have been sitting down instead of standing up,' or 'He should not have been aggressive in that scene but passive.' [50]

It is difficult at this point to make a case for Towne's exceptionalism as contributor to the above texts, primarily because they are part of a production line system dominated by generic forms that was developed and finely tuned in Hollywood in the 1930s and continued throughout the 1960s (and was imported into television, largely controlled by the same financial interests) despite the upheaval in the film industry. However it is clear that Towne's accession to major television series, which already boasted on their rota of screenwriters some of the key genre fiction writers working at the time in the United States, offers proof of the level of trust he was already capable of inspiring in some of the industry's key network personnel. It can also be seen that he proved this trust in those moments in the screenplays where he departs from the strictly generic conventions required by the narratives and expresses the innermost longings of his characters, whose conflicted situations are caused by their being trapped by their occupation and betrayed by those closest to them. We can also see his strengths as a trusted adapter of franchised material and well-known novels, as well as an uncanny ability to inject in the most banal of teleplays a brand of humour and a sense of his control over story structure: action (story or plot), character, dialogue, genre, setting, theme, and tone (point of view). In his attempts to formulate a backstory for the title character in Poe's *The Tomb of Ligeia*, we can see Towne attempting what Robin Wood terms 'coherence,' in the sense of "the internal relationships that give a work its structure." [51] He also comes within reach of some of his later tropes – the references to mythology in the story of 'Ligeia' and of course Verden Fell's obsession with his lost love's eyes.

In any auteurist analysis or criticism a sense of continuity and stylistic evolution is sought and traced through the main body of the author's work. While Towne's identity as a screen author might therefore be difficult to adduce in a decade in which he exercised very little authorial control over these elements, it is, as we have seen, possible to note signs of his distinctive approach to each of these aspects of screenplay structure in terms of narrative preoccupation and structural coherence. In other words, a style has begun to emerge. If authorship can be attributed at the level of the individual or the multiple or the collective, the screenplays we have examined so far would appear to indicate that while evident, Towne's signature is not yet sufficiently developed to have become the most outstanding voice in the authorship model which is in any case rendered a more subtle problem by his involvement in the adapting of materials. [52] In short, while we might not yet see an archetypal pattern or even a canonical text, we can already identify some of those formal elements of Towne's major theme, which are

---

[50] Rainer, 1974: 234.

[51] Robin Wood's essay, 'Big Game: Confessions of an Unreconstructed Humanist,' appears in his 2006 collection, *PERSONAL VIEWS*, 27. He continues: "All art must strive towards coherence, which is simply another term for significant articulation." *Op.cit.*, 28.

[52] Richard Dyer. *STARS*. London: British Film Institute, 1998, 151.

beginning to emerge, even through the restricted generic forms which he had already mastered.

Towne's awkward handling of the material may have embarrassed him latterly but the model of the love triangle in *Last Woman...* would serve as a useful indicator for later subject matter; meanwhile, Corman's trust was repaid five years later with *Ligeia*, one of Towne's most literate and best filmed screenplays. Of no lesser importance is Towne's work for television, a medium which privileges the screenwriter.

A Time for Killing (1967) (screenplay) (uncredited)

Towne's Western script, which was circulated around Hollywood in the mid-60s, was the work which attracted the attention of Warren Beatty and gained Towne a reputation. *A Time for Killing* (aka *The Long Ride Home*) was originally destined to be made by Corman for Columbia but it was rewritten substantially by others, not to Towne's liking, which is ironic given the lucrative future in script doctoring that lay ahead of him. The film as shot has been described as "a typically brutal, post-Leone Western" which is set in the post-Civil War era. A Confederate prisoner is executed by a firing squad composed of Negroes. Other Confederate prisoners are enraged and break out of jail, chased by Glenn Ford, headed toward the Mexican border. The script would finally be reworked and shot by low budget specialist Phil Karlson, by which time Towne had removed his name from the credits. Even Monte Hellman withdrew from editing the film. But it served its purpose and opened doors to a niche in Hollywood, which Towne must have dreamed about as a neophyte screenwriter.

What distinguishes Towne's work in this period is his (customary) early exposure to generic forms; and coupled with this, his leaning towards emotional realism reflected through his characters and the way they used dialogue, which was relentlessly contemporary, if occasionally pretentious, yet endlessly quotable, a fact that appealed to an actor-producer such as Warren Beatty. He had read and was impressed by Towne's Western screenplay and legend would have it bumped into him at the office of their mutual psychoanalyst. He hired him to work on the screenplay of *Bonnie and Clyde*, a film of enormous importance to the seismic shift now taking place in the industry and the culture.

Chapter 3 1967-1975: NEW HOLLYWOOD

Bonnie and Clyde (1967) (Special Consultant)
The Last Detail (1973) (screenplay)
Chinatown(1974) (written by)
Shampoo (1975) (written by Robert Towne and Warren Beatty)
The Yakuza (1975) (screenplay)

The Screenwriter as Collaborator

Prologue

The Sixties was the era when Hollywood fell behind – in every way possible: aesthetic, commercial and technological. Instead of setting trends, for the first time it was following them. As David A. Cook puts it,

> Its decline resulted from the American industry's obstinate refusal to face a single fact: that the composition of the weekly American film audience was changing as rapidly as the culture itself. Between the mid-fifties and the mid-sixties, that audience shifted from a predominantly middle-aged, modestly educated, middle- to lower-class group to a younger, better educated, more affluent, and predominantly middle-class group. The new audience in America, as all over the world, was formed by the postwar generation's coming of age. It was smaller than the previous audience, and its values were different.[318]

Between 1965-1970, American cinema was fully engaged in a transition,

> with regard to its thematic content, formal procedures, and industrial organization, which were driven by the most divisive moment of social and political unrest in American history since the Great Depression of the 1930s. [319]

Thus the demographics had changed and yet the studio output was slow to react despite inflation, which was putting up the costs of production. By 1962, when studio revenues had slid down to 900 million dollars (their lowest ever), the big epics were still being ground out, most infamously *Cleopatra* (1963), which gave Elizabeth Taylor her biggest payday and saw Fox Studios pause for thought - until they recouped massively two years later by taking a punt on *The Sound of Music* (1965). Demographics were thus altering irrevocably and Hollywood was being confronted with a new, 'youth audience.' As Schatz puts it, "Hollywood was understandably queasy about this younger audience because it lacked the very qualities that the entertainment industries demanded: size and homogeneity. Without the massive numbers and shared traits which could identify this subculture as a 'mass', as a specific public, standardizing products for that audience would be difficult indeed." [320]

---

[318] David A. Cook. *A HISTORY OF NARRATIVE FILM* (2nd edition). New York and London: W.W. Norton & Co., 874.
[319] Mark Shiel in *CONTEMPORARY AMERICAN CINEMA*, edited by Linda Ruth Williams & Michael Hammond. Berkshire: Open University Press, 2006, 12.
[320] Schatz, 1983, 195.

James Monaco surmises that the changing face of American cinema in the 1970s was as much to do with the casting of unpredictable types as any other contributory factor:

> … we can discern some patterns in the map of actors that suggest a turning away from the macho type, which has dominated the male character of films for far too many years, toward a more complex type capable of realistic, human interactions with the new actresses.

He continues:

> … the tradition of the romantic, good-looking hero with sensitivity, culture, and style seems to have died out. [321]

This phase of Towne's career covers possibly the most aesthetically significant era of contemporary American filmmaking, the era of the auteur in American cinema and is therefore the most complex and rewarding for further investigation into the mode of multiple authorship in the screenplays of Robert Towne. The concerns of this chapter have to do therefore with the particular signature that now attaches to Towne's work; how this manifests in terms of the strength of a writer/director like Roman Polanski, or a visual and dramatic stylist like Hal Ashby, or a very strong star/writer/producer such as Warren Beatty. Towne's association with Beatty and director Arthur Penn on *Bonnie and Clyde* would prove to be perhaps the most significant of his career, not merely in terms of his status but in the orientation of his screenplays which inevitably point towards death.

Kristin Thompson states that

> There is no doubt that in the early 1970s the auteurist directors set out deliberately to change Hollywood in what at least some of them perceived as a subversive way. [322]

Just how Towne would contribute to the success of this subversion is traced in this section, in which he collaborates with some of the most celebrated directors of the era. Towne's friendship with Jack Nicholson, a self-styled blue collar intellectual, would prove singularly important in the fashioning of character roles in two of his most acclaimed works, *The Last Detail* and *Chinatown*.

Part of the contradictory project of auteurist study is the necessary attribution of credits to the *other* people whose 'signature' is readily identifiable in film texts. In 2002, the President of the 15th USC American Scripter awards could refer to the New Hollywood era without apparent irony, announcing, "we are excited that Robert Towne, whose distinguished career has defined an era in American film, will chair this year's selection committee." [323] Towne's collaborations with Warren Beatty; Francis Ford

---

[321] James Monaco. *AMERICAN FILM NOW: The People The Power The Money The Movies*. New York: Plume Books, 1979, 98.

[322] Kristin Thompson, 2001, 5. Thompson argues that this generation did not actually change the rules of storytelling, "Rather, some of the younger directors helped to revivify classical cinema by directing films that were wildly successful."(8). David Thomson also argues for Towne as a classical storyteller: "… if Towne is an outstanding example among Hollywood writers, then he does seem to rate craft, conceptual vividness, and on-screen workability above everything else. That is one way of saying that the American movie has not risked narrative structure in the last twenty years." Thomson, 1981, 86.

[323] Regina Leimbach, President of the Friends of the USC Libraries, quoted in Robert Towne

Coppola; Jack Nicholson; Roman Polanski; and Hal Ashby, delineate the possibilities of individual, collective and multiple authorship in the various projects which are included here and bookend a critical phase principally concerned with directorial personality; commencing here with *Bonnie and Clyde* and closing with *Shampoo*. *Chinatown* (1971-1973) is this chapter's principal case study for two reasons: 1. it is the screenplay for which Towne is most renowned: as Mark Horowitz claims, "it is the lens through which all his other films are judged…" [324]; and 2., as Horowitz asks, "what if *Chinatown*, far from being quintessential Towne in theme, style, and structure, is really his most atypical and misleading work?" [325] These are the parameters of this particular case study, which examines the three drafts written by Towne between 1971 and 1973. Overall, this period cements the developing of the Towne brand, in other words, it is the culmination of the first phase of his career and his establishment as a celebrity screenwriter. It might also be termed the classical period of Towne's writing life.

Bonnie and Clyde (1967) [326] (Special Consultant)

1967 was the year that everything changed. As Peter Biskind puts it, two films "sent tremors through the industry." [327] One of those films was *The Graduate*, directed by Mike Nichols from the Charles Webb novel, adapted by Buck Henry (and Calder Willingham). The other was *Bonnie and Clyde*.

> … we don't take our stories straight any more.
> -   Pauline Kael on *Bonnie and Clyde* [328]

Bonnie and Clyde could be said to belong to a subset of the gangster genre, the 'love on the run' cycle which numbers some classic examples: *You Only Live Once* (1937) made by Fritz Lang; *They Live By Night* (1948) directed by Nicholas Ray; and *Gun Crazy* (1950), directed by Joseph H. Lewis. It was also predated by *The Bonnie Parker Story* (1958) a low-budgeter which fails to mention Clyde Barrow. The outlaw genre was obviously reconfigured from the earlier Western examples – Billy the Kid or Jesse James had proven popular stories in that genre, while the gangster genre itself boasted any number of examples, taking their lead from real-life criminals such as Al Capone and John Dillinger.

Looking back on this period, Towne would declare of his approach to writing:

> I like to write films that are drawn from real life, and yet have a prior cinematic reality … I like to take a myth and make a new myth. [329]

Named Selection Committee Chair for Scripter XV, www.businesswire.com, 25 November 2002 accessed on www.findarticles.com, 21 March 2007.
[324] Horowitz, 1990: 52.
[325] Horowitz. *Op.cit.*, 54.
[326] The screenplay, production history, background, critical reception and cycle of outlaw films *Bonnie and Clyde* influenced are explored in the author's 'Riding the New Wave: The Case of *Bonnie and Clyde*,' in *Senses of Cinema*, 38, January-March 2006. Accessible on www.sensesofcinema.com.

[327] Biskind. *Op.cit.*, 15.
[328] Pauline Kael, in her review for *The New Yorker* (which was rejected by *The New Republic*) reprinted in *5001 NIGHTS AT THE MOVIES*. New York and London: Marion Boyars, 1993, 112-113.
[329] Gene Siskel, 'Hollywood's Mr Fix-it,' *Sunday News*, Leisure section, 13 June 1976.

His work can now be read as an intertwining of collaborators and influences, a collage of circumstances and industrial change. As James Monaco reminds us,

> Colloquially, we tend to oppose myth and reality. The phrase, 'that's a myth' suggests is untrue, unreal. But in fact, myth and reality are closely interconnected. Real myths, those artistic evidences of our collective unconscious, spring directly from roots in reality, they heighten reality and condense it. [330]

The thirty-year anniversary of the release of *Bonnie and Clyde* was marked by a celebratory documentary 'American Desperadoes: The Story of *Bonnie and Clyde*'. The original screenwriters, David Newman and Robert Benton, were extensively interviewed about the origins of the film and its progression to the screen. Also interviewed were director Arthur Penn and star/producer, Warren Beatty. Nobody mentioned Robert Towne – and yet it was he – not Benton or Newman (who were not allowed on the set of the film) who completely rewrote the screenplay at the behest of both Beatty and Penn.[331] It is his work on this film that created his legendary role as Hollywood's leading script doctor.

Newman and Benton were journalists at Esquire magazine in the early 60s when they discovered a mutual love of the films coming out of Europe, especially from France. The newly minted screenwriters were always consciously trying to evoke the mythology inherent in the tale, "… because we saw *Bonnie and Clyde* as kind of emblematic of the times we were living in. We began to sense that something was going on in this country and that all our values not only culturally but psychologically and mythologically and romantically, that everything was shifting in a really interesting way." [332]

Figure 4 *Bonnie and Clyde* flysheet poster

---

[330] James Monaco. *AMERICAN FILM NOW: The People, The Power, The Money, The Movies.* New York: Plume Books, 1979, 251.
[331] Other than the predictable final shootout, *The Bonnie Parker Story* (1958) bears no other resemblances to the later film, especially in terms of visual style, where it remains strictly in the B-movie tradition of American International Pictures, its production company.
[332] Speaking on *American Desperadoes*, BBC, 1997.

After a couple of frothy mod-ish comedies (*Promise Her Anything*, *Kaleidoscope*) and believing *What's New Pussycat?* (1965) to have been stolen from him by his friend, the producer Charles Feldman (under the influence of Woody Allen), Beatty wanted to strike out on his own as producer to find the correct vehicle for his particular style. He acquired the Robert Benton and David Newman screenplay for Arthur Penn to direct, with himself in the leading role.

Newman and Benton claim that Penn was interested in the fact that Barrow had turned bisexual while in prison, but believed that this fact would alienate the audience, reasoning that his motivation could be interpreted as perversion, while the writers agreed that something sexual should be amiss in his persona – hence the impotence, a counter to the happily Freudian phallic symbolism of the gun. Radical as the film was, it still has its critics, mainly because of director Arthur Penn, who arguably never achieved the same aesthetic relevance afterwards in his career:

> Arthur Penn was so bent on creating representative folk heroes that he missed the real story, which was far more intriguing than fiction, and would have pushed the boundaries of film subject matter even further. [333]

Towne's script for *The Long Ride Home* aka *A Time for Killing* (eventually directed by Phil Karlson) had found its way into Beatty's hands and impressed him enough to hire him to completely rewrite the Newman/Benton script. Towne's official account of events is that he was asked to do the shooting draft, on location. [334] Towne was apparently called in when the debate had reached 'an impasse.' In order to satisfy both Penn and Beatty, Towne apparently had to rewrite some scenes as many as fifty times. [335]

> I was rewriting scenes time after time. The movie was impromptu in the sense that there was rewriting going on constantly, but once Arthur was satisfied with a scene, once the rewriting was done to everybody's satisfaction, there was no deviation whatsoever from those   lines. There was less improvising in *Bonnie and Clyde* than in any other movie I have worked on. [336]

---

[333] Ellis Amburn. *THE SEXIEST MAN ALIVE: A Biography of Warren Beatty.* New York: Harper, 2002, 99.

[334] Robert Towne, 'A Screenwriter on Screenwriting,' in David Pirie (ed.) *ANATOMY OF THE MOVIES Inside the Film Industry: The Money: The Power: The People: The Craft: The Movies.* London, Windward, 1981: 150-151. Towne summarized for Peter Rainer: "I think that the original script... was an enormously talented script that got sidetracked by the fact that it originally had a ménage a trois. It was taken out – by the original writers – at the request of Warren (Beatty) and Arthur (Penn) and the script sort of fell apart. So my task was to create a relationship between two of the people instead of three, and to give a kind of inevitability to what happened to them. There was a lot that was rewritten; there was a lot that was the same. I was called in because the decision was made that the writers had gone about as far as they could go. I was in Dallas three weeks before they started filming and I was there when the company left." Rainer, 1974: 166. Newman and Benton were all but forgotten, while Towne was on the set at the North Park Motor Inn, Dallas; Midlothian; Point Blank; Pilot Point and Ponder, Texas, available for rewrites and even changing line readings during filming.

[335] Amburn. *Op.cit.*, 89. He told Brady: "In rewriting someone or in adapting a work, you can come to feel it's your very own, too. Or you can feel that you are in the service of somebody else's material that you love very much, and you want to work." *Op.cit.*, 407.

[336] Towne, in John Brady. *Op.cit.*,395.

The specifics of the rewrite according to Towne were to do with the idea of the ménage à trois amongst Bonnie, Clyde and C.W., as proposed by Newman and Benton. One of the problems was that the studio would not go along with it; another, was that the 'permissive society' had not quite arrived; finally, it didn't really lead anywhere (in reel, as in real life, perhaps). And then there was Beatty, who was against it for both personal and genre reasons. As Towne put it, "If you're going to do a movie about shifting relationships, like Truffaut's *Jules and Jim*, it is tough to do a gangster movie at the same time." [337]

The Changes to the Original Script

Towne's first problem was to alter the three-way relationship: that was removed, and C.W. Moss becomes a more comical character. Bonnie goes to see her mother before going to the mortician in the Newman and Benton script. Towne suggested that this episode happen prior to her visit, "so that the impetus of having a good time, only to find out that the guy is a mortician, strikes Bonnie, who is the most sensitive and open of the group, and makes her say, "I wanna go see my Mama." It scared her. Pacing like that gives the character a little drive, makes her want to *do* something as a result of it." [338] When Gene Wilder admits to his professional occupation and dampens the spirit of joie de vivre in the car, Bonnie caps the moment saying, "Get him out of here." The feeling of doom is heightened and the moment underlines Bonnie's sense of her mortality, giving her character a greater arc.

Clyde now concludes the scene at Bonnie's mother's house by saying, "We're gonna end up living by you," and Mrs Parker replies, "You try to live three miles from me, and you won't live long, honey." This tagline, added by Towne, confirms the idea that Bonnie can't go home any more, and, that, in Towne's words, "she is being thrown back on Clyde for a ride that is going one way." [339] This is no longer the happy occasion intended in the Newman/Benton version.

Towne adds a later scene in a hotel room, when Bonnie remarks to Clyde that she thought they were really going someplace. She is clearly disillusioned. Clyde returns, "Well, I'm your family." Their mutual need is intensified.

Realism was key for this version of the film. As Towne himself says, " 'When I was a kid, I noticed four things about movies: the characters could always find parking spaces at every hour of the day and night, they never got change in restaurants, and husbands and wives never slept in the same bed. Women went to sleep with their makeup on and woke with it unmussed. I thought to myself, I'm never going to do that. In *Bonnie and Clyde* – although I don't think it was my doing – Bonnie counts out every penny of change, and C.W. gets stuck in a parking space and has a hard time making a getaway'." [340] Towne is expressing his desire for authenticity which is paradoxically rooted in his nostalgia for both the artifice of classic cinema(in which realism is always cinematic code for 'real') and the times in which his favourite films originated. Realism as a cinematic code is more complex and ideologically bound and it is both outside Towne's stated ambitions for his work and the parameters of this study; however it is a significant frame of reference inasmuch as it codifies his influences – films 'torn from the

[337] *Ibid.*
[338] Towne in Brady. *Op.cit.*, 396
[339] *Ibid.*
[340] Towne interviewed by Peter Biskind. *Op.cit.*, 33.

headlines,' the work of Jean Renoir, the desire for plausibility. According to David Thomson, he even spent time with Clyde Barrow's nephew, who bore his uncle's name

> … and picks up anecdotes about Clyde's skill with cars and the way 'he could cut a corner square when he drove.' [341]

According to Matthew Bernstein's interpretation, Towne's additions to the screenplay were crucial to making Bonnie appear more sympathetic. He added Mrs Parker's line ("You best keep runnin', Clyde Barrow"); as well as Bonnie's own lines to Clyde:

```
                    BONNIE
     You know, when we started out, I really
     thought we was really goin' somewhere.
     But this is it. We're just goin', huh?
```

This conforms to the overall sense of classical form that Towne crafted to unify the sense of the pre-existing drafts. [342]

The larger problem, for Towne, was the choice to be made as to when it was appropriate for Clyde to down his gun and have a heterosexual relationship. Yet the homosexual undertone in Clyde's demeanour is still apparent, despite Beatty's protestations. According to Peter Biskind's account,

> Beatty liked to play against his image, but he said, 'Let me tell you one thing right now: I ain't gonna play no fag.' He thought the audience wouldn't accept it. 'They're going to piss all over my leg,' he said, using one of his favorite expressions." Penn's attitude to Newman and Benton was that they couldn't make a French movie: "'You're making a mistake, guys, because these characters are out there far enough. They kill people and rob banks. If you want the audience to identify with them, you're going to lose that immediately if you say this guy is homosexual. It's going to destroy the movie.' [343]

The details and textures for which Towne were hired are emblemised in a line he wrote for the dying Buck Barrow:

```
                     BUCK
        Clyde, Clyde, the dog got my shoes.
```

This kind of detail, says Ellis Amburn, proved that Beatty was not only a formidable star-maker but

> demonstrated that he could control inspired below-the-title work horses. [344]

[341] Thomson. *WARREN BEATTY AND DESERT EYES: A Life and a Story.* New York: Vintage Books, 1987, 254.
[342] Matthew Bernstein, 'Perfecting the New Gangster: Writing *Bonnie and Clyde*,' *Film Quarterly*, Vol. 53, No. 4: 23; 24.
[343] Biskind. *Op.cit.*,32. Speaking at the American Film Institute, January 22, 1975, transcript at the Louis B. Mayer Library, 23.
[344] Amburn. *Op.cit.,* 97.

It also reminds us of Towne's obsession with detail and fetish objects: shoes would be a signature device in *Chinatown* and *Without Limits*. He shared a love of detail with his star/producer: Thomson comments of Towne's perceived influence in the film's complex weave:

> ... when Clyde first meets Bonnie he tells her to make a small alteration in her hair, dropping a cutesy curl for free fall. It does improve her, and it shows us Clyde as a producer of history. Maybe the scene comes from Towne seeing Beatty stroll among actresses adjusting hairstyles here and there, like a sultan becoming a genius. A film is full of details, and Beatty has learned in his movies so far that sometimes people are too tired or too casual or too bad to chase down all the details. [345]

The compass of *Bonnie and Clyde* orients to beauty and death, and the two are conjoined in those final, shocking images which are imprinted on the collective memory, all the preceding little deaths leading up to this final, orgasmic shoot-out (another ironic counterpoint to Clyde's impotence):

> The death scene is the climax, and it is graced and consented in by the rapid exchange of knowing close-ups as they look and see what is coming. Naming is no longer necessary. Death is greeted as something as rare as ecstasy because of the great outlawry. Being famous has been shown as the most certain way to beauty. The only way. [346]

The irony underlying this ending is underscored by the protagonists' lack of consciousness – they seem to drift towards the hail of bullets in a casual, unpremeditated way. This sensibility would inform Towne's later writing of *Chinatown* – when Jake drifts into a problem he has no hope of understanding, in a world where he could never hope to gain entry. Towne was undoubtedly influenced on another level, that of Penn's shooting style, which frequently utilises mirrors, windows and doorways as framing devices. *Chinatown* is based entirely on Jake's inability to see what is in front of his eyes and this is punctuated by this image system which must surely derive from Towne's observation of Penn. [347]

Structurally speaking, of course, this was a writing challenge for Towne:

---

[345] Thomson, 1987, 253. Towne expanded on the nature of his involvement when speaking at the American Film Institute, 22 January 1975: "It was a long process. I was on the film from about three weeks before we started shooting all the way through the shooting of the film... I don't know what would have happened if it had been arbitrated, you know, if it had gone to the [Writers] Guild. At this point I couldn't begin to say. It depends upon – I don't remember specifically. The rules are that 33 per cent of it has to be changed, and I really can't say what the final result would've been because it's such a long time and I can't remember everything that was done. But there was a certain feeling of guilt on everybody's part because Benton and Newman were asked not to come down while the shooting was going on. And I think that Warren really – everybody felt a little bad about that. And I didn't really think that much about it. And probably none of it would've ever been examined so closely if the film had not enjoyed the success that it had. But once it had, it kind of created a funny little problem for everybody in that way." AFI transcript in the Louis B. Mayer Library, 22; 24.

[346] David Thomson, 1987,,273

[347] In his author study of the director, Robin Wood says of *Bonnie and Clyde*,"every shot bears the director's signature ... there is nothing in *Bonnie and Clyde*, stylistically, technically, thematically, which was not already implicit in *The Left-Handed Gun*." *ARTHUR PENN*. London: Movie Magazine, 1967, 72.

…you always knew they were going to die. I mean you knew it before you went to see the movie. And if you didn't, you knew it very early on. So the real suspense in that film was not if they were going to die, but how, and if they were going to get something resolved between the two of them before they died. You know? And so in order to do that, I mean you had to structure their relationship going inevitably toward their particular fate which was death at the end of the road that they were travelling. [348]

This statement underpins Towne's commitment to the framework of the genre in which he was writing but it also stresses his belief in a moral code, something that would be a hallmark in his work. Impressed as he was with Newman and Benton's writing of the legendary outlaw tale, Towne admits, crucially (if contradictorily):

… I thought it was a terrific script when I first read it, but it was kind of unformed… Remember the scene with the undertaker and Velma? You know? It's a terrific scene which was really right from the original script. That was probably the one scene that was never touched at all. [349]

Beatty supervised every conceivable aspect of the production. The dailies were printed in black and white to save on costs, which were increasingly being borne by Beatty, leading to his having a disproportionately large share of the eventual rentals. In conversation with David Thomson, Towne declared his admiration for Beatty the producer. [350] Warners released it in second-string theatres in August 1967, to a slew of bad reviews in what was then the slowest period for audiences, Summertime. Such was the impact of the Time and Newsweek reviews that Warner Brothers withdrew the film from release. When Beatty ultimately persuaded Warners to re-release it, with an ad campaign using copy provided by Beatty himself *Newsweek* recanted their original review and lauded the film as the harbinger of a New Cinema.

---

[348] Towne speaking at the American Film Institute, 22 January, 1975. Transcript at the Louis B. Mayer Library, 23-4.

[349] *Ibid.*

[350] This information is in Thomson, 1987, and Towne is also quoted, 254. See also Biskind. *Op. cit.,* 45-50 for details of release.

Figure 4 Escaping the law

I am sorry to say I consider [*Newsweek*'s] review grossly unfair and regrettably inaccurate … I am sorrier to say I wrote it. [351]

At the forefront of the plaudits for the film was Pauline Kael's review for *The New Yorker* which locates the film in American film history not least because of its cultural significance:

> *Bonnie and Clyde* is the most excitingly American movie since *The Manchurian Candidate*. The audience is alive to it. Our experience as we watch it has some connection with the way we reacted to movies in childhood: with how we came to love them and to feel they were ours – not an art that we learned over the years to appreciate but simply and immediately ours. When an American movie is contemporary in feeling, like this one, it makes a different kind of contact with an American audience from the kind that is made by European films, however contemporary. Yet any movie that is contemporary in feeling is likely to go further than other movies – go too far for some tastes – and *Bonnie and Clyde* divides audiences, as *The Manchurian Candidate* did, and it is being jumped on almost as hard.

Kael teases out the differences between *Bonnie and Clyde* and the earlier examples by pointing out that the audience's worldview had changed from the Thirties or Forties when real hardship made the average moviegoer essentially sympathetic to people involved in a life of crime. The film had a somewhat confusing effect on its

---

[351] Joe Morgenstern in *Newsweek* as quoted in Amburn. *Op.cit.*, 103. The turnaround in the film's critical fortunes coincided with its release to great fanfare and acclaim in the United Kingdom. Bosley Crowther was fired from *The New York Times* following his negative review: he was obviously out of step with the zeitgeist but was probably due for retirement in any case. (See Raymond J. Haberski, *FREEDOM TO OFFEND*. Lexington: University of Kentucky Press, 2007).

audience, something that Kael dissects as "… the absence of sadism – it is the violence without sadism – that throws the audience off balance at *Bonnie and Clyde*. The brutality that comes out of this innocence is far more shocking than the calculated brutality of mean killers… There is a kind of American poetry in a stickup gang seen chasing across the bedraggled backdrop of the Depression (as true in its way as Nabokov's vision of Humbert Humbert and Lolita in the cross-country world of motels) – as if crime were the only activity in a country stupefied by poverty." [352]

What is significant about this analysis is its precise delineation of the film's contours proceeding from myth (and its insistence upon 'America'), deconstructed through reality, and back towards myth via a sense of misplaced nostalgia, mostly rooted in cinematic and photographic representations of reality. This would have a formative effect on the forthcoming phase of Towne's writing career, and Kael herself would play a vital part in making his name part of the vanguard of the American New Wave (although here she gave all credit to Newman and Benton). The larger mythical discourse of the film is emblemised by Bonnie's self-eulogising doggerel verse [353]; and the newspaper headlines – a device perhaps borrowed from *The Left-Handed Gun* (1958), also directed by Penn, from Gore Vidal's play; and eventually paid homage by Towne in *Chinatown*, and David Webb Peoples in *Unforgiven* (1992).

David Thomson in his (unauthorised) and semi-fictional biography of Warren Beatty highlights the film's appeal, somewhat aping Kael's style of analysis:

> This is the crucial American movie about love and death, lit up by fresh-air faces
> that have been burning underground for years, too much in the dark to admit, yes,
> we're in love with death, let's fuck death. But *Bonnie and Clyde* surpasses its early, easy
> claim that violence is aphrodisiac (Bonnie stroking Clyde's casually offered, groin-
> crossing gun) and reaches the far more dangerous idea that death brings glory
> and identity. [354]

There may have been a handful of writers, but David Thomson is in no doubt as to who is the true author of *Bonnie and Clyde*:

> What makes the movie so lastingly fascinating is the glimpse we get of a great seducer
> setting himself the hardest task, of withholding his most celebrated force and asking us
> to see that reputation, the mystery of being known, is what most compels him. It is the
> producer's film, the imprint of his views about the world and himself.[355]

Towne commented to Peter Rainer of working with Penn and how it affected his approach to work:

> He kept having me rewrite myself. I revered Arthur. We had a great working
> relationship, probably the best I've ever had. It was a real learning experience. I also
> got tagged as a rewrite man subsequently, the guy who could come in and fix up a
> script. I suppose I'd rather have a reputation for fixing things than messing things up.
> I do love to take apart scripts. I've learned that I have a certain facility for looking at

---

[352] Kael. 1993, 112-113. It is interesting to note that Kael, just as Towne had, refers to the significance "the way we reacted to movies in childhood."

[353] An allusion to the letters exchanged in *Jules and Jim*.

[354] David Thomson. *Op.cit.*, 267.

[355] Thomson. *Op.cit.*, 271. Despite his later, complimentary appraisal of Towne, we must assume a certain partiality in Thomson's reading of his subject.

a script and saying what didn't make it work and what could make it work and then doing it. It doesn't make you an artist, it's a skill." [356]

Towne's acknowledging of the importance of his collaborators is crucial in forming a picture of his writing practice and his understanding of the nature of the industry. He was working in a genre, but one conscious of its own formation and evolution, and alongside him were fellow professionals whose trust in him forced him to produce some of his best work, as well as influencing his approach to later screenplays.

Villa Rides (1968) (screenplay by Robert Towne and Sam Peckinpah)

Despite his insider status, Towne's reputation was not yet such that he could afford to pick and choose his projects. He became involved in a production which was initially to be written and directed by Sam Peckinpah but the star, Yul Brynner, hated Peckinpah's treatment of the book by William Douglas Lansford in which an American pilot's path crosses that of the revolutionary. [357] Peckinpah made use of the research facilities he had been given at Paramount for the duration of *Villa*'s writing, however, and gathered up books, articles and photographs of Mexico, circa 1913. The material was central to his next film, the unmistakably brilliant and ultimate Peckinpah Western, *The Wild Bunch* (1969) about a gang of bankrobbing yanquis soldadas caught up in the revolution. Meanwhile, other than the above comments, Towne has never spoken of his involvement with the project, save to liken moviemaking to warfare in conversation with John Brady:

> The guy who becomes an expert is the guy who doesn't get killed. Ah, here's
> Pancho Villa, the greatest expert on guerrilla warfare in history. It's because he
> [Villa] didn't get killed. Everybody else got shot, and he survived, so he's an expert. [358]

The guerrilla described by Peckinpah was a flawed idealist but a key scene involving the hanging of a teenage boy was said to have upset Brynner. The film was directed by Buzz Kulik and is no great credit to any of the practitioners involved, even if there are some bright moments with good scenes given to Robert Mitchum and Charles Bronson. Peckinpah hated the resulting film, to the extent that it barely warrants a mention in *IF THEY MOVE, KILL' EM!* It might however be inferred that Towne's subsequent writing was influenced by Peckinpah's preferred theme of male loyalties.

Drive, He Said (1971) (uncredited)

In 1971 Towne found himself in Oregon doing rewrites on Jack Nicholson's directing debut, *Drive, He Said.* Nicholson had been busy in one of the leading roles for Bob Rafaelson in *Five Easy Pieces* so it was 1970 before he could begin shooting on his film. He had also committed to *Carnal Knowledge* for director Mike Nichols. Thus he began *Drive…* without a complete script. Jeremy Larner adapted his own book but Nicholson wasn't happy with it and had begun writing a second draft himself. [359] He

[356] Rainer, 1974: 166.

[357] "After *Bonnie and Clyde* I went to Spain to do another rewrite on something called *Villa Rides!* (1968) with Robert Mitchum and Charles Bronson. It was one of those 'pay or play' situations, meaning Paramount had to go ahead with the project and make the best of a bad job." Towne in Pirie. *Op.cit.*, 151. According to Paul Seydor, who re-evaluates his earlier Peckinpah book, it was Brynner who brought in Robert Towne, "declaring Peckinpah knew nothing about Mexico." Paul Seydor. *PECKINPAH The Western Films: A Reconsideration.* Urbana and Chicago: University of Illinois Press, 1999, 182.

[358] Brady. *Op.cit.*, 423.

brought in Robert Towne to complete his vision on set, with the added bonus of an acting role for his screenwriter friend – that of a cuckolded, broad-minded professor. The film was completed on time for Nicholson to report to the East Coast for Mike Nichols. He edited *Drive…* on weekends and downtime from shooting *Carnal Knowledge*. *Drive…* is an exposé of Sixties left-liberal attitudes, set on a campus infected with radicals and replete with ready-made mythological references which must have appealed to Towne: a leading character called Hector (who of course as the eldest son of the king, led the Trojans in their war against the Greeks, fought in single combat with Achilles and stormed the wall of the camp and set it alight). And, as if we don't 'get it,' Hector's major is Greek. The radical elements were complete with the casting in the lead role of William Tepper – a dead ringer for producer Bert Schneider, whose famously radical approach to production would lead Hollywood out of the old-style studio system but would embalm him in the mid-Seventies forever.

As usual, there is a romantic element that interferes with male friendship: Gabriel is the guerrilla, played by Michael Margotta. Hector is besotted with Karen Black, married to Towne's professor in the film. Her name, Olive, signifies her role as peace-maker in the narrative.

> GABRIEL
> Do something man. Do something before
> they take it all away from you. That's
> what they're gonna do. Don't count on
> anything else.

Gabriel runs away to escape the draft. Hector is the warrior in love – he is in touch with nature (his surname, is, after all, Bloom.) He communes with the trees in the forest, stays in a log cabin and is generally at one with everything that is not 'the Man.'

The film is structured around Hector's basketball games – the opening titles are underlined in a stunning sequence by the use of cult musician Moondog's music - later paid homage by the Coen Brothers in *The Big Leboswki* (1998). The filming style in slow motion corresponds with much of *Visions of Eight* (1973), which would itself be an influence on Towne's own film style in his directing debut, *Personal Best*.

The existential angst expressed by Hector echoes the feelings expressed by Mace in Towne's earlier script for *The Chameleon*:

Hector claims:

> HECTOR
> I feel so disconnected.

He later adopts Bartleby's attitude with his coach, stating:

> HECTOR
> I'd prefer not to.

---

[359] Reclusive screenwriter and director Terrence Malick also did a rewrite – prior to making *Badlands* (1973).

The film was entered in Cannes and Nicholson's efforts were the subject of scorn. It opened in New York on 13 June 1971 where it got mixed reviews. BBS apparently offered more money to promote it but were deflected by Nicholson himself, who was depressed at the critical reception. But as biographer Jack Shepherd astutely points out, its lyricism, message and sub-Godardian construction have held up considerably better than Nicholson himself believed:

> Because it explored rather than exploited the conditions of the social and
> political unrest of its day, it's still an interesting film, while its commercially
> successful counterparts now seem inconsequential and even silly. [360]

Nicholson waited another 18 years to direct again, and that was due to the breakdown in his relationship with Towne on *The Two Jakes* (1990).

Cisco Pike (1972) (uncredited)

Towne's additions to writer/director B.L. Norton's screenplay remain unremarked upon, but it is certain that aspects of the story, about a rock star turned drug dealer (Kris Kristofferson) blackmailed by a crooked cop (Gene Hackman) into selling heroin, played into the outline of his treatment for *Tequila Sunrise* (1988). Towne was reportedly so unhappy with the film of his screenplay that he had his name taken off.

The Godfather (1972) (uncredited)

This phase of his career progressed as Towne worked with what could be described as major American auteurs, and includes his minor but crucial work on the adaptation of the Mario Puzo novel, *The Godfather* (1971). It would immediately precede that period of his greatest fame and success. The garden scene was written under extreme duress, overnight, on the set; its purpose was to express the love between father (Marlon Brando) and son (Al Pacino), a love that went unspoken throughout the entire screenplay and yet such a scene would be essential to underpinning the entire film's arc of emotional realism, in this adaptation of what was generally considered trashy, potboiler material. As a screenwriter himself (of Academy Award-winning abilities), Coppola immediately understood the significance of Towne's contribution in creating a dramatic scene of which Coppola judged himself incapable of producing. He told Marjorie Rosen, "The art of adaptation is when you can lie or when you can do something that wasn't in the original but is so much like the original that it should have been." [361]

Towne says of his work on the film,

> Mainly, Francis was perplexed. In the book there wasn't any resolution between
> Vito Corleone and his son Michael – their relationship. He needed a scene between
> the two of them. Francis kept saying, "Well, I want the audience to know that they
> love each other." He put it that way. [362]

---

[360] Donald Shepherd. *JACK NICHOLSON An Unauthorized Biography.* London: Robson Books, 1991, 87.
[361] Coppola speaking to Marjorie Rosen in 'Francis Ford Coppola,' *Film Comment*, July 1974: 47; quoted in Jeffrey Chown. *HOLLYWOOD AUTEUR: Francis Coppola.* New York: Praeger Publishers, 1988, 80.
[362] Towne in Brady. *Op.cit.,*398.

Respectability forms an essential virtue in the world of Don Corleone. Coppola has said that the character was a synthesis of two Mafia chieftains, Vito Genovese and Joseph Profaci. Genovese, like Vito, ordered his soldiers never to deal in drugs, even if he himself did exactly that on the side. Genovese once threatened Joseph Valachi in words that could have been spoken by Brando's Don: 'You know, we take a barrel of apples, and in this barrel of apples there might be a bad apple. Well, this apple has to be removed, and if it ain't removed, it would hurt the rest of the apples.'

His solution? The scene takes place in the garden, where the Don is transferring power to his son and the dialogue is indirect but the subtext is unmistakably that of a father not merely giving his son his blessing to take over the reins of the family business, but communicating a wealth of love to him also.

Towne says of his involvement:

> … dialogue should never spell out to an audience what a scene is about…
> I looked at the footage that had been filmed and talked to Marlon and Al; eventually I wrote the scene so that it was ostensibly about the succession of power, about youth taking over and the reluctance of the old to give way. The older man is telling his son to be careful in the future and mentions some of the people who might pose a threat, while the son reassures him with a touch of impatience – 'I can handle it.' And you can tell the father's obsessive concern for these details reflects his anxiety that his son is having to adopt a role that the old man never wanted him to have, as well as the father's reluctance to give up his power. Underlying all this is the feeling that they care for each other. A scene like that takes a long time to write. [363]

Chapter 29 in Puzo's novel consists of an opening paragraph describing Michael's difficulties; this is followed by a description of the Don's death in his beloved garden, and the ensuing obsequies. Towne's scene is 92C in the available screenplay:

```
            DON CORLEONE
Barzini will move against you first.

            MICHAEL
How?

            DON CORLEONE
He will get in touch with you through
someone you absolutely trust.  That
person will arranged a meeting, guaran-
```

[363] Robert Towne, 'A Screenwriter on Screenwriting,' in David Pirie *ANATOMY OF THE MOVIES Inside the Film Industry: The Money. The Power. The People. The Craft. The Movies.* London: Windward Books, 1981, 151. He explained to Gene Siskel: "I had a long meeting with Francis that day. He was very nervous. Then I met with Al and Marlon that same day. Then I sent to a deli and brought home some San Pelegrino [sic] bottled water, and wrote from 10 at night until 4:30 in the morning. Francis picked me up at 7. We were both very nervous. Francis is a friend of mine. This was a very big movie, the biggest he'd ever worked on. The budget had been expanded to many millions of dollars. He didn't say much when he picked me up, something like, 'Did you have any luck?' "When we got to the set he showed the scene to Al, and then he showed it to Marlon. Marlon read both parts aloud. He liked it. They rehearsed it. And Francis shot it." 'Hollywood's Mr. Fix-it,' *Sunday News,* June 13, 1976: 9.

```
                tee your safety …

He rises, looks at Michael…

                … and at that meeting you will be
                assassinated.

The DON walks on further

                    DON CORLEONE
                Your wife and children … you're happy
                with them?

                    MICHAEL
                Yes.

                    DON CORLEONE
                Good.

MICHAEL wants to express something … hesitates, then:

                    MICHAEL
                I've always respected you…

A long silence.  The DON smiles at MICHAEL.

                    DON
                And I… you.
```

(The Godfather: 139)

Basically, Towne's strategy was to extrapolate the sense of the situation described by the omniscient narration and translate it into dialogue. This moment expressing love completely belies the massacre to come. Other, less celebrated alterations were to Pacino's speech about how he would kill McCloskey; and the scene in which he and Diane Keaton pass the limo and Pacino leaves her to discuss family business.

Asked what he thought of the auteur theory, Towne said,

A movie is always collaborative. I believe the auteur theory is merely one way it is easier for historians to assign credit or blame to individuals. [364]

The Last Detail (1971) (screenplay)

While the late Sixties were a dark era for America on the political front at home and abroad, they proved a time of great cinematic experimentation – while the studios

---

[364] Brady. *Op.cit.*, 426-7. As a corollary to this it is interesting to note that the story of Towne's friend John Fante's novel *THE BROTHERHOOD OF THE GRAPE* has a structure not unlike that of THE GODFATHER, with a tough patriarch governing three sons, the least likely of whom, Henry, a writer living in Redondo Beach, inadvertently takes over the family business after "one last job." Fante's *ASK THE DUST* would eventually be Towne's fourth outing as writer/director in 2006.

were drained of money. In the wake of *Bonnie and Clyde* (1967), many more American filmmakers took up the baton from European filmmakers and tried to make 'art' from a necessarily commercial product. David A. Cook comments, "it had seemed for a time that America was headed for a major cinematic (and social) renaissance. But neither came to pass." He adds that neither Arthur Penn nor Sam Peckinpah made a film to equal their late Sixties achievements (although, in the case of Peckinpah, it could be argued that *Bring Me the Head of Alfredo Garcia* (1974) and *Cross of Iron* (1977) are equal, if not superior, cinematic pleasures). [365]

The Last Detail could be said to be part of the new wave of American cinema that was begun with *Bonnie and Clyde*:: Peter Biskind claims it as part of the first wave of those films produced by "white men born in the mid- to late '30s (occasionally earlier)... Peter Bogdanovich, Francis Coppola, Warren Beatty, Stanley Kubrick, Dennis Hopper, Mike Nichols, Woody Allen, Bob Fosse, Robert Benton, Arthur Penn, John Cassavetes, Alan Pakula, Paul Mazursky, Bob Rafelson, Hal Ashby, William Friedkin, Robert Altman, and Richard Lester." Those whom Biskind would classify as second-wavers are the 'movie brats', Martin Scorsese, Steven Spielberg, George Lucas, John Milius, Paul Schrader, Brian De Palma and Terrence Malick. [366] The revolution may have been televised but it was also being preserved on celluloid and the output of these writers and directors has meant that ever since the Seventies has been seen as the last gasp of the golden age of cinema.

One of the complicating issues concerning the reading of any film text is a consideration of the times in which it was produced, and the industrial situation of the film business. As a consequence of the outer culture, concerned with youth issues and the Vietnam War, feminism and problems in the Nixon administration (which would later blow up into the infamous Watergate scandal), it is appropriate to give equal consideration to the impact these had on the decisions taken at Columbia Pictures regarding *The Last Detail*. While it was obvious that the potential audience could not be actually offended by the material, the excessive use of the word 'Fuck' was an issue for studio brass. The overwhelming changes that dominated studio decisions had been imminent since about 1965. As Schatz points out, "the rules of filmmaking and the marketplace changed so drastically" between then and 1975. [367]

Adaptation had already been proven to be a Towne speciality. *Detail* would require some specialised treatment. After doctoring and appearing in *Drive, He Said*, for debutant director Nicholson, Towne was hired for the project by producer Gerald Ayres, who recalled, "'He had this ability, in every page he wrote and rewrote, to leave a sense of moisture on the page, as if he just breathed on it in some way. There was always something that jostled your sensibilities, that made the reading of the page not just a perception of plot, but the feeling that something accidental and true to the life of a human being had happened there'." [368]

[365] David A. Cook. *A HISTORY OF NARRATIVE FILM* (2nd ed.) London & New York: W.W. Norton and Co., 1990, 886.

[366] Biskind. *Op.cit.,* 15 .

[367] Thomas Schatz. *OLD HOLLYWOOD/NEW HOLLYWOOD Ritual, Art and Industry.* Ann Arbor, Michigan: UMI Research Press, 1983, 201.

[368] Peter Biskind. 1998, 31. Ayres' first film had been CISCO PIKE, on which Towne had done some script doctoring.

Towne took to the job with gusto when Ayres persuaded top brass at Columbia Pictures to take him on, on the basis of his Special Consultant credit for *Bonnie and Clyde*. The project was a favourite of Nicholson's, whose star was rapidly on the rise:

> Part of the incentive of the project was that Jack's part would be equal and set against that of the other Navy lifer, a black sailor. It would be an actor's showdown between Nicholson and Rupert Crosse, his and Towne's mutual friend. [369]

The Novel

Darryl Ponicsan's novel was first published in the United States in 1970. It tells the story of petty officer Billy 'Bad Ass' Budduksy who receives orders to escort a petty thief to the brig (prison) and decides to show him a good time before he is behind bars at the Portsmouth, New Hampshire, Naval Prison. The 'thief' isn't much of a criminal at all: he tried to make away with forty dollars from the favourite charity of the General's wife and didn't succeed. Buddusky reckons they can deliver the boy very quickly and parlay the trip into a holiday but his conscience gets the better of him and he turns the trip into a sentimental education for Meadows. When it appears that Buddusky might suffer from the association with Meadows, he cuts his ties with the young sailor and abandons him to his fate. However, Buddusky and his fellow gaoler, a black sailor called Mulhall (or 'Mule') fail to report Meadows' inevitable escape attempt and after delivering him they go AWOL before their planned return to base but Buddusky is killed in the ensuing fracas. The trip turns out to have been his last detail for the American Navy.

The novel consists of nine chapters and an epilogue; the Signet paperback movie tie-in edition published by the New England Library runs to one hundred and forty-two pages.

> Inevitably, while we were making the film, we considered changing the ending so that Nicholson *would* let the kid escape. But I thought that would really be letting the audience off the hook. The audience must be left with the problem, because ninety nine out of a hundred people in the audience – maybe a hundred out of a hundred – would have done what Nicholson did in the movie and taken the kid to prison, rather than risk their own skin. So I thought it would be completely dishonest of us to send the audience out of the theatre with a warm glow thinking: 'Gee the world is full of nice people.' [370]

The overall shape of the screenplay for *Detail* is that of the novel, albeit in necessarily shortened form. The original screenplay is 135 pages long (the revised draft runs to 131 pages) and the finished film runs approximately 110 minutes. Many of the scenes (up to 45 pages of them, in fact) were shortened or dropped altogether from the released version of the film. All of the revisions to the first draft are dated 15 August. Towne is mainly faithful to the principal thrust of the book, namely the relationship between Buddusky and Meadows. He says: "Nicholson is flattered by the fact that this young, rather sick kid looks up to him as a surrogate father figure. So Nicholson takes him places and shows him things. But when it looks as though all of this might really cost Nicholson something, he just turns around and says 'It's my job.' Even though he is aware his attitude is fundamentally corrupt and cowardly." [371]

---

[369] Patrick McGilligan. 1995, 236.
[370] Robert Towne, 'A Screenwriter on Screenwriting,' in Pirie,1981, 151-152.
[371] *Ibid.*

Towne radically altered Ponicsan's Camus-loving protagonist with his beyond-beautiful wife and recast him as a more ultimately compromised man, adding him to the gallery of unformed underachievers that populates his screenplays: J.J. Gittes in *Chinatown*, George Roundy in *Shampoo*, Mac in *Tequila Sunrise*. All of these men are compromised in their need for the means to survive. Of these characters, it could be said that Buddusky (certainly in Towne's interpretation of the original character as conceived by Ponicsan) is actually the least tragic (he does not succumb to the fate administered in Ponicsan's novel, thereby rendering the title meaningless!), the most pragmatic – and the most well-adjusted. Towne's interpretation of Buddusky aligns him in the vanguard of New Hollywood in its politicised, anti-authoritarian heyday. While his work on the film was undoubtedly influenced by his producer and director (particularly, it seems, by Ashby), it copperfastened his position as upcoming screenwriter in the early Seventies. [372]

In a letter dated November 24, 1971, it is clear that director Hal Ashby has a purist's approach to the material, and the perspective of a poet in sympathy with the principals:

> ...What else ultimately is there but time in, a clean record, new ports and
> a good time? That's a question Billy is forced to ask in *Detail* and it makes
> him miserable. [373]

A survey of the changes made to the novel gives an insight to the respective authorial agents and how they treat the text. They are as follows:

The character of Buddusky in the novel is more highbrow and evidently intellectual than the person portrayed by Nicholson in the film. He no longer reads Camus; nor was he ever married to the classy New Yorker. According to Towne, this character change was the start of several other consequential changes to the novel.

> Buddusky in the novel is sort of a closet intellectual who secretly reads Camus but tells
> the fellas he's reading skin books, and who has an amazingly sophisticated, attractive
> ex-wife in New York for a fellow who is a lifer in the Navy. I felt this was dangerous
> for the script because if he is running around in New York with this beautiful girl, and
> his shore patrol buddy, who is black, doesn't have any girl, it would be implausible. It
> was also unrealistic. I know from my own experience in the service that the uniform is
> enough to turn any girls off... [374]

---

[372] The Hal Ashby files at the Margaret Herrick Library, AMPAS, yielded several pieces of correspondence between Gerry Ayres and Towne concerning excerpts of the novel, which Towne could consider, as well as concern about treatment of Navy personnel in the script and the use of the vernacular. A message dated October 26, 1972 reads: "Dear Robert: I am enclosing excerpts from the novel. Some of them may spark ideas for last minute strokes on the screenplay. I want to repeat the obvious – our screenplay as it stands is monstrously skilled in its tempos, its harmonies. New motifs could be disruptive, I understand. Still, let's give one last look at the enclose, as well as excerpts from Darryl's version of the screenplay, and discuss it when you arrive in Toronto." There are 10 pages of excerpts/quotations, concluding with a note: "There needs to be a resolution to the question of whether Mule has a girl, where she is and where in the screenplay we learn of her." The entire missive is CC'd to Hal Ashby.

[373] Hal Ashby in a letter to Robert Towne, 24 November, 1971, in the Ashby Collection, as before. Excerpts in Appendix 3.

[374] Towne in Brady. *Op.cit.*, 420.

As a consequence of this decision the party scene doesn't take place at his ex-wife's apartment – instead it happens in Greenwich Village.

Buddusky and Mulhall no longer have a sense of guilt over their escorting of Meadows to the brig; rather they are unhappy, but not exactly exercised by the experience.

The scene with Meadows' alcoholic mother and her lover is dropped; although they visit the house, it is in a state of disrepair and her slovenliness and the empty bottles tell their own story, perhaps revealing Towne's feeling about family and absence:

```
Buddusky opens the screen door and tries the door.  It
opens.  Only as it does, he realizes that Meadows has his
hand on his arm, trying to stop him.

From the front door all three can see the living room
behind the blinds and a glimpse of the kitchen beyond:
it's all a mess, wine bottles, cigarette butts floating
in cheap dago red, stubbed out in plastic dishes with
dried egg yoke, scattered underwear, etc.  It's sloppy
and alcoholic.

                       MEADOWS
               (after a long moment)
     Aw, hell - I don't know what I would've
     said to her anyway …
```

(The Last Detail,, sc.55: 66)

Towne creates a fight scene at the Port Authority washroom that doesn't exist in the novel.

> I wasn't merely trying to create physical action. It was part of the education of this boy Meadows. What do they do? They get him in his first fight, they get him laid, they take him to places he hasn't been, they get him drunk. And getting in your first fight is really part of that. [375]

The tug of war that occurs between Buddusky and Mule is heightened, once again in a scene that has no direct origins in the novel, when Mule asserts himself. Towne says: "It was fun, exhilarating, and Buddusky's way of having the final answer in the argument. That was the reason for the scene." [376]

Towne added the episode in the restaurant where he encourages Meadows to order his cheeseburger the way that he wants it: [377]

---

[375] Towne in Brady. *Op.cit.*, 421.

[376] *Ibid.*

[377] This is probably a tribute to both Nicholson and writer Carole Eastman aka Adrien Joyce for their collaboration on FIVE EASY PIECES a couple of years earlier with its infamous chicken salad sandwich scene. Eastman/Joyce was a classmate of both at Jeff Corey's workshop. Thank you to Tom Stempel for pointing this out.

Buddusky looks at it closely.

                    BUDDUSKY
          Ain't melted at all. Send it
          back.

                    MEADOWS
          No, it's okay, really.

                    BUDDUSKY
          Send the goddam thing back.
          You're paying for it, aren't
          you?
                    MEADOWS
          It's all right, really.

                    BUDDUSKY
          Have it the way you want it.
          Waiter?

                    MEADOWS
          No please –

                    WAITER
          Yes, sir?

                    BUDDUSKY
          Melt the cheese on this for the
          Chief here, will you?

                    WAITER
          Certainly.

The waiter takes it away.

                    BUDDUSKY
          See, kid, it's just as easy to
          have it the way you want it.

CLOSE ON MEADOWS
biting into his cheeseburger.

                    BUDDUSKY
          See what I mean?

Meadows nods. Buddusky looks over to Mule, pleased with
himself.

     The following line was not included in the revised draft page dated 15 August
and may have been ad-libbed on-set to express Meadows' newfound confidence:

                    Goddam! Hey! Where's those malts
                    at?

(The Last Detail: 33-34)

The ice-skating scene was added, but the ice rink is pointed out in the novel.

Of course, the ending was changed. Instead of going AWOL after delivering Meadows to the brig and Buddusky dying, in the screenplay Buddusky and Mule just walk away, none the worse for wear. This perhaps falls into what Ricoeur calls the 'contingencies' of narrative, wherein he states, "rather than being *predictable*, a conclusion must be *acceptable*. Looking back from the conclusion towards the episodes which led up to it, we must be able to say that this end required those events and that chain of action. But this retrospective glance is made possible by the teleologically guided movement of our expectations when we follows the story. Such is the paradox of the contingency, 'acceptable after all,' which characterises the understanding of any story." [378]

This alteration by definition changes the point of the novel written by Ponicsan. Towne explained the change speaking at the American Film Institute at a seminar held on 22 January 1975:

> That was my decision, actually. Completely. And there was some argument about it…
> I wanted to tell a story about typical people, not atypical people. [379]

Towne's rationale for the major changes to the novel necessarily alters the 'play' of the various elements. It also comes from his own experience in the service and his observation of people's behaviour as he explains:

> My main decision was to do a story about *typical* people instead of atypical
> characters…
> With Buddusky, in order to make his behavior typical in this fashion, he had
> to be a more *typical* lifer in the Navy. In the novel, though, he was a man
> of rather extraordinary sensibilities who deliberately talked like a sailor at
> times, but underneath it all had a sophisticated Whitmanesque appreciation
> of the sea, the joys of physical labor, and all that shit. From my point of view,
> that was wrong… I think the characterization may be a little harsher than the
> novel. But more realistic, too." [380]

It is said that there were a number of endings shot:

> There was talk about it. No. A lot of people suggested that the picture end at
> that moment when the gates close behind him in the jail. There's a clang. And
> there was talk about where exactly it should end. But there was never more than
> one ending shot. I mean it's a question of cutting it off before then. But never

---

[378] Paul Ricoeur, 'The Narrative Function,' in John Thompson (ed.), *HERMENEUTICS AND THE HUMAN SCIENCES Essays on language, action and interpretation*. Cambridge: Cambridge University Press, 1982, 277.

[379] Towne in interview, AFI transcript: 12. Pauline Kael's review would state, "It's doubtful if there's any way to extract an honest movie from a Ponicsan novel." Kael, 'The Current Cinema: Nicholson's High,' *The New Yorker* 11 February 1974: 95.

[380] Brady. *Op.cit*: 420-421.

more than one ending. [381]

In order to better present Buddusky's point of view, which dominates the structure of the novel, Towne says, "I wanted to show the tug-of-war between him and Mule Mulhall. In fact, I wanted *more* of the back-and-forth stuff between the two of them to come out in the screenplay, but it may have been vitiated by the fact that Rupert Crosse, for whom the screenplay was written, died, and Otis Young is a different kind of actor than Rupert was." [382]

The spotlight of the film now shifted more completely to Nicholson, since the script's emphasis was now changed. Nicholson simply did not have the same kind of relationship with Otis Young, Crosse's replacement. It was now truly a star vehicle. Meadows was played by Texan newcomer Randy Quaid, who towered over Nicholson, lending even more comedy to the situation.

The influence of Jack Nicholson on modern American cinema cannot be underestimated, and the overweening influence that he has had on the writing of Robert Towne should be interrogated. As critic Stanley Kauffmann pointed out: "Any future history of American film must, if it is to be adequate, treat Jack Nicholson as more than a star." [383] Towne was in awe of Nicholson's improvisatory powers and he has admitted

> It's hard *not* to think about Jack even when I'm not writing for him. His work
> literally affected the way that I work, totally independent of doing a movie
> with Jack. [384]

Pat McGilligan quotes Gerald Ayres: " 'Jack is so courageous, not protective of himself in star ways. Not only was he conscious of that disparity, but he used it in the movie, playing off of it'." [385] Nicholson relished the role, using his experience of growing up around the Jersey shore and watching sailors to build up the nuances of 'Bad-Ass'.[386]

Undoubtedly Nicholson's powerful presence lends Buddusky a charismatic edge and his own interpretation of the speaking style (complete with New Jersey accent), completes the edgy tone that is granted a horrible culmination when he attacks Meadows. Nicholson apparently sees himself as something of a blue-collar intellectual, while Towne admits to having tailored roles for his friend. Towne's part in creating the Nicholson image has never been thoroughly examined yet it was through the creation of this role (and later, that of J.J. Gittes in *Chinatown*) that much of the Nicholson star persona is based: his role as muse to Towne would be to their mutual advantage in *Chinatown* (1974).

Pauline Kael would observe astutely of Nicholson's pairing with Towne:

[381] Towne in interview, AFI transcript: 17.

[382] Brady. *Op.cit.*, 421-422.

[383] In *The New Republic,* 23 February 1974.

[384] Towne in Brady. *Op.cit.*, 401. David Thomson comments: "Jake Gittes, the character, was not just the finest fruit of association; he was the shared ideal of a friendship – shrewd, funny, sad and error prone." From: 'The Towne,' in Thomson, 1997, 101.

[385] McGilligan. *Op.cit.*, 243.

[386] According to McGilligan, the bird tattoos were his idea. McGilligan also comments that, "it was one of his top jobs, as revealing of his depths as the Rafelson films, a crucial clue to the hard-shelled, soft-centered person that was emerging." McGilligan. *Op.cit.*, 245.

The role of Buddusky, the tattooed signalman, first class, is the best full-scale part he's had; the screenwriter Robert Towne has shaped it to Nicholson's gift for extremes." [387]

Towne explains the rationale for his intentional shift in tone from the novel:

… Buddusky felt guilty about what he had done, but he wasn't going to go AWOL or get killed over it. Both men know that they've done something wrong, but they can't face it. So all they can say to each other is, 'Well, I'll see you later.' They don't want to stay with each other… We would help people to a point, but if they really threatened us we would throw them in the pokey no matter how horrible an act it was, just to save our jobs, our reputations, anything. I don't necessarily think they were bad guys; in fact, I think they were good. Most people are decent. But given a situation like that, they took the path of least resistance . [388]

This attitude ties in with Towne's avowed desire to keep material 'real', to carry on the tradition of psychological realism that appears to motivate the majority of his output, not merely in terms of classical Hollywood melodrama which has so influenced him, but in terms of how people *are*. This is primarily based in the reality of character and also tends to dictate the unhappy or compromised endings which are a feature of his narrative, not to mention the unsuccessful relationships between men and women which permeate his work. His phrase, 'the path of least resistance' would come to characterise the most typical male protagonists of his oeuvre. It also expresses his fascination with people trapped by their occupations. He states:

'Most people just do their job, whether it's shove Jews in ovens or take a kid who's stolen forty bucks and rob him of eight years of his life. You're nice about it. You're polite … I'm just doing my job… The ending of that screenplay is more consonant with my sensibility than the ending of *Chinatown.*' Not surprisingly, Ponicsan is said to have hated it. [389]

Ultimately, Towne changes the book's anti-authoritarian stance. He says, "'I wanted to imply that we're all lifers in the Navy, and everybody hides behind doing a job'." [390]

In terms of how Towne can relate that to this material, he has stated that the ending is in fact inevitable if you examine the script closely: the "tunnel at the end of the light," as he describes it must follow the affection displayed between the three men -

You know, it's just kind of elemental. If you're plotting something like that, it's kind of basic in a way that you would want to do that. In a melodrama like that, if there are kind of confrontations between good and evil more or less, if evil is too triumphant, it throws you out of your ability to identify with it, than if its

---

[387] Pauline Kael's comments are reprinted in *5001 NIGHTS*. New York and London: Marion Boyars, 1993, 408.

[388] Towne in Brady. *Op.cit.*, 422-423.

[389] Horowitz, 1990: 57. Ponicsan wasn't the only one to hate the ending: critic Frank Rich expressed the opinion that "Towne's resolution … nosedives into a useless pessimism, one that negates nearly all that has gone before." 'The Details are all right – and almost completely cold,' *New Times,* 08 March 1974: 62. Charles Champlin described it as "existential pessimism … But it is a downer, ferociously so." 'Ponicsan Films Plumb the Depths of Navy Life,' *Los Angeles Times,* Calendar, 09 December 1973: 33.

[390] Brady. *Op.cit.*, 421.

victory is only qualified.

I believe in that. It's a lie – I'm making no relationship to anything I do – but if you read a great tragedy like King Lear, what makes it so effective is that – all the little kindnesses along the way, the Fool, Cordelia, the virtuous daughter. Ultimately, so much of it gets destroyed, and so much of it – they get destroyed, they die – but it makes really, it lends kind of reality to the presence of the evil. You know, that kind of thing. Whereas, if it just seems to take place in a vacuum, if it's just so relentlessly cruel… [391]

This statement seems to reinforce two strategies operating in Towne's work ethic at this time: the relentless drive towards authenticity; and the desire to create a screenwriting structure that veers away from the limited possibilities in classical Hollywood representation. It is also worth quoting because of the contrast that could later be drawn with his more linear and perhaps simplistic representations of good and evil in screenplays that he would produce for both the Simpson/Bruckheimer and Tom Cruise stables in the 1990s, particularly *M: I – 2*.

Interviewed by Gene Siskel, he said, "I like to write films that are drawn from real life, and yet have a prior cinematic reality." [392] Described by *Newsweek* magazine as a 'classic craftsman,' he is quoted as believing that "'People want to escape into stories with strong narrative lines. A well-made screenplay has to go somewhere, not just ramble around. A good script should have air in it, to allow everybody latitude. If you don't want to totally alienate directors and actors and drive them crazy, don't tell them what they're feeling'." [393]

The final page of the screenplay is a lesson in lucid screenwriting – visually expressive and concise, with understated dialogue:

```
The two stare at each other for a long moment.  Then they
look away, each inadvertently gazing down opposite ends
of the street.  Until the very last exchange they don't
look at each other.

                    BUDDUSKY
        So where you goin'?

                    MULE
        Norfolk.

                    BUDDUSKY
        I mean now.

                    MULE
        Don't know - stop off in
        Baltimore maybe.  You?
```

---

[391] Towne, speaking at the American Film Institute, 22 January 22 1975. Original transcript read by the author in the Louis B. Mayer Library: 18. It should be recalled that Towne himself served in the US Navy fifteen years previously.

[392] 'Hollywood's Mr. Fix-it,' *Sunday News*, June 13, 1976.

[393] 'Hot Writer' appeared in *Newsweek*, October 14, 1974.

```
                    BUDDUSKY
                 Go back to New York.

There's a sticky pause.  They look at each other.

                      MULE
                 Well, see you in Norfolk.

                    BUDDUSKY
                 Yeah, maybe our orders came thru.

They walk away from each other.

                    THE END.
```

(The Last Detail, Revised First Draft: 135)

The revised pages dominate Hal Ashby's copy of the script and are dated 15 August: pages 2-12; 18-21; 24-33; 36; 39-40; 48; 51; 53; 54-63; 71-72; 80-100; 103-110; 119-122; 124-131. A number of other pages are revised but without dates: 13; 34; 47; 77-78; 111-2. However, these alterations were minor and the finished film is remarkably faithful to Towne's first draft.

One of the factors influencing the difficulty in financing the script was the use of the vernacular. Towne says in an article for *Sight and Sound*, "I was thinking of the things that weren't in movies that could make them more like real life when I came to write the script for *The Last Detail*. So I was determined to include the swearing in the army. I hadn't heard it in the movies before but I knew it was important – it was an expression of impotence. These guys were going to buckle under to authority, and their only way of defiance was to whine and swear." [394]

Columbia Pictures read Towne's script and backed down from the project on the basis of the excessive use of the word 'fuck'. Towne wouldn't change a word. Peter Biskind_quotes studio executive Peter Guber: "'The first seven minutes, there were 342 'fucks'. At Columbia, you couldn't have language, couldn't have sex. If you made love, it had to be at 300 yards distance, no tongues'.." Biskind then quotes Towne on the issue:

---

[394] Robert Towne, 'I Wanna Make It Like Real Life,' in *Sight and Sound*, February 1999, Vol.9, Issue 2: 58-59. In an interview for the American Film Institute, he says: "All the socially taboo language was necessary. From the time Rhett Butler said, 'Frankly, my dear, I don't give a damn,' in *Gone With the Wind*, it has usually been the case that socially taboo language in film was for dramatic emphasis. But in fact, in *The Last Detail*, it was used for exactly the opposite reasons. In the army you swear a lot precisely because you are impotent. When Columbia said that wouldn't it be better to have twenty 'motherfuckers,' I said no, because then you'd lose the point that these men can't do anything more than swear. The repetitiousness is an index of their inability to do anything else." Robert Towne, 'Dialogue on Film,' in *American Film*, 1975 Vol.1, No.3 December 1975: 43. In a letter from Gerry Ayres to Robert Towne dated 17 October, 1972, he expresses some concern about the treatment of Navy personnel and changes requested by the legal department. The memo also gives an insight into the influence of broadcasters on the film industry as Ayres points out that 'hell' and 'damn' are mostly acceptable, and urinals can be shown but the word 'whorehouse' and the phrase 'wonderful world of pussy' couldn't be broadcast. From the Hal Ashby Collection.

'"Now that movies were opening up, this was an opportunity to write navy guys like they really talked. The head of the studio sat me down and said, 'Bob, wouldn't twenty 'motherfuckers' be more effective than forty 'motherfuckers'?' I said, 'No.' This is the way people talk when they're powerless to act; they bitch.' Towne refused to change a comma, and Nicholson backed him up." [395]

Biskind quotes Gerald Ayres on director Hal Ashby: ' "I thought this was a picture that required a skewed perspective, and that's what Hal had. He felt to me like a brother in the fraternity of the self-styled underground of the early '70s. He was distrustful of people from the studios he considered bombastic or authoritarian. But if somebody came to the door and said, 'I've been driving a bus, and I've got a great idea for a scene,' he'd say, 'Okay, do it'." [396] Ashby was persuaded to read the script a second time and agreed to shoot it. Biskind says, "Actors, at least those who didn't much like to be directed, loved Ashby. Nicholson called him one of the greatest 'non-directors' of all time. 'He would become their dad,' says [Charles] Mulvehill. 'He'd stroke them, he'd try things, he'd let them try things, he created an atmosphere that was totally permissive – and yet he was no fool, he knew when something wasn't working, he'd move it along as well.' He'd let them try almost anything they wanted, saying, 'I can get behind that.'" [397]

Figure 5 Bad Ass runs the whole show

And yet Ashby's keen understanding of the film's characters led him to shoot the film as they were permanently imprisoned – as Maynard says, "To symbolize this

---

[395] Biskind. *Op.cit.*, 175. In a lengthy letter from Gerry Ayres to Towne dated 24 November 1971, he says: "As for the profanity, I do not want to act as an editor and go through and make deletions. I want your discretion to direct you to deletions and substitutions. I can tell you only that Columbia has asked for ½ to ¾ of the profanity to go out of the script." Ayers goes on to suggest that Towne use "some rough poetry… not in the idiom of Arthur Miller but more in the idiom of Steinbeck." Ayres proceeds to give a highly detailed interpretation of how he sees the adaptation progressing, from the portrayal of Billy to the underlining of what he calls the "pivots" of the screenplay ie plot points. He concludes: "Bob, I have so often praised the excellence of your screenplay, I know that you will not take these long pages of criticism [6] as a mark against that excellence. Though these pages are long, I'm not sure the rewrite needs to be. Many of the things mentioned are already in the grain of the screenplay. It is my feeling they could profit from clarification and emphasis."(The Hal Ashby Collection.)

[396] Biskind. *Op.cit.,* 174-175. Ayres was asked at the time why Ashby, and stated: "'He's intelligent, sensitive, capable. How many Hollywood directors do you know whom you can say those things about?'" Bridget Byrne, 'We Didn't Want Some Sweet Faced Kid: Fighting for *The Last Detail*,' *Los Angeles Herald Examiner*, 10 February 1974.

[397] Biskind. *Op.cit.,* 179

constriction, Ashby employed fewer rhythmic montages [than usual] and used more dissolved and tight shots." [398] However, according to Biskind, Towne didn't like what Ashby was doing: "He didn't like what he saw, didn't like Hal's pacing. 'The good news about Hal was that he would never allow a dishonest moment between people,' says Towne. 'But, gentle soul that he was, he almost considered it a moral imperative never to interfere with the actors. He would never pressure the performers, provoke a clash on the set. He left his dramatizing to the editing room, and the effect was a thinning out of the script'." [399]

McGilligan declares of Ashby's directing style, that he

> had a visual simplicity whereby he let the scene more or less create itself. His style was to observe through an open frame and to let the actors move freely through that space. His close-ups were modest, his pullbacks and other camera moves unobtrusive. Almost patriarchal, Ashby would lean back in his chair on the set, saying nothing, watching. To the casual observer the man in charge might seem almost invisible." [400]

However Towne would ultimately prove to be a careful observer of Ashby's techniques, including his astute use of location, and utilise them when he eventually made his own directing debut.

Diane Jacobs' assessment concludes that *Detail* is "the most visual of Ashby's early films. The dark, dirty quality of the photography is important; the fade-ins and – outs and superimpositions suggest that one scene, one spot on the map, is really no different from the next. The world looks ugly and cold; the colors, especially the institutional yellows, reinforce the tawdriness of these men's lives. Many of the sequences take place in buses and trains where we see no further than the bright blur of a windowpane, and much of the action takes place at night." [401] She correctly notes that the ice-rink scene is probably the most 'open' and yet it is clearly circumscribed by the boundaries of the rink itself. However Ashby's stylistic punctuation is revealed in the shots of the brig, where the bars so neatly demarcate Meadows' future: a wide-angle lens is on the staircase and the giant figure of Meadows is dwarfed. The film's pattern has been moving towards this point all along, via trains, buses and even ice-skates. Now it has reached a dead halt.

The first edited version presented to Columbia had jump cuts straight out of Godard. This did not help the film's reception at the studio, where the level of profanity in the script was still being debated. Editor Bob Jones even did a three and a half hour version, stripping out the film's humour. The release was delayed for six months but Ayres at least persuaded the studio to enter it at the Cannes Film Festival. Towne explained the heavily edited scene in the hotel room as being the result of

---

[398] John Maynard, '*The Last Detail*,' Biography, AFTRS Network Events 2002, accessed online.

[399] Biskind. *Op.cit.,* 180

[400] McGilligan. *Op.cit.,*243.

[401] Diane Jacobs. *HOLLYWOOD RENAISSANCE.* New York: Delta, 1980, 227. One review of the film concludes: "It is dark in its message and gray to the eye. Locations are all washed out as though there were a thin membrane of filth spread across everything except the leads, who pop out colourfully like three strawberries in a bowl of Cream of Wheat." James Pallot and the editors of CineBooks. *THE FOURTH VIRGIN FILM GUIDE.* London: Virgin Publishing, 1995, 439.

… an editing problem. I mean what happened, I feel, was that in the playing of that scene as it went on a long time. I mean the scene was a long scene as written and I really think they just – Maybe if they'd talked a little faster, the editing would have been a little better… I think they could have talked faster on the train, too. They might not have had the same editing problem. I don't mean to be glib about this… There was more written than was said. Because I mean these guys – Randy and Jack are in the scene, a couple of terrific actors really, and I think they went on at their own pace. And you can get lulled into saying, 'Well maybe if you could do it a little quicker.' So the editing was really because of that… particularly the train and in the hotel which were long scenes." [402]

Despite Ashby's sympathy for the material, it was clear that Towne was already coming to the conclusion that he ought to have a more direct role in the translation of his ideas to the screen.

Richard Schickel in *Time* magazine grasped the essence of the project: "Dramas about male bonding have glutted the market recently. No one connected with this adaptation of Darryl Poniscan's novel can be accused of enormous originality. But there is an unpretentious realism in Towne's script, and director Ashby handles his camera with a simplicity reminiscent of the way American directors treated lower-depths material in the '30s." [403] This interpretation understood Nicholson's desire to be an old-style star; Towne's desire to cultivate material in the classical Hollywood style around his persona, albeit with the contemporary inflexions that New Hollywood plausibility demanded; and the ideal teaming of Ashby, Towne and Nicholson in a project which had had the potential to be a strictly run of the mill buddy picture.

Genre

Broadly speaking, *Detail* could be said to be a service picture, and then a Navy comedy. However few of these types of film are set in peacetime (the musical *On the Town* is an exception to this rule.) It is difficult to place this film in a single, recognisable category. James Monaco says that "movie genres are simply formulaic patterns, some stricter than others." [404] It could be called a buddy movie yet there are three principals, thus deviating from the norm. It might also be called a comedy drama, a road movie or a rites of passage film. In his *GOOD MOVIE GUIDE*, critic David Parkinson manages to classify *Detail* in a group which he categorises 'All Boys Together' films. [405]

Some of the biggest films in 1973 (the film was released in December) could be similarly classed as Buddy movies, with a twist: *Serpico, The Sting, The Three Musketeers* and *American Graffiti*. It might be argued however that none of these films (with the exception of *Graffiti*) demonstrated such a lightness of touch that they could bring up complex social issues and resolve them within the neat exchanges of dialogue that characterises *The Last Detail*.

[402] Towne speaking at the American Film Institute, 22 January 1975, transcript at the Louis B. Mayer Library: 13. This expresses Towne's innate frustration at the way his work was interpreted and his powerlessness to interfere with production. It helps us understand his motivation to direct his own work.

[403] Richard Schickel, 'Not Fancy, Not Free,' *Time*, 18 February 1974.

[404] James Monaco. *AMERICAN FILM NOW*. New York: Plume Books, 1979, 54.

[405] David Parkinson. *GOOD MOVIE GUIDE*. London: Bloomsbury Publishing Ltd., 1990, 7-8.

One of the problems confronting cinema in general is the preponderance of male writers, directors and studio heads. This is undoubtedly a contributing factor in the excessive number of prostitutes on the big screen (whether or not they have a heart of gold) whose goodly characters both serve to give a man a great time and assuage him of any doubts as to how great he actually is anyhow. The character of the prostitute in *Detail* is a case in point: both sweet and absurdly kind to Meadows, she is portrayed by Carol Kane, an actress with kewpie-doll looks and unusually long, golden hair. She is also, however, a realist, and ensures she will get paid for 'another try', when the inexperienced Meadows gets over-excited too soon. Thus the cliché becomes enriched and humanised with the reality of paying for sex.

Figure 6 Bad Ass bargains with the whore (Carol Kane)

INT. WHOREHOUSE BEDROOM - NIGHT

The four of them. Meadows looks disconsolate. He sits on the bed - his jumper still on, a towel around his middle.

            GIRL
    Look, those are the rules,
    doesn't matter if it's ten
    hours or ten seconds.

            BUDDUSKY
    Okay, honey, we'll stake him
    to another shot.

            MEADOWS
    Gee, I'm sorry.

(*The Last Detail:* 116)

Towne wanted to avoid cliché at all costs when writing the screenplay, which is why he insisted on the coarse language which proliferates in the film.

EXT. THE ALCOVE

Buddusky immediately removes the SP from his peacoat and begins to put the .45 belt on the inside. Mule, a little reluctantly, does the same. Buddusky takes out the keys to the cuffs.

BUDDUSKY
Look, Meadows. Your word worth anything?

The next two lines were dropped from the script; then:

Mule waits, a little apprehensive about what's coming next.

MEADOWS
… sure it is, as good as the next guy's.

MULE
The next guy's a prick.

(*The Last Detail* 32)

It's a throwaway line, delivered with no particular emphasis, but underlining Towne's commitment to typical, not atypical, characters. Some telling observations have been made by critics. Biskind claims that, along with Towne's other work of this period, *Detail* is concerned with 'innocence and experience, purity and corruption.' [406]   Diane Jacobs comments, "expressed here … is the idea that it's far simpler to be kind to strangers than to close friends or lovers. Bad-Ass couldn't get along with his wife. The only women he or Mule seem drawn to are whores. And yet, Bad-Ass is very willing to be generous with a kid whom he'll know for a week at most. Similarly, Mule, who even has doubts about helping Meadows, goes out of his way to assist a strange woman in a train station with her packages." [407] Jacobs also categorises this in terms of Ashby's oeuvre: "The idea that although we travel in pairs or in small groups we are ultimately alone is marvellously suggested through the easy rapport of these men." [408] This is an important comment in light of what can now be recognised as the markers of Towne's

[406] Biskind., *Op.cit.,* 393. We can link this with the idea of loss as Towne's central theme.

[407] Jacobs. *Op.cit.,* 227.

[408] *Ibid.*   Peter Thompson is of the opinion that "in its bitterly cynical script by Robert Towne, Ashby was able to execute a variation on the theme of much of his work which asks 'How does one live?' *The Landlord* and *Harold and Maude* both suggested individualistic approaches from an external view while *The Last Detail* internalised the question. Life for its characters was a series of prisons, many of their own making. To symbolize this constriction, Ashby employed fewer rhythmic montages and used more dissolves and tight shots." (from the AFTRS Network events website to announce the Tuesday 04 June event celebrating *The Last Detail.*)

screenwriting style – his evocation of Hawks' preferred world of men, troubled in their professional roles and finding comfort in their own friendships; the lack of family – or here, when family is useless, drunk and absent.

Finally, perhaps, the book and the film both concern themselves with the compassionate exchange between these three men. When Buddusky eventually realises that his act of kindness is actually a sort of cruelty, showing Meadows everything that will be denied him for the next 8 years of his young life, he cuts his ties and has him face up to reality.

At least one critic commented on the film's masculinity: "Buddusky has grafted the [John] Wayne ethic to his own rebellious and sadly defeated life…. He has the toughness, even flashes of the same man-to-man comradeship, but unlike Wayne's heroes, he isn't free – he's just a poor slob of a sailor, obedient to the core, however resentfully, when you come right down to it." [409] Darryl Ponicsan's material might not have been termed misogynist per se, although it could be charged that along with *Detail* his other novel, *CINDERELLA LIBERTY*, which he himself adapted for the screen, might just constitute an overtly masculine worldview – however realistic. Certainly the same could be said of any of the novels of James Jones. Towne's use of the vernacular in his adaptation undoubtedly reinforces criticism and as already pointed out, caused many problems in bringing the film to fruition. Nicholson's presence, while in itself a guarantee of excellence, also brought his formidable intuition with character. He improvised the following during the shooting of the Greenwich Village party scene with Nancy Allen:

```
                BUDDUSKY
      You know what I like about it? One of
      my favorite things about this uniform
      is the way that it makes your dick look.
```

Nicholson ad-libbed many endpoints and punctuations to dialogue throughout the film, though none so overtly sexual as this.

It is pertinent to note that the more contemporary entries here faced charges of misogyny, something that was levelled at *The Last Detail* by a number of reviewers. However, it is also worth remembering that at the time of the film's release the feminist movement was at its peak. This note of caution necessarily becomes part of the cultural mythology surrounding the production and reception of films, especially since the kinds of films being produced in this era were changing – although as usual the male domination of the industry continued unchecked. As Monaco suggests,

> throughout the sixties, as the film industry began to recover its health, the pattern of genres expanded… the two most important formal developments of the sixties don't fit into the classic genre pattern at all; they cut across lines. The Buddy film shifted the decades-old tradition of attention on a single hero to a focus on a pair of heroes, perhaps in response to the lack of powerful male leads like Bogart, Cooper, Gable or Wayne… Far more important than the vogue of the Buddy film (which seems to have subsided in the late seventies) was the rise of the Black film. [410]

---

[409] 'Superb and Raucous: Jack Nicholson in *The Last Detail*,' *Glamour*, April 1974.
[410] Monaco. *Op.cit.*, 55-56.

Detail cuts through both these generic patterns, and its significant use of Mulhall gives the film a political edge when he admits to a girl at the Greenwich Village party to having done a tour of duty in Vietnam. Thus the negro's patriotic sense of duty (presumably borne out of economic necessity, since he comes from a family of sharecroppers) conflicts with (what would presumably be) the privileged hippie scene, home to anti-Vietnam War protesters.

```
Henry's off to pour himself another drink.


                    GIRL
          Well, how'd you feel about going
          to Vietnam?

                    MULE
          - the man says go, we got to do
          what the man says.  We livin' in
          this man's world.

The girl shakes her head.

                    GIRL
                 (softly)
          Oh, baby.
```

(The Last Detail: 97)

and later, at the party:

MULE AND GIRL

```
Henry is back with his drink.

                    GIRL
          Well, tell me this - how come
          you don't see more black officers?

                    MULE
          - cause you got to have a recommendation
          from a white man usually … white man's
          not about to recommend no black man to
          be over no white man, even if he qualifies …

                    GIRL
          … then how can you stay in? …
                    HENRY
          - nothing, nothing that Nixon does
          disturbs you, is that right? Just
          answer is that right?

                    GIRL
```

```
          Henry, stop that.
               (to Mule, quietly)
          … how can you stay in?


                    MULE
               (a long moment, then: )
          … it's okay.
```
(The Last Detail. 98-99)

The first sequence above actually preceded the second sequence in the screenplay; but Ashby changed the order of many of these excerpts from the party scene, presumably to undercut the supposed radicalism of the hippies and to demonstrate a more straightforward and ultimately sympathetic reality that is the lifers' existence. The above sequence certainly gains in poignancy when viewed onscreen and creates a straightforward dialogue with the poses of youth culture (which seem vaguely ridiculous and even cynical viewed thirty years later, when viewed in opposition to the contrary and dignified stance of Mulhall.)

Authorship

It is notable that in many statements regarding the writing of this film, Towne uses the phrases 'real' or 'true to life'. Psychological realism – or authenticity - is more important to him than plot structure (or, at times, although not in terms of this film, comprehensibility, if you read his critics) and, in this regard, he could be said to be in a line of nineteenth century writers going back to Frank Norris in the United States, and Zola and the French Realists. This, despite the fact that his ironic, compromised anti-heroes often occupy potentially mythic surroundings.

Horowitz notes that "in his original screenplays Towne prefers a loose approach to storytelling." [411] A fact that perfectly suited Hal Ashby's laidback style: "I prefer to be much looser with a script and pick up things as I go along. That has to do with my own thing about spontaneity in film. Not describing what the characters look like is always better. I never get any lock-in on what people look like when I'm reading a script … I read them in general just to see what the idea is, to start with – what the hell kind of story we're trying to tell and why. I look to see what the rhythms are, and I try to hear certain things which give me an idea of how it starts to come to life. From that point on, it depends upon how good the writer is. That's why Bob Towne reaches the point where the stuff becomes magic. It comes to life very easy off the page with Bob." [412]

What is significant about Towne's writing style and Hal Ashby's style of directing, is their common reliance on character to dictate the scene: Ashby was notorious as one of the least dictatorial directors to have major successes in the Seventies. He was open to the suggestions of both actors and writers and, ironically perhaps, in those *auteur*-driven days, served every script well, rather than imposing a severe pictorial or cutting style that could be easily identified from one film to the next. It is precisely his honouring of the intention of the story (rather like John Huston) that frustrates the purists, but made him the ideal collaborator for Robert Towne, who could be said to have adopted a similar 'attitude' and indulged their shared penchant for realism crossed with melodrama when it came to directing his own work for the screen some years later.

---

[411] Horowitz. *Op.cit.,* 53.
[412] Ashby in 'Dialogue on Film,' *American Film*, May 1980: 60. See also Appendix 3.

Peter Biskind's account quotes producer Charles Mulvehill on Ashby: "'A lot of times producers never even showed up. Hal wouldn't deal with them. So after a while, they said, 'Fuck it.' He particularly disliked the creative producers who brought scripts to him. It really frustrated him that he couldn't originate material. By getting rid of them, he could assert authorship over the project'." [413]

In terms of the screenplay's relationship with the original novel, it is said that Ponicsan was not happy with the outcome. There is no doubt that the intention of the novel was altered in its transposition to the screen - but as Miller points out, what usually happens in adapting a work for film is that "a novelist's personal, corrosive vision is merely softened by the filmmaker." [414]   In the case of DETAIL that position was reversed. When Towne himself was asked if the film was close to how he had conceived it, he replied that in many ways it was. [415]

The New Centurions (1972) (uncredited)
aka *Precinct 45: Los Angeles Police*

Joseph Wambaugh's debut novel about the experiences of rookie officers in the Los Angeles Police Department proved of immediate interest to Stirling Silliphant (the credited writer): the prolific powerful Oscar-winning writer-producer acquired the rights and it was given to Richard Fleischer to direct. Certain problems with the adaptation began to surface, and Towne was called in as co-writer.

There are clear distinctions between the novel and the finished screenplay: The most telling is the blending of two rookie officers, Gus and Roy, into one, called Roy. Kilvinsky doesn't occupy such a prominent part of the novel, nor does he return to Los Angeles, as he does in the film. However, he does shoot himself and leaves Gus a few thousand dollars in his will. Several scenes in the screenplay are constructed from very minor allusions (in the case of the Oregon 'fruit', a mere paragraph, told in anecdotal form by an officer) or the outcome altered: for instance in the novel, the black man suspected of a felony is not killed; Gus/Roy dies in the film; in the novel Roy's death is the last thing we see. The most significant alteration is probably the excision of the Watts Riots which form the combustive (and logical) penultimate episode in a novel which has its finger on the pulse of the changing racial stratification of Los Angeles in the 1960s.

The changes to the novel, which is sprawling and takes place over five years rather than the one year described in the film, owe much to the strengthening of the throughline which is chiefly delineated through Roy's experiences and his relationship with his wife and Kilvinsky. Unfortunately it is not possible to specify who decided upon the changes as there were no production notes or copies of the screenplay drafts available. The excision of the Watts Riots sequence is possibly most pertinent for the consideration of Towne as auteur, inasmuch as his association with Warren Beatty's liberal political worldview perhaps disappointed students of his subsequent screenwriting work, which didn't cleave to any particular ideological leaning. Whether the choice was his or the team's is open to speculation, however, overt politicising beyond that which occurs in the subtext is absent on the whole from Towne's signature.

413 Biskind. *Op.cit.*, 178-179.
414 Gabriel Miller. *Op.cit.*, xii.
415 Towne was speaking at the American Film Institute's Harold Lloyd Master Seminar in 1998. The text of this interview is available at the AFI's website, www.afi.com.

Kilvinsky maintains his incarnation as written by Wambaugh, the ageing mentor and veteran cop, while Roy Fehler becomes a jaded version of him within one year, forgoing his ambition to return to college and study law. While it is not possible without access to either Silliphant's or Towne's drafts to delineate the precise input Towne had to the finished film, it can be seen that throughout Towne's work there is a tendency to construct strong student/mentor relationships (*Personal Best* and *Without Limits* are exemplary of this) and this may be one way in which he contributed to the writing of the adaptation. The early set up at the academy is glossed over and the bulk of the film takes place at the Los Angeles district police station where it is set, with the regular morning meetings the hook which sets each episode in motion (rather like television's *Hill Street Blues* some ten years later.) Clearly, the exclusion of the Watts Riots removes the social message which underpins Wambaugh's writing.

However due to Towne's unhappiness at the finished film – he claimed that the first twenty minutes made him dizzy – he would eventually disown his work and he asked for his name to be removed from the credits, which it duly was. That of Stirling Silliphant remains.[416] Towne said a couple of years after the film's release, "It was a really bad movie, which hurt because I really like Joe Wambaugh. It should have been a great movie." [417] Years later, when Britain's National Film Theatre held a retrospective of Towne's work, they included the film in the event. Adrian Turner notes that despite Towne's disavowal of the finished film, he still had pride in the screenplay:

> … he [Towne] said the best line he ever wrote was in *Precinct 45 – Los Angeles Police*.
> The line turned out to be 'No,' but Towne wasn't being facetious. He just
> boiled everything in the scene down to that single word.
> 'Are you better?' asks a nurse of Stacy Keach who had been shot and whose life is
> in ruins. 'No.' Take a look at it. [418]

---

[416] 'On the Scene: The Screenplay's the Thing,' *Playboy*, March 1975.
[417] *Wayne Warga, 'Writer Towne: Under the Smog, a Feel for the City,'* Los Angeles Times*, 18 August 1974: 22.*
[418] 'Cut To: Robert Towne,' *National Film Theatre programme*, May 1988: 4.

<u>*Chinatown* (1971-73) (written by): A Case Study of Authorship in a Screenplay</u>

Towne has achieved a strikingly personal cinema, and even in productions where several people could be credited as author, particularly *Chinatown* (1974), his signature and vision can be readily identified. His career acts as a lens by which to view over time the shifts in an industry whose storytelling style nonetheless remains for the most part within what has been termed Classical Hollywood Cinema, defined by David Bordwell as "an artistic system…[dependent on] flexible but bounded variation." [419]

Towne described to Joel Engel the impact of having seen photographs of the city he remembered one Sunday afternoon in the late Sixties:

> I came upon a bunch of photographs, one of a green Plymouth convertible under a streetlight in front of J.W. Robinson's [department store]; one of a Packard convertible in front of a Pasadena mansion; one taken near the train station. They were accompanied by prose from Raymond Chandler's novels, describing Los Angeles. I'd never read much Chandler, though I did after that. In reading these words and looking at these pictures, I realized that I had in common with Chandler that I loved L.A. and missed the L.A. that I loved. It was gone, basically, but so much of it was left; the ruins of it, the residue, were left. They were so pervasive that you could still shoot them and create the L.A. *that had been lost. That touched me.* [420]

Towne was engaged in an ecological battle close to his home in the late Sixties. He writes "[I]… got involved in an ecological battle concerning some land in the Santa Monica mountains. There were pay-offs in City Hall, so we lost and the land went under." [421] This experience directly informs the main line of action in *Chinatown*

He started taking long walks in the coastal hills and rediscovered the place where he had grown up.

> *Chinatown* began when I discovered I had a stronger feeling for Los Angeles than I had ever realized. Its genesis took place over a long period of time. I first became aware of it quite suddenly when I was walking up in the Santa Monica mountains. Like everybody else in Los Angeles, I had never thought of doing any walking until an old friend of mine talked me into it, and I found that I loved it. One day we were walking up in the Palisades when I suddenly felt as if I was about ten years old. It was an overwhelming feeling, and I couldn't understand where it came from. Until I realized that up there on the Palisades it was still like the city I remembered from childhood. Back then, you could smell the

[419] David Bordwell. *THE WAY HOLLYWOOD TELLS IT.* Los Angeles: University of California Press, 2006, 14.
[420] Towne in Joel Engel. *SCREENWRITERS ON SCREENWRITING The Best in the Business Discuss Their Craft.* New York: Hyperion, 1995, 215. The photographs in the article were taken by John Waggaman, the text written by Laurence Dietze.
[421] "The destruction of the valley community was so blatant I could hardly believe what I read. I was bowled over by it. It reminded me of our useless battle to save a part of the Santa Monica mountains. And at this point *Chinatown* began taking shape in my head. I began to write a story about a man who raped the land and his own daughter. One, at least, was in the name of progress." Towne in Pirie (ed.). *Op.cit.*, 152. Such was Towne's dedication to the conservation cause that the Benedict Canyon Association gave him an award for 'his devotion to the preservation of the santa Monica Mountains, this canyon, this city, and a whole variety of good causes.' *Canyon Crier*, February 2, 1975.

city: the pepper trees, the eucalyptus, the orange blossoms. It was a delight. [422]

Chinatown is the major work in Towne's career. If the overarching theme of Towne's work is, as Norman Mailer correctly adduced, that of loss, then it is in *Chinatown* that this theme is most acutely expressed.

> I was suddenly filled with a tremendous kind of sense of loss, of what that city was... that had been gone. And you could see it just sort of... little pockets of time that could throw you right back into the past. And I knew that it was still possible to photograph the city in such a way as to recreate that time, much in the way that those street lamps existed. And I suppose, in a way, that was the beginning. [423]

Perhaps one of the most astute observations on the effect that *Chinatown* has had on an understanding of Towne as screenwriter comes from Horowitz, who poses the question, "What if *Chinatown* far from being quintessential Towne in theme, style, and structure, is really his most atypical and misleading work?" [424] He correctly identifies Towne as a classicist, above all a psychological realist, whose roots and inspiration lie in the nineteenth century European novel (and whose greatest cinematic hero is Jean Renoir). *Chinatown*'s apparently clear, crystalline structure, its precise plot, its dark sensibility, are allegedly pure Polanski, as Towne himself admits: "except for Arthur [Penn], Roman taught me more about screenwriting than anybody I've ever worked with, both in spite of and because of our conflicts. Roman is great at the elucidation of the narrative – to go from point A to B to C. In that sense, he is excellent." [425]

Content, History and Theme

In 1971 Towne found himself in Oregon doing rewrites on Jack Nicholson's directing debut, *Drive, He Said*, when he came across the prodigious account of California's history by Carey McWilliams:

> Here, in fact, was all America. America in flight from itself, America
> on an island.
>> - Carey McWilliams, *SOUTHERN CALIFORNIA: COUNTRY:*
>> *An Island on the Land* [426]

---

[422] *Ibid.*

[423] Towne. *Writing CHINATOWN*, BBC. He also recounts this experience in 'Growing Up in a City of Senses,' *Los Angeles*, May 1975: 49-50.

[424] Horowitz. *Op.cit.*, 54.

[425] Brady. *Op.cit.*, 410. The section on *Chinatown* to follow should confirm that the core of the work is Towne's and argues that Polanski's insistence on cuts actually works against the logic of the story.

[426] In the First Draft of the screenplay Towne uses the following description as an allusion to this subtitle. At Rancho Del Cruce, Cross, Evelyn and Jake meet and it is described as follows:

```
-     a   miniature California encompassing desert, mountains,
and canyons that tumble down palisades to the windward side of
the island.
```

(*Chinatown* First Draft: 96)

And Towne wrote the screenplay in a sort of exile from the mainland on Catalina Island in the company of his dog, Hira, whom he got from the Chinatown policeman who helped inspire the screenplay, along with regular counsel from his close friend Edward Taylor. See Towne in Pirie, 1981, as before; and Towne in John Boorman and Walter Donahue eds., *PROJECTIONS 6*. London: Faber and Faber, 1996, 109. His love of the island metaphor is described by Thomson, 1997, 100.

A section of the chapter 'Water! Water! Water!' tells the story of the Owens Valley tragedy: Dubliner William Mulholland, a former sailor and lumberjack, got work labouring on a pipe-building scheme on the Los Angeles River. He had a vision to bring water to the city from the High Sierras and floated a $1.5 million bond on the prospect of a 233-mile aqueduct after defrauding the farmers in the Valley who believed that an irrigation project was being planned. He was backed by notorious businessman Harry Chandler, publisher of the *Times*, who, along with a number of other financiers, bought up many of the holdings in the San Fernando Valley in 1905 and 1910. The engineering triumph was opened in 1913. "There it is! Take it!" [427] Mulholland cried as the first waters spilled out of the San Fernando Reservoir. (The whole disgraceful episode is thinly disguised in Mary Austin's 1917 novel *THE FORD*.) The McWilliams book led Towne to pursue his interest in the water crisis, a story memorably told by Morrow Mayo, in *LOS ANGELES* (1933), a work that is regarded as the greatest hatchet job on that city. For Towne's purposes, proceeding from reality to form a mythical monster, William Mulholland and Harry Chandler (of *The Los Angeles Times* family) intertwined to became the characters Hollis Mulwray and Noah Cross. Slowly the story of *Chinatown* began to evolve, as the images of the city he loved combined powerfully with his sense memory of his childhood landscape; and his recent dealings with City Hall blended into the history of Los Angeles and its depiction by Raymond Chandler. He explains:

> I didn't feel I would be able to tell it with an appreciable audience as a Frank Norris polemic about water and power in California so I decided to telescope it into a few months in the 1930s. [428]

A search for his beloved dog inspired the riverbed scenes.

> I was suddenly filled with a tremendous kind of sense of loss, of what that city was... that had been gone. And you could see it just sort of... little pockets of time that could throw you right back into the past. And I knew that it was still possible to photograph the city in such a way as to recreate that time, much in the way that those street lamps existed. And I suppose, in a way, that was the beginning.[429]

Robert A. Rosenstone urges caution when judging history on film: "The academic or *Dragnet* historian ('Just the facts, Ma'am') looking at film has to face difficult questions: What criteria are applicable for judging visual history? How does film contribute to our sense of the past? The easiest answer (and most irrelevant because it ignores the change in the medium) is to assess how true a work remains to 'the facts.' But you do not have to see many films to know such an approach is ridiculous in the extreme." He continues: "… all history, including written history, is a construction, not a reflection… history (as we practice it) is an ideological and cultural product of the Western World at a particular time in its development… history is a series of conventions for thinking about the past." [430]

[427] Towne used this as the prefatory quote to the screenplay's first two drafts.

[428] Speaking on BBC TV. Towne remarks in his Preface and Postscript to the published version of the screenplay, "It wasn't the compendium of facts in the Chapter 'Water! Water! Water!' or indeed in the entire book. It was that Carey McWilliams wrote about Southern California with sensibilities my eye, ear, and nose recognized." *CHINATOWN*. Santa Barbara, California: Neville, 1982.

[429] Speaking on BBC TV.

[430] Robert A. Rosenstone. *VISIONS OF THE PAST: The Challenge of Film to our Idea of History*. . Harvard University Press, 1995: 7; 10.

While *Chinatown* does not set out to fulfil these criteria it actually amplifies its subject and places it in a complex context, making history come alive, just as Rosenstone suggests. *Chinatown* sheds light on a society riven by class conflict and real estate wars, raising for discussion issues of civil liberty, corruption and duty. In the end, the lesson of *Chinatown* as parable is simple – history repeats itself, and the future is indeed sown in the past. *Chinatown* may use the story of the Owens Valley for inspiration but as Towne admitted, he wasn't writing an historical film. [431]

The screenplay might be said to have had its canonical status assured in the mid-Seventies with the analysis afforded it by Syd Field: since *SCREENPLAY* was published in 1978, the script has been extolled as a model text by teachers at film schools all over the world. [432]

Principally utilising the filter of genre construction, the following section examines aspects of the three drafts of the screenplay. [433]

---

[431] Towne in Brady. *Op.cit.*, 414. Abraham Hoffman, in his article 'Myth, History and Water in the Eastern Sierra' says that Towne got it wrong: "CHINATOWN, of course, created its own myths and distortions. While it successfully recreated an era of political intrigue and mystery, it obscured basic facts by setting the story in the 1930s instead of the early 1900s, murdering the Mulholland character, and even injecting incest into the plot. I have found that in talking to anyone whose interest in the water controversy was whetted by seeing CHINATOWN, I first have to strip away all of the fictional devices in the film in order to start discussing the history. And, of course, some people are disappointed that there wasn't any incest after all." Abraham Hoffman on E Clampus Vitus website, Lost Dutchman Chapter 5917 Arizona, internet article. Paul Ricoeur posits the problems or possibilities of the dimensionality of narrative: on the one hand there is chronology and on the other a configurational aspect which derives from the telling of the story and is non-chronological. He states: "The full recognition of the continuity between narrative and history presupposes, however, that we dispense with these two other assumptions: that the art of narrating is necessarily linked to the blind complexity of the present as it is experienced by the authors themselves, and that this art is subsumed to the interpretation which the agents themselves give of their actions…To narrate and to follow a story is already to 'reflect upon' events with the aim of encompassing them in successive totalities." Paul Ricoeur and John B. Thompson, 'The Narrative Function,' 1981, 279.

[432] Syd Field. 1994.

[433] Cohan and Swires state that, "The advantages of analysing a story in terms of its genre are several. First of all, a genre identifies the cultural semiotics of a story, thereby making its narrative signs publicly intelligible…. Second, calling attention to the way in which the story conforms to but also subverts a generic paradigm highlights the contradictions in and disruptions of the very meanings which the genre promotes as a cultural semiotic… Third, analyses of the specific way in which a story reproduces the paradigmatic structure of a genre makes evident the historical timeliness of its sexual and class meanings." *Op.cit.*, 79-90.

Figure 7 *Chinatown* one sheet

<u>Genre, New and Old</u>

Towne says of *Chinatown*'s generic impetus:

> It was a conspiracy after all, a huge conspiracy, so I determined to turn it into a mystery. It was a genre that has so many traditions that if you are able to invest that tradition with a reality that [it] has not had it would be kind of jolting.[434]

Towne's evident feeling for reality and naturalism, above and beyond the bounds of generic limitations, is partly the reason Pauline Kael called him "a great new screenwriter in a structured tradition – a flaky classicist." [435]

Towne has long acknowledged his debt to the pulp fiction which informs film noir and especially the seminal influence of Raymond Chandler and Dashiell Hammett on the writing of *Chinatown*. Hammett's particular contribution to the pulp jungle was primarily a series of novels, beginning in the Twenties, depicting the machinations of the Continental Op., a singularly unprepossessing private eye. RED HARVEST was probably the first of the hardboiled genre, first published in 1929. It was quickly followed by THE MALTESE FALCON, which in its third cinematic adaptation, by John Huston, became probably the seminal hardboiled film with the genre's basic plotline and constellation of characters. Sam Spade, possibly the screen character closest to Jake Gittes, is acknowledged by Towne as a direct influence, and one that is especially notable since Nicholson's persona is based around this character, and Towne wrote the script with his friend in mind. Towne says,

> I created the detective J.J.Gittes around his personality.[436]

---

[434] Towne speaking on *Writing Chinatown*.

[435] Pauline Kael. 1992, 442. The strict dictionary definition of flaky connotes 'dodgy,' 'unreliable.'

[436] Towne in Engel. *Op.cit.*, 216. I took a lot of things from Jack Nicholson in life for the character of Gittes in *Chinatown*... Things that happened. I used his idiosyncracies,but, more importantly, I tried to use his way of working. I've seen him work so much that I feel I know what he does well. In fact, I don't even think about it. I just do it. I saw Jack work and improvise two or three times a week for maybe five straight years. It's hard *not* to think about Jack even when I'm not writing for him. His work literally affected the way that I work, totally independent of doing a movie with Jack." Towne in Brady. *Op.cit.*, 401. David Thomson comments: "Jake Gittes, the character, was not just the finest fruit of association; he was the shared ideal of a friendship – shrewd, funny, sad and error prone." From: 'The Towne,' in Thomson, 1997, 101.

Schatz says of this world "the arena of action – and especially of social action – is expanded to include both sides of the tracks." [437]   Hammett's first true cinematic impact was based on the adaptation of *THE THIN MAN* by MGM in 1934 – it did a roaring trade and the studio immediately decided it had a franchise on its hands. As played by William Powell and Myrna Loy, the wisecracking gumshoe and his ritzy, sassy, martini-swilling wife were a major hit. It was one of the most prolific and successful film series ever, spawning several sequels which departed significantly from Hammett's original creation. Michael Eaton comments, "as in the schema perhaps most prominently at work in the novels of Dashiell Hammett, there is only a mystery because other characters will not tell the investigator the truth." [438]

Gittes' position is wholly undercut (literally and metaphorically in this City of Senses) by the slashing of his nose (because that's what happens to "nosy fellows") by "a midget" (played in the film by the director), and he is obliged to wear a cartoon band-aid on his nose for the remainder of the film.[439] Stephen Cooper says of the sensory damage which ironically comments on Gittes' futile quest,

> *Chinatown* and *The Maltese Falcon* differ significantly in the way that each establishes the protagonist's ability to sniff out, as it were, a lie. Nor is the nasal metaphor at all out of place. Caught comically off guard, Gittes must hustle to rectify his mistake, and in the process he nearly loses his nose… leaving both eyes free to probe, even while suggesting a tragicomic impairment of the detective's investigative-generative faculties.[440]

Raymond Chandler is acknowledged by Towne as "more of an inspiration in terms of his feeling for the city than anything else. His heroes tend to be tarnished knights whereas I wanted to make Gittes (played by Jack Nicholson) more vulgar and crass and venal than anything that had been done before – a guy who deliberately specialized in sordid divorce work and then rationalised his own seamy job."[441] Chandler was actively engaged as a screenwriter in the 1940s – but by Paramount and his contract did not permit him to work on the adaptation of *The Big Sleep* (1946) - which was made by Warners and adapted by Leigh Brackett and Jules Furthman. [442]

> The realist in murder writes of a world in which gangsters can rule nations …
> in which hotels and apartment houses and celebrated restaurants are owned by

---

[437] Schatz, 1983, 78.

[438] Michael Eaton. *CHINATOWN*. London: BFI Film Classics, BFI Publishing, 2000, 38.

[439] Towne has written of himself, "Like my struggling detective, Gittes, and my dog, Hira, I have always been, to some extent, led around by the nose." Robert Towne, 'Chinatown – A Screenwriter's Eulogy for Los Angeles,' *Architectural Digest*, April 2000.

[440] Stephen Cooper, 'Sex/Knowledge/Power in the Detective Genre,' *Film Quarterly*, Vol. XLII, No.3, 1989: 28. Cawelti concludes that the private eye is simply unable to control or comprehend the depths of evil to which he is suddenly exposed: "*Chinatown* places the hard-boiled detective story within a view of the world that is deeper and more catastrophic, more enigmatic in its evil, more sudden and inexplicable in its outbreaks of violent chance. In the end, the image of heroic, moral action embedded in the traditional private-eye myth turns out to be totally inadequate to overcome the destructive realities revealed in the course of this story." Cawelti. *Op.cit.*,503

[441] Towne in Pirie. *Op.cit.*, 152.

[442] His screenwriting credits include an adaptation of *DOUBLE INDEMNITY* by James M.Cain which was co-written with director Billy Wilder.

men who made their money out of brothels, and in which a screen star can be finger man for the mob…

       - Raymond Chandler, *The Simple Art of Murder* [443]

Genre could be said to exist in different stages of development. We should refer once more to Thomas Schatz, whose *HOLLYWOOD GENRES* (1981) encapsulates many of the aspects of writings on the subject, and reminds us that genres evolve, from a pure, conventionalized form that becomes a purely self-conscious form.[444]

In terms of the dialogue that exists between an audience and the making of a genre film, Schatz refers to Leo Braudy whom he quotes as follows: "'Change in genre occurs when the audience says, 'That's too infantile a form of what we believe. Show us something more complicated'." [445] Schatz concludes, "The genre film reaffirms what the audience believes both on individual and on communal levels. Audience demand for variation does not indicate a change in belief, but rather that the belief should be re-examined, grow more complicated formally and thematically, and display, moreover, stylistic embellishment." *Chinatown* occurs at a time when the genre is at a mature, self-reflexive stage, shot in Panavision and full colour in the glare of the Californian sun, confident enough to shine a torch into the darkest recesses of the water-logged, power-crazed brains of those who shaped the state and particularly Los Angeles. Stephen Cooper puts it another way: "like other structures of power, the detective genre over time develops its internal contradictions to such an extent that the genre's own eventual unravelling is self-assured… Removed from the era which it evokes (1930s Los Angeles) by some thirty to forty years, *Chinatown* cannot fail but to have a longer perspective on the genre."[446]

Paul Schrader says that "film noir's techniques emphasize loss, nostalgia, lack of clear priorities, insecurity; then submerge these self-doubts in mannerism and style. In such a world style becomes paramount; it is all that separates one from meaninglessness." [447] If meaninglessness is the alternative to grim reality, then noir must be defined by its innate pessimism: Schrader says its over-riding theme is "a passion for the past and present, but also a fear of the future. The noir hero dreads to look ahead, but instead tries to survive by the day, and if unsuccessful at that, he retreats to the past."

---

[443] Quoted by Paul Jensen. 'Raymond Chandler: The World You Live In,' *Film Comment*, Volume 10 Issue No 6, 1974: 18-26

[444] Schatz, 1981, 37. He quotes Foçillon, who observes that there is an experimental stage, a classic stage and an age of refinement which could be called a baroque or self-reflexive age.

[445] Schatz continues: "Thus the end of a genre's classic stage can be viewed as that point at which the genre's straightforward message has 'saturated' the audience… we no longer look through the form (or perhaps 'into the mirror') to glimpse and idealized self-image, rather we look at the form itself to examine and appreciate its structure and cultural appeal.
"A genre's progression from transparency to opacity – from straightforward storytelling to self-conscious formalism – involves its concerted effort to explain itself, to address and evaluate its very status as a popular form." Schatz, 1981,38.

[446] Cooper. *Op.cit,* 24-27. Towne comments: "I was trying to do not necessarily a Chandler or a Hammett but, instead, how it actually might have been. Inevitably you use the genre; otherwise you would tell a very straight flat story about the scandal. The genre made the horror *greater*. You're reaching a broader audience." Peter Rainer, '*Chinatown*'s Robert Towne,' *Mademoiselle*, November 1974: 234. Dancyger and Rush say of film noir, "as a genre that depicts the worst in human beings, it brings out the best in writers and directors. An interesting irony." *Op.cit.*, 35-36.

[447] Paul Schrader, 'Notes on Film Noir,' *Film Comment*, Vol.8,No.1, Spring 1972: 8-13.

Thus, noir could be appreciated as a response to a particular set of social conditions, principally those associated with a nation in the aftermath of World War II, but also those accumulated tensions from the years of the Depression, i.e. a 'Social Moment' or stressline in the graph of the United States' well-being. B. Ruby Rich refers to it as etching "a metaphor of light and shadow into the popular psyche; rain-slicked streets, feelings of loss, fear, and betrayal; male bonding, femmes fatales, post-war malaise, atomic pressures, Communist threats, melodrama and gangsters all coalesced under its banner. Capone met Mabuse in the darkness… Americans flocked to noir to pacify themselves with its equally tangled narratives and unreliable narrators." [448] *Chinatown* opposes film noir by taking place in dazzling sunshine, in rain-starved streets and drought-ridden desert.

Chinatown could be said to be "an adaptation of the tradition. Here, the knight is afoot in his own time and place, Los Angeles in the thirties, but like the clownish knight of the seventies, he is still made to look ridiculous … [Gittes] is no clown, but something of a gifted amateur, quite clever it is true, but far out of his league when trying to outsmart some very professional evil-doers. He is an amateur for the same reason Marlowe is a clown: his high morals and stamina, what you might call his good American enterprise, no longer produce automatic good results. Virtue may still be its own reward, but it is not likely to solve cases." [449]

In terms of the kinds of hero proposed by film noir, the modern man is "an endangered species, unable to control the forces around him, caught in a vice between impulse and guilt." [450] He is in a sense a chess piece, manipulated and misled by all around him – but he usually triumphs.

> Folks ain't safe a minute in this town. When I come here twenty-two years
> ago we didn't lock our doors hardly. Now it's gangsters and crooked
> policemen fightin' each other with machine guns, so I've heard.
> - Raymond Chandler, *FAREWELL MY LOVELY* (1940)

While similarities in *Chinatown* are to be seen in the film of *The Big Sleep* (1946) (adapted by William Faulkner, Leigh Brackett and Jules Furthman from the novel, by Raymond Chandler), in what was perhaps the first instance of Towne's self-conscious act of homage to classical Hollywood (the private eye hired by a wealthy family; the seemingly unsolvable mystery; the nymphomaniac little sister; the drugs; the cross and double-cross; the powerful father; the innuendo about horse-riding in a conversation between Marlowe and Vivian); they can also be seen across other novels produced by Raymond Chandler: a survey of the story elements of *THE LONG GOODBYE*, first published in 1953, which itself would receive a contemporary adaptation by Robert Altman and veteran screenwriter Leigh Brackett in the year prior to the release of *Chinatown*, (it was released on 07 March 1973; *Chinatown* was released on 20 June 1974) indicates a plethora of story elements which can be interpreted as components mapped across the narrative of *Chinatown*:

---

[448] B. Ruby Rich, 'Dumb Lugs and Femmes Fatales,' *Sight & Sound*, November 1995, Vol.5, No.11: 6-10. However Prof. Tom Stempel disagrees – films noirs were outgrossed by virtually every other genre, as can be seen in his figures on moviegoing in *AMERICAN AUDIENCES ON MOVIES AND MOVIEGOING*. Lexington: University Press of Kentucky, 2001.

[449] Bill Oliver, '*The Long Goodbye* and *Chinatown*: Debunking the Private Eye Tradition,' *Literature/Film Quarterly* Summer 1975 Vol. 5 No. 2: 241.

[450] Mitchell S. Cohen, 'Villains and Victims,' *Film Comment*, Vol. 10 Issue No 6, 1974: 29.

Figure 8 Jake Gittes (Jack Nicholson), that very nosy fellow

Philip Marlowe is manipulated by his client (Terry Lennox – who's really Paul Marston), who is apparently murdered/or commits suicide, when he flees to Mexico with Marlowe's aid; Jake Gittes is manipulated by his client (Evelyn Mulwray – who's really Ida Sessions), who is then murdered when she is attempting to flee to Mexico with Gittes' aid. Ida Sessions herself is murdered when she attempts to ask Gittes for help.

Marlowe regularly dines at the Hollywood Boulevard restaurant Musso and Frank's [a longtime favourite of screenwriters.]; in *Chinatown* Gittes regularly dines at the Hollywood Boulevard restaurant The Pig & Whistle. Lennox's wife Sylvia is the daughter of one of the most powerful men in Los Angeles, Harlan Potter, who controls the content of the city's newspapers; Evelyn Mulwray is the daughter of Noah Cross, one of the most powerful men in Los Angeles, and he controls the content of newspapers as well as City Hall, the Department of Water and Power, and so forth. Sylvia Lennox is promiscuous; Evelyn is promiscuous. Roger Wade is being drugged by a doctor; **Evelyn's sister/daughter is being drugged.** Sylvia Lennox has her face blown off; Ida Sessions, the fake Evelyn Mulwray, has her face blown off.

Another suspicious doctor is running an old people's (or 'dying-in') home whose occupants have no idea that their assets are being robbed; the Mar Vista is full of clients whose homes have been stolen by Noah Cross. Another suspect sells up a small tract of land with no idea of its value to real estate developers; the farmers' land north of Los Angeles is being intentionally drained of water to render it 'worthless.' In the second part of the still-incomplete *Chinatown* trilogy, *The Two Jakes*, real estate development forms the narrative spine.

Sylvia Lennox has a sister who tries to put Marlowe off the scent after meeting him in Musso and Frank's; the real Evelyn Mulwray tries to put Jake off the scent after meeting him in The Pig & Whistle. In the film *The Long Goodbye* (1973), director Mark Rydell plays an unhinged psychopath called Marty Augustine; in *Chinatown*, a similar role is played by the film's own director, Roman Polanski.

Eileen Wade doesn't seem particularly bothered when her husband Roger dies; Evelyn doesn't seem particularly bothered when her husband Hollis is murdered. Marlowe's mature worldview is especially scathing about the abuse of power; Gittes becomes disabused of powerful men through the story's machinations. Much of the book is set in Idle Valley; Much of *Chinatown* is set in the San Fernando/Owens Valley.

When Marlowe meets Potter, he receives a lecture on the uses of power; when Gittes meets Cross, he receives a lecture on the uses of power. The point of view narrative which drives both stories is distinguished by a mature, jaundiced perspective of Los Angeles.

Towne, however, departs from this particular Chandler work in two crucial ways: Jake Gittes is a self-conscious dandy; and he specialises in divorce cases, something the mature Marlowe only takes on when he desperately needs the cash. So Marlowe is actually elegant while Gittes is seedy but aspires to elegance.

> The one thing a film noir private eye would never do, where those cynical gumshoes
> drew the line, they would not take matrimonial cases, meaning adultery.
> In *Chinatown* J.J. Gittes boasts that adultery … is his métier. [451]

In *The Long Goodbye*, Chandler also represents his burned-out, self-hating, alcoholic novelist self in the character of Roger Wade; whereas there would appear to be no such equivalent for Towne in the screenplay for *Chinatown*: rather the entire screenplay represents Towne's elegy for the (lost) city he loves.

Aside from plotting devices and character borrowings, we might briefly surmise Chandler's contribution to literature as the creative use of metaphor, something Towne does superlatively with his insertion of both incest and water (and by implication, power) into the *Chinatown* narrative. In a narrower sense, Chandler's descriptions of his preferred location, Southern California, are indelible. The poetic use of California and particularly Los Angeles, as his preferred location, would, following *Chinatown* become a hallmark of Towne's work. Towne incorporated, via the original screenplay by Benton and Newman, the popular legends and mythology surrounding the real-life Bonnie Parker and Clyde Barrow: this interpolation of myth, fact and legend would receive a crucial re-imagining in *Chinatown*. Towne's own fondness for legendary characters can be seen in the brief newspaper allusion to Seabiscuit (the little horse that could) in the barbershop scene; this remains as a mere visual reference in the film but his track success actually dictated much of the scene's content as it was originally written by Towne in the first two drafts. Jake's characterisation was lost, with the excision of the original, which was intended to

---

[451] Robert Mc Kee, *Filmworks: Chinatown*, BBC, 1993. The 3rd draft of the screenplay opens with a virtual diorama of pornography and shocking stolen intimacy– the fruits of spying on a cheating wife for a client. It is a conscious echo of the opening of the modish 1969 adaptation by Stirling Silliphant of Chandler's THE LITTLE SISTER, *Marlowe* (the director, in a nice touch, was Paul Bogart) in which the private eye is updated to the Swinging Sixties and played by James Garner who would essay the type again – in the film, *They Only Kill Their Masters* (1972) which is a similarly complicated mystery owing a debt to THE LONG GOODBYE; and for TV, most popularly in the long-running series *The Rockford Files*. Script analyst Meg Wolitzer states: "The opening should always be something that people will remember; it should never be merely a random moment in the middle of a scene. There needs to be a real reason that we are eavesdropping on the scene right now, as opposed to five minutes earlier." Meg Wolitzer. *FITZGERALD DID IT: The Writer's Guide to Mastering the Screenplay*. New York: Penguin, 1999, 63.

form the link between his admiration for Seabiscuit – a classy character – and his desire to help Evelyn (a thoroughbred.) Instead, Polanski's cutting of the action diminishes the scene's function. [452]   (Jake's own 'legendary' status in the city is derided by a fellow customer in the same scene who alludes to the seamy nature of his work, which brilliantined hair and natty dressing cannot overcome.)

Overall, the conscious adapting of the story of Los Angeles and its history of water problems indicates a deep understanding on Towne's part of the power of myth; in fact, *Chinatown* now seems to have seeped into the public consciousness to the extent that it represents for most people the true history of that city's acquisition of a water supply. [453]

The plot of *THE LONG GOODBYE* is somewhat confusing; *Chinatown*'s three complex drafts are the stuff of legend (principally amongst those who haven't read them); ironically, the third – alleged shooting – draft would excise several crucial story elements, including Evelyn's backstory with Escobar and her character's development; Ida Sessions' motivation; and the ending, which still makes more sense than Polanski's last-minute rewrite with Nicholson, which is how the film concludes. These will be systematically examined here, draft by draft. Central to an understanding of the three drafts is the struggle that Towne describes which has to do with the labyrinthine nature of the plot (echoing the Byzantine levels of corruption), the deep structural conflict and the mythological approach to the past via the generic fiction which had already cast Los Angeles as a locus of corruption and decadent power.

Towne acknowledges that he had problems putting the script together from the start:

> … I was constantly trying to organize it. I wrote at least twenty different
> step outlines – long, long step outlines. Usually I have a pretty clear idea of
> where the screenplay is going, even if I don't know every step of the way. [454]

Chinatown belongs to the genre of the detective film – not only inspired by Hammett and Chandler in a literary sense but belonging squarely in a group of films that, although termed film noir (surely now understood as a trans-generic visual style rather than a pure genre), have certain tropes that were highly evolved by the time it was made, in 1973. Virginia Wright Wexman asserts that the pattern of the film is ultimately that of the hard-boiled subset: *"Chinatown* both exemplifies this genre and comments on it," she states. [455] The key year for this style of film however was 1946. Schatz says that the film noir and the hardboiled detective combined to create what he terms, 'American Expressionism.' Film noir is a style that can be found in melodramas, Westerns, gangster films, and psychological thrillers, which are a genre proliferating with the work of Hitchcock. Schatz claims that it is a style that can also be located outside traditional genre

---

[452] Towne in Brady. *Op.cit.,* 415-416.

[453] Interviewed by Rob Davis, urban studies professor and author, Steve Erie commented "What I tell Robert Towne, the screenwriter, is that it's lousy history. It's a great movie. There's none better. It's got everything. Sex, power, greed, you name it. It is American gothic. But as an understanding of how L.A. grew, it plays fast and loose with the facts." *Los Angeles Times*, 06 May 2006.

[454] Towne in 'Dialogue on Film,' *American Film* Vol.1, No.3 December 1975: 44.

[455] Wexman, 1985, 93.

territory, for instance *Sunset Blvd.* (1950), *Hamlet* (1948) and *The Lost Weekend* (1945). . *Chinatown* then probably belongs, loosely, to that subset of the genre called 'detective noir.' [456]

The screenplay honours its debt by its formal analogy with detective noirs characteristic of 1941-1946; it refers to the post-war realistic period (roughly from 1945-1949) through its complexion of historical events; but mostly in its tone and thematic concerns it is related to the period of 1949-1953, a phase which, as Paul Schrader says, was

> the most aesthetically and sociologically piercing. After ten years of steadily shedding romantic conventions, the later *noir* films finally got down to the root causes of the period: the loss of public honor, heroic conventions, personal integrity, and finally, psychic stability. The third-phase films were painfully self-aware; they seemed to know they stood at the end of a long tradition based on despair and disintegration and did not shy away from that fact. [457]

Schatz describes the narrative time scheme of the detective noir as follows:

> In this process of investigation and revelation, the detective necessarily is preoccupied with the past, with unravelling the events and motives which led to the crime and his eventual employment. [458]

Of course, in a textual sense, we can add another layer of time and investigative narrative procedures to the process, by inscribing Towne's own research and position as a subjective interpreter of the past, projecting events of the 1910s to a time two decades' hence, and then doubling back from the 1970s, layered into the detective narrative which controls the generic form. [459] Nostalgia may have been a contributing a factor to its terms

---

[456] Schatz, 1981, 112.

[457] Schrader *Op.cit.*, 12.

[458] Schatz. 1983, 144.

[459] The film can also be read as an expression of the straining relationship between culture and entertainment at the time of its production. Robert Sklar points out that while films such as *Chinatown* (and others such as *The Conversation, Mean Streets, Taxi Driver, The Godfather Part II* and *Nashville*, for instance) belong to an era in which iconoclastic films examine critically national and political institutions "that the dominant 'political energies' of the era are barely represented in even the most political of commercial fiction... Film subjects and forms are as likely - more likely – to be determined by the institutional and cultural dynamics of motion picture production than by the most frenetic of social upheavals." The true benefit of this era of society and film/studio culture in transition was for the filmmakers themselves, particularly the directors, whose status was augmented in what Sklar describes as "a generational transformation. The great figures of Hollywood's studio era, a generation born at the turn of the twentieth century, were retiring from the scene... The prestige they retrospectively accrued conferred enhanced status on the director's role in filmmaking ... abetted by growing familiarity in the United States with French New Wave polemics... The similarities between the 1930s and the 1970s went beyond crisis to consolidation. The 'age of turbulence' in 1970s filmmaking was succeeded by an 'age of order'." The time-loop metaphor from the 1970s to the 1930s, and back again, extends to the industry proposing the film, as Sklar locates the major difference in the eras in "the revolution in distribution. The story of filmmakers and the films they made in the 1970s is inseparable from the story of how their films were delivered to theatres." Sklar. *Op.cit.,* 322-323. Sklar says, "the years 1972 to 1976 indeed marked a period not only of cinematic innovation but of a critical and analytical approach to national institutions rarely seen in mainstream American filmmaking." (322).

of construction but *Chinatown* was not history, rather 'an anachronism.' *Chinatown* is not interested in the Great Depression, more in the eternal problem of political corruption, what McKee calls "social cement... the glue that holds society together." [460] James Monaco probably best surmises the effect in calling *Chinatown* "canny pastiche," continuing

> ... Towne revived the Marlowe/Spade type in a period setting, and gave Jack Nicholson's J.J. Gittes an historical mystery to investigate that had some contemporary relevance. Southern California water politics are still very interesting. Add John Huston (director of *The Maltese Falcon*) as the villain and you have a film with very sharp resonances. [461]

The screenplay also occasions a time-loop in existential style by referring to Gittes' former time on the beat as a cop, implying that *Chinatown* is more than just a state of mind, but a state of chaos, ever imminent and bound to repeat itself. [462]

Ryan and Kellner locate *Chinatown* in the mid-Seventies noir revival – along with *The Long Goodbye* (1973), *Night Moves* (1975) and *The Big Sleep* (1978) and, perhaps, *Klute* (1971) – which "can be said to instantiate the emerging reality of political liberalism – that it was powerless against the entrenched economic power blocs of the country. It could do nothing against steep price rises and the bleeding of the country by oil companies. It is in the tragic figure of the noir detective, determined to do right yet incapable of changing the basic realities, that the liberal ideal, with all of its well-deserved self-pity, finds its strongest expression at this point in time."

The authors argue that the revival could be traced to *Bonnie and Clyde* and *Point Blank* (and *Marlowe*) and "could be said to coincide with the breakdown of conservative moral and social boundaries that characterized the sixties." They continue that in contemporary noir films, "it is difficult to sort out good from evil in a clearly boundaried way. Normal institutions like motherhood are corrupt; and the trust usually associated with family relations is betrayed. The supposedly innocent delve into incest, but their death is not in any way justified as moral retribution.

The moral dilemma is often due to the incursion of the past, the return of the repressed. Noir flashbacks often highlight the power of past guilt in determining the present, and this abreactive form undermines the 'eternal present' of Hollywood film, the appearance that everything occurs in a nonhistorical space. The narrative turns in these films are part of a general moral rhetoric which confuses simplistic conservative moral judgments by overturning the logic of moral responsibility. If individuals are evil, it is usually because they are examples of a class structure."

They conclude, that "the mid-seventies noir revivals are distinguished by a sense of pessimism devoid of even the individual triumphs that the traditional *noir* detective enjoyed." [463] The arc of *Chinatown* certainly falls into that mode of pessimism, while the

---

[460] McKee, *Filmworks: Chinatown*, BBC TV, 1993.

[461] James Monaco, 1979, 281. Huston's presence may have been more than tricky showmanship; cast as the film's centre of evil, this may be an insider's gloss on Huston's reputation – certain authors have suggested in recent years that his departure from Hollywood in the Fifties was connected with a dark side not previously acknowledged as some works on the Black Dahlia murder claim.

[462] Which of course it would – in the sequel, *The Two Jakes*.

familiar flashback is limited to a reference to Jake's past which is more fully explored in the first two drafts of the screenplay.

Cawelti suggests that it could be linked with seemingly diverse films such as *Bonnie and Clyde* (1967), *Blazing Saddles* (1974), *The Wild Bunch* (1969) and *M*A*S*H* (1970), as examples of postmodernism, "through their frequent allusion to the narrative conventions of American film." [464] He says that *Polanski's* [my italics] methodology is to "set the elements of a conventional popular genre in an altered context, thereby making us perceive these traditional forms and images in a new way." [465] He concludes that

> *Chinatown* uses both humourous burlesque and nostalgic evocation as a basis for its devastating exploration of the genre of the hard-boiled detective and his myth. [466]

The Screenplay

Howard and Mabley, and Linda Cowgill, in their discussions of *Chinatown*'s structure, state that the screenplay uses the full panoply of story elements at its disposal: metaphor (*Chinatown* itself); planting and payoff, again, chiefly *Chinatown* itself, but also the loaded phrases "bad for glass" and "apple core," both repeated motif-style; unity of action (the pursuit of knowledge); dialogue (Gittes is the wise guy; ironically, Evelyn has a stutter, betraying her past; Noah bulldozes people); point of view (almost entirely from Gittes' perspective); exposition (masked, as Jake thinks he's making progress in his detection, through the drought, the farmers, politics and the past); characterisation; cause and effect relationships (the story starts from Scene 2 and all subsequent scenes are action/reaction); and finally rising conflict (orchestrating the actions between the protagonist, Gittes, and his true antagonist, Noah Cross). [467] All of these elements are in the First Draft, albeit in somewhat different form.

Dancyger and Rush sum up their writing on the film noir genre by stating that it "symbolizes our nightmares." [468] They provide a list of the genre's characteristics which now provides a useful grid against which to measure *Chinatown*'s being considered as film noir.

---

[463] Michael Ryan and Douglas Kellner. *CAMERA POLITICA The Politics and Ideology of Contemporary Hollywood Film.* Bloomington and Indianapolis, Indiana University Press, 1988: 83. Furthermore, Garrett Stewart identifies the film by linking it with *The Long Goodbye*: "one can feel *The Long Goodbye* lurking behind it with the latent force of a foregone conclusion…The full satiric thrust of *Chinatown*, with its evasive and symbolic plot, is clear only if we see it pointing forward in time (and a short step backward in film history) to the metropolitan blight of *The Long Goodbye*, that deep cultural malaise which *Chinatown* serves accurately and eerily to prognosticate. *Chinatown* becomes, and is hardly diminished by being, an exploratory flashback for *The Long Goodbye*, a premise and a prevision. Polanski's film emerges as what we might term an 'antecedent sequel,' and this is a paradox worth braving in order to get closer to the heart of Polanski's black parable, and of Altman's before him." Stewart, as before: 25-6.

[464] John G. Cawelti, '*Chinatown* and Generic Transformation in Recent American Films,' in *FILM THEORY AND CRITICISM: Introductory Readings* (4th ed.) edited by Gerald Mast, Marshall Cohen and Leo Braudy. Oxford and New York: Oxford University Press, 1992, 504. We might also call this the demythologising project of the era's more serious filmmakers. And perhaps Cawelti is indulging in some revisionist historicising of his own in terms of his interpretation.
[465] *Ibid.*
[466] Cawelti, 1992, 510.
[467] Howard & Mabley. *Op.cit.,*, 177-188; 77-94; Linda Cowgill. 1999, 87-94, etc.
[468] Dancyger and Rush. *Op.cit.,* 49.

Chinatown is classically unified by its dramatic action – Jake Gittes is in pursuit of a solution to the mystery posed by the fake Mrs Mulwray and the water scandal. In the style of the Poe story, 'The Purloined Letter,' the evidence is right under his nose but he doesn't see it. [469]   On page 51 Jake asks Escobar how come he's so keen to make Mulwray's death look like an accident: he is nosing towards the truth and gets punished.

"The desperate central character lives on the edge; he merely exists… the personal behavior of the central character in the film noir is anything but heroic." [470] Unlike the typical noir hero, Gittes is not 'at the end of the line', a prerequisite for many narrative arcs in traditional noirs. He is however haunted by his past, when something happened in *Chinatown* – "the girl died." He is somewhat inept at his job, which has no honour, marginal or otherwise; his attempts at humour border on the grotesque; and he is surprisingly dim-witted for a man who makes his living as a 'snoop.'   Towne himself claims,

> The characters I write about are men who control events far, far less than events control them. My characters get caught, they try even though they don't prevail or even significantly influence events. These guys muddle through. [471]

In Jake, Nicholson seemed to have found his ultimate vehicle, according to biographer Patrick McGilligan:

> Jack seemed at the pinnacle of his craft, playing Jake Gittes, for all the nose bandages and clever wardrobe, from the inside out, a swaggering fool for love. He would never seem as weary nor as poignantly betrayed. Nicholson took his place alongside Bogart and the other immortal screen detectives. [472]

Chinatown breaks the primary rule for Chandler's Marlowe by having Gittes take on matrimonial work which gives him a very good living – even his barber says he's "like a movie star." Towne said in interview at the Edinburgh Film Festival, "As much as I admire Philip Marlowe and loved Chandler's evocation of the city, successful private detectives were not tarnished knights who refused to take divorce work and dressed

---

[469] Acknowledged as an influence by Towne speaking at the AFI in 1994. Accessed online www.afi.com. Of course Dupin *does* see the letter.

[470] *Ibid.*

[471] Speaking with Kenneth Turan, 'Robert Towne's Hollywood Without Heroes,' *New York Times*, 27 November 1988.

[472] McGilligan, 1995, 266. Nicholson turned down all subsequent acting roles which would require him to play detective to ensure his legendary turn – excepting of course, *The Two Jakes*. Danny Leigh comments: "Of course you could always connect the dots between the dark revelations of Robert Towne's script and the murk of Nicholson's own background (specifically, the discovery that his elder sister was actually his mother). Such literal-mindedness would, however, unfairly diminish the power of the character Nicholson created: studiedly cynical but profoundly disappointable, whip-smart but not quite sharp enough to get out of the way of the Mulwrays and their toxic secrets. The film may have afforded him the chance to use both his charm and his temper, yet its most indelible memory of him remains his final scene, mute and impotent, undone. In the rush to garland director Roman Polanski and writer Towne for *Chinatown*'s deathless appeal, the contribution of its star should not be neglected." Danny Leigh, 'Don't Fence Me In,' *Sight & Sound*, Vol.13, No.5, May 2003: 14.

shabbily. They were peepers, hired to catch people *in flagrante delicto*, and have photographs taken and do all the correspondence [sic] stuff that is made fun of in divorce cases. There were several models for Gittes in the past of whom I knew, so I made my detective a dapper guy who would basically take only divorce work." [473]

Chinatown Draft by Draft

What follows is an examination of each of the three drafts extant of the screenplay. They are variously related to both each other and the finished film, so as to extrapolate the core work and linkages, excisions and alterations that came about in the development and pre-production phases.

The First Draft

The first page of the First Draft opens on the LA riverbed in October 1937 with Hollis Mulwray and the Mexican boy:

SUPERIMPOSE <u>L.A. RIVER OCTOBER 1937</u>

It's virtually empty. Sun blazes off its ugly concrete banks. A man sits in a dark sedan on the flood control road fifteen feet above the bottom of the river and sweats. He's fiddling with a feathered jig and wire leader as he stares down at the dry riverbed.

HOLLIS MULWRAY

Stands in the centre of the riverbed, powerlines and sun overhead, the trickle of brackish water among the weeds at his feet. He seems intent on something.

Suddenly there is a squishy sound. Mulwray turns downstream and sees a Mexican boy riding a swayback horse into the river at a point where it fans out and the concrete ends in clay banks.

The sound of the horse's hooves pop like champagne corks as the animal moves along the riverbed through the mud.

The visual and auditory details, the insinuation in the opening juxtaposition – a dry riverbed – these are Towne trademarks. It is important later on in this draft to note such items as the fact that Towne indicated that Gittes' POV be used for the spying scene at the El Mirador Apartments – a photographic statement usually attributed to Polanski:

As the angle widens it is possible to see one veranda below an empty chaise lounge with Gittes' hat, shirt, sunglasses, and camera case lying scattered about.

WITH GITTES' POV [474]

---

[473] 'Robert Towne: On Writing,' in Boorman and Donohue, eds. *Op.cit*, 111.
[474] It's important to notice that this again is Jake's point of view, a situation Polanski would

Has climbed so that he's nearly even with the Mulwray veranda. He stares through a grillwork and a puff of bright bougainvillea for a limited view of Mulwray.

(Chinatown 1st draft: 17)

On page 18 Jake mentions "the Biscuit at Santa Anita," Towne's emblematic representation of Gittes' empathy for 'the little fellow with the big heart.' This would later be minimised as a motif at Polanski's behest, thereby diminishing an aspect of Gittes' complex characterisation.

The Chinaman joke is in this draft, another instance of Towne's insistence on the contemporary vernacular as well as foreshadowing the dénouement. [475]

For Dancyger and Rush, typically in film noir, "'the by-product of this [central, sexual] relationship is violence." [476] The real Evelyn Mulwray is introduced on page 21, spinning the action into Act II when obstacles multiply in an arc of rising conflict caused by Jake's involvement with Evelyn and by extension her father's wrongdoings. Linda Cowgill observes that the film is built on a classical series of action and reaction, cause-and-effect relationships; rising conflict is bound into these relationships beginning with the publication of the photographs of Hollis and the girl, which prompts the real Evelyn Mulwray to take action and confront Gittes – this sets in motion a series of attacks leading Gittes to Hollis Mulwray and then his true antagonist, Cross.[477]

Jake's sensory deprivation is key to his character arc in a series of incidents which lead him by his nose: page 59 sees him at Hollenbeck Ridge; at 62 he's in the flood channel and on 63 he meets the infamous Small Man who calls him a "nosey fellow" and "kitty cat" and he has his nostril slit. Pages 65-6 have Escobar lure Jake to 555 ½ Cerritos Apartments where Ida Sessions (the gloriously fake Evelyn) is found dead, with Jake's phone number on her wall, incriminating him. Escobar asks Jake about his nose and says, 'See you kitty cat,' in a conscious echo of the Small Man (Haze). Duffy, Walsh and Jake wonder what it can all be about - Jake concludes "it's gotta be more than a dam." [478]

---

supposedly insist upon being the main narrative focus throughout the shooting draft.

[475] Towne says of the off-colour joke which Jake inadvertently repeats in front of the real Evelyn Mulwray: "I would probably have been roasted today for the 'Chinaman' joke, but aside from its intrinsic entertainment value and because I like racist jokes, it was emblematic of the time: a kind of naked racism that was rampant in the thirties that was not disguised. It's like the attitude to women, which was, 'Sophie, go to the ladies' room, you can't hear this.' Those are attitudes that did exist and I think it's important in doing any period piece really to try not to revisit that time and kind of clean it up and make it as it is now with our allegedly enlightened attitudes. The other side of it was that people were not nearly so much victims; they could call someone a name and they wouldn't sue you for it. They would either punch you out or do something else. So, it sets up the time, and it also sets up the crudeness of the man. It's an attempt really to suggest what this pimp in his suit is like when he is involved with a woman of some substance and elegance." Towne in Boorman and Donahue, eds. Op.cit., 115.

[476] Dancyger and Rush, 49.

[477] Cowgill. Op.cit.,88-91.

[478] The irony is that it really isn't about more than a dam – but the dam is a figure for mass corruption at a civic level, a topic that remains somewhat under-explored in all three drafts and becomes even less comprehensible under Polanski's influence when he excises most of the heavies.

At the beach, Paradise Cove, Evelyn tells Jake that she's been having an affair with a married man, wanted by police. On 85 they both hear the water outfall from the palisades. All of this contributes to what Dancyger and Rush describe as the palpable "sense of aloneness in the central character." [479]

Act III begins with Jake almost bumping into an ice truck (p.153) in another example of Towne's use of visual juxtaposition and thematic insinuation (literally an example of on the nose writing). He meets Byron Samples on Sunset Beach by a sign for fish marked 'Bait.' Samples is reading the Times' obituaries. On page 156 'Kitty Cat' Haze turns up, "fishing for change." At the police station Jake makes a citizen's arrest on him.

Dialogue

The dialogue also expresses some unusual aspects of characterisation. As the film's parentage can be located both in the classic detective noir of *Falcon*, directed by Huston and starring Ida Sessions' inspiration and the baddest femme fatale of them all, Mary Astor as Brigid O'Shaughnessy; and *The Big Sleep* (1946), a film whose convoluted plot so confused its own author, Raymond Chandler, that even he didn't know who had committed one of the murders by the time the film was through. There are clear similarities between the latter and *Chinatown*, with the stifling greenhouse of *Sleep* played in opposition to the Oriental gardens of *Chinatown*; the smouldering rich girl tempted to the bad played by Lauren Bacall posing in ironic counterpoint to the mask-like presence of the tragic Evelyn Mulwray; the wheelchair-bound Sternwood vis-à-vis the omnipotence of Noah Cross; the 'little sister';

Figure 9 Jake on the prowl with Evelyn Mulwray (Faye Dunaway)

and the restaurant scene, replayed almost shot for shot in *Chinatown* with Sam Spade ultimately a more knowing and cosmopolitan hero than the impotent, weak J.J. Gittes, when he uproots Lauren Bacall's confidence even after a conversation rife with doubles entendres. [480]

Dancyger and Rush's second point is that "the central character thinks that his chance at a better, richer more vital life can only be found in another character – usually a woman."

However Evelyn Mulwray does not conform to the classic femme fatale, betrayed by a stammer to indicate her underlying insecurity. On page 50 Escobar tells Jake that a

---

[479] Dancyger and Rush. *Op.cit.*, 49. This interpretation could be based on the idea that neither Jake nor Evelyn speaks truly even in an intimate situation.
[480] Which she initiates, enquiring as to whether he likes to ride out in front or from behind.

friend of his cousin "had a little something to do with her. In fact, I think he knocked her up." (Evelyn admits p. 146 that she was pregnant when she married Luis aka Lou Escobar himself - not a friend of Escobar's cousin or the cousin as it would be claimed Jake – along with Yelburton at Water and Power, initially when Jake's visits the Department of Water and Power (pp.28-29). "In addition," say Howard and Mabley, "he has Mulvihill and the little man (played by the director) opposing him on the one side and Escobar and the police hemming him in on the other. And he has to solve the mystery of who the girl is and what she has to do with the rest of it. Behind all that, there is a full history between Cross and Mulwray to fathom, along with a burgeoning plan for the northwest valley that is actively being kept secret." [481]

Dancyger and Rush argue that "the relationship between the central character and his savior is a highly charged, sexual relationship." [482] In *Chinatown*, Jake's act as a successful private eye is worn down – first, with his broken nose (he is led around by his nose by people lying to him); second, with his attempt to be a saviour himself in his attempt to rectify the damage visited upon Evelyn (although we learn that it is he who is in need of being saved himself because of a past mistake.) On page 79 Jake tells Evelyn that Hollis was murdered. Then he tells Evelyn what he knows and embroils her in the job, film noir fashion. He concludes, "It's why I think he was killed" (p.80).

As Robert McKee points out, Evelyn is a fully rounded character, "a poignant, tragic figure herself." [483] She is explicitly described as having Oriental-type features which immediately links her with 'otherness' and Jake's repressed past, in *Chinatown*: Orientalism and Jake's past immediately connotes a sense of adventure which is otherwise lacking in Jake's character; it also links Evelyn with Hollywood's cycle of Orientalist fantasies produced between the wars and with their implications of transgression and miscegenation, mystery, fear and desire. The Orient is the root of all evil in film noir: a trope that Towne consistently invokes in his evocation of Gittes' world. The Los Angeles of *Chinatown* is an alien space, populated by Japanese gardeners, Chinese housemen, Mexican police, and a Spanish-speaking girlfriend whose plaintive emotions are hidden by an Oriental mask – a profile in the 'boosterism' to which Barney Hoskyns alludes and a symbol for the class barriers that wealth would not eradicate. (And of course, there is *Chinatown* itself, a rich metaphor for venality and a mythical place made real by the gaudy neon heralding its streets at the film's close.) [484]

---

[481] Howard and Mabley. *Op.cit.*, 179-180.

[482] Dancyger and Rush, *ibid.*

[483] McKee, as before.

[484] See Barney Hoskyns, WAITING FOR THE SUN: *Strange Days Weird Scenes and the Sound of Los Angeles*. London: Penguin, 1997. David Thomson, in his playful book of parodic backstories for film characters, *SUSPECTS*, presents J.J. Gittes as the progeny of a nineteen year old Eurasian in a San Francisco whorehouse, lending the character we know from *Chinatown* even more poignancy as he attempts to protect a brothel keeper, Iris Ling, but resigns from the LAPD in disgust when she is abused in a dispute with a Tong gang. He mixes legend with fact when, awaiting the anticipated biography by Gore Vidal, his notes on Noah Cross include the known-facts about John Huston, that he retires to Galway, Ireland, "where he bred, rode and talked to horses." He also, poetically, states that "Katherine Mulwray killed herself when she was eighteen: she was found drowned in the Hollywood Reservoir." *SUSPECTS* by David Thomson. London: Picador, 1985, 1-6. Of course this doesn't fit in with the later story of *The Two Jakes*, in which she assumes a different life as the wife of Jake Berman. Towne's penchant for the vernacular (another example of his insistence upon authenticity) had already been much in evidence in *The Last Detail* and would be repeated in *Personal Best* and elsewhere.

Cohen says that crisply delineated alternatives of womanhood present in traditional noir are "treachery-immorality, fidelity-purity." He says the women come in three basic types: "the girl next door, the deceptive seductress, and the beautiful neurotic." They reflect the fear that homecoming GIs had in terms of not just domestic relations but also of the workplace. "What these films, and others like them, are about is the hidden, dangerous nature of woman beneath her beguiling façade." [485] Ida Sessions, the fake Evelyn, fulfils the femme fatale profile and comes to a grisly end. Evelyn, who departs significantly from the stereotype, has a different ending in this draft to the one in the shooting draft.

In contrast to the smartass repartee of Jake, Julian Cross, Evelyn's father, uses language to overpower people. Evelyn reveals on page 92 that Hollis owned the water supply, while on page 94 she then reveals that Noah was Hollis' partner. On page 94 they take the seaplane from San Pedro to the Albacore Club, where, on the same page, Julian Cross' first word is "horseshit." The scene between the three is lengthy, running from pages 95 through 103. Cross says of Escobar,

```
Sure, he's got to swim in the
same water we all do.
```

The metaphor, subtext and imagery are inbuilt in character, dialogue and setting.

Location & Visuals

In *Chinatown* the formal dimension is lent rigour by the juxtaposition of desert and water; in the film Hollis Mulwray is framed as a frequently distant figure in the landscape, Gittes is shot in close-up, while Cross is usually in lush, expensive surroundings: the image system is clearly delineated in all drafts of the screenplay. Thomas Schatz describes the Los Angeles depicted in the screenplay as "the metaphoric center of urban duplicity and corruption." [486] Not only that, the city serves as metaphor for an America in crisis.

Dancyger and Rush also stipulate that "the key root of the problem with the relationship is the city, the stand-in symbol for modern life." [487] As we shall see, Los Angeles is not only the location, it serves as the theme. In the first draft (and the second) modernity is visualised as a threat – the modern dirty sprawl is in fact the final image. The authors continue that "the city saps the generosity out of the relationship. All that is left is deception and betrayal." [488] The fact that the relationship at the narrative's core is bound up with both characters and place in a double spiral of lies is part of its ingenuity and craft.

Theme

Towne's great gift is not only excellent visuals but precise, everyday dialogue. A three- page scene (52-55) introduces a concept familiar from the finished film – the possibility of drowning in a dry river bed: Jake talks to Morty the mortician about the local drunk found in an empty L.A. River storm drain – this is carried through to the second draft and the shooting (third) draft: the theme is encapsulated in the line

---

[485] *Ibid.*
[486] Schatz, 1981, 149.
[487] Dancyger and Rush. *Op.cit.*, 49.
[488] *Ibid.*

```
                        MORTY
        Yeah?  Ain't that something?
        Middle of a drought, the water
        commissioner drowns -- only in L.A.
```

(*Chinatown*, 1st draft : 43)

This seems to sum up the film's theme early on, it remains in the shooting draft (p.45) and the film and is planted to signpost the line that really encapsulates the story: pages 56-59 are mainly concerned with office banter but with the inclusion of a crucial line stating the theme after Jake admits he lied:

```
                        WALSH
                     (lightly)
        It's Chinatown.
```

Howard and Mabley, in their analysis of the film's structure say, "Stated most simply, the theme of *Chinatown* is '*Chinatown*' – that is, the state of mind of thinking you know what's going on while you really don't." To that extent, the film's theme is also its metaphor. [489] Michael Eaton says that *Chinatown* is more than this – "it is the ultimate organising principle of the story." [490] '*Chinatown*' crops up again in a heavy underscoring of the theme when Evelyn tells Jake she doesn't want him to go to the police (p.86). It occurs again when Jake refers to the Tong Wars (p.89) On p. 147 Jake tells Evelyn about the little slave girl...

```
                        GITTES
        .. well, baby, as far as I'm con-
        cerned, this year you're Chinatown.
```

Tone

The prevailing character of the screenplay is evident in dialogue, setting and overwhelming dramatic irony. The lengthy meetings between Jake and Evelyn conform to detective fiction but not necessarily to the film genre. These would be excised from the Third Draft.

The love scene as filmed between Gittes and Evelyn is played in classical mode and culminates in their sleeping together, something that Towne did not entirely want:

> I thought it was important to continue the mystery of the woman as he was getting more and more fascinated with her and was falling in love. [491]

Towne's overt belief in the mystery of women would be expressed in other work, as we shall see.

---

[489] Howard and Mabley. 1993, 181.

[490] Eaton. 2000, 40.

[491] He continues: "Roman [Polanski] just didn't like it that way. I think perhaps, he preferred identifying with the character when the woman praised him for making love well. I don't know – I'm only conjecturing." Towne, 'Dialogue on Film,' as before, 47.

Dancyger and Rush point out that there are usually no children in film noir. In *Chinatown*, the child, Katherine, is an unfortunate, if innocent, product of an unnatural relationship and perversely the one good thing remaining in Noah Cross' depraved life. In the film, the look of unblinking ecstasy on Cross' face, when he realises she is now his forever, is chilling.[492]

Myth/Countermyth: The Classic Detective

Horowitz comments that the script's ambitions

> were as grand as they were apocalyptic. It promised to lay bare the sinister roots of modern capitalistic society by proposing a countermyth to the traditional American story of benevolent founding fathers. Evelyn Mulwray's father, the all-powerful Noah Cross, begat modern Los Angeles by bending man as well as nature to his will…. Cross was the paragon of unrestrained capitalism, monstrous and heroic, destructive and creative. No meat was unfit for his insatiable appetite. He was the secret id of modernity, the Oedipal nightmare turned on its head: Dad kills son and rapes daughter. He was unstoppable." [493]

Towne himself admits

> I think all detective movies are a retelling of Oedipus. I mean those kinds of detective movies where the detective in looking for the solution to the crime finds he's part of the crime, he's part of the problem.[494]

Cawelti places *Chinatown* in a mode of generic transformation which appropriates the 'aura' of the traditional hard-boiled film but subverts its thematic and narrative elements: he says that "the presence of color, along with increasing deviations from established patterns of plot, motive and character give us an eerie feeling of one myth colliding with and beginning to give way to others." [495] He points out that, "the film deviates increasingly from the myth until, by the end of the story, the film arrives at an ending almost contrary to that of the myth. Instead of bringing justice to a corrupt society, the detective's actions leave the basic source of corruption untouched. Instead of protecting the innocent, his investigation leads to the death of one victim and the deeper moral destruction of another. Instead of surmounting the web of conspiracy with honour and integrity intact, the detective is overwhelmed by what has happened to him." [496]

The term burlesque is significant inasmuch as it is a twofold technique, the "breaking of convention by the intrusion of reality and the inversion of expected implications," and intended to comment on conventional genres, a tradition which dates to Aristophanes. [497] In *Chinatown*, a visual trope inextricably linked with noir, calls our attention to the film's parodic potential on the first page of the screenplay:

---

[492] Dancyger and Rush, as before. The ingenious casting of John Huston also plays on what the audience knows about Jack Nicholson's then-relationship with Huston's daughter Anjelica. The on-set joke about Jake/Jack sleeping with his daughter Evelyn/Anjelica has been recounted several times.

[493] Horowitz. *Op.cit*, 52-53.

[494] Robert Towne. *Writing Chinatown,* as before.

[495] Cawelti, 1992, 499.

[496] Cawelti. *Op.cit.*, 501.

[497] Cawelti, 1992, 506.

Figure 10 Evelyn and Jake get closer in the bathroom

```
            GITTES
     All right, enough is enough --
     you can't eat the Venetian
     blinds, Curly.  I just had
     'em installed on Wednesday.
```

(Chinatown 3rd draft: 1)

This is an example of ironic three-act structure embedded in the dialogue as a formative tool… Thus, the dramatic irony which underpins the entire story (the audience is always ahead of Jake) is telegraphed from page one: the *blind* private *eye*.

The other techniques of generic transformation are the cultivation of nostalgia (a conscious act in the screenplay which nonetheless refuses resolution, symbolic or actual, in any draft); and "the use of traditional generic structures as a means of demythologisation." [498]　　The double-edged structure of *Chinatown* utilises one mythological form to comment on others – the genre itself; and the city, which nourished it. We are reminded of what Towne had said to critic Gene Siskel: "I like to write films that are drawn from real life, and yet have a prior cinematic reality … I like to take a myth and make a new myth." [499] Towne's innovativeness therefore lies not merely in his deploying of the conventional elements of classical genre and its mythical dimension - a fundamental aspect of the structural interpretation of films to be found in Jim Kitses' *HORIZONS WEST*, for instance [500]; but it also lies in his simultaneous demythologising of the genre. In other words, he was using the genre to comment on itself. Virginia Wright Wexman acknowledges this in her commentary arguing that *Chinatown*

---

[498] Cawelti, 1992, 507

[499] Gene Siskel, 'Hollywood's Mr Fix-it,' *Sunday News*, Leisure section, 13 June 1976.

[500] Kitses, 1969.

proposes an ironic reinterpretation of the private-eye genre in w
pattern of heroic self-determination played out by Gittes is cont
conscious critique of the formula carried by the film's images, a
hero's control over his world as an illusion. This critique overpc
generic structure at the story's conclusion, instating another, mo:
which the conventional form had previously hidden. [501]

The roots of *Chinatown* have another origin, outside of cin
Towne now utilised his extensive knowledge of Greek drama to exp

> There is no fairer duty than that of helping others in distress.
> -   *Oedipus Rex*, Sophocles

Oedipus Rex is the original detective story, a closed murder mystery that Aristotle called the most perfect example of tragic drama. Longinus wrote, "Would anyone in his senses regard all the compositions of Ion put together as an equivalent for the single play of the *Oedipus*?" The play is probably about one single thing: discovery. Michael Tierno describes it as being "about what happens when you try to escape destiny." [502]

> ... better dead than living and blind.
> - *Oedipus Rex*

Barthes defines the function of myth as the translation of history into nature:

> What the world supplies to myth is an historical reality, defined, even if this goes back quite a while, by the way in which men have produced or used it; and what myth gives in return is a *natural* image of this reality.

If that is the case, then one might surmise that Towne turns history *and* nature into myth using the structure of the bourgeois narrative.[503]

Towne himself has stated:

> Detective movies have certain things in common with dreams and with Oedipus Rex. ... As far as Oedipus goes, Oedipus determines to find the killer of the king and he has the killer in front of his eyes – basically himself – from the very beginning, though he doesn't see it. Similarly, most detective movies that are satisfying, generally speaking, have the villain appearing almost from the beginning, and only the detective doesn't see it. He is blind to what is right in front of his face. ... In a classic detective movie, generally speaking, the hero, like Oedipus, shares to some extent the responsibility for the crime, by either a failure to see it or hubris of some kind that he can solve a problem. In attempting to solve it he becomes part of the problem, and this is the case in *Chinatown*. [504]

---

[501]   *ROMAN POLANSKI*, Boston: Twayne Publishers, 1985, 95-96.

[502] Michael Tierno. *Op.cit.,* 55. Kevin Boon says that "what makes OEDIPUS a great tragedy in Aristotle's philosophy is that the line of action renders Oedipus' actions inevitable." Kevin Boon, 'Poetics and the Screenplay: Revisiting Aristotle,' *Creative Screenwriting*, Vol.8, No.3, 2001: 71.

[503] See 'Myth Today,' in Roland Barthes, *MYTHOLOGIES*. London: Granada, 1983, 142.
[504]   Towne in Boorman and Donahue, eds. *Op.cit.,* 113-114.

s the flaw in his character – fatal arrogance, hubris, if you want to call it
at way, the kind of hubris that allowed Oedipus to believe he could avoid his fate.
He was blind even though he could see. Gittes' particular arrogance is a failure to
see that the killer was right in front of his eyes from the very beginning. [505]

Towne's deployment of this is key to the structure of the screenplay, as a number
of critics have observed. [506]   John McGowan's commentary quotes Barthes, who
counsels that power is mythically obscured in our culture:

> … the movies themselves also retain a dim awareness that the mysteries of sexuality
> and of power keep avoiding their gaze, which promotes the recurrent paranoia
> evidenced in films such as *Chinatown* and *Body Heat.*. Surely someone or something must
> be withholding this knowledge that the art form keeps searching out
> so ardently. *Chinatown* and *Body Heat*, unable to examine how power is created through
> social processes or by the resources of film as an art form, fall back on differences in
> personality to explain differences in power… Oedipus at the movies sees that power
> rules over him, sees his own weakness, but remains blind to the ways in which power is
> created by men in specific instances to serve specific purposes. [507]

There are, then, certain broad structural, thematic and objective similarities
between the great mythical drama, *Oedipus Rex* and *Chinatown*:

---

[505] *Ibid.* Tom Stempel explains Towne's writing strategy in these terms: "Towne keeps the show
going by a very simple mechanism: Whenever things threaten to slow down, Gittes tells Mrs.
Mulwray she has been lying to him, and she replies that *now* she is going to tell him the truth.
Count the number of times she does this in the film. This is part of Towne's skill in telling you
only as little as he can get away with at any given point in the film. You do not need a lot of
exposition, and most of what Towne gives you in the first half of the movie is not true anyway."
SCREENWRITING. San Diego: Tantivy Press, 1982, 140-141. Gittes' recognition is of the
fourth type identified by Aristotle (invented by the will of the writer) – she just tells him what's
really been going on. Kevin Boon, *op.cit.:* 75

[506]   Charles Altman suggests that plot follows the Oedipal configuration in his 'Psychoanalysis
and Cinema: The Imaginary Discourse.' See Bill Nichols, ed., *MOVIES AND METHODS*,
Volume II. Berkeley: University of California Press, 1985,519; John McGowan aligns *Chinatown*
with the later noir *Body Heat* (1981) and says of the screenplays' trajectory that "Both films move
toward the revelation of one all-powerful master criminal as controlling the world in which the
hero lives. And in both films the criminal's power is so complete that he or she literally gets
away with murder." John McGowan, "Oedipus at the Movies,' *Southern Humanities Review*, 1986,
No. 20: 8-9. See also Deborah Linderman, 'Oedipus in *Chinatown*,' *Enclitic*, 1981-198, No. 5: 190-
203; and Wayne D. McGinnis, '*Chinatown*: Roman Polanski's Contemporary Oedipus Story,' in
Literature/ Film Quarterly Vol.3, No.3, 1975: 249-251. Both Sigmund Freud and Claude Lévi-
Strauss analyse *Oedipus Rex*, with the latter looking at different versions of the myth than Freud,
who confines himself to Sophocles' version. Freud describes it as a 'a tragedy of sex'; theorist
Paul Ricoeur calls it 'a tragedy of truth.' John Belton traces the links between Oedipus and
detective fiction and states, "Sophocles construes the epistemological dilemma which
characterizes the genre's interplay between the rational desire to know and the irrational
repression of knowledge as an internal one, situating it within his detective hero who is also the
criminal he seeks, whereas Poe and other, modern practitioners of the genre externalise it, pitting
the rational detective figure against an irrational counterpart." ('Language, Oedipus and
Chinatown,' *MLN*, 1991 No. 106, Vol. 5: 936.)
[507] John McGowan, *Ibid.*

Both take place against a backdrop of a drought, a waste land plagued by its own ruler. Both protagonists think they are working for the good of the public. Both protagonists exhibit a fatal flaw – hubris, believing that they can change fate. Both protagonists believe that the crime committed was because of greed or power but discover that it was due to utterly irrational evil. Both stories are about incest: Oedipus with his mother, Evelyn is raped by her father. Both stories involve the murder of a father figure.

Both are ultimately stories of discovery: Oedipus realises he has unwittingly) committed incest, while Gittes discovers that Evelyn has committed incest with her father, and that her father is the rapist of the Owens Valley, along with his murdered former partner, Hollis Mulwray. Both protagonists become unwitting victims despite every effort to avoid their fate: while Oedipus gouges out his own eye in light of his discovery, Gittes is forced to watch the police shooting through Evelyn's (damaged) iris. Both dramas are told with a great degree of irony – centered on the dissonance between what is known to be true and what is discovered to be true. Both focus on blindness and seeing and *Chinatown* has an array of penetrative visual organs and opticals in its text, highlighting the discrepancy between seeing and knowing/understanding and creating an epistemological system of framing devices, echoing Jake's limited range of knowledge. However, as John Belton points out, blindness is displaced onto Evelyn by a policeman.[508] Both stories are about the limits of human knowledge. Both can be understood as allegory, with Oedipus/Gittes the powerless scapegoat for a society in crisis.

Cawelti points out in his analysis of the finished film that "*Polanski's* [my italics] version of Los Angeles in the 1930s reveals the transcendental mythical world of the sterile kingdom, the dying king and the drowned man beneath it – the world, for example of Eliot's 'Wasteland' and before that of the cyclical myths of traditional cultures." [509] Thus, we could say that the through-line connecting *Oedipus Rex*, Eliot's 'The Wasteland' and *Chinatown* is simply that dramatic belief which holds that the health of a land's ruler reflects directly on the security of the *polis*, a key element in all Athenian Greek tragedies.

That Towne self-consciously likens his work on *Chinatown* to not just the tradition of Greek drama, but also that of detective fiction, pulp fiction and classical Hollywood, illustrates his keen awareness of the panoply of influences under which he constructed the screenplay – the combination which ironically gives rise to his own, unique, cinematic voice, binding classical storytelling in a form that is populist cinema and pulp fiction. This lends ballast to Horowitz's claim, but it also challenges his assertion that it is atypical in the canon.

Metaphor & Motif

Fetishes are placed in orderly fashion throughout Towne's work: in *Chinatown* they proliferate according to an examination of the image system based on the subtext of the film: water, power and vision. (They might also derive from a play on the multiple meanings of the words 'private eye' with all the consequent sensory deprivation visited upon Gittes and his lover throughout the film.)

---

[508] Belton, 1991: 940.
[509] Perhaps he really means *Towne's* version. Cawelti, 1992, 503. As Kawin says, "There is something plainly wrong about giving a director credit for the insights and the structural imagination of a writer…" *Op. cit.*, 299.

The city is barely seen however except in a heat haze of blistering sunshine – so many scenes were shot by bodies of water as a result of the changes to drafts one and two of the script that many of the interiors were shot on soundstages while the exteriors were by ponds, reservoirs, dams, the ocean, orange groves and vast gardens backing onto the mansions of the wealthy.

> I read some of the Department of Water and Power's own accounts which rationalised and justified what happened. At one point if I hadn't called the picture *Chinatown* I'd have called it *Water and Power*.
>
>   - Robert Towne [510]

The fetish objects in *Chinatown* provide an image system and poetic based on these principles and they control the narrative – with the principal system perhaps based on the homophone of 'see'/'sea.'

Water vs. drought: the sea, The Department of Water and Power, the dam, the tidepool (pond), saltwater, Noah, Gittes' 'baptism' in the torrent of water at the reservoir. Absent from the final film are the overseas trip by aeroplane to meet Noah Cross and a scene with a water diviner, prior to meeting the farmers. The potency of water is linked to sexual profligacy, abundance and containment ("he oughta be able to hold your water for you"). The film is, after all, concerned with the revelation of a villain's sexual power, a magical essence beyond mere social organisation or approbation as the conclusion declares the immunity of Julian/Noah Cross. In terms of vision, Towne deploys tropes of blindness, seeing falsely, spying, voyeurism, *Mar Vista*... The visual tropes used throughout the film and some of the drafts reflect on this system – Jake's precious Venetian blinds, mirrors, windows, broken spectacles, binoculars, bifocal lenses (split vision), cameras, rearview mirrors, Curly's wife's blackened eye, Evelyn's flawed iris, busted tail-light and so on. The framing devices separate the 'private eye' from the spectator's eye.

Power is explicit as metaphor and motif: Cross OWNS the Dept. of Water and Power – in this film water IS power. Fish are used as symbol: : albacore, Jasper Lamar Crabbe, Byron Samples with his bait; fish hooks...and Cross is repeatedly associated with fish. Horses: love of racehorses connects Jake with Cross in the first draft, where Cross announces of one of his stable, "Bred her myself," (p. 73), a Freudian slip which of course connects to the incest subplot.

The Old Testament is referred to by bodies of water, floods, drought, the Ark, the desert, and the names - *Evelyn, Noah,* not in the screenplay but changed for the film[511]:

---

[510] Robert Towne speaking on BBC TV's *Writing Chinatown*. In fact a film called *Water and Power* was made by Pat O'Neill in 1989 and its subject is also that of Los Angeles' origins. See Scott MacDonald. 'The City as Motion Picture: Notes on Some California City Films,' *Wide Angle*, Vol. 19, No. 4, October 1997: 121-128.

[511] The cruciform imagery that proliferates throughout the film is evidently attributable to the coining of the principal powerholder in the film – the ironically (and classically emblematically) monikered, Noah Cross. 'Noah', as symbolically potent as it appears, was actually chosen to replace 'Julian Cross', Towne's original and preferred name, which couldn't be used because somebody by that name really existed. (Towne said that if he ever wrote it as a novel he would return to his original choice of name. That name is still on the final draft of the shooting script which was used for production.) Brady. *Op.cit.,* 417. Yet the name 'Noah' could not be more appropriate for a film whose narrative thrust and thematic sensibility is driven by water and power and, ultimately, pointless sacrifice. It is nothing if not an interdiction – to water, power,

The fact that Evelyn (or 'Eve', the first woman) is the mother of a child produced by incest also indicates the story is a take on fabled beginnings. Like his hero Jean Renoir, Towne constructs his screenplays so that his characters are defined by moral relationships. [512]

Sensory damage reflects as juxtaposition against the shiny Art Deco surfaces - to Gittes' nose, Evelyn's eye – first it's flawed, then she is shot through it. Colour in the film is expressed in a limited palette, beige to dusty sand to brown, until the finale, shot on the neon-lit streets of Los Angeles. Flowers – associated with 'otherness' are also quoted. Fruit is clearly a statement of plenty. And everybody except Jake seems to smoke – which is reflected in the final image of the first and second drafts – the polluted modern city.

Robert McKee would hold that another level of poetic system holds true and this is 'political corruption as social cement' but strictly speaking this is of course not visual. In *Chinatown*, however, the poetic and the visual are inextricably intertwined. [513] This is the brilliance of Towne's interweaving of theme in relation to classical dramatic structure, which is why the last line of the film (if not Towne's) is so appropriate – "Forget it, Jake. It's *Chinatown*." [514]

Dancyger and Rush's rule, that "sexuality and violence coexist, and seem to be cause-and-effect" is echoed in what Towne would describe as his major writing problem: deciding which aspect of the *Chinatown* story to prioritise:

> The struggle in my mind initially was quite a technical one – which story do
> you tell first, or which strand of story do you want to start pulling off the ball first?
> The water and power scandal or the incest? And maybe it's because America's a
> puritanical country I felt the way to drive home the outrage about the water and the
> power was to sort of cap it with the incest and to sort of put the nail in the coffin, the
> man who is raping the land is incidentally doing the same thing with his child. And I
> felt that would be a better way of actually making the point, the monstrosity of it
> because it's that violation, exponentially, that would be visited on the future indefinitely
> and in fact it has been.[515]

---

knowledge. John Huston had earlier played Noah in *The Bible* (1966), which he directed.

[512] "Towne prefers ambiguous, morally compromised characters because they're real." Horowitz, 1990: 54. As Garrett Stewart reminds us, Noah is a figure of America's 'monstrous paternalism.' "This modern psychopath and water-prophet, who once owned the city's water supply, is now proprietor of the Albacore Club and eats whole fish for lunch, drowns his upright son-in-law in a miniature backyard tidepool… and, in a demonic parody of the original Noah's role in repopulating the earth after the Flood, has even begotten on his daughter a second anemic daughter." Stewart, as before: 31. Cross, moreover, could be likened to Freud's notion of the primal father, as Cawelti notes: "but against his overpowering sexual, political and economic power, our hero-Oedipus in the form of J.J. Gittes proves to be tragically impotent, an impotence symbolized earlier in the film by the slashing of his nose and the large comic bandage he wears throughout much of the action." John G. Cawelti. *Op.cit.*, 503.

[513] McKee, as before.
[514] "In a great film, theme declares itself in the climax. It is the sum of all the dramatic elements, of characterization, mood, action and, most importantly, transformation, which come together in the shape and end result of a particular climactic movement." Linda Cowgill. *Op.cit.*, 68.
[515] Dancyger and Rush, as before. Towne on 'Writing *Chinatown*,' a/b. In the Preface and Postscript section to the published screenplay, Towne writes: "There are probably as many kinds

Towne had already his major antagonist in the story – and Cross is the figure (actually and representationally) of sexuality and violence, conjoining Dancyger and Rush's eighth element in their characteristics of noir as generic form.

On page 39 Jake asks Evelyn if she knew that Hollis withdrew $30,000 cash "the day after the news broke in the papers." Jake explains that his matrimonial work is his "meetiay" and says he doesn't think Escobar is being rewarded. Evelyn denies knowing anything about the water scheme. Cross tells Jake how Hollis Mulwray "made this city" (p.102) On page 104 Evelyn and Jake stop at a roadside stand at Sunland and two pages later a guy shoots at Jake and the farmers catch him, thinking he's with the Water Department. [516] Jake says he's checking out the irrigation policy – which is met with an Older Farmer's response that they've "been sending out men to blow up my water tanks." Jake just wants to meet Haze.

At the Hall of Records (page 110) Jake looks for the plat books on the North West Valley. [517] A "coatless man" whose screeching tires herald his arrival turns out to be Byron Samples. In the lot Jake spots fish hooks hanging from Samples' sun visor. Jake visits Ida Sessions' old apartment building, claiming to be her bereaved brother. He matches a feather to one in his hat brim. The "kitty cat" man is back – with Byron Samples. A scuffle ensues. Jake helps Samples with his injury and gets him ice.

Jake gives Evelyn the list of names; her 'friend' hasn't left town yet. Up on the Alta Vista Road, Jake looks out at the Valley – his list covers 47,000 acres – except they're mortgage trustees with no accompanying information. He leaves Evelyn at Marmion Way Apartments but she's staying at the Montecito apartments under the pseudonym 'Miriam Wells'. Jake asks her if she heard who won the seventh at Santa Anita [continuing Towne's beloved association with Seabiscuit] and he complains about the weight the horse had to carry (p.127).

---

of crimes as there are hatreds and fears in the human heart. Whatever the crime in *Chinatown*, greed wasn't represented by money – land and water respectively did that. But I suppose the central crime of *Chinatown* – the wanton destruction of the past – wasn't a crime at all. Its perpetrators were far more likely to have Junior Highs or streets named after them than they were likely to go to jail. The truly murderous act in the movie was laying waste to land and to fragile communities as tho they were an incidental part of Noah Cross' grand vision – a vision about as grand and expansive as cancer. It was a rape worse than Cross could visit on his own daughter – hurting the land he inevitably hurt all children, affected where they'd live and what they'd see and even what they'd breathe. When a crime can no longer contain or content itself with the past and insists on visiting the future it's no longer a crime – it becomes a sin, and very difficult to punish.
"The murdered Mulwray, who Cross had so outraged by making him a partner to his blasphemy was posthumously honoured for the very thing he loathed and for which he was murdered – like other public sins of far greater scope humanity is sometimes at a loss unable to punish, they are reduced to rewards." *CHINATOWN*, Santa Barbara, California: Neville, 1982.

[516] This is a conscious echo of the scene in *Bonnie and Clyde*.
[517] As Towne remarked at the AFI, "trying to tell a story out of things that would normally seem boring – going to the Hall of Records and looking up in a plat book – these are things that are not normally put in movies. But if you put them in a movie and scrupulously follow them out, you will find that they have drama because the important thing about drama is not its size but its action." Speaking at the Harold Lloyd Master Seminar, 1994. Accessed online at www.afi.com.

Page 128-9 are in Jake's bathroom, with the steam rising. Cross pays him a visit. He has bruises from a spinal injury when he was shot 15 years previously. Escobar's cousin Ayala supposedly has a hold on Evelyn. Evelyn arrives but leaves abruptly the moment she sees her father. Cross gets an injection from his doctor. (p. 137) Jake drives to the Mulwray house where he is told that the pond is saltwater and sees what was a starfish: "Jesus is he a mess." He recounts Cross' conversation with him:

EVELYN

.. oh.. what I really did was
keep me from killing myself.

Cross apparently had a breakdown. Evelyn admits she was pregnant when she married Luis. Jake says he heard about Seabiscuit. It appears that Evelyn is selling up (p.150). She tells Jake that Hollis drowned" 'but it wasn't in the Oak Pass Reservoir... not all that salt water in his lungs, no." Jake looks in the saltwater pond. Evelyn comments that Hollis "didn't move himself." When Jake returns to his office he discovers that Duffy has quit. Walsh tries to tell Jake that he doesn't know what's going on. Gittes agrees:

GITTES

Yeah - I don't want any part of it
so I agreed not to say nothin'
one way or another.

(*Chinatown* 1st draft:161)

Walsh says he was "very condescending." He got $500 for talking to Escobar. Jake asks Walsh what's his cut? It turns out to be $250. Jake takes to the Pacific Coast Highway with Sophie, his secretary. A delayed item in the obituary column showed that Clarence Speer died at the Mar Vista Inn two weeks prior to his purchase of 18,000 acres.

At the Mar Vista Inn Gittes asks, "Do you accept anyone of the Jewish persuasion?" (p.163) [518] On the Inn's bulletin board, Jake sees all the names listed in the Hall of Records plat book and declares, 'Sophie you are looking at the owners of an empire.' (p.164) He locates Emma Tannenbaum [a name later changed to 'Dill'] and Palmer tells him that they are the charity of the Albacore Club. Jake sees Escobar at City Hall and tells him the Albacore Club are behind the murders of Mulwray and Sessions. Escobar affects interest (p.167).

Jake has an address at 29th Street, San Pedro. Evelyn gives him three minutes to see if Ayala is there. It's Curly's house – and his wife has a black eye. Jake runs through the back yard and jumps into his car, which is being driven by his secretary, Sophie (pp.169-171). At Montecito he goes to Bungalow 5 and into a dirt road to Montecito Gardens. He sees Evelyn on a sofa – she looks up as she sees him. The doctor previously caring for Julian at his ranch shows up and tells Jake that Evelyn is under sedation (p. 172). Jake asks Evelyn where is Luis? She says he's been dead for five years.

---

[518] In later drafts, Jake would be accompanied by Evelyn on this trip. It is rumoured that it was this exchange that cost the film the Academy Award for Best Picture.

(p.173) She's been protecting somebody. Jake asks, "who?" In walks 'Miriam Wells,' last seen with Mulwray. She speaks to Evelyn in Spanish. She tells Gittes she's protecting her from her father (Cross). (p. 174)

Evelyn says that 'Miriam' thinks she's Hollis' daughter. Jake asks who killed Hollis. The doctor says, "I killed Mulwray – by accident... they quarrelled down at the house when Evelyn was up here with her daughter." (p. 175) Doc explains that Hollis found out that Julian was behind the water project and struck him and he apparently "drowned." Julian tried to make it look accidental. Ida Sessions was a witness. Hollis found out through his assistant. So, Jake concludes, Evelyn killed her father over Mulwray? Doc says, "No -- not because of that."

EVELYN
I didn't want my father to find her
and I was right – once he found
out from Hollis who the girl was, he
wouldn't stop looking for her. I had
to stop him – he would have told her.

GITTES
Stop him from what?

EVELYN
Finding his daughter.

Gittes stops. He looks at Miriam below him, chattering
happily in Spanish with the maid. Then back at Evelyn,
who stares evenly at him.

GITTES
But I thought – she was your daughter...

EVELYN
.. she is..

(*Chinatown* 1st draft: 177)

This draft concludes along Alta Vista Drive, Jake looking at " ... the tangle of traffic, ugly buildings, foul air and noise." (180)

The Relationship of the First Draft with the Third (Shooting) Draft

In short, while the structure and thematic resonances are similar, it is evident from the final (third, alleged shooting) draft that many of the scenes have been retained in their original version, but ordered in different and perhaps more impactful sequences; and that what has been identified by Syd Field as the first turning point, the introduction of the real Evelyn Mulwray, happens at exactly the same point in the narrative; however her hiring of Gittes is postponed until Act III. [519] The second turning point remains the

---

[519] However, as Rachid Nougmanov reminds us, films must engage the viewer (and scripts the script reader) within the first 10 minutes ('Setup') – therefore the hiring of Jake by the fake

same but the third act is more prolonged due to the involvement of Escobar, who is given the revelatory line that the girl is Cross' daughter. The subplot with Walsh and Duffy betraying Jake would be sacrificed; as would the Byron Samples subplot, lessening the story about Ida Sessions: overall, the number of obstacles faced by Jake is decreased. The climax also changes in future drafts and here Towne is working in full film noir mode with an explanatory voice over. The theme of *Chinatown* is emphatically stated, which it would not be in future drafts.

The Second Draft aka 'The Polanski Rewrite' [520]

According to Lamar Sanders, the rewriting process is an intuitive one, which involves four stages: figuring out the main line of action; figuring out the major image of the story and its sub-images; figuring out what is the story's central thematic concern and how it might connect to the imagery at the story's heart; and knowing when and what to cut and what to substitute for something else. The basic lesson in this process is to cut out anything which is not affected by something else in the script. [521]

The changes to the first draft are then as follows: Gittes is hired to do a job; Gittes tries to clear his name; Gittes wants to find the truth; Gittes wants to save Evelyn. These apparently simple alterations give the film its main line of action and are organic to the plot and each other, coming from certain basic, latent associations in the material. The main image in this draft is water – but popular perception is that this was *apparently* missing from the first draft.

In his own (ghosted) autobiography Polanski recalls the script somewhat misleadingly as:

> ... brimming with ideas, great dialogue, and masterful characterization, it suffered from an excessively convoluted plot that veered off in all directions. Called *Chinatown* despite its total absence of Oriental locations or characters, it simply couldn't have been filmed as it stood, though buried somewhere in its 180-plus pages was a marvellous movie ... Unfortunately the character of Gittes was overwhelmed by the intricate and almost incomprehensible plot. The screenplay required massive cuts, drastic simplification, and the pruning of several subsidiary characters, all of them beautifully drawn but contributing nothing to the action. [522]

Evelyn Mulwray might well be the start point for the action and occurs in what he describes as the first of five acts, in the classical style; and the *second* appearance of the real Evelyn Mulwray (p. 32 in the Third Draft) is therefore the first turning point because it represents a twist in the action. In his terms, this is in fact in Act II, which he labels 'Intrigue,' and occurs from pp.10-30. (The other Acts are: 'Learning,' pp.32-57; 'Trouble,' pp.58-91; and 'Confrontation' pp.91-118.) In Andrew Horton, ed. *SCREENWRITING FOR A GLOBAL MARKET: Selling Your Scripts from Hollywood to Hong Kong.* Berkeley and Los Angeles: University of California Press, 2004, 145-150.   According to Robert Benedetto, "Towne conceded that if his first draft had been filmed as it was, it would have been a mess." He is quoting the *Los Angeles Times* Calendar Weekend, July 8, 1999: 10. Benedetto's article, 'The Two Chinatowns: Towne's Screenplay Vs. Polanski's Film,' appeared in *Creative Screenwriting*, Volume 6, December 1999: 49-54.

[520] Undated, this is the copy held in the Margaret Herrick Library at AMPAS as, allegedly, the first draft, and is identical to that draft known to be the Second Draft in the Louis B. Mayer Library at the American Film Institute in Los Angeles.

[521] This is adapted from a lecture '*Chinatown* – The Rewriting Process,' by Professor Lamar Sanders at the University College Dublin/New York University Scriptwriting Summer School held in Dublin on 19 July 1993; as transcribed by this author.

[522] *ROMAN* by Polanski. London: Pan Books, 1985, 351.

One of the sacrifices to Polanski's decision-making was the removal of the character of Byron Samples – Mulwray's assistant and Ida Sessions' boyfriend: so that subplot was lost and her appearance is as mysterious as her disappearance. Samples had also accompanied Jake to the rest home. The limitation of Lou Escobar's character also shortchanges the backstory; while Cross becomes ever more venal, with the previous explanation of Mulwray's death as an accident symptomatic of his original character as somewhat more deluded, physically frail and guilty.

Polanski discussed his ideas with Towne and left for Rome. Towne's next draft "was almost as long as before and even more difficult to follow. If *Chinatown* were ever to become a movie, it would mean two months of really intensive collaboration, pulling the screenplay apart and putting it together again." [523]

Towne's management of story information should be noted: he conveys difficult but important backstory via newspaper headlines and flyers, allowing Jake to pursue action efficiently.

There is an exchange of plot and extra information which did not survive to the shooting draft.

```
            DUFFY
Then there was something really funny –
her husband it seems, shot her father.
            WALSH
Before or after he married the daughter?
```

(*Chinatown* 2nd draft: 26-27)

This information is credible because Duffy claims that Andy Escobar told him – which subdues Gittes – Escobar used to pick avocadoes for Cross. On page 28 we discover Evelyn is suing Gittes for $600,000 although he says it's a million. Gittes announces to the boys,

```
Evelyn Mulwray's no better than anybody
```

---

[523] Polanski recalls his contribution as follows for Jon Tuska: "Whenever I was trying to do something interesting, I realized that it was a vain effort and I was going against the grain. It looked as though I was trying to jazz up certain things, so I just abandoned that approach and made it a straight suspense story." Jon Tuska, editor, *CLOSE-UP: THE CONTEMPORARY DIRECTOR*. Metuchen, New Jersey & London: The Scarecrow Press, Inc., 1981, 398. Towne commented of his early drafts: "I remember that the second draft was very clumsy, and I was forced to embark on a third draft. One of the things about the first and second drafts is that Gittes is told by Evelyn, when she feels backed up against the wall, that she is seeing somebody else, that she's seeing a married man and that's her reason for not wanting to go to the police. It was a little lame in the third draft, a little vague in the shooting script, but in the earlier drafts it was very clear. Gittes says, 'OK, I'm going to the police unless you tell me what is going on.' And she gives him the most plausible reason to her mind that he would accept, because it involved a certain amount of culpability on her part: She's a married woman, and she's making it with somebody else. Because he thinks that she's being honest with him, and because he's been kind of a sucker, he decides to go along with her. Then he becomes slowly jealous of this mythical character. So when he goes to see who she's seeing – when he follows he her – he thinks he's going to find her lover. Which I felt would have been much more interesting." Towne in Brady. *Op.cit.*, 411.

```
                else in this town.  They're all a bunch of
                whores and phonies, aren't they, boys?
                Aren't they?
```

Duffy and Walsh nod and grunt assent — "Yeah, Jake.
Sure, Jake."

(Chinatown 2nd draft:28)

    Two boys playing at the reservoir notice there are white boils on the surface of
the water. One of them gags when he notices Mulwray's body (pp.34-36) Evelyn
attends the coroner's office where Escobar speaks to her: she says there is no possibility
he would have taken his own life. Gittes deliberately drops a coin when she is asked
about hiring him to spy on her husband: Escobar is angry with Gittes but allows him to
remain (p. 39). Outside, Evelyn thanks Gittes for going along with her. She'll send him
a check —

```
                          EVELYN
            To make it official I hired you.
```

(Chinatown 2nd draft: 41)

    The scene at the coroner's office is much the same as before: keen to cover up
Mulwray's death, Escobar says it's out of respect for his civic position but he doesn't care
because Mulwray did in so many people himself. Escobar explains that Mulwray built a
dam that broke; he was dirty and took bribes, he didn't care about the 500 people he
drowned. (p. 42) Escobar calls them a 'bunch of dumb Mexicans.' (p. 43). Gittes refers
to Escobar knowing Evelyn when she was young. The scene with Morty and Gittes is as
before: "only in L.A." Jake pulls the flyer marked 'Save our city!! Los Angeles is dying of
thirst!!' from his windshield after picking up an ice cream (p. 45) On the following pages
he talks to an old man who was friends with Leroy the drunk and doesn't know he's dead
(p.46). On page 51 Jake is back at the office and tells the guys he lied to Escobar.

```
                          WALSH
                        (lightly)
            It's Chinatown.

                          DUFFY
                  (almost contemptuous)
            Another twist.
```

(Chinatown 2nd draft: 51)

    This is an instance of Towne's effective use of dialogue as commentary — every
time a character lies to Jake, they say, "It's *Chinatown*." And Jake is spun in another
direction, fighting another obstacle. The phrase is used as a kind of Greek chorus, in the
classical style and it also indicates (subtextually, to the reader) Gittes' mounting
suspicion: Walsh has seen the check from Evelyn on Jake's desk and Jake is furious. He
asks the guys is it possible somebody asked them to get him to lay off the case. They
deny it.

Escobar calls Jake and gets him to come down to 555 ½ Cerritos – to see the murdered body of 'Mrs Mulwray' ie Ida Sessions (pp. 53-57). Jake meets Evelyn at the Brown Derby as in the First Draft and is interrupted by Mrs Match (p. 59) "another satisfied client" as Evelyn calls her.   On page 61 Jake declares that Mulwray was murdered, Ida Sesssions was murdered and "your husband's little blonde is probably dead." (p. 61):

> GITTES
> I goddam near lost my nose! And I
> like it. I like breathing through it.
> So before I lie anymore for you I want
> the truth. Let's take a ride to the
> beach and talk.

(Chinatown 2nd draft: 51)

These lines would remain in the Third Draft but the following scene would not: Jake takes Evelyn to the beach and explains what he thinks is going on. They watch a family and children playing on the sand.   Evelyn says she didn't kill her husband (p.61). As in the First Draft, she claims to be having an affair with a married man and says that she loves both men. Gittes asks if there's anything else she's not telling him. She says he's sadistic. (p. 65). They hear an outfall of water from the palisades (pp.66-7). Back at the Derby's parking lot:

> EVELYN
> Mr. Gittes, because I don't want you
> to go to the police – doesn't mean I
> don't want to find out what happened
> to Hollis.

Gittes sighs.

> GITTES
> It's *Chinatown* …

> EVELYN
> What does that mean?

> GITTES
> Don't ask me to explain it right now.

(Chinatown 2nd draft: 67)

Once again, the line indicates his growing suspicion that someone is lying to him. Page 68 was missing from the draft I read at the Margaret Herrick Library but on p. 69 in the office Jake says to Duffy he's dropping the whole Mulwray thing and Duffy replies, "Glad to hear it, Jake." Jake is cleaning a .38 on his desk and he isn't smiling.

P. 69A starts with Jake in San Pedro and taking a seaplane out to Catalina to meet Julian Cross (p. 70) who explains he owned the Water Department with Hollis Mulwray. Cross – who comically mispronounces 'Gittes' and makes it sound like an

164

insult - says he'll pay him \$10,000 to find out what happened to Hollis (p. 73). Jake tells him he and Escobar worked *Chinatown* together.   Then Cross says Escobar used to work for him, too (p. 73) Cross says he's concerned if Jake is extorting money from his daughter (p. 74). The scene ends with Cross clearly moved by a beautiful horse called Lambchop and Jake's return on the plane (p. 77). Jake visits City Hall but Lou Escobar isn't there (p. 77A).

Jake visits Evelyn pp. 78 onwards and finds a bottle of clear liquid, a hypodermic and a rotting peach (p. 79) in the bathroom. Then, in a change to the First Draft, the place is shot up by Escobar and his men. Jake doesn't know why Evelyn called him – she says he's an old friend and contrary to Jake's claims wouldn't have ransacked the place himself.   That night he takes her out and they see a beautiful Mexican girl driving an old Model A pull up beside them: Evelyn teases him about the girl's legs and then acts somewhat coquettishly herself.

Jake visits Yelburton at the Dept of Water and Power and Yelburton concedes they have been diverting a little water at night "to irrigate avocado and walnut groves in the northwest valley. As you know, the farmers there have no legal right to our water, and since we've been so short ourselves, we've had to cut them off. The city comes first – but, well, we've been trying to help some of them out, keep them from going under" (p. 89) He asks Jake to keep that information under his hat. (p. 90) Jake sees Mulvihill outside – he's "beating up customers that don't pay their bills" Jake suggests (p. 91) At the hall of Records Jake gets the plat books for the northwest valley (pp. 92-92B.) At Evelyn's house he sees an Indian motorcycle and tells her, "I rode one of those all over *Chinatown*" (p. 93) and they drive up to Sunland and on page 94 the famously lost rainmaker scene begins:

Gittes looks up as some lavender smoke drifts into FRAME. He gazes off to the far end of the dried field. There a MAN has mounted a strange machine and lifted the lid off it, and a large mounted fan has been blowing the lavender smoke in their direction.
And:

He tips his hat and heads back across the field in the direction of the lavender smoke. Half-way across he turns back and calls out:

96

CONTINUED: (2)
                    RAINMAKER
          But the rains will come. It's going
          to be torrential, a flood, an apocalypse.

He waves gaily and continues on – Eveyln waves back just as gaily. Gittes watches her.

(*Chinatown* 2nd draft: 96)

This scene is intensely visual and strikingly linked with the film's content and theme – perhaps so obviously that Polanski would insist on its being dropped on the shoot (it survived to the next screenplay draft in shorter form.)

Again from the First Draft, Jake and Evelyn go to the orchard which has evidently had water and where he is shot at and the farmers confront him and ask if he's with the Water Department or Haze? Jake doesn't know the name. The farmer tells him that the water dept. has actually been sending men out to blow up water tanks. They go to the farmer's house where the man's wife serves them tea and food and Jake asks if they recognize any of the names on his list from the hall of records (p. 100) They don't. Jake meets the Small Man who sliced his nose and who calls him kitty cat again (p. 101) after visiting Arroyo Realty in the valley – Danny Haze. Men from the realtors approach the farmers but apparently they can keep their property. Back at the Mulwray house, Jake apologizes for the loss of the motorcycle (p. 103) Jake notices that Evelyn has something in her eye. She says that there's a flaw in the iris. This scene dissolves to a post-coital situation here and in the Third Draft (and film) the edited version of which bothered Towne.

<pre>
                         GITTES
          Mrs. Mulwray?

                         EVELYN
          - yes?

                         GITTES
               (with a certain insouciance)
          I hope it's something I said.
</pre>

(Chinatown 2nd draft:105)

They enjoy an amicable exchange and on page 108 Jake says, "It's *Chinatown* all over again" and tells her about the Tong Wars: he attempted to help a Chinese girl who wanted to marry her boyfriend. Trouble was her dowry was fifty pounds of stolen opium - her boyfriend "was the biggest dope dealer east of Hong Kong," and Jake was arrested as an accessory after the fact. He lost his job. Escobar got promoted (p. 109). Again, this may have been too redolent of the detective noir and too expositional to suit Polanski's reading and wouldn't feature in the Third Draft where it is simply subtext

<pre>
                         EVELYN
               (looking steadily at Gittes)
          So now I'm Chinatown?

                         GITTES
               (more than that)
          it's a thought.
</pre>

(Chinatown 2nd draft: 110)

It is now obvious that Towne's writing strategy is to utilise the word '*Chinatown*' to indicate each time a character is duping Jake – thematically inscribed each time (now it is overtly contextualised in Jake's backstory so the Orient is once again the root of noir-ish evil).

The house is being watched. Jake tells her the names on the list belong to people whose properties have been bought up by the city. In the morning Jake asks the Oriental gardener to move – the pond is overflowing badly.

> GARDENER
> Salt water bad for glass.

Gittes stares at the pond. He can't quite believe what he's heard.

> GITTES
> That's salt water?

The gardener nods vigorously.

> GARDENER
> Mr.Mulwray makee tide pool - bring in
> sea water - but velly bad for glass.

Gittes kneels. Clinging to the edge of the pond, he can now see - as he could have before if he had looked closely - a starfish.

CLOSE STARFISH

It has one leg missing. The fifth point on the star is just beginning to grow back.
GITTES

touches the creature and it moves. He then looks up slowly, glances at the newly repaired decking that he had seen Evelyn work on - glances at the wall, now repaired - the mortar still a little darker than that on the rest of the wall.

THE GARDENER
breathes an audible sigh of relief. The waters have begun to recede back into the pond.

(Chinatown 2nd draft:114-5)

And Jake finds a pair of bifocals with one lens shattered.

This key scene – heavily thematised with notions of vision, insight, scales falling from the eyes – would remain more or less intact in the Third Draft.

The third act begins once again with Evelyn hiring Jake – she will give him $5,000 if he can find out who killed her husband. At the office Jake apologises to Duffy for what he said the day before. He meets Cross at the Albacore Club – this time without Evelyn - and Cross tells him about his wife dying of diabetes and being left to bring up Evelyn alone. He gives Jake a $1,000 check. Jake flies out. (pp.119-124) Jake asks Byron Samples to quit following him and dumping water in the ocean. Samples tells him a Clarence Speer, one of the names on the list, went into escrow and three weeks earlier hired Ida Sessions to pose as Mrs Mulwray – but four weeks earlier he died at the Mar Vista Inn in Venice (p. 126) Walsh and Duffy hustle Jake into the freight elevator at the office but Jake overpowers them: it transpires that Walsh was paid $250 to betray Jake.

Samples tells Jake that Mulwray told him (Samples) that he would let him resign if Ida could come to his (Mulwray's) house to meet someone – but he never named that someone. At the Mar Vista Inn and Rest Home Gittes questions the manager, Palmer, and finds Emma Tannenbaum, one of the names on the list. She's sewing a quilt with a gray game fish against a white background, with the initials A.C. beneath the fish. Jake asks her where she got it. Another lady responds: "apple core." (p. 134) Palmer tells Jake the home is the charity of the Albacore Club. Jake tells Palmer it was Cross who recommended it to him. (p. 135). Jake pulls up at the Sweetzer Arms and sees Evelyn and a girl – the one Jake had shot with Mulwray at the apartments, his alleged girlfriend. The girl calls to Evelyn – "Mama." Evelyn stops when she sees Jake. Evelyn tells Jake they were getting ready to leave. (p. 137)

138

CONTINUED: (2)

                    EVELYN
          Maybe our friend was right.

                    GITTES
          Our friend?

                    EVELYN
          The rainmaker – it's starting to pour.
          What did he say? It would be torrential?..

                              (*Chinatown* 2nd draft:138)

This is not just expositional and literal but metaphorical and probably too much so for Polanski's tastes.

Jake thinks Escobar is leaving with them. Evelyn says she wants to protect the girl. Jake tells her Julian killed Hollis at the house. She says she'll talk to Julian. That night in Hollywood Jake leaves Sophie minding Maria (the girl) in Samples' car. He returns to his apartment where he's met with a fist – Escobar's – for selling out Evelyn. Escobar shows him Mulwray's bifocals – Duffy and Walsh handed them in that morning. Evelyn is to be arrested for murder. Escobar mocks Jake's idea of drawing the line. (p. 142) Jake pulls out Julian's check and it falls like confetti to the floor. Escobar asks, "where is she?" Jake thinks he's referring to the girl and calls her Escobar's daughter, which stuns Escobar. Escobar wants Evelyn. "Do I have to spell it out for you? Maria is Julian Cross' daughter." (p. 143)

```
                    GITTES
        - but I thought she was Evelyn's

                    ESCOBAR
        She is!
```

Gittes sits slowly on the arm of the sofa, staring
blankly in front of him.

(Chinatown 2nd draft: 143)

Jake admits Evelyn has gone to see Julian. Escobar says, "she's gone to kill him." (p. 144). They go after her with Mulvihill, in the driving rain along the coast. Evelyn is dazed and waiting for Julian's approaching seaplane at the oilfields and the screen goes blank when she blinks. She pulls out a .45 and fires at her father on the beach, first hitting the radiator of the car. At the oil fields the "rain is now falling in relentless sheets. Evelyn is stalking Cross, Mulvihill looking for her." (p. 149) Julian has fallen near the sign marked 'bait' Mulvihill tries to shoot at Evelyn but a shot from either Jake or Escobar knocks him into the mud, off his feet (p. 150) Evelyn shoots Julian.

The last pages of the Second Draft read, as before, as a highly detailed visual description of Jake's convertible driving in a rainstorm along Alta Vista Road, now renamed Mulwray Drive, accompanied by his voiceover, explaining the 'double Cross' that winds up the narrative - Evelyn got a four-year prison sentence for killing her father and has now disappeared; while the bigger scandal was buried. Jake learns from Saul that the second thing a man should always do himself is to put on his own hat. He looks out across the lush, Biblically replenished valley beyond, which dissolves into the valley today, a "contemporary sprawl – the tangle of traffic, ugly buildings, foul air and noise." (p. 153)

Overall, Towne's screenplay can be seen as a direct descendant and adaptation both of the complex Chandleresque tradition in fiction; however, although this version of the screenplay is shorter, it is actually somewhat more difficult to follow.

The Other Second Draft (152 pages)

As a researcher conducting work in an area long worked over by others, this author never envisaged the discovery of anything new in writing about *Chinatown*. However, in November 2003, while attempting to buy luggage on Hollywood Boulevard, it was my peculiar good fortune to locate an apparently legitimate copy of the Second Draft of the screenplay – and one markedly different from that assumed to be the second draft. This numbers 152 pages and is dated 7th September 1973. It is, in fact, almost word for word a replica of the acknowledged shooting draft – the Third Draft, which was to be finessed one month later. It is labelled 'Second Draft' and contains all of the same scenes of the Third Draft, with some lines of dialogue excised and other minor changes. It also includes the rainmaker scene and Jake's trip by seaplane to Catalina to visit Julian Cross' estate, albeit Evelyn does not accompany him in this version, as she does in the 'Polanski Rewrite'. This, then, is probably the 'official' second draft for the studio and financiers, given that it is marked, 'Produced by: Robert Evans' and 'Directed by Roman Polanski.'

Widely available, and said to be the shooting draft, this nonetheless differs slightly from the finished film as is noted. Towne told John Brady,

> I was struggling through the first and second drafts simply trying to figure out the story for myself. The second draft was so complex that a shooting script based upon it would have run close to three hours. I would have had to do a radical rewrite in order to simplify it... in the film I missed that kind of progressive jealousy by Gittes – his thinking that she was involved with someone else. [525]

Polanski recalls his collaboration on the final draft rather prosaically:

> I made it really a subjective narrative. I was very rigorous about the construction. I believed – and still do – you can't just settle one single problem in one scene, that each scene has to settle several problems of the plot. [526]

Towne remarks:

> What I wrote was good, but Roman, I now think was right in recognizing that it was excessively complex. [527]

---

[525] Towne in Brady. *Op.cit.*, 412. He continued: "There comes a point where you're confused, you don't know where you're going. Then it helps to talk. It was really true of *Chinatown*. I got lost so many times." 'Dialogue on Film,' as before: 42.

[526] Roman Polanski, *Scene By Scene*, BBC TV. Wright Wexman writes of Polanski's interpretation of Towne's writing in the recurring use of deep-focus three-shots that it "undercut generic expectations by defining shifting power relationships in which Gittes is not always visually as privileged as his cocky, tough-guy attitude assumes. Though Huston had employed a similar strategy of three-shots in *The Maltese Falcon*, Bogart almost always dominated the other characters in the frame by virtue of his superior height or positioning. Nicholson, however, is not so favoured by Polanski." She continues, "Gittes's scenes with police officers Escobar and Loach and with civic officials Yelburton and Mulvihill typically find the hero either boxed in or pushed to the side of the frame: visual expressions of his ultimate helplessness in the face of greater numbers." She notes that Gittes is frequently watching, from the side of frame: "spying is, after all , his business." Wexman. *Op.cit.*, 99. It also plays into the overriding tone of dramatic irony so pervasive in the film text: the blinding lack of insight on the part of the self-appointed voyeur. Wexman writes of Polanski's framing of Evelyn Mulwray that she "is also portrayed in this way. When Escobar interviews her in the morgue, he stands to her right. To escape his disturbing questions, she tries to turn away, only to be startled by Loach, who is lurking on the left side of the broad Panavision composition." Wexman. *Op.cit.*, 96. The positioning is reversed at the film's climax when Gittes inadvertently causes Loach to kill Evelyn. The use of Panavision literally endows the film with a 1970s perspective on the carefully-wrought *mise-en-scène*, a distancing perspective that broadens and distends perception of a moral and destructive wasteland as well as imposing an ironic epistemological structure (the unseeing J.J. Gittes.) At approximately fifteen and a half minutes into the film his position in the text is vitally undermined by Polanski's visuals when the image of Hollis Mulwray and his 'girlfriend' is imposed on Gittes' camera lens. This then introduces the separation or experiential discrepancy between the spectator and Gittes, presenting a play on the notion of point of view or focalisation in the filmic text.

[527] Towne in Engel. *Op.cit.,* 201-202.

The principal alterations to the script's second draft are as follows: Mulwray, who is corrupt in the first draft, is made a virtuous man in this draft – which raises the dramatic stakes. He drowns, but not at the Doctor's hands; Gittes is in every scene and all those scenes which might have taken place ordinarily on the street are now located at bodies of water; Sophie's role is diminished; the incestuous relationship between Cross and Evelyn is no longer revealed by Escobar but by Evelyn: on the sister/daughter scene which is probably the most shocking and revelatory, Towne comments:

> I think the single most valuable thing Roman suggested was the scene in which somehow Gittes had to get the information out of Evelyn that she had had her father's child. I tried it different ways, but I couldn't see how on earth he would get something so devastating and personal out of her. Roman said it should occur during a confrontation between the two of them and I agreed, but I said I just couldn't see any way to do it. And Roman just said, 'Oh it's easy. Have him beat it out of her.' It was such a simple solution. [528]

The Escobar and Samples subplots are now largely eliminated. Polanski wanted Gittes and Evelyn to sleep together, something that Towne didn't want to happen in the way that it finished onscreen but Polanski comments:

> I thought it was important that they have some intimate relationship which changes the rapport between them for the second part of the picture. Something serious stands between them, events are working against them. If they don't have this relationship, it doesn't matter so much. [529]

In fact, Towne wanted Jake to be impotent – a fact that would not only be thematically resonant but would be yet another self-consciously mythical character function.[530] Instead, Polanski, supposedly to spite Towne, shot the scene in a very perfunctory fashion, cutting to a mocking, post-coital cigarette. The third draft doesn't include the scene.

Field notes that the screenplay's dramatic question is stated on page 5 (by the phony Mrs Mulwray) and then restated on page 10 (by the farmer at City Hall: "You steal the water from the Valley, ruin the grazing, starve my livestock – who's paying you to do that, Mr Mulwray, that's what I want to know!" And so does J.J. Gittes. Noah (in the film he is no longer Julian) Cross is given the line of dialogue that encapsulates the line of action:

```
                    CROSS
      Either you bring the water to L.A.
      or you bring L.A. to the water.
```

(*Chinatown* 3rd draft: 139)

This, says Field, is the dramatic 'hook' of *Chinatown*.[531] He concludes, "the water scandal is woven through the screenplay, and Gittes uncovers it a piece at a time. That's why it's such a great film. *Chinatown* is a voyage of discovery." [532]

---

[528] Towne in Pirie, 1981, 153.

[529] *Scene By Scene With Roman Polanski*, BBC TV.

[530] And would also create a conscious link with Clyde Barrow, in another allusion to *Bonnie and Clyde*.

[531] Field. *Op.cit.,*119.

Cross sums up the text and subtext of the story:

```
                    CROSS
        The future, Mr. Gittes -- the
        future.
```

(Chinatown 3rd draft: 140)

This explicit threat – modernity – would dominate the text of the sequel, *The Two Jakes*. In fact, Jake states to Curly the subject of the film on p.3 of this draft: "I'll tell you the unwritten law, you dumb son of a bitch, you gotta be rich to kill somebody, anybody and get away with it." It was dropped, along with many other pieces of dialogue, but none so forceful or explicitly thematic. [533]

Field is quite right in calling to our attention two recognizable act breaks in *Chinatown* despite the unusually long second 'act': Act One ends when the real Evelyn Mulwray presents herself to Gittes at his office (approximately seventeen minutes into the film, 23 pages into the script's third draft), transforming Gittes' quest, because she threatens to have his license revoked and without this he can't work as a detective. This is what Field calls a 'plot point', hooking into the action and spinning it around.[534]

Act Two is exceptionally long, and ends when Gittes discovers the shattered bifocals in the tidepool (implicating Evelyn in Mulwray's death.) Field says: "The plot point at the end of the second act is also an incident, episode or event that 'hooks' into the action, and spins it around into Act III. It usually occurs at about page 85 or 90 of the screenplay." [535]

Field is keen to stress the legacy of three-act structure in comprehending the way screen stories are written. Field says that the first plot or turning point occurs *usually* around page 25-27 of a screenplay while the second takes place somewhere between pages 85 and 90. He identifies Jake's discovery of the bifocals in the Mulwray fish pool as the screenplay's second turning point (p.122, third draft.). [536] While some commentators (and screenwriters) would take issue with the prescriptive notion, there is no doubt that it is based on observation, but it has had the perhaps unfortunate effect of becoming a standardised method or formula for aspiring screenwriters (and studio executives).

---

[532] Field. *Op.cit.*, 92.

[533] According to Viki King, this is exemplary screenwriting, because page 3 should have "a line of dialogue … that introduces a central question." *HOW TO WRITE A MOVIE IN 21 DAYS: The Inner Movie Method*. New York: HarperPerennial, 1988, 34.

[534] Field. *Op.cit.*, 13. Field's identification of Evelyn Mulwray's entrance to Gittes' office as the first turning point may be a case of misrecognition however; it could be a false premise as this story point might also be identified as the narrative's inciting incident.

[535] Field. *Op.cit.*, 13-14.

[536] Field. *Op.cit.*, 119. The second turning point might also be identified as Jake agreeing to work for Noah Cross, which happens about 65 minutes into the film and on p.81 of the third draft. Field concedes this in *THE SCREENWRITER'S WORKBOOK*. New York: Dell Publishing, 1984, 131-145.

Act III of *Chinatown* is now very short and forms the story's resolution. Gittes has a character arc that sees him develop from being a cool outsider to an emotionally involved lover – traditionally we would expect him to be fulfilled at story's end, whereas *Chinatown*s conclusion destroys him. Dancyger and Rush describe this as 'ironic three-act structure' because it defies the usual arc of transgression-recognition-redemption popular in American cinema. Ambiguity is privileged over a happy ending and a darker reality prevails, refusing us the release of the triumph of good over evil. [537]

> Then there was the ending, a famous locus of dispute that quickly deteriorated into mutual abuse. [538]

The third draft possesses the ending that was shot. Polanski justifies his change to Towne's original ending as follows:

> … if it all ended with a happy ending we wouldn't be sitting here talking about this film today. If you want to feel for Evelyn, if you want to feel there is a general lot of injustice in our world, if you want to have people leaving the cinema with a feeling that they should do something about it in their lives; if it's all dealt for them by the filmmakers, they just forget about it, and that's it… I wrote that scene the night before we shot it because we had a falling out about this ending with Bob [Towne]. At that time he didn't believe that it was the right approach, he said many times since that it was. So the film almost came to the final stretch and we still didn't have the ending! [539]

Towne claims:

> I came up with an alternative ending about four or five days before shooting. I brought it over to him [Polanski], and he said, 'Well, it's too late. We're going to shoot in a week and I can't change anything. I just can't do it.' That was the last we spoke during the picture. It was very quiet, subdued, although we'd had several fights in which I'd blown up and yelled at him, and he at me .[540]

It is arguable that the new ending changed fundamentally the philosophy of the script: no longer did J.J. Gittes save the world from Noah Cross and get the girl; instead it is clear that he still has no idea of the depths of evil into which he has found himself hurled and has rather precipitated a series of events so vicious as to be quite incomprehensible to him. (It could be debated that Gittes still fits into the Townean mould of the compromised man, trapped by his occupation.) Towne hated it initially and went public in his vociferous reaction, but years later agreed that it was logical, emotionally correct, and made the film great. He is quoted by William Goldman as follows:

---

[537] Dancyger and Rush. *Op.cit.,* 35-36; 40. See also Howard Suber's THE POWER OF FILM on cinema's bittersweet endings. Los Angeles: Michael Wiese Productions, 2006. Thanks to Prof. Tom Stempel for providing the reference.

[538] Peter Biskind. *Op.cit.,* 166.

[539] Polanski speaking on *Scene By Scene*, a/b; according to William Goldman, "Towne thinks if Faye Dunaway had had sex with her pop, John Huston, today they would end up on Oprah Winfrey, or, if Oprah wouldn't have them, then Geraldo. Towne feels there is so little shame in our world now, it damages the possibility of drama at this level." Goldman. *WHICH LIE DID I TELL? FURTHER ADVENTURES IN THE SCREEN TRADE.* London: Bloomsbury, 2000, 233.

[540] Towne in Brady. *Op.cit.,* 410.

Looking back at it now, I'm somewhat chagrined at my anger at Polanski. There were a lot of things. There has been a lot of talk about his ending, which is what's in the movie now, and what I wanted, which was virtually as dark and maybe, I think, a little more literary. Evelyn Mulwray killed her father. And had to go to jail. And Gittes was going to talk about it. She was going to be fried, because the identity of her daughter had to be protected. So it made a mess of it anyway. But in retrospect, Roman was right. The movie needed a stark ending after such a complex story. [541]

Ultimately, while *Chinatown* has some of the elements necessary to fulfil the conditions explored above, it is more properly a pastiche and examination of the style, according to the tenets laid out by Dancyger and Rush.

Chinatown and Multiple Authorship

In his discussion of Raymond Chandler's work, Paul Jensen describes the world of the writer's stories as one of "pervasive corruption and duplicity." Chandler's detective is an outsider,

His function defines his existence; to be active and to care is to live; but to lose detachment is to court disaster.

Jensen comments on conventional endings:

… the final emphasis is therefore what is revealed about human nature, about the things people choose to do, are driven to, or tolerate. [542]

Towne says,

I don't think that it's altogether fair or correct to say simply that it didn't turn out the way I'd imagined when writing…In hindsight, I've come to feel that Roman was probably right about the ending, that I don't think that what I had in mind could have been done; that an end with that ambiguity and ambivalence that I had in mind simply could not satisfactorily be done as the tag to a movie with that much complexity; the end had to have a level of stark simplicity that at the time I thought was excessively melodramatic. Roman rightly believed that the complexities had to conclude with a simple severing of the knot. [543]

However, a linear interpretation of the story makes his original decision aesthetically correct and dramatically logical. It is now clear that the screenplay Towne constructed played genre *against* myth and it is here that Towne's innovation lies. Thus we have Towne's admission of the possibility of reading the film as a product of contested authorship – an artistic collision, perhaps. One could claim, perhaps, that it was the triumph (or clash) of Polanski's modernist sensibility over Towne's traditional classicism. Virginia Wright Wexman says that *Chinatown* "marks the culmination of Polanski's career. In no other film has he so successfully fused his diverse creative and cultural influences." [544] She espouses Andrew Sarris' view that Polanski works best in

[541] Goldman, 2000. 223.

[542] Paul Jensen, 'Raymond Chandler: The World You Live In,' *Film Comment* 1974 Vol. 10 No. 6, 1974: 18-19.

[543] Towne in Engel. *Op.cit.* 201.

[544] Virginia Wright Wexman. *ROMAN POLANSKI.* Boston, Twayne Publishers, 1985, 91. Mark Cousins disputes Polanski's links with the New Hollywood: "Polanski was never attracted by the stylistic freedoms of the New Wave filmmakers and here, as in ROSEMARY'S BABY, he filmed with wide-angle lenses, bright lights and precise framing, the opposite of both [Gordon] Willis'

collaboration, and in fact it is clear that he acknowledges this himself in his frequent writing collaborations with Gérard Brach. With Evans and Nicholson contributing to the way the film was made, Wexman says, "in such a situation, a major part of the director's role is to synthesize the creative contributions made by a variety of talents." [545] Cinematographer John A. Alonzo said that Evans had always had in mind a classic kind of film. [546] Pat McGilligan says that when the chips were down, Jack Nicholson backed Polanski. [547]

Following Polanski's intervention, there are major problems with the film's logic and sense of character development – we have no real idea of who Ida Sessions is; we don't understand the backstory between Evelyn and Escobar; and the mythic sense that drives the original story is lost in favour of ellipsis: the rainmaker scene is shortened in this draft but is excised entirely from the film; as is the flight to Catalina – a trope for Los Angeles, that island in the desert surrounded by water – lessening the story's overall mythic impact. The lengthy exchanges between Jake and Evelyn, so true to the sensibility of the Forties classics that influenced the writing, were also lost, thereby sacrificing character development. The repetition of the line "it's *Chinatown*" has gone; and the Seabiscuit motif. None of these story holes is in Towne's first draft and in fact its supposedly legendary confusion is non-existent; it is an exemplary piece of intricately plotted, Forties-style detective fiction. [548]

Polanski's place in the traditional directors' Pantheon is both marginalized and augmented by his private life. This predicates the reception of all his films, and preclude an 'impartial' reading (if that is ever possible) of any of his works, most of which he is responsible for co-writing or at least he ensures he is credited as such. One of his biographers, John Parker, claims, "… his films consistently allude to his own personal mythology, reflecting his private dramas set against the backdrop of society at large." [549]

He is viewed as a master of black comedy, a satirist, a bitter and twisted individual – in fact his re-emergence with *Chinatown* was viewed with bemusement (and in some quarters bewilderment) since in the perversely Puritanical United States, the murder of his eight-months pregnant wife was seen as a byproduct of Polanski's own Satanic tendencies - he had, after all, directed *Rosemary's Baby* (1968) and for Robert Evans, no less. Hence the general assumption that Polanski wielded the seniority on *Chinatown*, since it is a widely held view that there are two ways a writer can have his personal worldview expressed cinematically – through one single character (usually a secondary figure, who becomes the film's 'moral guiding voice' and of course, ironically, it is Cross who expresses the thematic subtext in *Chinatown*); and, through the ending: which, in the case of *Chinatown* the film, was definitely Polanski's.

---

approach on *The Godfather* and the whole film noir cycle." Mark Cousins. *THE STORY OF FILM.* London: Pavilion Books, 2006, 350.

[545] *Ibid.*
[546] 'Behind the Scenes of *Chinatown*,' *American Cinematographer* Vol. 56, No. 5, May 1975: 528.
[547] McGilligan, 1995, 251.
[548] For an alternative case study of *Chinatown* which also focuses on the changes to the screenplay which led it to becoming rather illogical, see Lovell and Sergi. *Op.cit.*, 90-99.

[549] John Parker. *Op.cit.*, 271.

Figure 11 Noah Cross (John Huston) meets Jake

Pauline Kael's commentary on *Chinatown* partakes of this reading of Polanski:

> ... [he] turns the material into an extension of his world view; he makes the L.A.
> atmosphere gothic and creepy form the word go. The film holds you, in a suffocating
> way. Polanski never lets the story tell itself. It's all over-deliberate, mauve, nightmarish;
> everyone is yellow-lacquered, and evil runs rampant. You don't care who is hurt, since
> everything is blighted. And yet the nastiness has a look, a fascination.[550]

Always possessed of a seemingly darker sensibility than Towne, whose creative
influences could be said to be his great friends, Warren Beatty and Jack Nicholson,
Polanski's experiences had been governed by the rather more pernicious figures of Adolf
Hitler and Charles Manson. [551] Tom Milne in his review disagrees, claiming,

> Cynics, as someone commented of Hemingway, lean so far backwards to avoid
> sentiment that they inevitably overbalance; and once their defences are down, there
> is no limit to the romantic imagination. It is in this subterranean passage of *Chinatown*
> that Polanski rejoins his more overly personal self of WHAT?, wryly commenting on the
> sad fact that art and life so seldom coincide. [552]

Towne himself has stated:

> That movie is truly an amalgam of me and Roman. [553]

Virginia Wright Wexman teases out the differences between Towne and Polanski
in her study of the director's work, when she points out that Towne had earlier expressed
admiration for Bogart

---

[550] Pauline Kael, 1993, 135.

[551] Polanski is consistently obliged to chide interviewers about their insistence that his tragic life
have an effect on his art.

[552] Milne, *Op.cit.*, 243.

[553] Towne in Engel. *Op.cit.*, 201.

in terms of the American star's readiness to combat fascism and his ability to commit himself to people and causes. By contrast, Towne saw the more modernist figure of Belmondo as someone to whom 'nothing matters beyond him – no clash of alien ideologies, no human sufferings beyond or within his ken; only the moment. [554]

A similar bias toward 'commitment' – though atypical of Polanski – colours *Chinatown*. "Moreover," continues Wexman, "in the character of Evelyn Mulwray, Towne created a figure of dignity and sensual warmth that goes far beyond the pathetically diminished caricatures of women that Polanski himself often favors." [555] She says, "… where Towne is biased towards the romantic, commercial and political, Polanski tends to be cynical, elitist and anti-social." Wexman states of Robert Evans' role that he "played a pivotal role in this process of balance and accommodation between the director's modernist leanings and the more traditional approaches of his co-creators." [556] She suggests that, "because of Towne, Polanski was forced to relate his thematic concerns to a context of politics and ecology." [557]

Schatz comments that "the very basis for 'classic Hollywood realism' is its capacity to render technique invisible by filtering narrative information through the perceptions of its central character(s), thereby accommodating the psychology of the viewer – or, rather, of countless viewers simultaneously." [558] Polanski's 'invisible witness' shooting style forces the spectator to partake in proceedings to an uncomfortable degree, to the extent that he is complicit in the morass of bad behaviour that tugs away at the film's atmosphere, which is undercut with the threat of violence. Towne says, "Many people have called the movie violent. But it actually has very little violence in it." [559]

Occasionally the shooting style departs from the classical mode as John A. Alonzo recounts:

> Polanski did some rather daring things in *Chinatown* – like shooting Faye Dunaway without diffusion, so that you could see the scar on her face. That would never have been done in the 'classic' period. Greta Garbo and all those beautiful people would have looked perfect. He also had the great guts as a director to allow his leading man, Jack Nicholson, to go through half the picture with stitches in his nose. No one would ever have done that to Humphrey Bogart. [560]

We might then say that Polanski is interrogating the whole aesthetic underpinning the classic realist tradition. The continuing misperception (sometimes even by Towne) that the entire film is from the perspective of J.J. Gittes (instead, we see what

---

[554] Wright Wexman, 1985, 92.

[555] *Ibid*. Robert Benedetto is probably more accurate in his claim that, "Towne's *Chinatown* is, in essence, a eulogy for the lost LA of his childhood – a paradise lost through corruption and greed. Roman Polanski's *Chinatown* is something quite different. His film is a dark parable about human nature, expressing a fatalistic world view shaped by his childhood in Nazi-occupied Poland and reinforced by a repeated series of personal tragedies. Towne's story of a city plundered for money and power is still present in the film, but only to serve Polanski's theme of the omnipresent heart of darkness and man's powerlessness in the face of it." Benedetto, *Op.cit.*, 49. Benedetto ultimately sides with Polanski as the *film's* author.

[556] Wright Wexman. *Op.cit.*, 92.

[557] *Ibid.*

[558] Schatz, 1983, 3.

[559] Towne in Engel. *Op.cit.*, 223.

[560] Alonzo. *Op.cit.,* 565.

he *does*), is a tribute to the understanding of the director's masterly command of the medium and his keen appreciation of the genre, which, according to Schatz, privileges "the isolated subjective vision of the detective." [561]

Towne has said of the director,

> There were certain battles where I had a limited amount of success, but basically Roman would get his way. Bob Evans's position - he is right in this – is that you take Roman as he is, or you fire him. Roman's strength is that he is what he is, and it's also his weakness, because someone like this can be terribly rigid and subject to ossification.[562]

Kael concludes that

> … Towne's temperament comes through, too, especially in Nicholson's Jake Gittes, the vulgarian hero who gives the picture much of its comedy: Gittes gets to tell wittily inane, backslapping jokes, and to show the romanticism inside his street shrewdness. [563]

If we return to Horowitz's admonition that *Chinatown* was atypical of Towne and that all of Towne's (subsequent) work would be viewed through the lens provided by *Chinatown*, then it is imperative to draw certain conclusions from this case study.

Conclusions

Let us return to Pauline Kael's description of Towne as 'flaky classicist.' In purely definitional terms, to be flaky means 'irrational,' 'eccentric,' or in layman's terms, 'dodgy.' [564] Essentially she is accusing him of ploughing the familiar furrow of classical Hollywood, albeit without the style imbued by studios of the period. She is also perhaps alluding to the common perception of him as disorganised, as manifested in the illogical

---

[561] Schatz, 1983, 80.

[562] Robert Towne, 'Dialogue on Film': 47. Towne elaborated for Peter Rainer: "There is a natural antipathy between director and writer because there's a power transference that takes place that both have to be sensitive to… But I think that it's good when a writer can work on a movie when it's being shot. I think it's helpful to the director and the actors. Writers should always be on movies, but rarely are. All I ask is that I be allowed to make my contribution to the ongoing process. Classically, a director gets the script from the writer and then says, 'Get that asshole out of here. We don't need him around.' If you think enough of a writer to gamble a year and a half of your life on what he's done, then presumably you should think enough of him to keep him around while you're doing it. This is done about as often as there are really good movies made. You learn to seek out the people who want you to make a contribution." Rainer, 1974: 234. Jack Nicholson's [unauthorised] biographer, Patrick McGilligan, claims that when the chips were down, the actor backed Polanski: "Nicholson's growing importance was illustrated by his contract: a reported $500,000 plus a percentage of the gross. But Jack stayed out of the screenplay arguments, although he was around for dinners and talks. His instincts were more those of an actor than a filmmaker in these situations, his focus on his own part, not the snarls of the script. Working with temperamental talents was Towne's strong suit, usually spurring him to great diplomacy and greater achievement. But Jack's way of staying noncommittal undercut his old friend and had the net effect of reinforcing the traditional hierarchy in Hollywood and throwing his considerable weight behind the director – Polanski." McGilligan, *JACK'S LIFE*, 251.

[563] Kael. *Op.cit.,*135.

[564] http://encarta.msn.com./dictionary).

structure of some of his work. While Kael might be perceived to be criticising Towne, it might also, in strictly Kael terms, be a kind of back-handed compliment to a man attempting to emulate the filmic style of those of her favourite writers of the 1930s and 1940s, which she always admitted to preferring to any other phase in Hollywood history.

It is evident that in exploring the history of his hometown Robert Towne had in fact begun the excavation of his great theme, which would be demonstrated time and again in his future work, and had so often been part of the landscape of his screenplays until *Chinatown*: loss. He had also inadvertently discovered his great character, and one that would dominate his finest work: Los Angeles. They can of course be connected by simple wordplay and in fact Los (t) Angeles was the subject of another part of the *Chinatown* trilogy, *Two Jakes* aka *The Two Jakes*, as well as the later work, *Tequila Sunrise*, which might be said to be a riff on draft 2 of *Chinatown*. The city and its surroundings would also be the subject of his next, great work: *Shampoo*, whose opening scenes of lovemaking in the dark would echo the pornographic photographs which greet Gittes at the opening of *Chinatown* (Towne has a habit of cannibalising his own work.[565]) He adheres to the narrative paradigm that dominates any survey of the oeuvre: the failure of the hero. He also utilised the persona of Jack Nicholson in creating his characters on several occasions and creates an extra-familiar nexus of relationships. He also proceeds from a premise grounded in reality towards a kind of mythological resolution, real and imagined. Therefore we can conclude that Horowitz is both correct and incorrect: the draft of *Chinatown* shot by Polanski is probably the least typical draft of the story that Towne created inasmuch as the overt (or overly obvious) elements of myth are mostly excised and streamlined in favour of alleged story logic, which we see is wholly questionable as an aesthetic decision. Yet the mythical subtext remains in the visuals, which are described in great detail in the text. [566] However, all three (and in fact, four) drafts of the screenplay proliferate with Towne's preferred theme, his story premise, his characters, his dialogue, wry humour, use of the demotic, his constant sense of conflict, his narrative arc, visual style and fetish objects. The screenplay purveys both the real and the deconstructing of the real.[567] The fact that Towne's work would all be viewed retrospectively through the lens of this particular film is, however, indisputable. He admits that Polanski taught him a great deal about the craft of filmmaking:

---

[565] Wood writes in his study of *Bonnie and Clyde* that "the credit-sequence provides an admirable starting-point for the film, with its juxtaposition of actual photographs … and a song…. It implies the need to transcend or escape from commonplace reality and the lack of any spiritual or intellectual training for finding a valid alternative." Wood, 1967, 82. This opening sequence had an obvious impact on Towne and he would revisit it in writing *Shampoo* [with Beatty] and *The Two Jakes*.

[566] Horowitz. 1990: 54. As Garrett Stewart observes, "ordinary narrative suspense, the train of multiplying clues and partial discoveries, is to a large extent replaced by a sense of atmospheric foreboding divorced from plot, and more importantly by a suspension in the symbolic details themselves, a consistently withheld relevance that defines the true plotline of the film." Stewart, as before: 28. See Lovell and Sergi, as before, 91-92, for the consequences of the changes enforced by Polanski.

[567] This subject is further examined in William Galperin. ''Bad for the Glass'': Representation and Filmic Deconstruction in *Chinatown* and *Chan is Missing*,' *MLN*, No. 102 (5) 1987: "*Chinatown*'s subversive energies come chiefly, then, from being a different kind of 'realist text.' For such 'realism,' as expatriate filmmakers have frequently underscored, involves that peculiar 'doubling' or dualism by which films can resist their conventions by continuing to bear them." (1156) Galperin refers to *Chinatown*'s "bifocal vision." (1158)

As I look back on it, Roman taught me an awful lot. But it was an agonizing process. [568]

Perhaps Horowitz sums it up most accurately when he states "Towne's and Polanski's artistic agendas diverged at times, and Polanski, as director, had his way at the crucial moments." [569]

Cultural relativity is a major part in the reception of *Chinatown* and its continued relevance as a film. How did this become a part of its mythology? The world surrounding and producing the film was charged with an end to absolutism: Thomas Schatz contextualises it as a time of

> substantial revaluation of American ideology, and the detective-hero necessarily reflected the change in values. As did his '40s prototype, the screen detective of the 1970s accepted social corruption as a given and tried to remain isolated from it, still the naïve idealist beneath the surface… No longer a hero-protector, the detective in more recent films is himself the ultimate victim… Perhaps the clearest image of the contemporary hard-boiled detective's ineffectuality appears in the closing moments of *Chinatown.* [570]

The Left cycle of films that emerged in the late Sixties typically glamorised its outlaw heroes; but Jake Gittes is humiliated, mocked, lied to, misled, and ultimately overmatched. The detective is rendered obsolete in the face of global corruption and an entire genre is disavowed. [571] As Ray suggests perhaps,

> … Hollywood mobilized renovated versions of its traditional genres and heroes to satisfy the audience's schizophrenic impulses toward irony and nostalgia. [572]

Hence, the character of Jake Gittes, perhaps the prototypical Towne (and Nicholson) and atypical Polanski hero, ultimately compromised into tragedy not merely because of the diegesis but because of the film's multiple authorship, with Polanski's necessarily bitter (if parodic) worldview grafting onto the screenplay a horribly twisted ending to the classic presentation insisted upon by producer Evans from Towne's narrative. The undercutting of generic convention serves the purpose of destabilising the inadequate myth which supposedly underlies the culture of America itself.

---

[568] Towne speaking at the AFI's Harold Lloyd Master Seminar, October 1994. Accessed online at www.afi.com.

[569] Horowitz. *Op.cit.,* 53.

[570] Schatz, 1981,149.

[571] Dilys Powell remarked in her review, "… Jack Nicholson has done something startling with personality. He has effaced it." *THE DILYS POWELL FILM READER.* Manchester: Carcanet Press Ltd., 1991, 255.

[572] See Robert B. Ray's analysis of the Left and Right cycles of this era of filmmaking. *A CERTAIN TENDENCY OF THE HOLLYWOOD CINEMA, 1930-1980.* Princeton, N.J.: Princeton University Press, 1985, 296-325. He states: "The extent of intentional manipulation in Hollywood's revised tactics is ultimately irrelevant. While Classic Hollywood's use of the traditional American mythology had certainly not been innocent, its 'sincerity' (to use Godard's description) had reflected the culture's own naïve relationship to the world. By contrast, the contemporary period's self-conscious reworkings accurately mirrored the audience's increasingly ironic attempts to deal with historical events in the traditional terms." (298)

It is in fact a much more radical work than has previously been described. In refusing to privilege or advocate the individual protagonist, Towne's screenplay (in all drafts) actually negates the mythology which underwrites the text – not merely the mythology of the private eye but the mythos of America itself, and the powerful metaphor that '*Chinatown*' became, without ever being visualised in his first draft: it is instead verbalised and internalised as theme, trope and endgame. A common assumption about the film is that Polanski is the modernist and Towne the classicist, seeking a form of redemption – but the first ending was nothing less than downbeat compromise and is, simultaneously, probably truer to the film noir form, and more deadly, in terms of its dread of the future, than Polanski's Gordian closure in the literal location of the title; while Polanski's preferred, elliptical shooting style resulted in a narrative that, on close examination, makes no sense, dropping backstory in favour of quick cuts.

Robert Evans, whose patronage of and belief in Towne ensured that *Chinatown* was made according to the highest standards possible, should not be overlooked: he initiated the project, guided it, mastered the art of collaboration with the group of temperamental perfectionists writing, directing and starring in it, and enforced its classical excellence and may have elevated it to its now canonical status.[573] Everyone involved, therefore, brought distinctive authorial preoccupations to *Chinatown*. Evans says: "Till this day, Towne vents his anger toward me. How *could* I have sided with Roman? Poor Robert, for all his *schreien* he copped his one and only Oscar for this 'fucked up' *Chinatown*. Subjectivity rarely allows the artist the proper perspective he needs to judge the merits of his work. An overview is needed, showing your canvas for the objective eye to critique." [574]

The film is, then, a triumph of authorship for screenwriter *and* director *and* producer *and* actor, a forceful collaboration that demands to be read in terms of Hollywood pragmatism and artistic dues; a superb exercise in, and refutation of, genre and studio filmmaking, that provides a scathing insight into venal behaviour; a damning analysis of modernity, development, and the pure greed that built the city of Los Angeles. It is, quite simply, a great, if flawed, film – if it were not, the screenplay would have been ignored - and remains widely viewed as the quintessential achievement of 1970s American cinema, whose credits state more forcefully than any other commentary the true story behind the film:

'Written by Robert Towne

---

[573] Polanski was not present for the editing as he left to direct an opera at Spoleto; Evans dumped the score Polanski commissioned and hired Jerry Goldsmith who composed a now classic soundtrack. Towne attended the editing at Evans' house and throughout post-production. Polanski also had to have the print reworked following Evans' attempts to create a sepia image from the negative, GODFATHER- style.

[574] Robert Evans. *Op.cit.*, 265. David E. James makes a case for the producer as author in his study of Andy Warhol in *ALLEGORIES OF CINEMA: American Film in the Sixties*. New Jersey: Princeton University Press, 1989, 84: "… Warhol showed how that function controlled and determined all others in the communications industry. In doing so, he called into question the rhetoric of romantic authorship, clarifying film as commodity production writing itself as textual production. He thus brought into visibility what such romantic rhetoric had obscured: that making film is a social and material act taking place in history."

Produced by Robert Evans
Directed by Roman Polanski.
Starring Jack Nicholson.'

It may be, as Christopher Sandford's biography of Polanski suggests, that this was the perfect fusion of Old Hollywood and New Hollywood. [575] Ultimately, it remains the personal statement of its writer, Robert Towne. It was of course the first part of a planned trilogy, which would only ever see a second film in *The Two Jakes* (1990), a compromised version of Towne's original (as are perhaps *all* screenplays), *Two Jakes*. Ironically, it would be the triptych of *Chinatown* itself, 1971-1973, which would perhaps comprise Towne's compendium of regret. This is clarified in an interview which he gave twenty years after the film had been released, and four years after the release of its troubled sequel, *The Two Jakes* aka *Two Jakes*, which was directed by Jack Nicholson:

> ... I thought at the time I was going to direct it...
> the only way that a writer can have control over his work ... full
> control ... and even then it's illusory, is by directing. [576]

This is an admission which has never been probed by an interviewer and is the only time on record that Towne uttered this ambition in relation to *Chinatown*. Perhaps he meant it as the truth; or perhaps it was a necessary part of his rewriting of that part of his career which has unfortunately remained at the centre of any discussion of his work.

The screenplay has recently been voted the third best of all time by the Writers' Guild of America. And, as we have observed through the drafts, to the extent that Horowitz suggests, *Chinatown* is the lens through which all of Towne's work is viewed (retrospectively), we have here a model which strongly backs up this claim. We can see that Towne successfully integrates myth (that of the private eye) and reality, in a narrative which is ready-supplied by the city of Los Angeles, classical Hollywood and contemporary literature and remains a constant in Towne's work. Let us remind ourselves of Monaco's assertion, that "... myth and reality are closely interconnected. Real myths, those artistic evidences of our collective unconscious, spring directly from roots in reality, they heighten reality and condense it." [577] For Towne they were the

---

[575] Christopher Sandford. *POLANSKI*. London: Century Books, 2007, 252-253. Chris Petit's review ponders the unmentionable – what would Polanski's career have been like if he hadn't been so short?! *The Guardian*, Review, 16 October 2007. Accessed online at www.books.guardian.co.uk/reviews. Robin Wood, discussing Howard Hawks, comments, "however frustrating it may be for the scholar to find his attempts at sorting out the specific details of authorships defeated by the sheer complexity of the interconnections, this dense cross-fertilization is one of the greatest strengths of the American cinema." And: "One has the sense that Hawks's achievement, the richness of his art, depends on the complex cross-fertilizations of Hollywood genre cinema." 'To Have (Written) and Have Not (Directed),' reprinted in Nichols, (ed.), 1982, 301; 305. Lovell and Sergi state: "The evidence does not suggest that the coherence of the film depends on the 'vision' of one person. The involvement of the contributors with each other is like a spider's web with the script at the heart of it... If there is one element around which all the contributions cohere, it is the script." As before, 97.

[576] Towne speaking at the Harold Lloyd Master Seminar, AFI, 1994. Accessed online at www.afi.com.

[577] Monaco, 1979, 251.

complementary parts of a storytelling spiral: it was a model from which he would only intermittently depart over the following thirty or so years.

As a finished film, it probably represents the best case for collaborative authorship in the Towne career, given the parts played by Evans, Polanski and Jack Nicholson in the shaping of the material and the way in which it was filmed. It is certainly the most complex, yet also the most relentlessly personal of Towne's screenplays, disguising his father as Julian/Noah; paying homage to his beloved films noirs, detective fiction and his city of dreams and nightmares; taking the mythical American bourgeois aspiration to task and trussing it up in a Biblical nightmare of rape, drought, pillage and incest. Despite the variety of talent involved in bringing Towne's story to the screen, and paraphrasing Robin Wood, we might suggest that *Chinatown* is simply a great work of art that actually transcends the personality and values of the people behind it. [578]

The Parallax View (1974) (uncredited)

Towne was hired as a script doctor again. Warren Beatty's paranoid conspiracy melodrama wasn't supposed to happen, in the way that it did. It wasn't Beatty's production; it was his first work after the McGovern campaign; he argued constantly with director Alan J. Pakula; then there was a writers' strike and Beatty got heavily involved in the rewrites And nobody would have known of Towne's eventual rewrite of Beatty's rewrites if Peter Bart, head of MGM at the time, hadn't wound up giving the game away, albeit many years later, to Peter Biskind, a trusted chronicler and historian, whose notorious *EASY RIDERS, RAGING BULLS*, opened a kind of Pandora's Box of dubious anecdotes, half-truths and downright lies to a public eager for the cocaine-fuelled romance of Seventies cinema, a touchstone for the auteur years. Robert Towne broke the strike.

> "In that book Peter Bart mentioned *The Parallax View*, which he had no fucking right to do... it was during a strike. Bart was an executive at the time, he should have known better." [579]

Towne followed David Giler, who succeeded the original writer, Lorenzo Semple Jr., in adapting the eponymous novel. Giler and Semple split the credits, despite its having been heavily rewritten by Towne. In his faux-biography, David Thomson recounts Beatty's involvement with Robert Kennedy's campaign for election in the Winter of 1967, until the candidate's assassination, an incident that would haunt Beatty

---

[578] Robin Wood. *PERSONAL VIEWS*, 248. Towne described the reasons for his problem with the imposed ending as follows: "At Roman's insistence there were alterations to *Chinatown* I'll always be uncomfortable with. For example, I felt at the time it would be more consistent with the tone of the film if it ended with Evelyn killing her father and being punished by the law. I felt that if there was a tiny ray of hope at the end then all the malevolence would stand out all the more sharply. It would underline the tragedy. I wanted it to be fatalistic but I was worried that Polanski's ending would be too overwhelming. And I was always against setting the final scene actually *in Chinatown*. In my version Chinatown wouldn't have figured in any material sense at all because I wanted it to stand as a symbol. I felt the metaphor would sustain itself, and to bring in the location was heavy-handed." Pirie, 1981, 153. Towne's acknowledging of the importance of tone and metaphor in his work should be noted.

[579] Towne commenting on Peter Bart's remarks in *EASY RIDERS, RAGING BULLS*, in an interview with Michael Atkinson of *The Guardian*, 'A Lot of What Has Gone Wrong Was the Result of Choices I Made,' *The Guide*, 29 May 1999: 6.

and influence his decision-making on *The Parallax View*, which Semple claimed was 'fatal' to the source novel's intentions and calls it "a combination of the very obscure and the very obvious." [580] Save for the above, Towne has never commented.

Shampoo (1975) (written by Robert Towne and Warren Beatty) [581]

James Monaco makes the claim for *Shampoo* that it is "Robert Towne and Warren Beatty's existential statement about the New Hollywood." [582] However in an economic analysis of the industry, Douglas Gomery states "that in terms of economic structure and power, little changed in the American film industry during the Seventies, despite all the pundit's claims." [583] The seven companies that had always dominated the business continued to do so, and maintained their power he says "through revenues rather than by making all the films. During the Seventies the majors earned 90% of the revenues with only about one-third of the Motion Picture Association of America rated films. The other two-thirds had to settle for 10% of the revenues." [584] The international distribution network continued to underpin the powerful structures that ran the American film business. The majors were still making A and B films and often screened double features. This was the era just before mass releasing, which dominates the American industry today, and a film could still do well on word of mouth alone.

The old style of platforming films in certain key cities no longer worked and the studios were keen to capitalise on what could be perceived to be a more national culture, courtesy of television's penetration. Interest rates had risen since the onset of Vietnam and it was crucial to take advantage of quick releases in order to pay off heavy loans. Fast distribution was now a priority and as Sklar points out, "the potential overrode the risk." 1975 would prove the key year for this strategy and it was *Jaws* that hit the jackpot, with a massive TV campaign to herald the saturation exhibition schedule. [585] It was also the year in which *Shampoo* was released.

A number of factors, and people, contributed to the writing of *Shampoo*. Towne was in London with Warren Beatty and Julie Christie in 1969 and saw a Restoration Comedy which reminded him of his TV script, 'So Many Pretty Women, So Little Time': 'The Country Wife' was being revived at the Chichester Festival, with Maggie Smith in a leading role. With its origins in sexually explicit Greek theatre and taking its more immediate inspiration from the contemporary scabrous social comedies of Moliére, Restoration Comedy's origins clearly lay in the satyr play and its popularity undoubtedly derived from the immediately preceding period which was dominated by Puritanism. [586]

---

[580] Thomson, 1987, 334-341. 'A Screenwriter on Screenwriting: Lorenzo Semple Jr.,' is in Pirie. *Op.cit.*, 156-157. Towne's essay precedes Semple's in the book.

[581] The origins, production history and screenplay are comprehensively examined by Elaine Lennon in 'The Edge of Melancholy: *Shampoo*,' in *Senses of Cinema*, 37, Oct-Dec 2005. Accessible via www.sensesofcinema.com.

[582] James Monaco, 1979, 296.

[583] Douglas Gomery, 'The American Film Industry of the 1970s: Stasis in the ' "New Hollywood",' *Wide Angle*, 1983 Vol. 5 No. 4: 52.

[584] *Ibid.*

[585] Sklar. *MOVIE-MADE AMERICA: A Cultural History of American Movies.* New York: Vintage Books, 1994, 324.

[586] *THE BEDFORD INTRODUCTION TO DRAMA* (2nd ed.) defines the satyr play as, "a comic play performed after the tragic trilogy in Greek tragedy competitions. The satyr play provided comic relief and was usually a farcical, boisterous treatment of mythological material Boston: Bedford Books, 1993, 1394). Pauline Kael's review of the film alludes to the theatrical

Character names in the play are typically emblematic and witty, while Wycherley's London is full of debauchery, populated seemingly exclusively by whores, flirts, seducers and cuckolds. The story concerns a man, Horner, who convinces his friends that he has been rendered a eunuch by his doctor (Doctor Quack), so that they will trust him with their wives. Foolishly, as it transpires. A variety of couplings and misunderstandings ensues against a comical depiction of contemporary London society, told over five acts with a brief prologue and epilogue.

Towne had been dating a divorcee whose ex-husband was legendary Beverly Hills hairdresser Gene Shacove (Hugh Hefner's stylist), whom Towne had (incorrectly) presumed to be homosexual, yet who still did his ex-wife's hair. Towne described the hairdressing fraternity as

> A whole subculture of wildly heterosexual guys with a great sense of design, who worked on human heads instead of pieces of paper. I was fascinated by it, thought it was a terrific subject. [587]

---

dimension of the film: "The balletic, patterned confusion of *Shampoo* is theatrical, and Los Angeles – more particularly, Beverly Hills, the swankest part of it, a city within a city – is, indisputably, a stylized theatrical setting. But a bedroom-chase construction isn't stagey in Beverly Hills: *Shampoo* has a mathematically structured plot in an open society. Los Angeles itself, the sprawl-city, opens the movie up, and the L.A. sense of freedom makes its own comment on the scrambling characters. Besides, when you play musical chairs in the bedrooms of Beverly Hills, the distances you have to cover impose their own comic frenzy. As in a Feydeau play or some of the René Clair and Lubitsch films, the more complicated the interaction is, the more we look forward to the climactic muddle and the final sorting out of couples. The whirring pleasures of carnal farce require our awareness of the mechanics, and the director, Hal Ashby, has the deftness to keep us conscious of the structure and yet to give it free play. The plot isn't arbitrary; it's what George, who can never really get himself together, is caught in. The mixed pairs of lovers don't get snarled at the same parties by coincidence; they go knowing who else is going to be there, wanting the danger of collisions." Kael notes the differences between Towne's contemporary staging and classic theatre: The actors are much more free than in the confines of classic farce. They're free, too, of the stilted witticisms of classic farce: Towne writes such easy, unforced dialogue that they might be talking in their own voices." 'Beverly Hills as a Big Bed,' reprinted in *REELING: Film Writings 1972-1975*, London and New York: Marion Boyars, 1992, 437-438.

[587] Towne in Joel Engel. 217-218. Beatty and producer Charles Feldman had been close for a number of years. In the 50s Feldman had bought the rights to a Czech play about a Don Juan, called 'Lot's Wife', as a vehicle for Cary Grant, who turned it down. Then Feldman decided it was right for Beatty (who didn't want Feldman's girlfriend, Capucine, to have a role in the film.) Beatty's catchphrase to women on the telephone was, 'What's new, pussycat?' and Feldman took that as a title for the screenplay by I.A.L. Diamond. Neither Beatty nor Feldman was happy with Diamond's work and gave the project to Woody Allen, who boosted his own role at Beatty's expense. And Capucine reappeared. Beatty walked and the deal with Feldman was off, but the film was made and was a huge hit. See Peter Biskind's article, 'The Man Who Minted Style,' in *Vanity Fair*, April 2003: 100-111; and also David Thomson, *WARREN BEATTY AND DESERT EYES A Life and a Story*. New York: Vintage Books, 1987. Gene Shacove would serve as technical consultant on the film.

Unlike Restoration Comedy, *Shampoo* ends badly, with a negative coda offering a chill reflection on the contemporary environment, despite its ostensible setting in the previous decade.

The Writing

Beatty initially hired Towne to write a draft for a fee of $25,000 while they were making *Bonnie and Clyde*. Towne experienced writer's block in 1968 and 1969 and it led to difficulties with Beatty. By 31 December 1969 Towne still had not produced a draft. Beatty went ahead and made *McCabe and Mrs Miller* (1971) with director Robert Altman and co-star Julie Christie. Allegedly, he and Towne didn't speak for months.[588] When shooting was wrapped, Beatty wrote his own draft of the script while holidaying on Sam Spiegel's boat – but Towne had turned in a draft the previous January, which Beatty thought lacked a proper structure. So, there were two versions of the script and Beatty agreed to work with Towne.

Beatty had demonstrated a great deal of courage when he produced *Bonnie and Clyde* and he appears to have asked Towne for a co-writing credit on *Shampoo* – and got it.[589] Towne took time over the writing and the film was going to be made at Paramount, with Robert Evans hiring Hal Ashby to direct. Ashby, Evans and Towne holed up for a week in December 1973 (at the time of the release of *The Last Detail* and possibly subsequent to Towne's revision of *The Yakuza*) and worked on a draft. It is said that Towne felt his control of the script had been diluted.[590]

Tone and Character

Towne has commented that his script for the film was largely influenced by Jean Renoir's *La Règle du Jeu*. [591] The people populating *Shampoo* are as follows - George Roundy, the naïf hero; Jill, George's fiancée; Jackie, Lester's mistress, George's ex; Felicia Karpf, George's lover, married to Lester Karpf, businessman, Jackie's lover; Lorna Karpf, Felicia and Lester's daughter; Norman, George's boss at the salon; Johnny Pope, director, dating Jill. While there is no obviously direct correlation between the cast of

---

[588] Hal Ashby said that of Beatty that "when Towne had finally written the script and given it to him to read, he was so angry with it that he sat down the next day and wrote his own version. I read both versions, and I told him I thought it would make an interesting film because of the interactions between the characters. And he and I sat down and we took pages from each one just to get an overall idea." Ralph Appelbaum, 'Positive Thinking: Hal Ashby Interview,' *Films and Filming*, July 1978: 16. It is notable that Beatty apparently turned down the scripts that would become the cornerstones of Robert Redford's career: *Butch Cassidy and the Sundance Kid*, *The Sting*, *The Way We Were*; and *The Great Gatsby*, which Towne also turned down as a writing project in favour of *Chinatown*.

[589] Beatty has said however, " It was Towne that offered me the screen credit. I would have been happy to go to arbitration. The story had no political context with Robert, no Nixon, no nothing. All of that is 99% me, my work. We used to meet every fucking day and I'd have to tell him the goddamn story. It's absolutely not true that every line of dialogue is his. It's an outrageous lie. Both party sequences were written by me, none of those were in Towne's original draft at all. That's half the movie. This idea of his being upset about credit is insane. Half the fuckin' time he didn't show up on the set, he'd be at the doctor." Biskind. *Op.cit.*, 305.

[590] Hal Ashby never took writing credits on those films he directed but it should be noted that, as with *The Last Detail*, he was known for the care he bestowed on screenplays he was shooting. David Thomson says this was particularly the case with *Coming Home*. Thomson, 1981, 83.

[591] Towne introduced a screening of *La Grande Illusion* in Los Angeles in the winter of 2006 as a way of acknowledging his debt to Renoir who, before he himself died, had intended screening *Shampoo* and following it up with a public question and answer session.

characters in 'The Country Wife' and that of *Shampoo*, the inspiration for Roundy is quite clear in that of Horner, and Mr and Mrs Pinchwife are probably a mirror image of the cuckolded Lester and Felicia Karpf. [592] The name 'Jackie' is probably intended as an iconic reference to the former Jackie Kennedy, now Onassis, whose departure from the United States following Robert Kennedy's assassination chimes nicely with the sentiment (and setting) of the film.

Ashby agreed to direct *Shampoo* despite knowing that Beatty wouldn't allow him much control of the project. Ashby's previous films had not been hits and he respected Beatty. Beatty was responsible for hiring key cast: Julie Christie, Goldie Hawn, Lee Grant and Jack Warden - who would feature in virtually all of Beatty's projects, right up to *Bulworth* (1998). In the meantime, *Detail* was released in time for Oscar nominations in December 1973 and proved very popular. It was at this time that Asbhy, Towne and Beatty set about rewriting *Shampoo* in Beatty's suite at the Beverly Wilshire. The film went into production in January 1974.

It is to Beatty's credit, as David Thomson points out, that *Shampoo*'s

> great insight is to see how far the Beverly Hills hairdresser is a servant who may have more power, knowledge and intimacy than lovers or tycoons. For he conjures appearance: when George softens and enhances Jackie for the party, when he lifts her out of weary, common attractiveness into beauty, it is the greatest gift that movies or LA know. It is the generosity that could seduce anyone there – the accurate understanding of how they might be beautiful… This is not just cosmetics; it is only grace that makes people feel better about themselves. [593]

The film moves quickly, as though time were running out, from its opening moments on black with The Beach Boy's song 'Wouldn't It Be Nice' ironically underscoring George and Felicia making love (*Wouldn't it be niiiice? …. We could be married, then we could be happy, wouldn't it be niiice?*)

The characters are drawn in equal measure subtly and periodically, with George announcing grandiloquently to Felicia, 'I'm a star,' but the editing echoes his nervous narcissism, with his worst moment, outside the Bank of America, allowed to exist simply, a long shot at the back door with George trashing his non-existent financial statement. [594]

Diane Jacobs claims that "Ashby's editing is flawless" with its fast movement and ensemble shots. As she points out, "only a few scenes – one between Beatty and Christie in a bathroom is memorable – are attenuated. Like the characters whose lives it glimpses, the film moves at a frenzied pace and is careful not to reveal too much of itself for fear we'll notice the scores on the underbelly and stop laughing." [595] The film is shot cleanly and crisply, drenched in Southern Californian sunshine and reeking of wealth. The effect is maximised by setting the film over a twenty-four period in the fashion of

---

[592] Roundy reminds us of the Roundhouse production but it also connotes the circular shape of the screenplay; inspiration from *La Ronde*; and the fact that George goes round in circles, getting nowhere, as Jackie tells him (see dialogue originating on p.80-81 of screenplay.) Jackie and Jill might be seen as a play on the nursery rhyme, which has its narrative and rhythmic inevitability. Felicia might be seen to be plundering happiness wherever it can be found. Jacobs describes the screenplay as "a cross between a Sheridan comedy and a game of Clue." Jacobs. *Op.cit.*, 229.

[593] Thomson, 1987, 351-352.

[594] The only financial statement George makes is "I do Barbara Rush."

[595] Jacobs. *Op.cit.*, 230.

operatic and Aristotelian principles and a repeated word, 'great,' which is rendered entirely meaningless it is repeated so falsely, so many times: it has the virtue of being a leitmotif for the feelings it is inevitably suppressing.

Figure 12 George (Warren Beatty) gives Jackie (Julie Christie) a blow dry

Critical Method: Plot and Character

A protagonist (or hero, if indeed the protagonist is heroic) is the driving force of any story. In the Aristotelian formulation, 'we are what we do.' In other words, behaviour is character, character is behaviour. In the Stanislavskian method, the energy of a character is often a product of tension, between what a character wants and what they feel they should do. As promulgated by Lee Strasberg, 'Method Acting' as it came to be known via the Group Theater and the work of Elia Kazan, came to be the most formidable influence on American screen (and stage) acting style for many years (and it has never really left the consciousness.) Acting is no longer acting, it is behaviour, linked to an inner life. While this may have led to unseemly actorly excesses, it coincided with a huge social change owed in equal parts to Freudian analysis and the uncertainties of the post-World War II era.

While Towne claims, rather ingenuously, not to be aware of screenplay structure, the key points of the screenplay are the emotional turning points that have to do with George's relationships with Jill and Jackie. Any screenplay's structure is gauged according to the shifting perception of the protagonist, therefore we can 'read' the text of *Shampoo* according to George's growing realisation of his own (increasingly grim) situation.

> It's a movie about people who seem to be looking for things they don't really want, people who are accepting views of themselves they don't really want… Only George hasn't accepted somebody else's view of himself. He's very sweet: he never seduces anybody. He's really the girl in the movie. [596]

Given that George is the protagonist, or chief character, he is the one person about whom the story's events are centred and the person who is chiefly affected by anything that happens. (Pauline Kael says of him, "George, the sexual courier, servicing a

---

[596] Towne quoted in Gene Siskel, 'Movies: Robert Towne – script, scalpel, action. Oscar,' *Chicago Tribune*, 9 May 1976, Section 6: 6.

garden apartment as ardently as a terraced estate, is a true democrat... the only one of the characters who isn't completely selfish; he's the only one who doesn't function successfully in the society. The others know how to use people, but George, the compleat lover, does everything for fun. Making love to a beautiful woman is an aesthetic thing with him, and making her look beautiful is an act of love for him. He's almost a sexual saint... Towne's heroes... are hip to conventional society, and they assume that they reject its dreams. But in some corner of their heads they think that maybe the old romantic dream can be made to work." [597]) In making the choice about who the protagonist might be, the writer is choosing something that will determine the entire nature of their story. The protagonist can be viewed in two ways – in close-up; and in relation to the social world about them. Not only that, but the protagonist must grow over the course of the story, if only in knowledge about their own particular situation. Lawson advises that the protagonist must be active in order to drive the plot; that he must be committed to something and forced to take action because of that commitment. [598]

What must then be addressed is what is at stake for the character and how much he might lose over the course of the story: the more he has to lose, the more conflict there is – and conflict is the stuff of drama. Kristin Thompson comments that "protagonists in classical Hollywood films seldom change quickly, and when they do change, they usually acquire desirable traits which they retain to the end ... plots in which central characters gradually reform or mature are common in American films." [599]

Figure 13 George rides through Beverly Hills on his BSA

While gently laughing at its characters, however, *Shampoo* does not condemn them. As Thomson says, "it is always on the edge of melancholy, as if it knew the horror of aging and decay. Its ambiguity grows out of the very level way in which so many characters are seen. No one is rejected, or seen as without faults." [600]

So what is the underlying, unifying idea behind *Shampoo*? The following scene appears to encapsulate the film's message regarding sexual politics and hypocrisy:

INT.BISTRO

---

[597] Kael, 'Beverly Hills as a Big Bed,' as before, 437.
[598] Adapted from John Howard Lawson, *THEORY AND TECHNIQUE OF PLAYWRITING* (reprinted by Garland, New York, 1985, 168).
[599] Kristin Thompson, 2001, 50.
[600] He calls it "a lucid moral disaster, with resemblances to comedy of confusion." Thomson. 1987, 352.

SID ROTH has been eyeing Jackie.

                    SID ROTH
          Aren't you hungry, Miss Shawn?

Jackie looks at Roth. Roth shoots his cuffs and smiles.

                    JACKIE
          Not for rubber chicken, no.

Sid Roth smiles. Jackie smiles back.

                    SID ROTH
                 (intime)
          Well maybe I can get you something.

                                        CONTINUED

                    JACKIE
          That's very sweet of you, Mr Roth.

                    SID ROTH
          Sid.

                    JACKIE
          Sid. You must be a very important
          executive.

                    SID ROTH
              (almost a whisper)
          Well, whatever I am, I think I can
          get you whatever you'd like.

                    JACKIE
          You do?

                    SID ROTH
          Yes.
                    JACKIE
                 (same tone as Sid's)
          - - well, more than anything else - -
          - - I'd like to suck his cock.

She points to George. George chokes on the last of a
piece of chicken. Sid Roth is stunned. He doesn't know
what to do. George is coughing badly. Jackie slaps his
back.

                              (*Shampoo*: 94-95)

Figure 14 Publicity shot from the results dinner

Warren Beatty is quoted as saying,

> The subject of *Shampoo* is hypocrisy, the commingling of sexual hypocrisy and political hypocrisy. The reason Julie's line made for such an explosive moment was because it shredded that hypocrisy. [601]

Reportedly, when David Begelman saw this scene he was appalled, and asked Beatty to remove it: Beatty refused, saying it was the film's best line. The screenplay however makes three mentions of prostitution, and the idea of receiving money for sex is implied throughout. [602]

The first turning point in *Shampoo* could be said to be when George is turned down for a loan at the Bank of America:

```
INT.BANK OF AMERICA - DAY

                    GEORGE
      How do you expect to lend me money
      if you don't know the first thing
      about my business?
                    PETTIS
      I don't.
```

(Rewritten scene from *Shampoo*: 19-20)

This has the effect of making him turn to Lester Karpf for financing, and he meets Jackie again. This sets Act Two in motion.

What could be determined as the midpoint sequence in *Shampoo* takes place approximately between 51 and 53 minutes in terms of running time, and on pages 80/81 of the script.[603]

---

[601] Biskind. *Op.cit.,* 302.

[602] Jackie says Lester is great because it's great to wake up knowing your rent is paid; George tells Jackie her hairstyle makes her look like a hooker; when Lester calls Jackie a whore, George says you could call everyone that. George distances himself from any such accusation, however, saying that he doesn't fuck for money, he does it for fun.

[603] Please note that the copy of the script being used for this analysis bears several substantially

In this scene, the following exchange takes place between Jill and George:

                    JILL
        Well are they going to give you
        the loan?… I don't know why I
        bothered to ask. The only way
        you're ever going to get money out
        of a bank is to rob one![604]

                    GEORGE
        What are you so mad about?

                    JILL
        Oh, just fix my hair. You break
        your neck to go up to Jackie's,
        when do I get my hair done?

                    GEORGE
        She asked me to do her hair.

                    JILL
        Does that mean you have to do
        whatever anybody asks? Why am I
        always at the end of the line when
        you're passing out favors?

                    GEORGE
        You want me to do your hair, I'll
        do your hair.

                    JILL
        And stop kissing everybody's ass
        that comes into that shop. That's
        not going to put you in business,
        that's gonna make you a kiss ass.

                    GEORGE
        I'm trying to get things moving.

                    JILL
        Oh grow up! You never stop moving.
        You never go anywhere! Grow up!
        Grow up!

                    GEORGE

different scenes than those in the film as released and was the one used by casting agent Jane
Feinberg. Therefore I am merely repeating the dialogue in this scene, as spoken in the film,
without adding any physical descriptions or commentary.
[604] This is of course a nod to Beatty as Clyde Barrow.

```
Honey … I just can't take it any
more.  I want to get up early and
run my own business.  I want to
take you out to a movie on the
weekend.  I'm trying, honey, I
just can't get out of my own way.
```

(Rewritten from *Shampoo*: 80-81)

Thematically, this is the stage where George is beginning to alter what he *desires* with a dawning realisation of what he might actually *need* in order to have a really fulfilling life; it is also the point that Jill begins to realise that she would be better off without him. Thus the midpoint serves in microcosm to deal with the film's principal concerns and draws out the protagonist's situation in relation to the narrative structure. This exchange of dialogue dramatises the problem.

Figure 15 Jill (Goldie Hawn) doesn't allow Richard Nixon to distract her from George

According to contemporary screenwriting manuals, based on years of observing Hollywood screenplay structures, a character's graph is represented by a rising arc of self-awareness, with a catharsis that betrays the protagonist's ultimate need, which has been masked by their desire all along. However when a protagonist is heedless and amoral, like George, it can cause a problem with critical (or even audience) reception. (This did not seem to affect *Tom Jones* (1962) however, possibly due to its period setting and its emphatic delight in sheer bawdiness.)

According to Trottier,

> Plot grows from character because everything starts with a character who has a goal. [605]

We return to the notion of the emplotted character seeking his own identity. George is seeking, however inadvertently or passively, to unseat that disturbance in his own life – the women around him who want more from him than he is able to provide – but as he unwittingly rids himself of their presence in the process of attempting to achieve his aim, a salon of his own, he (logically) finds himself alone. He gets what he neither wants, nor needs.

---

[605] David Trottier. *THE SCREENWRITER'S BIBLE: A Complete Guide to Writing, Formatting, and Selling Your Script.* Los Angeles: Silman-James Press, 2005, 29.

In the *Time* magazine review of *Shampoo*, Jay Cocks states his problem with this seemingly superficial protagonist:

> As played, deftly, by Beatty, George is an affable con man who goes no deeper than his own hypocrisy. [606]

Kristin Thompson states that that portion of a film lying between setup and climax "often follows a trajectory that depends on more than simply throwing obstacles in the protagonist's path – that trajectory includes modifications of existing goals or even the formation of entirely new goals." [607] It is certainly noticeable that George achieves greater moments of depth when he confronts his own emptiness, and comes to terms with the consequences of leading a pleasurable life as a stud/satyr, but is that not an element of character structuring?

Lawson says that

> It is the sometimes conflicting dynamic between what a character acknowledges to be his goal and his unconscious motivation that drives a story forward. [608]

George is a man of principles, however: when Lester Karpf accuses him of being 'anti-Establishment' he is horrified: "I'm not anti-Establishment!' And when Jackie confronts him about his involvement with Felicia Karpf, he says, "I don't fuck anybody for money, I do it for fun."

When he asks Jackie why she left him, why she didn't settle down with him, she replies,

```
                    JACKIE
          You're always so happy.   About
          everything!
```

Diane Jacobs comments,

> fortunately, Towne and Ashby stop here, short of pathos or (more likely) bathos. There's a wonderful line in [Paul] Mazursky's *Next Stop, Greenwich Village* where the actors tells the poet, 'I'll tell you something: underneath that pose, there's just more pose.' This is not quite true with George. Beneath the pose, there's trouble, but we sense that the trouble is not particularly interesting; his behavior is the stuff of comedy, of social satire – not of tragedy. And thus, we leave him and his society probed a bit, but essentially unchanged and surviving. [609]

This outcome is true to Towne's repeated bittersweet, compromised endings.

The Scene Sequence

Shampoo is structured around two important social gatherings, in a pair of scene-sequences that operate to bring many of the film's concerns to the fore.[610] One is the

---

[606] From Lawrence Quirk. *THE FILMS OF WARREN BEATTY*. New York: Citadel Press, 1990, 193.
[607] Kristin Thompson. *Op.cit.*, 52.
[608] Lawson. *Op.cit.*, 168.
[609] Jacobs. *Op.cit.*, 230-231.
[610] And rumoured to have been written by Beatty.

bistro party for the election returns, the other is the counter-culture party at Sammy's, where further truths are unveiled. Cowgill describes scene sequences as a group of scenes "structured in cause and effect relationships, showing the protagonist of the sequence trying to accomplish something. They are also structured around the confrontation of an obstacle, complication or problem. Characters have to deal with this problem and produce a plan of action to do it." [611] Syd Field describes a sequence as, "a series of scenes tied together, or connected, by one single idea." [612] They can be variable in their length, structure and focus and can either encompass events leading to a problem or can begin with the problem and then build towards some kind of solution. Both of these techniques are evident in the major scene-sequences in *Shampoo*.

The second turning point in the film takes place again in a scene between George and Jill after she has caught him *in flagrante delicto* with Jackie at Sammy's party and confronts him back at her apartment. He finally lets loose with a valedictory speech that explains his philosophy:[613]

GEORGE

Let's face it, I fucked 'em all. I mean,
that's what I do. That's why I went to beauty
school. I mean, they're always there – and
I don't know what I'm apologising for, so
sometimes I fuck 'em. I go into that shop and
they're so great looking, you know…
and I'm doin' their hair and they feel great
and they smell great … you know, and I could be
just on the street or stop at a stop light
or go into an elevator or there's a beautiful
girl … I don't know …
I mean, that's it – it makes my day – makes me
feel like I'm gonna live forever. As far as
I'm concerned with what I'd like to have done
at this point in my life? I know I should've
accomplished more but I got no regrets – Jesus
– aahhh… maybe that means I don't love
them. Maybe that means I don't love you. I
don't know. Nobody's gonna tell me I don't
like 'em very much.

(as transcribed from the film)

This takes place approximately 86 minutes into the film and, as originally written in the script, on page 130.

Towne says of the on-set problems with the scene:

---

[611] Cowgill. *Op.cit.*, 174.

[612] Field. *Op.cit.*, 96.

[613] Matthew Wilder says this scene is "probably the single strongest moment of Towne's and Beatty's careers. George's crack-up in front of his favorite girlfriend (Goldie Hawn), a scene in which George's and Beatty's inabilities to tell the truth on every imaginable level merge in a Pirandellian conceit of staggering genius." 'Your Guide to the Stars: Robert Towne Maps the Psychology of the American Bad-Ass,' www.citypages.com, Vol.27, No. 1315, 15 February 2006.

There were three of us behind the camera. If one of us wasn't satisfied with a take, it was done over. In the celebrated scene between Warren and Goldie where she asks, 'Were there other women?' and he replies, 'Well, there were a few times at the shop – Let's face it, I fucked them all ...' Originally, he said, 'Grow up, everybody fucks everybody.' Warren was towering over Goldie, so it seemed like he fucked everybody and was lecturing her about it. I called for a reshoot. Hal thought it was okay, and Warren, being the prudent producer, was reluctant, but I insisted, and then he got mad at me for not having realised that it was fucked up before we shot it. I went for a walk with my dog Hira and realised that Warren had to be sitting down and Goldie towering over him, and that his this speech had to be personal. It had to be torn out of him, so I did a rewrite.[614]

George seems almost surprised when Jill tells him to leave but he drives home where Lester is waiting for him with two hoods. Lester might be willing to finance George's shop, despite all that has happened. George then goes to the salon where he discovers that Norman's son (a soldier, on his way back to active duty) has been killed in a car crash. (This was originally going to be Mary's son, who was serving in Vietnam.) George then realises what he must do – and begs Jackie to marry him. She leaves for Acapulco, with Lester. [615] " The last page of the original screenplay bears the legend:

```
TO BE WRITTEN:
        A page and a half epilogue between
Mrs. Jackie Karpf and George in his quite
successful shop in 1974.
```

It was never shot.

George is left rather like Jake Gittes: essentially unable to comprehend his situation, and oblivious of the sweeping effect his entanglement with the mystery of the women in his life. This is consistent with Towne's earlier remark about Evelyn Mulwray in *Chinatown*. [616]

Metaphor & Motif
The obvious symbolic motif in the film is the hair and hair styling: these moments in the salon and in Jackie's house provide intimacy and an opportunity to create subtext. (Pauline Kael says that when George asks Jackie if she wants him to do her hair, it's his love lyric.) When Lester is confronted with his infidelity at the bistro, all

---

[614] Towne in Biskind. *Op.cit.,* 194. His last comment may be telling of his admiration for Polanski's technique in the sister/daughter scene in *Chinatown*. Ashby said of Towne: "I don't know a writer that's as good as Bob Towne. I don't know anybody that even comes close to him. He's in a whole other league." He continued on *Shampoo*: "It comes to life better than the reading of it. I prefer to be much looser with a script and pick up things as I go along. That has to do with my own thing about spontaneity in film." 'Dialogue on Film,' *American Film*, May 1980: 59.

[615] David Thomson, in his typically fantastical way ventures another ending: "*Shampoo* might end more challengingly if it had a vision other than the producer's, or one that could be colder in looking at him. It might end more challengingly if the forlorn George was cheered up by the film's most frightening character, the Carrie Fisher part, in a blunt, unadorned, unalleviated scene of sexual excess, a home movie of them getting it on, with her sucking George's ankle and Warren's faraway face watching, nearly deserted." Thomson. *Op.cit.,* 355-356.

[616] See 'Dialogue On Film,' as before: 47.

he can think of saying to his wife and his mistress is that their hairstyles are 'fabulous.' (The irony of course is that George has cloned all his lovers – their hairstyles are identical.) At the film's climax, George's hair is a mess, Jackie's is great. Even Lester looks like he might have had the layering George recommended in desperation at the bistro.

George rides a BSA motorbike, which immediately marks him out in a city that is famed for its freeways – and his mode of transit (or narrative transition) is in stark contrast to the silver Rolls Royce preferred by Lester Karpf, and the signal red Porsche driven by director Johnny Pope, his rivals in love. It might even suggest that he is working class. [617] George's dumb luck is brought home to him with the news that Norman's soldier son is killed in a car crash, caused by another driver.

When we first meet George, he is having sex with Felicia and eats a red apple – a symbol straight out of fairytales (again, an ironic verbal reference) like Snow White. When George meets Felicia's precocious daughter Lorna, she offers him a baked apple: a clear invitation to sin. When Jill is considering her future with George, she pauses at a fruit and vegetable stall outside the grocery store. She takes up a green apple – and leaves it aside. This is also an ironic play on the Sixties/Seventies idea of 'fruit', with its homosexual connotations, which George uses to his advantage in 'gaying up' in front of his lovers' husbands (a spin on Horner's role of pretend-eunuch in Wycherley's play.)

Jill's apartment is characterised by Towne as 'good-little-girl tidy' (p.125) in contrast to the mess at Jackie's, who nonetheless has George's heart.

Lester says of George's own apartment, on page 132 of the script:

> LESTER
> (continuing)
> You live like a pig.

And on page 137:

> LESTER
> Jesus, what a way to live. You
> don't have a clean glass in the
> house...

Of course this thread of cleanliness as symbol, which of course is packed into a film about hair (and washing, combing through and styling) is completed at the film's climax when Jackie is finishing packing for Acapulco at her place. George finds her and the cleaners arrive shortly thereafter: the underlying idea, that it's finally time to clean up her act (and clean out the clutter from the closets), couldn't be more clear. The leitmotif for the film could well be *South Pacific*'s 'I'm Gonna Wash That Man Right Out of my Hair' but the film is bookended by The Beach Boys' 'Wouldn't It Be Nice,' which emphasises the yearning beneath George's braggadocio.[618] A number of late Sixties hits

[617] Chuck Kleinhans, '*Shampoo*: Oedipal Symmetries and Heterosexual Satire,' *Jump Cut*, No. 26 December 1981: 6. "George [goes] constantly from woman to woman – a movement underlined with numerous transition shots of him on his motorcycle. (One of the few instances in recent Hollywood film where transportation transition shots actually have a theme and character-revealing importance.)"(7).

had been named in the original script, but the film's final music was scored by Paul Simon with just a few excerpts of pop songs underlining the various scenes' lessons: The Beatles' 'Sergeant Pepper's Lonely Hearts Club Band' forms the backdrop to Sammy's party, a piece of music that diametrically opposes The Beach Boys' (supposedly) innocent desires, coming as it does from the mature side of The Beatles' body of work and subsequent to their mind-altering meetings with Ravi Shankar, the Maharishi and LSD: it perfectly expresses Towne's ongoing interest in the conflict between innocence and experience. The ultimate irony is that it is George, the insatiable lothario who is revealed as an innocent, his conquests the victors.

A Cultural Myth

Thomas Schatz has written of cinema's role in perpetuating myth that

> ... a myth is both true and false, both a clarification and a distortion of real-world experience and the human condition. It is, finally, a formalized means to negotiate the present via concepts and images which are the residue of human history. [619]

Shampoo is more than just a film of seductions and betrayals, as David Thomson would have it. The idea of capturing a specific time, and place, was something that had caught Towne's imagination in *Chinatown* and was now about the different atmosphere characterising the city with which he was so familiar as well as layering in political and cultural mythology to a specific time and place – 1968, and now.

Pauline Kael says of the film in her review,

> ...the picture is a sex roundelay set in a period as clearly defined as the Jazz Age... Maybe we've all been caught in a time warp, because the Beatles sixties of miniskirts and strobe lights, when people had not yet come down from their euphoria about the harmlessness of drugs, is already a period with its own bubbly potency. The time of *Shampoo* is so close to us that at moments we forget its pastness, and then we're stung by the consciousness of how much has changed. *Shampoo* is set in the past for containment, for a formalized situation, just as Ingmar Bergman set his boudoir farce, *Smiles of a Summer Night*, in the operetta past of the MERRY WIDOW period. What the turn-of-the-century metaphor did for Bergman the 1968 election, as the sum of an era, does for *Shampoo*. [620]

The film thus utilised its boomerang effect to discuss the contemporary as well as the past, rather like *Chinatown*. As Diane Jacobs puts it, "where *The Last Detail* is about people society calls losers, *Shampoo* is about people society calls winners." She continues,

> everyone in the film – from the 'scoring' executive to the 'scoring' hairdresser – aspires to success in bed and in the bank. We are given only the most fleeting glimpse of something beyond the struggle to get rich and conquer when George learns that Norman's son has died – and he's momentarily troubled. [621]

In fact, this is the third part of Turning Point 2, triggering George's final desperate attempt to win back Jackie. The conclusion of the film however is true to the intention of 'The Country Wife,' where Horner acknowledges his shortcomings.

---

[618] Towne would later have The Beach Boys' songs on the soundtrack to *Tequila Sunrise*.
[619] Schatz, 1981, 261-266; David Thomson, 1987, 397.
[620] Kael, 'Beverly Hills as a Big Bed,' reprinted in *REELING,* 437.
[621] Jacobs. *Op.cit.,* 228-229.

James Monaco comments on the film's 'existential statement about the New Hollywood', that "myth begins to overtake reality. The characters work, their significance politically and culturally doesn't: it's too little, too late." [622]

Part of the (negative) mythology surrounding *Shampoo* has of course to do with the fabled sex life of its star and producer, Warren Beatty. (On the other hand, his legendary reputation makes the jokes about gay hairdressers all the more potent and nourishes the text in ways that the casting of no other actor could perhaps achieve.) *Shampoo* was cast to perfection, adding Lee Grant as the other woman with whom George is sleeping regularly, and all three actresses are at the height of their powers both in terms of the roles they play and the way they are presented. Beatty himself has said of the film,

> One could attack *Shampoo*, for instance, propagandistically. My God, you
> certainly could – the feminist movement could attack it, the serious forward-seeking
> optimist in American politics could attack it, capitalists, communists, everybody could
> attack it – because it doesn't seem to put any of its characters in a very admirable,
> positive light. But I think what has happened is that American filmmakers of the mid-
> 1970s have drawn negative conclusions from their basic perceptions, and that's what
> the films are about. [623]

Pauline Kael, the tastemaker critic eventually taken up by Hollywood and installed by Beatty with her own (disastrous) production deal at Paramount, said of the film that it was "the most virtuoso example of sophisticated kaleidoscopic farce that American moviegoers have ever come up with." [624]

The screenplay establishes a nostalgic note primarily because of George's naïveté – a fatal component of his character and a key motif threading throughout Towne's body of work: loss of innocence, innocence *destroyed* by experience. This is emblemised in the final shots of the film, when George is left standing pathetically (perhaps emotionally castrated) on the hill, watching his dreamgirl being driven away. [625]

This negative coda haunts precisely because it is connected with his naiveté – his innocence would be revisited in a very different environment by Towne with what he would hope to make his directing debut, *Greystoke*.

A Political Text: The Divided Self

A political and social reading of the film is connected with the way in which romance was perceived in films of the time. As critic David Denby wrote, romance was dead by 1973. [626] Ryan and Kellner comment that,

> the liberal critical spirit that motivated the decline of romance is strikingly articulated
> in *Shampoo*,

---

[622] Monaco. *Op.cit.,* 276.

[623] As quoted in Quirk. *Op.cit.,* 21.

[624] '[Beverly Hills as a Big Bed,' as before.

[625] As Matthew Wilder states, "One of the script's most striking qualities is the way in which Beatty's persona is protected from the overall wave of melancholy and distaste that rides across the large ensemble cast…" *Op.cit.*

[626] David Denby, "Rear Window: Delivering His *Personal Best*," *Premiere*, December 1988.

which they say is

a satire of the Republican style of political sleaze as well as being a post-Watergate
'I told you so' that presupposes the subsequent revelations of Republican corruption
as an ironic context for Agnew's moralistic pontifications. Though critical of
conservative attacks on 'permissive attitudes', the film nonetheless is itself critical of
sexual promiscuity.

The writers continue that the film possesses 'deflationary rhetoric', and that it

offers no metaphoric idealizations. Its rhetorical mode is more metonymic.
Rather than pretend to reveal a moral truth, it constructs meanings through
he juxtaposition of material worldly elements ..., or the satiric displacement within
the narrative of the same event so that the various contexts transform its meaning...
These debunking strategies prevent idealization, and they point toward the material
basis which leads a woman to choose one man over another.

The authors conclude,

... an ideal of a genuine romance serves as an implicit criterion for judging both
female opportunism and male cynicism. The failure of romance is associated with the
success of conservative capitalism and the undermining of human relationships by the
cash nexus.
As *Shampoo* illustrates, the undermining of romance is linked to the shearing away of self-
delusion and pretension regarding the materiality of social life. If conservative delusion
and idealization are based on the suppression of materiality, liberal and radical critiques
of those delusions promote a counterideological awareness of the power of materiality in
determining social interaction, especially such fragile, delusion-fraught dimensions of
social life as romance. [627]

This aspect of the film's text is inevitably linked to the character not merely of
the protagonist, but to that of Beatty, whose hands layered the text in the same way that
George's layer his lovers' hair; and to Hal Ashby, whose humanist worldview seems
reactionary in the twenty-first century but whose input to *Shampoo* (and *Last Detail*) seems
indelible, contriving to make of this production a series of collaborative decisions.[628]

A transition in culture can be read through the prism of the films which are
produced within it. Yet films being made in the studio system were simultaneously a
retreat from, and an analysis of, the present. Robert Sklar argues that "the years 1972 to
1976 indeed marked a period not only of cinematic innovation but of a critical and
analytical approach to national institutions rarely seen in mainstream American
filmmaking." [629] Since a filmic text can be read as an expression of the straining
relationship between culture and entertainment at the time of its production, we are
reminded of Sklar's claim of

a generational transformation. ... The similarities between the 1930s and the 1970s
went beyond crisis to consolidation. The 'age of turbulence' in 1970s filmmaking was
succeeded by an 'age of order'.

---

[627] Michael Ryan and Douglas Kellner write about the politics of *Shampoo* in *CAMERA POLITICA*, 1988, 152-3.
[628] As Bruce Kawin remarks, "... some films do reveal the workings of a particular stylistic imagination, one that tends to recur in other films made by the same artist(s)." Kawin. *Op.cit.*, 299.
[629] Sklar. 1994, 325.

He locates the major difference in the eras in "the revolution in distribution. The story of filmmakers and the films they made in the 1970s is inseparable from the story of how their films were delivered to theatres." That era, he claims, "makes one of the strongest cases for the link between social turmoil and creative dissidence in film. Just as the United States was not prepared to endure a long constitutional crisis over the Nixon Presidency, however, the question that 1974 posed was whether the film industry was willing to sustain itself on dissidence." [630] In *Shampoo* the political lead was taken by its producer and star, noted Democrat, Beatty; while Ashby, the director hired, could always be depended upon to supply a left-leaning, countercultural sensibility.

At a crucial moment in the bistro scene held during the election returns, Felicia is dragging George to the Ladies' Room and their departure from right to left across the screen reveals Pope and Jill, sitting to either side of a television set, where Spiro Agnew is declaiming:

> Exactly what can a President do to affect the moral tone of a country? A President can end the permissive attitudes, non-critical of an individual who decides for himself whether to obey or not…

While Pope asks Jill why George might have gone into the Ladies' Room with Felicia, Richard Nixon intones in the background:

> In our administration the American flag will not be a doormat for anybody…

For all the film's political advocacy, nobody in the film is seen to vote on Election Day (perhaps that was Towne's note of authenticity.)

Jacobs makes the claim for *Shampoo* that it dispelled any doubts there might have been about Ashby's versatility as a director because the film "is as different in tone and subject matter from *The Last Detail* as it is compatible in approach." [631] Of course, *Shampoo* was really created by three distinct people and Beatty was not the least of them. Of him, Towne once commented, "Warren will not knowingly go down a crooked road," which might indicate there were some problems in assembling this elaborate ensemble farce.

Towne was undoubtedly happy with the finished film and says,

> Of all the movies I've done and have not directed, *Shampoo* probably came closest in tone to the way I would have done it had I directed it. [632]

Despite his apparently compromised position in a production initiated and guided by Beatty, the film bears Ashby's clever yet delicate framing, and his generous sensibility. And yet Towne was actually never off the set. And despite - or, perhaps, because of - the fact that he was collaborating with some of the era's great auteur directors, Towne's authorial voice could be heard throughout his work and as distinctive as that of his co-authors'. Indeed, as Bordwell states, "character-driven films of the New

---

[630] Sklar. *Op.cit.*, 322-323. Quoted in full on page 195.
[631] Jacobs. *Op.cit.,* 228.
[632] Towne in Engel. *Op.cit.*, 219.

Hollywood like … *The Last Detail* and *Shampoo* made filmmakers aware of alternatives to the 'externally' driven protagonist." [633]

In terms of the critical perception of the film's authoring, Thomson offers, "it shows how in American film the producer can be the artist." [634] Kael says of Ashby that his "control keeps *Shampoo* from teetering over into burlesque. His work doesn't have the flash of an innovative, intuitive film artist, but for the script Towne has prepared, Ashby, the craftsman who serves the material, is probably the only kind of director." [635] Towne never again wrote a film so expressive of his country's political schizophrenia; both Ashby and Beatty were committed to what might retrospectively be called the New Hollywood project and their subsequent work reflected their ideological beliefs, which suggests that, as Towne confirms, this was truly a tripartite work of collaborative authorship on a work of elegiac power, haunted by the failure of its selfish characters to transform a cultural revolution into a political statement. [636] Towne's writing was now at its critical and commercial peak; the themes, characters and styles which he had developed throughout his apprenticeship in the 1960s had emerged fully-formed in the context of American auteur cinema: a morally ambivalent protagonist, trapped by his occupation; a strongly articulated sense of loss; innocence destroyed by experience, in a narrative which would end in bittersweet compromise.

The Yakuza (1975) (screenplay) [637]

It is not clear when precisely Towne became involved but it was at the behest of the studio (Columbia and Warner Brothers). In terms of Sydney Pollack's output as director, the film's theme, namely, "survival in the face of appalling odds," seems to belong to what one critic describes as "familiar Pollack territory", echoing the filmmaker's concern "with the loser rather than the winner." [638] The reviewer finds that the relationship between Kilmer and Eiko is a "mirror-image" of that between Robert Redford and Barbra Streisand in Pollack's previous film, *The Way We Were* (1973). Thus, in typical *auteur*-critical fashion is located the strand connecting *The Yakuza* with other films in the Pollack canon – character and theme, bringing together elements of the director's worldview, as evidenced in his entire output. Similarly, in the review published by *Films and Filming*, the writer finds "the theme of survival has remained the one consistent strand throughout all his films." [639]

Once director Sidney Pollack was on board, Robert Towne was hired to completely revise the screenplay by Paul and Leonard Schrader; and he shares credit with Paul Schrader on the finished film, while Leonard Schrader is relegated to story credit.

---

[633] David Bordwell. 2006, 84.

[634] Thomson., 1987, 355.

[635] Kael. *Op.cit.,* 441.

[636] Towne was speaking about the film at the Galway Film Fleadh in July 2006. In fact, the film was subject to a lawsuit by a writer who claimed it was stolen from her work, but the first decision, to award a six-figure in damages to the claimant, Bernice Mann, was subsequently reversed. See Stephen Farber, 'Plagiarism or Coincidence? Hollywood's Battle for Ideas,' *New West*, 27 August 1979: 55; 57-59.

[637] The background, production history and complete textual analysis of the screenplay by Elaine Lennon in 'A Question of Authorship: *The Yakuza*,' can be found at www.sensesofcinema.com, Issue 37, Oct-Dec 2005.

[638] 'The Yakuza,' *Films Illustrated,* Vol. 4, No. 47, July 1975: 405.

[639] 'The Yakuza,' *Films and Filming*, Vol. 21, No. 12, September 1975: 37.

Towne's draft is dated 18 December 1973 – which means he must have written it during production on *Chinatown*. Thematically the film must have appealed to him – the idea of a loyalty between two men that refuses to die, despite its unpleasant ramifications (Kilmer and Tanner, Kilmer and Ken); the blending of East and West in a formal gangster film that bases its structure around the traditional yakuza film – this would have proved highly attractive in the aftermath of rewriting *Chinatown*, which refers to many aspects of Orientalism without providing historical referents; [640] a resurrected romance which proves impossible (this also has its echo in *Chinatown*); and the mentor-student relationship between Kilmer and Dusty, a trope that Towne would pursue in his sports films.

The primary problem with the narrative is its exposition, which frequently appears awkward and results in explanatory voiceovers over montages of action and travel in the film. This is ironic, given Towne's views on screenplay construction:

> Generally speaking… scripts are too talky. And when there's a problem, it's usually because the script lacks clarity. Sometimes when creative people are insecure they can get esoteric. But striving to be understood – that is the mark of anybody who's really gifted. I always ask myself what the scene is really about, not the events, but the subtext, and try to do it as simply as possible. [641]

The formal mirroring structure evidenced in the oppositional narrative gives the screenplay the kind of balance detected by Wollen in analysing a group of films directed by John Ford, in his seminal work of author-structuralism. [642]

Towne described the Schrader screenplay at the American Film Institute speaking there on the film's release:

> I took it to be my task in reworking it, in the structural changes I made and in the dialogue changes and the character changes, to make it, from my point of view once you accepted the premise, credible that this American would go over there, would do this, would get involved in the incidents that he got involved in the script which would involve recovering a kidnapped daughter and then ultimately killing his best friend and killing 25 other people along with it and immolating himself. And I thought that in my reading of it, I just didn't feel that he was provoked in the right way to do all that. It's hard to make it credible that somebody would do that, and I tried to make it, from my point of view and the point of view of the director, more plausible. Not absolutely plausible, but plausible in the framework of this kind of exotic setting…

He concludes:

> When I had read it, I said these are the things that I felt should be done, and they agreed with me, so I did them. But it was pretty much agreed upon with the director and myself. [643]

---

[640] Pauline Kael says the film "offers Oriental decadence" and "cheap mythology." "The Rear Guard," 24 March 1975, reprinted in *REELING: Film Writings 1972-1975*. New York and London: Marion Boyars, 1992. 471; 472. She says of Towne's contribution that he "may have improved the dialogue (though it's hard to believe it could have been much worse), but he failed to simplify the plot." (470).

[641] Quoted in 'Your Write to Win,' *The Times*, 14 April 2003: 14.

[642] Peter Wollen. *SIGNS AND MEANINGS IN THE CINEMA*. London: Secker and Warburg, 1972.

The genre evolved from the traditional yakuza film and took its various elements, themes and ethical codes into a modern Japan. It was principally made by the Toei Studios from the mid-Sixties and approximately one hundred films a year were produced. One of the genre's fans was a writer called Yukio Mishima. *The Yakuza* is of course also linked with noir, given that its protagonist, Harry Kilmer (Robert Mitchum) could be said to be in a line of prototypical noir detective heroes – an anachronistic throwback, cynical, world weary, and double-crossed, but with a heart that is steadily revealed to be alive and kicking through the revelatory scenes of his former relationship with Eiko. Interestingly, the script extract published at the top of Schrader's article is not credited to anyone but is marked with the copyright of Warner Brothers Studio. It is almost exactly a replica of Towne's draft, pages 138 –141. [644]

In terms of genre convention, Schrader points out that

Yakuza films are litanies of private argot, subtle body language, obscure codes, elaborate rites, iconographic costumes and tattoos.

Schrader claims that

It is not difficult to be a standard yakuza-eiga screenwriter… The only requirement is that he be able to work fast. [645]

Figure 16 *The Yakuza theatrical* poster

Structurally, the screenplay is a clever byplay between an elaboration of conventional narrative exposition and evocations of the *yakuza* rituals, most of which are founded on violence and honour codes. Rather than obscuring the experience for the viewer, this form of exposition lends itself to the creation of an astonishing character –

[643] Speaking at the American Film Institute, 22 January 1975 transcript at the AFI, Louis B. Mayer Library: 10-11.
[644] Paul Schrader, '*Yakuza-Eiga* A Primer,' *Film Comment*, January 1974: 13. American Film Institute, January 22, 1975: 9-10.
[645] Schrader. *Op.cit.,* 15.

Tanaka Ken, whose entire post-WW II existence appears to have been founded on an extraordinary personal sacrifice in order to retain his honour and repay his debt to Harry Kilmer.

The story concerns Harry Kilmer (Robert Mitchum), an ex-GI whose WWII buddy in Japan, George Tanner (Brian Keith) needs his help when his daughter is kidnapped by the eponymous *yakuza* after he has reneged on a deal. Kilmer doesn't realise that he is being used as bait and travels to Tokyo with Dusty (Richard Jordan), Tanner's young sidekick. His trip brings him into contact with Tanaka Eiko (Kishi Keiko), his former girlfriend whom he rescued from a life of penury, along with her infant daughter (Hanako). She now runs Kilmer House, a nightclub built with Tanner's money. Harry needs to see her brother, Tanaka Ken (Japanese star Takakura Ken), to extract a favour, but discovers he has retired from his life as a *yakuza*. Harry is too embroiled in the situation to leave Tokyo before finishing his business there. He discovers the unpalatable truth of Ken's relationship with Eiko – they are husband and wife – and realises that Ken walked away because he saw that Harry had saved her from a far worse fate when he, Ken, had been a victim of the war: ('Ken is a relic left over from another age and another country.') In the same way that Hanako explains certain of the peculiarities of the Japanese to Dusty, Wheat is also a 'translator' of history and relationships in the film. The translations and explanations of one culture to another take place primarily at Wheat's apartment, which serves as a sort of locus of cultural détente in the film. Paradoxically, it is here that Hanako is killed, perhaps suggesting that such détente is impossible.

The events take place against a background of contrasts – between Japan old and new, both in terms of how it has changed since WWII and the age-old rituals of the *yakuza*, and the differences between Japan and the United States, which Dusty discusses with Harry:

```
                    DUSTY
          When an American cracks up, he
          opens a window and shoots up a
          bunch of strangers, he shoots
          out -- When a Japanese cracks
          up, he closes the window and cuts
          inward --
                    (MORE)

                                        (CONTINUED)


              DUSTY (cont'd)
              (does mime of hari-
              kari with his
              fingers)
          Everything's the reverse, isn't
          it?  When an American has an
          orgasm he says 'I'm coming.'
          When a Japanese has an orgasm,
          he says, 'I'm going.'

Kilmer smiles.
```

Character and Theme

Ken's supposedly inscrutable character is the emotional pivot to Kilmer's laconic style (virtually pioneered by Robert Mitchum in his cinematic persona): the stinging rebuke delivered by Ken to Kilmer is reversed when Ken confronts rival yakuza in a nightclub restroom where he surprisingly defends Kilmer in another scene which effectively builds on his enigmatic persona:

Figure 17 The enigmatic Ken

<pre>
              OLDER YAKUZA
          (in Japanese et seq.)
      Tanaka-san. Someone will pay us
      to rough up that American, but
      we don't want any trouble with
      you.
</pre>

Ken, looking in the mirror, does not turn and face the Yakuza.

<pre>
                                    (CONTINUED)

                  KEN
      He is family.

                  SUNGLASSED YAKUZA
      Bullshit. He's an American.

                  KEN
      Family.
</pre>

(The Yakuza: .93-4)*

Later on, he continues to jibe Kilmer:

<pre>
                  KEN
      -- What have you been doing all
      these years, Kilmer?
</pre>

The question really is an acceptance of Kilmer's position and Kilmer recognizes it as such. They turn together and start to walk back.

<pre>
                  KILMER
      -- Quite a few things -- police
      work, private investigations,
      real estate, investments...
</pre>

```
                    KEN
          --You've done well?


                    KILMER
          Depends on how you figure that
          kind of thing.


                    KEN
               (not unkind)
          -- Yes.  You have no family, do
          you?

KILMER AND KEN

The way Kilmer says this it's a confession.

                    KILMER
          -- No.
```

(The Yakuza: 108)

The film thus turns on the notion of 'family,' which forms a strong motif in the film's action and could be described as the screenplay's theme:

Harry has no family; Harry is hired to rescue Tanner's daughter; Harry is reunited with Eiko, with whom he had a relationship, and who also has a daughter; Eiko's 'brother' Ken owes Harry a debt; Ken has an older brother, Tanaka Goro, *oyabun* or advisor to the clans, whose own son is a violent *yakuza*, turning against his own father and family; Ken hasn't spoken to Goro in many years; in the same way that Harry is ultimately Tanner's pawn, Goro's position as counsellor is being threatened by Tono, Tanner's 'enemy in the *yakuza* war, who turns out to be his ally. Thus Harry and Goro are also linked. Ken is actually Eiko's husband, and he is so grateful to Harry for saving her life and that of their daughter, Hanako, that he steps aside, in an extraordinary sacrifice of his own personal happiness; Ken has retired from the *yakuza*, his alternative 'family'. He, like Harry, has no family. Harry kills Tanner. Ken and Eiko's daughter Hanako is killed by Goro's son in *yakuza* crossfire in Wheat's apartment, in a parallel to Tanner's daughter's kidnapping, which catalysed the whole story. Ken kills Goro's son in revenge. Ken kills Tono. Harry makes a sacrifice to honour Ken, and in doing so becomes a part of Ken's family at last: his brother.

Family means biological; friend; fellow gangster; fellow soldier. This motif is a strong feature of the dialogue:

```
                    KILMER
          -- Yeah, Ken has a habit of not
          speaking to relatives, doesn't
          he?  Do you have his address?
          Could I see him?
```

(The Yakuza: 70)

We might infer from this theme – that the script 'belongs' to Schrader (Paul) because if we accept his position as a screenwriting auteur, that theme more properly belongs as a consistent theme in his oeuvre, than to that of Robert Towne.

Change is also a strong feature in the story – for instance, Kilmer doesn't drink any more (in an alteration to dialogue at the bottom of p. 53); and Japan has experienced total modernisation:

> KILMER
> Everywhere I look I don't
> recognize a thing.

(The Yakuza: 30)

Ken's authoritarian manner is revealed in his relationship with his students:

> KEN
> Get rid of thinking you must
> have a certain attitude. Get
> rid of thinking. Don't expect
> to win... don't expect to lose.

KEN AND STUDENTS

Takano and the others absorb this.

> TAKANO
> But Sensai, what should I
> expect?

Ken's eyes widen slightly. He straightens up a hair. It's almost the change of an animal that has scented something on the wind.

> TAKANO
> (continuing)
> Sensai?

> KEN
> Expect nothing.

(The Yakuza: 46)

It is Hanako who explains the concept of 'giri' or duty (also translatable as 'burden'), to Dusty, who is of course performing his official duty for Tanner, to whom Harry is also 'dutiful.' When Dusty realises Tanner's treachery, he swears allegiance to Harry instead because Harry has earned his respect. The symmetry continues in the sense of history repeating itself: firstly, Ken returned in 1951 to find his wife living with Kilmer; now Kilmer has returned to Japan to find Eiko unquestioningly loyal to Ken, whom Kilmer discovers was her husband all along; secondly, the unswerving loyalty that leads Kilmer to help out an old friend and then kill him, is echoed in Ken's loyalty to his old *yakuza* friends, whom he must kill. The formal mirroring structure is strengthened in the budding relationship between Hanako and Dusty, which comes to an untimely end. And of course, Kilmer is a mirror-image of Ken, while Tanner is a mirror-image of Tono: "characters on a chessboard, each programmed to make a certain number of set moves; the Yakuza code dictates such, and nobody questions its right to direct his or her life. For Kilmer it is a welcome discipline, and a not unfamiliar one. The tension in the film springs from the fascinating moves of each character across the board, the sudden outbursts of violence signalling the loss of one or more pieces from the game. Nothing could be further from the Western gangster film: personal feelings play little part – moral obligation is everything." [646][647] Ken cuts off his little finger as apology to Goro; likewise, Harry cuts off his little finger as apology to Ken.

> KEN
> No man has a greater friend than
> Harry Kilmer.

(The Yakuza: 140)

With the exception of scene ordering in certain sequences, the released film is remarkably faithful to the screenplay draft credited to Towne. Certain scenes have been dropped entirely, however, including an in-flight samurai movie during Harry's journey to Tokyo, which may have been a reference too far. Perhaps in order to bring greater symmetry to the story, Eiko's son is also excised from the story proposed in the screenplay – in fact it is he (Taro) who gets killed at Wheat's apartment, and Hanako who survives. He no longer figures as a character at all, while Hanako's death provides a thematic rhyme to the kidnap of Tanner's daughter. In a highly symbolic screenplay (the opening titles explain the origin of the word, 'yakuza' being formed from the numbers eight, nine and three), Hanako's death also signifies the death of Ken and Eiko's marriage, and, ironically, the impossibility of Eiko's marriage to Harry. Hanako's role in the story is highly significant – she has a warmer, more straightforward welcome for Harry than her mother; she explains *yakuza* rituals to Dusty, who falls for her immediately; and her ultimately violent demise (an ironic antithesis to her name which she explains means 'flower child', in a casual reference to the American anti-war protesters during the then ongoing Vietnam war: Dusty is a Vietnam veteran) proposes a softening of Ken's apparently implacable character. It is also important to note that Hanako is a teacher of the English language and can thus communicate equally – translate - to both 'sides' of the story. (This is especially true in consideration of the film's other through-line, duty.)

> YAKUZA SONG
> A Yakuza pays his debts,
> A Yakuza does his duty,
> A man without debt,
> A man without duty,
> Is not a man.

---

[646] '*The Yakuza,*' *Films and Filming,* Vol. 21, No. 12, September 1975: 37.

[647] In a furthering of the film's attempt to formally blend East and West, this song is followed by 'My Darling Clementine,' that staple of the Western film genre, and all the nightclub audience sings along. This of course reminds us that the central abduction here is a deliberate reference to *The Searchers* (1956.) The review of the film in *Time Out* points out that "there emerges the familiar and increasingly explicit relationships of countless American Westerns." *THE TIME OUT FILM GUIDE,*2nd ed., edited by Tom Milne. London, Penguin Books, 754.

Schrader meanwhile produced an article called 'Yakuza-Eiga' for *Film Comment* in January 1974, a 'primer' for an understanding of Japanese gangster movies. It traces the genre's history from the samurai film and elucidates its themes, conventions and stylistic elements. This article is in line with other of his critical writings, for instance his famous piece on film noir, published by the same journal. [649] Since the pages of *The Yakuza* as printed are exactly the same as the screenplay available under the name of Robert Towne, which gives rise to the question, exactly what did Robert Towne contribute to the screenplay, given the avowed theme, that of family?

Asked why he took on the project, Towne replied:

> Trying to imagine someone reaching the point where he'll kill 25 people. Trying to make it credible that this American would go to Japan to recover a kidnapped girl, kill his best friend and 25 other people and mutilate himself. In reading the original script, I didn't feel he was provoked in the right way to do all that. I tried to make it more plausible. [650]

Figure 18 Kilmer's final shootout

It is known that Towne totally rewrote the screenplay – what is called 'a page one rewrite.' In Peter Biskind's account, Paul Schrader later felt guilty about the credits situation on the film:

> "I had always treated Leonard badly. Taking sole screenwriting credit on *The Yakuza* wasn't very nice. Treating him as an employee wasn't very nice.

---

[648] Paul Schrader, 'Notes on Film Noir,' *Film Comment*, Vol.8, No.1, Spring 1972.

[649] National Film Theatre programme May 1988: 8. He was quoted from the AFI seminar January 22, 1975, when he added, "When I had read it, I said these are the things that I felt should be done, and they agreed with me, so I did them. And then where they disagreed with me, we went around with it. But it was pretty much agreed upon with the director and myself." Interviewed at the American Film Institute Seminar, January 22, 1975, transcript at the Louis B. Mayer Library, AFI: 11. Evidently the subject of Japanese gangsters still fascinates Towne: *Variety* announced 11 May 2006 that Raymond De Felitta was to helm Towne's screenplay *Street of Dreams*, based on the career of Japanese American gangster, Montana Joe. 'Welcome to the Street of Dreams,' accessed online at www.variety.com.

[650] Biskind. *Op.,cit.*, 426.

Throughout all that, he had one thing that I didn't have, which was Japan. And then came *Mishima*, and I stole Japan from him. To do *Mishima* was his idea." [651]

They never spoke again. As for Towne, he spoke elliptically about the situation in public:

> …it's an original script by Paul Schrader and his brother Lennie. Now exactly who did what I'm still vague on. [652]

While we have noted the film's familiarity for audiences who knew the work of Sydney Pollack, and that of Paul Schrader, the film however also sits easily in the Towne canon with its thematic concerns about male friendship, rivalry and loyalty; the mentor/student relationship; a certain nostalgia for the past; and a comfortable restriction by generic formula which also poses an alternative structure to the notion of family, a social arrangement rarely seen in Towne's work. [653]

Towne's reputation as the top script doctor continued unabated. These jobs were usually short fixes which were well paid and centred around his group of highly powered friends.

As David Thomson surveys Towne's career,

> He isn't really getting anywhere until he does a Western, *A Time for Killing*, and takes his name off *that* because he loathes the way it's rewritten. But Warren Beatty likes the script (scripts are passed around, like pictures of women), and so when *BONNIE AND CLYDE* comes along, it's Robert who does the rewrites on the original Robert Benton-David Newman script. Do you see how paranoia and dependency can become like illness in this scheme of sometimes secret, unacknowledged rewriting? How do you know you are not being interfered with? How should you not be awed and resentful of the great and powerful men who hire you and act like your friends? [654]

Towne himself comments on the pain of the rewriting process:

> How *many* times something has to be rewritten just to get the right tone. When you're rewriting a picture, you're rewriting the scenes that didn't work, the one

[651] American Film Institute, January 22, 1975,transcript at the Louis B. Mayer Library, AFI: 9.

[652] Michael Sragow asks how do Pollack's collaborators fit within the director's oeuvre: he says, "Surprisingly snugly… Pollack's movies have often focused on off-center friendships and romances featuring strong women." Interviewed by Sragow, Pollack says, "Every director who's successful gets offered five hundred scripts. So you make a choice. And you keep making choices from the moment you pick a project. Even when there are ten names on a script, the reason is that you couldn't get what you wanted from the first screenwriter so you went to the second one, got a little bit more, incorporated what you wanted, left out what you didn't." This, says Sragow, is why Pollack was called a 'writer-fucker' by William Goldman. Michael Sragow, 'Ghostwriters: Unraveling the Enigma of Movie Authorship,' *Film Comment* 19, March-April 1983: 14. (Pollack hired Towne to doctor Goldman's adaptation of his own novel, *MARATHON MAN*.) Sragow concludes that "a director like Sydney Pollack deserves all the praise he gets for keeping a complicated movie coherent, but he still needs screenwriters around to get scenes down on paper before he puts them on film." (18).

[653] David Thomson, 'Trouble in Chinatown,' *Vanity Fair*, November 1985: 60.

[654] Rainer, 1974: 234.

that didn't make thought plausible, or a character change that isn't adequately dealt with. You're dealing with the most difficult scenes. When a director is directing a difficult scene, he often goes through a lot of takes. This happens for a writer too. [655]

It is perhaps one of the richest ironies of Towne's life that he came to minister resuscitation to so many screenplays by other people when he spent so many years in ill-health, plagued by what eventually was discovered to be a series of allergies. An early article wondered would he wake up long enough to capitalise on his successes, given his predilection for sleeping twelve hours at a time. [656] Towne himself says of the craft,

> Some people may think there's something pejorative about the term 'script doctor.' But on the whole it's better to have a reputation for fixing things up than for messing them up. I have enjoyed the role, and conceivably would and will do it again. If for no other reason than you force yourself into somebody else's world and you learn things at every level that you don't if you are doing original material. It's a way of revitalizing yourself. You learn things from other people. In rewriting someone or in adapting a work, you can come to feel it's your very own, too. Or you can feel that you are in the service of somebody else's material that you love very much, and you want to work. We all have rescue fantasies. Somebody may have a terrific idea, but they've screwed it up, and you'll fix it.[657]

Perhaps it is politic to leave the final word to the doctor:

> It's misleading, though, to talk about script doctoring or polishing as though it were a specialized art. All scripts are rewritten, whether they be yours or somebody else's. The only question is whether it is rewritten well or badly. But everything is and should be rewritten. [658]

This philosophy – or justification, more properly – is a part of Towne's pragmatic approach to cinematic collaboration, for himself and others. In years to come he would be 'doctored' himself.

The Missouri Breaks (1976) (uncredited)

Jack Nicholson arrived on the $8 million set of *The Missouri Breaks* to discover that his role had been minimized in his absence, due to Marlon Brando's influencing of director Arthur Penn. 'Poor Nicholson was stuck in the center of it all, cranking the damned thing out,' Brando said, 'while I whipped in and out of scenes like greased

[655] Jesse Kornbluth, 'Will Success Keep Bob Towne Awake?' *New York*, 21 April 1975: 73.

[656] Towne in Brady, 1981, 407. He told Brady: "When you're rewriting, very often you're doing the scenes that don't work. The toughest scenes in a piece of material may not only have been the toughest for the writer who worked ahead of you, but may also be the most difficult scenes to solve, period. So they are the ones you have to keep redoing." Critic Gene Siskel called him 'Hollywood's Mr. Fix-It,' in the Leisure section of the *Sunday News*, 13 June 1976, where Towne told him: "Today, everybody thinks they're an auteur, and they don't want their work tainted. Today's scripts try to be more penetrating, and they're usually not as much fun. The older screenplays had a marvellous kind of snowshoe effect as they tried to cover a wider territory... I feel a little chary about my visibility [as a script doctor]... it does satisfy a sort of rescue fantasy I think we all have. Yes, it's like the relief pitcher in baseball coming into the game with the bases loaded. I do enjoy working things out."

[657] Towne in Brady, 1981, 406. He admitted to Michael Atkinson, "There's no question, a lot of it was done for cash." *Ibid.*

[658] Shepherd. *Op.cit.*, 110.

lightning.' [659] Shepherd states, "With an $8 million budget, Arthur Penn directing, and Marlon Brando and Jack Nicholson starring, *The Missouri Breaks* had to be great. It wasn't. It was interesting but too disjointed and episodic to come anywhere near its potential. Jack thought it could have been saved in the editing, but his opinion was disregarded. He didn't like the film, and he told director Penn so. According to Jack, Penn was offended and stopped speaking to him." [660] It is unclear as to what Towne's contribution might have been.

Marathon Man (1976) (uncredited)

William Goldman adapted his own novel, which was directed by the late British director, John Schlesinger. Unknown to the author, Towne was brought in for last-minute alterations to the script, including the bedroom scene with Hoffman and Marthe Keller which was in any case re-cut, removing much of the pointed dialogue supplied by Towne.[661]

Orca aka *Orca- Killer Whale* (1977) (uncredited)

This re-imagining of *Moby Dick* was clearly created in the backwash of *Jaws*, which had created a new kind of cinema – the blockbuster phenomenon. While it isn't clear what Towne may have contributed, it is interesting as a timely comment on his concerns with *Greystoke*, as he was in the midst of completing the research on that, his most beloved creation, which also deals with modernity and nature in conflict. Directed by Michael Anderson, from a script co-written by producer Luciano Vincenzoni with Sergio Donati, the film is distinguished by two things – a score by Ennio Morricone, and a convincing and moving evocation of the killer whale. Shark hunter Nolan (Richard Harris) is responsible for killing a pregnant female whale. Seen on deck his vessel by her mate, the Captain is destined to find his justice at sea by the vengeful male, who immediately knocks his ageing assistant and mentor Novack (Keenan Wynn) into the sea and eats him.

The film earned terrible reviews but hindsight actually reveals a very well-structured story with engaging characters, contemporary ecological concerns and a far more convincing enemy than JAWS could essay. Its main theme of survival, that of man in a beast's world, and vice versa, was obviously a temptation too hard for Towne to resist at the time that he was desperately trying not only to write but also direct *Greystoke*, conflating his internal and external authorial skills.

He maintained his profile with high-paying jobs doctoring scripts, yet his heart lay with personal projects which would eventually cost him his reputation. Towne's problems in finishing the screenplay for *Greystoke* meant that somehow the story got lost and he would once again gain a reputation for procrastination. The first eighty or ninety pages were completely free of dialogue and he realised he would have to direct it himself. This is when he started to focus on another idea, about female track athletes.

Conclusions

While Towne has inexorably been connected with the New Hollywood generation, his writing style can also be seen to have a character and form consciously identifiable with an earlier era, reminding us of Kristin Thompson's admonition that the

[659] Shepherd. *Op.cit.*, 112.
[660] According to a number of sources including Towne himself, speaking at the Galway Film Fleadh, July 2006.
[661] Kristin Thompson. *Op.cit.*, 8.

New Hollywood generation did not alter classical Hollywood storytelling, rather they revived it.[662] As Robert B. Ray suggests

> The radical fashions of the 1960s and 1970s concealed the obvious: the traditional American mythology had survived as the generally accepted account of America's history and future. [663]

However, *Chinatown,* that perfect fusion of Old and New Hollywood, was actually a canny rewriting of the founding mythos and the idea of the individual as hero, demonstrating the vestigial traces of authorship that could be detected in the generic reinterpretation represented by *Bonnie and Clyde* and its Nouvelle Vague forebears; while *Shampoo* might more accurately reflect what Ray describes as "its audience's ambivalent relationship to the period's development" (some seven years after the election in question). [664]

Nonetheless, despite Towne's numerous collaborations, or perhaps what Kael referred to as 'cross-fertilising accidents,' a coherence deriving from dramatic elements can be seen across the cinematic texts, suggesting that the controlling intelligence in these films, far from being the singular expression of the director's vision, is in fact the product of multiple, collaborative authorship.[665] Richard Combs cautions that "the critical ideal of an auteur who is always making personal statements in defiance of the system is an unperceptive way of looking at the complex equation of movies." [666] The continuity in style exhibited by Towne in this phase of his career is evident in the picaresque style of *Shampoo*, rather like that of *The Last Detail*, in which the episodic adventures of the antihero are followed.

As Wollen reminds us, "it is possible to speak of a film auteur as an unconscious catalyst." [667] That Towne's voice is still identifiable suggests that this is a model for further exploration within the terms outlined.

In *Shampoo* the Lothario is left without a girlfriend; the future mapped out by Towne was left out in the editing with George alone to ponder what might have been if he could only get it together, utterly deflating the hope embedded in comedy's conventional conclusion of marital union. If *Shampoo*'s opening on black to the sound of orgasmic grunts echoes that of *Chinatown*'s diorama of adulterous photographs, its reflective coda expresses its authors' [Towne co-wrote, somewhat controversially, with Warren Beatty] nostalgic longing for a time that may have been more hallucinatory than real; its existence however proves the narrative's real purpose – a post-coital elegy to a time of aggressive promiscuity and political unrest. That tension, between past and

---

[662] Robert B. Ray. *A CERTAIN TENDENCY OF THE HOLLYWOOD CINEMA, 1930-1980*. Princeton, N.J.: Princeton University Press, 1985, 296.

[663] *Ibid.*

[664] Kael, 'Raising Kane,' as before, 62. Love says that, "collaborative authorship is so common, and so often disguised, as to constitute a central concern of attribution studies." Harold Love. *ATTRIBUTING AUTHORSHIP: An Introduction.* Cambridge: University Press, 2002, 37.

[665] Richard Combs, 'Cinema's Vision Thing,' *The Listener*, 13 September 1990: 37.

[666] Peter Wollen, 'The Auteur Theory,' (extract), 1972 excerpt, reprinted in Caughie, (ed.), 1981, 147. And in *The Yakuza* we can detect a series of structuring oppositions across the text of the type that Wollen finds in the films directed by John Ford.

[667] Bruce Kawin. *Op.cit.,,* 293.

present, is doubly reflective here, commenting on politics and private lives, but it is explored throughout Towne's screenplays.

Towne's writing was at its critical and commercial peak; the themes, characters and styles which he had developed throughout his apprenticeship in the 1960s had now emerged fully-formed in the context of American auteur cinema: a morally ambivalent protagonist, trapped by his occupation; a strongly articulated sense of loss; innocence destroyed by experience. Despite - or, perhaps, because of - the fact that he was collaborating with some of the era's great auteur directors, Towne's authorial voice could be heard throughout his work and as distinctive as that of his co-authors'. Towne received critical recognition and had a champion in Pauline Kael, who had inadvertently burdened him with the onus of cultural significance following his work on *Bonnie and Clyde*.

As Bruce Kawin reminds us, "the special merit of the auteur theory is that it is capable of acknowledging the collaborative structure of the cinematic enterprise and the evidence of patterns of coherence that have the integrity of authorship." [668]

This period in Towne's career is also notable for his popular acceptance. Furthermore, at the peak of the New American Wave, when the self-proclaimed auteurs had established themselves as cinematic spokesmen for a generation, Towne was nominated for an Academy Award three times for his screenplays, and won once, for *Chinatown* (1975). In purely narrative terms, this era would also determine Towne's preoccupation with his major theme: loss - the loss of idealism, self, integrity, the real/.mythical Los Angeles, the girl. Throughout the oeuvre this theme is modified in terms of betrayal. A subtext to this would be the main narrative lines pursued in his screenplays: myth and realism (and the subject of corruption). At times these would be conflated, as in *Bonnie and Clyde* and *Chinatown*. At other times, a mythical (or Hero's Journey) structure would be pursued in an otherwise realistic work such as *The Last Detail* (1971) and *Shampoo* (1975). Principally this period is of interest for the recognisable markers of his personal writing style and the mutually beneficial influence his various collaborations had in the Seventies, when, as Gomery puts it, "the U.S. motion picture industry operated inefficiently, underemployed resources and distributed its rewards to a few corporations." [669]

While Towne had been part of the vanguard of the New Hollywood filmmakers, he was prepared to articulate a keen sense of shared anti-authoritarianism, most successfully in his reworking of *The Last Detail*, ensuring that he took over definitively from Ponicssan at the film's shockingly banal ending. He had shared script doctoring duties on *The Parallax View* (1974) and participated in Republican-bashing in the disillusioned *Shampoo* (1975), as well as writing what was quite possibly the greatest film of the 1970s, *Chinatown*, which had laid bare the corruption behind the building of his beloved Los Angeles.

---

[668] Douglas Gomery, 'The American Film Industry of the 1970s: Stasis in the "New Hollywood",' *Wide Angle*, 1983 Vol. 5 No. 4: 57.

[669] Stuart Byron in *Film Comment*. Vol. 16, No. 1 Jan/Feb 1980. As quoted by Ryan Gilbey in *IT DON'T WORRY ME: The Revolutionary American Films of the Seventies*. New York, Faber & Faber, 2003: 233.

Towards the end of the Seventies it was possible to view those auteurs' achievements as inadequate:

'The decade has been the worst in history for American films.' [670]

Clearly, Robert Towne was a writer with a strong vision, who realised that the visual impact of his writing was not fully his. We could accord him Richard Corliss's attribute of a Promethean, linking him with some of the greats of an earlier era, Herman J. Mankiewicz and Abraham Polonsky. [671] Towne now took the serious step of finally contemplating his debut as director of his own screenplays.

Acknowledgements:
Thank you to Professor Charles Barr for a copy of Robin Wood's *ARTHUR PENN*; Randi Hokett and Jennifer Prindiville for arranging everything at the Warner Brothers Archives at the University of Southern California; and to Judy Noack and Shannon Fifer of the Warner Brothers legal department in Los Angeles; Kathleen Dickson at the British Film Institute archives for arranging a print of *Drive, He Said*; and to Tom Stempel for the tour of the locations for *Chinatown*.

---

[670] Corliss, 'The Hollywood Screenwriter': 6.
[671] Jesse Kornbluth, 'Will Success Keep Bob Towne Awake?' in *New York*, 21 April 1975: 73.

Chapter 4 1976-1989: TO HAVE (WRITTEN) AND HAVE NOT (DIRECTED)

Greystoke: *The Legend of Tarzan, Lord of the Apes* (1977) (screenplay, as P.H. Vazak)
Personal Best (1982) (written and directed by)
The Two Jakes (1990) (characters) (written by)
Tequila Sunrise (1988) (written and directed by)

The Screenwriter as Director

Prologue

In 1975 Towne was interviewed by Jesse Kornbluth: he had been tirelessly promoting *Shampoo* on the road with Warren Beatty for a solid month and the *New York* article announced that Towne had just optioned John Fante's *ASK THE DUST*. It would be perfect for Warren Beatty or Jack Nicholson. In the meantime, he had a long overdue Tarzan script to finish, *Lord Greystoke*…[672]

> I like to write films that are drawn from real life, and yet have a prior cinematic reality … I like to take a myth and make a new myth. [673]

Perhaps Towne was inspired by his work on *Bonnie and Clyde* to make this statement – or to make this a statement of his career's intent. His work can now be seen as an intertwining of collaborators and influences, a collage of circumstances and industrial change. As James Monaco reminds us,

> Colloquially, we tend to oppose myth and reality. The phrase, 'that's a myth' suggests is untrue, unreal. But in fact, myth and reality are closely interconnected. Real myths, those artistic evidences of our collective unconscious, spring directly from roots in reality, they heighten reality and condense it. [674]

Whereas previously we have seen Towne as writer for hire and collaborator, as well as script doctor, here we shift focus in terms of authorship, perhaps attempting to combine the at times conflicting demands of internal and external authorship. The legacy of the auteur theory was a generation of Hollywood directors who came to believe their own publicity. In his collaborations with some of the most interesting and powerful directors and stars of the era, Robert Towne had greatly underlined their fame and status and perhaps felt that he had contributed sufficiently to the elaborating of other people's careers. Following his Academy Award successes in the mid-Seventies, he decided to turn to directing, however the rights to *Greystoke* were taken from him as collateral by David Geffen, the new production head at Warner Brothers.

> He whom Hollywood would humble, it first indulges. It is, perhaps, the most basic law of the business.[675]

---

[672] Gene Siskel, as before.
[673] James Monaco,1979, 251.
[674] Richard Schickel's biography of *BRANDO* is quoted by Alex Cox in 'How to Kill a Film Star,'*The Guardian*, Film & Music, 25 May 2007: 7.
[675] Towne, 'On Directing,' as before, 124-5. And, as we have acknowledged, he had always intended directing *Chinatown*.

Towne's decision to direct came about as a result of his long-held desire to shoot his screenplays the way he saw them. He commented,

> Your whole work career is preparation – as a writer and having been on sets from almost the time I started writing. Specifically, I think that when you write it, you've sort of prepared it. A screenplay is really an attempt, ideally, to describe a movie that has already been shot, only it hasn't been shot. I think that has an awful lot to do with the preparation of it. [676]

In the three films Towne directed between 1980 and 1998 there is a strong sense of his desire to conflate myth with reality, yet holding to his elemental idea: the ultimate defeat of the protagonist in his or her chosen occupation; the importance of male friendship; and, finally, his signature theme - loss. *Tequila Sunrise* (1988) would mark a return to his favoured location, Los Angeles.

> The state of things is such right now that for me it's impossible to be satisfied working for someone else. I want to direct from now on. I was unable to direct for a number of years for personal reasons so I had to write, but that's no longer the case – so I can do both now. [677]

The strategies employed in this chapter focus on the influence of his collaborators such as Hal Ashby on previous films; his own homages to, or borrowings from, classical Hollywood, particularly the films of writer/director Howard Hawks; and the infusing of the sports genre with a narrative line increasingly important to him, the relationship between student and mentor embedded in mythological form. Inasmuch as we are discussing the proposition that *Chinatown* (1971-1973) is the major work and the lens through which all of Towne's other work might be viewed, we can certainly see the continuing use of fetish objects such as flowers, cigarettes and lighters, animals, drinks, shoes, as motif; a discursive approach to the city of Los Angeles, of which *Chinatown* is the virtual founding cinematic mythos; the role of water as major cinematic affect; and an abundance of mythical references. A major organising principle of his sports film narratives, and one that was first overtly illustrated in *Greystoke*, is the hero's journey model which is here examined in detail, specifically in relation to his directing debut, *Personal Best*, a production beset by industrial action and financial and personal difficulties from the start. Towne would streamline and simplify this mythical code of storytelling in his future screenplays. For now, he was departing from the more realistic approach he had utilised in collaborations with Nicholson, Ashby, Polanski and Beatty, despite the fact that in some of those screenplays he had, ironically, clung to a circular, and mythical, storytelling shape.

Ultimately, we now see that what distinguishes Towne from his screenwriting contemporaries is his coherent vision, maintained and re-stated in those screenplays which he directs himself. This is the lens through which he views the world. Therefore this chapter gives credence to that strand of auteurist study which might be termed 'personal vision.'

Barry Langford defines the notion of auteurism as follows:

---

[676] Towne in conversation at the Edinburgh Film Festival quoted in *PROJECTIONS 6*. London: Faber & Faber, 1996, 132.
[677] Langford. *Op.cit.*, 9.

Auteurism seeks to (and claims to be able to) identify submerged patterns of continuity – thematic preoccupations, characteristic patterns of narrative and characterisation, recognisable practices of mise-en-scène and the like – running through films with (usually) the same director. Establishing such individuating traits makes a claim for that director's creative 'ownership of the films he has directed: the director earns a status as a creative originator – an *auteur* – along the traditional lines of the lone novelist or painter. [678]

Directing encompasses the application of visuals, technical work, cameras, music, performance and editing techniques to narrative and in the case of the writer turned director, we are in the realm of authorial intention being manifested in directorial expression. This unity of vision, the stamp perfected in his screenplays, is ultimately translated to the films he directs so that while the films stand alone in their own right, they also build on his previous body of work to cohere into something unified, allowing us to ask the question, is he in fact an auteur.

The industrial context of the late Seventies, when Towne undertook his mission to translate his work as screenwriter had changed, as we have previously noted. Between 1970 and 1975,

> The new relationship between distributors and producers … fundamentally altered the notion of independent production in American cinema. All film productions, even in Hollywood, became 'independent' by definition, such that it was no longer clearly meaningful to speak of it as 'independent', at least in any artistic or ideological sense. [679]

The 'movie brat' generation was now benefiting from the changes: not merely from the critical fallout that came their way from the auteur theory but also in terms of the subject matter they could tackle (including the expansive mutating of genres) and the concomitant power they might now wield with their enhanced box office and studio status:

> They benefited from a new degree of autonomy and authority accorded to the film director by the major studios for whom, following the popularisation in the US of auteurist approaches to cinema, the film director now possess not only a greater degree of intellectual and artistic weight but also important box-office drawing power. [680]

As Gilbey reminds us, Coppola spent an inordinate amount on *Apocalypse Now*; Spielberg made *1941*; and Scorsese made *New York, New York*. By 1980, the retrospective glance proved highly unkind. [681] Diane Jacobs' contemporary survey notes,

> In certain respects today's director actually suffers from the gradual attrition in the expansive structure of heyday studio oligarchy. 'I think what's changed,' [Paul] Mazursky told me, "is that the great monolithic figures, the Harry Cohns, Jack Warners, those great mastodons that were strong and powerful, angry and

[678] Mark Shiel, 'American Cinema 1970-75,' in *CONTEMPORARY AMERICAN CINEMA*, eds. Linda Ruth Williams and Michael Hammond. New York and London: McGraw-Hill and Open University Press, 2006, 132.

[679] Shiel. *Op.cit.,* 139-144.

[680] *Ibid.*

[681] Diane Jacobs. *HOLLYWOOD RENAISSANCE: The New Generation of Filmmakers and Their Works.* New York: Delta Books, 1977 & 1980, 3.

primitive, are not there anymore. They left a stamp on so many movies that my childhood was probably a vision of those men. Somewhere along the line Jack Warner must have been an auteur. That quality is gone from Hollywood today." [682]

Shiel pinpoints the industrial transition post-1975:

Put simply, Hollywood had become accustomed to the new routine of making fewer films for a smaller total audience, but bigger pictures and for a larger audience per picture than ever before. This new routine would underpin its economic success for a whole generation to come, although it would do nothing to guarantee the artistic or intellectual value of the films produced. [683]

Now, as Towne prepared for his directing debut, it is quite possible he stunned everyone in his choice of subject, with what appeared to be a total departure on every conceivable level.

Greystoke (1977) (screenplay, as P.H. Vazak)

If you're a writer, you spend a lot of time getting the shit kicked out of you by directors. When you become the director, you suddenly realize why directors have to do that. You think: this is really a job for a sadist. Maybe I'll learn to enjoy it. Other sadists do.

- Robert Towne [684]

TARZAN OF THE APES is clearly in the tradition of the *'enfant sauvage'* narrative, dating from the findings of Carolus Linnaeus in 1758 and the subsequent documenting of the Wild Child of Aveyron in 1797. While never claiming to be an intellectual, Rice Burroughs said of his interest in 'the albino ape', "I was mainly interested in playing with the idea of a contest between heredity and environment. For this purpose I selected an infant child of a race strongly marked by hereditary characteristics of the finer and nobler sort [the English aristocracy], and at an age which he could not have been influenced by association with creatures of his own kind I threw him into an environment as diametrically opposite that to which he had been born as I might well conceive." [685]

---

[682] Shiel. *Op.cit.*, 155.

[683] Speaking at the Edinburgh Film Festival.

[684] Quoted by John Taliaferro, Introduction to *TARZAN OF THE APES*. New York, Modern Library Paperback, Random House, 2003, xiv. "There is something basic in the appeal of Tarzan which makes me think that he can still hold his own as a daydream figure, despite the sophisticated challenge of his two contemporary competitors, Ian Fleming and Mickey Spillane. For most adults, Tarzan (and John Carter of Mars) can hardly compete with the conspicuous consumer consumption of James Bond or the sickly violence of Mike Hammer, but for children and adolescents, the old appeal continues. All of us need the idea of a world alternative to this one. From Plato's *REPUBLIC* to Opar to Bond-land, at every level, the human imagination has tried to imagine something better for itself than the existing society ... In its naïve way, the Tarzan legend returns us to that Eden where, free of clothes and the inhibitions of an oppressive society, a man can achieve in reverie his continuing need ... to prevail as well as endure." Gore Vidal, Biographical Note to *TARZAN OF THE APES*. New York: Modern Library Paperback, Random House, 2003, vii.

[685] Biskind. *Op.cit.*, 392-393. Biskind is perhaps making a criticism typical of auteurism: what Stuart Klawans says is "the translation of a film's explicit subject matter into a representation of the processes of filmmaking and of the filmmaker's life." *FILM FOLLIES: The Cinema Out of*

The novel is a great adventure – the greatest, perhaps, since Jules Verne, whose work influenced Rice Burroughs to add science fiction to his oeuvre. Above all, *TARZAN OF THE APES* is a great romance.

> I have come across the ages out of the dim and distant past from the lair of the primeval man to claim you – for your sake I have become a civilized man – for your sake I have crossed oceans and continents – for your sake I will be whatever you will me to be.
> - Tarzan to Jane in *TARZAN OF THE APES*, 259

Towne had long been fascinated by the tale, probably for its heroic and mythic resonances, and he read a great deal on the subject. Other examples of the wild child narrative deriving from the ideas of evolution and Social Darwinism in the air in Burroughs' era are <u>Mowgli</u> from Rudyard Kipling's *JUNGLE BOOK*, and work by the likes of Jack London and Robert E. Howard.

Peter Biskind's scurrilous account of Seventies Hollywood goes so far as to negatively interpret the story of *Greystoke* as a gloss on Hollywood:

> Like every Hollywood movie, on some level it was about the business. After all, he [Towne] was a defenseless screenwriter, at a disadvantage against the ferocious carnivores around him, condemned to live on scraps from the table of friends – Beatty, Nicholson, Evans and Calley – who were way more powerful than he. Indeed, for him, Hollywood was the planet of the apes. As he grew older and more wily in the ways of the town, became mesmerized by the theme of innocence and experience, purity and corruption, which was, after all, the preoccupation of *The Last Detail, Chinatown* and *Shampoo*. [686]

On the one hand, Biskind overlooks the idea that in fact every great writer utilises their personal experience to embellish or even amplify a fictional reality to the level of art: that may be one of Towne's better achievements; on the other, he is enlivening the idea that has evidently taken phantasmagorical shape in Towne's own mind – that *Greystoke* is a great lost work and one that is central to his career. It is this reading that this author believes to be true in terms of Towne – that it is the emotional midpoint of his career, were his oeuvre to be measured out in acts, with *Bonnie and Clyde* as the first turning point, *Two Jakes* aka *The Two Jakes* as the second. It is clear that, due to both horrendous personal problems (a custody battle which would prevent him leaving the state of California) and professional turmoil (a quasi-Faustian deal with David Geffen to save *Personal Best*) Towne gave up a project which was teeming with problems – a film about apes.

Interviewed in *Playboy* in March 1975, Towne states that he was adapting portions of the original Rice Burroughs novel 'into something more akin to his own concerns about the natural world and its possible destruction. "If I ever made millions, I'd do something eccentric – like trying to save an endangered species from extinction." Why not?' asks the [anonymous] author. 'He's done it with screenwriters.' [687] Towne had lately been appointed as special creative consultant to Warner Brothers to help develop feature properties. [688] It is clear why Towne would announce to *Newsweek* magazine,

---

Order. London: Cassell, 1999, 66.
[686] 'On the Scene: The Screenplay's the Thing,' *Playboy*, March 1975: 156.
[687] As reported in *Variety*, February 4, 1976.

"The original myth showed that an English lord could conquer nature on the Dark Continent ... This lord will have a communion with nature." [689] Essentially Tarzan was the story of a primitive man entering Victorian society. The subject of Tarzan from the gorillas' point of view was certainly innovative, and Towne took the project to John Calley at Warner Brothers after Peter Bart had made it clear to the writer that Paramount was only interested in seeing the next draft of *Chinatown*. A couple of years later, in November 1977, Towne travelled to Africa to scout locations for *Greystoke*.

The novel is told in 28 chapters; while the story is split evenly into two sections – the first dealing with Tarzan's birth to the Claytons and then his upbringing, following their deaths, by Kala and his eventual realisation that he has outgrown his 'family.' He is then 'reborn' as a nobleman. This division also governs Towne's basic structural choice in his translation; albeit it is split into three sections, the final, incomplete part dealing with Tarzan's world being disturbed and his sojourn in the land to which he is rightful heir.

The screenplay, *Greystoke*, is one of Towne's finest pieces of writing: filled with delightful, poetic description, mythical resonance and brilliant juxtaposition, it is a model of screenplay craft and detailed camera movement. The 04 August 1977 draft available consists of (an incomplete) 187 pages plus a further three outlining Towne's final pages for the screenplay. The first 30 pages set up the framing story with D'Arnot and introduce Tarzan as the hunter-sidekick to the supposedly dead Frenchman; the next 45 pages create a dense picture of the trip to Africa which goes so badly wrong; pages 76-119 delineate in fascinating and powerfully emotive detail the white boy's life amongst the apes – this is the only lengthy portion of the screenplay which was eventually filmed by director Hugh Hudson and released in 1984; while the remaining pages introduce D'Arnot and his fortuitous meeting with 'Tarzan' (119-171) – whom he brings 'home' to England (172-187). Thus, while Towne disingenuously denies any knowledge of screenplay structure, the innate shape of *Greystoke* conforms to that 'discovered' and recommended by screenwriting analysts and experts, the classic 'three act' structure, which derives from Aristotle's edicts on the subject, the three 'unities' of time, place and action. And it conforms to the spirit of the originating source material.

Towne's take on the material wasn't so much consciously mythical as classically realist: he wanted to make the story entirely human and probable. As Robert Arnett points out in a commentary on the screenplay,

> The style of *Greystoke* is almost anthropological in its treatment of the ape
> world and colonial exploration. The style of the story stands in direct contrast to
> other Tarzan movies. Towne certainly does not intend for this be [sic]
> Johnny Weissmuller swinging from vines on the MGM backlot. The style in
> Towne's version is one that makes the story concept plausible. The Tarzan
> myth, it seems, could have some truth to it. Towne's style places emphasis on
> realism in the depiction of the apes and the humans. [690]

---

[688] As quoted by Robert Arnett, 'The Screenwriter as Artist: Three Lost Masterworks by Robert Towne,' *Creative Screenwriting*, Vol. 7, No. 3, May-June 2000: 47.

[689] Robert Arnett, 2000: 48.

[690] He continues: "And that ability in the shorthand an idea, where somebody says 'Well, I'm not sure but go ahead and do it.' That willingness to gamble on the hunch of the filmmaker is gone. You know, there are too many other people who will second-guess every second, the creative

Arnett's observation is apposite, given that Towne acknowledges the huge influence of the work of Dr. Jane Goodall on his adaptation, in particular, her book, *IN THE SHADOW OF MAN*, first published in 1971: interviewed for *Creative Screenwriting*, he recalled, years later, "… I remember when I wanted to do *Greystoke*. I called up a friend and said, 'Let's do it.' And he says, 'Oh, damn man, that's going to be a problem' – because an associate of his had [met resistance trying to put together a *Tarzan* film]. Oh no, come on – Jane Goodall, *SHADOW OF MAN*. We could actually do it now as it really happened. [And my friend said] 'You're right, screw it, let's do it.' [691] Her influence and perception of these animals suffuses the following excerpts from *Greystoke*, which is utterly visual and written as camera directions: [692]

343   DROOPY LIP

      cannot resist moving above the child and dropping down on him. He bounces on the branch the child is holding.

      The child loses his grip, falls a few feet -- easily grasps another branch. He looks up to Droop Lip who hoots derisively.

344   THE CHILD

---

executives that came along and read the material and then sit around. That visceral response, that 'Try it, and if you screw up, then it's your ass, but go ahead and try.' Storytelling is fun and impulsive. 'Wouldn't it be great if we did this and did that?' When you have to wait five damn years to find out if it'd be great the impulsiveness is gone." 'Surviving the Game: An Interview with Robert Towne,' by Daniel Argent, *Creative Screenwriting*. Vol. 7, No. 3, May/June 2000: 44.

Goodall's chief discovery is beyond dispute – that we share more than 99% of our genetic makeup with gorillas. In more recent years, however, Goodall has acknowledged what many long suspected to be true: that her observations were based on a false premise and that human co-existence had in fact altered chimpanzee behaviour to the extent that in another four sites on the African continent it was intensely aggressive, violent, and in the case of the Gombe Reserve, murderous – Frodo the friendly chimp beat one of his companions to death. The first chimp that Goodall befriended she named David Grey*beard*.

[691] Towne would comment to Alex Simon: "When you write like that, each moment is so subject to interpretation, that it's almost impossible to communicate to someone else what it is that you see." 'Mr PRE Comes to Towne,' *Venice*, September 1998: 35. Conrad Hall commented: "What a pity he didn't get a chance to direct that film!… We shot a scene with an orang-utan and a gymnast in a gorilla suit – like in *2001: A Space Odyssey* – and they looked like a child and his mother holding hands and walking through the forest together. Robert loved what I shot. They got into some real beefs, which I caught on film. The orang-utan would bite and wrestle and grab and run away and climb trees, and the 'mother' would climb after him, and together they'd go swinging through the trees. It looked very violent. There were real bites, and the gymnast had to fight for life. That's what made it real. And I was on the perimeter kicking dust up and making it look more violent." Michael Sragow, 'Return of the Native,' *New Times Los Angeles*, 3-9 September 1998: 17. The fact that Towne used an orang-utan might suggest a certain deficiency in his research.

[692] Biskind.*Op.cit.,* 393-4.

stares up at the young ape and gives a low-pitched panting bark -- an obvious threat. He moves swiftly toward the teasing ape.

345   DROOPY LIP

feigns alarm. He screeches, does a somersault to a lower branch.

346   THE CHILD

follows and the two move more swiftly through the trees until Droopy Lip tumbles onto the ground and the child follows, jumping onto the young ape and they go rolling and screeching down an embankment in a fierce mock battle until they hit the edge of a small lake.
The two of them break abruptly. They get to their knees and stare at the lake. It is particularly beautiful -- a placid crystalline surface with shafts of sunlight playing on it.

The child stares at the surface, then gives a "hu" of surprise.

He sees the reflection of Droopy Lip and next to him he sees his own reflection. Droopy Lip also looks and is equally fascinated. He touches the reflection of the child and the image shimmers on the surface of the water. Then it clears and the images become sharp again. The two turn to one another in wonder, then look back at their images on the water.

The image is shattered by a leopard that lands in front of them, having leapt from the trees behind them.

The leopard goes for the child, cutting off its retreat to land as it does.

91

347   THE CHILD

tumbles forward into the pond, disappearing under the surface.

348   THE LEOPARD

immediately turns its attack on the ape who screeches and starts to scramble up the embankment.

In two strides the leopard leaps on the ape's back.
She drags it screaming and tumbling back to the
water's edge. There she completes the kill by
biting the back of the young ape, severing its
spinal cord.

The ape lies paralyzed when the leopard turns its
attention to the splashing in the water.

Towne has taken the anthropological lessons of Goodall to heart and describes
with infinite sympathy the chimpanzees' own capacity for empathy in this midpoint
sequence. What matters in this sequence is not merely the struggles delineated between
the various beasts, but the planting of crucial information: Tarzan's differences from his
'family' and his potential, indicated by his cleverness in staying in hiding, below the
surface of the water.

349   THE CHILD

has surfaced. It begins to paddle fiercely to the
far side of the lake.

Meanwhile, the screams of the paralysed ape have
brought the rest of the troop, which comes crashing
through the trees.

350   THE LEOPARD

reacts to the SOUNDS of the troop and immediately
goes to its prey, dragging it off, not wishing a
confrontation with the entire troop.

351   KALA

in the trees sees the spectacle below, and calls out
frantically to her child who is in the water. He
doesn't respond. In desperation, she drops out of
the trees, lumbers to the water's edge, calls out
again.

352   THE CHILD

lies sprawled on the opposite bank. He now looks
back.

353   KALA

continues to call but is afraid to go more than a
few feet into the lake. She glances around him
nervously.

92

354   THE CHILD

       returns her call, promptly plunges back into the
       lake and begins to paddle toward her.

355   KALA

       is so astonished she stops calling altogether.

356   THE CHILD

       continues his steady paddling and reaches the
       embankment where Kala stands and they embrace.

Tarzan is already a worry to his 'mother', Kala. The
power of the descriptions - brilliantly lucid
juxtapositions - Tarzan is dripping wet in the jungle,
dry on the side of the embankment; Tarzan flying through
space, Tarzan lying beneath the water;' these show a
strong grasp of basic cinematic visuals - contrast,
conflict, and colourful action.

                                           DISSOLVE TO:

357   THE CHILD

       moves along the floor of the forest. He's dripping
       wet. He scrambles up a tree trunk.

358   IN THE TOP

       he begins to move it back and forth. The trunk
       groans. When he has it at its widest possible arc,
       he lets go. The trunk catapults him through the
       air.

359   THE CHILD

       flying through space. He crashes into a stream.
360   UNDERWATER

       he twists and turns and shoots to the surface.
       There he paddles about happily.

361   KALA

       remains on the embankment by the stream. She eats
       some bark and watches uneasily as her charge goes
       flying from the trunk top and cannonballs into the
       water again. Clearly it bewilders her.

        now lies on the embankment. His hair is sleek and
        glistening, his eyes clear, his skin white -- in
        vivid contrast to his earlier welt-ridden and dirty
        body.

Every shot is either connected to or in contrast with
that preceding and following it, each action building
toward Kala's realisation that her child is indeed
different to the average ape.

This is the beginning of the midpoint sequence, that
portion of the screenplay which serves in microcosm as
the crux of the work's concerns. It is, if you will, the
heart of the film, following the rather conventional
first act, which delineates the journey of the young
Englishman and his pregnant wife and their suffering at
the hands of a mutinous crew and culminating in the
protagonist's psychical acquisition of his true self – an
albino ape.

The middle chapters of the book delineate Tarzan's increasing realization that he
is growing away from his adoptive 'family' and he has successfully taught himself the
English language through the insect-like shapes he has studied so assiduously in the
jungle cabin. He leaves the jungle to seek out people of his kind and is 'reborn' as a
nobleman in his encounter with his 'successor', Clayton, Lord Greystoke, and Jane
Porter, educated by D'Arnot. This use of screenplay structure exemplifies the midpoint
sequence as described by Linda Cowgill in Chapter 1.

In the screenplay this sequence continues as the child makes his way following 'a
strange scent on the wind' which brings him to a cabin:

369   THE CABIN - MED. SHOT

        Jungle vegetation has half-reclaimed it. Vines with
        bright colored flowers snake in through the rotting
        window staves -- the chimney top has collapsed into
        rubble.

370   THE CHILD

        is mesmerized by the structure. He takes the last
        few steps to the entrance. He touches the door,
        moves along the cabin wall to one of the windows.
        He peers in.

                                                        94

371   THROUGH THE STAVES AND FOLIAGE

a dim but suggestive outline of the room can be SEEN.

372   THE CHILD

shakes the staves. They creak but they don't give.
He moves along the wall -- spots the opening at the
top of the collapsing chimney.

He swiftly climbs to the roof - makes his way toward
the chimney, but as he does, the roof gives way.
The child disappears with a grunt of surprise.

373   INT. CABIN

The child holds onto a cross beam, looking down at
the contents of the cabin as he dangles in the air.

He lets go of the beam and drops to the floor. There
he hits some mildewed sail-cloth. Dust rises. He
sneezes violently. He sneezes again.

He slowly moves about the room, moving past:

Mildewed rag-bag of bones by the cabin wall. He all
but ignores them.

The cradle which he brushes against. It rocks. He
jumps back -- makes a threatening face and sound. It
stops. He pays no attention to the tiny skeleton
beneath it.

Portrait of his father in uniform of the Old Stream
Guards. It is on sideboard, its ornate silver frame
now black with tarnish. He stares at it but doesn't
respond to it.

Oil lamp decorated with a snow scene.
A horse-drawn water cart in carved and painted wood.
He sniffs these last two -- sneezes again.

Swivelled mirror, painted with storks and bulrushes,
mounted on tiny dressing table. Cobwebbed combs and
brushes lie before it.

374   THE CHILD

stares at his dusty reflection. This he recognizes.
He makes a face and some noises at his image. He
touches the mirror, looks behind it.

This is a classic midpoint sequence as described by Cowgill, locating the very heart of the story – family, community, identity and belonging - amidst some of Towne's favourite tropes (landscape, water, building frames), and contains the very essence of Lacanian psychoanalysis – the initial misrecognition and then identification in the mirror sequence (attempted with a rather different intention and outcome by The Marx Brothers some years previously.)   It also foreshadows what is to come when he is found again by his human family.

95

374   CONTINUED:

> Then, suddenly, his eyes are drawn back to the portrait. He moves back to it -- this time gazes intently. He picks it up and goes back to the mirror.
>
> He holds the portrait up so he can see it beside himself in the mirror. It disturbs him -- he starts to shake -- throws the portrait over his head with a threatening bark -- turns away from the mirror. He turns back -- screams into the mirror. Then stops -- stares suddenly at his face again. It is expressionless. He moves away -- freezes. Grows pale. His breathing becomes shallow.
>
> He leaps onto the desk. The desk collapses, throwing him against the door -- where the impact trips the latch and sends him tumbling through the door to the outside.

(*Greystoke*: 94-5)

This acquisition by Tarzan of his 'self' demarcates the screenplay into the two distinct halves which reflect the novel's structure: Europe, then Africa and the clash of nature versus civilisation, an ecological and anthropological excavation of the type that Towne himself had attempted in *Chinatown*. (It is also all that truly remains of Towne's script in the film directed by Hugh Hudson, subtitled, *The Legend of Tarzan, Lord of the Apes*, released in 1984.)

The cabin symbolizes Tarzan's inner life, the life of the mind, that is the key to his survival – the value that is the whole screenplay's through-line. This entire dialogue-free section of the screenplay which juxtaposes so vividly the world of the apes and the naïve hero, with the world of humans [which he eventually enters, armed with deadly weapons], would be retained by the makers of the film in its most successful sequence – for that was the sacrifice that was made, the death of one child, so that another could live in this 'psychical' phase of self-discovery. Ironically, it is probably this that discouraged producers from taking on the project by a neophyte director, given that his popular reputation was for endlessly quotable dialogue. Towne never had to make the one difficult decision which would influence the production's relative practical difficulties – who would play the apes? Actors in gorilla suits? (And he passed on the chance to do an adaptation of his sick friend John Fante's novel, BROTHERHOOD OF THE GRAPE.) He did some script doctoring to help out other friends instead. Towne's brilliant midpoint evocation of a child's life turned out to be probably the emotional midpoint of his screenwriting career.

The last few pages of the available screenplay consist of a step outline to the conclusion, suggesting the final 35 pages in which Tarzan, following the death of Lord Greystoke, and having recovered from a potentially fatal childhood illness, returns alone to the jungle, his *natural* home, to live with his true family of apes:

```
Back in Africa.  The Aberdares.  The fig tree – Tarzan
alone or Tarzan and Silver Beard.  They play, pull down
figs.  Presently Silver Beard cocks his head- there are
the sounds of apes.  He beckons Tarzan.  He displays in
annoyance.  Tarzan embraces him and lets him go off into
the forest alone.
```

(Greystoke: Outline p.175 – concl.)

Towne's problems in finishing the screenplay for *Greystoke* meant that somehow the story got lost. The first eighty or ninety pages were completely free of dialogue and he realised he would have to direct it himself: it is difficult in these circumstances to see the attraction for any major studio. This is when Towne started to focus on another idea, about female track athletes and he eventually lost the entire project to David Geffen in order to complete financing on *Personal Best*. Anthea Sylbert was forced to say to her fellow executives at Warners, "let's look at it this way. From the practical side, isn't it better to have Towne do a movie that's controlled, right here, with adults, rather than off in Africa with babies, and live chimps, and mechanical chimps. It seems to me that not only does this make creative sense, but it probably makes business sense." [693]

On 14 February 1980 David Begelman announced a new production – *Tarzan*, to be directed by John Derek and starring his wife Bo. According to *Variety* on that date, "status of another Tarzan pic long-ago announced to be written and directed by Robert Towne, remains unclear." [694]

However impractical it may seem to the observer given the clear production difficulties implicit in Towne's screenplay, it is clear from his own repeated references to that period of his life that *Greystoke* has come to symbolise something of a tragedy for Towne:

Usually it's just movies, but the loss of *Greystoke* is inconsolable. Just inconsolable.

- Robert Towne, 1998 [695]

In protest, Towne put his dog's name, P.H. Vazak, on the screenplay for the film instead of his own, from a screenplay which was 'co-written' with Michael Austin. Hira

[693] *Variety* 14 February 1980.
[694] Rebecca Ascher-Walsh, 'Testing *Limits*,' *Entertainment Weekly*, 18 September 1998: 24.
[695] Towne, speaking to Michael Dwyer, 'Call the Script Doctor,' *The Irish Times*, 22 July 2006: 7. P.H. Vazak died shortly after his nomination for an Academy Award.

was the first dog to have been nominated for a screenwriting achievement. He didn't win. Towne has stated, "I felt bad about that because I think my dog was entitled to a better film. He was a wonderful dog." [696]

Heaven Can Wait (1978) (uncredited)

Here Comes Mr Jordan (1941) was Warren Beatty's new project, a remake of the Robert Montgomery and Evelyn Keyes comedy hit for Columbia Pictures which Beatty wanted to write and co-direct (with Buck Henry) with Muhammad Ali in the leading role of a boxer killed in an accident whose heavenly abode holds no attraction.[697] He wants to return to earth for some unfinished business. Beatty returned to the title of the originating play and co-wrote the screenplay with Elaine May (and her writing partner, Peter Feibleman) adapting the original screenplay by Sidney Buchman and Seton I. Miller, from Harry Segall's story (all three had won Academy Awards for their work.) Beatty asked Towne to do a script polish but Towne was preoccupied with *Greystoke* and apparently contributed just one scene to the rewrite.

Reds (1981) (uncredited)

Warren Beatty's pet project took him several years to put together. The screenplay was written in London's Dorchester Hotel by Beatty and English radical playwright, Trevor Griffiths after Griffiths' first draft was judged 'too political.' This draft was also deemed unacceptable and Griffiths allegedly abandoned the project at this point.[698] Beatty favourites Robert Towne and Elaine May were supposedly brought in to polish the screenplay, a recreation of the autobiography of John Reed (1997-1920), American journalist and communist revolutionary, *TEN DAYS THAT SHOOK THE WORLD*, which was first published in 1918. In fact, Towne contributed the outline and the line, "Don't leave me." [699] The project reunited him, however briefly, with Nicholson, who agreed to play Eugene O'Neill. Towne commented to Michael Sragow,

> Whenever I help out Warren, whether it's on *Reds* or *Heaven Can Wait*, I only feel
> I'm helping him get his own vision on the screen. I wouldn't think of taking writing
> credit for friendly suggestions. Did Tiffany sign every lamp, or Fabergé every egg? [700]

Towne's perception of his work, that of master collaborator, is evident here. However, simultaneously, he was cultivating his position as writer/director, indicating a conflict (or readiness to compromise) that was economically necessary for his survival.

Personal Best (1982) (written and directed by)

> *Personal Best* didn't take long, about a month.
> > - Towne on scriptwriting, at the Edinburgh Film Festival

---

[696] Despite the title, the production had no connection with *Heaven Can Wait* (1943), directed by Ernst Lubitsch from Samson Raphaelson's screenplay.

[697] Donald. Shepherd. *JACK NICHOLSON: An Unauthorized Biography*. London: Robson Books, 1991. 141.

[698] Towne interviewed by Michael Atkinson, *ibid.*

[699] Michael Sragow, 'Ghostwriters: Unraveling the Enigma of Movie Authorship,' *Film Comment*, 19, March 1983.

[700] Kenneth Turan, 'Robert Towne's Hollywood Without Heroes,' *New York Times*, 27 October 1988.

Athleticism has often denoted homoerotic activity in Hollywood cinema – but with the lifting of censorship laws, the change in the Production Code and the pervasiveness of frontal nudity in Seventies Cinema, a penchant for pounding on running tracks no longer signified covert sexuality. Yet for Robert Towne, a lifelong devotion to sport could finally see the light of day in his directorial debut, a gift from newly installed studio chief David Geffen that would prove decidedly double-edged, paradoxically centring on a relationship between lesbian athletes, *Personal Best*. Why make the leap to directing? He told critic Kenneth Turan some years later: "... even if someone is scrupulous about your text, tone is finally what's important, and you can't get that if you're not willing to be there and insist on it." [701]

> Male or female, how do you compete with a body you have already surrendered
> to your opponent?
> - Advertising for *Personal Best*

The specifics of the story were rumoured to be based on a scandal in the US track team, a claim that Towne has never corroborated or denied. But he did venture that the characters were

> combinations of characters... in casting certain people, the minor characters,
> the athletes themselves became the characters. But the coach and the girls
> were all based on certain characters or combinations of them. [702]

The story might have been prompted by a chance meeting with athlete Jane Frederick in the weight room at UCLA in 1976. Biskind makes the claim for it that "it was still another story about innocence despoiled, primitive grace, pre- or sub-verbal natural man, or in this case, woman." [703] The film is unique in its two female leads (perhaps only *The Turning Point*, 1977, could boast a similar contemporary story of female rivalry and love/hate); in its utilising of the mythological (even fairytale) as narrative arc; and in its eliciting of an extended response among queer film theorists.

Figure 19 *Personal Best* dvd cover art

Towne wrote the screenplay at his bungalow on the Warners lot, racing ahead in order to beat a threatened actors strike. The film would go ahead despite the Americans not leaving for the Moscow Olympics. Nicholson turned down the role of coach and the part was offered instead to Scott Glenn. Towne then cast Mariel Hemingway (*Manhattan*) in the leading role of Chris Cahill, hurdler turned pentathlete, and Patrice Donnelly, a hurdling star, as Tory Skinner, a brilliant pentathlete. Hemingway trained for

---

[701] Towne. *Op.cit.*. 129
[702] Biskind. *Op.cit.*, 394.
[703] Speaking at the 1998 Floating Film Festival

over a year in order to convince as a track veteran, whereas this was to be Donnelly's acting debut.

> Strictly speaking, a movie about athletes wouldn't interest me… What interests me are issues…The issue in *Personal Best* I think was: How do you compete against someone you love? And the answer was: You don't, you compete against yourself.
>
> - Robert Towne [704]

Synopsis:

At the 1976 Olympic trials, successful Pentathlete Tory_Skinner meets hurdler Chris Cahill, who is depressed at her poor performance. The two women spend an evening together and, after getting stoned and engaging in an arm-wrestling contest, they become lovers. Tory's trainer, Terry Tingloff, is reluctantly persuaded to take Chris in hand, and she is eventually selected to run in the 1978 World Student Games in Cali, Colombia. She falls ill after eating fruit from a street market, and Tory nurses her through the night. The next day, Chris performs well while Tory does badly. Later, Terry proposes that Chris train for the Pentathlon. She is reluctant to compete directly with her lover and Tory is resentful at first, but on Chris' birthday, gives her a Pentathlon training record book as a gesture of reconciliation. Later, Tory suggests that Chris lengthen her approach to the high jump, but accidentally moves the mark too far, causing Chris to injure her knee. Suspecting foul play, Chris spends the night at Terry's place, and then leaves Tory. She meets water polo player Denny Stites and they become friends, eventually lovers. [705] At the 1980 Olympic trials in Oregon, Chris spots Tory, from whom she is now completely estranged; against Terry's orders, she goes to wish her luck. As the Pentathlon proceeds, Tory falls behind and, in the last event, the 800 metres, Chris helps her out by forcing the pace, thus tiring out Tory's main opponent, Charlene Benveniste, at the expense of her own performance. As a result of the race, however, both women qualify for the Olympic team. [706]

The 22 February 1980 edition of the script differs somewhat from the released film. Running 168 pages, it elides whole sequences – for instance the Maple Leaf event in Toronto pp. 43-6 is excised and replace with the Cali, Colombia World Student Games of 1978 - and brings forward conversations from one scene and cuts them into another, so that the finished film, while having the main shape of the screenplay, also loses many of the more subtle aspects of characterisation on the page. It was probably written during the actors' strike because the film had commenced shooting in Summer 1979. Towne's personal relationship with his wife deteriorated at this time and there were substantial rumours about the nature of his relationships with both Mariel Hemingway and Patrice Donnelly, as well as the use of cocaine on the set, something which Towne has never denied. The film was Hemingway's first role since making *Manhattan* (1979) for Woody Allen. [707]

---

[704] Towne himself had played water polo at college.

[705] Taken from *Monthly Film Bulletin*, Vol. 50 No. 594, July 1983: 193.

[706] During the strike Towne confessed his affair with Patrice Donnelly to his wife, who started divorce proceedings and launched a legendary custody battle for their daughter (Katharine, now an actress). When the film finally resumed shooting it was several months later.

[707] See Dancyger and Rush. *ALTERNATIVE SCRIPTWRITING: Writing Beyond the Rules, Second Edition*). Boston and London: Focal Press, 1995.for the genre characteristics of sports films, 67-68.

Personal Best conforms to the generic categories of the sports film as follows: Mariel Hemingway is a gifted athlete, testing herself within the confines of her chosen career; the film however is not dealing with one of the top three popular sports subjects, boxing, football or baseball, but it does deal with a subject familiar to audiences from the Oscar-winning *Chariots of Fire* and perhaps *Golden Girl*, from a few years previously. That the protagonist's internal struggle is the real antagonist does not especially hold true for Hemingway's character, since she must deal with the overweening good cop/bad cop influence of mentor Scott Glenn, who is her male lover, as well as dealing with her attraction to her fellow competitor, another woman, all of which contributes to her unravelling emotional state. Family is not an aspect of this narrative - Towne makes the interesting decision not to revert to the backstory after the introduction to the self-evidently troubled home - but the track activities are crucial to the unfolding story and the coach, fellow athletes and romantic relationships create an alternative to a family structure in the traditional sense, somewhat in the manner of a fairytale (whose subtext is always the reforming of family). The person who espouses the motivational outlook which finally drives her to succeed is her final male lover, Denny Stites (Kenny Moore), who encourages her to do her '*Personal Best.*' [708]

The 1980 Moscow Olympics was the event that mysteriously inspired a glut of Hollywood productions, yet ironically was decreed off-limits to U.S. athletes. Towne said of the disastrous decision that it could render the conclusion of his film devoid of meaning. Nonetheless, if the real-life athletes couldn't compete officially, some of them got work as extras on several other track and field films. Thus, when Towne was writing and preparing *Personal Best* it would become part of a minor if short-lived genre. In terms of its dramatic narrative, the central relationship in the film is lesbian, a minor genre which had its examples. Commenting on *Personal Best* in the film adaptation of Vito Russo's book *The Celluloid Closet,* 'sexpert' Susie Bright makes that point quite succinctly, explaining certain of the lascivious critical comments on reception:

> There's a whole world of difference between how an audience looks at two
> men getting it on and two women getting it on. There's a comfort with female
> nudity and female girlishness and kind of girly bonding, that it can be sexy and it
> can be completely palatable, even erotic. Women don't find it threatening and men
> often find it completely unthreatening or titillating. [709]

The history provided both by Russo's book and the documentary that followed is summed up in the phrase, 'writing movies between the lines,' a situation exacerbated by the introduction of the Hays Code (also known as the Production Code). As one commentator during the documentary notes, "it didn't erase homos, just made them harder to find." [710] It wasn't really until the Eighties that homosexual characters began truly to be represented in their own right: however they became victimisers, for instance in *Cruising* (1980) and *Windows* (1980).

Writer/Director
The principal element that distinguishes the director's authorial contribution above the screenwriter's might be condensed into the pictorial, especially in the case of the writer/director. Towne's visual choices are certainly influenced by his previous

---

[708] *The Celluloid Closet* (1993)
[709] *Ibid.*
[710] Speaking at the Edinburgh Film Festival.

collaborators, especially Hal Ashby; however it is evident that in his decision to make what is essentially a sports drama that other aesthetic choices would drive his filmmaking style. It is certainly the case that he had a highly developed visual style as can be seen in all his screenwriting; and particularly in the case of *Chinatown* that the visual imperative of the film was Jake's point of view, which is clearly delineated in the script. In *Greystoke* the degree of visual description clarifies his statement that in writing a screenplay he is describing something that has already been shot. It is pertinent to quote from the work since it exemplifies his visual precision and focus on movement, obviously here the emphasis being the depiction of the women's physicality, a trait that is echoed in the variety of close-ups, long shots and varied shooting and editing rhythms.

Page one reads as follows:

```
FADE IN:

EXT. EUGENE STADIUM - DAY

A TARTAN TRACK

twenty inches away.  Superimpose:  OLYMPIC TRIALS
EUGENE OREGON 1976.  Droplets hit the speckled yellow
surface and sink into it.  O.S. an announcer with a
vaguely apocalyptic tone calls out the lane assignments
for the finals for the women's hundred meter hurdles.
More droplets hit the surface. VIEW SHIFTS and CAMERA
TILTS UP to show:

THE WOMEN AT THEIR BLOCKS

for the start of the race.  The droplets of perspir-
ation hitting the track are from CHRIS CAHILL, on the
inside lane, closest to CAMERA.  She's sweating so much
she looks as though she's already run the race.  The
announcer completes the lane assignments.

EXT. EUGENE STADIUM - DAY

THE STARTER

steps into position, his red-sleeved arm raising the
pistol.

CHRIS
sees him out of the corner of her eye.

                    THE STARTER
          Runners to your marks -

ALONG THE BLOCKS

rear legs scrunch up against the rear block.
```

CLOSE — CHRIS

breathing heavily

BEFORE HER

are ten hurdles. Sun glinting off the track makes them
shimmer. The roar of the crowd seems to grow — then
abruptly trails off into a hiss, with whispers of
"Gun's up! Gun's up!" — then silence.

> THE STARTER'S VOICE
>   — get set —

(CONTINUED)

CONTINUED:

ALONG THE BLOCKS

everyone is poised to explode.

THE GUN

goes off.

THE HURDLES

Racing toward CAMERA are the eight finalists. Two of
them hit hurdles — one of the girls goes sprawling.

PENNY BRILL

moves thru the field after a slow start. With each
hurdle she seems to pick up speed, grow more aggressive.

AT THE SIXTH HURDLE — CHRIS

sees Penny skim by her. It throws her off stride and
she begins to tie up.

AT THE FINISH

Penny Brill crosses first, Chris Cahill is fifth.

THE RUNNERS

continue down the chute, all in varying states of
ecstasy.

(Personal Best: 1-2)

Thus from the starting blocks we have inscribed in dynamic fashion the metaphor of competition– the stress on Chris' energy levels (she seems to have run the race before it has started) emphasises her youth (and relative inexperience) as well as her willingness to make an effort to succeed. Her competitive drive is etched on the rivulets of sweat coursing down her face. This sets up the dramatic arc for her character in an interesting and active way. Page one also serves to illustrate the degree to which Towne is conscious of auditory expression on film, matching sound effects to the visuals, which are cut vividly to demonstrate the degree of effort the hurdlers are forced to make. It is also notable that Towne uses the word 'ecstasy' to describe the women's response to their intense experience, as though the race itself is foreplay for a bigger, sexual drama. The visual effect is such that the viewer feels not merely empathy but virtual participation.

If we are to begin to assess the evolution of Towne's directing style, and hence his assumption of the mantle of another aspect of authorship, we might see here the shadow of *Shampoo*, whose first scene, the aftermath of George Roundy's lovemaking with Felicia, takes place in the dark. (The directorial decision to go along with Towne's idea, to shoot the scene in the dark with the sound effects, emphasises Towne's own keen awareness of the importance of sound effects on film audiences, with the heightened sense of auditory detail and scene-setting.) Towne's theme – that of loss – is heavily underscored throughout the narrative as every aspect of the protagonists' lives is a competition – on and off the track people have the potential to win or the misfortune to lose.

Towne used three directors of photography and acknowledged his debt to *Olympia*, the Leni Riefenstahl film. He used different camera speeds to emphasis motion, which for him signified character: he admitted to being influenced by Robert Reagar's swimming coverage. He reversed Riefenstahl's technique, sometimes going from a speed of 120 to slow to heighten tension (the shot putt sequence) in "an attempt actually to underscore the way in which the athlete himself moved." [711]

David Bordwell and Kristin Thompson's photographic analysis of the Leni Riefenstahl documentary film demonstrates the elements common to it and the Towne production. According to the authors, Riefenstahl was limited in the way in which she could organise the shoot around the real-life athletes and "overcame this limitation by creating a variety of ingenious devices that could allow her camera crew to film from a distance (including using airships and aeroplanes) and from unusual angles. In this way, the solution to technical problems ended by enhancing the stylistic variety of the film." [712]

Two of the stylistic components evident in *Olympia* may also be seen in *Personal Best*: the compositional framing wherein an object low in the foreground heightens the depth of the background; and the juxtaposing of alternating film speeds and editing rhythms which lends the films a fluidity and balances the more fundamentally dramatic aspects of the story in the case of *Personal Best*. These elements prove that Towne's interest in the cinematic went beyond the mere duplication of action: he was keen to inscribe into his shooting methodology a style that reflected not only the philosophical

---

[711] David Bordwell and Kristin Thompson. *FILM ART An Introduction, Fifth Edition*, McGraw-Hill, 1997: 368.
[712] Towne, 'On Directing,' 123-124.

ideals of the sport but also a visual expression of what the athlete might herself be experiencing.

Towne ascribes a great deal of importance to the size of shot and style of movement in communicating character:

> ... I think film does this, through movement rather than the traditional thing where character is revealed through action. In film, the character is as often as not in movement.

Towne continues:

> Part of what I am saying is that I saw, literally, the development of character in motion... I did not see a distinction between athletic action and character, and so much of the point of it was about the nature of competing and about the nature of how you square that with yourself in terms of someone you really care about, either defeating them or going ahead and trying to realize yourself the best way you can. These are two fundamentally different approaches to competition. That was the point of the film. [713]

This conjoins Towne's philosophy as a writer with his filmmaking practice as he completes the project of authorship: the innate link between a character's personal situation or occupation, and their position in life (and in a race).[714] The arm-wrestling scene in Act I provides an apt metaphor for the struggle between the central characters and indicates Towne's deep understanding of the importance of visual language and symbolic gesture.

Personal Best provided a rare opportunity for feminist critics to engage in a queer reading of a mainstream film. Christine Holmlund says it is part of a new subgenre, the 'femme film,' part of a group of films which offered a change in the traditional cinematic representation of lesbianism. [715] Its release provoked an exchange of lengthy justifications and rebuttals in the pages of film journal *Jump Cut*, when Linda Williams' defence of the film was answered by Chris Straayer discussed its portrayal of lesbianism on screen, and also made the crucial distinction between the interpretation of the film (or any film dealing with lesbian issues) from the perspective of a lesbian/feminist reading.

Williams makes the point that

> ... the combination of sports and sex was a stroke of genius. Those who would normally be shocked or at least irritated by a lesbian relationship in any other context find it quite 'natural' among female athletes who, it is presumed, are simply more physical than other people. The film thus capitalizes on public awareness of, and curiosity about, lesbian athletes like Billie Jean King while evading any real presentation of lesbian identity. [716]

---

[713] Director Nicolas Roeg says, "it's the film itself that will complete his [the screenwriter's] job." Quoted in *THE FILMS OF NICOLAS ROEG* by Neil Sinyard. London: Letts, 1991, 2.
[714] Christine Holmlund, 'When is a Lesbian Not a Lesbian? The Lesbian Continuum and the Mainstream Femme Film,' *Camera Obscura*, 1991: 25-26, 145-178. The other films are *Lianna*, *Entre Nous* and *Desert Hearts*.

[715] Linda Williams, '*Personal Best*,' *Jump Cut* 27, July 1982: 10-11.

[716] Chris Straayer, '*Personal Best*: Lesbian/Feminist Audience,' *Jump Cut* 29, February 1984: 40. Straayer provides a brief overview of feminist film theory, referring to books like *POPCORN*

Straayer responded to the points made by Williams, commenting that she had not investigated 'the question of female viewer response.' [717] Straayer argues that Williams is in danger of perpetuating homophobic myths by her insistence on the female/lesbian/audience imbibing the pre-arranged 'male' viewpoint in the absorption of images. [718] Straayer interrogates Chris and Tory's relationship, noting that lesbian existence is necessarily a meta-identity that involves passing between two worlds, the heterosexual one and the lesbian community. This identity is forged from an acknowledgement of the self and an understanding of that identity created by others for you, what Straayer defines as 'a co-exisiting awareness.' [719]

This diversion into queer criticism is useful because it draws attention to the fact that it is not necessarily the content but the structure – the way the story is told – that is ultimately important: Towne's authorial choices, reflected in his directing style, are what is of interest. Culturally speaking, *Personal Best* came about at a time of social and economic upheaval for women when the peak of the feminist movement was on the wane and it expresses real male confusion at the newly empowered opposite sex as well as awe (perhaps not very subtly expressed) at women's physical prowess in performing traditional male sports.

Towne told Dale Pollock of *The Los Angeles Times*,

"What I'm interested in is how you deal with a society that encourages competitions, and still care about other people. These two women are in love with each other. In order to place emphasis on who they're making love to, you have to show it. But there are only two minutes of sex in the film; there are two hours of competition." [720]

Perhaps we should leave the last words on the queer interpretation to the writer since it is he who is pursuing the theme and content: Towne responded to criticisms of the film as follows in an interview conducted by Gregg Kilday for the *Los Angeles Herald-Examiner*:

VENUS and *FROM REVERENCE TO RAPE*, which popularised the notion in the early 1970s at the height of the feminist movement, and then discusses Laura Mulvey's seminal article, 'Visual Pleasure and Narrative Cinema,' whose Freudian/Lacanian approach coloured film theory for at least a decade and which itself provoked a wealth of commentary. Straayer however comments that further discussions of identification in cinema preferred not to use the psychoanalytical model because of its innately sexist premise and refers to Arbuthnot and Seneca's discussion of *Gentlemen Prefer Blondes* in *Film Reader* No. 5 in which the authors engage positively with the film's female role models and concludes, with the authors, that "identification is not in itself a male operation." *Op.cit.*, 41.

[717] *Ibid.*

[718] *Ibid.*

[719] Dale Pollock, 'Towne: Toughing it Out to the Finish Line,' January 29, 1982, *L.A. Times*, Calendar: 1.

[720] February 5, 1982: D4-5. Elsewhere, Towne said it was about "two children … discovering who they are with their bodies." Jack Kroll, 'Chariots of Desire,' Newsweek, 99.6, 08 February 1982: 60. Holmlund states that, "Production publicity further displaced the issue of homosexuality by emphasizing Donnelly's status as an ex-pentathlete and Hemingway's assiduous athletic training for her role." Holmlund. *Op.cit.*: 150. Following a deconstruction of the swift transitions from lesbian to heterosexual sex scenes, she concludes, "the moral of this story is: a lesbian, and especially a femme, is *not* a lesbian when there's a man around." (154.)

"…To me, anyway, women's track is a little more revelatory, a little more theatrical…

"That [lesbianism] isn't the subject of the movie… there is one love scene in the film compared to more than 30 minutes of the various competitions. What I wanted to do is just make their sexual relationship very matter-of-fact. The feeling and the caring between the two women is what's important. I mean, I'm offended when Barbara Walters interviews Billie Jean King and asks her if she's a lesbian. It's just too simplistic." [721]

We should recall that in creating the role of Evelyn Mulwray, Towne had sensed there was a part of femininity that would always remain essentially inaccessible to the male psyche, and here, with both Chris and Tory, he would express this in such a way as to make the male characters curious, ignorant, and even admiring, of their sensibility. The pursuit of love and the pursuit of one's *Personal Best* is the narrative throughline; sexual success and personal compatibility are, it seems, some of the benefits of being a winner. The flipside of losing in competition was also that one could win in love – a theme that would persist in *Without Limits*.

Mythology and The Female Hero

Towne's interrogation of the female hero here is quite unique in American cinema and is further evidence of his pursuit of the mythological in screen stories. Carol Pearson and Katherine Pope question the portrayal of female characters in literary history. They posit the notion that female heroes have traditionally fallen into two categories: on the one hand there is the woman as heroine wherein she is virgin, mistress or helpmate (corresponding with Joseph Campbell's goddess, temptress or earth mother – someone who is part of the male journey but does not exist as a whole person). On the other hand, however, Pearson and Pope claim that there is place for a female hero, along the lines of tradition male heroes: they categorise her as sage, artist or warrior and she becomes the primary character in her own story. [722]

In Pearson's THE HERO WITHIN: *Six Archetypes We Live By*, the author extends the analogy as a useful metaphor by which to understand female development. In taking the archetypes (usually understood as male) of Innocent, Orphan, Martyr, Wanderer, Warrior and Magician, she creates a gallery of portraits representative of character qualities and stages of personal evolution. This is a hero's journey parallel to that posited by Carl Jung, a journey of individuation, in which the archetypes manifested in our daily lives help define and expand the ego's boundaries. [723] At the centre of this

[721] Pearson and Pope. WHO AM I THIS TIME? *Female Portraits in American and British Literature*. New York: McGraw-Hill Co, 1976.

[722] Pearson describes the stages as follows: "Each of the archetypes carries with it a worldview, and with that different life goals and theories about what gives life meaning. Orphans seek safety and fear exploitation and abandonment. Martyrs want to be good, and see the world as a conflict between good (care and responsibility) and bad (selfishness and exploitation.) Wanderers want independence and fear conformity. Warriors strive to be strong, to have an impact upon the world, and to avoid ineffectiveness and passivity. Magicians aim to be true to their inner wisdom and to be in balance with the energies of the universe. Conversely, they try to avoid the inauthentic and the superficial." Carol Pearson. THE HERO WITHIN: *Six Archetypes We Live By*. San Francisco: Harper and Row, 1986, 4-5.

[723] Pearson. *Op.cit.*, 153. Maureen Murdock defines the heroine's journey in terms of a redefining of the heroic (male) quest – creating balance by integrating the masculine and feminine aspects of our nature. The ultimate boon is the reclaiming of the Goddess – a projection of the female principle, that needs restoring to our culture. This model also entails the three components of

idea is the individual, who at various stages of personal development exhibits some of the tendencies described above, and ideally, 'ascends' to the stage of Magician when her journey is completed. This implies a return to a state of innocence, but the journey brings with it lessons, which, when learned and absorbed, transform the hero into a wise and loving individual.

In simple screenwriting terms, this gives us a way in which to understand the transformation of character in Towne's classical interpretation: the circular journey of a hero from Innocent to Magician provides a benchmark of psychological accuracy by which to measure that arc which in an ideal fictional work guides the reader or viewer to a deeper understanding of story.

The author summarises the journey (or the effect of the understanding that such a model provides) as follows:

> As we become more and more who we are and hence link up with whom we feel a deep connection, we have more, and satisfying, intimacy with others. The reward for the hero's inevitably solitary journey, then is community – community with the self, with other people, and with the natural and spiritual worlds. At the end of the journey, the hero feels and *is* at home in the world. [724]

Towne's characters frequently take circular journeys: in *The Last Detail* he altered the ending so that Bad Ass would end up back where he started; similarly, George Roundy, whose name signifies his particular character's destination; and in *Chinatown* Jake is right back where he started. The particular journey taken by the heroines in *Personal Best* is strikingly different from the way athletic women were portrayed in Hollywood in the 1930s and 1940s – Sonja Henie and Esther Williams were not placed in competitive narratives and remained essentially non-threatening (as well as heterosexual.) In the 1950s, Katharine Hepburn would play opposite Spencer Tracy in *Pat and Mike*, with the inevitable promise that he would 'straighten' her out. [725] The Sixties would see only one female athlete's story on film, in *Billie* (1965). [726] Ultimately, all of these models involve what Aristotle termed 'recognition', or the realisation of one's true nature: in an extension to this dramatic idea, Towne takes it further – and not for the first time in his work, *Chinatown* being another example – insofar as 'recognition' comes in *Personal Best* it is in the form of Chris finally seeing *other people's* true nature. In this case, Chris realises that Tory is mortally jealous of her achievements and therefore she can never be her equal. Waking up to this realisation completes the second act of *Personal Best*. (In terms of what Dancyger and Rush delineate as the restorative screenplay structure in American cinema, Act One takes the form of transgression, while Act Three takes that of Redemption.) [727]

---

the hero's circular journey – Separation, Initiation and Return; Maureen Murdock. *THE HEROINE'S JOURNEY: Woman's Quest for Wholeness.* Boston: Shambhala Publications, 1990, 69.

[724] A trope that is enriched by the contemporary revelations about both actors' complicated homosexual private lives.

[725] Information courtesy of Demetrius W. Pearson, 'The Depiction and Characterization of Women in Sport Films,' in *Women in Sport and Physical Activity Journal,* V.10; N.1, 31 March 2001: 103. Article copyright Women of Diversity Productions, Inc. Database copyright. © SoftLine Information, Inc. 2001. Accessed online.

[726] Dancyger and Rush. *Op. cit.,* 33.

Integrating both models as paradigm, Pearson's and Murdock's, the character arc of Chris Cahill can be described as follows:

1. Chris begins as Innocent but is quickly initiated as
2. Orphan when she moves away from home and is 'adopted' by the older, lesbian pentathlete Tory Skinner.
3. Chris's Martyr phase allows her to commit to her relationship with Tory and she is encouraged to be a part of a team under the tutelage of Terry Tingloff (Scott Glenn.)
4. Chris and Tory are both jealous of each other's attractiveness to men and the jealousy manifests in the 'unconscious' damage to Chris' hopes when Tory advises her to attack the high jump differently. Under the influence of Denny, with whom Chris becomes intimate, Chris begins to find herself. This could be said to encompass the Wanderer phase of her development.
5. Chris then becomes a Warrior, battling for self-definition on and off the track.
6. When Chris meets Denny Stites, the former Olympic medal winner he inducts her into the world of both heterosexuality and the philosophy of '*Personal Best.*' It is now that Chris enters the Magician stage of her individuation and is able to sacrifice her own Gold medal chances in order to allow Tory to compete as an equal at the Moscow Olympics – which they cannot in any case attend.[728]

As Pearson asserts, we occupy what might be termed a 'Warrior culture,' in which "the hero/villain/victim myth informs our culture's basic secular belief system. The ritual that underlies the Warrior myths is found, of course, in war, but it also is played out culturally in our sports, our business practices, our religions, and even our economic and educational theories. In the realm of sports, we have seen over the *centuries* a progression from gladiatorial contests in which the loser actually was killed, to football, baseball, or soccer, in which the antagonist simply loses." [729] Thus, we could read the leading characters in *Personal Best* slightly differently if we see Tory as oscillating between the roles of mentor, villain and victim, in that order, throughout the unfolding story. Murdock describes a woman's descent to the Goddess (often described as depression in medical terms) as the beginning of her deep need to reconnect with the feminine – we could read Chris's relationship with Tory as a necessary precursor to her role as girlfriend to Denny. [730]

Using Murdock's model, we can read those periods of injury to Chris as an emotional and psychological opportunity to revise her goals. That she ultimately chooses

---

[727] The website www.managing-creativity.com, in its guide to writing a screenplay using the tenets of the hero's journey, offers this advice: "a) Once you know the apotheosis - the seminal insight the hero has - then you can build your story up to and beyond that point. Knowing the hero's apotheosis allows you to decide what the hero's restrictions will be and how to overcome them (atonement with the father). Knowing the hero's apotheosis allows you to decide the hero's inner resolve and actions upon the enlightenment (ultimate boon)."

[728] Pearson. *Op.cit.,* 77.
[729] Murdock. *Op.cit.,* 69.
[730] She asserts that "Women have to find autonomy before they can achieve wholeness. Examining the meaning of autonomy often involves discarding old ideas of success… The rewards of the outer journey can be seductive, but at some point the heroine awakens and says no to the heroics of the ego. They have come at too high a price." Murdock. *Op. cit.,* 69.

heterosexuality over lesbianism is partly a reaction to Tory's opportunistic sabotaging of her career but can also be read as a realisation that she can thrive better with a man as her romantic partner. This fits into Murdock's reworking of the traditional model.[731]

<pre>
                    CHRIS
         I watched your long jump - great,
         tremendous height. I love that
         feeling, flying thru the air,
         that's the way I started, the long
         jump ..

                    TORY
         Yeah?

                    CHRIS
         -yeah, anyway, congratulations.

Tory looks at her, touched both by the sincerity of the
compliment and Chris' try for composure.

                    TORY
         Thank you. I was into it and -
         some days you get lucky and, aww
         fuck, I'm so sorry -

She reaches out and to shoulder lightly. Chris nods and
then bows her head and abruptly begins to shake with sobs
- silently at first.
                    TORY
              (continuing;
               matter of fact)
         Hey, let go - it's got to come out
         sometime.

Chris' sobs become audible and wracking. Tory starts to
reach to her, thinks better of it, sits back and stares
out the front window.
</pre>

(Personal Best. 12)

Chris then occupies the more conventional role of the hero, with Tory alternately playing Mentor, Villain and Victim as Chris learns to assert herself and (literally) raise the bar, forcing Tory to acknowledge her superiority, but using her own generosity of spirit to allow Tory to reclaim her former glory as an athletics star. [732]

Ironically, then, in *Personal Best* it is the lesbian relationship which initially helps Chris to progress but then stifles her, seemingly in an accident but probably intentionally

---

[732] Egri. *Op. cit.*, 50.

as Tory changes Chris' work pattern in her strongest event. Tory then becomes the stereotypical 'husband', jealous of the wife's success and keen to keep her in the domestic environment, far from any opportunity for outshining him in the workplace. Towne's screenplay keeps Chris on a constant journey of change, conflict and self-knowledge which is deeply rooted in this mythological foundation, reflecting on his classical education but also on the mundanity of an unequal relationship. As Egri reminds us,

> Constant change is the very essence of all existence. Everything in time passes into its opposite. Everything within itself contains its own opposite. Change is a force which impels it to move , and this very movement becomes something different from what it was. [733]

Towne's focus on change prepares us for Chris' transitions, both personal and professional, which are always intertwined and interdependent. The strength of the screenplay lies in its powerful depiction of independent-minded characters whose ultimate conflict is inescapable:

> The real unity of opposites is one in which compromise is impossible. [734]

Initially, Tory is Chris' greatest supporter, encouraging her when she is feeling down about her potential as an athlete:

TORY
You can be great.

Chris' eyes grow moist.

CHRIS
You really believe that?

TORY
(quiet conviction)
I know it.

(*Personal Best*: 22)

We could, then, also interpret Tory as a Shapeshifter,

> ... the person who starts out as the hero's love interest shifts shape so far that she becomes the Shadow, bent on the hero's destruction. [735]

Towne is famous for the creation of morally ambiguous characters, Tory's mutability fits into that model, as well as mirroring the script's classical structure of circularity – and the shape of the track itself. Tory's jealousy of Chris' achievements (the

---

[733] Egri. *Op. cit.,* 119.

[734] Vogler. *Op. cit.,* 85.

[735] David Denby, 'Rear Window: Delivering His Personal Best,'"in *Premiere*, December 1988: 78. Aristotle's view of dialogue's power lies in its revelation of character: "What a personage says or does reveals a certain moral purpose; and a good element of character, if the purpose so revealed is good. Such goodness is possible in every type of personage, even in a woman." *ARISTOTLE The Art of Poetry*, Tr. Ingram Bywater, 55.

student overtaking the mentor) leads to conflict approximately 70 minutes into the film and immediately precedes the event that leads to the severing of the relationship:

```
                TORY
    There's only one thing left to
    do. See other people.

                CHRIS
    I just - need you.
```

Towne's reputation has largely been created on the basis of his powerful, truthful dialogue. Chris' stating of her need is more acceptable in a female than a male character. As David Denby says, Towne "writes just about the best realistic dialogue in modern movies." [736] This particular exchange is part of what is arguably the biggest emotional scene in the film and is not in the screenplay. The incident which irrevocably alters the relationship between Chris and Tory occurs on page 100 of the screenplay (and around 75 minutes in to the film):

```
                TORY
    Don't do me any favors.

                CHRIS
             (taking her arm)
    I said I'll try it.
                TORY
    So try it.
```

```
She disengages her arm and walks off.  Chris is upset.
She turns and moves to the forward tape, not noticing
that it in fact was Tory's mark - not hers.  She con-
centrates for a moment, and takes off in the bounding
three step move, but the final step is much farther away
from her take off point than she realized.  She almost
leaps to reach it, hits the take off and col-lapses
screaming to the ground.

TORY

Walking away, turns back to see Chris jackknifed in
agony.  She hurries to her.
```

(Personal Best: 100)

This leads to the most conflicted and hurt dialogue between Chris and Tory.

```
                TORY
             (to Chris)
    I wish it had been me ..
             (she takes Chris'
```

---

[736] In the film she actually says "Don't let *him* do this to us," meaning Coach Tingloff.

                                        hand)
                   - could you look at me at least?

Chris looks up, stares blankly at Tory. Then withdraws
her hand - ostensibly to adjust the bag under her knee.
Tory's having a hard time controlling her growing
desperation.

                         TORY
              You know I'd do anything to avoid
              hurting you.
                         (silence from Chris)
              ..all I've ever tried, I mean I
              was trying, I was trying to ..
              help.
                         (more silence)
              Dammit, don't play the dumb Indian
              with me. Say something.
                         (lowers her voice,
                         pleading)
              Don't let them do this to us![737]

                         CHRIS
                         (looks up slowly)
              Do what? What's he doing?

                         TORY
              What did I do? C'mon, spit it
              out for once in your life. Did
              I hurt you on purpose?

                         CHRIS
              Take your hands off me.[738]

                         TORY
              Did I? did I? did I? did I?
              did I? did I? You're so fucking
              gutless. Do you have a fucking
              thought in your fucking head?

                         CHRIS
              - my thought is that at this point off
              we're both better off with a dumb
              Indian.

                                        (*Personal Best*. 103)

     (It is notable that the significant conversation between Chris and Denny -
allegedly an alter ego for Towne himself - about her past relationship with Tory is also

[737] This line is dropped in the film.
[738] Speaking at the AFI's Harold Lloyd Master Seminar in 1994. As before.

altered from the exchange delineated on pp. 134-5 of the screenplay.) For Towne, conflict is the centre of all drama, emphasising his classical style:

> … that involves some sort of conflict and that creates compression all by itself. Just the use of conflict. [739]

In *Personal Best* the stakes are constantly raised through action and dialogue as the conflict between Christ and Tory escalates. Finally, it is Chris who demonstrates the more courageous character – she stands up to Tingloff, reconciles with Tory, and has an equal relationship with Denny Stites, whose requisite awe at her athleticism is (perhaps unfortunately…) expressed in the 'crotch' shots which earned Towne such criticism. [740] Their first encounter at the Cal Poly pool is however one of cinema's great 'meeting cute' scenes and based on one of Towne's own real-life encounters:

```
After a few strokes, Chris' body can be seen under the
water's surface coming up on Denny's left - kicking and
stretched out, it is spectacular.  The GOGGLES stop mov-
ing from air to water and remain IN THE WATER, holding on
Chris' legs and upper body.  As the GOGGLES move past
they remain underwater looking BACKWARD toward Chris,
until there is a sudden JOLT.

DENNY

has crashed into the wall.  He surfaces, shakes his head,
and grabs the gutter.

CHRIS
approaches, kicking.  She's seen him hit the wall but has
no idea why.

                    CHRIS
            - you all right?

                    DENNY
            What?  Yeah, fine.

                    CHRIS
            (reaching the wall)
            - fog's amazing.

                    DENNY
            (more stunned by her
            than anything else)
```

---

[739] Pauline Kael says however, that "Towne's cameras make love to women… [they] never ogle the women's bodies." She calls it "one of the best dating movies of all time." 'The Man Who Understands Women,' 112, 118; 119. A rebel lesbian reading yields a different interpretation: "… as the sheer beauty and grace of women in air, laid out maybe, but not laid back…" Theresa Catalano, '*Personal Best:* A Critique of the Movie,' *Women and Therapy*, 2.4, Winter 1982: 88; quoted in Holmlund. *Op.cit.*, 155, 164.

[740] Murdock. *Op.cit.*, 60.

```
                    - really


                         CHRIS
              - well, be careful.


She pushes off and kicks back down the pool.  Denny some-
what reflectively cleans his goggles and watches her go.
```

(Personal Best: 114)

This meeting happens when Chris has finally become who she *really* is, according to the tenets of the mythological model. Murdock says that,

> The heroine must have the courage to demythologise her partner and take back responsibility for her own life. She must make hard decisions and earn her autonomy. When a woman is liberated or liberates herself from the belief that her fulfilment comes at the hands of a man, then she can find a partner who is an equal and enjoy true romantic love. [741]

Thus, the screenplay for *Personal Best*, far from utilising the seemingly radical lesbian relationship at its heart to critique contemporary culture or even sporting cliché, could be interpreted as falling into the traditional storytelling model, which Vogler maintains is the most emotionally and financially rewarding for audiences and studios alike. However, most radical of all, perhaps, is the idea that the screenplay suggests and forms its organising paradigm: even lesbians are human and suffer from professional jealousy, and sometimes women really can thrive in more conventional, heterosexual relationships in which their male partner truly enables them to undertake their personal journeys. [742]   That is the underlying message of *Personal Best*.

Character and Authorship

The relationship between Tory and Chris could also be read as that of Mentor/Student, a Towne trope, which becomes threatening to the Mentor when the Student's true (and greater) talents are revealed. Structurally this is reflected when Tory injures herself in the long jump (Chris' former Personal Best sport prior to the high jump, which had been Tory's) and their roles are reversed – as well as perhaps a form of poetic justice. However when Chris visits her, instead of being bitter, Tory advises her as to how she should play the 800 meters. They achieve closure on the winners' stand, when, Chris wearing red, and Tory wearing blue, Tory expresses her reaction to Denny:

```
                         CHRIS
              - what do you think?


Tory tries to say something  everything – then nods to
the stands where Denny is.


                         TORY
              - well – he's awful cute ... 743
```

---

[741] Crucially, of course, Denny will never compete with Chris so their relationship will always be a level playing field.

[742]   "…for a guy!" is added onscreen.

[743]   The change to the then-familiar vernacular, "Are you shittin' 'me?"   may have been

248

```
              CHRIS
       (delighted, manages
        a nod)
     ... I know!... 744
```

(*Personal Best*: 168)

Terry Tingloff and Denny Stites also play the role of Mentor to Chris in this new Oedipal drama: atonement with the father in *Personal Best* is sublimated for Chris through her relationships with these men. This structure is a powerful motif in Towne's oeuvre and can be seen in his later screenplay, *Days of Thunder* (1989), which might be seen as a dry run for, or even a first draft of, the later film, the Steve Prefontaine biography, *Without Limits* (1997), which he would direct himself, from a screenplay by himself and Kenny Moore (playing Denny here), who was one of Prefontaine's teammates. *Without Limits* contains, as we shall see, perhaps Towne's most balanced relationship between athlete and mentor.

Vogler states that mentor-hero relationships can be marred by conflict, as is the case in *Personal Best*. [745]

This is one way of interpreting the structure of the breakdown of Chris and Tory's relationship when Tory advises Chris to lengthen her pace on the approach to the long jump. However, the film's actual coach/mentor, Tingloff, turns out to be a 'bad coach' – in contrast with the benign Bill Bowerman in *Without Limits*. [746]

The film still offers other facets of Towne's characteristic screenwriting, for instance his penchant for 'off-colour' jokes:

```
Tingloff looks up, smiles.

              TINGLOFF
     You know what you're like?  There's
     a joke about a faggot who makes a
     pass at a Marine in the men's room
     on the fortieth floor of the Empire
     State building.  The marine throws
     the faggot out the window.  When
     he gets down to the street, the
     marine passes this faggot in the
     gutter who struggles to one elbow
     and says, 'Yoo-hoo ... I'm not mad.'
```

---

improvised by the actress.

[744] Vogler, *Op. cit.,* 142.

[745] Entire stories, such as *Goodbye Mr Chips* (1939), can be built around the idea of the Mentor as Hero; whereas the Mentor can also be portrayed as an Evolved Hero – someone who has enough experience to teach others – as Vogler points out, "Mentors spring up in amazing variety and frequency because they are so useful to storytellers. They reflect the reality that we all have to learn the lessons of life from someone or something. Whether embodied as a person, a tradition, or a code of ethics, the energy of the archetype is present in almost every story, to get things rolling with gifts, encouragement, guidance, or wisdom." Vogler. *Op.cit.,* 144.

[746] *Ibid.*

> Just go home and kiss and make up
> or eat each other or whatever you
> do, will you? Ah, I think I
> actually made you mad. Then why
> don't you hit me? It would be nice
> to see you have the balls to hurt
> somebody. Go ahead, hit me.

(*Personal Best*: 110)

Towne is defensive against criticism of the running footage: "It's not athletic footage, damn it… it's drama, it's part of their lives. It's a war not between genders, but between how you love someone and how you serve yourself. That's an inherently schizophrenic conflict. "The answer is in the title. There <u>is</u> an inner standard. You just have to learn to accept it." [747]

The Project of Authorship and *Personal Best*

Part of the project of cinematic authorship, certainly insofar as it has traditionally been mooted, is finding those traces of a director from film to film which establish his trademarks, a dominant vision, if you will. [748] Towne as director is confident that as a *writer* he is expert at scene construction, and the building of scene sequences, a tool intrinsic to his craft. In terms of narrative skill, then, he puts the dramatic emphasis on mythic elements in *Personal Best*, allowing them to be offset by humour as counterpoint, with the mentor/student relationship a major structuring dramatic component which would form the basis of two more of his screenplays – *Days of Thunder*, and *Without Limits*, which he would also direct. [749]

His directing technique is certainly aided by the years watching Hal Ashby up close: he likes to frame wide shots, allowing scenes to happen within their own space and without too many cuts. He allows actors great freedom yet due to the action sections he is not afraid of utilising the traditional aspects of the sports director's battery, perfected in years of television coverage and extended in documentary features such as *Tokyo Olympiad* (1965) and *Visions of Eight* (1973): quick cuts, slow motion, cutting on action; lyrical and comic interludes; as well as auditory effects such as heartbeats and heavy breathing.

Most surprising of all perhaps is the occasional abstract cut, for instance in the very opening shot of *Personal Best* when the viewer is assaulted with the alien sounds of an

---

[747] Robin Wood describes this recurrence of theme and attitude in terms of Hawks' work: "The films are linked by the whole structure of their scenarios, by the pattern of the character relationships, and by passages of closely similar (at moments near-identical) dialogue." Wood, 'To Have (Written) *and Have Not* (Directed),' in Bill Nichols, Bill (ed.). *MOVIES AND METHODS: An Anthology: Volume I.* Berkeley, California: University of California Press, 1982, 300.

[748] In *Chinatown* Towne had offset genre against myth, a tool he had skilfully adapted from his work on *Bonnie and Clyde*.

[749] Pollock, 1982: as before. David Thomson says of *Personal Best*, "No one could say it was as sharp as Robert's best scripts – it was sweeter, but less alive. It did moon just a bit over the lady athletes, as if a naturalist were celebrating gorgeous animal bodies. The eye loved it, but the talk was tame; and Robert has never been as good on women as he is with dry, potent men who sniff sex and challenge in the air." Thomson, 'Trouble in Chinatown,' *Vanity Fair*, November 1985: 125.

athletics track, accompanied by enormous close-up images of huge droplets hitting the ground. It isn't until the camera abruptly pulls back that it is possible to interpret the setting. Likewise, later, when Tory and Chris are running in the dunes, it is in long shot against the white sands so that it appears the women are running to stand still. Such moments turn the meaning of the film into something other than the sum of its parts, perhaps attempting to attain a gloss on Chris's Native American heritage where the concept of time is strikingly different than that of the white man's tradition. Ultimately, *Personal Best* can be appreciated as a lucid and sensual male celebration of women's physiques. Towne was particularly proud of his technical achievements on the film and said of the sound effects in the shower room when Tory nurses Chris during her bout of food poisoning.

> "That sound is more evocative than anything I could have written… I'm a great believer in written dialogue, but what I see and what I hear I have come to realize increasingly is more important than any line of dialogue. It shows the limitations of the written word. It's not a palpable thing – it's an *idea*." [750]

So Towne was not just balancing the terms of internal authorship in the screenplay itself; he was adjusting his creative skills in terms of the final, finished product – the adaptation of his writing into moving pictures. Overall, as his critics claimed, Towne was now writing palpably softer material, with compromised endings – because these were the stuff of life itself.

He commented on the experience of making the film:

> I don't think anybody has control in a movie. The one thing that you know when you are finally in that position – I had final cut and I was the writer and, out of necessity, became the producer and director – is that moment when you theoretically have control is the moment when you realize that you have no control. Anything can happen. Control is a loose term. Intention, now that's a different matter. What always surprises you is that no matter how carefully you write something, if you are not in constant communication with the director, the number of ways in which every single moment and every single shot can be misinterpreted is just amazing. [751]

In many ways, this statement summarises the concerns of the writer-director in terms of authorship. While on the one hand Towne was always accepting of the limitations (and potential) of collaborative filmmaking, he was now realising the somewhat mixed benefits of at least nominally being seen as the controlling artistic intelligence behind a production. He is also acknowledging here the advantage of having a good relationship with a director – the better to express *his* intention as screenwriter. [752] However the conflating of internal and external authorship had come at the price of *Greystoke*, a loss which would forever underscore his writing and perhaps his view of the world.

The Mermaid (1983) (screenplay)

Towne's next script, for high-powered producer Ray Stark, and the equally daunting Warren Beatty, was a comedy project called *The Mermaid*, announced in *Variety*

---

[750] Towne, 'On Directing,' as before, 127-128.

[751] This is perhaps why the films of Paddy Chayefsky's work rarely expressed the powerful writing behind them.

[752] Michael Sragow. *Op.cit.*, 11.

on October 29, 1982. Its 120 pages recount the story of a yacht salesman, Gaer, who finds new meaning in his life when the titular creature enters his existence. The project was cultivated around Beatty's amiable screen persona and is self-evidently set at one of Towne's favourite locations, the ocean. Typically, the film ends with the not entirely 'watery finale' pinpointed by Pauline Kael – Gaer finally attains a stable domestic existence, on his spinnaker, with a pregnant siren.

He said to Michael Sragow that he wasn't sure he wanted to put his name on the screenplay unless he could see his work 'carried through': "We talked about this up-front: I told Ray he could buy my work, but he couldn't buy my name'." [753]

Towne's sensibility was certainly in tune with current box studio demands; however the project was scooped by Touchstone Pictures' (the new live-action Disney imprint) *Splash* (1984). Thus, *The Mermaid* never made it to the screen, although Towne's public profile was undoubtedly enhanced that year by his being featured on the PBS series, *Screenwriters: Word Into Image*, along with his contemporaries, William Goldman, Neil Simon, Paul Mazursky, Eleanor Perry and Carl Foreman.

Deal of the Century (1983) (uncredited)
Towne's involvement in this William Friedkin-directed satire of the arms industry starring Chevy Chase has only recently come to light. Coolly received, it is difficult to assess what Towne's contribution might have been.

Swing Shift (1984) (uncredited)
'Rob Morton' does not exist. He is composed of four different screenwriters, the principal amongst whom was Nancy (*Coming Home*) Dowd. Others were Bo Goldman and Ron Nyswaner. Goldie Hawn produced *Swing Shift* (1984) for herself but could not find a single writer to fashion a workable screenplay – so she hired several writers, who are united pseudonymously rather in the manner of Alan Smithee, that repository of all things directorially suspect. Director Jonathan Demme allegedly suffered almost as much as the screenplay (he in fact renounced the film completely) and the process has been described as 'a Hollywood tragedy.' At some point, Robert Towne became one quarter of 'Rob Morton.' [754] It led to him casting Kurt Russell in *Tequila Sunrise* five years later.

8 Million Ways to Die (1986) (uncredited)
8 Million Ways to Die was as they say in publishing, "a hot property," and a prize-winning novel by Lawrence Block. The story is told in thirty-four chapters over three hundred and fifty pages and is a "New York novel" in the best sense of that term, as is evident from the title which refers to the narration of *The Naked City* (the film and TV series): Scudder is a recovering alcoholic, haunted by an incident from his past as a cop in which a child was caught in police crossfire, and his daydreams are writ large on newspaper headlines which etch his moral quandaries in our memory. Early in the story he is told to quit drinking or die: this novel is pivotal in the Scudder series in its exposition of his deep-rooted problems and his strength of character. He attends Alcoholics Anonymous meetings and always passes on the opportunity to tell his story – right until the last moment, when he has achieved some form of justice for the murdered callgirl, and he can finally go easy on himself. He cries.

---

[753] The grisly tale of the rewrite is recounted in 'Swing Shift: A Tale of Hollywood,' by Steve Vineberg, in *Sight & Sound*, Winter 1990/1991. Accessed online.
[754] James Riordan. *STONE: The Controversies, Excesses and Exploits of a Radical Filmmaker*. London: Aurum Press, 1995, 142. This would be the book found beside Don Simpson's body in 1996.

The eventual film would be unrecognisable in plot elements, style, tone and story from the original novel. Oliver Stone optioned the book as a directing prospect for himself. He brought the project to producer Steve Roth, with the proviso that he would write and direct once the financing came through. The financing on the film never worked out and ultimately Hal Ashby was hired to direct, much to Stone's chagrin.

The reuniting of Towne and Ashby should have been cause for celebration but the production was dogged with problems from the beginning. Stone wasn't directly told that he was being taken off the film; according to what he told biographer James Riordan, "He gave it to Robert Towne behind my back. Robert later called me and was very nice about it, but it wasn't his fault. Hal wanted it totally changed. He was on a completely different wavelength than I was." [755]

The rewriting process was evidently long and painful, as can be seen from the number of drafts produced by Oliver Stone alone, and his subsequent drafts with David Lee Henry (aka Lance Hill.) When it came to the writing by Towne, the files at AMPAS would suggest that the core decisions on the production were taken in tandem with the production team and Ashby in extensive story conferences. [756] This gives an insight into the range of inputs that occur prior to a screenplay being presented by a writer. It is also an indication of the concerns that occurred to the producers – Folder No. 214 contains worries about the level of ethnic-oriented jokes in the material; Folder No. 225 contains an expression of worry by Towne's wife Luisa that all the colored people in the script will be villains after Towne suggests that Chance no longer be accepted as a 'friend' by Scudder.

For Towne, the project was probably some relief in the turmoil of *Two Jakes/The Two Jakes*. There are records of extensive story meetings, following a nine-page document written by Towne on the subject matter of the novel, entitled 'Easy Does It.' These meetings commenced on 29 June 1985, some three weeks after the sixth Stone/Henry draft had been delivered. There are also pages from another draft, done perhaps by Ashby himself, after the delivery of the third Stone/Henry draft. The Hal Ashby file in the Special Collections section of the Margaret Herrick Library at the Academy of Motion Pictures, Arts and Sciences contains 15 sets of transcribed notes from those

[755] Detailed notes taken at AMPAS 03 November 2003 on the first (undated) draft provided by Stone, running to 140 pages. A revised draft dated 01 November 1984 runs to 131 pages. A March 1985 draft runs to approximately 127 pages and is heavily annotated, with 'Hal Ashby Copy' marked on the cover. Another draft, dated 22 April 1985, and queried as having been written by Hal Ashby (unlikely) is marked 22 April 1985, again with many annotations and some handwriting. A draft dated May 1985 is attributed to Oliver Stone and David Lee Henry (aka Lance Hill) and it is 117 pages long. All of these drafts were allegedly based on two novels by Block, the eponymous book plus another, earlier novel, entitled *A STAB IN THE DARK* (1981). However, author Lawrence Block believes that Stone purchased the earlier Scudder novel because he believed they were the only two in the series. (According to a letter from Block to this author, 22 March 2004). There is no evidence in the Stone drafts that any elements from *STAB...* were ever used in the screenplay's construction. Ashby's memos on the film are to be found at the Margaret Herrick Library in the Academy of Motion Pictures, Arts and Sciences.

[42] Cliff Rothman, 'Roth files vs. PSO in $2.3 million suit,' *The Los Angeles Times*, 27 March 1986. The tone and content of a memo from Ashby to Chuck Mulvehill, 19 July 1985, indicate a troubled preproduction phase, characterised by distrust on the part of PSO of the director, whose insecurities are beginning (understandably) to come to the fore in the light of the budget cuts proposed by the company without consulting with him.

meetings, dating 29 June through 10 July 1985, variously involving Towne, his wife-to-be Luisa, Peter Bart and Hal Ashby. At this point it is evident that the draft Towne is proposing is vastly different to that written by Oliver Stone and it has already been transplanted from New York City to Los Angeles, rendering the title utterly without meaning (the reasons for relocating the production and story to California would seem to have been primarily financial). It is clear that Towne's take on the script shows an interest in investigating the effects of addiction and his take on the Block material is vastly different from that evident in the original Stone manuscript.

The extent of the labour on the screenplay can be seen just from the pages produced by Towne and the dates on which they were written.

The screenplay by Robert Towne up to page 32 is dated 15 July 1985. Then the screenplay by Robert Towne is dated August 1985 and runs to 123 pages (17 pages shorter than the draft produced by Oliver Stone). Page one is dated 30 July 1985. The extent to which the production was created through discussion between the various parties is evident. (The temptation to use the term 'written by committee' is overwhelming.). The story note pages relevant to the discussion about the tanning salon scene alone seems to have preoccupied the creative team yet is merely an incidental factor in terms of plot action and story resonance.

Ashby's memos on the film are to be found at the Margaret Herrick Library in the Academy of Motion Pictures, Arts and Sciences.

The production ended in disaster, with Roth suing PSO for 'fraud and breach of contract' to include his and Ashby's firings and the re-firing of Ashby after Roth posted money for him. Ashby took his own dispute to the Directors Guild where he apparently came out ahead – he had, after all, been an Oscar-winning editor and hadn't even been allowed in the editing room of 'A Hal Ashby Film'.[42]

In a letter to this author, Block declared his distaste for the resulting film:

I thought the decision to transplant such an intrinsically New York story to LA was ill-advised. I thought the plot changes were senseless. I think the direction by Hal Ashby might have been good---Jeff Bridges says they shot some awfully good scenes--- but as they took the cut away from him, it wound up being a mess.
I don't have a problem generally with adaptations. Changes are often essential to make what worked on the page work upon the screen, and I recently adapted a book of my own (HIT MAN, to be filmed as Keller) and made sweeping changes with a free hand. But I don't think I'd have liked Eight Million Ways to Die even if I hadn't written the book. I just don't think it was much good. I don't know how much Robert Towne's rewrite had to do with the movie's failure---the Oliver Stone draft was a piece of crap all on its own---but he certainly didn't save it, did he? [757]

This, then, was an adaptation which Towne did not master and marked the final decline in Ashby's one-time stellar career. [758] The screenplay does not conform to the

[757] Letter via electronic mail from Lawrence Block to Elaine Lennon, 22 March 2004.
[758] According to Peter Biskind, "the director changed some details while he was staging a scene and, according to the producer, Steve Roth, 'Robert went ballistic. Psychotic. He thought he was the greatest thing since sliced bread. He was this raging egomaniac with a whole group of sycophants around him. He was envious of Hal being a big director, and he thought he did him this big favor in rewriting the movie. It was the ugliest fight I ever saw in my life. Hal was down

model of Towne's work as described, outside the hero being trapped by his occupation – although the return to Los Angeles, while not Towne's ultimate decision, certainly marks out his preferred setting.

Tough Guys Don't Dance (1987) (uncredited)

Norman Mailer made his directing debut with an adaptation of his own novel, starring friend (and fellow pugilist) Ryan O'Neal. The screenplay proved problematic and a studio-demanded rewrite involved Towne. The film never received widespread distribution and Mailer never made another film.

The Pick-Up Artist (1987) (uncredited) (producer)

Towne assisted (apparently for less money than usual) Beatty's pet project for his latest protégée, Molly Ringwald, a teenage sensation discovered by John Hughes, still attending high school in Los Angeles. James Toback, another writer/director apparently constantly indebted financially to Beatty was the writer/director. Toback would eventually write *Bugsy* for Beatty, where he cast wife-to-be, Annette Bening as his leading lady.

The Bedroom Window (1987) (executive producer)

Towne executive produced this for fellow writer-director Curtis Hanson. It's unclear whether he contributed to the impressive Hitchcockian screenplay.

Fatal Attraction (1987) (uncredited)

James Dearden wrote an extremely accomplished short film in the early Eighties, entitled 'Diversion' aka 'Head On.'. Years later he fashioned a feature screenplay from the original idea and it drew the attention of several interested studios but Sherry Lansing at Paramount financed the production. Last-minute changes were made by Robert Towne to the infamous *Fatal Attraction* (1987). It is not clear however if he was responsible to the controversial ending, which differed substantially from the original as written by Dearden, and was added following preview screenings.

Frantic (1988) (uncredited)

Polanski's Parisian film starred Harrison Ford as an American doctor whose wife is kidnapped moments after the couple's arrival in the city. A fast-paced, witty thriller, this is nonetheless second-rate Polanski, with the original screenplay by himself and regular collaborator, Gérard Brach, who had become an agoraphobe and was no longer familiar with the contemporary Paris setting the screenplay was supposedly depicting. Towne was brought in to spice up the dialogue to the Cold War Hitchcockian thriller, which also featured additions by Jeff Gross, who had worked on the screenplay for two months and was never credited. [759]

The Two Jakes (1990) (characters) (written by)

Two Jakes was the second screenplay of the projected trilogy that had its beginnings in *Chinatown* (1974). It was the continuing story of the making of Los Angeles, a cinematic mythos for which Towne could claim true authorship in the three

---

on his luck at that point. All kinds of accusations about drug abuse had been levelled at him. Towne was vicious. Said he was over-the-hill and gone. A cripple. 'I'm not gonna be fucked by this guy one more fucking time.' What was sad was these guys genuinely liked each other. They took an entire relationship and threw it away. I don't think they ever spoke again'." *Op.cit.*, 428-9.

[759] Christopher Sandford. *POLANSKI*. London: Century, 2007, 365-367.

drafts of *Chinatown*. The singularity of his voice, expressed through the literal voice of Jake Gittes, and the landscape of a diseased city, being trampled by developers and criminals, threaded through the perception of him as the actor's screenwriter.

Despite the financial disaster and the breakdown of Towne's friendship with both Evans and Nicholson, Jack Nicholson was never in any doubt as to the merits of the screenplay:

> Because of Robert's [Towne] influence, it's [*The Two Jakes*] a very literary piece. No car chases, no dead innocent bystanders while I'm supposed to worry if they catch the Russian dope addict. I hate those movies. I mean, back in the [Corman] days, Monte Hellman was the first guy that showed the dead body on the screen. They used to just drop out of the bottom of the frame like death didn't count, and I think that can be culturally degrading. Just like guys driving through the fruit stands and up on the sidewalk, cars are blowing up left and right, and we're supposed to care about the people in the script, I don't buy it. [760]

The Two Jakes screenplay, revised from the original 1984 draft titled *Two Jakes*, was delivered by Robert Towne in December 1988, the month that *Tequila Sunrise* was released. It differs somewhat in detail from the film, and excludes Towne's poetic, half-hopeful ending – the January 1949 snowfall in Los Angeles that really happened. (It was *Chinatown* all over again, but in this case the ending was shot and then changed.) The film boasts a self-effacing, semi-parodic voiceover narration by Jake Gittes (not written by Towne) that appeared to make the plot less, instead of more, comprehensible, despite its noir-ish language yet it bore a sadness that Danny Leigh calls "an unmistakably caustic tang of regret." [761]

The screenplay starts similarly to *Chinatown*, and in fact bears many structural similarities to the second draft of that screenplay: a routine case of marital infidelity is tied up with a land grab – this time, for oil (hinted at by Evelyn's fatal shooting of her father on an oilfield at the climax of the first draft); Gittes is hired by (what might as well be a fake) Jake Berman and is fooled by almost everyone he encounters, framed as an accessory to murder. The first draft has scenes in Mexico City, where Gittes attempts to find Katherine Mulwray and locates the orphanage where she was brought up before her marriage. In the 1988 draft, examined here, this changes to a search for Khan, her butler, in Los Angeles. Once again he misunderstands everyone around him.

[760] Jack Nicholson quoted in *Premiere*, September 1990: accessed online.
[761] Danny Leigh, 2003: 15.

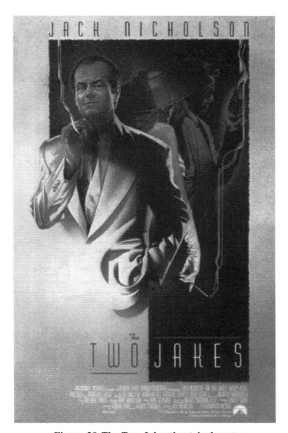

Figure 20 *The Two Jakes* theatrical poster

<u>Synopsis:</u>
Act I

It is 1948. Jake Gittes is now a wealthy specialist in divorce work (the first we see of him is his two-tone 'co-respondent's' shoes). He is hired by property developer Julius 'Jake' Berman to spy on his beautiful wife Kitty, whom he suspects of having an affair. Gittes rehearses Berman and he and his assistant Walsh set up a recording device in the room next to the love nest at the Bird of Paradise Motel. To their horror, Berman bursts in on the couple as arranged, but fatally shoots the man in question. The victim turns out to have been his business partner, Bodine, and the man's widow, Lillian, accuses Gittes of conspiring with the Bermans to take Bodine's share of the business, a housing development in the San Fernando Valley.

The tape made by Gittes becomes the subject of attention from Berman's lawyer, Cotton Weinberger; Lou Escobar, now police captain, and his associate, Loach, whose father killed Evelyn Mulwray in *Chinatown*; and mobster Mickey Nice. Chuck Newby, lawyer for both the Bodines and oil tycoon Earl Rawley, suggests that Gittes prove that Berman murdered Bodine in order that Lillian will get her husband's share of the housing lot. Gittes listens closely to the tape recording and hears Lillian refer to Katherine Mulwray, who disappeared after Evelyn's death. He meets Kitty Berman at the San Fernando lot – property that should rightly be Katherine's. Later, he is seduced by Lillian Bodine – who also wants the tape. Walsh finds deeds to prove that Katherine Mulwray gave the rights

257

to the sub-division to Berman – via Mickey Nice, but retained the mineral rights for herself. Gittes follows a man who is tailing Berman – and is led to Earl Rawley, who is drilling for oil, supposedly in the direction of the ocean. However a local geologist, Tyrone Otley, informs Gittes that in fact Rawley Petroleum is diverting its sea drilling in the direction of the sub-division: a deadly pursuit since the land is the site of gas deposits. (Berman dismisses Otley earlier on by saying, "every kid in the subdivision knows there's gas in the water.") When Gittes lights up his cigarette, a gas explosion is triggered and he drifts into a troubled sleep, having nightmares about Evelyn Mulwray. He wakes up to the sight of Kitty Berman's face.

Act II

Gittes realises that Berman had smuggled a gun into the hotel room through a moving company. He plays golf with Berman, who tries to persuade Gittes to hand over the tape. He inadvertently reveals to Gittes that he is terminally ill. Gittes confronts Kitty Berman with the truth behind Bodine's death and she asks him to give the tape to the police: he finally realises that she is really Katherine Mulwray and that Berman did his utmost to protect her because Bodine had discovered her real identity. Bodine was planning to blackmail Berman in order to hand over the mineral rights to the sub-division to Rawley and himself.

Act III

At the sub-division, a melancholy Berman reveals he had kept his distance from Katherine because of his imminent death, pushing her into Bodine's arms. What appears to be excrement starts bubbling up through every part of the model home's plumbing and the earth begins to shake: Gittes informs Berman of the vast oil wealth on the lot. Berman is astonished and asks for a light. Mickey insists and Gittes hands Berman a Rawley Petroleum Ronson lighter. Nice tells Gittes to get out... From his rearview mirror, Gittes sees the model home explode: he and Mickey feel the earth rumble and look towards the sea where an oil well burns and crashes into the water. Kitty listens to a recording made by Berman to explain his actions. Gittes doctors the recording and makes it impossible to bring a case against Berman: the case is laughed out of court and the charges of pre-meditated murder are dropped. She and Gittes part tenderly. Snow falls in Los Angeles: it's January 1949.

The screenplay bears the intricate plotting which is the signature of Towne's original draft screenplays for *Chinatown*; as in *Chinatown* the entire, layered plot and image system is only clarified in the final moments; *The Two Jakes* (revised from Towne's original draft, *Two Jakes*, which was not available for this study), also conveys background information quickly, this time, through black and white stills (in *Chinatown* it is often conveyed through newspaper headlines or flyers); and, as in *Chinatown*'s original incarnation, the film has the Forties film noir voiceover, which, however, was added to the film at the behest of Jack Nicholson, the director (see below.)

Theme, Metaphor and Motif

The use of cigarettes and lighters is another fetishistic component of Towne's writing – *Tequila Sunrise*, which could be read as a gloss on the theme, if not the story, of *The Two Jakes*, also uses a lighter to trigger something explosive – the memory of a seemingly dead friendship (pp. 30, 38, 126). The gas explosion that forms turning point one injuring Jake (p. 39) is echoed in the explosion that forms the story's climax, as Jake Berman takes a pointedly ironic Rawley Petroleum Ronson from Gittes (for the second time) and literally blows himself and Rawley's oil prospect to smithereens (p.126) as the gas and oil begin to surface through the plumbing of the model home – a pleasant metaphor for the way the base elements surface in Towne's narrative structure, prefigured by the earth tremor on p. 2. The explosion on p.39 causes an explosion of a different sort in Jake's mind, triggering a complex multi-layered flashback derived from scenes in the earlier film, suggesting the explosive nature of the revelations in that narrative and their return to the surface here. (Tremors and temblors prefigure every major false lead or revelation in the screenplay, including pp. 19, 20 and p.122). A three-and-a-half page montage of *Chinatown*'s key scenes make up Jake's disturbing dream/nightmare sequence, signifying the screenplay's debt to the original (pp.40-43, not included in the film, instead transposed into a montage of newspaper cuttings of the same events; and echoing the fade out in *Chinatown* itself when Jake is knocked unconscious.)

The climax is foreshadowed by this explosion in lighting his cigarette at the beginning of Act Two; and in Earl Rawley's rather *Apocalypse Now*-esque line, "I love the smell of sulphur" (p.78): excrement is explicitly acknowledged as the byproduct not merely of the irresponsible tideland drilling but the past actions of the story's characters – pp. 37, 124 and of course echoes Noah Cross' love of horseshit (*Chinatown*, 3rd draft: 75.)

Figure 21 Jake Gittes lights up Jake Berman (Harvey Keitel)

Cross, the amoral potentate, is replaced by the oil baron Rawley, who is bent on committing the raping of the earth's natural resources in order to run the economic machine that is the modern city. Rawley consistently plays to Gittes' vanity by calling him 'John,' unlike the more sinister Cross who calls him 'Gits.' Rawley's role is greatly minimised from the screenplay and as played by Richard Farnsworth, he lacks the sheer menace evinced by John Huston in the earlier film.

Chinatown is visited early on, when Jake tries to find Khan and a game of Mah Jong and the numbers 2-3-7 lead him to the Pacific Coast bungalow that once belonged to Katherine Mulwray. These atmospheric scenes are not included in the film but *Chinatown* is revisited with a straight cut to Gittes at Khan's present home, the old Mulwray bungalow, whose tiered foundation reflects the layers of excavation at the story's core:

> Stairs lead from the cracked and broken rubble of one floor to the weed-infested foundation of another. The stone chimney hangs against the sky like a crumbling spine. The plumbing is twisted and charred on each floor, blacked and charred remains of wooden siding can be seen. Khan indicates to Gittes that he climb the crumbling stone steps. Gittes does, stopping at the first floor, wildflowers growing beneath the cracked tile at his feet, the sea far below the sumptuous plain of flowers and nursery trees.

<pre>
                    KHAN
          … she is here…
</pre>

And:

<pre>
                    KHAN
               (fingers them)
          … the fire changed her from a
          sunflower to a flower of the
          twilight --
</pre>

His hands move from the bright sun-colored poppy to the pale lavender one.

<pre>
                    KHAN
               (continuing)
          --so she could hide from those
          who wished to find her. Someday,
          when she's forgotten, perhaps the
          twilight flower will become a
          sunflower again.
</pre>

Khan remains kneeling, fingering the delicate crepe of the pale lavender-bordered poppy.

<pre>
                    KHAN
               (continuing)
          …until then, she will live
          here, with me.
               (looking up to Gittes)
          Come back whenever you wish to see
          her.
</pre>

(*The Two Jakes*: 51-2)

In this typically Townean scene sequence, which takes place instead in a greenhouse in the film, losing the notion of the layers of the past suggested by the burned out building, Towne conveys through three sets of imagery the film's principal concerns, which all lead back to Katherine Mulwray: the fire motif; the flowers, connoting the Otherness linked to the Orient, as in *Chinatown*, and the scorched earth – the seeds were scorched by Katherine to generate her own, unique breed, which connects her with her father/grandfather and his penchant for (incest and) horsebreeding; and the idea of hiding and secrecy, which of course are all linked to Gittes' own basic need – to look after Evelyn's sister/daughter. And of course the scene is an echo of the 'bad for glass' scenes in *Chinatown*, replete with Jakes' usual misinterpretation of the facts.

The overarching theme – digging up the past – is writ large: Towne is eternally inspired by the power of landscape and sets one scene (following the scene with Khan and Gittes) in the La Brea tar pits, complete with sinking mastodon sculpture (p. 54) which leads to Tyrone Otley's body:

> One thing makes Los Angeles different from most places… and that's two things
> - a desert with oil under it and, second, a lot of water around it. Hollis Mulwray
> and Noah Cross moved the water onto this desert. Now we have to move people
> the way they moved water, 'cause this city land is no city at all until you can
> get to it! … The nature of the game is oil. [762]

The scenes with Otley are changed in the finished film – he gives a public lecture on the tar pits - and he isn't murdered: instead, he meets with Gittes in the gay club.

The metaphor of looking is again a constant in the screenplay's construction:

> To pry into people's personal lives and uncover personal treacheries and infidelities.
> I think it's the perfect avenue to uncover the far more pervasive treacheries and
> breaking of faith within the society itself. [763]

The truth is always revealed in black and white photographs (pp. 17, 92, 100, 122), whereas the audio recordings are misleading – although they prove a sensual soundtrack to Jake's sleep while he is being watched (pp.21-22). Here, it's Gittes' genius for spying that leads him to his character's need – Katherine Mulwray, as she is namechecked in the recording made at the Bird of Paradise Motel, Redondo Beach (p. 23), whose titular pattern is literally replicated on an easy chair (p.94). Yet he finds himself manipulated by everyone until he discovers the X-rays (the most intimate photographic proof) of Berman's unhealthy lungs. The earthquake leading to Berman's self-immolation triggers its own aftershock in the water, another example of Towne's favourite symbolic element. Flowers, such an important referent of "foreignness" in *Chinatown*, also have their place here (poppies, gardenias, morning glories, Katherine's pendant), and contribute to Gittes' eventual realisation that Kitty Berman is Katherine Mulwray as Khan explains the significance of the burnt wildflower (a victim of a scorched earth policy, a fertile symbol in itself), which stands for Katherine, a fragile, delicate, Oriental flower of two colours – dying her hair from red to blonde at Max Factor's - damaged and struggling to survive. Towne's liking for shoes is a nod to an early scene from *Strangers On a Train*, when Gittes discovers Berman shares his penchant for chic two-tone lace-ups (p. 3). Duality and mirror-imaging is at the core of the narrative.

The "unnaturalness" of the land grab is explicitly linked to homosexuality (Rawley asserts that Otley is gay; and talks about his "unnatural direction," p. 79). Phallic symbols and language proliferate and the insinuation that Gittes is gay (he is led to a gay

---

[762] James Greenberg, 'Forget it Jack, It's *The Two Jakes*,' *American Film*, 15 (5) 1990: 22.
[763] Samuel G. Freedman, '*Two Jakes* Picks Up the *Chinatown* Trail,' *The New York Times*, 05 August 1990: 18.

club by Rawley) is laughed out of court. (Dialogue includes "suck on this;" and "cocksucking") and images of dogs (p.26-7 and p. 69) are explicitly sexual, linked to Lillian Bodine's rapacious lusts – another version of a kind of Brigid O'Shaughnessy figure, she is described as "a painted cat" (p.12); she is also a trope for the men's desire for oil and easily replaces Jake's girlfriend, who is dispatched in a telephone call and never seen or heard from again, pp.24-5 (although in the film she follows Jake into Katherine's house and, misinterpreting the situation, breaks off their engagement). The images of the erect oil derricks are clearly linked to this idea (commencing p. 18). Machinery versus nature is an important and overarching visual tool in the narrative; just as wealth and business acumen were pitted against personal charm and sexuality in *Shampoo*.

Time is problematic: as *Chinatown* had its own doubling metaphor familiar from the detective noir, so *The Two Jakes* redoubles again, not just in the two principal characters – linked by heartbreak, secrecy, illicit photography and recordings, as well as a penchant for two-tone shoes - but also on the previous film, the previous characters, the loop between the two, the concern with the abuse of power, the two beautiful if neurotic women, and the growing transformation of Los Angeles, a city now rapacious and unlovely in its modernisation. Of course the ending was changed. [764]

> GITTES (VOICEOVER)
> Time changes things... But the footprints
> of the past are everywhere. You can't
> forget the past any more than you can
> change it.

As Samuel G. Freedman commented on the film's release, it is "burdened by – memory itself," its creation "every bit as complicated as its narrative and every bit as inextricably bound to its precursor." [765] The title refers to the doubling replete in the narrative as a whole – two Jakes, two Katherines (Kitty), two-toned shoes, two-coloured flowers, two-coloured hair (Kitty's).

Nicholson stated of his character in the same article,

The power of memory is his central motivation. When the spectre of the past rises, when it comes into his life, all of the life he's developed since falls away from him. Gittes is pretending this is just another job, that he's not obsessing about his past. But you can see by the way the others around him react – his secretary, his assistants – that this is an obsession. He tried to do something good once – of that he's sure – and he doesn't want to lose that. He can try to subvert the past. He can try to bury it in old files. But time is continuous and circular. [766]

Unlike *Chinatown*, the conclusion of *The Two Jakes* sticks to genre convention and redemption, salving Gittes' conscience and allowing him to be the saviour he secretly longed to be back in *Chinatown*, making good on his past mistakes which he has already partly atoned for with his wartime heroics; while Berman (sounds like vermin), the bearer of disease (let's call it modernity, an echo of Cross' implied threat, "the future"), does the

---

[764] "... when it was filmed, it became clear that it was the kind of scene that played better on paper than on the screen." James Greenberg. *Op.cit.*, 25.

[765] Freedman. *Op.cit,* 1.

[766] Freedman. *Op.cit.,*18.

right thing and uses the earth's elements to end the oncoming tragedy of unstoppable modernisation – which, of course, he could not possibly be empowered to halt, perhaps the story's ultimate irony. But he can at least guarantee his wife's wealth and provide a good example to Gittes. One of the more perceptive reviewers commented that the film wasn't a sequel, *per se*, "it's an atmospheric evocation of the postwar period in L.A., a hardboiled look at the passage of time, but most importantly, it functions as a mediation on *Chinatown*, not as a 'sequel' or 'follow-up' feature in the sense that we're accustomed to.' [767] Robert Arnett rightly calls the screenplay "a poem of postwar America." [768]

Nicholson alluded to this when speaking about the film in 2007:

> I kind of bulked up a bit. I wanted to look like a guy settling in. America was wanting to get moving again after the war. It's classic saga writing. Gittes, who was kind of a ne'er-do-well, disrespected guy, now has been in the naval intelligence. He owns the the building he works in. He's in a country club. These are classic character developments and why Robert's writing is so perceptive and good. I was most pleased that Roman felt that *The Two Jakes* was a perfect fit for what it was intended to be. It's the middle section really. The middle part of a trilogy has more of a pastoral to it. [769]

Figure 22 Jake attempts to quell the unquenchable lusts of Lillian Bodine (Madeleine Stowe)

---

[767] Edmond Grant, '*The Two Jakes*,' *Films in Review*, 41 (1/2), 1991: 43.

[768] Robert Arnett, 2000: 50. Michael Eaton says that "what is impressive about *Chinatown* is still reincarnated in its sequel: the dialectic between a highly charge and melodramatic emotional core and a real, recognisable and even politically delineated depiction of the world in which the story is set... its is the economic machinations that underpinned the post-war development of Los Angeles that *The Two Jakes* is interested in." 'Condemned to Repeats,' *Sight & Sound*, Vol.1, No.8, December 1991: 4.

[769] Nicholson was speaking to Josh Horowitz on MTV, November 2007; accessed online at www.mtv.com/movies/news/articles/1573487/story.jhtml, 06 November 2007. Coincidentally, Towne himself worked in Naval Intelligence in the 1950s.

The film's release was postponed from Christmas 1989 to the following March. Then Paramount delayed it yet again, until August 1990. No reasons were given but allegedly the editing was posing problems. It was said that it might even take until December for Nicholson to painstakingly cut the film, in the same way that he had done with *Drive, He Said*, especially because of its $30 million budget.

The story seems to ape the elliptical shape that resulted from Polanski's intervention on *Chinatown*'s shooting draft but on reflection owes much more to the first draft of that screenplay, as Arnett avers. [770] The voiceovers are not in the screenplay written by Robert Towne but perhaps express Nicholson's own humorous take on the character this time around, when *Chinatown* itself has entered the lexicon (and thereby convention) and the well-meaning Gittes is a byword for haplessness. Nicholson revised Towne's revisions and during post-production resorted to hiring a magazine journalist to write the voiceover narration, which, as McGilligan asserts, "was completely at odds with anything Robert Towne had ever written." [771] The screenplay relies on many references to the previous film; however, it doesn't expose properly the relationship between Gittes and his fiancée; and the other Jake, Berman, remains slightly out of focus throughout; while the conscious echoes (Jake's injury; his gullibility; Mickey Nice's immaculate shoes; Khan; the Beach Club; the use of the term "kike" and, paradoxically, some Yiddish vernacular) may ultimately blunt the impact of the story which so clearly owes *Chinatown* its existence. Nor does Rawley work as the villain. Perhaps Towne was making a statement about the incompatibility of oil and water in this scrupulously elemental excavation of his hometown. And Rawley's speech about Los Angeles clearly paves the way for a third episode as well as laying out the trilogy's theme:

> RAWLEY
> One thing makes Los Angeles
> different from most places, John,
> and that's two things -- a desert
> with oil under it and, second, a
> lot of water around it. Hollis
> Mulwray and Noah Cross moved the
> water onto this desert. Now <u>we</u>
> have to move people the way they
> moved water, 'cause this city land
> is no city at all until you can
> get to it!

(The Two Jakes: 83)

The directing style, both painterly and subjective (with far more over-the-shoulder and point-of-view shots than *Chinatown*, exudes a warmth lacking in *Chinatown*, where the sun always shines but never penetrates the brittle 1930s sheen. According to Patrick McGilligan's (unauthorised) biography, Nicholson was under particular pressure following lurid revelations about his private life that Fall and this had an inevitable effect on his atypical on-set behaviour.[772] Speaking in December 1988, Towne said:

---

[770] Robert Arnett, 2000: 49.

[771] Patrick McGilligan, 1995, 374.

[772] Patrick McGilligan, 1995, 372-3.

The life that you have on a movie is so concentrated. We form extremely close relationships, not unlike the intensity of friendships in high school. Then we go off to our own respective worlds and movies. In my world, people routinely trade on friendship as an excuse to get what they want in business. Without realizing it, we corrupt our basic values by talking about friendship when we're really talking business. What constitutes friendship and betrayal is the issue, after all. In the case of Jack, Robert and myself, it was happily resolved." [773]

Sadly that was not in fact the case; Towne's next screenplay (*Tequila Sunrise*) would dwell on the incompatibility of certain friendships when business interests force former allies to take different paths. Towne has commented about his absence from *The Two Jakes*, which could at least partly be attributed to his commitment on *Days of Thunder*:

In the case of *Chinatown* I knew in every respect what the film was going to be like. I watched the dailies. I fought with Roman every day and ate dinner with him every night. We even agreed about where we disagreed. Here I didn't have the same sense. The most truthful answer is that I don't know how I feel about *The Two Jakes*. [774]

Producer (and former Jake) Robert Evans gives the story a different twist in the telling in his memoir:

… not only did Robert Towne not deliver a completed script, but went to Bora Bora with his wife, claiming he would only complete the remaining 20 percent from there. The only line of communication with Towne was to call the main hut between certain hours of the day. The 'staff' would then try to locate him because Towne's hut had no direct phone line. That was the last we ever heard from Robert Towne. What a friend. [775]

As Richard Combs points out in his insightful interpretation, "… a more interesting test and proof of friendship than anything in the film is the way Nicholson has allowed Towne to emerge as the real auteur." [776] The next chapter in the proposed LA trilogy, *Cloverleaf* (as in freeway interchange), would supposedly take place in 1959, in a city clogged with freeways and smog. Only Towne knows if it has been written. [777]

---

[773] Towne in Anne Thompson, *ibid.*

[774] Freedman. *Op.cit.,* 19. He expanded on this comment in interview with Alex Simon; "I honestly haven't seen it in its final form. I saw a few early versions. The one thing I don't want to do is criticize someone else's work, because a lot of people work to make a movie. Margot Asquith, who was a wonderful woman married to the British Prime Minister, once said, in talking about the aristocracy and the life that they lived, 'it doesn't really matter what we do, as long as we don't scare the horses.' And I think that was good advice. Why point out the degrading, small ways in which we hurt each other? In the long run, it won't really be the truth anyway." 'Mr PRE Comes to Towne,' *Venice*, September 1998: 35.

[775] Robert Evans. *Op.cit.,* 390. Evans had become a suspect in the *Cotton Club* murder. He was now, officially, "notorious."

[776] Richard Combs, *The Two Jakes* Review, *Sight and Sound,* Vol.1, No.8, Dec. 1991: 54.

[777] According to Jack Nicholson, "I would imagine Robert has some kind of outline. I can tell you it was meant to be set in 1968 when no-fault divorce went into effect in California. The title was to be GITTES Vs. GITTES. It was to be about Gittes' divorce. The secrecy of Meg Tilly's character was somehow to involve the most private person in California, Howard Hughes. That is where the air element would have come into the picture." Speaking with Josh Horowitz on

Tequila Sunrise (1988) (written and directed by)
    Kristin Thompson outlines the main orientation of the Hollywood narrative:

> Hollywood favors unified narratives, which means most fundamentally that a cause should lead to an effect and that effect in turn should become a cause for another effect, in an unbroken chain across the film. [778]

For Bordwell and Thompson,

> The tight binding of the second line of action to the love interest is one of the most unusual qualities of the classical cinema, giving the film a variety of actions and a sense of comprehensive social 'realism' that earlier drama achieved through the use of parallel, loosely related subplots…
> Psychological causality, presented through defined characters acting to achieve announced goals, gives the classical film its characteristic progression. The two lines of action advance as chains of cause and effect. [779]

A key influence on the shaping of *Tequila*'s narrative was the screenplay for *Casablanca*, which could be defined as a classic melodrama. – the form preferred by Hal Ashby, and the one which Thomas Schatz identifies as probably the most classically 'realist' of generic forms. [780]   Sidney Lumet defines melodrama as "when the plot moves characters." [781] Towne conceded to Kenneth Turan:

> I think melodrama is always a splendid occasion to entertain an audience and say things you want to say without rubbing their noses in it. With melodramas, as in dreams, you're always flirting with the disparity between appearance and reality, which is a great deal of fun. And that's also not unrelated to my perception of life working in Hollywood, where you're always wondering, 'What does that guy really mean?' [782]

Tequila Sunrise is a hybrid of the romance, action and the police/detective movie genre. It might be more generically precise to call it a romantic thriller. At the time of writing it he described it as being "about the difference between love and friendship." [783]

Perhaps the clearest template for *Tequila Sunrise* as genre is that proposed by *Casablanca*: a romantic drama about friendship, loyalty and love, set against a backdrop of intense action, the Second World War, when lives were truly at risk and the subtext of the action is 'what is a human life worth?' A melodrama, in other words. This allusion is verified by the film's director of photography, Conrad Hall.[784]

> Robert wanted a romantic film … and I of course wanted to give it to him. I thought it should have the tone of a film like *Casablanca*. Robert is an incredible story teller.

MTV, as before.
[778] Kristin Thompson, 2001, 12.
[779] Bordwell and Thompson. *Op.cit.*, 17.
[780] Schatz. 1983, 276.
[781] Sidney Lumet. *MAKING MOVIES*. London: Bloomsbury, 1996, 111.
[782] Kenneth Turan, 'Robert Towne's Hollywood Without Heroes,' *New York Times*, 27 November 1988.
[783] Richard Trainor, 'L.A. Graft: Robert Towne and the Stalled *Chinatown* Sequel,' *Sight and Sound* 55, 1986: 223.
[784] Hall shared Towne's TV history, since both men worked on *The Outer Limits* series in the 1960s.

He acquaints you with a certain story and setting and opens up your juices so you are able to give it back to him with appropriate images. [785]

For Towne, *Tequila Sunrise* enabled him to return to the surroundings of Redondo Beach, where he spent much of his childhood: the entire film is set in South Bay, that stretch of coast lying between Terminal Island and Santa Monica, featuring crucial scenes at San Pedro Harbour, across the channel from where Towne docked as a Navy man in the 1950s, returning to his home town.[786]

Cinematographer Conrad Hall was also familiar with the area, having spent much of his student years at USC surfing on Hermosa Beach.

'The whole area along the South Bay has a dazzle of light created by things like smog and aerial haze from the ocean... I wanted that incredible atmosphere on the screen.'

Mostly written on set, from the original screenplay by the Epstein brothers and Howard Koch (and Casey Robinson), based on the play, 'Everybody Comes to Rick's,' by Murray Burnett and Joan Allison, from day to day the cast of *Casablanca* didn't know what scenes they were shooting and nobody knew the ending until the day of shooting. Forty pages of script were available which Hal Wallis thought were good enough to start the production; then Koch was brought in; while Robinson wrote the Paris flashback. However it remains, if decidedly *post hoc*, a masterpiece of screenwriting, blending war heroics and suspense with romance, wit and thrilling character studies. Rick is a perfect blend of epic and romantic hero, holding to blame what Andrew Horton calls his 'core experience' – the liaison in Paris with Ilsa, who dumped him - for his present non-committal nature. [787]

The screenplay boasts some of the greatest lines written for cinema, including probably the most widely misquoted film dialogue of all time. In terms of construction, it is based on two lines of action: the 'letters of transit' which helps European émigrés leave Africa and Rick's supposedly dispassionate interest in the cause of the French Resistance, and his relationship with Ilsa, the wife of Laszlo. It also boasts five subplots, all of which are introduced in Act One, helping to draw attention away from its stage origins – virtually the entire first thirty-five minutes of the films take place in Rick's – a potentially fatal flaw.

In the same way that *Casablanca* is constructed around shifting triangular relationships (and many of their encounters take place in a public space – Rick's *Café Americain* in *Casablanca*, Vallenari's in *Tequila*...), *Tequila* ... has a constantly moving paradigm at its core: 'Mac' McKussic (Mel Gibson) and Nick Frescia (Kurt Russell), Nick and Jo Ann (Michelle Pfeiffer), Jo Ann and Mac, Mac and Carlos (Raul Julia). In all of these relationships truth, loyalty, friendship and love are being tested, constantly being rearranged in series and having knock-on effects on the next relationship. To this we might also add the triangle proposed by Mac, Jo Ann and Sandy Leonard (renamed Andy in the film), whose dealings with both of them lead Nick to presume the restaurant is a

[785] Marc Daniel Shiller, 'Triangle of Mistrust in *Tequila Sunrise,' American Cinematographer*, January 1989: 49.
[786] Shiller. *Op.cit.*, 50.
[787] Andrew Horton. *WRITING THE CHARACTER-CENTERED SCREENPLAY*. Berkeley and Los Angeles, University of California Press, 1999, 9-11.

front for drug smuggling; Mac, his cousin and the Sin Sisters; Mac, his ex-wife Shaleen and their son, Cody; and so forth. In other words, this structure lends itself to conflict and greater permutations of conflict in various directions. This is a hallmark of Towne's writing, as far back as his first screenplay, *The Last Woman on Earth*, written when he was just twenty-two years old. Ilsa is like Jo Ann, and the earlier Evelyn, in representing that unknowable quality of femininity which Towne had earlier referred to when speaking about Evelyn Mulwray – in that sense she is part of the continuum of his female characters who boast that ineffable quality – the mystery of women. [788]

The entire film is constructed on two levels: the forward movement of the investigation and Mac's decision to act; and the backward motion to a past crime – familiar as a trope from the detective noir, when Mac and Nick's friendship was replaced by that of Mac and Carlos - when Mac took the fall for a minor marijuana arrest in Mexico. This is the doubling narrative shape, moving back and forth, familiar from the detective noir genre that also cleaves to *Chinatown* and *The Two Jakes*. It is this debt – to a friend – that dictates the constant rearranging of contemporary relationships in the film. Thus the film is posited on an unravelling double spiral, DNA-like, hinged on the possibility of love with a beautiful woman, reflected on Towne's own biography - his second wife, Luisa Selveggio, had been the proprietor of a venue called Valentino's which the writer had frequented in the midst of his divorce from Julie Payne. [789]

The main line of the film is complicated by the subplot, which introduces conflict for the principal characters. This could be said to occur when Maguire (J.T. Walsh) brings in Jo Ann to question her about the goings-on she might have witnessed at her restaurant:

> MAGUIRE
> In other words you're telling us you never
> have to satisfy any personal requests from
> Mr. McKussic.

The implication, however vague, is unsavory. Jo Ann's
face becomes a mask.

> JO ANN
> No, Mr. Maguire. He usually orders right
> off the menu -- who are you and what's
> this all about?

> *(Tequila Sunrise*: 28)

Critic Stephen Schiff rationalises Jo Ann's choice between the two men (which on the surface would not appear to be a terribly enviable decision):

… the romantic triangle at the center of the movie is like a working model of

[788] Towne, 'Dialogue on Film,' as before: 47.
[789] Inasmuch as Towne's career might be said to ape that of Howard Hawks, the character of Jo Ann is based on Luisa Selveggio; in the same way that the character played by Bacall in *To Have and Have Not* was based on Hawks' wife of the time, Slim Keith, who had spotted Bacall on a magazine cover. Bacall was famously the cause of Bogart's marriage breakup although Hawks had planned on having her for a mistress first. Likewise, Bacall's character inspired Gail Hire's character in the later *Red Line 7000*.

Towne's moral principles. Jo Ann cares no more for the customary definitions of right and wrong than Towne does; between cop and drug dealer, whom will she choose? The answer is: the man who, as the writer puts it, 'lies the least.' Towne's characters always invent their own morality, and part of what makes his work at once utterly compelling and utterly true to the American grain is the way his people persuade us of that morality...[790]

This relates to Aristotelian postulates, as Michael Tierno reminds us that

To Aristotle, 'character' refers strictly to the moral quality of a person revealed through his or her thoughts and the actions stemming from these thoughts... [791]

Screenplay analyst Linda Cowgill states "If the character's want doesn't drive the story, his need must." [792] Narrative motion, complex motivations and the weblike construction of *Tequila Sunrise* can be understood by exploring the dissonance between the wants and needs of the romantic leads, in a screenplay which never moralises about anyone's reasons why. (Another nod to Jean Renoir).

Rick Blane wants to pursue his neutral role but his need for the truth alters his course of action:

Until he knows it, he is incapable of moving on, of becoming involved with other people, of returning to his true, former self. This need drives Rick within the plot. [793]

[790] Schiff. *Op.cit.,* 41.
[791] Tierno. *Op.cit.,* 94.
[792] Cowgill. *Op.cit.* 45.
[793] Cowgill. *Op.cit.,* 46.

Figure 23 Mel Gibson (Mac) on the set of *Tequila Sunrise* with Robert Towne

His discovery that Ilsa was already married to Laszlo in Paris drives him (and the plot) to the climax which sees Rick display his partisan role. Similarly, Nick wants to pursue the drugs line leading from Mac to Carlos but in doing so encounters both Jo Ann and his own loyalty to a dear friend. Ultimately, he makes a sacrifice which both counters Jo Ann's cold-eyed view of him and confronts the audience's preconception of him as a policeman on the make. We can see that both Ilsa and Jo Ann are the respective moral centres of their films, the pivots around whom the principals make extreme and life-changing decisions. Cowgill explains:

> What a character needs is often the psychological key to understanding his inner
> obstacles; it therefore deepens the levels and meaning of the story. How the
> character copes with these inner obstacles forms the basis of his development through
> the film because the psychological or emotional problems force the character into
> corners which demand new and different responses if he is to conquer the outer
> obstacles and attain his goal. [794]

Of course the urbane, sardonic and dispassionate (even cynical) Rick Blane in *Casablanca* is ironically revealed to be an enormously compassionate, politically motivated, humane man capable of enormous sacrifice - even risking his life, and losing the love of his life - for other people. Cowgill describes the effect:

> At its best, drama examines the costs of the protagonist's actions, usually in terms
> of personal relationships. Part of the drama comes from what he leaves behind or
> forsakes in order to gain his goal... In *Casablanca*, Rick recommits to life and
> the good fight, but loses Ilsa. These costs are trade-offs; gains come from losses,
> losses from gains. Audiences then ask of these trade-offs: 'Are they worth it?' [795]

---

[794] Cowgill. *Op.cit., 47.*

Cowgill correctly identifies Ilsa as a strong agent for change in *Casablanca.* [796]   In *Tequila Sunrise*, Jo Ann doesn't have quite the same role, since Mac has already made the decision to quit drug dealing. However she has a symbolic role in that she acts in the role of benefactor and supporter, as well as lover, and takes his son Cory angel hair pasta when the boy is ill and home alone. In simple story function terms, she is an ally. The influence of Howard Hawks and his work can be seen in the way that Jo Ann comes between Nick and Mac, splitting the narrative line into two strands of love interest and unconsciously spurring both men to doing the right thing. [797]

Jo Ann, however, is much feistier and probably cleverer than any of Hawks' heroines and her wordplay is on a par with anyone conceived by Towne for the screen. If we view Jo Ann's role in relation to Nick, we see that her capacity as agent for change is enhanced, which then leads to the conclusion that we are dealing with a split protagonist: Mac and Nick – who are literally split apart since Mac befriended Carlos, after the drug bust in Mexico all those years ago – and this eases our understanding of the screenplay's construction, which is after all about the nature of broken friendship, and how it might best be repaired.

Figure 24 *Tequila Sunrise* poster art

The Dramatic Hook

The entire screenplay is constructed around Mac's need to do his old drug buddy Carlos one last favour. (The irony is that Carlos is setting him up.) This need is ultimately replaced by his need for Jo Ann – he wants to reject her and even hits her several times in the cigarette boat, so desperate is he to try to deny his love for her. He is responding to her in the same way that he has responded to drink and drugs – like another addiction that he doesn't want to acknowledge.[798] The empathy we have for Mac may stem from the identification that the author had for his protagonist:

> Anytime you're involved in legal matters, as I was with my divorce and *Personal Best*, you feel like a criminal, which made it particularly easy to identify with McCussick. [799]

Towne commented of the character Nick Frescia, "He is the hero, while Gibson's Mac is the film's emotional center. Kurt has the Bogart part: he loses the girl, saves his friend, and he's the one with the last line in the movie." [800] Towne said of Jo

---

[795] Cowgill. *Op.cit.,* 49-50.

[796] Cowgill. *Op. cit.* 58.

[797] This analysis is derived from Robin Wood, 1982, 297-305.

[798] On page 90A Mac declares to JoAnn, "It's tougher to quit than you think." The metaphor of cleaning up and her role in this is reinforced on page 95A when, after their lovemaking, Jo Ann's clothes are whirling around in the dryer.

[799] Turan. *Ibid.*

Ann that he was looking for "someone with that kind of sang froid, that kind of infuriating beauty. You wonder if this girl ever gets upset at anything…"[801] Towne was therefore continuing his infatuation not merely with classical Hollywood generic forms but with the star system itself.

> 'You know I always felt that the South Bay was like a different country…
> I felt that these characters belonged in that setting.'[802]

Thus the film was armed with a powerhouse trio of romantic leads, aided by superb support in the form of J.T. Walsh as Hal (formerly Al) Maguire and Raul Julia as Carlos/Escalante. Maguire (as cop/villain), Carlos/Escalante (as friend/villain), Andy/Sandy Leonard (failed drug dealer and lawyer to both Mac and Jo Ann) and Lindroff (Mac's cousin, Carlos' victim) form a rich, dualistic array of supporting characters whose roles and traits are well-served in this complex narrative. Likewise, Arturo and Nino. Each has startling functions and lines to perform. To quote Andrew Horton,

> Each minor character exists in her/his own right but acts as a means
> of further defining/expanding/exploring the main determining
> character. They thus enrich and complicate the main narrative.[803]

Towne cast friend and fellow director Budd Boetticher as the judge, mainly to repay him for the use of Fifties bullfighting footage on TV ("a particularly bloody corrida": p. 117) in the background to a crucial scene between Mac and Carlos (another example of Towne's preference for animal symbolism); and as compensation for losing the role of Earl Rawley in what would have been his version of *The Two Jakes*.[804]

Metaphor & Theme

Just as *Chinatown* features water as a major metaphor and part of the narrative, there are very few scenes in *Tequila Sunrise* that don't allude to or include this element, which forms a subtext to the entire story. The film is set in the South Beach area of Los Angeles and takes place variously at Hermosa Beach, Redondo Beach and Manhattan Beach, concluding at San Pedro Harbour, a location familiar from Towne's childhood. The entire film might be read as a recasting of his own private dramas and the cross- and double-cross and Janus-faced behaviour of some of his former friends (and perhaps himself). That the film is about drug dealing obviously gave Warners pause for thought, but as Towne reasons, "I needed an unsavoury profession for a man who was trying to escape it. The film is set in Southern California; what can you do, a stock swindle? The frightening thing is that nice and charming people do terrible things. Life would be a lot easier if every drug dealer looked like the Night Stalker."[805]

---

[800] Turan. *Ibid.*

[801] Turan. *Ibid.* Rumours abound that the star and her director did not exactly see eye to eye.

[802] Shiller. *Op.cit.*, 49.

[803] Horton. *Op.cit.*, 56.

[804] This forms a further, if tenuous, link with the New Hollywood, as *Westbound*, directed by Boetticher, is the film within a film in *À Bout de Souffle (Breathless)*, which was such an influence on *Bonnie and Clyde*

[805] Turan. *Ibid.*

Dialogue

Despite the generic construction of the screenplay for *Tequila Sunrise*, which owes much of its structure to the 1940s melodrama, as well as Howard Hawks' collaborative adaptations of *THE BIG SLEEP* and *TO HAVE AND HAVE NOT*, Towne's leisurely approach allows for excellent, layered dialogue, with more than a hint of sarcasm and byplay between the actors, particularly Nick and Jo Ann.[806] Nick's somewhat superior attitude to Mac also gives him the opportunity to trade one-liners, such as:

```
        NICK (to MAC)
Yeah, but a hometown boy like you could do
a lot for South Bay cops, you're a legend
around here.  Not only that, you're white.
They figure when they print your picture
in the paper they'll be able to see it.
```

(Tequila Sunrise: 14)

The film contains some of Towne's most brilliant and brittle exchanges, allowing for an expansiveness of character that is all too rare in contemporary Hollywood cinema. Director of Cinematography Conrad Hall says that

> *Tequila Sunrise* is a story told primarily in words rather than images. The story comes out through the dialogue between the characters. Robert wrote such exquisite words for the characters to use. I felt that it was a picture that should be shot from the waist up – or even tighter. It's basically people talking to one another. [807]

This breadth of expression gives Nick Frescia one of the longest monologues outside of Ron Shelton's *Bull Durham* (in which Kevin Costner eulogises the beautiful things in life) and gives an insight into a man torn between duty to the law and loyalty to a friend:

```
            FRESCIA
Mac knows what he feels - - he's crazy
about you and he doesn't want to get
caught.  For a crook, it's crystal clear.
On the other hand, for a cop it's
confusing.  Mac's my friend and I like
him.  Maguire's my associate and I hate
him.  I probably have to bust my friend if
I'm gonna do my job.  Now I hate that, but
I hate drug dealers, too, and somebody's
gotta get rid of Carlos.  How do I do
that?  Maguire, the creep, wants me to
bust Mac any way I can, even if it means
```

---

[806] *To Have and Have Not*'s debt to *Casablanca* is summarised by Robin Wood; but, as he says, a comparison between the two "could furnish material for a further long essay in itself." In Nichols, 1982, 297-303.

[807] Shiller. *Op.cit*, 51.

manufacturing evidence. Then he wants to
coerce Mac into turning over Carlos - - I
don't approve of this approach. I think
I'll stay away from blackmail and try
'selective surveillance.' What the hell
is that? Well it's not too complicated.
                    (MORE)

                                        (CONTINUED)

                    FRESCIA (CONT'D)
With my powers of deduction, I walk into
your restaurant, take one look at you, and
realize that no matter how good the food
is, Mac's not here to eat. He's in love.
He's always been piss-poor at hiding his
feelings and you're gorgeous.[808] Then I
have to wonder if you're not as smooth
about concealing your feelings as you
are at taking care of your customers. I
know you're not in the drug business, but
maybe you've got guilty knowledge that
can help me do my job. I check you out
- - you've had, as near as I can tell,
three affairs in the last seven years - -
one with a lifeguard who was more a high
school buddy than anything else, the
other a painter from Venice, who did some
frescoes in your restaurant, and the third
a married man where you broke off the
relationship almost immediately. You are
not exactly wild and unpredictable in
this area. So I figure if you're willing
to get involved with me you're probably
not involved with Mac, but given his
interest in you you're likely to find out
what's going on in his life as anybody
else - - whether you cater a party, or he
brings people in here[809] - - what I didn't
figure is that you're not like me. You're
not devious. You're honest and kind and
principled and I trust you - suddenly I'm
ashamed. You're the most beautiful thing
I've ever seen, I'm nuts about you. Now
- - I've only got one question - - and it's
not about Mac. I don't want to know what
you know about Mac. I just want to see
you tonight. Will you? See me?

                                (Tequila Sunrise. 82-3)

---

[808] Kurt Russell doesn't say this line in the film.
[809] This phrase is not in the film.

This speech, lengthy as it is, embodies those things that Linda Cowgill states are necessary to screenplay structure:

> A screenwriter uses the answers to the questions of want, why and need to define the protagonist, antagonist and other main characters as well as to build a plot. The other main characters' wants and needs should conflict to various degrees with the protagonist's wants and needs; they should become obstacles and complications for the protagonist to deal with and overcome. [810]

It is worth noting with reference to the length of this 'speech' as written and shot by Towne - and Kevin Costner's declaration of love and the sweet things in life ("I believe…," a take on the oath of allegiance) to Susan Sarandon in *Bull Durham* (1988) - that the only contemporary filmmaker writing dialogue (or to be more precise, monologues) of this nature could be deemed to be Ron Shelton – another writer who occasionally directs his own material. We might conclude that it may well be the privilege of writer/directors such as Towne and Shelton to exceed the normal boundaries of film dialogue only when they are helming their own screenplays. [811] Nonetheless, it boasts alliterative assonance in the first three lines; a poetic conceit ("guilty knowledge"); and an almost embarrassing display of self-effacement.

It is clear from Nick's speech that he is driven both by his want (for Jo Ann, who is falling in love with Mac) and his need to do his duty, despite his loyalty to Mac. He also has a deep need for truth. This conflict – the obvious disparity between what he wants and what he needs - is at the heart of the screenplay. As Towne himself states, "… those cases where people are sometimes talking and you realize it's not good and you change the nature of the scene into something that is … that involves some sort of conflict and that creates compression all by itself. Just the use of conflict." [812] Hence the importance of the speech, despite its unconventional length. It also enhances Nick's character: although he is ostensibly the good guy and Mac is the bad guy, it is he, Nick, who is physically more suspect and oleaginous, and he also denies to Mac that he told Jo Ann about the party (which he thought was for Carlos but is actually for Cody):

```
                    McKUSSIC
        By the way -- you told Jo Ann about the
        party.


                    FRESCIA
        No, Mac.  You got it backwards.  She
        told me.


                    McKUSSIC
        Yeah?  Then she got it backwards.
```

---

[810] Cowgill. *Op.cit.*, 46.

[811] Thanks to Tom Stempel for initiating this discussion in Los Angeles, 2003. It is also a reminder of Pauline Kael's statement that Towne's characters have 'sides' and they like to tell anecdotes: Pauline Kael, 'Beverly Hills as a Big Bed,' as before 1992, 442.

[812] Speaking at the AFI's Harold Lloyd Master Seminar, as before.

FRESCIA
Well, it's understandable -- you
confronting her like that -- she probably
got flustered. After all she's not used
to that sort of thing. She's a very
traditional girl. Wish Cody happy
birthday for me--

(*Tequila Sunrise*: 62)

This exchange exemplifies the shifting pattern of loyalties, cross and double cross, which characterises the narrative, culminating in Maguire breaking his word to Frescia and attempting to murder McKussic in cold blood, and Carlos' attempted betrayal of McKussic. The wordplay is rooted in conflict and rising action, escalating into more confusion and more conflict. Ultimately, we see that Frescia mends his ways at the film's conclusion, when he brings Mac and Jo Ann together courtesy of Woody in Harbour Patrol (played by longtime Towne crony and co-writer on *Without Limits*, Kenny Moore.) Towne commented: "Critics failed to see that Mac is sympathetic only to make Nick more heroic. The drug dealer is the exemplar of decency, which makes it difficult for the cop to make a choice. Nick is corrupted by his profession; the girl chooses the man who is least corrupted, the caring drug dealer." [813]

The Scene Sequence

Tequila ... is built along the lines of a classical Hollywood screenplay of cause and effect linearity. "... Suddenly you're back in a '40s movie, with grown-ups dressed up. There you are without even trying. I backed into it." [814]

The story has a forward movement which involves an investigation by the LAPD and the DEA, and a backward motion averting to a past crime in Mexico, which led to Carlos substituting for Nick as Mac's best friend. This structure is the centre of the screenplay's unravelling double spiral hinged on Nick and Mac's love for Jo Ann, as well as the concurrent spiral of friendship involving Carlos/Escalante. There is a series of triangular relationships constantly rearranging themselves according to the various internal dynamics and conflicts, and shifting the paradigm (and meaning) of friendship. Mark Finch, in his review for the *Monthly Film Bulletin*, finds that the film's generic underpinnings are not difficult to locate:

> Certain genre foundations are clearly visible, like Mel Gibson's drug dealer who, as
> has many a gunfighter before him, wants to give up the business but is trapped by
> other people's expectations. And the triangle has that old Hawksian characteristic
> of two men who can't disentangle themselves from their own friendship sufficiently

[813] Towne in Anne Thompson, *ibid.* Stephen Schiff claims, "Towne's characters always invent their own morality, and part of what makes his work at once utterly compelling and utterly true to the American grain is the way his people persuade us of that morality. Like Fenimore Cooper's heroes (not to mention Hemingway's and Hammett's and Mailer's), Towne's characters shrug off conventional mores in favor of a code that is somehow loftier and more stringent, an unarticulated ethic that reveals itself only in its heroes' day-to-day behaviour – in their deeds." Stephen Schiff, 'Talk of the Towne,' *Vanity Fair*, January 1989: 41.

[814] *Ibid.* Towne is referring to the melodramatic mode, which as Barry Langford attests, is a fundamental component of Hollywood storytelling, with its Manichean emphasis on morality. Langford. *Op.cit.,,* 29-50. This mode can be seen as a dominant figure in the Towne oeuvre.

to be sure what they feel about Michelle Pfeiffer's restaurateur – updated only to the extent that she is more impatient with the situation than any Hawks woman would have been. [815]

In this, as in many of his other screenplays, Towne orders sequences around the fetish objects that tie the characters and story together: water, drugs, a lighter, a highly decorative trophy gun. (In another nod to *Chinatown*, he also has Carlos/Escalante go fishing for albacore on his way home.) In order to explain this, let's look at one particular sequence in the film which lasts approximately 16 minutes onscreen and commences on page 48 of the screenplay with Jo Ann in a booth at Vallenari's with Frescia. He still suspects her of criminal behaviour and a relationship with Mac. He is shocked when she says Mac has never even asked her out.

```
Frescia picks up a Zippo and lights a cigarette.  When he
sets it down, the raised brass lettering that is worn
nearly to the aluminium surface boldly reads R.U.H.S.


                         JO ANN
                (tapping the lighter
                with a fingernail)
             -- What's that mean?

                                            (CONTINUED)


                         FRESCIA
                Redondo Union High.


                         JO ANN
                (teasing)
                You smoked in high school?
                         FRESCIA
                (with a wink)
             -- We were a bunch of rowdies, Jo Ann --


He touches her wrist.  She jumps a little.


                         JO ANN
             --How about an espresso?


                         FRESCIA
                What?


She goes over to the bar and the espresso machine.


                         JO ANN
                I've got to lock up and I'll never do it
                like this…
```

---

[815] Mark Finch, '*Tequila Sunrise*,' *Monthly Film Bulletin*, Vol. 56, No. 664, May 1989: 153.

She doesn't see the rain-spattered envelope by the cash register. She's just gotten smacked in the eye with a water drop. She looks up toward the roof.

(*Tequila Sunrise*: 50-51)

The sequence continues to the cellar where the skylight falls in and drenches Nick. He and Jo Ann embrace in the raindrops. Meanwhile, back at Mac's, he watches the rain with a picture of Nick and himself at Redondo Union High as a backdrop (explaining the 'McGuffin' Zippo which triggers the meaning of this entire sequence – friendship and loyalty.) At Lomita Station, Maguire asks Frescia where Mac's party is being held – he doesn't know. At the restaurant Arturo observes with suspicion when Jo Ann takes Frescia's call and she agrees to lunch with him at the weekend. The next three parts of this montage are cut – they include restaurants where Jo Ann can dine as well as 'checking out the competition.' She and Frescia have lunch at a taco stand. Later at Mac's back yard a children's party is taking place, complete with magician. Jo Ann arrives and notes the ping-pong table set up on the second floor [this being the equivalent of 'As Time Goes By' in *Casablanca* – a paean to a time impossible to recapture; here, it bears meaning for the impossible friendship between Mac and Carlos.] Mac is aware that the place is being watched from the beach by twenty-five cops.

> McKUSSIC
> (quietly)
> Are you going to tell me <u>that's</u> a surprise?

> JO ANN
> -- No. Mr. Frescia said there was a possibility the police would be watching you.

> McKUSSIC
> Did he say why?

Jo Ann finally looks at McKussic.

> JO ANN
> --Yes. Do you want me to be specific?

> McKUSSIC
> I'd appreciate that.

Mac steps back inside and Jo Ann follows.

> JO ANN
> (very uncomfortable)
> He said… you were a serious drug dealer and that you promised to quit but that you lied and were -- still doing it--

> McKUSSIC
> He called me a liar? What a bummer --

```
                     well, I can't blame you.

                          JO ANN
               Blame me for what?

                          McKUSSIC
               Telling Nick about the party --
                    (tapping the envelope)
               --I counted that kind of fast --

CONTINUED:

He abruptly walks away and heads up the stairs.

                          JO ANN
               --I didn't tell Mr. Frescia about the
               party. He told me.
```

(*Tequila Sunrise*: 57-8)

Page 76 was dropped from the filmed version – Jo Ann loses her temper and says "it would have been more insulting if I'd refused to cater the party. I didn't know it was your child's birthday, you didn't order the cake from us, I didn't even know you had a child." She wishes Cody a happy birthday. Mac and Lindroff pace the beach wondering how Frescia knew about the party before Jo Ann. Frescia can't believe that Maguire has enlisted the Harbour Patrol in the operation. Mac calls Frescia from the beach and asks for a meeting. At dusk Mac and Frescia are sitting on a child's swing set at the beach – and the sequence involving the lighter, the issues of truth, loyalty and friendship are explored in a dialogue that takes place silhouetted against the warmth of the evening sun. Mac says that if Frescia wants to go after Carlos, 'be my guest. Just don't let me catch you using me to do it.'

```
                          McKUSSIC
               By the way -- you told Jo Ann about the
               party.

                          FRESCIA
               No, Mac.  You got it backwards.  She
               told me.

                          McKUSSIC
               Yeah?  Then she got it backwards.

                          FRESCIA
               Well, it's understandable -- you
               confronting her like that -- she probably
               got flustered.  After all she's not used
               to that sort of thing.  She's a very
               traditional girl.  Wish Cody happy
               birthday for me.
```

(*Tequila Sunrise*: 62A)

It is typical of Towne's tricky writing style (some might call it convoluted), and reminiscent of *Chinatown*'s construction, that all the strands of the complex dialogue, imagery, theme and story, and the real hero of the piece, are not fully clarified until the final moments of the film.

A Musical Theme

Composer Dave Grusin is a constant in Towne's work, going back to *The Yakuza*. His contribution to *Tequila Sunrise* is to 'fill' those moments not embellished by the quintessential Southern California sounds that Towne chose to delineate his film. [816] Grusin composed two songs for the soundtrack – 'Tequila Dreams' featuring Lee Ritenour and a theme for Jo Ann – 'Jo Ann's Song,' which features a solo by saxophonist David Sanborn.   The film's title is, of course, inspired by The Eagles' eulogy to the early 1970s California lifestyle – ironically, the line that gives rise to the film's name is dropped from page 50:

```
                    JO ANN
Sooner or later you hear everything in a
restaurant-- [817]


          FRESCIA
He's never asked you out?


          JO ANN
The only thing he's ever asked me for is
another Tequila Sunrise, you're
still suspicious!
```

(*Tequila Sunrise*: 50)

Several pages later, Mac wants to drown his sorrows (with the eponymous drink) at home following Cody's surfing accident.

The dangers of liquid – all kinds of liquid – provide a strong thematic undertow to the material and are never far from the surface story. The soundtrack is built around the sounds of the summer – Southern Californian music is at the root of the film's attractiveness and the songs reflect the story's themes. Opening the film is Bobby Darin's recording of the Charles Trenet song, 'Beyond the Sea' ('La Mer'), which not only introduces us to the South Beach location, it also heralds the film's dénouement, at a body of water in full tide. Its lyric represents Mac's aspiration to a life beyond that which he has been trying in vain to escape. Later, 'Don't Worry Baby,' a Beach Boys song sung here by the band with the Everly Brothers, underscores Mac's fear when he can't see Cody on the surfboard by the pier and dives straight into the ocean to save his life. Not on the official soundtrack, but perhaps the most important musical item of all in terms of its symbolic significance, is 'The Star Spangled Banner.' This is playing on

---

[816] A personal observation: Grusin's score feels too contemporary (ie 80s) and works against the tone of the material as written, acted and directed. A producer might have stepped in at this point and chosen a more classical theme (as Evans had done on *Chinatown* when he hired Jerry Goldsmith against Polanski's wishes) in order to give the film a more tragic undertow.

[817] This might well be Jo Ann's echoing of Rick's classic world-weary line of feigned indifference in *Casablanca*, "I stick my neck out for nobody."

the radio during the standoff between Mac and Carlos on the cigarette boat – after the clock sounds three A.M. The Biblical reference is inescapable – Carlos is Judas to Mac's Jesus. (This scene is on page 131A of the screenplay.) It alludes to F. Scott Fitzgerald's declaration that, "in a real dark night of the soul it is always three o'clock in the morning." Not only that, but the song emphasises that if Mac hasn't made a decision over his 'retirement' from the drugs scene, he has made a patriotic choice – the United States over Mexico, the new life [and what is America but the opportunity to remake an old life in the land of the free, home of the brave] over the old-world lure of Mexico with its connotations of drug-smuggling, revolution [already essayed by Towne with Peckinpah] and gun-running.

The mythical resonance of the screenplay is completed when Mac escapes from the ocean's life-threatening riptide (again, a warning issued on radio) and 'walks on water' to be born again with Jo Ann (pp.136-142), in a change to the original ending by forces outside of Towne's control – Towne wanted Mac to die. [818] He said to Michael Sragow, "Gibson's character was supposed to be a moth in the flame. The real high for him was never doing the drugs but the danger of dealing the drugs. I made the guy too earnest and hangdog. He should have been more like the race horse attached to the milk truck – he hears a bell and he's off!" [819]

Instead, Mac is not only born again, 'baptised,' as it were, in the Pacific Ocean, he gets the girl. This is a highly ironic outcome, given Towne's original opposition to Polanski's fatalistic resolution in *Chinatown*. However, it is not true to say that this is a happy ending, per se. More correctly, it is a bittersweet or 'mixed-emotion' ending. As Andrew Horton says,

> The cliché is that Hollywood likes happy endings. But most of the films we like best have mixed-emotion endings and fall somewhere in the middle between a 'closed' (completed) ending and an 'open' (life goes on, and we are not sure how it will work out) closing. In *Casablanca* Rick loses his true love and gains himself … suggest[ing] something lost and something gained. [820]

We are unsure as to whether Mac has quit drug dealing – like Frescia, he is a character torn by the disparity between what he wants and what he needs, and this traditional dramatic strategy, here presented with Towne's typical ambiguity, drives his story – his way out from the job is to sell leaky irrigation, hardly the act of a moral man; and for Frescia, it is not an unqualified success, despite his involvement in the set up (rather like Rick at the conclusion of *Casablanca* – losing his true love but regaining a sense of self.) [821] Water as symbol is crucial in the sexual narrative drive too: the pipe

---

[818] This actually reflects the character arc of Rick Blaine: " …In *Casablanca*, Rick is reborn: he changes from a bitter ex-partisan to a recommitted patriot" Cowgill. *Op.cit.*, 50.

[819] Michael Sragow, 'Return of the Native,' *New Times Los Angeles*, 3-9 September 1998: 17. He said to Joel Engel on the same subject, "It had great tone, because the tone that was lost came from this guy who wanted out of the dealing game... There was excitement, and the action was fun; he couldn't help himself. That meant that, in the end, either he or the girl was going to get killed. There's no other way out. It would have been a great movie. …[Warners] will always feel that they made more money because of it, and I will always feel that they would have made more money if they hadn't. He would have been a more romantic figure had he died. After his death, the character played by Michelle Pfeiffer takes care of his kid." Engel, 1995, 220-1.

[820] Horton. *Op.cit.*, 128.

[821] Roger Ebert's review contains an astute observation about Towne's plot construction: His review contains an astute analysis of Towne as writer: "In his movies, the plots turn and twist

bursting in Vallenari's, christening Nick and Jo Ann's first clinch; the hot tub scene at Mac's beach house, where he and Jo Ann are watched and eavesdropped, Playboy Channel-style by the police; the final, romantic embrace in the ocean when Mac is picked up by Woody and Jo Ann runs into the surf to meet him, watched by Nick. Mac's Biblical-style 'resurrection' is complete and the motivations for all the characters are fully revealed.

Directing

Cinematographer Conrad Hall and Towne enjoyed a particularly close collaboration with the result that the film is suffused with an unusual level of warm, sunny tones and black contrasts to bring out the light. Towne stated that

> I wanted to feel the daytime atmosphere in these funky beachy backyards…
> Conrad is able to capture it so well. He is a master of a desaturated daytime look.' [822]

American Cinematographer reported that Hall and Towne both wanted the same 'look':

> I wanted California to look hot so that the audience could feel the glow of light that the beach creates,' Hall maintained. 'I felt at first that the colors were too bright for the California beaches. By overexposing them some more in the printing, I was able to pale them out. I'm not sure that California will look as hot as I might have liked, but at the same time I know that it won't look so clean and well saturated either. [823]

Hall explains the rationale behind the decision to employ the Color Contrast Enhancement process in *American Cinematographer*. [824] However, as an addendum to this reportage, the magazine's Editor says that 'at the last moment, the producers decided not to use the CCE process in the release prints.' [825] It does however prove that Towne was choosing his collaborators with a great deal of care in his attempts to achieve the desired result, that the images on the screen match the vision he inscribed in the screenplay: that it express his *voice*.

The production designer, Richard Sylbert – another associate on *Chinatown* – built Vallenari's, the restaurant where much of the action takes place, in a warehouse in Santa Monica. The film expressed yet another phase in Californian mythology for Towne:

> The road houses and places like Lowry's had collapsed, just in the last five to seven years. The advent of these restaurants is almost emblematic of a way of life. [826]

---

upon themselves. Nothing is as it seems. No character can be taken at face value. We learn more about the characters when they're not on the screen than when they are. And even when we think we've got everything nailed down, he pulls another rabbit out of his hat, showing us what fools we were to trust the magician." *Chicago Sun-Times*, 02 December 1988.

[822] *Ibid*.

[823] *Ibid*. In a sense one could argue that the heat of the image serves to alter the tone of the material.

[824] Shiller: 49-50.

[825] *Ibid*.

[826] Towne in Anne Thompson, *ibid*. This of course enriches Towne's theme of loss in his effort to recapture a city overwhelmed by the modern. Sylbert continued the visual tone of his *Chinatown* palette by painting the walls of Vallenari's in a sandy yellow of the type that adorns Paramount Studios.)

Not only was Vallenari's like Lowry's (and Valentino's), it alluded to *Chinatown*'s own noir influences – including the films of Howard Hawks, which it recalls in the scene between Jake and Evelyn in the restaurant: in *Tequila*, the restaurant scenes between Mac and JoAnn and Nick and JoAnn are direct physical quotes from *To Have and Have Not* and (perhaps more surprisingly, but not in the light of the later *Days of Thunder* screenplay), *Red Line 7000* (1965).

It could be argued that Hall's contribution to the film mirrored the influence that we can detect in Towne's work from his years with Hal Ashby, the 'non-directing' director, by which we mean a director who allows actors and not visual flourishes to dictate the scene –

> … I wanted to save movement for times when there was a particular reason. I used movement to try to get to know someone better by moving closer to them, as you would see in real life. In *Tequila Sunrise* there is hardly any movement with the camera at all. I learned that lack of movement doesn't necessarily make for a static picture. The drama is always moving forward. It's a visually quiet picture and that's good for this material. [827]

Town is again emphatic in his belief that movement translates into story value and character revelation.

<u>Authorship</u>

Movement illustrating character echoes what Towne had already said about his work on *Personal Best* and indicates the degree to which he had integrated it in his cinematic praxis. The film would eventually gross a highly respectable $41,292,551.

Tequila Sunrise may well be the quintessential Towne script – a meditation on the value of true friendship between men, both trapped and ultimately compromised by their respective occupations; a hymn to a place the writer loves; a reworking of a genre infused with great character detail, metaphors and motifs; and expansive sequences that elaborate on textual concepts, slowly but surely building up to a mission statement: *be true to yourself.* In a way, the film's subject matter is a throwback to Towne's earliest filmed screenplay, *The Last Woman on Earth* – a woman comes between two possessive men in an area filled with danger - what is South Beach if not fraught with danger both natural (the riptides washing both Cody and Mac offshore) and unnatural (drugs and guns)? The watery ending, in every sense, may have been foisted upon him by the studio but it continues to link his filmmaking with that of Hal Ashby – in her review of *8 Million Ways to Die* (1982*),* Pauline Kael refers to Ashby's penchant for 'visionary, watery finales,' perhaps further muddying the authorship argument with its implication of cross-fertilised themes from auteur to author. [828]

The noir love triangle' in *Last Woman…* had been filled out with the actor Edward Wain (aka Robert Towne) playing a lawyer; in *Tequila Sunrise*, not one, but two characters feature who look like the young Robert Towne in that film – Arye Gross as drug-dealing lawyer Andy/Sandy Leonard and Arliss Howard, playing McKussic's cousin, Lindroff. At the time of the film's release, Towne claimed to be writing two screenplays – a third instalment in the *Chinatown* trilogy, and another, perhaps about no-

[827] Shiller. *Op.cit.*, 51.
[828] Pauline Kael, *The New Yorker*, 19 May 1986.

fault divorce in California, a traumatic experience in Towne's own recent past. The entire story of *Tequila Sunrise* betrayed Towne's bewildered hurt at the price paid for lost loyalties and friendships, however misguided. It also betrayed his penchant for melodrama with noir elements, rather like *Chinatown*. Sometimes art imitates life, imitates art. Read (or viewed) alongside *The Two Jakes*, it is clear that the films are companion pieces, sharing the same concerns, the same kinds of characters, the same rueful acceptance that this, too, shall pass. [829]

Towne here deploys the full panoply of structural and diegetic materials at his disposal. Complicating the issue of Towne's authorial signature in his homage to Forties Hollywood, Howard Hawks and *Casablanca*, and the concept of the screenwriter as author in general, is the fact that Towne allegedly did not in fact originate the idea for *Tequila...* on his own. The first treatment and twenty-five pages of the screenplay were written in 1980 in collaboration with Peter Peyton, who successfully sued Towne and Warner Brothers in Los Angeles Superior Court, shortly after the film's production commenced in March 1988, for $250,000, the amount he claimed he was promised in an oral agreement with Towne in exchange for a producing credit (which he never received) and allegedly having agreed to waive credit for his screenplay contribution. [830] However it could also be said that the idea behind the film was cannibalised from his earlier work on *Cisco Pike*.

> CARLOS
> You son of a bitch! How could
> you do this? Friendship is the
> only choice you can make in life
> that's yours.

(Tequila Sunrise:129/30)

Conflict was certainly the theme and the reality of the film's writing: Towne was still in litigation with Warners while finishing the screenplay (according to *Variety* on 05 May, 1982.) Peyton won his lawsuit, despite the fact that Towne had clearly lifted many of the plot points from his own rewrite of *Cisco Pike*, a decade previously. [831]

The issue of authorship is *further* complicated by the emergence of the script doctor's script doctor – on New Year's Day 2006 *The Los Angeles Times* carried an interview with a lecturer in English at Orange Coast College, Anna Waterhouse, by Dana Parsons, under the headline, 'This Reward Wasn't in the Script.' [832]

---

[829] Richard Combs, *The Two Jakes* Review, *Sight & Sound*, Vol.1, No.8, Dec. 1991: 54.

[830] *Variety*, 23 March, 1988. Peyton was in fact associate producer on *Personal Best*.

[831] Anne Thompson, 'Towne Crier,' *L.A. Weekly*, 16 December 1988. As noted, Towne likes to cannibalise his own work.

[832] *The Los Angeles Times*, 01 January 2006, accessed online. The possibility that the script had been doctored was brought up in one contemporary review: "... *Tequila Sunrise* gives the disquieting impression of a film that has been much worked over by a script doctor, but the original premises or possibilities of which have long ago been lost sight of, or were too slight to begin with. This kind of groundless elaboration, with characters and plot detail treated with loving circumspection, but basically floating in a void of their own, was noticeable over ten years ago in *Shampoo*. There it had some thematic justification... But *Tequila Sunrise* promises something more integrated, a romantic triangle in the specific environment of Los Angeles' South Bay, with

Ms Waterhouse, it transpired, had worked for several years as a consultant to Robert Towne. Specifically, she had consulted initially on *Tequila Sunrise* and subsequently, *Mission: Impossible* and *Without Limits*. She said of the screenplay for *Tequila*, "I found things in it that needed to be fixed," Waterhouse says. "Lines that didn't quite go, some technical things I didn't think would happen in those circumstances."

In a letter to this author, Ms Waterhouse, herself a working screenwriter, states:

I think to use the term 'script doctor,' when it comes to my work on Robert's scripts, is to be a bit misleading. He didn't need surgery -- simply, as I stated in the interview, someone to serve as editor (to cut and restructure) so he could focus on writing without immediately engaging his own internal editor. It gave him the freedom to, for example, write dialogue without worrying if it went on too long, or even if said dialogue would be better placed elsewhere. He was always active in the process -- he never simply handed me his work to do with as I chose. He wrote, I read, then I suggested -- and he agreed, disagreed, or came up with other ideas, which we would then discuss.

She adds:

The truth is, Robert is a fascinating combination of the solitary writer and the ultimate collaborator. What he creates, he creates on his own. But he loves nothing better than to share his writing (reading scripts out loud, for example, to friends, co-workers and family) in order to get that immediate input (where do they seem rapt? where does he lose them?) that a stage actor is privy to. In the same way, he prefers to have someone he trusts read over his scenes. Since I left (in 2001), his favorite collaborator has been his wife, Luisa. (She would, no doubt, have been his favorite collaborator all along, were it not for the fact that their daughter was small, and it was hard for Luisa to have the time and focus that the work necessitates.) [833]

Whilst not forthcoming about the precise nature of her contribution to Towne's screenplays, presumably because of its confidential nature, Ms Waterhouse points to an aspect of Towne's professional character which might be traced throughout his oeuvre: his willingness to take on board outside opinion and integrate the audience's need for story logic into his writing. (In fact Robert Evans had long ago lamented Towne's penchant for telling stories to his friends but taking years to present them in screenplay form.) [834] The collaboration with second wife Luisa Towne certainly can be verified by her surprising presence and participation in the story meetings for *8 Million Ways to Die* according to the production memos seen by this author at the Margaret Herrick Library. [835] This of course adds weight to the debate *against* the singularity of any claim that might be made for his unique authorship.

Writer/director Philip Dunne cautions that

...the director of a picture is seldom its author...

---

two of the characters negotiating an old friendship from opposite sides of the law, an old debt turning in new guise, and some bittersweet reflections on the manipulative or inscrutable nature of love." Richard Combs, *Monthly Film Bulletin*, August 1974, Vol.41, No.487: 171-172.

[833] Letter from Ms Waterhouse to Elaine Lennon 31 January 2006.
[834] Evans. *Op.cit.*
[835] Part of the Hal Ashby Collection sourced courtesy of the staff of that library in November 2003. These meetings were of course akin to the story conferences part of the classical studio praxis, as described in Brady. *Op.cit.*, 13, and elsewhere.

I have no wish to begrudge any director the credit he deserves; I only deplore the fact that the Auteur Theory enriches him in prestige while it robs the writer of the credit he has earned. [836]

Rumours abounded that this film was re-cut against Towne's wishes. In fact, the ending was dramatically altered from Towne's screenplay: Mac was supposed to die, while Nick would get the girl. In other words, another ending was changed – an ongoing feature of Towne's screenplays, and, like *Chinatown*, this was against his wishes. Nonetheless, it is, as can be seen, a highly complex piece of mythic and character-centred genre writing, thematically rich and awash with astringent dialogue. It may well be his masterpiece. A director's cut would be something to relish.

Conclusions

Ira Konigsberg urges caution where attribution is concerned: "It would be foolish to underplay the importance of all those who contribute to a film. Film is a composite art, and it is often difficult to distinguish where the contribution of one person ends and that of another begins. It is also an art as much dependent on technology as the people involved. But for these very reasons, the role of the director looms large: he is the technologist and the artist, the creative mind who must give to all these disparate elements unity, design, and coherence. It is his vision and sensibility that should stamp the film and infuse it with spirit and meaning." [837]

In his attempts to translate to the screen the drama he had created on the page, Towne proved that he had a visual style of his own – surprisingly abstract at times, light in tone (and reminiscent of his collaborations with Hal Ashby), and consistent in terms of the themes he had previously explored. [838] In terms of the narrative paradigm which seems to have dictated his approach to screenplay structure, he has retained the principal elements or 'internal coordinates' [839] – the man trapped by his profession and compromised within his relationships; the theme of (unheroic) failure and ultimately, loss; the recurring visual motifs which amount to fetish objects throughout his oeuvre; all the while working within his beloved classical Hollywood structure, with its problematic studios, producers and stars, whose power he has always assiduously cultivated, perhaps in his own drive to become an acknowledged cinematic author. He did not however attempt the kind of overtly political narrative for which he had become

---

[836] Dunne. *Op.cit.,* 47. In his own case, he concludes that he is in fact a better director than screenwriter yet asks himself the question, "Why didn't I, as director, force me, as writer, to cut all those unnecessary words?" (335).

[837] Ira Konigsberg. *FILM DICTIONARY: The Complete Film Dictionary* (2nd ed.). London: Bloomsbury, 1997, 98.

[838] It is probably wise to try to avoid what Ryan Gilbey describes as "the auteurist bias of film theory, where every work must constitute a piece of the same puzzle, or risk going without favour." *Op.cit.,* 231. On the other hand this cinematic abstraction forms a link in the chain of auteurist cinema: *Bonnie and Clyde* lifted slow motion and abstract editing devices from the New Wave style – without of course repudiating the Classical Hollywood that Godard was parodying, pasticheing and denying, all at once. The assimilability of American cinema is perhaps the subtext to this argument. See Robert B. Ray, *A CERTAIN TENDENCY OF THE HOLLYWOOD CINEMA, 1930-1980.* Princeton, N.J.: Princeton University Press, 1985, 247-295.

[839] William Luhr and Peter Lehman. *AUTHORSHIP AND NARRATIVE IN THE CINEMA: Issues in Contemporary Aesthetics and Criticism.* New York: GP Putnam's Sons, 1977, 26.

famous in the New Hollywood era, suggesting perhaps that *Chinatown* aside, his concerns lay far from those of his powerful collaborators.

Thus while acknowledging that it is possible to identify a producer or star or director as author of films based on screenplays written by Robert Towne, this phase is important inasmuch as it represents an attempt to locate his authorial signature on those films of which he is not only the author according to their structural elements but also accounting for their translation to the screen. This necessitates the overriding assumption that as a screenwriter he is an auteur, in other words, that his work overall contains an identifiable consistency of thematic concerns or controlling principles, major character archetypes and other structural elements, from text to text. In Wood's terms, the consistency of Towne's theme and character reinforces his claim to auteur status, with his 'dominant personality' a constant determinant of his work. [840]

His career as director has been replete with irony: in order to make his directorial debut, he sacrificed both his marriage and perhaps his best piece of writing; to make his fine genre thriller, he gave up his best male friendships in a series of mutual betrayals, which, ironically, fuelled the narrative; and his greatest piece of contemporary mythic filmmaking, *Without Limits*, would come at a time in his life when he admitted he didn't even know how much it cost to make a film. And then there are the collaborative writing relationships, both credited and uncredited. While a fact of life in the Hollywood industry, it certainly compromises the case for Towne as an auteur. Unlike New Hollywood contemporaries such as Coppola, however, he did not misunderstand the machinery of the business. [841] If an auteur is the person who has the most control over its final outcome, then Towne has at least occasionally admitted that he has lost such control at crucial moments. At the very least, his is a highly significant determining influence, despite (or perhaps, because, of) the history of altered endings to his screenplays. The greatest dramatic irony is perhaps the fact that his career now had the compromised (and formerly successful) shape of that of his protagonists: he was a man whose (potentially) greatest artistic triumph, *Greystoke,* was also his greatest loss, and one from which it is doubtful he has ever truly recovered. His biography is inextricably intertwined with his professional output not merely in terms of subject matter: the shadow of *Greystoke* has dictated his subsequent career choices, and yet, despite its central place in his career, it is none of the things for which he was acclaimed: it is, rather, an expression of hope, an articulation of humanity, a primal scream for freedom; above all, it is a great romantic adventure. Robert Towne's *Greystoke* is yet to be made.

Acknowledgements:

The Hal Ashby Collection, Margaret Herrick Library, Academy of Motion Picture Arts and Sciences; special thanks to Greg Walsh for article research.

---

[840] Wood in Nichols, 1982, 301.

[841] Jon Lewis claims that the "… success of auteur films in the 1970s did not, as Coppola had hoped it would, give auteur directors increased access to film financing. Instead, directors became increasingly dependent on studio financing to produce and distribute such 'big' films." *WHOM GOD WISHES TO DESTROY … : Francis Coppola and the New Hollywood.* Durham & London: Duke University Press, 1995, 22.

Chapter 5   1990-2000: CONSOLIDATION

Days of Thunder (1990) (screenplay) (story by Robert Towne & Tom Cruise)
The Firm (1993) (screenplay by Robert Towne & David Rayfiel)
Mission: Impossible (1996) (screenplay by Robert Towne)
Without Limits (*Pre*) (1998) (screenplay by Kenny Moore and Robert Towne; directed by Robert Towne)
Mission: Impossible 2 aka *M:I 2* (2000) (screenplay)

The Screenwriter for Hire

This is the period of consolidation in Hollywood, when the Summer's tent-pole blockbuster had easily become a part of every studio's development schedule. Towne hitched his career to that of several stars – Tom Cruise, and producers Don Simpson and Jerry Bruckheimer, seemingly content, at least for the first half of the decade, to take on unchallenging subject matter and highly paid rewrites.

We have said that in the traditional, classic filmmaking style, Towne's screenplays mostly fall within the pattern of transgression, recognition and redemption, albeit with key exceptions (*The Last Detail, Chinatown*). This is what is described by Dancyger and Rush as 'restorative act structure' and might be said to demonstrate a specifically American way of redemption. We might also say that within that pattern Towne has kept within the rubric of the three-act structure without consistently using all of that structure's elements (midpoints, redemptive finales). [842]

In his 90s screenplays, which are primarily genre-based, we see this structure continue, albeit with an equally integrated pattern of those motifs which became part of his screenwriting signature in the Seventies work. In short, we see the industrialised Towne screenplay, fine-tuned to the studios' blockbuster requirements and somewhat shorn of the extraordinarily personalised themes of the earlier works yet at the same time expressing the intrinsic desires of the characters in perhaps more subtle and compressed fashion.

Jim Collins examines the cultural context of cinematic genericity in the late Eighties, early Nineties by analysing the pre-conditions formed by "the interplay of cultural, technological and demographic factors," and pointing out that the genre film was now being rewritten as a hybrid *across* genres. [843] This 'hyperconsciousness,' says Collins, affects not just the narrative formulae of films, "but the conditions of their own circulation and reception." [844] Those conditions could perhaps prove oppressive for a screenwriter who strove to write the classical Hollywood film: as Tom Shone points out,

> The blockbuster era would require a different set of skills from Hollywood's actors:
> a gift for the one-liner, not the speech; for more graphic powers of delineation at
> the service of pacier narrative; and for the powers of imagination required to act
> opposite special effects. [845]

[842] Dancyger and Rush, 1995, 17-42.
[843] Jim Collins, 'Genericity in the Nineties: Eclectic Irony and the New Sincerity,' in Collins, Radner, and Preacher Collins. *FILM THEORY GOES TO THE MOVIES (AFI Film Reader)*. London: Routledge, 1993, 245.
[844] Collins. *Op.cit.,* 248.
[845] Tom Shone. *BLOCKBUSTER: How Hollywood Learned to Stop Worrying and Love the Summer*.

The implications for the screenwriter are clear, as, he claims, the blockbuster may now be "the quintessential American form, for many countries have film industries, but only America makes blockbusters." [846]

According to Peter Biskind,

the blockbuster syndrome probably started with *The Godfather* in 1972 and got an added boost from JAWS in 1975 but really took off with *Star Wars*. Once it became clear that certain kinds of films could reap immeasurably greater returns on investment than had ever been seen before, studios naturally wanted to turn the trick again, and again, and again: enter the Roman-numeral movie, product of the obsession with surefire hits. Blockbusters were expensive to make, and the more they cost, the safer and blander they became, while the smaller, riskier, innovative projects fell by the wayside. [847]

Story 'guru' John Truby counsels on writing the blockbuster that it is more than the much-vaunted notion of 'high concept':

Blockbuster films are usually based on a high concept, but they also extend the high concept through theme and opposition…
Blockbuster writers hit all the beats of their genre, but they twist each one so that the story seems original. [848]

Given his stated predilections, how does Towne's narrative style fit into the notion espoused by the literary-influenced film theorists of the 1970s and the industry's contemporary needs? Towne repeatedly cites Jean Renoir as the filmmaker he most admires; he has also claimed to be greatly influenced by the work of the nineteenth century French realist novelists, among them Zola, Flaubert and Balzac.[849] Bordwell comments that

What's surprising is that today's screenwriters create more psychologically complex characters than the genre has typically required.
In action films, we're told, spectacle overrides narrative, and the result works against the 'linearity' of the classical tradition. All the stunts and fights make the film very episodic. But these claims are untenable because narrative and spectacle aren't mutually exclusive concepts. Aristotle long ago indicated that spectacle (opsis) is a manner of showing forth plot (mythos.) Every action scene, however 'spectacular', is a narrative event, and it can advance characters' goals and alter their states of knowledge. [850]

London: Simon & Schuster, 2004, 113.

[846] Shone. *Op.cit.*, 57.

[847] Peter Biskind's article 'The Last Crusade' appeared in Mark Crispin Miller (ed.), *SEEING THROUGH MOVIES*. New York: Pantheon, 1990, 130. Although in Summer 1990 studios dumped their action blockbusters momentarily, following the shock successes of *Pretty Woman* and *Ghost*. Shone, *op.cit.*, 201.

[848] John Truby, 'Secrets of Blockbuster Moves, II,' accessed online at: www.writersstore.com/article.php?articles_id=14.

[849] Horowitz says that Towne "shares this deference to existing forms with Renoir, who also moved freely from costume drama to war films to Hollywood melodrama to Technicolor musical, always leaving the conventions of the form as he found them. His interests, like Towne's, lay elsewhere: in the moral relationships of the characters." 1990: 54.

[850] Bordwell. 2006, 104.

Bordwell refers to the principles of classical unity in the action film as laid out by William Martell; he concludes by labelling the contemporary style "intensified continuity"; and identifies four strategies of camerawork and editing utilised to express narrative unity – "rapid editing, bipolar extremes of lens lengths, reliance on close shots, and wide-ranging camera movements." [851]

The visual tics and motifs Towne puts on paper compare very favourably with the realised vision on the screen and in interview with Bernard Weinraub of *The New York Times*, Towne claimed, "… I made up my mind that when I wrote movies it was going to be real." [852] He said to the *New York Times*, "The one thing you can work with is the emotional life of your hero." [853] How that intention could be translated "in what constitutes narrative action and visual entertainment" in the Nineties is the focus of this section. [854]

Days of Thunder (1990) (screenplay by Robert Towne; story by Robert Towne & Tom Cruise)

Days of Thunder was, in its makers' eyes, the first feature film to be based around the subject of stock-car racing. The National Association for Stock Car Auto Racing was hoping that the organisation would benefit from the association with Simpson-Bruckheimer in the same way that the Navy accrued wonderful publicity following the huge success of *Top Gun* (1985).

```
                HARRY
            (acidly)
In other words all you have to
worry about is getting beat by
other drivers.
```

(*Days of Thunder*: 17A)

However, stock car racing had featured in several films prior to *Thunder*, some of which would lend *Days of Thunder* plot elements, perhaps commencing with the 1960 film *Thunder in Carolina* (Darlington Films) featuring Rory Calhoun as a competitor in the Southern 500 who purposely crashes his car in order to save a fellow driver and former protégé. Howard Hawks had returned to the world of motor sport in 1965 with the drama *Red Line 7000* (Paramount), starring James Caan in his first leading role. (However, there are significant similarities between certain of that film's characters and Towne's earlier work on *Tequila Sunrise* (1988), as we have already seen.) Thus, as would be levelled at him on other projects, Towne, or Towne and Cruise together, had liberally 'borrowed,' whether consciously or otherwise, from a well-established, if little respected, sub-genre in the sporting spectrum. In the early 80s Ronald Bergan summarises this kind of racing as follows:

[851] William Martell. *SECRETS OF ACTION SCREENWRITING*. In Bordwell, 2006, 109; 54-55; 121-138.

[852] Weinraub. *Op.cit.*, 1.

[853] Rick Lyman. 'Villains and Heroes,' *The New York Times*, 26 May 2000: E26.

[854] Collins. *Op.cit.*, 257.

At the other end of the spectrum from Grand Prix racing are the demolition derbies and stock car races. The drivers operate at the lowest and least publicized levels of sport. Most exponents of the 'stox' circuit build their own cars, although they are, on the whole, men of modest means. The car has to be strong enough to hit a fence at 60mph, turn two somersaults and keep going. The best cars can cost over 10,000 dollars to build and the drivers don't earn big money. The gritty independence of the participants, the risks involved for mean gains were presumably what attracted Howard Hawks to the sport in his *Red Line 7000* (1965) and supplied the perfect metaphor in *The Last American Hero* (TCF 1973). [855]

The narrative template for the motor racing film is as follows: an independent-minded racer wishes to pursue his chosen sport but his bloody-mindedness scares off potential team bosses until someone takes a chance on him. His aversion to romance is cured by a tempestuous relationship with a spirited woman who ultimately wants to settle down with him, leaving him to choose between her and the sport, until a near-fatal accident makes the choice for him and he realises that life without a woman is meaningless. Bergan puts it this way:

> The moral point often made in car race pictures (and in boxing ones) is that all the risk and effort of the hero's profession is not worth the sacrifice of personal happiness (ie female, fraternal and family responsibilities). The hero must realize that his life is empty, that he has been exploited, and that the spectators are a bloodthirsty mob hoping to see him killed. Before this view is expressed, the director and the audience have revelled in the dangers, thrills and fatalities for 70 minutes. [856]

Days of Thunder arose from Tom Cruise's wish to make another action film – something along the lines of *Top Gun* (1985), in which his superstardom was enshrined and assured by producers Don Simpson and Jerry Bruckheimer. He got the idea while doing practice laps at Daytona with veteran racer Paul Newman after they had wrapped production on *The Color of Money* (1986). [857]

During the production of *Thunder* Simpson and Bruckheimer announced their 'Visionary Alliance' with Paramount Pictures, which allowed them total control over a $300 million, five-year deal. Simpson was a hands-on producer, obsessed with story and keenly analytical in terms of the frame-by-frame impact of a film on its audience. Bruckheimer stated:

> I don't think there's ever been pressure to produce a big film. What we try to do is make effective films, and films that we are real proud of. To satisfy myself, there's always pressure, creative pressure to do something different, unique.[858]

---

[855] Bergan. *SPORTS IN THE MOVIES*. London: Proteus Books, 1982, 83.

[856] *Ibid.*

[857] According to Charles Fleming it may also have been suggested by Ned Tanen, the film executive. Charles Fleming. *HIGH CONCEPT: Don Simpson and the Hollywood Culture of Excess*. London: Bloomsbury, 1998, 146.

[858] Jerry Bruckheimer, *Premiere*, June 1990: 84. Shone claims that "all the clues to Simpson's later success with Bruckheimer lay with the movies he saw made at Paramount under [Barry] Diller's stewardship." Shone. *Op.cit.*, 175. (Interestingly, Michael Eisner tried to steer Simpson, whom he had just promoted to Head of Production, towards an adaptation of Romain Gary's *White Dog*, to which Robert Towne was at one point committed; instead, Simpson opted to make a little romantic film called *An Officer and a Gentleman*.

From Towne's perspective, aside from the happy coincidence of a shared agent at CAA, Paula Wagner, it may be, as Michael Sragow shrewdly suggests, that Tom Cruise's old-fashioned star persona inspired this screenwriter who had been so inspired by his friends Jack Nicholson and Warren Beatty. [859] As for Cruise, he loved racing from the time he was sixteen when he took his mother's car and went drag-racing down a New Jersey street. [860] Quoting Towne's own preface to the Grove Press edition of *Chinatown* and *The Last Detail*, Sragow reminds us of Towne's own feelings on 'star quality':

> "'For gifted movie actors affect us most, I believe, not by talking, fighting, fucking, killing, cursing, or cross-dressing. They do it by being photographed. It is said of such actors that the camera loves them. Whatever that means, I've always felt their features are expressive in a unique way: They seem to register swift and dramatic mood changes with no discernible change of expression'." [861]

According to Sragow, two things convinced Towne to take on the idea: Cruise; and the racing itself – "he fell in love with the stock-car world." [862] For Wagner, what drew her to bring Cruise and Towne together was Towne's "mental and spiritual daring, his love to try new things." [863] The story of the brash young man who in facing his own mortality, finally grows up, never really came to fruition – it would be a more tragic tale that would bear the weight of Towne's sinewy brilliance years later in *Without Limits*. For now, the 'need for speed' was paramount. Cruise would be introduced here much as he had been when previously paired with director Tony Scott in *Top Gun* – on a motorcycle, reeking of gritty rebellion and steadfastness. In fact, for a spell, the film was being called *Top Car*. In Bruckheimer's mind, Towne was "*The Godfather* of verisimilitude. If the script called for a bloodhound, and [*Days of Thunder* director] Tony Scott brought out a dog that wasn't a bloodhound, Robert went nuts. He's a stickler." [864]

Figure 25 *Days of Thunder* poster art

An on-set report from Daytona in *Premiere* magazine describes the preparatory work involved prior to shooting *Thunder*, including the scouting of locations and the racing scene, conducted by Simpson, Bruckheimer and Towne for a year beforehand.

---

[859] Towne had also served as 2nd A.D. on Corman's production *The Young Racers* (1963) and might well have cultivated a taste for the track on that set. Fleming suggests that Towne had previously tried and failed to cast Cruise in a film called RUSH – this suggests that at some point Towne may have been involved in the eponymous production directed by Lili Fini Zanuck adapted from Kim Wozencraft's novel and released in 1991. This remains to be confirmed. *Op.cit.*, 147.

[860] Tom Friend, 'Man with a *Mission*,' *Premiere*, June 1996: 71.

[861] Michael Sragow, 'Return of the Native,' *New Times Los Angeles*, 03-09 September 1998: 17.

[862] *Ibid*. He brought Towne to see a race at Watkins Glen and Towne was hooked.

[863] *Ibid*.

[864] Sragow. *Op.cit.*, 18.

Don Simpson attended the Bob Bondurant School of High Performance Driving with Tom Cruise. Towne loved the racers themselves, whom he described as "the best people on earth, so gutsy and super-glamorous and everything else." [865]

The relationship with producers Simpson-Bruckheimer didn't run completely smoothly for Towne, as *Variety* 'dished' on 07 July 1992, when tempers frayed as Towne left the production to do rewrites on *The Firm* (ironically, another Cruise project).[866]

Towne said of Simpson, "Don would fume and carry on beyond unreason, go into black rages... But if you told him he was so full of shit, he'd say, 'OK, I stand corrected,' and turn on a dime. He was great that way." [867] The problems accruing to the entire production seem symptomatic of the conditions surrounding studios' need to have their tent-pole film ready for release.[868]

Based around Cruise's obsessions and his appearance, the screenplay seems to offer many things in common with *Top Gun*, including a linked destiny with a supposed antagonist (Rowdy Burns, the Anthony Edwards role from *Top Gun*) whose dumb luck allows Cruise to shine; and a real antagonist (Russ Wheeler, essaying Val Kilmer's role from *Top Gun*) whose admission that Cruise is better than him allows the audience to enjoy Cruise putting him against a wall. The role of mentor would go to Robert Duvall as Harry Hogge, a typically tricksy, obsessive Towne character whose repressed past catches up with him: he is now working with the son of the racer whose death he may have inadvertently caused the previous year. [869] This is echoed in Cole's admission that

[865] Michael Sragow. *Ibid.*

[866] "What really smarted the producing duo was they had just agreed to shell out over $300,000 from their Disney discretionary fund to help pay Towne the $1 million fee he'll collect to adapt their recently acquired Paul Lindsay book 'Witness to the Truth.' Simpson and Bruckheimer gave their blessing to the vet screenwriter to work on the film. Towne's fast-track mandate to help Pollack get 'The Firm' in shooting shape for a newly set late October/early November start (a month later than originally planned), forced Don and Jerry to postpone their research trip to Detroit with the screenwriter until later this month." 'Dish', *Variety,* 07 July, 1992.

[867] Sragow. *Ibid.* Simpson/Bruckheimer dissolved their company September 1995, apparently on account of Simpson's unreasonable behaviour. Simpson would die of heart failure on his toilet seat January 1996, after the production of *The Rock* had wrapped, found with a copy of the latest Oliver Stone tell-all biography (quoted elsewhere in this volume) at his feet. His own tawdry life would be exposed in Charles Fleming's *HIGH CONCEPT*, which offers many insights into *Thunder*'s troubled production. Simpson himself was to play racer Aldo Benedetti, but he was so terrible his part was reduced (at his own behest) to the delivery of a mere line, in the guise of a TV pitlane interview.

[868] As Richard Combs states, "It's possible that the current Hollywood business set-up, the deal-making and packaging, does militate against directorial freedom more than the studios did. Its greatest restriction, though, may just be in making each film such a huge investment of both time and money." 'Cinema's Vision Thing,' *The Listener*, 13 September 1990: 37.

[869] Matthew Wilder recognises this achievement: "Towne works a unique alchemy. The producers' and star's formula – cocky kid learns to play by the rules, then tastes victory – gets a Townean makeover that turns *Days* into a Howard Hawks-style melodrama: Cruise's uppity racer comes to respect a wise elder..., collaborates with a onetime rival ..., and appreciates the balance between duty and risk. Damned if Towne doesn't make something stirring and even shrewdly observed out of the relationships between these three swaggering archetypes." 'Your Guide to the Stars: Robert Towne Maps the Psychology of the American Bad-Ass,' www.citypages.com, Vol.27, No. 1315, 15 February 2006.

his own father was a crook who was financing Cole's racing through junk bonds and stolen yachts. Once again, Towne was treading Oedipal territory; the relationship is also an echo of that in *Personal Best*; and a precursor to that of *Without Limits*, which features an athlete finding a father figure in his track coach (and was originally supposed to star Cruise.) Cruise's role here as Cole Trickle (a name part elemental, part tribute to NASCAR veteran, Dick Trickle) is typically iconoclastic and his entry is on a motorbike, an homage to *Top Gun*, his biggest hit to date, and another Simpson/Bruckheimer/Scott production.[870] Towne said of the story that it

> becomes the struggle of a driver to replace his belief in his own infallibility with the true courage of a man who recognizes that even if some things are beyond his control he must go on to face them if he is to race, to win, to live his life. [871]

An obsession with eyesight and vision (familiar from *Chinatown* and *Ligeia*) also dominates the film's thematic concerns – Cole's crash occasions his brief loss of eyesight but brings him into contact with Dr Claire Lewicki, the beautiful neurosurgeon whose first race is the one to bring Cole his triumphant victory at the film's climax (the sexual innuendo accorded through this and the name 'Trickle' is unfortunately inevitable; while Trickle's incomprehension that a woman could be a doctor is played up in a scene where he is presented with a stripper dressed like a state trooper and he believes that Lewicki is similarly a prostitute hired for his pleasure). It is she who helps Cole gain insight into himself, after performing brain surgery on him, at the same time that his antagonist/friend, Rowdy, is losing his eyesight.

```
            COLE'S VOICE
Well, I can't see anything –
          (a funny laugh)
– I'm blind... I feel okay, Harry
but I'm blind.
```

(Days of Thunder: 58)

Their destinies are linked finally when Cole takes Rowdy's car to victory after Rowdy's career is prematurely ended. The narrative is decorated with vehicles, flowers, feet, shoes ("ever since you and Rowdy crashed at Daytona and Rowdy got sick, you been waitin' for the other shoe to drop, waitin' on somethin' bad to happen to you..."), animals ("We end up looking like a monkey fucking a football out there!") – the usual Townean motifs that underscore his themes; in this case, once again, a man trapped and then transformed by the mastery of his occupation. This description gives some ballast to the critical reviews - which were little short of damning - but nonetheless demonstrates Towne's narrative strengths despite the conditions in which the film was made. Roger Ebert voiced the opinion that "Cruise is so efficiently packaged in this product that he plays the same role as a saint in a Mexican village's holy day procession: it's not what he does that makes him so special; it's the way he manifests everybody's faith in him." [872]

The screenplay would even include a description of the physics of down-drafting, which plays a crucial role not only in the way Cole achieves victory, but how Steve Prefontaine *loses* in the 1972 Munich Olympics, in perhaps Towne's finest achievement as

---

[870] And perhaps a tribute to Towne's great naïf, George Roundy.

[871] Janet Maslin. 'Tom Cruise and Cars, and a Lot of Them,' *New York Times*, online archive.

[872] Roger Ebert, '*Days of Thunder*," *Chicago Sun-Times*, 27 June 1990.

director, the later *Without Limits*. It is the kind of colour detail for which Towne had been hired dating back to *Bonnie and Clyde*:

```
                    PUNCH
        Cole Trickle, did you have any
        idea you could go wide open on
        that last turn and make the car
        stick like that?

Cole is all smiles.

                    COLE
        Knew it all along.
```

(Days of Thunder: 44)

Despite Towne's reworking of the genre – Cole collaborates with his competition, he changes tactics in order to win - the script wasn't ready for the shoot, but the studio was "desperate for a summer movie. We knew the script wasn't ready, but we needed a movie for Memorial Day. We needed to work off this tremendous overhead we were paying Don and Jerry. We had a window [of availability] on Tom Cruise. Suddenly we all felt more fondly about the script." [873] It was scheduled to open opposite *Dick Tracy*, the new Warren Beatty production. Such were the circumstances in which films were now being made; it was a long time since *Last Detail* was held back from general release because Columbia worried about shocking its audience and costing the studio its relationship with potential broadcast outlets.

Figure 26 Tom Cruise, Don Simpson and Michael Rooker on the set

The shoot went ahead despite accompanying weather problems. The tent-pole hit was not looking good and the boardroom at Paramount was extremely concerned. On the production, Simpson stayed off-set and in his hotel room all day long, becoming increasingly despondent. The film would mark the beginning of a downward spiral for him that would last five years culminating in a most unglamorous death.

```
                    ROWDY
        Okay.. then I gotta ask you to do
        somethin'.

                    COLE
        Hell, name it.
                    ROWDY
        Drive my car.
```

[873] Lance Young, senior production executive at Paramount, speaking to Simpson's biographer, Charles Fleming. *Op.cit.,,* 143.

```
Cole looks like he's been smacked in the face.

                    COLE
        What're you talking about?

                    ROWDY
        Daytona.
```

(Days of Thunder: 106)

Towne wrote many scenes to order overnight and also did much of the second unit coverage. (And, allegedly, it was he who talent-spotted Nicole Kidman for the film.) Nonetheless, the screenplay is a canny blend of sports psychology, personal tragedy and action. [874]

Ever the PR, Simpson would not be publicly deterred and openly praised Towne, perhaps a little tongue in cheek:

> One person deserves the sole credit for the script… and that's Robert Towne. Whatever's on screen came out of his (Towne's) mind, heart and soul. He kept writing until one week before we finished. I never saw anyone that talented work that hard. Towne deserves more credit than he's gotten – if there's an award above an Oscar he should get it. [875]

In fact, the film only went ahead because Simpson would not make it without Towne. [876] Test screenings confirmed Simpson's suspicions that the film didn't hang together - the initial cut didn't even have Cruise reaching a checkered flag. The finale was reshot, to Tony Scott's loud objection – but under his direction. New scenes featuring Cole's recovery from injury were also shot. Sid Ganis , copresident of Paramount admitted that " There was almost no story, and there was no ending. It was just cars going around a racetrack. We shouldn't have started without a script." [877]

The next version of the film was a box office success but the critical reception was hardly favourable, despite reliable turns by Robert Duvall as Harry Hogge and Randy Quaid as the team owner. Interviewed by Michael Sragow, Towne commented: "What everybody learned… is never to lock a film so early into an opening date ever again. The fact is, the editors had four weeks to go through two or three million feet of film." Sragow himself added to this the crux of the film's problem – "the racing scenes focused on spectacle and not on the narrow parameters the drivers operate within, and whatever nuances and colors Towne and Cruise worked to achieve ended up on the cutting-room floor." [878] There were to be no Oscars, despite Simpson's eternal public optimism.

---

[874] Towne says of the action genre, "If there is a romance, will the girl survive?" In *Days…* it seems the girl was played by Cruise.

[875] He may have been referring to the fact that amid the chaos of production, Cruise was repeating lines dictated through his headset by Towne as he drove around the track. Army Archerd, 'Just for Variety,' *Variety*, 09 May 1990.

[876] Fleming. *Op.cit.*, 143-144.

[877] Quoted in Fleming. *Op.cit.*, 148.

[878] Sragow. *Ibid.*

<u>The Firm</u> (1993) (screenplay by Robert Towne & David Rayfiel)

David Rayfiel had been helping Sydney Pollack on material, sometimes uncredited, dating back to the Natalie Wood vehicle, *This Property is Condemned* (1966).[879] As commentator Michael Sragow previously averred, that, "a director like Sydney Pollack deserves all the praise he gets for keeping a complicated movie coherent, but he still needs screenwriters around to get scenes down on paper before he puts them on film." [880]

Figure 27 *The Firm* dvd cover

The novel is indeed gripping and the changes made to the structural elements don't inflict any harm to its familiar Townean theme – power, the abuse of power, the corruptibility of ordinary people. (Or what Nick James calls "festering immorality." [881])

The power wielded by Bendini, Lambert and Locke, is both legitimated by its normal clientele and made coercive by the stranglehold (social, familial, professional) waged on the young associates once they make partner (it's too late to leave – the wife is usually pregnant or a mother by the time the truth is told; the lure of filthy lucre has become too enticing; their social status has been incomparably enhanced by association: everyone else in the firm has done it and those who have tried to leave on learning of the Mafia ownership have died in 'mysterious circumstances'.) Thus, aside from the undoubtedly welcome paycheque and the opportunity to continue a fruitful working relationship with superstar Cruise, Towne was working fertile territory. How Mitch McDeere turns the tables on his mentors, all the while begging his betrayed wife's forgiveness, taking on his imprisoned felon brother and bringing on board Tammy, the Elvis impersonator's cheating wife grieving her murdered boyfriend/employer, is an exercise in brainpower and courage that is both audience-pleasing and cunning. The alterations made to the novel raise the stakes in expert fashion, shifting the balance between Avery and Mitch in see-saw manner until the final, excruciating showdown. The odd thing about this legal thriller novel and its subsequent transposition to film is that it had actually started out as a screenplay – but unlike most of its genre, had no courtroom scenes.

Towne comments: "He [Rayfiel] had done an early version of it that he and Sydney felt was structurally not working, and both he and Sydney, who are friends of mine, called me. We all worked out an outline, or a new treatment, frantically. And then

[879] Gavin Lambert. *NATALIE WOOD: A Life*. New York: Alfred A. Knopf, 2004, 227.
[880] Michael Sragow, 'Ghostwriters: Unraveling the Engima of Movie Authorship,' *Film Comment*, 19, March 1983. In fact, as Towne admitted, Pollack lives across the street from him, and when he asked him for help Towne thought it was to lift a garbage can, because it was collection day in Pacific Palisades. Michael Dwyer, 'Call the Script Doctor,' *The Irish Times*, 22 July 2006: 7.
[881] Nick James, 'The Firm,' *Sight & Sound*, Vol.3, No. 10, October 1993: 45.

I was pretty much left to myself to write all night, with the two of them revising during the day." [882]

The screenplay draft by Towne mainly follows the narrative through-line of the novel with some exceptions. The principal elements changed from the novel are as follows:

Eddie Lomax is not assassinated in front of Tammy, his secretary/lover in the novel – he is hired to do a 'peeping tom' job and executed beside a motel. It is Tammy, and not Abby, who seduces Avery Tolleson in Grand Cayman. In the film it is switched to Abby, lending credence to her hurt at Mitch's betrayal in the firm's honeytrap with a Cayman Islands prostitute. Abby and Mitch separate after the initial FBI deal is made in the novel.

The long-drawn out and complicated cat-and-mouse, hide-and-seek structure of the novel's climax is dropped in favour of a more linear narrative which similarly involves the Morolto family, the FBI, the police and the firm's partners. Mitch strikes a deal with the Moroltos, allowing them to sue the firm.

These alterations seem minor in the light of the novel's length and level of detail (forty chapters told over four hundred pages) but every significant change lends greater impact and heightens personal conflict, helping create cycles of greater drama in the screenplay and finished film.

In his interview with Towne, Joel Engel commented that he thought their ending was an improvement on Grisham's, and Towne agrees:

> I thought so too. That was the thing that I had the hardest time convincing them of. They thought that that was going to let the Mafia off the hook. My arguments were manifold. You can't just let a guy take the money and run; it's disgusting. He should learn to care about something. Yeah, they said, that's true, but it'll look as if he's just afraid of being killed. I said that it wouldn't. Then Sydney said, 'Well, I don't know. If you could just have a scene where these Mafia guys were talking about trying to kill the lawyer, and one of them says, 'If I could get my hands on that – ' And then the lawyer walks in at that moment.' I said, 'Sydney, that's what I'm talking about.' 'That might work,' he said. So I wrote the scene. Now if this scene didn't work, there was no ending for the movie. [883]

However, the problem ending for the hero in Grisham's book carries its own punishment – life on the run, permanently afloat in the Cayman Islands under the witness protection programme. He has made a Faustian deal. In the film, Mitch is basically unharmed. There were other accommodations to be made – also, probably at the behest of Cruise's star persona, which usually demands a high degree of audience-pleasing action. On page 119 of the screenplay he slams a chair through Dunbar's window when the firm has rooted him out:

```
Mitch picks up one of the heavy leather chairs in front
of Dunbar's desk and HEAVES it out the window.  It
explodes like a bomb.  Kicking away the glass, Mitch
```

---

[882] Joel Engel. *Op.cit.*, 207.
[883] Engel. *Op.cit.*, 207-8.

```
looks down on the alley.    Twelve feet below him is the
Cotton Truck.   He jumps.
```

(The Firm: 119)

One of Towne's proudest achievements in the adaptation was in turning Avery, played by Gene Hackman, from a hardboiled villain into a malleable, emotional character.

A practical problem arose during the shoot which required consultation with Towne:

> When Sydney was shooting *The Firm*, he ran into problems right in the middle
> of shooting that had to be solved with a new scene. I had written a sequence
> where Tom [Cruise] was to hold a fire hose and jump down the stairwell to get
> away from the villains there. Well, Sydney couldn't find an open stairwell. They
> did have a building that had a boiler room. Faxing back and forth, we finally came
> up with Tom taking the briefcase and pummelling poor Wilford [Brimley].
> Sydney would describe the room in a fax, I'd send some notes, he'd send some back,
> and that's how the scene developed. [884]

This admission proves two things in terms of the writer/director relationship: the extraordinary respect Pollack retains for Towne's abilities; and also the extent of their co-dependency. It certainly proves Michael Sragow's assertion about Pollack, quoted earlier in this section. [885]

It is impossible to know, given the credits situation, who might have initiated these changes, but Towne is one of the three credited writers, despite, as he says, never having seen a draft by David Rabe. The film's credits would read "David Rabe and Robert Towne & David Rayfiel," a perhaps misleading credits attribution, presumably based on the Writers' Guild rule of one third, so that Rabe could be properly paid. However the ampersand between Towne and Rayfiel properly indicates that they co-wrote a draft.

Part of the project of reclaiming the screenwriter in the name of authorship (or more strictly speaking, auteurism) is utilising those tools already established in the name of the director's place as prime site of cinematic expression; thus in this situation we simply assume that Towne's prior form, his pattern of writing and those structural elements which he brought to his body of work, are those which are evident here and which both drew him to the work and caused him to be hired for the rewrite in the first place. The issue of 'whose' screenplay it might be is merely compounded by the ongoing opacity of the Writers' Guild in these matters.

> … I never saw his [David Rabe's] screenplay. The first writer on an adaptation
> is assumed to have written the work. It's not a good rule. David Rayfiel is
> another matter. [886]

What did Towne think of the overall result? "I've had to push stories more than I wanted to. There are hybrids – *The Firm*. It has a lot of good stuff in it, and has stuff

---

[884] Engel. *Op.cit,* 210.
[885] Michael Sragow, *Film Comment*, 19, March 1983.

[886] Engel. *Ibid.*

that is wonky. It's a combination of trying to work with material that you can only go so far with, or, given the constraints of the time, one could dream some part of it as a night dream and some, being unable to wait, as a daydream. I think that's the process, generally speaking, for me." [887] Todd McCarthy's review pinpointed something in Towne's career perhaps elided elsewhere: if *Chinatown* is the signature Townean text, it is notably anti-authoritarian and equally viable as a 'conspiracy thriller,' the likes of which is emblemised by *Three Days of the Condor* (and also *The Parallax View*, one of three conspiracy thrillers directed by Alan J. Pakula in the Seventies.) [888] This suggests that the underlying theme of Towne's work, despite the circumstances behind his being hired on *The Firm*, was a key reason for his involvement in the project. [889] The mentoring relationship between Mitch and Avery is also continuous with previous such relationships in Towne's screenplays, including that which immediately precedes it, *Days of Thunder* (which of course also features Cruise and is a favoured motif in *his* oeuvre.) Therefore Towne had once again continued his pursuit of relationships with Hollywood's powerful men in working once again with Cruise, while still retaining the respect of a reliable director and prior collaborator whose own status in Hollywood as both producer and director has never been in doubt. In terms of authorship we might refer to Bordwell and Thompson's assertion, that

…the director has most control over how a movie looks and sounds.[890]

As Lovell and Sergi remind us, it is their qualification *'most'* which interests us here. [891]

Pollack had already worked with Towne, as we have already seen, on the substantial rewrite of *The Yakuza*, and it was by all accounts a happy collaboration. That either man can separately be called 'auteur' of the work seems confusing, because it seems to fit into their respective oeuvres in terms of theme, which Robert Riskin considered the most exacting proof of 'authorship.' [892] In terms of *The Firm*, the novelist, John Grisham is certainly 'author.' Lovell and Sergi emphasise that controversial aspect of auteurism which is its implication of *quality*:

Because an individual personality … can be detected in the films he directs. It is this presence that separates a good film from a bad one. The position depends on identifying most films as anonymous; a personality cannot be detected in them.

And they significantly depart from this position, suggesting,

It would be better to return to the old version of credits with only a 'directed by' credit for the director.[893]

---

[887] Engel. *Op.cit.,* 204.
[888] Todd McCarthy, Reviews, *Variety*, 12 July 1993: 52.
[889] *Variety* reported that Paramount rewarded Tom Cruise, Sydney Pollack and Scott Rudin with $100,000 Mercedes convertibles for making the film a hit. Towne didn't get one, "though his deft doctoring was credited with saving the movie. He too was said to be unhappy [John Grisham didn't get one either]. The press chided Par for giving autos to overpaid stars, and Rudin reportedly sold his back to the studio." 'Buzz,' *Variety*, 03 January 1994.
[890] Bordwell and Thompson, *FILM ART: An Introduction*. New York: McGraw-Hill, 2001. 33.
[891] Alan Lovell and Gianluca Sergi, *op.cit.,* 114.
[892] Ian Scott. *IN CAPRA'S SHADOW*. Louisville: University Press of Kentucky, 2006, 125-126; 128.
[893] Lovell and Sergi. *Op.cit,* 115.

And they continue:

> The authorship of a film always has to be established, it cannot be taken for granted. It is likely to be collective; the most likely candidates for inclusion are director, producer, star and writer. Other candidates are always possible. [894]

That position is perhaps easier to maintain in consideration of the blockbuster genre which suffuses the industry in the 1990s. It is a crucial issue in determining Towne's contribution to contemporary cinema; however he is a writer who has persisted in his view that writing a film is always a matter of collaboration if not total compromise. [895] From an assessment of the screenplay and the opacity of its various contributors it is difficult to make an assured statement about the authorship of the film *The Firm*.

Love Affair (1994) (screenplay by Robert Towne & Warren Beatty) [896]

An unhappy collaboration with Beatty, the adaptation of the classic Hollywood weepie was designed as a tribute to the great movie romances and to the relationship Beatty had embarked upon with actress Annette Bening. Bening had been his co-star in *Bugsy* (1991) and was now Mrs. Beatty. Writing in *Esquire* that July, it was announced that Towne was "currently working on a screenplay with Warren Beatty." [897] *Love Affair* would be his Valentine to her, wrapped up in Golden Age Hollywood valedictions, from Leo McCarey's 1939 tearjerker (scripted by Delmer Daves and Donald Ogden Stewart from an original story by McCarey and Mildred Cram), to *An Affair to Remember* McCarey's 1957 remake, and Nora Ephron's latterday homage, *Sleepless in Seattle* (1993). The project was taken on at the behest of the legendary Steve Ross, Time-Warner boss and Hollywood dealmaker extraordinaire. The screenplay would be an easy one, allowing Beatty time with his new daughter to Bening. As re-envisaged by Towne, who struggled for a year to breathe life into a first draft, Beatty plays an entirely Beatty-esque character, a sports reporter who meets the kindergarten teacher while on a storm-ridden layover in the South Seas – which, incidentally, boasts the island home of his wonderfully feisty and aged aunt (played by Katherine Hepburn).

According to Corie Brown, the 'quickie' turned out to be a nightmare for Towne – it took him a year to deliver a first draft, "in which Towne … was to have a little fun with Beatty's Mr Suave persona. Beatty wasn't laughing." While Towne tinkered with the drafts he was offered a rewrite of *The Firm*, for Sydney Pollack, for a straight million dollars to be paid through his agency, CAA. A momentary diversion was at hand when unlikely couple Whoopi Goldberg and Ted Danson announced their intention to remake *An Affair to Remember*, bringing Beatty's plan out into the open and allowing Towne to escape, although his million was halved when Beatty took money Towne owed him, enforcing their previously agreed deal that Towne repay him $800,000. According to this account, Towne did not repay his remaining debt. [898]

---

[894] *Ibid*.

[895] (Or, ultimate collaboration.) Thomson, 1981, 85. Clifford Odets once said, "When you start seeing the other person's point of view, that's when you're in ultimate danger." Speaking to Stewart Stern, in Patrick McGilligan, (ed.) *BACKSTORY 2: Interviews with Screenwriters of the 40s and 50s*. Berkeley: University of California Press, 1991, 305.

[896] As there was no original material extant this screenplay unfortunately remains unexamined.

[897] Robert Towne, 'Why I Write Movies,' *Esquire*, July 1991: 86-7.

[898] Corie Brown, 'No Love Affair,' *Premiere*, February 1995: 46; 96.

The film ends just the way its predecessors did, romantically and wholly implausibly. One wonders how it would have turned out if Towne had had the last draft. He said to Michael Sragow: "I opened it up with Warren as a former football player getting a prostate examination. Then I put him on a fat farm. Warren didn't see it that way; he thought it was too funny and unglamorous." [899] Despite bringing back old collaborators such as Robert C. Jones and Conrad Hall, and with a cast of friends, neighbours and Hollywood legends, Beatty's project was not a commercial success.

Crimson Tide (1995) (uncredited)

The scene allegedly written by Towne in this blockbusting naval thriller takes place in the first half of Act II. As described by Syd Field, it runs as follows: "Hunter is the new member of the crew, so the captain, Ramsey, is trying to find out what his philosophy of war is, and what kind of 'man' his new CO is, what he believes in. The difference between 'you and me,' Ramsey explains, is that when 'I was taught, things were simpler in a war situation; I was taught how to push a button and told when to do it.' It's not a question of strategy, he states, but simply a matter of military and political procedure. And he quotes von Clausewitz. He pauses for a moment, then continues his observation: it's different now, he says; the brass, meaning the Pentagon, want you (referring to Hunter) to know 'why you're doing it.' The Denzel Washington character nods in agreement, then responds "that in a nuclear world the true enemy can't be destroyed, because the real enemy is war itself." Field concludes that

> This little dialogue exchange succinctly summarizes the differences in their
> philosophies of war. It also shows us the differences in their points of view, because
> it is this conflict that fuels the entire film. If the differences in their points of view
> had not been set up and established, the entire story would fail to work; there would
> be conflict, no mutiny attempt, no story, and the Alabama would just cruise the
> waters until the situation in Russia resolved itself. Basically, their differing points of
> view would be like two parallel lines moving toward infinity without ever connecting.
> That's not how you build and structure a screenplay. [900]

Towne remarks of his work on the film:

> I got a mad call one night from Don Simpson and Jerry Bruckheimer, and they needed
> a critical scene... I added that scene where they talk about the nature of war, and their
> opposition on that subject sets up the potential conflict between them for the rest of
> the film. I wrote that scene down the phone because they needed it straight away. [901]

Despite the fact that the scene plays very powerfully, Field adds:

> Some screenwriters might argue that the scene is too direct, too obvious, and they
> would either omit it or write it in a more subtle way. But some scenes in a
> screenplay have to be written directly, no matter how obvious, or expository, they
> are, and this happens to be one of them. It is set up to be paid off later so it can
> follow the natural law of cause and effect, action and reaction. If the essential seed
> of the screenplay is planted appropriately, in the right place and at the right time, it
> can blossom into a full-grown narrative, replete with the structural and

---

[899] Sragow, 1998: 18.
[900] Syd Field. *THE SCREENWRITER'S PROBLEM SOLVER.* New York: Dell Books, 1998, 281.
[901] Robert Towne interviewed by Michael Dwyer, as before.

character dimension. [902]

Mission: Impossible (1996) (screenplay)

Distinguished by the use of physical force and the presence of a single heroic protagonist, albeit sometimes partnered with another man of perhaps dubious intention and eminent corruptibility, the action genre is probably best figured in the James Bond series, which has adapted itself time and again to geopolitical changes and audience demands over its forty-year existence. Determined to preserve the masculinity fetishised by such films, they are usually populated with soldiers, policemen and government agents. [903] The action genre is most properly a hybrid – not quite a war or combat film, it usually has an ideological subtext (Us against Them). Neither an historical tract nor an overtly political message-bearer, it can be fairly contemporary or even offer what Alvin Toffler once termed 'future shock' in its documentary potential with stinging overtones - the extraordinary sequence of anti-Islamic films turned out by Hollywood in the mid- and late Nineties, such as *The Siege*, *Rules of Engagement* and *Executive Decision* (all criticised for their hostility to Moslems), turn out to have been stunningly prescient in the wake of 9/11 (and many previous incidents which had not even been acknowledged by global media commentators as part of a growing religious *intifada* against white, Western civilisation.)

Undoubtedly inspired by the James Bond series and the potential of a spy genre in a post-Cold War/Berlin Wall climate, the reawakening of old TV show *Mission: Impossible* (created by Bruce Geller) had all the ingredients for a hit – a literally killer cast, amusing stories, gadgetry galore and a huge star behind it – Tom Cruise. Cruise had already made a name for himself as 'Maverick' in *Top Gun*, which laminated his pass to Ronald Reagan's Star Wars Eighties Icons (numbering Sylvester Stallone, Bruce Willis, Arnold Schwarzenegger and Mel Gibson – all card-carrying Republicans); despite the evident homoeroticism of his role as fighter pilot for the United States Navy in this paean to kitsch sky Western gung-ho ethics. Cruise had further cemented his presence as action hero with *Days of Thunder*, however lamentable the reviews. However, with the end of Communism, the body politic was no longer quite to the forefront, nor was there quite such a desire to foreground the male body. Interestingly, while many of the Nineties action films would concentrate on destabilising and then re-formulating the white bourgeois American family, *Mission: Impossible*'s central conceit would be the job at hand - an intricate, tricky plot, visual gymnastics and fabulous gadgets – and mostly set in Europe, a nod to the genre's forebears. There remained only one problem with *Mission: Impossible*, the movie – and that was the script. It had been a Paramount property for eleven years until Cruise took it on. He recounted: "I said, 'I'd like to make a movie out of *Mission: Impossible*... and a lot of people were, like, 'What a ridiculous...,' And then *The Fugitive* came out and did great, so..." [904]

The film was co-written with David Koepp but the draft available, which is largely that of the feature as released, is in Towne's name only. It is difficult to surmise what his overall contribution was, given the series' generic roots, based on Bruce Geller's TV show. However the leitmotif of the film is contained within Ethan's name – Hunt, a creation unto the film. And the film, unlike the series on which it is based, separates him from his team, leading to an operation in which he is disavowed and spends the rest of

---

[902] Field, 1998, 282.

[903] See http://www.allmovie.com/cg/avg.dll?p=avg&sql=23:55)

[904] Tom Friend. *Op.cit.*, 71.

the story trying to clear his name – and, ultimately, that of his mother. This may have a parallel with Cruise's own background, in which his mother divorced Cruise's father after an acrimonious marriage and his mother reared him and his sisters single-handedly. (Cruise is apparently devoted to her.) However the more interesting allusion is to Everette Howard Hunt, the infamous CIA spymaster and member of the 'Plumbers,' that circle of Nixon's friends who masterminded the Watergate break-in. His reputation as a great insider and then as the enemy within gives subtext to Ethan Hunt's own alienated status in M:I's story arc and also lends a certain wry humour to Hunt's break-in at Fort Knox and the manner in which it is achieved – plumbing the depths. (Everette Howard Hunt's latterday infamy, as one of three supposed tramps on the grassy knoll at Dealey Plaza on 22 November 1963, and his naming of Lyndon B. Johnson as the chief culprit behind the JFK assassination, is not yet something aped by the franchise's screenwriters.) [905]   The overall theme, of corruption, is something that of course exercised Towne's writing sinews on a number of previous occasions.

Metaphor & Motif
The entire film is littered with animal references – from the restaurant meeting at Aquarium (Akvarium) (rejoining Towne's fondness for water motifs) with Kittridge (Henry Czerny); Ethan runs up a spiral staircase, which, photographed from above, looks like a seashell; to the idea of the disavowed Ethan as the mole (he literally burrows his way back into Langley – he has to be a mole to find the mole); and Ethan as prey – dangling like a fly into the spiderweb vault at CIA headquarters. [906]   Krieger's giveaway Judas sneeze is occasioned by the intrusion of a rat into the tunnel – thus putting the analogical symbol and the actual referent into the one shot so that we don't miss the crucial information – *Krieger is the rat...* The symbolism is absolutely clear throughout the dazzlingly constructed setpieces. Important threshold scenes take place on a bridge in Kiev – just as they did in Towne's *Man From U.N.C.L.E.* episode;   similarly the masquerade of diplomacy at the reception held at the American Embassy; and the

Figure 28 *Mission: Impossible* **dvd cover art**

entire theme (the enemy within) is also from '*The Dove Affair.*' Interestingly, Hunt's way out of his dilemma – selling the NOC list (again, an *U.N.C.L.E.* idea, but in that episode the list was microscopically written on the late President's dove pin) to an illegal arms dealer, Max (played with amusing hamminess by Vanessa Redgrave) – is rather like that of Mitch McDeere in John Grisham's THE FIRM, a conclusion that Towne would not envisage for the young lawyer in that adaptation but is a key McGuffin in a sequence of

[905] Erik Hedegaard, 'Secrets and Spies,' *Sunday Times Magazine,* 15 April 2007: 50-61.
[906] This scene is also an homage to *Rififi* (1954), which director and co-writer (along with Rene Wheeler and Auguste LeBreton, from the latter's novel) Jules Dassin himself parodied a decade later with *Topkapi* (1964), itself adapted by Monja Danischewsky from the Eric Ambler novel, thus spawning the comic caper/heist movie cycle of the 1960s.

entertaining McGuffins that keep *Mission: Impossible* thrilling from start to finish. (But, then, the name 'Ethan' is Hebrew for 'firm'!) This is entirely in keeping with the screenplay's reliance on the Bible for the transmission of information over the internet (a post-Cold War use of a pre-Cold War tool) – and the Book of Job is entirely appropriate for yet another Townean hero trapped and then enlivened by his occupation (job). It is a Gideon Bible from the Drake Hotel (a clue planted on page 12 of the script) which provides Ethan with the key to his predicament and the organisation's mole. The entire structure offers proof of Towne's desire to take a myth and make a new myth – from a pre-existing reality.

Another in-joke might have been in the naming of the CIA's prey at Kiev in Act One: 'Aleksandr Golitsyn' – written in Occidental style, 'Alexander Golitzen' is the name of a lauded set designer, supposedly responsible for over three hundred films, according to the classically Hollywood mode of authorship attribution, by virtue of being 'Head of Department.' Towne's penchant for things Irish (which also references Cruise's film *Far and Away*, 1992) is revealed in Jim Phelps' (Jon Voight playing the role made famous by Peter Graves) dialogue when he refers to a colleague flyfishing at the 'Oughterard Slough in County Kildare,' even if his geography's a little off. The whole theme of *Mission: Impossible* is emblemised in the term 'fishing expedition' and the sight of Ethan dangling in the Langley vault waiting to copy the diskette of NOC agents is nothing if not 'bait' writ large, completing the metaphor let loose when he explodes the fish tanks at Akvarium, literally flushing Ethan out into the paranoid open. The allusions to the metonymic *Chinatown* in all its drafts (or, at the very least, water…) proliferate throughout.

Genre and Authorship

A film such as *Mission: Impossible* is relatively difficult to assess in critical terms, a situation José Arroyo discusses in his analysis of the film:

> As yet we have no vocabulary adequate to describe or evaluate such films (which are now the dominant mode of Hollywood filmmaking) so we tend to dismiss them as popcorn. Your Mission, should you choose to accept it, is to take the Popcorn Movie seriously… the film is gleefully superficial. It doesn't fit easily into any traditional discourse of aesthetics. It seems to lack coherence, balance, internal consistency, and more importantly, depth. *Mission: Impossible* belongs in a long history of the Cinema of Attractions….[it] assaults the senses, by expressively conjuring a verisimilitude from the logically impossible. Like much current High Concept cinema, the film strives to offer a Theme Park of attractions: music, colour, story, performance, design, and the sense of improbably fast motion. The aim is to seduce the audience into surrendering to the Ride. [907]

However the political subtext links it to a genre occupied by such pseudo-political adventure-thrillers such as *North by Northwest*, 1959 (another famous train film), where the interrogation of dystopic East-West relations is individuated by the roles occupied by the hero and the antagonist and (as in *Mission: Impossible*) by the Janus-faced woman whose loyalties are divided and who brings them together and tears them apart (another Biblical lesson: Thou Shalt Not Covet Thy Neighbour's Wife, in this case, fellow agent and Phelps' wife, Claire, played by Emmanuelle Béart.)

As in Towne's usual styling of his male heroes, such as Jake Gittes in *Chinatown*, or Mac in *Tequila Sunrise*, his occupation has Ethan in a vise – he is trapped and then

---

[907] José Arroyo, 'Mission: Sublime,' *Sight & Sound*, Vol.6, No.7, July 1996: 19; 20.

ultimately transformed by transcending it, forced to recognise the dark consequences of his character's choices in order to finally do some good. This is an agent with a conscience, out to avenge his team's unnecessary deaths. One of the team was Cruise's old friend, actor Emilio Estevez, killed off in a brilliantly staged impaling incident in a Kiev elevator. (The two hadn't starred together since Francis Ford Coppola's adaptation of *The Outsiders*, over a decade earlier.)

But as Arroyo points out, this is to miss the greatest aspect of the film – the wonderful setpieces (scene-sequences in terms of Towne's deployment of dramatic structure) but also a lynchpin of Brian De Palma's wonderfully baroque psychosexual oeuvre. The film is structured around one or more scene-sequence in each country in which it is set: the bridge, the American Embassy and Akvarium restaurant scenes in Kiev; the *Topkapi*-inspired break-in at CIA headquarters at Langley; and the TGV train sequence, starting in London (commencing with a scene at Liverpool Street Station in De Palma's referential way, hinting at his own *The Untouchables* – another TV adaptation - as well as the train scenes from any number of Hitchcock films); and finally ending in Paris. Arroyo states that "their function as spectacle exceeds their function as narrative."

That is simply not true, since no scene in *Mission: Impossible* exceeds its narrative demands, a basic scriptwriting rule, and every scene is built in strict cause-and-effect style, with intricate metaphors and motifs underlying every action and line of dialogue creating action and reaction in escalating style. (It may, however, transcend them.) However Arroyo is noting the clever incorporating of one of the series' original influences (*Topkapi*, 1964).

Some of Towne's better moments are based on the use of the shift from omniscient narration to subjective narration, at its most ingenious when Jim, back from the dead, insists on his version of events in Kiev to an apparently gullible Ethan. Ethan, however, sees things [as does the audience] in his mind's eye – which is at all times logical. The difference between what we see and what we are told is palpable: it is the difference between a subjective lie and the objective truth, albeit from Ethan's point of view. It is a variant on both fundamental narrative strategising and the game that American children play in the schoolroom – Show and Tell. What we are shown and what we are told differs 180 degrees; and it is on this pivot that the film turns. (Rather like *Chinatown* and *Tequila Sunrise*.)

Cannily, Arroyo identifies the film's structural similarity to the musical – the overture introduces Tom Cruise under a mask, a theme of the film's charade-like exchange of roles and reliable identities throughout its convoluted narrative (what Philip Strick describes as De Palma's preparation for 'an unreliable universe' [908]); each scene-sequence is designed to different effect (funny/ingenious/suspenseful/self-referential/parodic), showcasing Tom Cruise's athletic movement (a factor also important to Towne in his choices as both writer and director); and the final showstopper reprises the Lalo Schifrin theme and brings the action quite literally to a knife-edge (the blade of double-dealing Krieger's helicopter) – foreshadowed by the hunting knife Krieger 'accidentally' let slip into the vault after Ethan's incursion, allowing the CIA to know who was there. Again, a knowing reference to the real-life spymaster's incursion into Watergate. "And like the musical, much of the beauty of and meaning in *Mission: Impossible* comes from the expressive use of non-representation signs: colour, music, movement." [909]

When De Palma joined the production the screenplay had yet to be written. The first writers brought on board were husband and wife team Willard Huyck and Gloria Katz. They were succeeded by Steven Zaillian (*Schindler's List*). Apparently, he and De Palma "mapped out a story line from scratch... Six weeks, every day. I mean, going over every way to go about this story, staring at each other across the coffee table until we came up with a scenario." [910] Zaillian couldn't commit for longer than six weeks; he was followed by David Koepp (who had written *Carlito's Way* for De Palma.) Koepp commented: "I had quit smoking, but starting on a spy plot started me again." [911] He returned to making his directorial debut (*Trigger Effect*). Then, Cruise called his collaborator, Robert Towne. The production was plagued with rumours of power struggles. David Koepp confirms this: "Yep, no shortage of opinions on this movie. No one was going to roll over and let the other's creative opinion rule the day... We all have egos." [912]

There are several levels of authorship in terms of an adapted television series, not the least of which is the extent to which the original series creator and team of writers developed and shaped narrative style and character and made the crucial decisions about the context in which the secret government operatives could be seen to work. However De Palma's virtuoso mise-en-scène is one of the key elements of his directorial signature, and, as Robin Wood points out (possibly dismissing Peter Wollen in the process),

> ...any emphasis in mise-en-scène implying an attitude, and a set of attitudes implying a thematic structure. [913]

In the case of both signatures, Towne's and De Palma's, we can see in *Mission: Impossible* groups of motifs familiar from both oeuvres, compatible both with the concept of collective authorship and the terms of blockbuster production in the 1990s. According to Syd Field,

> Different kinds of film require different kinds of transitions. An action or action-adventure film like *Apollo 13* or *Mission: Impossible* (David Koepp and Robert Towne), requires swift transitions, sharp, dynamic bridges that keep the pace flowing fast and smooth, so the reader and viewer are swept into a torrent of movement. [914]

Ian Nathan correctly identifies that "it certainly wasn't the movie we expected," in his review for Britain's *Empire* magazine, a title that is usually exacting in its demands of the Popcorn Movie:

> An actioner with only three proper action sequences. Still, they were corkers – the Topkapi (an inspiration for the original series) homage CIA disk-theft riff brings all De Palma's unabashed referencing skills into full focus. The team game that was the indelible series format is shunted into a sterling opening salvo in favour of a star-driven

[908] Philip Strick, '*Mission: Impossible,*' *Sight & Sound*. Vol. 6, No.7, July 1996: 48.

[909] Arroyo *Op.cit.,* 20.
[910] Brian De Palma speaking to Tom Friend, *op.cit.,* 72.
[911] *Ibid.*
[912] *Ibid.*
[913] Robin Wood, 2006, 236.
[914] Syd Field. *THE SCREENWRITER'S PROBLEM SOLVER.* New York: Dell, 1998, 155.

plotline – Cruise's point man is left to fend for himself in a world of moral fuzziness. And plot fuzziness. Screenwriters David Koepp and Robert Towne swotted up on their John Le Carré, instilling the storyline with the cool paranoia of post-Cold War spying. In a world without bad guys, you have to invent them. [915]

Tom Friend says that "the ending was so many rewrites in the making that writer Robert Towne had a perverse *déjà vu* from *Chinatown*." Cruise's take was different: "It was actually fun working on the script. We'd go, 'Okay, what would be the coolest thing we can think of to do here?' [916] Described as 'the movie that would not end,' Friend claims, "There were 4A.M. last-minute faxes volleyballed to Towne, to Koepp, to Towne again, begging for revisions, and all were mostly De Palma's doing. He had read Towne's original ending to the movie and he hated it, and had gone to Cruise with an alternate plan. 'Bob thought we could resolve the movie with a character revelation in a boxcar, leaning toward a *Maltese Falcon* type of ending,' says De Palma. 'I'd constructed a high-speed chase scene on top of the train, and I thought the movie needed this visceral ending to work. Of course, the cost was huge, and if we hadn't had my ending, we would've saved millions of dollars. Tom arbitrated, and, at one point, I said, 'Let's try Bob's.' But, in the end, Tom ultimately sided with me."

Figure 29 Ethan Hunt (Tom Cruise) instructs his team

Towne, told of De Palma's explanation, chuckles. "That's fine with me,' he says. 'It was a little more complicated than that, but what the hell. I went out and worked on his ending and kept some of the things I had. It was actually the same thing that happened with *Chinatown*." Cruise, being the man of the house as usual, was the liaison between the two. [917]

Apparently, Towne enjoyed the overall experience, as he relayed to the *Los Angeles Times* columnist, Liz Smith: "I have *never* experienced anything like *Mission: Impossible*. It has been so easy. Tom made me feel like I had been doing something wrong all these years because this was so great." [918] He continued: "It was a real challenge. But Tom just commandeered me… To see that much skill in the service of an old TV classic is truly amazing. I think it's as good as filmmaking gets, and this *Mission: Impossible* owes a lot to Tom's performance." (However one of the odder elisions in the screenplay and film is that Cruise's romance with Emmanuelle Béart's character peters out – either because Cruise is not traditionally adept at romance; or perhaps because it exceeded the requirements of the narrative as directed by De Palma.)

As Michael Sragow puts it, the challenge for Towne "was to sustain suspense in a format loaded with gimmicks and processes that warred with the characters. But he had fun with scenes featuring the three V's – Vanessa Redgrave, Ving Rhames, and Jon

[915] Ian Nathan, '*Mission: Impossible*,' *Empire* No. 92 February 1997: 102.
[916] Tom Friend. *Op.cit.*, 71; 73.
[917] Friend. *Op.cit.*, 73.
[918] Liz Smith, 'Making His Mission Possible,' *Los Angeles Times*, 07 May, 1996.

Voight – as well as the sequence in which Voight tells Cruise what he wants him to think happened, while Cruise, in his mind's eye, sees what *did* happen." [919]

The film opened to mixed reviews and unprecedented box office receipts.

<u>Con Air (1997), Armageddon (1998), Enemy of the State (1998) (uncredited)</u>
It's unclear precisely what Towne added to these blockbuster productions for the Bruckheimer stable. Says Jerry Bruckheimer of Towne's involvement with his company's productions: "He'll earmark certain scenes or themes that aren't dominant or prevalent enough and make the movie more cohesive and intelligent." [920]

<u>Without Limits (Pre) (1997)</u> (screenplay by Kenny Moore & Robert Towne)
Without Limits takes as its starting position the facts about Steve Prefontaine, and paints a leisurely portrait of someone who seems to be running away from himself - but at the very least he's doing it his own way. Born 25 January 1951 in Coos Bay, Oregon, Steve Prefontaine was the greatest middle distance runner America had ever seen. The son of German émigré parents, he started setting records at Marshall Field High School and was spotted by track coaches from several universities. He chose to go to Oregon State at Eugene, where he came under the watchful eye of Bill Bowerman, creator of the Nike shoe. Pre became the first rock 'n' roll track star, in Towne's words, egged on by partisan crowds roaring 'Pre! Pre!' as he raced in his inimitable style to the finish line.

> ...This isn't a true story but I
> will say it's a likely one.
> - Bill Bowerman's opening voiceover

Towne had first fallen under the spell of Pre's story when he cast former track star and *Sports Illustrated* writer Kenny Moore as Denny Stites in his directorial debut, *Personal Best* (1982). Moore had attended University and raced with the charismatic German-American and was full of stories about their competitive friendship until the star's tragic death in a car crash in 1975, when Pre was at the peak of his fame and was tipped for medals at Montreal the following year. He held most of the middle distance records at the time he died, and more than thirty years after his death he still holds the record for the Under-19s 5,000 metres in the United States.

Apparently it was in fact Moore who approached Towne with the idea of bringing the story of 'the James Dean of track' to the screen. He had regaled Towne with tales of Prefontaine during the troubled shooting of *Personal Best*: "Pre ran so hard… that no one had a chance of winning unless they dragged themselves through hell to do it." [921] Moore could help Towne fill in important factual details about the circumstances of certain track meets, the character of Bill Bowerman, and, perhaps most importantly of all, help convey those elements of Pre's character which led him to become the biggest track star in American history prior to the 'wonder years' of Carl Lewis.

When Towne was urging his friend to write the screenplay about Pre, Moore recalled,

---

[919] Sragow. *Op.cit.*, 18.
[920] Sragow. *Ibid.*
[921] George Christy, 'The Great Life,' *The Hollywood Reporter*, 15-21 September 1998: 103.

He said that I should go from journalism to scriptwriting, which is journalism and poetry – the *mot juste* of poetry with the good reporting that creates a sound picture of the world…It's a fitting definition if you're Robert Towne. Because poetry and journalism are structures – what makes drama is a dramatic sense, knowing what human beings respond to, how to make the audience fall in love or follow along or take sides. And I know that's what Robert is wading around in. [922]

Towne was keen to make a film about a genuine amateur :

in an insanely material time now, when athletes are getting $20 million a year and are more concerned about that than their performances, here was a guy who was enormously appealing, who had a pure love for the sport, who just wanted to shave a few seconds off the distance record… Steve was not a classical distance runner – he was relatively short, built like a fireplug, and was capable of dramatizing his feelings to the crowd and the world in virtually every step he ran. In a word, he was a spectacular showman. [923]

Without Limits appears to conform to those guidelines as espoused by authors Dancyger and Rush in proposing as protagonist 'a gifted athlete,' testing himself within the parameters of his chosen sport, who is himself his own worst enemy. [924] The pattern of Towne's screenplays has evolved over time – from the circular pattern he espoused, especially throughout the Seventies (emblematically represented by the version of 'La Ronde' played out in *Shampoo* to the more tragic linear shape – ending with death – as envisaged in the original screenplays of *Tequila Sunrise* and of course the present film under discussion, the biographical *Without Limits*. Dancyger and Rush locate the significance of the Biographical Film thus: "Underlying our fascination is our wish for immortality. In their own way, the subjects of biographical films (by their actions, achievements, character) have achieved immortality." [925]

Figure 30 Pre (Billy Crudup) acknowledges the fans

---

[922] Sragow. *Op.cit.*, 18.

[923] 'Giving Screenplays a Sense of Reality,' *The New York Times*, 08 September 1998: 5. Towne himself had earlier commented that screenwriting "is a very interesting kind of hybrid of two forms of writing … journalism and poetry. I think that screenwriting really demands every bit as much distillation and compression as poetry does and at the same time it demands the kind of verisimilitude and the kind of understanding of life that journalism has and the kind of observations that journalism has." Speaking at the AFI's Harold Lloyd Master Seminar, 1994. Accessed online at www.afi.com.

[924] Dancyger and Rush. *Op.cit.*, 305-306.

[925] Dancyger and Rush. *Op.cit.*, 70.

The origins of the production were clouded with confusion, according to Michael Sragow's account: Moore contributed to the 1995 Prefontaine documentary, 'Fire on the Track.' Towne got caught up in the story once again and tried to bring the story to the big screen with the documentary's producers and after showing footage to Cruise, Cruise declared his initial interest in starring in the production. However, the documentary team brought the project to Disney, locking in the Prefontaine family, while Towne, Cruise and Moore went back to Warner Brothers – the very company that had caused trauma for Towne on *Personal Best*. [926] Produced by Cruise/Wagner Productions (Paula Wagner had left CAA to work with her former client), Tom Cruise bowed out of the lead role, realising that he wouldn't be taken seriously as the teenage Pre.

Towne could be said to have been engaging in mythic construction from his time on *Bonnie and Clyde*: *Chinatown* is certainly built on mythic ideals, from its Biblical references to its circular shape. *Shampoo* similarly engages with the death of one mythical time – the Sixties – and its replacement with a more pragmatic, tragi-comic decade of counterfeit ideologies. Insofar as Towne could create his beloved *Greystoke*, it counters many of the legendary elements of the Rice Burroughs tale with a parallel story of survival, personal growth and achievement against an epic backdrop of change.

> Running is not about winning, it's about guts... To give anything less than your best is to sacrifice the gift...

> - Steve Prefontaine

Personal Best hinted at a more mythic structure, which in fact it ultimately evades by making the titular philosophy that of a minor character who is eventually sidelined (Charlene Benveniste) when the chips are down. While not a biographical film, *The Loneliness of the Long Distance Runner* (British Lion, 1962), directed by Tony Richardson and adapted from Alan Sillitoe's story, is an extraordinary exercise in sport as metaphor, something that runs throughout *Without Limits* as Pre attempts to confound traditional lore on how best to run. Time is the textual arrangement of event components of the story, according to Rimmon-Kenan. [927]

Without Limits opens during the 1972 Olympic Games at Munich, in which Pre faced the biggest challenge of his career to date, perhaps the race of his life, facing down the great Finnish runner, Lasse Virren. [928] It then flashes back to 1969, bringing us into Pre's origins and his entry to Oregon State University and the meeting with Bill Bowerman. That the race ends in defeat, and the film progresses steadily towards a fixed point – Pre's death in 1975 – is a major writing challenge. Towne described when and how he made the decision to structure the film in this way:

> I would say at the second draft, I decided to go that way. Certainly before

---

[926] Michael Sragow, 'Return of the Native,' *New Times Los Angeles*, as before: 18. Towne commented to Rebecca Ascher-Walsh, "All I know is that Tom went into [Warner co-chairman] Terry Semel's office, and when he came out, I had a $25 million budget." *Op.cit.*, 22.

[927] Shlomith Rimmon-Kenan. *NARRATIVE FICTION: Contemporary Poetics.* London and New York: Methuen, 1983.

[928] The emotional tone of these scenes is heightened by the massacre of the Israeli athletes by PLO terrorists.

pre-production started... I think that he [Hall] read the second draft when I changed from his death to the Munich race and I think that the writing actually improved all the way through the script, and I think that that structure committed itself to Conrad. [929]

Towne recalled his reasons for tackling the subject in the film's production notes:

Pre was special ...He was one of those extraordinary athletes who comes along every generation or so to shatter the records, shake up the world, die young and leave an inspiring legacy to push beyond the possible burning in our minds, to risk going beyond the limits, beyond the safe edges into the dangerous realm of pain and courage and pure strength of will, that enigmatic place inside each of us where our hopes and dreams live and breathe...
I'm always attracted to stories about people who are obsessed with their profession, who derive an unusual amount of identity with what they do and how well they do it. [930]

Metaphor & Motif

Towne consciously returns to the theme of the man both trapped and liberated by his occupation and links this idea with the concept of the student and mentor. [931] The screenplay's extensive use of motifs, both verbal and visual cues, strengthens the main narrative line of the film, which is the relationship between Pre and Bill Bowerman. "The coach is Oregon's version of Knute Rockne, a guy who invented the Nike shoe on his wife's waffle iron" said Towne. He elucidates his philosophy with a little more detail to Wade Major: "I believe that sport, at its best, is the development of a ritual with very specific rules that allow men to take out their hostility, their anger, their aggression by celebrating their respective skills and not by doing physical harm to one another. I don't know a better thing to do."[932]

We hear about Bowerman on pages 13-14 when Pre expresses dismay that he hasn't come to see him at his home. We then hear Bowerman in voiceover on page 15 when he invites Pre to attend the University. The pair finally meet on page 19: Pre's Germanic background is part of the dialogue fourteen minutes into the film, in a way that suggests he and Bowerman will be engaged in a battle, if not a war, inscribing the film's momentum with conflict that has an inevitable metaphorical connection with athletics:

```
                    MOORE
       When Bowerman commands, you obey.


                    PRE
              (with bravado)
       I'm not the German army and I'm not
       here to surrender. Besides, that's
       gotta be a bullshit story ...

Dellinger calls out:
```

[929] Harold Lloyd Master Seminar, AFI Oct 1998: 26-7.
[930] *Without Limits* production notes, courtesy of Warner Bros.
[931] This notion of being trapped has an ironic payoff with the capture and eventual murder of the Israeli athletes at the Munich Games.
[932] Wade Major, 'Back on Track,' Box Office Online.

Prefontaine!

PRE
(immediately)
Yessir!

(*Without Limits*: 18-19)

Thus are set out the rules of engagement: the story of an iconoclastic and stubborn runner who constantly locks horns with his kind-hearted but equally stubborn coach. (And a German-American against an American who steadfastly held his own against the Nazis; the younger man will have his own dreadful crucible at the Munich Olympics.) While this is hardly an original theme in terms of the sports film (and was a part of the more hackneyed screenplay, *Days of Thunder*), *Without Limits* is distinguished by the elegance in which its philosophy is parlayed, the witty banter exchanged between Pre and Bowerman, and the sheer power of the storytelling which is on the verge of mythic but always relegates Pre's behaviour to that of a flawed, albeit supremely gifted, human being. [933]

The verbal motifs deal principally with the philosophical argument that dominates Pre and Bowerman's relationship: their debate about talent, heart and limits. The human heart and its foibles occupy a prominent subtext in the story, with the Pre-Mary romance at its centre, but Bowerman recognizes that Pre's heart is the biggest of any runner and it is this unassailable physical asset which marks him out from other runners since he is actually much smaller in stature than any of his competitors.

Figure 31 Donald Sutherland as Bill Bowerman

This is how Towne introduces Pre (and the viewer) to Bill Bowerman:

[933] Cinematographer Conrad Hall commented to Michael Sragow: "I wasn't enthralled with the first draft, but in the rewrites I saw the possibilities of the coach and the runner and the kind of blind aggravation between them that causes the good things to come out." Sragow. *Op.cit.*, 19. The alternative production, *Prefontaine*, focuses on the struggles of an amateur athlete whose idiosyncratic talent marks him out in an era of conformity while runners struggled to break into the professional leagues. It demonstrates his significance to the amateur movement in aiding their struggle to achieve enough money to live on – in *Without Limits*, Pre is reduced to tending bar and living like white trash in a trailer park after the Munich Olympics. Critic Roger Ebert comments in his review of *Without Limits*, Towne's interest in mythical narrative shapes his view of the callow youth with the mysterious gift, perhaps to the detriment of making a social comment: "*Without Limits*," *Chicago Sun-Times*, 11 September 1998. The two productions were dependent on the same sources, as Towne explained at the Harold Lloyd Seminar, 1998: 12. (We might link this to the excision of the Watts Riot sequence in *The New Centurions* inasmuch as this might be interpreted as continued evidence of avoidance of social or ideological comment on the part of Towne in his work.)

Under the laugh of his teammates, Pre gingerly proceeds
into the next room to meet the great man. There's shoes
and lasts and rubber shavings, but no Bowerman.

                    BOWERMAN'S VOICE
              Over here.

Pre rounds the corner and looks down. Bowerman is
kneeling on the ground with a big grease pencil. Without
looking up, he slaps Pre's foot onto a piece of tracing
paper and begins to outline it.

(*Without Limits*: 19)

In fact in the film, Bowerman's opening line to Pre runs as follows:

              Take off your shoe. Your right one.

Thus is conjoined the major motif of the film, the apex of the relationship between Pre
and Bowerman – running shoes. Bowerman is presented mythically, as a man of
legendary bravado against a warring army; and, paradoxically, in a more kindly, fairytale
fashion, as a shoemaker:

Bowerman checks the outline. Pre glances around to the
shelves over Bowerman's 'cobbler's bench' to see shoe
lasts bearing the names of Dellinger, Bence, Moore,
Divine.

                         PRE
              You make everybody's shoes?

                       BOWERMAN
              Everybody that runs.

(*Without Limits*: 20)

Towne identifies the power of their interpersonal relationship as one of total
symbiosis:

> They weren't like teacher and student or father and son – unless you call Diaghilev
> and Nijinsky father and son. They were more like two prima donnas who clash,
> both sometimes right, both sometimes wrong, but better together than they could
> be apart. [934]

Vogler counsels when using this aspect of the hero's journey in screenplays:

> The audience is extremely familiar with the Mentor archetype. The behaviors,
> attitudes, and functions of Wise Old Women and Men are well-known from thousands
> of stories, and it's easy to fall into clichés and stereotypes – kindly fairy godmothers

---

[934] Sragow. *Op.cit.*, 19.

and white-bearded wizards in tall Merlin hats. To combat this and keep your writing fresh and surprising, defy the archetypes! Stand them on their heads, turn them inside out, purposely do without them altogether to see what happens. ... Audiences don't mind being misled about a Mentor (or any character) from time to time. Real life is full of surprises about people who turn out to be nothing like we first thought. The mask of a Mentor can be used to trick a hero into entering a life of crime... [935]

The conflict at the centre of the film turns on their differing philosophies in this re-running of the Oedipal theme. The following exchanges between the men encapsulate the story arc of the entire film. At the weight room, Bowerman talks to Steve:

                        BOWERMAN
            You know it takes about eight
            percent more energy to lead than
            follow. Frontrunners cut the wind
            for everybody behind them, then die
            in the stretch. In a close race
            the frontrunner never wins.

                        PRE
            He's not that good either.

                        BOWERMAN
            So what're you trying to do? help
            him out? give him a handicap?

                        PRE
            No. I hate to have people back
            there sucking on me.

                        BOWERMAN
            Then why do you let them?
            Doesn't look right there somehow.
            Never mind, we'll try it again
            later, thanks Mac. Why, Pre?

As Wilkins leaves:

                        PRE
            When you set the pace .. you control
            the race.

                                    (*Without Limits*: 29-30)

And later:

                        BOWERMAN
            Where does this compulsion come
            from?

---

[935] Christopher Vogler. *Op..cit.*, 141.

```
                    PRE
What compulsion?


                 BOWERMAN
Frontrunning.


                    PRE
Look, Bill, running any other way
is just.. chickenshit.


                 BOWERMAN
Chickenshit?


                    PRE
What else do you call laying back
for two and a half miles then
stealing a race in the last two
hundred yards?


                 BOWERMAN
Winning.
```

In the film the subsequent dialogue is slightly altered, with Pre concluding:

```
I don't want to win unless I've done
my best and the only way I know to do
that is to run out front and flat out.
Winning any other way is chickenshit.
```

(Without Limits: 45)

This is what is called 'on the nose' writing, that is, overly literal, and echoes some of Tom Cruise's dialogue as Cole Trickle in *Days of Thunder* when he attempts to distinguish the difference between courage and bravery. However, Pre's honesty is what drives him – and the narrative – and it is this truthfulness that characterises both his running and the film overall. Towne's easy dialogue and the humour underlying the scene's tone underscores the cinematic affect. The drama and the conflict turn upon an ideal expressed as winning versus losing; as in all of Towne's great work, the ultimate expression is of a sense of loss. Ironically, perhaps, for someone whose status as dialogue writer is that of elder statesman, Towne himself undervalues the skill:

People see it as sort of the California lotto; everybody thinks they can cash in …
Part of it is the fact that people think screenwriting is just dialogue – I can talk,
I can write dialogue…
What makes screenplays difficult… are the things that require the most discipline
and care and are just not seen by most people. I'm talking about movement
– screenwriting is related to math and music, and if you zig here, you know you have
to zag there. It's like the descriptions for a piece of music – you go fast or slow or

with feeling. It's the same.[936]

Towne ventured elsewhere:

> The Aristotelian postulate that character creates action gave rise to its corollary, that action is character. If it's thought of at all in Hollywood, it's usually translated to mean the more action for Arnold, the better… it has always struck me that in movies, far more than in any other dramatic medium, *movement*, not simply action, is most defining of character. [937]

Figure 32 Pre the frontrunner breaks out of the pack

Scene Sequence

As we have already seen, a favourite mode of Towne's writing technique is the scene sequence, that elongated complex of scenes expanding on character and story, and usually revolving around a fetish object. This type of sequence can last up to twenty minutes in a well-structured narrative. In a film based around a track athlete, the motif could only be feet – as in *Personal Best*. However the extra boon gifted to Towne in this set-up is Bill Bowerman's obsession with creating the perfect running shoe, based on Barbara Bowerman's waffle iron. Perhaps the strongest scene-sequence of Towne's writing career is contained in *Without Limits* from minutes 38 through 54. The order of scenes is slightly altered from the screenplay construction: this sequence revolves around Pre's habit of bequeathing Bill's running shoes on every girl he has a crush on until he meets Mary Marckx, who simply won't tolerate his callow behaviour. It has some of Towne's best dialogue, thematic exploration and finely wrought construction, which belies his declaration that he has no knowledge of screenplay formulae.

In the script they first encounter one another on page 37 when he has a date with her room-mate, Molly. He teams up with her instead:

EXT SPORTING GOODS STORE (DAY)

Pre's car is parked outside. In a moment he emerges carrying stacks of shoe boxes and walks a few doors down the street to Del's Coffee Shop where he enters.

INT DEL'S (DAY)

Mary's seated at a booth trying her best to sip a Coke while blushing madly, mortified at being the center of attention. In the crowded coffee shop Steve Prefontaine

---

[936] Weinraub. *Op.cit.*, 5.
[937] Towne, 1997: viii.

is on his knees before her, trying another pair of
running shoes at her feet.

>   PRE
>   How's *this* feel?

>   MARY
>   Yes. Fine. Good.

>   PRE
>   Don't say it if it doesn't fit.

>   MARY
>   It fits. It fits. Look, would you
>   mind getting off your knees?

But later:

>   A COUPLE OF COEDS
>   Hi, Steve. Hey, Steve, what're you
>   doing later?

Unfortunately Mary catches a glimpse of their feet – *both*
are wearing new running shoes remarkably like the type on
and around Mary's feet.

>   PRE
>   "Steve and Mary." Not bad. Think
>   it over.

>   MARY
>   I don't really think you're my type.

(Without Limits: 37-41)

This is the beginning of an extended sequence delineating their relationship in
parallel with that of Steve and Bowerman – in the same way that Bowerman and Steve
are educating each other in terms of each other's respective philosophies, Mary and Steve
teach each other also – as his attempts to make her fit into his life (and shoes) indicate,
and her resistance provides the dynamism that is the pre-requisite for their love affair.

Figure 33 Mary Marckx (Monica Potter) with Pre

The trip to a track meet in Iowa results in a sexual encounter that causes Pre
some terrible ligament damage to his foot. (This, perhaps, alludes to Pre's alleged lack of

prowess in other youthful pursuits such as football.) Pre knows the team desperately
needs his points and runs at Drake Stadium, regardless of any further damage he may be
inflicting on himself:

```
Bowerman has pulled off Pre's shoe and Kardong sees that
it's got half a cup of blood in it.  Kardong's look of
self-satisfaction has turned to horror, and something
close to fear.  As he watches Bowerman and Dellinger bag
Pre's bloody, bandaged foot in ice:

                     KARDONG
          He ran like that?  He's crazy!  He's
          a maniac!938
```

```
As  he wraps up Pre's foot, with deep and undisguised
affection:

                     BOWERMAN
          Oh yes..oh yes..
```

(*Without Limits*: 52)

Pre's conflict with Mary runs a parallel course to that with Bowerman – on a
quasi-philosophical level: this scene is played a little differently in the film but they
discuss her Catholic faith, which she displays through wearing a crucifix, and Pre
attempts to link it to his conviction with his running plan, pleading with her:

```
                     PRE
          It's the hardest thing in the world
          to believe in something.
```

Mary relates it to her religious convictions:

```
                     MARY
          Why do people do that, do you
          think?  Try to talk you out of what
          you believe?
```

(*Without Limits*: 54)

They embrace.

```
                     MARY
          ..I mean it!  You're not my type!..
```

(*Without Limits*: 55)

---

938 In the film Kardong addresses Pre directly.

This scene-sequence summarises the heart of the film: the father/son relationship enjoyed with Bowerman; the love affair with running which is the purpose of Steve's life; and the final, mature and truly equal relationship with the one woman who doesn't conform to his expectations and becomes his soulmate/solemate – in more ways than one.

Tone & Visual Style

It is perhaps ironic that in those films that Towne has directed from his own scripts, his writing technique has been foregrounded: Towne inherited from his close collaborations with the late Hal Ashby a subtle, unobtrusive directing style that allowed actors to shine. This seems to suit Towne's writing, since he disingenuously claims never to have consciously written to a specific style or structure, and allegedly has never actually read a screenplay manual. As already noted, Towne felt that Hal Ashby was the director who most accurately represented the content and *tone* of his work. Ashby was a great influence in the way that Towne set about bringing his scripts to the screen with himself as director: for both men, it was all about 'tone.'

Figure 34 Billy Crudup on set with Robert Towne

As to his insistence upon plausibility, the finished film makes excellent and subtle use of original footage merged with newly shot film of the actors. The film was praised for its technical verisimilitude: it was the first to utilise the Presto auto-focusser which automatically pulls pre-determined focus points – it is especially distinctive in the shots used with the athletes running straight to camera. However it was nonetheless a technical challenge to shoot, with only 8 days to shoot 4 races in Eugene, Oregon, Patrice Donnelly and Kenny Moore helped Billy Crudup with his running style to emulate Steve Prefontaine's appearance, to the extent that their footage of Munich (actually shot at Citrus College, Glendora) fooled people who had been at the actual race. Integrating the crowds footage was also a technical challenge in post-production.

However, as Towne would point out, the visual style of *Without Limits* was very simple – it was about how this particular man *moved*, echoing his thoughts on *Personal Best*:

> It's visual…and I've thought for a long time that so much more of character is
> revealed through simple movement than people realize. Just the way somebody
> moves tells you so much about them. Or their particular running style; it's
> fascinating. Also, it's inherently dramatic, as competition is, but with running you
> have your competitors and you have the clock, and they're really not the same thing.
> A runner has to make a choice to win or to beat the clock. One of Steve's idols
> was (Australian runner) Ron Clark, who considered it almost indecent or immoral
> to win a race without doing your best. [939]

---

[939] Interviewed by Scott Foundas of *The Daily Trojan*, 10 October 1998.

Ultimately, perhaps, *Without Limits* is perfectly expressive of its title and absolutely committed to hope – despite its final ending, from which there is utterly no return. Towne says of its inspiration:

> Everyone who saw him saw a man who was making his dream come true. So you thought: 'Maybe I can do that too.' He excited dreams in the crowd because he was so hell-bent on fulfilling his own. The awfulness of his death, as it was with people such as John F. Kennedy and Princess Diana, is the feeling that maybe the dream dies with the dreamer. But one of the reasons the film has a strong emotional effect on people … is that it is a way of saying that the dream did not necessarily die, that the dream never dies. The film gives people hope, even in tragedy. [940]

That sentiment is echoed in the trackside eulogy delivered by Bowerman:

```
              BOWERMAN
Of course he wanted to win.  Those
who saw Pre compete or who competed
against him were never in doubt how
much he wanted to win.  But HOW he
won mattered to him more.  Pre
thought I was a hard case.  But he
finally got it through my head that
the real purpose of running isn't
to win a race.  It's to test the
limits of the human heart.  That he did…
```

(Without Limits: 113)

The eternally optimistic spirit of Pre is emphatically declared in what would normally be a funeral oration delivered at a freshly dug grave. In the end, the teacher has learned from his student, after the student has learned what Bowerman tried to instil in him prior to the lesson hard won in Munich. It is an extraordinarily uplifting tale.

Sexual language pervades the work, as it does in much of Towne's oeuvre - Sragow calls it 'demotic frankness.' [941] This belies the Oedipal structure, a strategy Towne had employed not just in *Chinatown*, and to an extent, in *Shampoo*, but according to Towne, "Steve's father was not a critical figure in his life." [942] Once again, Towne was clinging to his desire to make authentic narratives. This simplifies the process of eliding the role of father/mentor, something he had already done in *Personal Best*. In *Limits*, Bowerman sires Pre, a running phenomenon, and a running shoe named after a Greek goddess: they both give wings to his dreams.

The irony of the subject, the desire to win, no matter what, was reflected in the fact that the film was barely released, two years after it wrapped, in September 1998. It got wonderful reviews from some of the US's most powerful critics, to no avail.

---

[940] Bruce Kirkland, 'Doing the Towne,' *Toronto Sun*, 28 January 1998.
[941] 'How *Chinatown* Screenwriter Robert Towne hooked up with Tom Cruise and John Woo to Script M:I-2,' www.salon.com 25 May 2000.
[942] Towne speaking at the Galway Film Fleadh, 14 July 2006.

> Any search for a hero must begin with
> what a hero requires – a villain.
> *M: I -2*

It seems that, once again, a number of writers (perhaps as many as eight) had attempted to write *Mission: Impossible 2* before it came to Towne's attention after an initial attempt prior to making *Without Limits*. Producer Paula Wagner declared that she wanted to make "a romantic action adventure film." [943] Tom Cruise remarked that he and Towne "had had ideas about if we ever did another *Mission...* which way we would take it." [944]

One of the basic problems with the first film was its overly complex story, and this, apparently influenced thinking on the second: "They didn't want to abandon all the complexity; they figured the puzzle was part of the pleasure of the series. But extra efforts were made to ensure that all crucial plot points were given enough space and time to register with the audience." [945]

Let us remind ourselves of one of the basic requirements of any screenplay: plot. Irwin Blacker says,

> *Plot is structure.* It is the most difficult part of scriptwriting. The crises
> selected in or selected out determine the quality of the script. A crisis in the
> wrong place, or a crisis needed but not present, can destroy a script.
> The plot is made up of scenes, incidents and crises, which are organized to
> develop the conflict from the moment it is locked through its complex parts to
> the resolution of the conflict. The order and selection of the scenes determines
> the plot and creates the structure of the script. [946]

Towne was basically brought in to create movement between the action scenes – he stated that "really what was involved was writing a story to fit the action. During this process Paula and Tom hit upon the excellent idea of asking John Woo to come on board as director." [947] While it was hardly the first film to go into production without a completed screenplay, it had its own uniquely convoluted situation in the figure of Woo and the established action sequences.

The influence of Hong Kong action films can be seen not just in the employing of Woo as director, but in the acrobatic stunts which are familiar from that genre (and made more audience-friendly in *The Matrix* trilogy, which itself followed on from the surprising success of *Crouching Tiger, Hidden Dragon*). Acknowledged as a modern classicist, chiefly as a brilliant director of balletic action sequences, Woo had hit the ground running in the United States with *Face/Off*, 1997, an ingenious camp classic starring John Travolta and Nicolas Cage. (In fact, Woo had made an earlier film, *Hard*

---

[943] Speaking on *Behind the Mission – The Making of M:I-2*. On the M:I-2 dvd.

[944] *Ibid.*

[945] Rick Lyman, 'Villains and Heroes,' At the Movies, *The New York Times*, 26 May 2000: E26.

[946] Blacker. 1986, 16.

[947] Speaking on *Behind the Mission – The Making of M:I-2*. On the M:I-2 dvd. *Screen International*, reported: "They said: 'These are the action sequences. What do you think of coming up with a story to fit them?' I said it was an insane idea, but I did it." Word of Mouth,' December 1, 2000.

Target,1993, with the infamous Muscles from Brussels, Jean Claude Van Damme, but nobody had noticed and so Woo's reputation remained unsullied.) "Basically it's a triangular love story," said Woo. "The good guy and the bad guy are both in love with the same girl." [948]

Towne revealed his motivation: "Ever since the end of the cold war, people have been looking for a villain... It's tricky writing for a franchise series like *Mission: Impossible* because there are certain things that you know you cannot do... The single biggest challenge is to convince the audience that the hero might die." [949] According to the same account, part of his inspiration came from watching '60 Minutes' "when he saw a segment about new boutique antibiotics that kill specific strains of viruses. He filed the idea away. A bit later he was reading an article in *National Geographic* about Eskimos and a weird strain of virus found frozen in the Arctic ice. The dime dropped. How's that for a villain? A pharmaceutical company that makes a super-killer virus just so it can sell people the antidote!' [950] How that might relate to the original story, credited to Ronald D. Moore and Brannon Braga, is open to speculation.

Genre and Symbol

However, the generic specifics central to an action film's structure require a romance line to create a subplot to the main narrative line. Towne said, " [Tom loves risks. And that's what drives Ethan.]...If there is a romance, will the girl survive?" In talking about Ethan's character, Towne reverts to the terminology of his beloved Greek mythology: "He looks like Icarus, but he is really Daedalus." [951] The mythology was explicit in the screenplay: the villain that needs a hero, the illness that requires an antidote, the Chimera that has to be killed by Bellerophon, the idea of Nyah as 'a Trojan horse' (p. 41) which is punctuated by a scene at the racetrack.

The coining of the name of the screenplay's female antagonist, Nyah Nordoff-Hall, owes much to Towne's play on the audience's prior knowledge and his own commitment to mythical storytelling, as well as his collaborator, cinematographer Conrad Hall. The writers James Norman Hall and Charles Nordoff are principally known for their novel trilogy *MUTINY ON THE BOUNTY* (*Botany Bay, Men Against the Sea, Mutiny on the Bounty*), which was the basis for the eponymous 1935 film and remains a well-loved adventure saga in the minds of Americans. (And James Norman Hall is the father of Conrad Hall.) As well as locating her in the realm of the mythic, this gives us a clue as to Nyah's destiny (to commit a form of treason to her former employer, also her former lover, in the course of a legendary adventure.) Nyah's profession is also a furthering of the animal motif introduced in the first film of the series – she is a cat-burglar. The orientation of the film towards the mythic is firmly figured in the patenting of the drugs, which clearly represent good and evil – the choice to be made by men who metaphorically hold the whole world in their hands. While perhaps not Towne's finest writing hour, the underscoring of the narrative with this level of symbolism creates firm links with the body of his work in general, neatly conflating both the mythic and realistic lines of his narratives, and underlines his own apprenticeship with genre fiction – the borrowing of influences; the intertextual referencing to classic Hollywood filmmaking; and the nod and wink to a knowing public, keen to participate in an adventure saga that

---

[948] Speaking on *Behind the Mission – The Making of M:I-2*. As before.
[949] Lyman. *Ibid.*
[950] *Ibid*
[951] *Ibid.*

owes much to the rather attractive madness inflecting the lives of explorers, geographic, scientific or even romantic, all for the love of patriotic discovery.

<u>Authorship and Origination</u>

Towne acknowledged to Michael Sragow the inherent difficulty of writing the screenplay:

> That took some working at it: to develop a language that at least had the simulacra of life -- if that's what you want to call it -- even if it wasn't real. That's what takes three drafts: to get that feeling for language, to get the right level of reality -- or its own level. [952]

He continues:

> I had always worried that *Mission* movies would always be over-involved in process and in the technological version of the Feydeau farce, with people pulling those masks on and off. But here I think we managed to use those things as metaphors for character. [953]

Of course the screenplay cannibalises the first film – the play of masks and identities - even an oxygen mask, in a nod of course to *Face/Off*, which Woo acknowledges as Towne's idea, [954] which has its ultimate payoff as Sean Ambrose (Dougray Scott playing the rogue agent much as Sean Bean had done in the James Bond film *Goldeneye*, 1995) takes off his mask to reveal Ethan Hunt and Hunt does the same, at different and crucial plot points. They 'face off' in a literal cliffhanging climax which echoes the film's introduction to Ethan, free-climbing in Dead Horse Point State Park. While the film doesn't divert our attention in its choice of locations – it does try to replay the excitement of the robbery when the IMF team tries to steal the virus and double-play involving Stamp and the pharmaceutical boss McCloy complicates the plot. The animal motif is repeated from *Mission: Impossible*, with references made in particular to Nyah either as a 'cat', or a 'monkey.' [955]

We see pigeons (carriers of messages – and disease) and horse-racing; and again, there is a reference to a rat in a maze (Stamp's dialogue on page 90). Some of the action takes place on Bear Island; doves accompany Ethan during the break-in; and Hunt, is, once again, prey. We have a reprise of helicopter scenes and a near-miss in an elevator to remind us of Emilio Estevez's death in the first film. As in *North by Northwest*, a series of different modes of transport is used – now an action movie trope. And, as in *Mission: Impossible* (and 'The Dove Affair') a transitional sequence takes place on a bridge. The Biblical analogy here is represented by the false 'resurrection' scene; and then the final, final shootout occurs, restoring peace after narrative disturbance: literally, a cliffhanger, replicating the opening as the DNA-like story spirals to its conclusion.

Wagner said of Towne that he "brings the nuance and complexity and a little bit of irony to the human interaction and to the characters." [956] The dramatic irony at the

---

[952] Sragow, 2000.
[953] *Ibid.*
[954] Speaking on *Behind the Mission – The Making of M:I-2*. As before.
[955] And cats are one of Towne's favourite on-screen animals, viz., the description of Lillian Bodine as "a painted cat" in *The Two Jakes* (p.12).
[956] Speaking on *Behind the Mission – The Making of M:I-2*. As before.

narrative's core is that a disease is being created in order to peddle a cure – perhaps a superficial riff on the theme of *Chinatown* with this dramatic twisting of the conflict into myth, a way of signposting the narrative endgame:

```
                    McCLOY
     I needed the Chimera in order to peddle
     Bellerophon.  For a hero to be appreciated,
     you need a monster.  Now, that's not so
     difficult to understand, is it?
```

(Mission: Impossible 2: 60)

The use of Ethan's own bloodstream as a petri dish literally makes him the embodiment of the conflict at the film's heart – the fight between good and evil.

In Anthony Hopkins, Towne finds a vehicle for some politically incorrect jibes, such as "Go to bed with a man and lie to him? She's a woman. She's got all the training she needs." While conforming to the needs of the blockbuster franchise, Towne's technique here also binds the two lines of action together, because in trying to save the girl, Ethan is also initiating the possibility of romance and humanising the hero-spy. [957]

Sragow suggests that it is necessary to have a good collaborative relationship with a director on "these romantic adventure-cum-suspense movies, they're always team efforts -- whether we're talking about Hitchcock and screenwriter Ben Hecht on *Notorious* or Hitchcock and screenwriter Ernest Lehman on *North by Northwest*," and Towne agrees that

> you have to have that teamwork -- you have to work with people so immersed in this world that they can give reality to the romance and adventure and suspense, or else it's all a lighter-than-air fairy tale. You have to ground it -- and to do that you have to help each other believe in it. [958]

However, linguistic problems hindered the nature of the collaborative process with Woo:

> He was involved every day in what we did; it's just, for the moment-to-moment work, his language skills are not such that he was able to achieve it. We would read to him and refer to him and he would make suggestions. But the actual involvement, in terms of the interplay, was with Tom and me. At the end of every day in Australia, Tom was there. And sometimes he would go up to [producer] Paula [Wagner's] room while I was writing; then he'd come down, take the pages, run back up the fire escape, and, I was told later, read the pages to whoever would listen to him and come back down. [959]

Sragow remarked to Towne:

S: It didn't take long before I thought of Hitchcock's *Notorious*.

---

[957] Woo remarked that it was his first film with a happy ending. Speaking on *Behind the Mission – The Making of M:I-2.* As before.

[958] *Ibid.*

[959] Sragow, 2000.

T: In a strange way you have both the villains in both those pictures deeply in love with the girl and you're meant to feel that. And I love that use of a triangle.

S:You even have a substitute for Claude Rains' protective, suspicious mother.

T: Yes, that Richard Roxburgh character. And we even have a racetrack! That was not intended; it's just suddenly we had this great racetrack down there. Sure there was an echo of *Notorious*. It's very rare to develop a love triangle as a subplot that happily exists and helps you advance the *plot* – that's a hard thing to do. But it also, not coincidentally, gives the heroine something to do for a change. Thandie Newton actually owns part of the story. [960]

Yet when Stephen Farber ('Mission: Familiar') suggested (perfectly reasonably) that Towne had lifted the film's plot from Hitchcock's *Notorious* (1946), hook, line and sinker, in the pages of *The Los Angeles Times* (31 May 2000, a week after Sragow's web article appeared), Towne responded with ire in the pages of same newspaper (05 June 2000). He defends with passion Farber's accusation, "Is there any reason why a movie couldn't have thrilling action scenes along with characterizations of substance and complexity?" The article exhibits Towne's defence of his craft as well as displaying a sensitivity to the politics of film criticism (in a town full of critics), and of course admits to what was fairly obvious to all concerned: just as *Tequila Sunrise* had been a tribute to *Casablanca*, *M:I-2* similarly paid 'homage' to *Notorious* (1946, written by Ben Hecht) one of Hitchcock's greatest works, in which an American agent, Devlin, played by Cary Grant, endangers the life of his true love, Ilsa (another Ilsa, again played by Ingrid Bergman), by asking her to spy on her Nazi husband, Claude Rains (yet another refugee from *Casablanca*). Not to mention Nyah's profession as cat burglar, a reminder of one of Hitchcock's greatest successes, *To Catch a Thief* (written by John Michael Hayes.) It is worth reading in full Towne's rebuttal, and to remember just how many similarities there are between his genre works and those in the Hollywood canon, particularly as written and directed by Howard Hawks. It makes his denial all the more bizarre. [961]

Cruise allegedly discarded screenplays by both Robert Towne and Frank Darabont, as well as Dan Gilroy and Dean Georgaris and one-time presumed director Joe Carnahan, for *Mission: Impossible 3*, which was critically lambasted upon its release in Summer 2006 (written and directed by J.J. Abrams & Alex Kurzman & Robert Orci) and spelled the end of Cruise's deal with Paramount Pictures in a controversial move by Sumner Redstone. [962] Instead, Towne spent the Spring of 2006 touring festivals with his long-anticipated adaptation of the late John Fante's beloved cult novel, ASK THE DUST, one of the principal inspirations for *Chinatown*. The film received extremely mixed reviews.

When they guest edited the Special Issue on Screenwriting for the *Journal of Film and Video*, in 1990, Dancyger and Rush stated that

[960] Sragow, 2000.
[961] Robert Towne, 'M:I-2 Author to Critic: Forget it Steve, It Isn't *Notorious*,' *Los Angeles Times*, 05 June 2000. As we have already noted, Towne was fond of 1940s melodramas. And if he plays the director's commentary on the DVD he will hear Woo acknowledge the debt.
[962] *Los Angeles Times*, www.calendarlive.com 01 May 2006. Interestingly, the story centred on Ethan Hunt's endangered bourgeois family which totally decentred the focus from the professional 'family' and changed the tone of the trilogy in the process. The first film had suggested that his (unlikely) rural family were in danger; this screenplay actively placed them in danger and to the forefront of the narrative, with very mixed results.

We feel that the challenge to screenwriters in the 1990s will be the development of narrative styles that borrow from other genres and even other art forms to go beyond the standard sympathetic character-driven, three-act models. [963]

In the previous decade Towne had finessed his collaborative efforts with stars, producers and directors in order to finance his own, more deeply felt work. And yet throughout the collaborative screenplays in the 1990s is the essence of his work: realism giving way to one myth and then the layering in of yet another myth; taking inspiration from classical Hollywood films and then fusing the ideas with contemporary praxis; and utilising the tools of metaphor and motif to yield unexpected depths in seemingly routinised genre productions. In terms of the changing nature of the film industry, M:I 2 would be just one of a number of sequels or prequels which would be number one top grossing films between 1990 and 2000. [964]

This phase of Towne's career might be summarised, as ever, as a balancing act. Towne's natural desire to be the 'controlling intelligence' behind a personal project was balanced with a pragmatic approach to collaborative cinematic authorship. In terms of his decade assisting on the screenplays of blockbusters, it can be seen that while participation in such projects enabled him to be financially secure in his private life, it also ensured that his responsibilities did not extend to the rigours of external authorship in a highly unpredictable industry. The term, the industrialised Towne screenplay, therefore, is not intended as scornful, merely a reminder that he was no longer working on equal terms with his collaborators; that the budget for the average blockbuster was of the high-risk variety; and that the demographics for Towne-led productions were perceptibly narrowed, as the lack of faith in the distribution of *Without Limits* demonstrated. As he himself discovered, "what you learn as a director is that the director has complete authority and no control." [965]

The requirements of collaborative authorship practices (ie compromise), seemingly unique to the production of blockbuster, in fact harked back to the production line processes familiar from the earliest days of filmmaking, suggesting once again issues of cinematic mastery, autonomy and credits, questions which have always complicated the idea of film authorship. Towne had referred in 1981 to 'rescue fantasies' and the revitalising possibilities available in salvaging a screenplay from other hands and giving it new life. [966] Perhaps most of his 1990s work for his collaborators represented a way of giving new form to his own career, which was once again that of the screenwriter for hire. However, his work still retains a stamp of what Wood calls 'significant articulation,' that mark of 'coherence' so necessary for auteurist evaluation. [967] Perhaps we should return to Corliss' layers of screenwriting – and attribute to some of Towne's 1990s output the term 'protean,' signifying the "gem-polishing of the gifted adaptor." [968]

---

[963] *Journal of Film and Video,* Special Issue on Screenwriting, guest edited by Ken Dancyger and Jeff Rush, Vol.42, No. 3, Fall 1990: 3.

[964] Introduction to 'The 90s and Beyond,' in Linda Ruth Williams and Michael Hammond (eds.). *CONTEMPORARY AMERICAN CINEMA.* London, Open University Press, 2006: 325.

[965] Towne in Engel. *Op.cit.,* 213.

[966] Towne in Brady. *Op.cit.,* 407.

[967] Wood, 2006, 28.

[968] Corliss, 'The Hollywood Screenwriter': 6.

If Towne's career now had a shape its contours were those of a circle – like so many of his protagonists, he was back where he started, a screenwriter for hire.

David Thomson states in *THE WHOLE EQUATION* that the lament of his book is:

> how someone who was once among the best writers in Hollywood, and who might have written a fine novel about the life and times of Jake Gittes and Los Angeles became the man who made a small fortune writing two *Mission: Impossible* pictures. [969]

The answer lies in the Hollywood machine. If Robert Towne were a genre, then his career was in its final phase of played-out conventions and self-parody. Towne's career now provides that most acute expression of the contours of post-1960 cinema: in short, decline.

---

[969] David Thomson. *THE WHOLE EQUATION: A History of Hollywood.* London: Little, Brown, 2004, 16.

CONCLUSIONS

This is the first academic study of the screenplays of Robert Towne. Its purpose was to explore in detail the process of a celebrated Hollywood screenwriter whose work displays an exemplary use of classical dramatic structure. It was also born of a desire to correct the usual accounts of filmmaking, which fail to recognise the contribution of the screenwriter. To (re) quote Lee Server, "… a director's cinema, a producer's cinema, a screenwriter's cinema. These are some of the variables of authorship in Hollywood." [970]

Given that the construction of a narrative sequence is classically ordered, the foundation of the research model utilised in this study was the framework for the principles of playwriting, as established by the Greeks. Because the typical Robert Towne scenario or story formula obtained within this model it could be analysed within the limits of the classical Hollywood format. The commonality within the Towne oeuvre meant that certain thematic and sometimes formal relationships lent it a set of components, which also fell within the elements of classical playwriting, despite its usual formation within the context of collaborative filmmaking practice. [971] The constitutive elements of Towne's screenplays therefore formed a matrix or grid against which his work could be measured, usually within the confines of the orchestral template suggested by Richard Corliss. The concept of the auteur, a figure of controlling intelligence, allowed this series of authorial patterns or internal coordinates to continue Corliss's suggestion, that the screenwriter could, like the director, be attributed the title 'auteur.' [972] Following on from Corliss, the visual elements of Towne's screenplays were considered, addressing a crucial component rarely attempted in conventional auteurist criticism. This was lent further ballast by Towne's own declaration that he had intended making his directorial debut with *Chinatown* (1974); and also by the sheer level of visual detail supplied by the screenplays themselves.

> The screenplay is not only the beginning for a film. It is the center of it, establishing the coherence that direction alone cannot provide. [973]

It was also born of a desire to correct the usual accounts of filmmaking, which fail to recognise its collaborative basis. Robert Towne's work in cinema has demonstrated a rare consistency with thematic subtext, character and literary fidelity. His great gift to actors has been the observational quality of his writing and his strong dialogue. His legendary screenplay *Chinatown* remains a touchstone not just of American cinema in the Seventies, it is a classic text in its own right. As a director he has attempted to communicate his own particular concerns, usually within what has come to be termed the classical Hollywood style, and leaning towards his own particular form of realism, ultimately tending towards a fatalism which could be termed mythic – this has had particular resonance in his early consultancy on *Bonnie and Clyde* and has been discussed in terms of its usage to greater or lesser degrees in *Chinatown, Shampoo, Greystoke, Personal Best* and *Without Limits*, forming a narrative continuity throughout the structure of much of his work, especially in the post-classical phase. Despite the sometimes appropriate application of Pauline Kael's withering term of 'flaky classicist' to his position as a

---

[970] Lee Server. *Op.cit.,* 10.

[971] Belton. 1987: 2-3.

[972] Corliss. 1975, 1

[973] Tom Stempel. *SCREENWRITER: The Life and Times of Nunnally Johnson*. New York: A.S. Barnes & Co., 1980, 192.

screenwriter, he remains a towering presence in Hollywood lore and *the* major contemporary figure in what Lee Server (and others) might welcome as a history of screenwriter's cinema, to which this study might in some small way contribute. [974]

The principal research question which dominated this study was the applicability or otherwise of the tenets of auteurism to screenwriting in general; and, in particular, to the screenplays of Robert Towne. This concept enhanced the appropriating of the elements of screenwriting as a theoretical tool by which to understand this particular level of cinematic narrative. The study's overarching theme of screen authorship is both strikingly contemporary and, ironically, somewhat outmoded. The dialogue between Andrew Sarris and Richard Corliss is witty, self-effacing and informed, but Corliss' appropriation of auteurism in the name of the screenwriter was flawed, not merely by his apparent failure to actually read any screenplays. His suggestion of a 'politique des collaborateurs,' was, however, a step in the right direction. Auteurism was essentially part of cinema's quest for legitimation.[975] The concept of authorship – or at least the critical and popular assumption of the director's overweaning contribution – continues to dominate most analyses of films, in terms of both criticism and film studies in general.

The argument for auteur cinema is finally evaluative and ultimately personal and subjective. The limitations in auteur study lie precisely in the ignorance of collaborative filmmaking praxis and the paradoxical denial of professionalism. However, screenwriting authorship provides another lens through which film studies can be further considered and defined. It might be said that Towne's writing falls into two distinct circles of Sarris' devising – his work as a masterful collaborator, in which he seems infused with the personality and concerns of his co-worker; and his work as writer/director, in which he returns to his own mythic forms and classical Hollywood tributes. Those circles overlap with the consistent usage of Towne's own narrative paradigm (the protagonist trapped by his occupation) and the inevitable theme of loss, in particular in those screenplays where he might be said to have more of a controlling influence than on his Nineties work where he was strictly for hire yet managed to infuse screenplays with his own concerns. It is useful to recall the words of his own script doctor, Anna Waterhouse, when she states, "The truth is, Robert is a fascinating combination of the solitary writer and the ultimate collaborator." [976]

The methodological implications of examining a single screenwriter in a complicated nexus of professional relationships derive not just from the issues of authorship examined in Chapter 1, but also from the idea that a group style or practice (as mentioned by John Belton) persists in Hollywood and has done since Robert Towne's career began. [977] Conflating the markers of authorship with the elements of dramatic structure for screenwriting establishes a matrix or grid of determinants, which identifies the screenwriter's signature within the collaborative structure and the cinematic text. Interpreted in terms of the tools of dramatic structure – action, character, dialogue, genre, location, theme, tone, visuals and sequence structure – Robert Towne's voice can be located systematically in those screenplays which he has written and co-written; and in those films which he has written and directed himself, because of his expert deployment

---

[974] Server. *Op.cit.*, 11.

[975] Robert Stam. 'The Author,' in Stam and Toby Miller. *FILM AND THEORY: An Anthology.* Oxford: Blackwell Publishers, 2000, 1.

[976] Letter to the author, 31 January 2006.

[977] Belton, 1987: 2-3. And Bordwell, Staiger and Thompson, *op.cit.*

of those traditional playwriting elements as they have come to signify classic Hollywood storytelling. As a theoretical tool it posed a number of problems, principally because of the issues that have developed within auteur theory (itself an outgrowth of popular film criticism); and also because of the direct transposition of certain assumptions in the cause of redeeming the screenwriter's role in the originating of screen stories (again complicated by issues of collaboration and adaptation). [978] Authorship debates evolved in the development of postmodernist theory as it applied in the sphere of film studies, resulting in a more widely understood concept of multiple or collaborative authorship, as suggested by the work of Jack Stillinger and Richard Dyer, amongst others. This has led to the possibility of asserting authorship attribution in terms of contributors other than those favoured by the original auteurist critics. In the case of Towne or any other screenwriter, it is possible to identify a signature through the textual markers of the screenplays. The progression of textual debate within film studies is continually as divided as it is divisive. While much theoretical writing is influenced by the decentering positions of Barthes and Foucault, in which authority (and intention) is removed from the author, it is fair to say that the dialogue long ago given a voice by *Cahiers du Cinéma* and Andrew Sarris is ever more resonant in contemporary terms. [979]

This approach suggests that the analysis of such work is in its infancy; and that future research would posit a series of analyses, across different eras of Hollywood history, in order to fully explore the pressures on screenwriters to conform not merely to studio orders but cultural expectations; and within that framework the extent to which they could express (or not) their own worldviews on their own terms. (And perhaps the degree to which this is 'blurred' or otherwise by the intervention of the director, to use Lizzie Francke's expression.) [980] This is another variant on auteurism and Patrick McGilligan's continuing series of oral histories of Hollywood screenwriters offers a revised consideration of the medium, from the point of view of the practitioner.[981] These accounts suggest a modified model of authorship, which could at the very minimum alter the balance of academic and general appreciation of the screenwriter's role in Hollywood history.

The link between this approach and that of other writers is twofold: firstly, this study appropriates a broad-stroke version of auteur-structuralism, mentioned in Chapter 1, which seeks to enact an intervention into an understanding of auteur theory and translates it into a series of filmic texts linked by their writer, but perhaps owing more to the (occasionally extreme) author studies by Robin Wood and the more recent forays into the sub-genre on the subject of the screenwriter's contribution and identity; and it utilises the kind of textual analysis familiar to screenwriting students from any number of contemporary manuals, making the crucial assumption that Robert Towne's deploying of dramatic structural elements (including Wollen's "core of repeated motifs") are the

---

[978] For, as Stillinger informs us, "critical appreciation of a masterwork requires it to be the product of a single organizing mind." Stillinger. *Op.cit.*, 138.

[979] "…the reader is the very space in which are inscribed, without any being lost, all the citations a writing consists of; the unity of a text is not in its origin, it is in its destination": Roland Barthes' essay, 'The Death of the Author,' was first published in the American journal, *Aspen*, and can be found in an anthology of his work, *IMAGE MUSIC TEXT*. New York: Hill and Wang, 1978; while Michel Foucault's 'What is an Author?' (which some might say attempts to answer the questions posed by Barthes and alludes to the idea of discourses created by cultural constructions or author-functions) is cited in the Introduction.

[980] Lizzie Francke. As before.

[981] The *BACKSTORY* series published by the University of California as previously cited.

markers of his particular style of authorship. This is systematically explored through the analytical tools supplied by screenwriting manuals. [982] A study of this type is delimited not merely by a word count: a larger study of the constraints and possibilities of Hollywood filmmaking (and all that this particular industrial framework implies) could only be supplied in synoptic form imposed by the length of the document. Film history, in the form of anecdotal accounts and production notes publicly available, provided scope for an interventionist text into the world of auteur theory and screenwriting as it might apply to the filmmaking process and served as the backdrop for much of the research. [983]

The initial purpose of this particular study was to redress the balance of film authorship in the name of the screenwriter; but also to highlight the difficulties in the attributing of credits in cinema. The overwhelming implication of this study is, finally, that the most meaningful contribution of auteurism to the study of screenwriting could probably be found in the orchestral mode of multiple authorship, to which I have alluded several times throughout the text, albeit necessarily prioritising Towne's role. Filmmaking is essentially a collaborative venture, which at times highlights a particular style of generic or personal writing - but this is, of course, dependent upon a necessarily sympathetic production team and cast. This should not downplay the fact that in the case of Robert Towne, he has frequently been the originator of not just the screenplays but those *essential ideas* onscreen to which his name has been attached as screenwriter. And, that in several notable cases, directors who would otherwise be credited as auteur filmmakers, sought his help in doctoring screenplays at crucial stages to ensure their films' completion. In other words, *his* filmmaking signature was essential for the enhancing of those of his *collaborators'*. It has been said of him, "He writes scripts for more than just a living. Life surrounds him in fogbanks of scenarios." [984]

> In dramatic writing, the essence is character change. The character at the end is not the same as the character at the beginning. He's changed – psychologically, maybe even physically.
>
> - Robert Towne

The great irony of Towne's career is his capacity to absorb the influences of those around him. That ability has also rendered him a master adapter, his literary translations sometimes occasioning his finest work. *Bonnie and Clyde* (1967) is self-evidently the major turning point in his work, taking off from legendary, if actual personae, and proceeding towards a mythical resolution, it would be the bedrock of his apprenticeship and apparently his filmmaking philosophy and storytelling style. It is also notable that since his association with Warren Beatty on *Shampoo* (1975), he has never

[982] As Wollen reminds us, "evaluation cannot be impartial" (1972 revision), 'The Auteur Theory,' (extract) reprinted in Caughie (ed.), 1981, 138-151. As he says, "What the auteur theory does is to take a group of films ... and analyse their structure." (144). This model should not appropriate Wollen's 'unconscious' auteur, however.

[983] A more broad-based approach of this nature, including screenwriters and other collaborators in filmmaking praxis, can be seen in Lovell and Sergi. *Op.cit.*, 2005.

[984] David Thomson, 'Trouble in Chinatown,' *Vanity Fair*, November 1985: 60. He continues on p. 129 of the same article: "I do think there is something in his very attractive, eloquent but crafty nature that could slip from being the uncredited master on other people's films to the thwarted author of unmade masterpieces. It is all part of the inherent tragedy of being a writer in Hollywood, of acting cheerful while being sick. And in Robert's case it would be more of a loss because he has occasionally broken into the kind of descriptive prose that shows what *Chinatown* and the Jake Gittes story could be – a book."

attempted a dramatic screenplay that might be said to have had overt social or political relevance; while Beatty went onto his most cherished project, *Reds* (1982) and later, *Bulworth* (1998), not to mention his own personal commitment to the Democratic cause. Director Hal Ashby, acknowledged by Towne as the best interpreter of his writing, also proved his political commitment through a variety of subsequent films such as *Coming Home* (1978). Towne never again sought to express himself in such a cinematic context. Indeed, it could be said that the relative disappointment of the last phase of Towne's career derives from the mistaken belief that his 1970s collaborative efforts are truly reflective of his personal worldview: yet this is to ignore a textual richness in the work that followed. As a director of his own material, he pays homage to classical Hollywood influences as well as a personal notion of heroism, which is rooted in traditional storytelling. As Michael Sragow says, "screenwriters… at their best … provide the ideas and even the imagery that galvanize their collaborators." [985] Left to his own devices, it is clear that Towne's world does not extend hugely beyond the circumference of Hollywood or the environs of Los Angeles, especially following the epic disappointment of *Greystoke* (1977), probably the true fulcrum about which his career might be said to turn; and yet the various drafts of *Chinatown* (1971-73) are probably more true to the spirit of radicalism and subversive of the concept of individualism than anything his collaborators ever produced: it is a deeply felt expression of political and personal *ennui* that originated in ecological politics and perhaps a kind of historical fetishism for the preservation of a mythical Los Angeles that only ever existed on celluloid and in the works of those vital exponents of the demotic, Hammett and Chandler.

Towne's latest film as director, released in March 2006, is his long-threatened (and poorly received) adaptation of John Fante's Depression-era novel, *ASK THE DUST*. Fidelity to the novel and directing subtlety is undermined somewhat by the principal casting over which Towne did not have final say. The attractions of the text are obvious: set in Towne's beloved hometown, this was a key work for him in gaining a deep understanding of his native city and inspired the writing, and especially the vernacular, of *Chinatown*. The romance of the starving, aspiring novelist whose mentor, H.L. Mencken (voiced by film critic Richard Schickel) guides him from short stories in *The Mercury* to his first full-length novel, forms the film's narrative arc. His fourth outing as director, its most successful elements are perhaps ironically those parts of the text which he as screenwriter has originated, proving that the point of departure from original texts represents at times for Towne his true calling: an extraordinary empathy with, and insight into, his fellow writers, particularly those for whom the long road of struggle is virtually a career strategy. Bandini/Fante's attempts to work in Hollywood can also be read as a trope for Towne's own retrospective desires to work in 1930s and 1940s Hollywood, a rich seam which he has mined both in terms of homage and influence, and also as a version of his own story in contemporary Hollywood.

Undivided authorship is a rarity; the model for a truer understanding of filmmaking praxis is more likely to reside in models of multiple authorship. The value of the auteurist proposal in its original incarnation lay in its recognising of certain directors' contributions to films; and in the elevating of Hollywood genres. [986] Its essentialism as an interpretive text however denies its wider applicability: theory cannot prescribe practice, only describe it *post hoc*; and auteurism, as Dudley Andrew points out, may well be

[985] Sragow. 1983: 18.
[986] Andrew Tudor. *THEORIES OF FILM*. London: Secker & Warburg, 1973, 122-123. As Stephen Crofts reminds us, "auteurism … was polemical and evaluative before it was analytical." Crofts, in Hill and Gibson, *op.cit.*, 314.

experiencing a renaissance. [987] Auteurist study retains its intrinsic value and relevance if it is applied to a wider variety of cinema practitioners, redressing the balance of film history through a more precise attribution of authorship and the evaluation of other cinematic signatures through the detailed examination of, as, for example, in this case, a single writer. Its great achievement was the evaluation of American cinema, still the world's dominant narrative force. As Robin Wood points out, the search for a structure "can draw attention to some of the possible sources of a successful work's vitality." [988] By exploring "the thematic and formal relationships between ostensibly different projects of a single" [screenwriter], a consistent pattern can be observed which suggests a personal vision or controlling idea, the constituent elements denoting a cinematic author. By addressing the visual aspects of these same screenplays the project of auteurism is extended into a formal discourse which extends its relevance to film studies. [989] For, as critic Richard Corliss stated, "auteur criticism is essentially theme criticism; and themes – as expressed through plot, characterisation, and dialogue – belong primarily to the writer." [990]

Identifying Towne as a typical (if not entirely quintessential) Hollywood screenwriter was based on an acknowledgement that his deployment of the tools of dramatic structure serves the classic Hollywood format designed to attract the maximum audience. Part of the recuperative strategy was the identification of the screenplay itself. [991] Towne's particular signature is a culmination of the markers of authorship based on the manipulation of those tools within the parameters of three-act structure as preferred by the studios.

Towne's formation as a writer happened during a fascinating time of apparent change in American cinema history. His relationships with some of the era's most powerful men inevitably influenced his work not just in tone but in subject matter: Warren Beatty, Jack Nicholson, Tom Cruise and Jerry Bruckheimer, are all major players in Towne's professional life. Despite the appearance of change, Hollywood remains a place where powerful men control film production; and they have never lost their power to beguile Robert Towne. The abuse and misuse of power and the theme of lost friendships provides the topical nature of much of his writing; it also suffuses his personal and professional history. His body of work is fortunately discussed in several works of popular screenplay analysis, which have helped create a picture of his role in the Hollywood hierarchy. His private and public lives are necessarily intertwined and provide a fascinating biography which to a large extent fall outside the limitations of this text but nonetheless merit further consideration as any full consideration of authorship

---

[987] Dudley Andrew, 'The Unauthorized Author Today,' in Stam and Miller, (eds.) *FILM AND THEORY: An Anthology*. Oxford: Blackwell Publishers, 2000, 20-30.

[988] Robin Wood, 'Hawks De-Wollenized,' in *PERSONAL VIEWS: Explorations in Film (Revised Edition)*. Detroit, Michigan: Wayne State University Press, 2006, 248.

[989] William Luhr and Peter Lehman. *AUTHORSHIP AND NARRATIVE IN THE CINEMA: Issues in Contemporary Aesthetics and Criticism*. New York: GP Putnam's Sons, 1977, 26.
[990] Corliss, 1974, xxi-xxii.
[991] "… a screenplay is a separate entity; it is not film, dialogue, an outline, or a cinematic tool. It is a literary structure written first to be read and then produced. And though pride of place is an arguable concept in the creation of a film, the pride of place in the creation of a screenplay is clear and definite; the creators is its writer or writers." Gary Davis, 'Rejected Offspring: The Screenplay as a Literary Genre,' *New Orleans Review, date unknown*. 90.

implies. (Not least because, like a novelist, he has regularly plundered his personal life to dramatise his stories.) The meta-narrative that constitutes Towne's career possesses the cumulative dramatic continuity and rising action obtained in a reading of his films: it is a story of deep male friendships, collaborations, ruptured loyalties, and reversals of fortune. The dominant story arc is one of loss. As Corliss has said, "the creation of a Hollywood movie involves a complex weave of talents, properties, and personalities." [992]

I spent a week in Los Angeles in late 2003 with the express purpose of speaking with Towne, following lengthy discussions with his agent: he didn't show up. The reason was clear when shortly thereafter the production of *Ask the Dust* was announced, finally greenlighted after Towne's promise to John Fante in the early 1970s. Unfortunately, although prepared for a brief meeting in 2006, he was not available for a full personal interview during his publicity tour for the released film; so my Ian Hamilton-like pursuit of the author was quashed, late in the day. (Although he did say he would meet me the *next* time I went to Los (t) Angeles.) His ambiguous, non-committal persona was shrouded in the bemused smile of an elder statesman, basking in the cigar smoke which hung around in the sunlight, glinting in his wake, like a punctuation mark of questionable emphasis. It was a fleeting glimpse of a spectral presence whose imprint is left in film negative. The meeting could perhaps best be described as uncomfortable, disturbing, even. To quote Towne himself, it was "nearly as miraculous as getting struck by lightning and living to tell the tale." [993]

The case for Towne as auteur will always be compromised by the fact that out of an extensive body of work, he is solely responsible for only four wholly original screenplays for cinema, namely, *The Last Woman on Earth*, *Chinatown*, *Personal Best* and *The Two Jakes*. [994] It is also clear that there has always been a tension between his internal and external authorship, yet the vestigial traces of his voice are evident throughout the oeuvre, collaborative and otherwise, perhaps making him a member of Corliss' honoured screenwriting élite: the author-auteur. [995]

We might also, therefore, make the claim for him that he is what Truffaut called "a man of the cinema", with the evidence of his signature embedded in the markers of screenwriting authorship as explored in this study. [996]

---

[992] Corliss, 'The Hollywood Screenwriter,' as before: 6.

[993] Towne, 1997, xv.

[994] *Shampoo* and *Days of Thunder* are excluded from this list because they were devised with other people, Beatty and Cruise, respectively; and *Tequila Sunrise* because of Peter Peyton's alleged involvement at an early stage as well as elements reworked from *Cisco Pike*, a screenplay credited to B.L. Norton.

[995] Corliss names ten men in this group - Ben Hecht, Preston Sturges, Norman Krasna, Frank Tashlin, George Axelrod, Peter Stone, Howard Koch, Borden Chase, Abraham Polonsky and Billy Wilder. He says of them: "To a degree rare in the commercial cinema, their personalities are indelibly stamped on their films. In their fidelity to idiosyncratic themes, plots, characterizations, styles, and moods, they won the right to be called true movie auteurs. Seven of the ten were eventually able to direct, thus nursing their visions onto the sound stage and through the editing rooms… even the failures of an auteur can be instructive: not only as critical fodder for a volume such as this, but also as proof that the American movie machine was resilient enough to endure the excesses and eccentricities of its most creative craftsmen." Corliss. 1975, 1.

[996] Truffaut, 'Une Certaine Tendence du cinéma français,' as before, 224-237. This signature gives Towne's body of work what Corliss calls "authorial personality." He also demonstrates another facet crucial to Corliss – versatility. 'The Hollywood Screenwriter': 6.

Capturing the work of a screenwriter is as difficult as Towne says it is to write a screenplay - *how do you describe a movie that's already been shot?*

A literary-style biography of this Hollywood author would be something to cherish: totally Hollywood, totally Towne.

THE END.

Appendix 1

The Screenwriter & Screenplay in Film History and Literature

The Screenwriter & Screenplay in Film History

In Hollywood, "history famously enjoys the same respect as writers and carrion." [997] Agnes DeMille recalls that

> The stories were generally settled in a day or two of conference…It was my
> father [Cecil B.] who, coming from the tradition of a literate theatre, suggested
> that it might be useful to write out in detail beforehand what they planned doing.

She also notes that when her father hung a sign bearing the words 'Scenario Department' on his office door it was the first time the expression was used in Hollywood. [998]

Terry Ramsaye's classic history of Hollywood notes that the industry's habit of adapting pre-existing works started at and immediately after the birth of cinema itself, noting that Porter's scenario for *The Great Train Robbery* was taken from a stage play (hence the name, 'photo*play*'). Its success as 'a story picture' led to the development of scenarios at Biograph Pictures, where a freelance journalist, Stanner Taylor, prepared scenarios in 300-word form which might be filmed at the rate of two per week.[999] Another journalist, Roy McCardell, was the first person to be specifically hired (also by Biograph) to write motion pictures.[1000] Ramsaye explains that

> The demand for screen stories was growing with the industry and rumours of
> easy money 'writing for the pictures' went through the gossip channels of the
> actor tribes, reaching picture patrons as well. The beginning of the scenario
> writing craze was in sight…
> The beginning of scenario writing began to evolve parallel to Griffith's development
> of pictorial narration. [1001]

The industry was already differentiated by 1908, with directing, acting, photography, writing and laboratory work all recognised as separate crafts: in fact screenwriting was already a well paid job, with anything from $5 to $15 being offered by the studios for 'picture ideas,' which now evolved from one-minuters into crude action stories. Every possible source was 'ransacked' to yield material for one-reel presentations, in an attempt to answer the overwhelming demand; the issue of copyright arose during the production of *Ben Hur* (1907) by Kalem. [1002]

Jacobs states that, as the industry developed and matured,

---

[997] Dennis McDougal. *THE LAST MOGUL: Lew Wasserman, MCA and the Hidden History of Hollywood.* Da Capo Press, 1998, rpt. 2001, 480.

[998] Agnes De Mille, 'Merely a Country Town,' from *DANCE TO THE PIPER* (1951), in Sylvester, ed., *op.cit.,* 15. De Mille says that in those days, 'directing was largely improvisation.' (14.)

[999] Terry Ramsaye. *A MILLION AND ONE NIGHTS: A History of the Motion Picture.* New York: Simon & Schuster, 1926; rept., London: Frank Cass & Co., 1964, 421; 455-456.

[1000] Stempel. 1991, 5.

[1001] Ramsaye, *Op.cit.,* 512.

[1002] From Lewis Jacobs. *THE RISE OF THE AMERICAN FILM: A Critical History.* New York: Teachers College Press, 1967, 59; 61; 67; 76; 122.

Like acting, photoplay writing developed under the stimulus of commercial rivalry… as competition intensified and pictures lengthened, directors felt the need of writers to create full stories and prepare them for efficient production. [1003]

During this period, Jacobs observes that

> The technique of screen writing itself … developed rapidly during these years, becoming more formalized and distinct from the literary and stage techniques. Screen writers became aware that above all it is necessary to think in terms of action, not description or dialogue: that the camera is the paramount consideration. [1004]

With the system of supervision initiated by Thomas Ince, the 'shooting script' became the order of the day while the increasing length of films necessitated the use of subtitles with the result that the writer's fame was "almost on a par with the star and the director," while the studio recognised that "a good scenarist, rather than a good author, was perhaps the greatest asset… It was presently realized… that the best results were obtained when the director and scenarist worked together," a system apparently devised by June Mathis, who "proved that the carefully prepared shooting script was essential to good results in an art that was becoming more and more a collective project." [1005]

Edward Azlant's comprehensive overview of American screenwriting from its earliest days to the 1920s indicates that as the studio system came about,

> written design was by its very written nature procedurally distinct from other aspects of production. Thus, in addition to the intrinsic factors of the narrative mode itself and the increasing length of films, the extrinsic factors of large-scale production and the evolving studio system surely helped institutionalise screenwriting. [1006]

He finds that by 1920, "the procedures of filmmaking were established." [1007] But, he claims, histories by scholars such as Kevin Brownlow and David Robinson serve to obliterate the vitality of early screenwriting and unfortunately inform future historians. [1008]

By 1938, Leo Rosten's study, *THE MOVIE COLONY,* found that only 17 screenwriters (as opposed to 45 directors, 54 producers and executives and 80 actors) earned more than $75,000 per year. [1009] Billy Wilder recalled of his days at Paramount that writers had to turn in 11 pages of script every Thursday. [1010]

[1003] Jacobs. *Op.cit.,*129.

[1004] Jacobs. *Op.cit.,* 203; 218.

[1005] Jacobs. *Op.cit.,* 219; 326-8.

[1006] Azlant. *Op.cit.,* 85.

[1007] Azlant. *Op.cit.,* 7.

[1008] Azlant. *Op.cit.,* 57.

[1009] Leo Rosten. *HOLLYWOOD: The Movie Colony, The Movie Makers.* New York: Harcourt, Brace & Co., 1941 referenced by Ian Scott *IN CAPRA'S SHADOW: The Life and Career of Screenwriter Robert Riskin.* Lexington: University of Kentucky Press, 2006, 234, quoting from McGilligan, *BACKSTORY 6.* Richard Fine's study covers similar territory for writers but in greater detail: *HOLLYWOOD AND THE PROFESSION OF AUTHORSHIP 1928-1940.* Ann Arbor, Michigan: UMI Research Press, 1985; reprinted as *WEST OF EDEN: Writers in Hollywood 1928-1940.* Washington and London: Smithsonian Institute Press, 1993.

[1010] Wilder speaking to James Linville in *The Paris Review,* 138, Spring 1996, 65. He comments "In the studio era, screenwriters were always on the losing end in battles with the director or the

John Gassner and Dudley Nichols' collections of prestigious screenplays preserved the film play in the public consciousness and allowed wider study. The 1943-44 volume, according to its editors,

> can make some claim to representativeness, in the sense that it exhibits the continued progress of some of Hollywood's more creative spirits. [1011]

The editors choose screenplays that in some way are 'well above average' even if they are not box office successes.

Brady points out that screenwriter employment was at a peak in the immediate post-WWII period "when some 560 writers were under contract in Hollywood, including 175 at MGM alone." [1012] And by 1945, as Otto Friedrich recounts, the Guild voted to strike in line with the anti-IATSE Conference of Studio Unions, a divisive move that would herald the factional split into left and right that would flare up during the HUAC hearings. [1013]

Credits

As Ramsaye reminds us, story rights and credits were an issue for production companies even in 1905, when "Selig and his motion picture confreres, George K. Spoor of Essanay and George Kleine, determined upon a plan to pool a hundred thousand dollars to corner the world's market on film story rights." [1014] Ed Azlant points out that,

> copyright entries prior to 1912 list only the producer. After 1912 copyright entries list a mixture of producers, screenwriters, directors, and authors of original properties. [1015]

According to Azlant, as early as 1910 the question of credit for scenario writers had been raised on the front page of Moving Picture World. [1016] The star system would also have an effect on screenwriters, as recognisable character traits could be utilised as vehicles for studio players. [1017]

---

studio... Back then, no writer was allowed on the set." (68)

[1011] John Gassner and Dudley Nichols, eds. *BEST FILM PLAYS OF 1943-1944*. New York: Crown Publishers, 1945, xii.

[1012] John Brady. *THE CRAFT OF THE SCREENWRITER*. New York: Simon & Schuster, 1981, 13. He quotes writer Allen Rivkin on the emerging spec script market: "Screenwriters took the gamble and left studio jobs to free-lance. The risk was great, but so were the rewards. By the late forties, writers began to make more money than they ever imagined was possible." (15)

[1013] Otto Friedrich. *CITY OF NETS: A Portrait of Hollywood in the 1940s*. New York: Harper & Row 1988; London: Harper Publishing, 1987, 248. The story of Hollywood's blacklisted screenwriters is told in a number of volumes, including Patrick McGilligan and Paul Buhle. *TENDER COMRADE: A Backstory of the Hollywood Blacklist*. New York: St Martin's Griffin, 1997. (No sooner was the blacklist ended than the auteur theory arrived: Brady, *op.cit.*, 16.)

[1014] Ramsaye. *Op.cit*, 653.

[1015] Azlant. *Op.cit.*, 16.

[1016] Azlant. *Op.cit.*, 99. He continues: "...the individual scenarist would never acquire that public distinction the article proposed. This complex obscurity would hang over the screenwriter indefinitely." (100).

[1017] Azlant. *Op.cit.*, 102.

Many of the issues of importance to screenwriters in the industry hinge on the whole notion of whose name is on the credits; what is perhaps ironic is that via the Writers Guild, writers more or less govern the allocation of these credits themselves. The Guild is asked to intervene in arguments over 150 times a year - and it would appear that 90% of the time, people feel they get their due recognition. [1018]

McGilligan reminds us of how the three-act play became the dominant form to influence screenwriting with the consolidating of the industry on the introduction of sound:

> ... the shooting script became the central need in studio filmmaking during the 1930s. Not only did it 'break down' the story and systematize the continuity but also it dictated how and what was to be shot. All scheduling and budgeting came down to the shooting script; that is where the money men got their hands on the elements of the story; that is where writers, typically, were left behind. [1019]

Lenore Coffee remarks that agents didn't become significant until the advent of the talkies until which time a 'charming informality' prevailed at the studios.[1020] Nancy Lynn Schwartz confirms this, stating that it was then, in 1933, the year of the formation of the Screen Writers' Guild, that John Howard Lawson recognised the significance of the issue of control

> ... so we opened up that first big meeting with a speech I made in which I said that the writers were the owners of their material. [1021]

In their first proposal for amendments to the Motion Picture Code, the Guild had, amongst other, seven demands, the fifth reading:

> that writers receive screen credit according to their contribution to a picture and that no contract violate this. [1022]

As Schwartz points out, the issue of credits would remain a thorny situation. In 1935 the Academy said that

> producers had a right to tentatively determine credits based on an assessment of substantial contributions, to be made by the producer. [1023]

[1018] Kirk Honeycutt, 'Whose Film is it Anyway?' in *American Film,* Vol. 6, No. 7, May 1981: 34. Michael Sragow comments, "Confusion of authorship is rooted in Hollywood history. Rarely ever did big studio movies spring from a single pen, which is one reason Dream Factory scribblers became well-known only when they got headstarts elsewhere." *Op.cit.* 9.

[1019] McGilligan (ed.) *BACKSTORY 1: Interviews with Screenwriters of Hollywood's Golden Age.* Berkeley: University of California Press, 1986, Introduction, 3.

[1020] Coffee, 'When Hollywood was a Village,' excerpted from *STORYLINE: Recollections of a Hollywood Screenwriter* (1973), in Sylvester, ed., 1999, 38.

[1021] Nancy Lynn Schwartz. *THE HOLLYWOOD WRITERS' WARS.* New York: Knopf, 1982, 24. Howard Dietz comments that agents "ceased being mere 10-percenters and were more or less in a position to offer their clients 10 per cent." 'The Growing Stature of Agents,' excerpted from *DANCING IN THE DARK* (1974) in Sylvester, 185.

[1022] Schwartz. *Op.cit.*, 30.

[1023] Schwartz. *Op.cit.*, 49.

Such was the state of relations between the Guild and the Academy that Dudley Nichols refused the Academy Award for *The Informer* one year later. During that ongoing dispute, Darryl Zanuck wrote to the then President of the Screen Writers Guild,

> …your article definitely promises the screenwriters that eventually they will be able to control the screen destinies of the stories they work on. I can imagine nothing that would kill this business any quicker. Moving pictures are not made by any one individual. Many minds are essential if success is to be desired. Many contributors are required… [1024]

This affirmation of multiple authorship was an expression of the collaborative nature of filmmaking and Zanuck himself was highly involved in the detailed development of scripts on the lot.

The Guild would eventually grant waiver on specific cases on credits (eg *Citizen Kane*) and waive its rights on residuals issues several times over the decades since its inception; most notoriously perhaps in 1952, to the monopolising talent agency MCA, as, under the guidance of Lew Wasserman it shifted its focus to production, particularly in television. The waiver finally ended a decade later. [1025]

In the early 1950s in the United States it was possible to claim the authorship of a film in the name of the director: in Lillian Ross's study of the making of *The Red Badge of Courage*, she describes John Huston as "one of the few Hollywood directors who manage to leave their personal mark on the films they make." [1026] She quotes the producer, Gottfried Reinhardt,

> "A picture, if it is a hit, is the director's hit… if it is a flop, it is the producer's flop." [1027]

Hortense Powdermaker's sociological approach to Hollywood is captured in her 1950 study. [1028] She observes of the scribes in their habitat:

[1024] Daryl F. Zanuck, 'Strong, Healthy, and Normal,' in Sylvester, 200.

[1025] This phase of the Guild's history is examined in detail by McDougal 1998, rpt. 2001. The book alludes to Ronald Reagan's collusion in the deals made by Wasserman prior to his support of Reagan's gubernatorial (and eventual Presidential) ambitions.

[1026] Lillian Ross. *PICTURE: John Huston, MGM, and the Making of The Red Badge of Courage*. 1952; rpt., London: Andre Deutsch, 1986, 3.

[1027] Ross. *Op.cit.*, 75. Reinhardt later states that, "'once a director is through [directing], you can usually do what you want with a picture".' 96. However the spine of the book is also the story of the screenplay for the film, also written by Huston, adapted from the Stephen Crane classic. At one point his producer, Reinhardt reluctantly admits, "We do not have a great picture …There is no story, because we do not show what the Youth is thinking. It is not in the script. John said he would put it on the screen. It is not on the screen." Ross. *Op.cit.*, 128. Reinhardt continues: "I never should have made this picture… I did it because I love the book and because I love John. And I thought that John would be able to show what goes on inside the boy. If we had narration for the picture – maybe with that we could show what goes on inside. But John kept saying, 'No narration.' Billy Wilder in *Sunset Blvd.*. had the nerve; after the man is dead, he has him do the narration. Joe Mankiewicz uses narration. Narration is good enough for them but not for John." 132. Loew's Eastern advertising manager Si Seadler described the film to Ross as "a flop d'estime." 214.

[1028] "The best way to understand writers, or any other people, is through their motivations. The primary one for Hollywood writer is the same as it is for everyone else there, namely, the inflated

The writer's social life is usually with other writers, occasionally with producers and directors, but almost always confined to people connected with the making of motion pictures. This means a withdrawal from the everyday life…

Writers vary in how much they play the Hollywood game. Some cultivate important people, entertaining and being seen at big parties and popular night clubs. [1029]

The focus on lucky 'breaks' she says precludes valuable analysis of the system, which she describes as "a complex set of power relationships of a highly personal as well as business nature, functioning outside of the studio as well as in it." [1030]

While Powdermaker's lead was rarely followed, she provides valuable (if apparently barbed) insights into a subculture rarely probed outside fiction.[1031]

By 1959 and 1960, when Robert Towne was writing his first screenplays, McGilligan notes that, "the studio contract writer could be said to be an endangered species." [1032] McGilligan comments of that era:

> The career climb for scriptwriters was perilous in the 1950s, and the creative atmosphere in the industry somewhat restrictive. A scriptwriter had to be determined – dead set on that sunshine and swimming pool (the perks were still attractive) – and *in love with the idea of writing movies.* That, if anything, was the fundamental difference between the scriptwriters of the earliest sound era and those of the 'next wave.' [1033]

---

salaries for which the industry is famous." Hortense Powdermaker. *HOLLYWOOD THE DREAM FACTORY: An Anthropologist Looks at the Movie-Makers.* Boston: Little, Brown and Company, 1950, 131.

[1029] Powdermaker. *Op.cit.,* 134. She concludes that writers place the same value as everyone else in the business on the lucky break, and returns her argument to the importance of paychecks: " The script on which he works is apt to be a confused jumble of many people's ideas and unrelated notions. The occupational satisfactions, traditionally a part of the writer's craft, are lacking. Even though the script writer's name may be among the list of credits for a movie, it is rare – unless he has taken on functions other than writing, or is in an exceptional position – for him honestly to feel that he has communicated anything of his own to an audience. He has ceased to be a writer in the real sense of the word. Instead, he takes dictation." Powdermaker. *Op.cit.,* 148.

[1030] Powdermaker. *Op.cit.,* 168; 155.

[1031] However, as Tom Stempel cautions, Powdermaker's work is littered with problems, a fact that she herself recognised some years later, when she admitted that her conventional, superior approach failed her as an anthropologist: "… I failed to identify with them or to get inside their roles." Powdermaker, *STRANGER AND FRIEND: The Way of the Anthropologist.* New York: Norton, 1966, 229; noted in Stempel, 1988, 69.

[1032] McGilligan, 1991, 1. This of course was in the wake of the HUAC hearings and the Soviet-style treatment of writers (and others) who were felt to be sympathetic to Communist causes, a situation which would itself give rise to issues of authorship as pseudonymous 'fronts' were established for those screenwriters obliged to work covertly for the studios. This is chronicled in, amongst other volumes, McGilligan and Paul Buhle. *TENDER COMRADE: A Backstory of the Hollywood Blacklist.* New York: St Martin's Griffin, 1997. Dalton Trumbo refers to 'documents establishing authorship' regarding his screenplay for *The Brave One* (by the non-existent 'Robert Rich') in 'It Will Be Broken,' a letter to the producer George Seaton, 20 January 1959, excerpted in Sylvester, ed., 1999, 462.

[1033] McGilligan, (ed.). *BACKSTORY 2: Interviews with Screenwriters of the 40s and 50s.* Berkeley:

Budd Schulberg, screenwriter, novelist and scion of the pioneering Hollywood Paramount family, says of the fictional projection of his former profession, he is "the irrepressible studio hack, part heel, part victim – an All-American, interchangeable with All-Hollywood in those hilarious and desperate days when Whitey-Pat Hobbies lived off the crumbs from the banquet tables of the queer people who combined the decadent flamboyance of Louis XIV with the stupidity of George III." [1034]

Aside from the classic stories of F. Scott Fitzgerald, the screenwriter as hero has figured in recent novels as diverse as *KAROO* (by the late Steve Tesich) who laments his experiences as script doctor; and *FORCE MAJEURE* (by Bruce Wagner), which serves as a shocking warning to any latterday Pat Hobby-types. The fiction of Gavin Lambert betrays as only an insider can the true horror of being beholden to the studio. [1035] In cinema, the (inevitably male) screenwriter has been represented variously by William Holden in both *Sunset Blvd.* (1950, Charles Brackett & Billy Wilder & D.M. Marshman, Jr.) and *Paris When it Sizzles* (1964, Julien Duvivier & Henri Jeanson and George Axelrod); and latterly in such examples as *Inside Monkey Zetterland* (1993, Steve Antin and John Boskovich), *Barton Fink* (1991, Coen Bros.) and *The Muse* (1999, Albert Brooks & Monica Johnson). The common thread linking together these films and novels is a sense of the absurd and a shared (and almost chronic) disbelief that such a ridiculously perverse world – Hollywood - even exists. They might therefore best be described as satires. Novelist Douglas Kennedy's Faustian parody *TEMPTATION* not only namechecks Robert Towne but offers a gloss on the plot of *The Last Woman on Earth*, the Devil's pathetically immature Beatnik statement on nuclear war. Kennedy then presents Towne as

---

University of California Press, 1991, Introduction, 4.

[1034] Budd Schulberg 'The Hollywood Novel - The Love-Hate Relationship Between Writers and Hollywood', *American Film*, Vol/No. *unknown*: 32. Richard Fine's *WEST OF EDEN: Writers in Hollywood 1928 - 1940* (Washington and London: Smithsonian Institute Press, 1993) was originally published in 1985 as *HOLLYWOOD AND THE PROFESSION OF AUTHORSHIP, 1928 - 1940* by UMI Research Press. Ian Hamilton's *WRITERS IN HOLLYWOOD, 1915 - 1951* (Carroll and Graf: 1990) charts broadly similar territory but with its central focus the experiences of literary figures such as Fitzgerald and Faulkner. Tom Stempel's *FRAMEWORK A History of Screenwriting in the American Film* (New York: Continuum, 1991) offers a concise and cogent account of the screenwriter in Hollywood's heyday, along with many useful thumbnail portraits of individual practitioners. He says that *Cahiers* critics "were over six thousand miles away from where American films were made and were wrong about how American films were made". He adds that, "the acceptance of the *auteur* theory had disastrous consequences for screenwriting in American films." (192). William Froug's interviews with many key screenwriters of the Sixties through the Nineties are collected in the volumes *THE SCREENWRITER LOOKS AT THE SCREENWRITER.* Los Angeles: Silman-James Press, 1991; and *THE NEW SCREENWRITER LOOKS AT THE NEW SCREENWRITER.* Los Angeles: Silman-James Press, 1991.

[1035] Steve Tesich. *KAROO.* London: Chatto & Windus, 1998. Bruce Wagner. *FORCE MAJEURE.* New York: Random House, 1991. F. Scott Fitzgerald's *PAT HOBBY STORIES* (New York: Simon & Schuster, 1995) are a droll gloss on Fitzgerald's own unhappy Hollywood experiences, examined by Ian Hamilton, 1990. Raymond Chandler wrote, "I wish I could write the Hollywood novel that has never been written, but it takes a more photographic memory than I have. The whole scene is just too complex and all of it would have to be in, or the thing would be just another distortion." 'Hollywood People Are Much Underrated: Chandler's Letter to Edward Weeks, 27 February 1957,' is excerpted in Sylvester, ed., 1999, 460.

... Justin Wanamaker, - the cutting edge radical screenwriter of the sixties and seventies who, in his twilight years, is now reduced to turning out lucrative, but generic, action scripts for Jerry Bruckheimer. [1036]

Thus has Towne not only entered the lexicon, but his elliptical career serves as a kind of parable or even a moral warning.

On a practical level, however, film is a medium of collaboration and the screenplay provides a template for production. As screenwriter Joan Didion points out,

> A finished picture defies all attempts to analyze what makes it work or not work: the responsibility for its every frame is clouded not only by the accidents and compromises of production but in the clauses of its financing ... to understand whose picture it is one needs to look not particularly at the script but at the deal memo. [1037]

A sadly limited number of screenwriters have committed their memories to paper and many of these are now unfortunately out of print; but many more writers' foreshortened anecdotes are currently preserved in Patrick McGilligan's invaluable *BACKSTORY* series of oral histories. [1038] These provide invaluable insights into the conditions governing the screenwriter's work situation, the deals done and the rationale behind many credit attributions.

Perhaps the best known contemporary memoir is William Goldman's *ADVENTURES IN THE SCREEN TRADE* in which his much misquoted aphorism, 'Nobody knows what movie will work,' has become a byword for insider industry stupidity. It is his statement 'Screenplays are Structure,' however, which has more pertinence for this particular study. [1039]

Authorship and the Screenplay

Authorship could be defined as, "an explicit way of assigning responsibility and giving credit for intellectual work." [1040] Eighteenth century critics were concerned with

---

[1036] Douglas Kennedy. *TEMPTATION*. London: Arrow Books, 2007, 221. The plot has Wanamaker defending the novel's protagonist against a charge of plagiarism, a charge which Towne himself was accused of more than once.

[1037] Joan Didion. *THE WHITE ALBUM*. London: Flamingo, 1993, 165.

[1038] Published by the University of California Press. Some of the writers who have preserved their experiences in print include Lenore Coffee, Frances Marion, Salka Viertel, Donald Ogden Stewart, Samuel Marx, Lester Cole, S.N.Behrman, Ben Hecht, Alvah Bessie, Garson Kanin, Howard Koch, Henry and Phoebe Ephron, Philip Dunne, John Gregory Dunne, William Goldman and Joe Eszterhas. A selection of excerpts from some of these works can be found in Sylvester (ed.) 1999.

[1039] William Goldman. *ADVENTURES IN THE SCREEN TRADE: A Personal View of Hollywood and Screenwriting*. Originally published 1983; rept, London: Warner Books, 1994, 195. Goldman capitalises the statement for emphasis. He claims that the auteur theory was responsible for the decline in quality of Alfred Hitchcock's output (103.) Robert Towne is namechecked as the script doctor who famously rewrote Goldman's own screen adaptation of his novel *MARATHON MAN* (245.)

[1040] President and Fellows of Harvard College, adapted from the paper version of *Faculty Policies on Integrity in Science*, 1996, Introduction.

the rules of rhetoric and the creativity of the author was at the centre of discourse: at the heart of all discussion was the making of meaning. Contradictions abound in this theoretical discourse due to the collaborative nature of the filmmaking medium, yet its convenience as a criterion of value supersedes any inherent contradictions in it as a tool of study.

As Maltby and Craven point out,

> Literary texts and paintings assert authorship as a principle of creativity. Hollywood's commercial aesthetics, on the other hand, not only advertises its products as being created by a multiplicity of personnel, but also concedes the authority to decide what a movie's content means to the individual viewer, who is provided with a host of opportunities to exercise that authority to maximize his or her pleasure from the movie. Within limits, Hollywood movies are constructed to accommodate, rather than predetermine, their audiences' reaction, and this has involved devising systems and codes of representation that permit a range of interpretations and a degree of instability of meaning. [1041]

The idea of authorship as an expression of the Romantic notion of the artist has a long history, albeit in literary media. In his account of the evolution of the Romantic idea, M.H. Abrams sums up the phenomenon in terms of 'Literature as a Revelation of Personality'. [1042]

Cinematically speaking, authorship as concept seeks to define cinema in terms of individual, personal aesthetics and vision – and, for reasons which will be outlined below, has usually been framed in terms of the careers of film directors. Essentially, its impact in terms of film criticism is to categorise film as part of an ongoing cinematic dialogue that a director is engaging in with his muse. It is true, however, that the screenwriter has not been entirely neglected. Indeed since Richard Corliss' *TALKING PICTURES* first appeared there have been biographies, oral histories (Patrick McGilligan's invaluable *BACKSTORY* series, published by the University of California) and a volume of literary biography devoted to the genus, not to mention several journals (*Creative Screenwriting*, *Scr(i)pt*, *Scenario* and *Written By*, the journal of the Writers' Guild of America (West).)

As previously stated, perhaps the only screenwriter to have been contractually guaranteed not just as much money as the director, but to have his screenplays shot

---

[1041] Richard Maltby and Ian Craven. *HOLLYWOOD CINEMA: An Introduction*. Oxford and Cambridge, USA: Blackwell Publishers, 1995, 43.

[1042] M.H. Abrams. *THE MIRROR AND THE LAMP: Romantic Theory and the Critical Condition*. Oxford: Oxford University Press, 1953, 226-256. In terms of a direct application of structure as a means of understanding artistic contributions to film, it is interesting to note the principles which the Rev. John Keble says characterize literary biography. Specifically in his own case, he sought to detect personality in the works of Greek and Roman Antiquity: The Canon of the Significant Theme; the Canon of Identification with the Hero; the Canon of Fervor; the Canon of Imagery and the Canon of Style (259-261). Abrams quotes Flaubert, who believed that, "The author in his work ought to be like God in the universe, present everywhere, and visible nowhere. Since art is a second nature, the creator of this nature ought to act in analogous ways, so that one may feel in all its atoms, and in every aspect, a hidden, infinite impassibleness." (262, from *Correspondence*, ed. Eugène Fasquelle (Paris: 1900, II, 155) [In the case of T.S. Eliot, he famously dismissed the significance of authorial biography when he referred to 'Shakespeare's laundry bills.']

exactly as written is Paddy Chayefsky. He didn't believe in collaboration unless it was intended to enhance his writing; he didn't think that becoming a director would help the screenwriter because he would lose his writing perspective. Despite his experience with *Altered States* (1980) his example remains the beacon for all screenwriters. [1043]

[1043] Chayefsky reportedly said, "The director is an assassin in terms of story. You have to stand ceaseless guard against the director's ambushes." Quoted by Joe Eszterhas. *HOLLYWOOD ANIMAL: A Memoir of Love and Betrayal.* New York: Random House, 2004, 41. However, Chayefsky did not attract what might be described as the best directors to his work – possibly because of the nature of his power in what has always been a collaborative medium

Appendix 2

<u>The Early Critics</u>

Azlant reminds us that, "it is belittlement, through avoidance or dismissal, that most often characterizes the treatment of screenwriting in early film theory." [1044] One of the reasons for this is, he says, "the scenario, being totally dependent on transformation into another medium for its perception as art, is incomplete." [1045]

Philip Lopate claims that

> One argumentative thread that ran through early film criticism was the attempt to justify the medium by defining its essence, singling out elements that seemed to make it unique. [1046]

American poet Vachel Lindsay was amongst the pioneers to seek out critical ground by which to discuss cinema as an art form. Lindsay's book is generally understood to be the first serious piece of film criticism and his unique contribution was his defence of film as art form, creating analogies between it and established forms such as painting and sculpture. [1047]

Hugo Münsterberg is perhaps the most significant of the early film theorists. Principally known for his significant contributions in the field of psychology rather than staking out aesthetic ground for cinema, although he sought to create an understanding of visual narrative's impact on the audience and could be said to have initiated reception theory as well as fielding questions about the transformation of reality. Cinema studies remained firmly based in the realm of the real until the 1960s and Munsterberg's own impact remained blunted by World War 1 yet his concern with cinema's moral influence continues to have ramifications today although he deprived the screenplay of any creative function in filmmaking. [1048]

Rudolf Arnheim's work was published in book form in 1932 and further examines the interstices between cinema's primacy as visual form and its representational possibilities, deriving from his scholarly work in gestalt psychology and visual perception. His work was important because he questioned the impact of sound technology on film aesthetics and inevitably his negative findings not only influenced filmmaking but criticism too, which was not to progress significantly for another twenty years. [1049]

[1044] Edward Azlant. *THE THEORY, HISTORY AND PRACTICE OF SCREENWRITING 1897-1920.* Unpublished doctoral dissertation at University of Wisconsin: 1980, 17.

[1045] Azlant. *Op.cit.*, 23.

[1046] Philip Lopate (ed.).*AMERICAN MOVIE CRITICS: An Anthology From The Silents Until Now.* New York: Library of America, 2006, xiv.

[1047] Lopate. *Op.cit.,* xiii.

[1048] Hugo Munsterberg. *THE PHOTOPLAY: A Psychological Study.* New York: Appleton, 1916; rept., New York: Dover, 1970.

[1049] Rudolf Arnheim. *FILM AS ART.* Berkeley: University of California Press, 1957. Maltby and Craven comment that "the movies' return to respectability began in the 1960s, and happened for a number of reasons," namely the emergence of television which replaced cinema as the moralists' bête noire; the growth in universities which necessitated new subjects; the vitality of

In 1937 Eric Rideout's *THE AMERICAN FILM* appeared, in which he stated,

In the final analysis it is to the director we look as the creative artist, as the unifying mind; the completed picture must be his personal interpretation of the theme.[1050]

This neglected work, which condensed a nation's cinema into the work of a chosen few directors, seems to predicate certain conditions for the work of Andrew Sarris decades later.

In terms of popular criticism, Lopate considers Otis Ferguson 'the first working critic who put everything together,' because

What Ferguson 'got,' while so many critics of his day were busy lamenting the low level of American movies, was the genius of the Hollywood system, the almost invisible craft and creativity of the average movie studio. [1051]

During and after World War II the writings of James Agee engaged in serious essay form with the potential of film for realism and a kind of morality within the aesthetic. While Agee was driven towards the documentary format, Robert Warshow attempted sociological readings of genre, most famously perhaps in his essay, 'The Gangster as Tragic Hero.' Both men were undoubtedly affected by the studies of Siegfried Kracauer.

We might see the emergence of a more content-based criticism in the work of Kracauer, who eventually compiled his work in *THEORY OF FILM*, published in 1960 and which concentrates on the still photograph.[1052] His masterpiece, *FROM CALIGARI TO HITLER*, written after he fled Nazi Germany, would underline the linkages between public fantasy and film nightmare. This focus on content would inevitably lead to a formalist response. [1053] The first voice perhaps to apply a painter's eye to film in this era was Manny Farber, who turned attention to directors such as Howard Hawks and Anthony Mann, before applying his modernist perspective to underground cinema.

British film criticism emerged in the pages of *Sequence*, edited by Gavin Lambert and Lindsay Anderson, whose commitment to the significance of everyday was proven in a series of landmark documentaries produced later in the decade. His article 'Stand Up! Stand Up!' challenged the complacency of British critics who adhered to the tenets of contemporary French criticism. [1054] Anderson wrote what might be described as an early

European art-house films; and, finally, the availability in translation of film theory from Europe. Maltby and Craven. *Op.cit.*, 420-421.

[1050] Eric Rideout. *THE AMERICAN FILM*. London: The Mitre Press, 1937, 2. Quoted in Koscarski, *ibid*.

[1051] Lopate. *Op. cit.*,xv.

[1052] Kracauer. *THEORY OF FILM: The Redemption of Physical Reality*. New York: Oxford University Press, 1960.

[1053] Kracauer. *FROM CALIGARI TO HITLER*. Princeton: Princeton University Press, 1947. He wrote, "It is my contention that through an analysis of the German films deep psychological dispositions in Germany from 1918 to 1933 can be exposed – dispositions which influenced the course of events during that time and which will have to be reckoned with in the post-Hitler era." Quoted in Lopate.*Op.cit.*,xvi.

[1054] Lindsay Anderson, 'Stand Up! Stand Up!' *Sight and Sound*, Autumn 1956; reprinted in

version of author-structuralism in his essay on *They Were Expendable*, directed by John Ford, stating that it:

> ... illuminate[s Ford] films which came before it and reveal[s] qualities in them which may up to now have gone unremarked. In this recognisable patterns emerge from the rather baffling diversity of Ford's films. [1055]

Movie would be published from May 1962, born out of a reaction against *Sight & Sound*, and including amongst its editors and contributors the likes of V.F. Perkins, Ian Cameron and Robin Wood and nailing its auteurist colours to the mast by declaring Howard Hawks and Alfred Hitchcock 'great,' while ranking the likes of Anthony Mann and Vincente Minnelli 'brilliant'.[1056] *Movie* also prided itself on close analysis of the films reviewed and in this way distinguished itself from *Cahiers*, being more or less associated with Leavisite principles and the Romantic tradition. However it never truly elaborated its philosophy at a theoretical level although maintaining a critical distance from the excesses of *Cahiers* and accommodating the possibility that effective authorship could lie outside the role of the director. [1057]

V.F. Perkins reluctantly admits, that "in outline, at least, the shape of a picture is controlled by the construction of its script." [1058]

Acknowledgements:

Thanks to Professor Charles Barr for the Ian Cameron article.

Anderson (edited by Paul Ryan). *NEVER APOLOGISE: The Collected Writings*. London: Plexus, 2004, 218-232.

[1055] Lindsay Anderson, '*They Were Expendable* and John Ford,' *Sequence*, No. 11: 1.

[1056] Pauline Kael declared that "if the editors of *Movie* ranked authors the way they do directors, Dostoyevsky would probably be in that almost untouchable category of the 'ambitious'." She dismissed the journal as "an intellectual club for the intellectually handicapped." Kael, 'Circles and Squares,' as before, 295; 310.

[1057] An early article by Ian Cameron typifies *Movie*'s purpose: "On the whole we accept this cinema of directors, although without going to the farthest-out extremes of *la politique des auteurs* which makes it difficult to think of a bad director making a good film and almost impossible to think of a good director making a bad one. ... provided he has any talent, it is the director, rather than anyone else, who determines what finally appears on the screen. The great weakness of *la politique des auteurs* is its rigidity: its adherents tend to be, as they say, totally committed to a cinema of directors. There are, however, quite a few films whose authors are not their directors. The various film versions of Paddy Chayefsky's works are all primarily Chayefsky movies rather than Delbert Mann, or John Cromwell, or even Richard Brooks movies. Given a weak director the effective author of a film can be its photographer ..., composer ..., producer..., or star..." Ian Cameron, 'Films, Directors and Critics,' *Movie*, No.2, September 1962: 4-7. Other than Chayefsky, it appears that *Movie* did not rate the screenwriter very highly, however. Perkins' *FILM AS FILM* simplifies the authorship problem when he states, "A film may have its own unity, with its relationships coherent and its balance precise. But that the ultimate unity can be entirely foreseen is a dubious proposition: the distance between conception and delivery is so great, and the path between them so tortuous and unpredictable." V.F. Perkins. *FILM AS FILM: Understanding and Judging Movies*, London: Pelican, 1972, 160.

[1058] Perkins. *Op.cit.*, 179.

Appendix 3

<u>Letter from Hal Ashby to Robert Towne 24 November, 1971</u>

I understand the theme of the picture to be about responsibility, the same type of 'brother's keeper' problem that is raised in Hemingway's The Killers. It is a unique look at responsibility since the principals are sailors and sailors... (as ideas) seem to avoid responsibility. There's something exhilarating – almost lyrically so – about leaving port and coming into port. Left behind are land responsibilities: wives, taxes, landbound folk who haven't experienced the initiation of sunrises and sunsets at sea, the weathering of high seas, the sense of being over deep water, the experiences that set the navy apart from other services.

No one is saying that sailors are walking Keats, but my experiences with them has shown a great pride... in the navy which may be great part drudgery but also great part emotionally unique.

What I'm saying is that the experience at sea gives the sailor a life apart from land responsibilities (it also affords a chance for some rough poetry which I'd like to see come into the screenplay, not in the idiom or [sic] Arthur Miller but more in the idiom of Steinbeck. There's something of the arrested adolescent to the sailor. Grab ass, the constant[sic] promise of new ports and a good time and a few laughs --- these become almost moral absolutes for a sailor. When Mule says (p. 73) that he can't have a good time. It ain't in him," I sense great pity from Mule as though the kid had failed the ultimate proof of being alive. What else ultimately is there but time in, a clean record, new ports and a good time? That's a question Billy is forced to ask in *Detail* and it makes him miserable.

Acknowledgements:
Courtesy of The Hal Ashby files at the Margaret Herrick Library, AMPAS.

.

Primary Sources

The Creature from the Haunted Sea (VHS) Hollywood Select

The Last Woman on Earth VHS) Sinister Cinema

The Chameleon VHS) MGM/UA Video
The Chameleon teleplay for *The Outer Limits* (story 39) written by Robert Towne.

The Dove Affair TX: TG4 July 2005
The Dove Affair teleplay for *The Man from U.N.C.L.E.* written by Robert Towne.

The Tomb of Ligeia TX: BBC TV

Bonnie and Clyde file kindly supplied by the Warner Bros. archive at the University of Southern California. This included the production history of the film, each draft of the screenplay and shooting script and studio memos. *There is no mention of Robert Towne.* I read the transcripts of Robert Towne's 22 January 1975 interview at the American Film Institute at the Louis B. Mayer Library, AFI in November 2003.

The Godfather by Mario Puzo and Francis Ford Coppola. Date unknown.

THE LAST DETAIL by Darryl Ponicsan
(New York: Signet Books, 1971)
The Last Detail screenplay by Robert Towne. Undated draft; the revised first draft (undated) in a copy in the Ashby Collection embossed with 'HAL' and 'Acrobat Films.' The first page bears what is presumably the production number of the film, 8986. This draft runs to 131 pages, with all the revisions dated 15 August.

Chinatown by Robert Towne, First draft, undated, pp. 180. This is the only draft held at by the James R. Webb Memorial Library at the Writers' Guild of America, West, Los Angeles where it is incorrectly labelled by hand 'Polanski Rewrite' as of November 2003.
Chinatown by Robert Towne, Undated draft, labelled pp.153. I read this at the Louis B. Mayer Library in the American Film Institute in November 2003. This is the draft written for Roman Polanski as director ie the Second Draft. It is also at the Margaret Herrick Library, AMPAS, again unlabelled, as of November 2003.
Chinatown by Robert Towne, Second Draft, dated 07 September 1973, pp. 152. I acquired this on Hollywood Boulevard. It is almost identical to the shooting draft and the number 3 is handwritten and circled on it.
Chinatown by Robert Towne, Third Draft, dated 09 October 1973, pp. 145. This has long been in the public domain.
CHINATOWN/THE LAST DETAIL by Robert Towne. New York: Grove Press, 1997. The published version of both screenplays with a foreword by Towne.

Shampoo screenplay by Robert Towne and Warren Beatty. Undated draft.
'The Country Wife' by William Wycherley in *THE PLAYS OF WILLIAM WYCHERLEY*, edited by Peter Holland. Cambridge: Cambridge University Press, 1981)

The Yakuza Draft by Robert Towne, dated 18 December 1973. This is the only draft available and it appears to be the one referred to by Paul Schrader *in* 'Yakuza-Eiga,' possibly for legal reasons imposed by the studio.

Greystoke by Robert Towne (aka P.H. Vazak), dated 04 August 1977. Incomplete version.

Personal Best by Robert Towne dated 22 February 1980.

The Mermaid by Robert Towne dated 24 September 1983.

Eight Million Ways to Die by Oliver Stone. Undated.
Eight Million Ways to Die by Oliver Stone. Revised, 01 November 1984.
Eight Million Ways to Die by Oliver Stone. Revised, March 1985.
Eight Million Ways to Die by Oliver Stone. Revised, 22 April 1985. By Hal Ashby?
Eight Million Ways to Die by Oliver Stone & David Lee Henry. Revised, May 1985.
Eight Million Ways to Die by Robert Towne, August 1985 (early pages are variously marked 15 and 30 July)
EIGHT MILLION WAYS TO DIE by Lawrence Block
A STAB IN THE DARK by Lawrence Block
'Easy Does It,' by Robert Towne, Folder No. 225, Hal Ashby File, AMPAS.
Step Outlines by Robert Towne. Undated.
Production notes, script drafts and two step outlines (undated), credited to Robert Towne, were read at the Hal Ashby File in Special Collections at the Margaret Herrick Library of the Academy Foundation at La Cienega Boulevard, Beverly Hills, November 2003.

The Two Jakes by Robert Towne, dated December 1988 (this is the revised version following the aborted 1985 production based on Towne's previous script, TWO JAKES, 1984.) A copy of the first version could not be located.

Tequila Sunrise shooting script by Robert Towne, dated 14 January 1988. The cover indicates that there were 12 revisions, the first dated 08 February 88, the last is recorded on 04 March 88.

Days of Thunder by Robert Towne, First Draft. Dated 20 November 1989.

The Firm screenplay by Robert Towne & David Rayfiel, 02 November 1992. Based on the novel by John Grisham.

Mission: Impossible shooting draft, revised by Robert Towne, 16 August 1995.

Without Limits (Pre) shooting draft by Kenny Moore & Robert Towne, 02 July 1996.

Mission: Impossible 2 by Robert Towne. Revised 04 December 1999.

FILMOGRAPHY

The Creature from the Haunted Sea (1960) The Filmgroup R/T: 76 mins
Screenplay by: Charles B. Griffith
Director: Roger Corman and Monte Hellman
Producer: Roger Corman.
Director of Photography: Jacques Marquette
Film Editor: Angela Scellars
Music: Fred Katz.
Cast: Antony Carbone (Renzo Capeto), Betsy Jones-Moreland (Mary-Belle), Edward Wain [Robert Towne] (Sparks Moran), Edmundo Rivera Alvarez (Colonel Tostada), Robert Bean (Jack), Sonya Noemi (Mango), Beach Dickerson.

The Last Woman on Earth (1960) The Filmgroup R/T: 71 mins
Screenplay: Robert Towne
Director: Roger Corman
Director of Photography: Jacques Marquette
Film Editor: Anthony Carras
Art Director: Floyd Crosby
Music: Ronald Stein.
Cast: Antony Carbone (Harold), Betsy Jones-Moreland (Evelyn), Edward Wain [aka Robert Towne](Martin)

My Daddy Can Lick Your Daddy (1962) (TV episode for *The Lloyd Bridges Show*) R/T: 22mins
Screenplay: Robert Towne
Director: John Cassavetes
Cast: Lloyd Bridges, Leila Goldoni, Gary Lockwood

The Young Racers (1963)
Screenplay: R. Wright Campbell
Director: Roger Corman
Producer: Roger Corman
Director of Photography: Floyd Crosby
Film Editor: Ronald Sinclair
Music: Les Baxter
Second Assistant Director: Robert Towne
Cast: Mark Damon, William Campbell, Luana Anders, Patrick Magee

The Lloyd Bridges Show (1963) TV episodes: 'A Personal Matter' (teleplay by Robert Towne); 'My Daddy Can Beat Your Daddy' (teleplay by Robert Towne)

Breaking Point (1964) TV episode: 'So Many Pretty Girls, So Little Time' (teleplay by Robert Towne)

The Outer Limits (1964) TV episode: '*The Chameleon*' (teleplay by Robert Towne)

The Man From U.N.C.L.E. (1964) TV episode: '*The Dove Affair*' (teleplay by Robert Towne)

The Tomb of Ligeia (1964)[aka: Tomb of the Cat/] 7,296 feet. A Roger Corman Production for American International Pictures. R/T: 82 mins
Screenplay: Robert Towne from Edgar Allan Poe
Producer/Director: Roger Corman
Director of Photography: Arthur Grant
Film Editor: Alfred Cox

Art Director: Colin Southcott
Music: Kenneth V. Jones.
Cast: Vincent Price (Verden Fell), Elizabeth Shepherd (The Lady Rowena/The Lady Ligeia), John Westbrook (Christopher Gough), Derek Francis (Lord Trevanion), Oliver Johnston (Kenrick)

A Time for Killing aka *The Long Ride Home* (1967) (Columbia Pictures Corporation) R/T: 88 mins
Screenplay: Nelson Wolford & Shirley Wolford and Halsted Welles; [Robert Towne - uncredited] from the novel THE SOUTHERN BLADE
Director: Phil Karlson [Roger Corman - uncredited]
Producer: Harry Joe Brown
Director of Photography: Kenneth Peach
Film Editor: Roy Livingston
Music: Mundell Lowe
Cast: Inger Stevens, Glenn Ford, Paul Petersen, Timothy Carey, Kenneth Tobey

Bonnie and Clyde (1967)(Tatira-Hiller Productions; Warners) R/T: 111 mins
Writer: David Newman & Robert Benton [Robert Towne – uncredited]
Special Consultant: Robert Towne
Director: Arthur Penn
Producer: Warren Beatty
Director of Photography: Burnett Guffey
Film Editor: Dede Allen
Music: Charles Strouse
Cast: Warren Beatty, Faye Dunaway, Michael J. Pollard, Gene Hackman, Estelle Parsons, Denver Pyle, Gene Wilder, Dub Taylor.

Villa Rides ! (1968) (Paramount Pictures) R/T: 125 mins
Screenplay: Robert Towne and Sam Peckinpah, based on the book *PANCHO VILLA* by William Douglas Lansford;
Director: Buzz Kulik
Producer: Ted Richmond
Director of Photography: Jack Hildyard
Film Editor: David Bretherton
Music: Maurice Jarre.
Cast: Yul Brynner, Robert Mitchum, Charles Bronson, Herbert Lom, Jill Ireland, Robert Towne.

Drive, He Said (1971) (BBS/Columbia) R/T: 95 mins
Screenplay: Jack Nicholson and Jeremy Larner, based on the novel by Larner [Terence Malick, Robert Towne - uncredited]
Director: Jack Nicholson
Producer: Steve Blauner, Jack Nicholson
Director of Photography: Bill Butler
Film Editor: Donn Cambern, Christopher Holmes, Pat Somerset, Robert L. Wolfe
Music: David Shire
Cast: William Tepper, Karen Black, Michael Margotta, Bruce Dern, Robert Towne

The Zodiac Killer (1971) R/T: 85 mins
Screenplay: Ray Cantrell and Manny Cardoza
Director: Tom Hanson
Cast: Hal Reed, Bob Jones, Ray Lynch, Tom Pittman, Robert Towne (Man in Bar No. 3)

Cisco Pike (1972) (Acrobat Productions) R/T: 94 mins
Screenplay: Bill L. Norton [Robert Towne - uncredited]
Director: Bill L. Norton
Producer: Gerald Ayres

Director of Photography: Vilis Lapenieks
Film Editor: Robert C. Jones
Music: Kris Kristofferson
Cast: Kris Kristofferson, Karen Black, Gene Hackman, Harry Dean Stanton, Viva, Joy Bang

The Godfather (1972) (Paramount) R/T: 171 mins
Screenplay: Mario Puzo, Francis Ford Coppola [Robert Towne - uncredited]
Director: Francis Ford Coppola
Producer: Albert S. Ruddy
Director of Photography: Gordon Willis
Film Editor: William Reynolds, Peter Zinner
Music: Nino Rota.
Cast: Marlon Brando, Al Pacino, Robert Duvall, Diane Keaton, James Caan

The New Centurions (1972) (Chartoff-Winkler Productions) R/T: 103 mins
Screenplay: Stirling Silliphant, adapted from the novel by Joseph Wambaugh [Robert Towne -
uncredited]
Director: Richard Fleischer
Producer: Robert Chartoff, Irwin Winkler
Director of Photography: Ralph Woolsey
Film Editor: Robert C. Jones
Music: Quincy Jones
Cast: George C. Scott, Stacy Keach, Jane Alexander, Scott Wilson, Rosalind Cash, Erik Estrada

The Last Detail (1973) (Acrobat/Columbia Pictures) R/T: 103 mins
Screenplay: Robert Towne, from the novel by Darryl Ponicsan
Director: Hal Ashby
Producer: Gerald Ayres
Associate Producer: Charles Mulvehill
Director of Photography: Michael Chapman.
Film editor: Robert C. Jones
Music: Johnny Mandel
Cast: Jack Nicholson (Billy 'Bad Ass' Buddusky), Otis Young, Randy Quaid, Carol Kane

The Parallax View (1974)(Columbia) R/T: 102 mins
Screenplay: Lawrence Giler and Lorenzo Semple, Jr from the novel by Loren Singer [Robert
Towne - uncredited]
Director: Alan J. Pakula
Producer: Alan J. Pakula
Director of Photography: Gordon Willis
Film Editor: John W. Wheeler
Music: Michael Small
Cast: Warren Beatty, Hume Cronyn, William Daniels Paula Prentiss

Chinatown (1974)(Paramount) R/T: 130 mins
Story and Screenplay: Robert Towne
Director: Roman Polanski
Producer: Robert Evans
Director of Photography: John A. Alonzo
Film Editor: Sam O'Steen
Production Designer: Richard Sylbert
Art Director: W. Steward Campbell
Costume Designer: Anthea Sylbert
Music: Jerry Goldsmith
Cast: Jack Nicholson (Jake Gittes), Faye Dunaway (Evelyn Mulwray), John Huston (Noah Cross)

Shampoo (1975) (Columbia Pictures) R/T: 112 mins
Screenplay: Robert Towne and Warren Beatty
Director: Hal Ashby
Producer: Warren Beatty
Director of Photography: Laszlo Kovacs
Film Editor: Robert C. Jones
Production Designer: Richard Sylbert
Music: Paul Simon
Cast: Warren Beatty (George Roundy), Julie Christie (Jackie), Goldie Hawn (Jill), Lee Grant
(Felicia Karpf), Jack Warden (Lester Karpf), Carrie Fisher (Lorna Karpf)

The Yakuza (aka *Brotherhood of the Yakuza*) (1975) (Warners) R/T: 112 mins
Screenplay: Robert Towne based on a story by Leonard Schrader
Director: Sydney Pollack
Producer: Sydney Pollack
Director of Photography: Duke Callaghan, Kozo Okazaki
Film Editor: Don Guidice, Thomas Stanford
Music: Dave Grusin
Cast: Robert Mitchum (Tanner), Takakura Ken (Ken), Brian Keith

The Missouri Breaks (1976) (United Artists) R/T: 126 mins
Screenplay: Thomas McGuane [Robert Towne - uncredited]
Director: Arthur Penn
Producers: Elliot Kastner and Robert M.Sherman
Director of Photography: Michael Butler
Film Editor: Dede Allen, Jerry Greenberg, Stephen A. Rotter
Music: John Williams.
Cast: Jack Nicholson, Marlon Brando, Randy Quaid, Mary Steenburgen

Marathon Man (1976) R/T: 125 mins
Screenplay: William Goldman, from his novel [Robert Towne - uncredited]
Director: John Schlesinger
Producer: Sidney Beckerman, Robert Evans
Director of Photography: Conrad Hall
Film Editor: Jim Clark
Music: Michael Small
Cast: Dustin Hoffman, Laurence Olivier, Roy Schneider, William Devane, Marthe Keller

Orca – Killer Whale (aka ORCA) (1977) (Paramount) R/T: 92 mins
Screenplay & Story: Luciano Vincenzoni and Sergio Donati [Robert Towne - uncredited]
Director: Michael Anderson
Producer: Luciano Vincenzoni
Director of Photography: J. Barry Herron, Ted Moore
Film Editor: John Bloom, Marion Rothman, Ralph E. Winters
Music: Ennio Morricone.
Cast: Richard Harris, Charlotte Rampling, Will Sampson, Bo Derek, Keenan Wynn

Heaven Can Wait (1978) (Paramount Pictures) R/T:100 mins
Screenplay: Elaine May and Warren Beatty, from the play by Henry Segall [Robert Towne - uncredited]
Director: Warren Beatty and Buck Henry
Producer: Warren Beatty
Director of Photography: William L. Fraker
Film Editor: Robert C. Jones, Don Zimmerman
Music: Dave Grusin

Cast: Warren Beatty, Julie Christie, Jack Warden, Dyan Cannon, James Mason, Charles Grodin, Buck Henry

Reds (1981) (Barclays Mercantile Industrial Finance, JRS, Paramount Pictures)R/T: 200 mins
Screenplay: Warren Beatty & Trevor Griffiths [Robert Towne, Elaine May & Peter Feibleman - uncredited]
Director: Warren Beatty
Producer: Warren Beatty
Director of Photography: Vittorio Storaro
Film Editor: Dede Allen, Craig McKay
Music: Stephen Sondheim
Cast: Warren Beatty, Diane Keaton, Edward Herrmann, Jerzy Kosinski, Jack Nicholson, Paul Sorvino, Maureen Stapleton, Nicolas Coster, Gene Hackman

Personal Best (1982) (Geffen Company for Warners) 11,403 feet. R/T: 126 mins
Screenplay: Robert Towne
Director: Robert Towne
Producer: Robert Towne
Executive producer: David Geffen
Executive associate: Edward M. Taylor
Director of Photography: Michael Chapman
Film Editor: Jacqueline Cambas, Jere Huggins, Ned Humphreys, Walt Mulconery, Bud S. Smith
Music: Jill Fraser, Jack Nitzsche
Cast: Mariel Hemingway (Chris Cahill), Scott Glenn (Terry Tingloff), Patrice Donnelly (Tori Skinner), Kenny Moore (Denny Stites)

Deal of the Century (1983)(Dream Quest Images) R/T: 99 mins
Screenplay: Paul Brickman, from the book by Bernard Edelman [Robert Towne, Robert Garland – uncredited]
Director: William Friedkin
Producer: Bud Yorkin
Director of Photography: Richard H. Kline
Film Editor: Jere Huggins, Ned Humphreys, Bud S. Smith
Music: Arthur B. Rubinstein
Cast: Chevy Chase, Sigourney Weaver, Gregory Hines, Vince Edwards

Greystoke: The Legend of Tarzan, Lord of the Apes (1984) (Edgar Rice Burroughs Inc. through Warners) R/T: 130 mins
Screenplay: Michael Austin. (Based on the original screenplay by Robert Towne, credited as P.H. Vazak)
Director: Hugh Hudson
Producer: Stanley S. Canter, Hugh Hudson
Director of Photography: John Alcott
Film Editor: Anne V. Coates
Music: John Scott
Cast: Ralph Richardson, Ian Holm, James Fox, Christopher Lambert, Andie McDowell

Swing Shift (1984) (Warner Bros. Pictures) R/T: 100 mins
Screenplay: 'Rob Morton' aka Nancy Dowd [Bo Goldman, Ron Nyswaner, Robert Towne - uncredited]
Director: Jonathan Demme
Producer: Jerry Bick
Director of Photography: Tak Fujimoto
Film Editor: Gib Jaffe, Craig McKay
Music: Patrick Williams

Cast: Goldie Hawn, Kurt Russell, Christine Lahti, Ed Harris, Fred Ward, Sudie Bond, Holly Hunter, Patty Maloney, Roger Corman.

8 Million Ways to Die (1985) (Fox) R/T: 115 mins
Screenplay: Oliver Stone & David Lee Henry [Robert Towne - uncredited]
Director: Hal Ashby
Producer: Steve Roth
Director of Photography: Stephen H. Burum
Film Editor: Robert Lawrence and Stuart Pappé
Music: James Newton Howard.
Cast: Jeff Bridges, Rosanna Arquette, Alexandra Paul, Randy Brooks, Andy Garcia

The Bedroom Window (1987) (De Laurentiis Entertainment Group) R/T: 113 mins
Screenplay: Curtis Hanson from a novel by Anne Holden (*THE WITNESSES*)
Director: Curtis Hanson
Producer: Robert Towne, Martha Schumacher
Director of Photography: Gilbert Taylor
Film Editor: Scott Conrad
Music: Patrick Gleeson, Michael Shrieve, Felix Mendelessohn.
Cast: Steve Guttenberg, Isabelle Huppert

The Pick-Up Artist (1987) (Amercent Films) R/T: 81 mins
Screenplay: James Toback [Robert Towne - uncredited]
Director: James Toback
Producer: David Leigh McLeod
Executive Producer: Warren Beatty
Director of Photography: Gordon Willis
Film Editor: David Bretherton, Angeo Corrao
Music: Georges Delerue
Cast: Molly Ringwald, Robert Downey, Jr., Robert Towne

Fatal Attraction (1987) (Paramount Pictures) R/T: 119 mins
Screenplay: James Dearden [Nicholas Meyer, Robert Towne - uncredited]
Director: Adrian Lyne
Producer: Stanley R. Jaffe, Sherry Lansing
Director of Photography: Howard Atherton
Film Editor: Michael Kahn
Music: Maurice Jarre
Cast: Michael Douglas, Glenn Close, Anne Archer

Tough Guys Don't Dance (1987) (Golan-Globus Productions) R/T: 110 mins
Screenplay: Norman Mailer from his novel [Robert Towne - uncredited]
Director: Norman Mailer
Producer: Yoram Globus and Menahem Golan
Director of Photography: Mike Moyer (and John Bailey, uncredited)
Film Editor: Debra McDermott
Music: Angelo Badalamenti
Cast: Ryan O'Neal, Isabella Rossellini, Debra Sandlund, Wings Hauser, Lawrence Tierney

Frantic (1988) (Warner Bros.) R/T: 120 mins
Screenplay: Roman Polanski & Gerard Brach [Jeff Gross, Robert Towne - uncredited]
Director: Roman Polanski
Producer: Tim Hampton, Thom Mount
Director of Photography: Witold Sobocinski
Film Editor: Sam O. Steen
Music: Ennio Morricone

Cast: Harrison Ford, Emmanuelle Seigner, Betty Buckley, Djiby Soumare.

Tequila Sunrise (1988) (Warners) R/T: 116 mins
Writer/Director: Robert Towne
Producer: Thom Mount
Director of Photography: Conrad L. Hall
Film Editor: Claire Simpson
Art Direction: Richard Sylbert
Music: Dave Grusin.
Cast: Mel Gibson (Dale 'Mac' McKussic), Michelle Pfeiffer (Jo Ann Vallenari),Kurt Russell (Det. Lt. Nicholas 'Nick' Frescia), Raul Julia (Carlos/Commandante Xavier Escalante), Arliss Howard (Gregg Lindroff), Arye Gross (Andy Leonard), J.T. Walsh (DEA Agent Hal Maguire), Ann Magnuson (Shaleen McKussic).

Little Nemo: *Adventures in Slumberland* (1989) (TMS/Hemdale) R/T: 85 mins
Screenplay: Winsor McKay and Ray Bradbury and Chris Columbus; story by Yutaka Fujioka and Jean Giraud [Richard Outten, Edward Summer - uncredited]
Story Consultant: Robert Towne
Director: Masami Hata, William T. Hurtz
Producer: Yutaka Fujioka
Music: Thomas Chase, Steve Rucker
Cast: Mickey Rooney, Rene Auberjonois, Bever-Leigh Banfield

The Two Jakes (1990) (Paramount) R/T: 137 mins
Screenplay: Robert Towne
Director: Jack Nicholson
Producers: Robert Evans and Harold Schneider
Director of Photography: Vilmos Zsigmond
Film Editor: Anne Goursaud
Music: Van Dyke Parks.
Cast: Jack Nicholson (Jake Gittes), Harvey Keitel (Jake Berman), Meg Tilly (Kitty Berman), Madeleine Stowe (Lillian Bodine), Eli Wallach (Cotton Weinberger), Richard Farnsworth (Earl Rawley)

Days of Thunder (1990) (Paramount) R/T: 108 mins
Screenplay: Tom Cruise, Robert Towne, from a story by Towne and Tom Cruise
Director: Tony Scott
Producer: Jerry Bruckheimer and Don Simpson
Director of Photography: Ward Russell
Film Editor: Robert C. Jones
Music: Hans Zimmer.
Cast: Tom Cruise (Cole Trickle), Robert Duvall (Harry Hogge), Randy Quaid, Nicole Kidman (Dr Claire Lewicki), Cary Elwes (Tim Daland), Michael Rooker (Rowdy Burns), Fred Dalton Thompson (Big John), John C. Reilly (Buck Bretherton).

The Firm (1993)(Warner Bros) R/T: 151 mins
Screenplay: David Rabe and Robert Towne & David Rayfiel, adapted from the novel by John Grisham
Director: Sydney Pollack
Director of Photography: John Seale
Film Editor: Frederic Steinkamp and William Steinkamp
Music: Dave Grusin.
Cast: Tom Cruise (Mitch McDeere), Jeanne Tripplehorn (Abby McDeere), Gene Hackman (Avey Tolar), Holly Hunter (Tammy Hemphill), Ed Harris (Wayne Tarrance)

Love Affair (1994) (Warners) R/T: 108 mins
Screenplay: Warren Beatty and Robert Towne
Director: Glenn Gordon Caron
Producer: Warren Beatty
Director of Photography: Conrad L. Hall
Film Editor: Robert C. Jones
Music: Ennio Morricone.
Cast: Warren Beatty, Annette Bening, Katharine Hepburn, Garry Shandling, Chloe Webb

Crimson Tide (1995) (Don Simpson/Jerry Bruckheimer Films) R/T: 115 mins
Screenplay: Michael P. Henrick from the story by Richard Schiffer and Michael P. Henrick
[Quentin Tarantino, Robert Towne - uncredited]
Director: Tony Scott
Producer: Jerry Bruckheimer and Don Simpson
Director of Photography: Dariusz Wolski
Film Editor: Chris Lebenzon
Music: Hans Zimmer
Cast: Denzel Washington, Gene Hackman, Matt Craven, George Dzundza, Viggo Mortensen

Mission: Impossible (1996) (Cruise/Wagner Productions, released by Warners) R/T: 110 mins
Screenplay: David Koepp and Robert Towne; story by David Koepp and Steven Zaillian; from
the television series created by Bruce Geller
Director: Brian De Palma
Producer: Tom Cruise, Paula Wagner
Director of Photography: Stephen H. Burum
Film Editor: Paul Hirsch
Music: Danny Elfman
Cast: Tom Cruise (Ethan Hunt), Jon Voight (Jim Phelps), Emmanuelle Béart (Claire Phelps),
Henry Czerny (Eugene Kittridge), Jean Reno (Franz Krieger), Ving Rhames (Luther Stickell)

Con Air (1997) (Touchstone Pictures) R/T: 115 mins
Screenplay: Scott Rosenberg [Robert Towne – uncredited]
Director: Simon West
Producer: Jerry Bruckheimer
Director of Photography: David Tattersall
Film Editor: Chris Lebenzon, Steve Mirkovich, Glen Scantlebury
Music: Mark Mancina, Trevor Ragin
Cast: Nicolas Cage, John Cusack, John Malkovich, Ving Rhames, Nick Chinlund, Steve Buscemi

Enemy of the State (1998) (Touchstone Pictures) R/T: 132/140 mins
Screenplay: David Marconi [Robert Towne – uncredited]
Director: Tony Scott
Producer: Jerry Bruckheimer
Director of Photography: Daniel Mindel
Film Editor: Chris Lebenzon
Music: Harry Gregson-Williams, Trevor Rabin
Cast: Will Smith, Gene Hackman, Jon Voight, Lisa Bonet, Regina King, Loren Dean

Armageddon (1998) (Touchstone Pictures) R/T: 151 mins
Screenplay: Jonathan Hensleigh and J.J. Abrams ; story : Robert Roy Pool and Jonathan
Hensleigh ; adaptation : Tony Gilroy and Shane Salerno [Robert Towne - uncredited]
Director: Michael Bay
Producer: Jerry Bruckheimer and Don Simpson
Director of Photography: John Schwartzman
Film Editor: Mark Goldblatt, Chris Lebenzon, Glen Scantlebury
Music: Trevor Rabin

Cast: Bruce Willis, Billy Bob Thornton, Ben Affleck, Liv Tyler,

Without Limits (1998)(A Cruise/Wagner production, released by Warner Bros.) R/T: 117 mins
PG-13, for brief sexual material and brief strong language.
Screenplay: Robert Towne and Kenny Moore
Director: Robert Towne
Producers: Tom Cruise, Paula Wagner
Executive producers Jonathan Sanger, Kenny Moore
Director of Photography: Conrad L. Hall
Film Editors Claire Simpson, Robert K. Lambert
Production design: William Creber
Art director: William Durrell
Costumes: Grania Preston
Music: Randy Miller.
Cast: Billy Crudup (Steve Prefontaine), Donald Sutherland (Bill Bowerman), Monica Potter (Mary Marckx), Jeremy Sisto (Frank Shorter), Matthew Lillard, Billy Burke, Dean Norris, Judith Ivey, Katharine Towne.

M:I II (2000) (Cruise/Wagner Productions, released by Warners) R/T: 126 mins
Screenplay: Robert Towne; story by Ronald D. Moore and Brannon Braga
Director: John Woo
Producer: Tom Cruise
Director of Photography: Jeffrey L. Kimball
Film Editor: Steven Kemper, Christian Wagner
Music: Hans Zimmer
Cast: Tom Cruise (Ethan Hunt), Thandie Newton (Nyah Nordoff Hall), Dougray Scott (Sean Ambrose), Ving Rhames (Luther Stickell), Richard Roxburgh (Hugh Stamp)

Television Resources:
American Desperadoes (BBC TV, 1997)
The Curse of Corman (BBC TV, 1990)
Filmworks: Chinatown (BBC TV, 1993)
The Celluloid Closet (1993)
Scene By Scene With Roman Polanski (BBC TV, 2000)
Writing Chinatown (BBC TV, 1997)

BIBLIOGRAPHY

Books:

Abrams, M.H.. *THE MIRROR AND THE LAMP*: Romantic Theory and the Critical Condition. Oxford:
Oxford University Press,1953.
Academy of Motion Picture Arts & Sciences and the Writers Guild of America, West. *WHO WROTE THE MOVIE AND WHAT ELSE DID HE WRITE? An Index of Screen Writers and their Film Works 1936-1969*. Los Angeles: 1970.
Allen, Richard and Murray Smith (eds.). *FILM THEORY AND PHILOSOPHY*. Oxford: Clarendon Press, 1997.
Alvarez, Al. *THE WRITER'S VOICE*. London: Bloomsbury, 2005.
Amburn, Ellis. *THE SEXIEST MAN ALIVE: A Biography of Warren Beatty*. New York: Harper, 2002.
AMERICAN SCREENWRITERS Edited by Randall Clark, Robert Morsberger and Stephen O. Lesser:
DICTIONARY OF LITERARY BIOGRAPHY Vol 26 . Gale, Detroit: 1984; 2nd ser.: 1986.
Gale, Detroit: 1984; 2nd ser.: 1986
DICTIONARY OF LITERARY BIOGRAPHY Vol. 44: AMERICAN SCREENWRITERS.
Amis, Kingsley. *THE JAMES BOND DOSSIER*. London: Pan Books, 1965.
Anderson, Lindsay (edited by Paul Ryan). *NEVER APOLOGISE: The Collected Writings*. London: Plexus, 2004.
Andrew, Dudley. *CONCEPTS IN FILM THEORY*. New York: Oxford University Press, 1984.
Andrew, Geoff. *THE FILM HANDBOOK*. Essex: Longman, 1989.
Aristotle. *ON THE ART OF POETRY*. Translated by Ingram Bywater with a Preface by Gilbert Murray. Oxford: Oxford University Press, 1920.
_____ . *POETICS*. Translated with an introduction and notes by Malcolm Heath. London: Penguin, 1996.
Auden, W.H.. *THE DYER'S HAND And Other Essay*. London: Faber & Faber, 1963.
Auiler, Dan. *HITCHCOCK'S NOTEBOOKS: An Authorized and Illustrated Look Inside the Creative Mind of Alfred Hitchcock*. New York: Avon Books Inc., 1999.
Bach, Stephen. *FINAL CUT: Dreams and Disaster in the Making of 'Heaven's Gate'*. London: Faber and Faber, 1985.
Bal, Mieke. *NARRATOLOGIE: essai sur la significations narrative dans quatre romans moderns*. Paris : Klincksieck, 1977.
Balio, Tino. *THE AMERICAN FILM INDUSTRY (Revised)*. University of Wisconsin Press: 1976, 1985.
Barr, Charles. *VERTIGO*. London: British Film Institute, 2002.
_____ . *ENGLISH HITCHCOCK*. Scotland: Cameron Books, 2000.
Barthes, Roland. *IMAGE MUSIC TEXT*. New York: Hill and Wang, 1978.
_____ . *MYTHOLOGIES*. London: Paladin, 1983.
Baxter, John. *SCIENCE FICTION IN THE CINEMA*. New York: A.S. Barnes & Co., 1970.
Bazin, André. *WHAT IS CINEMA? Vol. II*. Translated by Hugh Gray. Berkeley: University of California Press, 1971.
Beardsley, Monroe C. *AESTHETICS: Problems in the Philosophy of Criticism*. New York: Harcourt, Brace and World, Inc., 1958.
Behlmer, Rudy (ed.). *MEMO FROM DAVID O. SELZNICK*. New York: Viking Press, 1972.
Bergan, Ronald. *SPORTS IN THE MOVIES*. London and New York: Proteus Books, 1982.
Berman, Robert. *FADE IN: THE SCREENWRITING PROCESS*. Stoneham, MA; Westport, Ct.: Michael Wiese Film Productions, Focal Press, 1988.
Betrock, Alan. *THE I WAS A TEENAGE JUVENILE DELINQUENT ROCK 'N' ROLL HORROR BEACH PARTY MOVIE BOOK A Complete Guide to the Teen Exploitation Film, 1954-1969*. London: Plexus, 1986.

Biskind, Peter. *EASY RIDERS, RAGING BULLS How the Sex-Drugs-and-Rock'n'Roll Generation Saved Hollywood*. New York: Simon & Schuster, 1998.

Blacker, Irwin R. *THE ELEMENTS OF SCREENWRITING: A Guide for Film and Television Writing*. New York: Collier Books, 1986.

Blandford, Steve, Barry Keith Grant and Jim Hillier. *THE FILM STUDIES DICTIONARY*. London: Hodder Headline, 2001.

Block, Lawrence. *EIGHT MILLION WAYS TO DIE*. London: Orion Books, 1982.

_____ . *A STAB IN THE DARK*. New York: Avon Books, 1981.

Bogdanovich, Peter. *WHO THE DEVIL MADE IT And What Else Did He Make?* New York: Alfred A.Knopf, 1997.

Bookbinder, Robert. *FILMS OF THE SEVENTIES*. New York: Citadel Press, 1982.

Booker, Christopher. *THE SEVEN BASIC PLOTS: Why We Tell Stories*. London & New York: Continuum, 2007.

Boorman, John and Donahue, Walter (eds.). *PROJECTIONS 6*. London: Faber and Faber,1996.

Booth, Wayne. *THE RHETORIC OF FICTION (2nd ed.)*. Chicago: University of Chicago Press, 1983.

Bordwell, David. *NARRATION IN THE FICTION FILM*. Madison: University of Wisconsin Press, 1985.

_____ . *THE WAY HOLLYWOOD TELLS IT*. Berkeley and Los Angeles, Ca.: University of California Press, 2006.

_____ , Janet Staiger and Kristin Thompson. *THE CLASSICAL HOLLYWOOD CINEMA: Film Style and Mode of Production to 1960*. London: Routledge, 1994.

_____ and Kristin Thompson. *FILM ART: An Introduction*. New York: McGraw-Hill, 1997.

Brady, John. *THE CRAFT OF THE SCREENWRITER*. New York: Simon & Schuster, 1981.

Branigan, Edward. *POINT OF VIEW IN THE CINEMA: A Theory of Narration and Subjectivity in Classical Film*. Berlin, New York, Amsterdam: Mouton Publishers, 1985.

_____ . *NARRATIVE COMPREHENSION AND FILM*. London: Routledge: 1992.

BREWER'S CINEMA A Phrase and Fable Dictionary. London: Market House Books,1995.

Brownstein, Ronald. *THE POWER AND THE GLITTER: The Hollywood-Washington Connection*. New York: Pantheon Books, 1990.

Buckland, Warren. *DIRECTED BY STEVEN SPIELBERG: Poetics of the Contemporary Blockbuster*. London and New York: Continuum Books, 2006.

Burroughs, Edgar Rice. *TARZAN OF THE APES*. New York: The Modern Library, 2003.

Cameron, Ian (ed.). *THE MOVIE BOOK OF FILM NOIR*. London: Studio Vista, 1992.

Carroll, Noël. *INTERPRETING THE MOVING IMAGE*. Cambridge: Cambridge University Press, 1998.

Caughie, John (ed.). *THEORIES OF AUTHORSHIP: A Reader*. London: Routledge & Kegan Paul and British Film Institute, 1981.

Cawelti, John G. (ed.). *FOCUS ON BONNIE AND CLYDE*. Englewood Cliffs, N.J.: Prentice-Hall, 1973.

Chandler, Raymond. *THE LONG GOODBYE*. London: The Thriller Book Club, 1951.

Chown, Jeffrey. *HOLLYWOOD AUTEUR: Francis Coppola*. New York: Praeger Publishers, 1988.

Coffee, Lenore. *STORYLINE: Recollections of a Hollywood Screenwriter*. London: Cassell & Company Ltd., 1973.

Cohan, Steve and Linda M. Shires. *TELLING STORIES: A Theoretical Analysis of Narrative Fiction*. New York & London: Routledge, 1988.

Collins, Jim, Hilary Radner, and Preacher Collins, Ava. *FILM THEORY GOES TO THE MOVIES (AFI Film Reader)*. London: Routledge, 1993.

Cook, David A. *A HISTORY OF NARRATIVE FILM (2nd ed.)*. London & New York: W.W. Norton & Co., 1990.

Corliss, Richard. *THE HOLLYWOOD SCREENWRITERS*. New York: Avon, 1972.

_____ . *TALKING PICTURES: Screenwriters in the American Cinema*. Woodstock, New York: Overlook Press, 1975.

Corman, Roger. *HOW I MADE A HUNDRED MOVIES IN HOLLYWOOD AND NEVER LOST A DIME*. New York: Muller, 1990.

Corrigan, Timothy. *A CINEMA WITHOUT WALLS*. New Brunswick, New Jersey: Rutgers University Press, 1991; and London: Routledge, 1991.

Cousins, Mark. *THE STORY OF FILM*. London: Pavilion Books, 2006.

Cowgill, Linda. *THE SECRETS OF SCREENPLAY STRUCTURE*. California: Lone Eagle Press, 1999.

Cowie, Peter. *THE GODFATHER BOOK*. London: Faber & Faber, 1997.

Crane, Robert David and Fryer, Christopher. *JACK NICHOLSON: Face to Face*. New York: M. Evans & Co., 1975.

Crispin, Mark, (ed.). *SEEING THROUGH MOVIES*. New York: Pantheon, 1990.

Culler, Jonathan. *THE PURSUIT OF SIGNS*. London: Routledge & Kegan Paul, 1981.

Currie, Gregory. *IMAGE AND MIND: Film, Philosophy and Cognitive Science.*. Cambridge: Cambridge University Press, 1995.

Dancyger, Ken. *GLOBAL SCRIPTWRITING*. Boston, Mass: Focal Press, 2001.

_____ and Jeff Rush. *ALTERNATIVE SCRIPTWRITING: Writing Beyond the Rules*. Boston and London: Focal Press, 1991; *ALTERNATIVE SCRIPTWRITING: Writing Beyond the Rules, Second Edition*. Boston and London: Focal Press, 1995.

Dardis, Tom. *SOME TIME IN THE SUN: The Hollywood Years of Fitzgerald, Faulkner, Nathanael West, Aldous Huxley, and James Agee*. London: Andre Deutsch, 1976.

DeRosa, Steven. *WRITING WITH HITCHCOCK: The Collaboration of Alfred Hitchcock and John Michael Hayes*. London & New York: Faber and Faber, 2001.

Dick, Bernard F. *ANATOMY OF FILM (3rd edition)*. New York: St Martin's Press, Inc., 1998.

Didion, Joan. *THE WHITE ALBUM*. London: Flamingo, 1993.

Doherty, Thomas. *TEENAGERS & TEENPICS: The Juvenilization of American Movies in the 1950s*. Boston & London: Unwin Hyman, 1988

Dunne, John Gregory. *MONSTER: Living Off the Big Screen*. New York: Vintage Books, 1997.

_____ . *THE STUDIO*. New York: Farrar,Straus & Giroux, 1969.

Dunne, Philip. *TAKE TWO: A Life in Movies and Politics*. New York: Limelight Editions, 1992.

Dyer, Richard. *STARS*. London: British Film Institute, 1998 .

Eaton, Michael. *CHINATOWN*. London: BFI Classics, British Film Institute, 1997.

Egri, Lajos. *THE ART OF DRAMATIC WRITING*. New York: Touchstone Books, 1946; rpt.,1960.

Elsaesser, Thomas, Alexander Horwath and Noel King (eds.). *THE LAST GREAT AMERICAN PICTURE SHOW: New Hollywood Cinema in the 1970s (Film Culture in Transition Series)*. Netherlands: Amsterdam University Press, 2004.

Emerson, John & Anita Loos. *HOW TO WRITE PHOTOPLAYS*. Philadelphia: 1920; reprinted George W. Jacobs & Co, 1923.

Engel, Joel. *SCREENWRITERS ON SCREENWRITING*. New York: Hyperion, 1995.

Eszterhas, Joe. *HOLLYWOOD ANIMAL: A Memoir of Love and Betrayal*. New York: Random House, 2004.

Evans, Robert. *THE KID STAYS IN THE PICTURE*. London: Aurum Press Limited, 1994.

Fante, John. *ASK THE DUST*. New York: HarperCollins, 2002.

_____ . *BROTHERHOOD OF THE GRAPE*. London: Black Sparrow Books, 1988.

Fiedler, Leslie. *NO! IN THUNDER: Essays on Myth and Literature*. London: Eyre and Spottiswoode, 1963.

Field, Syd. *SCREENPLAY: The Foundations of Screenwriting: A Step-by-Step Guide from Concept to Finished Script (3rd ed.)*. New York: Dell Publishing, 1994.

_____ . *THE SCREENWRITER'S WORKBOOK*. New York: Dell Publishing, 1984.

_____ .*THE SCREENWRITER'S PROBLEM SOLVER*. New York: Dell Publishing, 1998.

Fine, Richard. *HOLLYWOOD AND THE PROFESSION OF AUTHORSHIP 1928-1940*. Ann Arbor, Michigan: UMI Research Press, 1985; reprinted as *WEST OF EDEN: Writers in Hollywood 1928-1940*. Washington and London: Smithsonian Institute Press, 1993.

Finstad, Suzanne. *WARREN BEATTY: A Private Man*. New York: Harmony Books, 2005.

Fitzgerald, F. Scott. *THE PAT HOBBY STORIES*. New York: Scriber, 1995.

Fleming, Charles. *HIGH CONCEPT: Don Simpson and the Hollywood Culture of Excess*. London: Bloomsbury Publishing, 1998.

Forster, E.M. *ASPECTS OF THE NOVEL*. London: Pelican, 1985.

Foucault, Michel. *THE FOUCAULT READER (ed. Paul Rainbow)*. New York: Pantheon Books, 1984.

Francke, Lizzie. *SCRIPT GIRLS: Women Screenwriters in Hollywood*. London: British Film Institute, 1995.

Friedrich, Otto. *CITY OF NETS: A Portrait of Hollywood in the 1940s*. New York: Harper & Row 1988; London: Harper Publishing, 1987.

Froug, William. *THE SCREENWRITER LOOKS AT THE SCREENWRITER*. Los Angeles: Silman-James Press, 1970.

_____ .*THE NEW SCREENWRITER LOOKS AT THE NEW SCREENWRITER*. Los Angeles: Silman-James Press, 1991.

_____ . *ZEN AND THE ART OF SCREENWRITING Insights and Interviews*. Los Angeles: Silman-James Press, 1996.

Frye, Northrop. *ANATOMY OF CRITICISM*. New Jersey: Princeton University Press, 1971.

Gary, Romain. *WHITE DOG*. London: Jonathan Cape, 1971.

Gassner, John and Dudley Nichols, eds. *BEST FILM PLAYS OF 1943-1944*. New York: Crown Publishers, 1945.

Gelmis, Joseph. *THE FILM DIRECTOR AS SUPERSTAR*. London: Secker & Warburg, 1971.

Gerstner, David A. and Janet Staiger (eds.). *AUTHORSHIP AND FILM: Trafficking with Hollywood*. New York: Routledge, 2003.

Giannetti, Louis. *UNDERSTANDING MOVIES (8th edition)*. New Jersey: Prentice Hall, 1999.

Gilbey, Ryan. *IT DON'T WORRY ME: The Revolutionary American Films of the Seventies*. New York: Faber & Faber, 2003.

Gledhill, Christine and Linda Williams, eds. *REINVENTING FILM STUDIES*. London: Hodder Arnold, 2000.

Goldman, William. *MARATHON MAN*. London: Book Club Associates, 1974.

_____ . *WILLIAM GOLDMAN: Four Screenplays*. New York, Applause Books, 1977.

_____ . *WHICH LIE DID I TELL? More Adventures in the Screen Trade*. New York: Franklin Library, 2000.

Goodall, Jane. *IN THE SHADOW OF MAN (Revised edition)*. London: Weidenfeld and Nicholson, 1988.

_____ . *JANE GOODALL'S ANIMAL WORLD: Chimps*. London: Collins, 1990.

Grisham, John. *THE FIRM*. London: Arrow Books, 1993.

Grobel, Lawrence. *ABOVE THE LINE: Conversations About the Movies*. New York: Da Capo Press, 2000.

Gulino, Paul Joseph. *SCREENWRITING: The Sequence Approach*. New York: Continuum, 2004.

Haberski, Raymond J., Jr. *IT'S ONLY A MOVIE! Films and Critics in American Culture*. Lexington: University Press of Kentucky, 2001.

_____ . *FREEDOM TO OFFEND*. Lexington: University of Kentucky Press, 2007.

Hammett, Dashiell. *THE GLASS KEY*. New York: Orion, 2002.

_____ . *THE MALTESE FALCON*. New York: Orion, 2002.

Hamilton, Ian. *WRITERS IN HOLLYWOOD 1915-1951*. London: Heinemann, 1990.

Hayward, Susan. *KEY CONCEPTS IN CINEMA STUDIES*. London and New York: Routledge 1996.

Heywood, Leslie and Shari L. Dworkin. *BUILT TO WIN: The Female Athlete as Cultural Icon*. Minneapolis and London: University of Minnesota Press, 2003.

Hill, John and Pamela Church Gibson (eds). *THE OXFORD GUIDE TO FILM STUDIES*. Oxford: Oxford University Press, 1998.

Hillier, Jim (ed.). *CAHIERS DU CINÉMA Volume 2 1960-1968: New Wave, New Cinema, Re-evaluating Hollywood: An anthology from Cahiers du Cinéma nos 103-207 January 1960-December 1968*. London: Routledge and Kegan Paul/British Film Institute, 1986.

_____ . *THE NEW HOLLYWOOD*. London: Studio Vista, 1992.

_____ and Peter Wollen (eds.) *HOWARD HAWKS: American Artist*. London: British Film Institute, 1996.

Hiltunen, Ari. *ARISTOTLE IN HOLLYWOOD*. Bristol: Intellect Books, 2002.

Hollows, Joanne, Peter Hutchings and Mark Jancovich (eds.). *THE FILM STUDIES READER*. London: Arnold, 2000.

Hollows, Joanne and Mark Jancovich (eds.). *APPROACHES TO POPULAR FILM*. Manchester: Manchester University Press, 1995.

Horton, Andrew. *WRITING THE CHARACTER-CENTRED SCREENPLAY*. Berkeley and Los Angeles: University of California Press, 1999.

_____ . (ed.) *SCREENWRITING FOR A GLOBAL MARKET: Selling Your Scripts from Hollywood to Hong Kong*. Berkeley and Los Angeles: University of California Press, 2004.

Hoskyns, Barney. *WAITING FOR THE SUN: Strange Days Weird Scenes and the Sound of Los Angeles*. London: Penguin, 1997.

Howard, David. *HOW TO BUILD A GREAT SCREENPLAY: A Master Class in Storytelling for Film*. London: Souvenir Press, 2004.

Howard, David & Edward Mabley. *THE TOOLS OF SCREENWRITING: A Writer's Guide to the Craft and the Elements of a Screenplay*. New York: St Martin's Press, 1993 .

Hunter, Lew. *LEW HUNTER'S SCREENWRITING 434*. New York: Perigee Books, 1993.

Jacobs, Diane. *HOLLYWOOD RENAISSANCE: The New Generation of Filmmakers and Their Works*. New York: Delta, 1977 & 1980.

Jacobs, Lewis. *THE RISE OF THE AMERICAN FILM: A Critical History*. New York: Teachers College Press, 1967.

James, David E. *ALLEGORIES OF CINEMA: American Film in the Sixties*. New Jersey: Princeton University Press, 1989.

Kael, Pauline. *THE CITIZEN KANE BOOK*. Boston: Little, Brown, 1971.

_____ . *REELING: Film Writings 1972-1975*. New York and London: Marion Boyars, 1992.

_____ . *5001 NIGHTS AT THE MOVIES*. New York and London: Marion Boyars, 1993.

_____ . *I LOST IT AT THE MOVIES: Film Writings 1954-1965*. New York and London: Marion Boyars, 1994.

Kaminsky, Stuart M. *AMERICAN FILM GENRES: Approaches to a Critical Theory of Popular Film*. New York: Dell Publishing Co., 1977.

Kapsis, Robert E. *HITCHCOCK: The Making of a Reputation*. Chicago: University of Chicago Press, 1992.

Kawin, Bruce. *HOW MOVIES WORK*. Berkeley, Ca.: University of California Press, 1987.

Kennedy, Douglas. *TEMPTATION*. London: Arrow Books, 2007.

Kerr, Walter. *TRAGEDY AND COMEDY*. New York: Simon and Schuster, 1967.

Kiernan, Thomas. *REPULSION: The Life and Times of Roman Polanski*. London: New English Library, 1980.

King, Tom. *DAVID GEFFEN: A Biography of New Hollywood*. London: Random House, 2000.

King, Viki. *HOW TO WRITE A MOVIE IN 21 DAYS: The Inner Movie Method*. New York: HarperPerennial, 1988.

Kipen, David. *THE SCHREIBER THEORY: A Radical Rewrite of American Film History*. Hoboken, New Jersey: Melville House Publishing, 2006.

Kitses, Jim. *HORIZONS WEST. Anthony Mann, Budd Boetticher, Sam Peckinpah: studies of authorship within the Western*. Bloomington, Indiana: Indiana University Press, 1969.

Klawans, Stuart. *FILM FOLLIES: The Cinema Out of Order*. London: Cassell, 1999.

Kolker, Robert Philip. *A CINEMA OF LONELINESS: Penn, Kubrick, Coppola, Scorsese, Altman*. New York: Oxford University Press, 1980.

Konigsberg, Ira. *FILM DICTIONARY: The Complete Film Dictionary (2nd ed.)*. London: Bloomsbury, 1997.

Lambert, Gavin. *NATALIE WOOD: A Life*. New York: Alfred A Knopf, 2004.

_____ . *MAINLY ABOUT LINDSAY ANDERSON: A Memoir*. London: Faber & Faber, 2000.

Langford, Barry. *FILM GENRE: Hollywood and Beyond*. Edinburgh: Edinburgh University Press, 2005.

Lapsley, Robert and Michael Westlake. *FILM THEORY: An Introduction*. Manchester: Manchester University Press 1994.

Larner, Jeremy. *DRIVE, HE SAID*. London: Mayflower Books, 1968.

Laurents, Arthur. *ORIGINAL STORY BY: A Memoir of Broadway and Hollywood*. New York: Alfred A. Knopf, 2000.

Lawson, John Howard. *THEORY AND TECHNIQUE OF PLAYWRITING AND SCREENWRITING*. New York: Putnam, 1949.

Le Carré, John. *THE NIGHT MANAGER*. London: Sceptre, 1999.

Lehman, Peter and William Luhr. *BLAKE EDWARDS*. Athens, London: Ohio University Press, 1981.

Levinson, Jerrold. *MUSIC, ART, METAPHYSICS: Essays in Philosophical Aesthetics*. Ithaca, New York: Cornell University Press, 1990.

Lewis, Jon. *WHOM GOD WISHES TO DESTROY … : Francis Coppola and the New Hollywood*. Durham & London: Duke University Press, 1995.

_____ .(editor). *THE NEW AMERICAN CINEMA*. Durham & London: Duke University Press, 1998.

Lewis, Jon E. and Penny Stempel. *CULT TV: The Essential Critical Guide*. London: Pavilion Books, 1996.

Lopate, Philip (ed.). *AMERICAN MOVIE CRITICS: An Anthology From The Silents Until Now*. New York: Library of America, 2006.

Love, Harold. *ATTRIBUTING AUTHORSHIP: An Introduction*. Cambridge: University Press, 2002.

Lovell, Alan and Gianluca Sergi. *MAKING FILMS IN CONTEMPORARY HOLLYWOOD*. London: Hodder Arnold, 2005.

Luhr, William and Peter Lehman. *AUTHORSHIP AND NARRATIVE IN THE CINEMA: Issues in Contemporary Aesthetics and Criticism*. New York: GP Putnam's Sons, 1977.

Lumet, Sidney. *MAKING MOVIES*. London: Bloomsbury, 1996.

Macdonald, Kevin. *EMERIC PRESSBURGER: The Life and Death of a Screenwriter*. London: Faber & Faber, 1998.

McArthur, Colin. *THE BIG HEAT*. London: BFI Classics, British Film Institute, 1992.

McCarthy, Todd and Charles Flynn (eds.). *KINGS OF THE Bs: WORKING WITHIN THE HOLLYWOOD SYSTEM An Anthology of Film History and Criticism*. New York: Dutton, 1975.

McCarty, John (ed.). *THE FEARMAKERS: The Screen's Directorial Masters of Suspense and Terror*. London: Virgin Books, 1995.

McClintick, David. *INDECENT EXPOSURE: A True Story of Hollywood and Wall Street*. London: Columbus Books, 1982.

McConnell, Frank. *STORYTELLING AND MYTHMAKING: Images from Film and Literature*. Oxford: Oxford University Press, 1979.

McCreadie, Marsha. *THE WOMEN WHO WRITE THE MOVIES: From Frances Marion to Nora Ephron*. New York: Birch Lane Press, 1994.

McDougal, Dennis. *THE LAST MOGUL: Lew Wasserman, MCA and the Hidden History of Hollywood*. New York: Da Capo Press, 1998, rpt. 2001.

McGee, Mark Thomas. *ROGER CORMAN: The Best of the Cheap Act*. N. Carolina and London: McFarland & Co., Jefferson, 1988.

McGilligan, Patrick, *CAGNEY: The Actor as Auteur.*. New York: A.S. Barnes & Co., 1975.

_____ .(ed.). *BACKSTORY 1: Interviews with Screenwriters of Hollywood's Golden Age*. Berkeley: University of California Press, 1986;

_____ (ed.) *BACKSTORY 2: Interviews with Screenwriters of the 40s and 50s*. Berkeley: University of California Press, 1991;

_____ *JACK'S LIFE: A Biography of Jack Nicholson*. New York: W.W.Norton & Co., 1995.

_____ . (ed.) *BACKSTORY 3: Interviews with Screenwriters of the 60s*. Berkeley: University of California Press, 1996.

_____ and Paul Buhle. *TENDER COMRADE: A Backstory of the Hollywood Blacklist*. New York: St Martin's Griffin, 1997.

_____ . (ed.) *BACKSTORY 4: Interviews with Screenwriters of the 70s and 80s*. Berkeley: University of California Press, .2006.

McKee, Robert. *STORY: Substance, Structure, Style, and the Principles of Screenwriting*. New York: Regan Books, 1997.

McWilliams, Carey. *SOUTHEN CALIFORNIA COUNTRY: An Island on the Land*. New York: Duell, Sloane & Pearce, 1946.

Maltby, Richard and Ian Craven. *HOLLYWOOD CINEMA: An Introduction*. Oxford, UK and Cambridge, USA: Blackwell Publishers, 1995.

Manfull, Helen (ed.). *ADDITIONAL DIALOGUE: Letters of Dalton Trumbo 1942-1962*. New York: Bantam Books, 1972.

Mast, Gerald, Marshall Cohen and Leo Braudy (eds.). *FILM THEORY AND CRITICISM: Introductory Readings, 4th Edition*. New York: Oxford University Press, 1992.

Mehring, Margaret. *THE SCREENPLAY: A Blend of Film Form and Content*. New York: Focal Press, 1990.

Meyer, Janet L. *SYDNEY POLLACK: A Critical Filmography*. Jefferson, North Carolina and London: McFarland & Co., 1998.

Miller, Gabriel. *SCREENING THE NOVEL: Rediscovered American Fiction in Film*. New York: Frederick Ungar Publishing, 1980.

Miller, Mark Crispin (ed.). *SEEING THROUGH MOVIES*. New York: Pantheon Books, 1990.

Miller, Toby. *SPORTSEX*. Philadelphia: Temple University Press, 2001.

Monaco, James. *AMERICAN FILM NOW*. New York: Plume Books, 1979.

_____ . *THE NEW WAVE*. New York and Oxford: Oxford University Press, 1991.

Montanari, Richard. *THE SKIN GODS*. London: Arrow Books, 2007.

Murdock, Maureen. *THE HEROINE'S JOURNEY: Woman's Quest for Wholeness*. Boston & London: Shambhala, 1990.

Naha, Ed. *THE FILMS OF ROGER CORMAN: Brilliance on a Budget*. New York: Arco, 1982.

Nash, Constance and Virginia Oakey. *THE SCREENWRITER'S HANDBOOK (Writing for the Movies)*. New York: HarperPerennial, 1993.

_____ . *THE TELEVISION WRITER'S HANDBOOK: What to Write How to Write It How to Sell It*. New York: Barnes & Noble, 1978.

Nichols, Bill (ed.). *MOVIES AND METHODS: An Anthology: Volume I*. Berkeley, California: University of California Press, 1982.

_____ . *MOVIES AND METHODS: An Anthology Volume II*. Berkeley, California: University of California Press, 1995.

Orr, John. *CONTEMPORARY CINEMA*. Edinburgh: Edinburgh University Press, 1998.

Pallot, James, et al (eds.) *THE FOURTH VIRGIN FILM GUIDE*. London: Virgin Publishing, 1995.

Palmer, Linda. *HOW TO WRITE IT HOW TO SELL IT: Everything a Screenwriter Needs to Know About Hollywood*. New York: St Martin's Griffin, 1998.

Parker, John. *POLANSKI*. London: Victor Gollancz, 1993.

Parkinson, David. *GOOD MOVIE GUIDE*. London: Bloomsbury Publishing Ltd, 1990.

Pearson, Carole. *THE HERO WITHIN: Six Archetypes We Live By*. San Francisco: Harper & Row, 1986.

_____ and Katherine Pope. *WHO AM I THIS TIME? Female Portraits in American and British Literature*. New York: McGraw-Hill Co., 1976.

Perkins, V.F. *FILM AS FILM Understanding and Judging Movies*. London: Pelican, 1972.

Pirie, David (ed.) *ANATOMY OF THE MOVIES Inside the Film Industry: The Money. The Power. The People. The Craft. The Movies*. London: Windward Books, 1981.

Poe, Edgar Allan. *THE EDGAR ALLAN POE READER*. Philadelphia, Pennsylvania: Courage Books, 1993.

Polanski, Roman. *ROMAN*. London: Pan Books, 1984.

Polenberg, Richard. *ONE NATION DIVISIBLE: Class, Race and Ethnicity in the United States Since 1938*. London: Penguin, 1986.

Ponicsan, Darryl. *THE LAST DETAIL*. New York: Signet, 1971.

Powdermaker, Hortense. *HOLLYWOOD: The Dream Factory*. Boston: Little, Brown & Co., 1950.

Powell, Dilys. *THE DILYS POWELL FILM READER*. Manchester: Carcanet Press Ltd., 1991.

Prover, Jorja. *NO ONE KNOWS THEIR NAMES: Screenwriters in Hollywood*. Bowling Green, Ohio: Bowling Green State University Popular Press, 1994.

Puzo, Mario. *THE GODFATHER*. New York: G.P. Putnam's Sons, 1969.

Pye, Michael and Lynda Myles. *THE MOVIE BRATS: How the Film Generation Took Over Hollywood*. New York: Holt Rinehart and Winston, 1979.

Quirk, Lawrence J. *THE FILMS OF WARREN BEATTY*. London: Citadel Press, 1979.

Ramsaye, Terry. *A MILLION AND ONE NIGHTS: A History of the Motion Picture*. New York: Simon & Schuster, 1926; rept. London: Frank Cass & Co. Ltd., 1964.

Ray, Robert B. *A CERTAIN TENDENCY OF THE HOLLYWOOD CINEMA, 1930-1980*. Princeton, N.J.: Princeton University Press, 1985.

Ricardou, Jean. *PROBLÈMES DU NOUVEAU ROMAN*. Paris: Seuil, 1967.

Richardson, John H. *THE VIPER'S CLUB*. London: Hodder and Stoughton, 1996.

Ricoeur, Paul. *TIME AND NARRATIVE Volume 1*. Chicago: University of Chicago Press, 1990.

_____ and David Pellauer. *FIGURING THE SACRED: Religion, Narrative and the Imagination*. Minneapolis: Augsburg Fortress, 1995.

_____ and John B. Thompson. *HERMENEUTICS AND THE HUMAN SCIENCES: Essays on Language, Action and Interpretation*. Cambridge: Cambridge University Press, 1981.

Rimmon-Kenan, Shlomith. *NARRATIVE FICTION: Contemporary Poetics*. London and New York: Methuen, 1983.

Riordan, James. *STONE: The Controversies, Excesses and Exploits of a Radical Filmmaker*. London: Aurum Press, 1995.

Rogers St Johns, Adela. *HOW TO WRITE A STORY AND SELL IT*. Garden City, New York: Doubleday & Co., 1956.

Rosenstone, Robert A. *VISIONS OF THE PAST: The Challenge of Film to our Idea of History*. Massachusetts, Harvard University Press, 1995.

Ross, Lillian. *PICTURE*. London: Andre Deutsch, 1986.

_____ and Helen Ross. *THE PLAYER: A Profile of an Art*. New York: Simon & Schuster, 1962.

Rosten, Leo. *HOLLYWOOD: The Movie Colony, The Movie Makers*. New York: Harcourt, Brace & Co., 1941.

Ryan, Michael and Douglas Kellner. *CAMERA POLITICA: The Politics and Ideology of Contemporary Hollywood Film*. Bloomington and Indianapolis: Indiana University Press, 1988.

Sandford, Christopher. *POLANSKI*. London: Century, 2007.

Sarris, Andrew. *THE AMERICAN CINEMA: Directors and Directions 1929-1968*. New York: Dutton,1968 and Da Capo Press, 1996.

_____ . *"YOU AIN'T HEARD NOTHIN' YET!": The American Talking Film History & Memory, 1927-1949*. New York: Oxford University Press, 1998.

Schanzer, Karl & Thomas Lee Wright. *AMERICAN SCREENWRITERS The Insiders' Look at the Craft, and the Business of Movie Writing*. New York: Avon Books, 1993.

Schary, Dore. *HEYDAY*. New York: Berkley Books, 1981.

Schatz, Thomas. *HOLLYWOOD GENRES: Formulas, Filmmaking and the Studio System*. Philadelphia: Temple University Press, Philadelphia, 1981.

_____ . *OLD HOLLYWOOD/NEW HOLLYWOOD: Ritual, Art and Industry*. Ann Arbor, Michigan:UMI Research Press, 1983.

_____ . *THE GENIUS OF THE SYSTEM*. New York: Pantheon Books, 1988; and London: Faber & Faber, 1996.

Scholes, Robert & Robert Kellogg. *THE NATURE OF NARRATIVE*. New York: Oxford University Press, 1966.

Schwartz, Nancy Lynn. *THE HOLLYWOOD WRITERS' WARS*. New York: Knopf, 1982.

Scott, Ian. *IN CAPRA'S SHADOW: The Life and Career of Screenwriter Robert Riskin*. Lexington: University of Kentucky Press, 2006.

Seger, Linda. *CREATING UNFORGETTABLE CHARACTERS*. New York: Henry Holt & Co., 1990.

_____ . *MAKING A GOOD SCRIPT GREAT: A Guide for Writing and Rewriting*. Hollywood: Samuel French, 1994.

_____ . *MAKING A GOOD WRITER GREAT: A Creativity Workbook for Screenwriters*. Los Angeles: Silman-James Press, 1999.

Server, Lee. *SCREENWRITER: Words Become Pictures*. Pittstown, New Jersey: Main Street Press, 1987.

Seydor, Paul. *PECKINPAH The Western Films: A Reconsideration*. Urbana and Chicago: University of Illinois Press, 1999.

Shepherd, Donald. *JACK NICHOLSON: An Unauthorized Biography*. London: Robson Books, 1991.

Sherwin, David. *GOING MAD IN HOLLYWOOD*. London: Penguin Books, 1996.

Shone, Tom. *BLOCKBUSTER: How Hollywood Learned to Stop Worrying and Love the Summer*. London: Simon & Schuster, 2004.

Simon, Neil. *REWRITES: A Memoir*. New York: Simon & Schuster, 1996.

Singer, Irving. *REALITY TRANSFORMED: Film as Meaning and Technique*. Cambridge, Mass. and London: MIT Press, 1998.

Sinyard, Neil. *FILMING LITERATURE: The Art of Screen Adaptation*. London: Croom Helm, 1986.

_____ . *THE FILMS OF NICOLAS ROEG*. London: Letts, 1991.

Sklar, Robert. *MOVIE-MADE AMERICA: A Cultural History of American Movies*. New York: Vintage Books, 1994.

Spoto, Donald. *CAMERADO: Hollywood and the American Man*. New York: Plume Books, New England Publishing, 1978.

Stam, Robert and Toby Miller. *FILM AND THEORY: An Anthology*. Oxford: Blackwell Publishers, 2000.

Steen, Mike. *HOLLYWOOD SPEAKS! An Oral History*. New York: Putnam, 1974.

Stempel, Tom. *SCREENWRITER: The Life and Times of Nunnally Johnson*. New York: A.S. Barnes & Co., 1980.

_____ . *SCREENWRITING*. San Diego, California: Tantivy Press, 1982.

_____ . *FRAMEWORK: A History of Screenwriting in the American Film*. New York: The Continuum Publishing Company, 1988.

_____ . *AMERICAN AUDIENCES ON MOVIES AND MOVIEGOING*. Lexington: University of Kentucky Press, 2001.

Stern, Stewart. *NO TRICKS IN MY POCKET: Paul Newman Directs*. New York: Grove Press, 1989.

Stillinger, Jack. *MULTIPLE AUTHORSHIP AND THE MYTH OF SOLITARY GENIUS*. New York: Oxford University Press, 1991.

Suber, Howard. *THE POWER OF FILM*. Los Angeles: Michael Wiese Productions, 2006.

Sylvester, Christopher (ed.). *THE PENGUIN BOOK OF HOLLYWOOD*. London: Penguin, 1999.

Taylor, Thom. *THE BIG DEAL: Hollywood's Million Dollar Spec Script Market*. New York: William Morrow and Co., Inc., 1999.

Tesich, Steve. *KAROO*. London: Chatto & Windus, 1998.

Thompson, Kristin. *STORYTELLING IN THE NEW HOLLYWOOD: Understanding Classical Narrative Technique*. New York: McGraw-Hill, 2001.

Thomson, David. *A BIOGRAPHICAL DICTIONARY OF THE CINEMA*. London: Secker & Warburg, 1970 & 1975; republished. as *A BIOGRAPHICAL DICTIONARY OF FILM*, London: Andre Deutsch, 1994.

_____ . *OVEREXPOSURES: The Crisis in American Filmmaking*. New York: William Morrow & Co., 1981.

_____ . *SUSPECTS*. London: Secker & Warburg, 1985.

_____ . *WARREN BEATTY AND DESERT EYES: A Life and a Story*. New York: Vintage Books, 1987.

_____ . *ROSEBUD*. London: Abacus, 1996.

_____ . *BENEATH MULHOLLAND: Thoughts on Hollywood and its Ghosts*. London: Abacus, 1997.

_____ . *THE WHOLE EQUATION: A History of Hollywood*. London: Little, Brown, 2004.

Tierno, Michael. *ARISTOTLE'S POETICS FOR SCREENWRITERS*. New York: Hyperion Books, 2002.

TIME OUT FILM GUIDE, THE. (edited by Tom Milne) London: Penguin, 1991.

Toolan, Michael. *NARRATIVE: A Critical Linguistic Introduction.* London: Routledge & Kegan Paul, 1988.

Towne, Robert. *The Chameleon* (Outer Limits) (1964)

_____ .*Chinatown* (1971-1973)

_____ . *Chinatown/The Last Detail.* New York: Grove Press, 1997

_____ . *Days of Thunder* (with Tom Cruise)

_____ . *The Dove Affair* (The Man from U.N.C.L.E.) (1964)

_____ . *Eight Million Ways to Die*

_____ . *The Firm* (with David Rayfiel)

_____ . *Greystoke* (1977)

_____ . *The Last Detail* (n.d.)

_____ . *The Mermaid*

_____ . *Personal Best* (1980)

_____ . *Shampoo* (1975) (with Warren Beatty)

_____ . *Tequila Sunrise* (1988)

_____ . *The Two Jakes* (1984)

_____ . *Without Limits* (with Kenny Moore)

_____ . *The Yakuza* (1973)

Trottier, David. *THE SCREENWRITER'S BIBLE: A Complete Guide to Writing, Formatting, and Selling Your Script.* Los Angeles : Silman-James Press, 2005.

Tudor, Andrew. *THEORIES OF FILM.* London: Secker & Warburg, 1973.

Turner, Graeme. *FILM AS SOCIAL PRACTICE.* London: Routledge, 1988.

Tuska, Jon (editor). *CLOSE-UP: The Contemporary Director.* Metuchen, New Jersey and London: The Scarecrow Press, Inc., 1981.

Vale, Eugene. *TECHNIQUE OF SCREENPLAY WRITING: An Analysis of the Dramatic Structure of Motion Pictures. Revised and Enlarged Edition.* (1944, 1972) Rept.,London: Souvenir Press, 1980.

Vidal, Gore. *HOLLYWOOD.* New York: Ballantine Books, 1990.

Viertel, Salka. *THE KINDNESS OF STRANGERS.* New York: Holt, Rinehart & Winston, 1965.

Vogler, Christopher. *THE HERO'S JOURNEY: Mythic Structure for Storytellers & Screenwriters.* Studio City, California: Michael Wiese Productions, 1992.

Wagner, Bruce. *FORCE MAJEURE.* New York: Random House, 1991.

_____ . *I'LL LET YOU GO.* New York: Random House, 2002.

Walter, Richard. *THE WHOLE PICTURE: Strategies for Screenwriting Success in the New Hollywood.* New York: Plume Books, 1997.

Wambaugh, Joseph. *THE NEW CENTURIONS.* London: Michael Joseph, 1972

Warner, Marina. *MANAGING MONSTERS: Six Myths of Our Time.* London: Vintage, 1994.

Weston, Jessie L. *FROM RITUAL TO ROMANCE.* Cambridge: Cambridge University Press, 1920.

Wexman, Virginia Wright (ed.). *FILM AND AUTHORSHIP.* London: Rutgers University Press; and New Brunswick, New Jersey: 2003.

_____ . *ROMAN POLANSKI.* Boston: Twayne Publishers, 1985.

Wicking, Christopher and Tise Vahimagi. *THE AMERICAN VEIN: Directors and Directions in Television.* New York: E.P. Dutton, 1979.

Willemen, Paul, David Pirie, David Will and Lynda Myles (eds.). *ROGER CORMAN: The Millennic Vision.* Edinburgh: Edinburgh Film Festival, in association with Cinema magazine,1970.

Williams, Linda Ruth and Michael Hammond (eds.).*CONTEMPORARY AMERICAN CINEMA.* London: Open University Press, 2006.

Wilson, George. *NARRATION IN LIGHT: Studies in Cinematic Point of View.* Baltimore: John Hopkins University Press, 1986.

Wolitzer, Meg. *FITZGERALD DID IT: The Writer's Guide to Mastering the Screenplay.* New York: Penguin Books, 1999.

Wollen, Peter. *SIGNS AND MEANINGS IN THE CINEMA 2nd ed.* London: Secker and Warburg, 1972.

Wood, Robin. *ARTHUR PENN*. London: Movie Magazine, 1967.

_____ . *HOWARD HAWKS*. London: Secker & Warburg/BFI, 1968.

_____ . *PERSONAL VIEWS: Explorations in Film (Revised Edition)*. Detroit, Michigan: Wayne State University Press, 2006.

Writers' Guild of America. *SCREEN CREDITS MANUAL*. Accessed online at www.wga.org.

Wycherley, William. (ed. Peter Holland) *THE PLAYS OF WILLIAM WYCHERLEY*. Cambridge: Cambridge University Press, 1981.

Articles & Dissertations:

Alonzo, John A.. 'Behind the Scenes of *Chinatown*,' *American Cinematographer* Vol. 56, No. 5, May 1975:526-529, 564-565,572-273,585-591

Alvarado, Manuel. 'Authorship, Origination and Production,' University of London Institute of Education Media Analysis Papers 1982.

Anderson, Lindsay. '*They Were Expendable* and John Ford,' *Sequence*, No. 11: 1-4.

Appelbaum, Ralph. 'Positive Thinking: Hal Ashby Interview,' *Films and Filming*, July 1978:10-19.

Archerd, Army. 'Just for Variety,' *Variety*, 09 May 1990.

Argent, Daniel. 'Surviving the Game: An Interview with Robert Towne,' *Creative Screenwriting* Vol.7, No.3 May-June 2000: 39-44.

Arnett, Robert. *A SEPARATE CINEMA The Screenplays of Robert Towne, Richard Price and Quentin Tarantino*. University of Southern Mississippi PhD 1997, pp. 296 (Proquest Dissertation Service); "The Screenwriter as Artist: Three Lost Masterworks by Robert Towne," *Creative Screenwriting* Vol.7,No.3 May-June 2000: 45-51.

Arnold, Gary. 'Towne's Long Trek to L.A. *Dust*,' *The Washington Times*, http://washingtontimes.com/ 25 March 2006.

Arroyo, José. 'Mission: Sublime,' *Sight & Sound*, Vol.6, No.7, July 1996: 19; 20.

Ascher-Walsh, Rebecca. 'Testing *Limit*S,' *Entertainment Weekly*, 18 September 1998: 21-24.

Ashby, Hal. 'Dialogue on Film,' *American Film*, May 1980: 53-60.

Atkinson, Michael. '"A lot of what has gone wrong was the result of choices I made'," *The Guardian*, The Guide, 29 May-04 June 1999: 4-6.

Azlant, Edward. *THE THEORY, HISTORY AND PRACTICE OF SCREENWRITING 1897-1920* (Unpublished doctoral dissertation at University of Wisconsin: 1980)

Bazin, André. 'On the Politique des Auteurs,' *Cahiers du Cinéma* in English I, January 1966: 8-18.

Benedetto, Robert. 'The Two *Chinatown*s: Towne's Screenplay Vs. Polanski's Film,' *Creative Screenwriting*, Vol. 6, December 1999: 49-54.

Bernstein, Matthew. 'Perfecting the New Gangster: Writing *Bonnie and Clyde*,' *Film Quarterly*, Vol. 53, No. 4: 16-31.

Biskind, Peter. 'The Low Road to *Chinatown*,' Premiere, June 1994: 68-78; 'Warren and Me,' Premiere, July 1990: 54-60; 104-105; 'The Man Who Minted Style,' *Vanity Fair*, April 2003: 100-111.

Boon, Kevin. 'Poetics and the Screenplay: Revisiting Aristotle,' *Creative Screenwriting*, Vol.8, No.3, 2001: 67-79.

Bowermaster, Jon. 'Daytona Thunder,' *Premiere*, June 1990: 83-84.

Braund, Simon. 'Hall of Fame: Peter Bogdanovich,' *Empire*, Issue 169, July 2003.

Brown, Corie. 'No *Love Affair*,' *Premiere* February 1995: 46-7, 96.

Byrne, Bridget. 'We Didn't Want Some Sweet Faced Kid: Fighting for *The Last Detail*,' *Los Angeles Herald Examiner*, 10 February 1974.

Cameron, Ian. 'Films, Directors and Critics,' *Movie*, No. 2 September 1962: 4-7.

Carey, Gary. 'Written on the Screen: Anita Loos,' *Film Comment*, Winter 1970-71: 50-55.

Carringer, Robert L. 'Designing Los Angeles: An Interview with Richard Sylbert,' *Wide Angle*, Volume 20, Number 3, July 1998: 97-131.

_____ . 'Collaboration and Concepts of Authorship,' in *PMLA*, March 2002 (116,2):370.

Carver, Benedict. 'Independent Force,' *Screen International*, 21 March 1997: 14-15.

Champlin, Charles. 'Ponicsan Films Plumb the Depths of Navy Life,' *Los Angeles Times*, Calendar, 09 December 1973: 1; 33.

Chinatown Review. *Cinema-TV Today* 17 August 1974: 14.

Christy, George. 'The Great Life,' *The Hollywood Reporter* 15-21 September 1998: 103.

CineAction. 'Rethinking Authorship,' No. 21/22, Summer/Fall 1990.

Cohen, Mitchell S. 'Villains and Victims,' *Film Comment*, 1974 Vol. 10 Issue No 6: 27-29.

Coleman, Todd. 'The Story Structure Gurus,' *Journal of Writers' Guild of America (West)*, June 1995, Vol. 8, No.6: 14-21.

Combs, Richard. *Chinatown* Review, *Monthly Film Bulletin*, August 1974 Vol.41, No.487: 171-172; *Tequila Sunrise* Review, *Monthly Film Bulletin* Vol.56, No.664 May 1989: 52-154; 'Cinema's Vision

Thing,' *The Listener*, 13 September 1990: 36-37; *The Two Jakes* Review, *Sight and Sound*, Vol.1, No.8, Dec. 1991: 53-4.

Cook, Page. *Chinatown* review, *Films in Review*, 1974, Vol.25, No.9: 560-563.

Cooper, Stephen. 'Sex/Knowledge/Power in the Detective Genre,' *Film Quarterly*, 1989 Vol. XLII, No.3: 23-31.

Corliss, Richard. 'Capra and Riskin,' *Film Comment*, November 1972: 18-21; 'The Hollywood Screenwriter,' *Film Comment* ,Winter 1970-71: 4-7; 'Love, Death and L.A...,' *Time*, www.time.com 13 March 2006.

Cox, Alex. 'How to Kill a Film Star,' *The Guardian*, Film & Music, 25 May 2007: 7.

Crofts, Stephen. 'Authorship and Hollywood,' *Wide Angle*, Vol. 5, No. 3, 1983: 16-22.

Crowdus, Gary. 'THE WRITERS GUILD OF AMERICA VS. THE BLACKLIST (Restoring the Credits of Michael Wilson and Other Screenwriters),' *Cineaste* Vol.21, No.4, 1, 1995: 29.

Curtis, Grant Clay. '*And God Stepped Aside*:   A Feature Length Screenplay. The Research, Methodology and Writing (Original Writing)(Central Missouri State University, MA: 1997)

Dare, Michael. 'How to Kill a Movie,' *L.A. Weekly* 16-22 May 1986: 31-33.

David, Ian. 'I'm an Auteur, So You Can Get Fucked,' *if Mag*, September 200036-37.

Davis, Gary. 'Rejected Offspring: The Screenplay as a Literary Genre,' *New Orleans Review*, date unknown, 90-94.

Davis, Rob. Steve Erie Interview, *Los Angeles Times*, 06 May 2006.

Dempsey, Michael. 'After the Fall: Post-Cimino Hollywood,' *American Film*, September 1981.

Denby, David. 'Rear Window: Delivering His *Personal Best*,' *Premiere*, December 1988.

Douglas, Ann. 'Day Into Noir,' *Vanity Fair*, March 2007: 242-247; 305-306.

Dunne, J.G. 'The Art of Screenwriting,' *Paris Review* 138, 1996.

Dwyer, Michael. 'Call the Script Doctor,' *The Irish Times*, 22 July 2006: 7.

Eaton, Michael. 'Condemned to Repeats,' *Sight & Sound*, Vol.1, No.8, December 1991: 4.

Ebert, Roger. *Days of Thunder* Review, *Chicago Sun-Times* 27 June 1990; *Tequila Sunrise* Review, *Chicago Sun-Times*, 02 December 1988; *Without Limits* Review, *Chicago Sun-Times*, 11 September 1998. Archived at http://www.suntimes.com..

Elley, Derek. *The Yakuza* Review, *Films and Filming*, Vol. 21, No.12, September 1975: 36-37.

Ellsworth, Elizabeth. 'Illicit Pleasures: Feminist Spectators and *Personal Best*,' *Camera Obscura*, 13/14: 45-56.

Elsaesser, Thomas. "The Pathos of Failure. American Films in the 70s: Notes on the Unmotivated Hero,' *Monogram*, 6, 1975: 13-19

Evry, Max. 'Robert Towne on *Ask the Dust*,' www.comingsoon.net, 1 March 2006.

Farber, Stephen. 'Plagiarism or Coincidence? Hollywood's Battle for Ideas,' *New West*, 27 August 1979: 55; 57-59; '*Mission*: Familiar,' *Los Angeles Times*, 31 May 2000.

Fawell, John. 'Cruel Fates: Parallels Between Roman Polanski's '*Chinatown*' and Sopohocles' '*Odeipus Rex*',' *The Armchair Detective* 1996, Vol.29,No.2,:179-185.

Finch, Mark. *Tequila Sunrise* Review, *Monthly Film Bulletin*, Vol. 56, No. 664, May 1989: 153.

Foreman, Carl. 'Confessions of a Frustrated Screenwriter,' *Film Comment*, Winter 1970-71: 22-25.

Foucault, Michel. 'What is an Author?' *Screen*, 20/1: 13-29.

Foundas, Scott. 'Right Down to *The Last Detail*,' *The Daily Trojan*, 10 September 1998.

Freedman, Samuel G. '*Two Jakes* Picks Up the *Chinatown* Trail,' *New York Times*, 05 August 1990.

Freeman, David. "The Great American Screenplay Competition," *Esquire* June 1985: 25-33.

Friend, Tom. 'Man with a Mission,' *Premiere*, June 1996: 68-74; 103.

Fuller, Stephen. 'Ben Hecht: A Sampler," *Film Comment*, Winter 1970-71: 32-39.

Galperin, William. ' "Bad for the Glass": Representation and Filmic Deconstruction in *Chinstown* and *Chan is Missing*,' *MLN*, No. 102 (5) 1987: 1151-1170.

Gomery, Douglas. 'The American Film Industry of the 1970s: Stasis in the "New Hollywood",' *Wide Angle*, 1983 Vol. 5 No. 4: 52 –59.

Goodwin, Chris. 'The Troubled Birth of *The Two Jakes*,' *The Sunday Correspondent*, 09 October 1989.

Goodwin, James. 'The Author is Dead: Long Live the Author,' *Quarterly Review of Film Studies*, Spring 1984: 113-119.

Gow, Gordon. *Chinstown* Review, *Films and Filming* Vol.21, No.1,October 1974: 38-9.

Grant, Catherine. 'www.auteur.com?' *Screen* 41,1, Spring 2000: 101-108.

Grant, Edmond. *The Two Jakes* Review, *Films in Review*, 41 (1/2), 1991: 43

Greenberg, James. 'Forget it Jack, it's *The Two Jakes*,' *American Film*, February 1990: 20-27.

Heath, Stephen. 'Comment on "The Idea of Authorship",' *Screen*, Vol.14, No.3, Autumn 1973: 86-91.

Hedegaard, Erik. 'Secrets and Spies,' *Sunday Times Magazine*, 15 April 2007: 50-61.

Hess, John. 'La Politique des auteurs : Part One : World View as Aesthetic,' *Jump Cut*, No.1 May-June 1974; 'Part Two: Truffaut's Manifesto,' *Jump Cut*, No. 2, July-August 1974.

Hoffman, Abraham. 'Lost Dutchman Chapter 5917 Arizona,' www.eclampusvitus.net.

Holmlund, Christine. 'When is a Lesbian Not a Lesbian? The Lesbian Continuum and the Mainstream Femme Film,' *Camera Obscura*, 1991: 25-26, 145-178.

Honeycutt, Kirk. 'Getting Credit + Screenwriting – The Scenario,' *American Film*, Vol. 6, No. 7; 1981; 'Whose Film is it Anyway?,' *American Film* Vol.6, No.7, May 1981: 34-39, 70-71.

Horowitz, Mark. 'Fault Lines and the Career of Robert Towne,' *Film Comment*, Vol. 26, No. 6, 1990: 52-58.

Houston, Penelope. 'The Return of Hecht,' *Sight and Sound*, 21, August-September 1951: 30.

James, Nick. 'The Firm,' *Sight & Sound*, Vol.3, No. 10, October 1993: 45.

Jensen, Paul. 'Raymond Chandler: The World You Live In,' *Film Comment*, Volume 10 Issue No 6, 1974: 18-26.

Journal of Film and Video, Vol.36, No.3, Summer 1984. Special Issue on Screenwriting, guest edited by William Miller; Vol.42, No. 3, Fall 1990. Special Issue on Screenwriting, guest edited by Ken Dancyger and Jeff Rush.

Kael, Pauline. 'Circles and Squares,' *Film Quarterly*, Vol. 16, No. 3, Spring 1963, 12-26; 'The Current Cinema: Nicholson's High,' *The New Yorker*, 11 February 1974: 95-6;

Kauffmann, Stanley. *The Last Detail* Review, *The New Republic*, 23 February 1974: 22; 33.

Kirkland, Bruce. 'Doing the Towne,' *Toronto Sun*, 28 January 1998.

Kleinhans, Chuck. '*Shampoo*: Oedipal Symmetries and Heterosexual Satire' *Jump Cut*, No. 26 December 1981: 12-18; www.ejumpcut.org/archive/onlinessays/JC26folder/Shampoo.html

Konow, David. 'Where Nobody's Dreams Come True,' *Creative Screenwriting*, March-April 2006: 64-68.

Kornbluth, Jesse. 'Will Success Keep Bob Towne Awake?,' *New York*, 21 April 1975: 73.

Kornits, Dov. 'Robert Towne – From *Chinatown* to Hollywood,' http://www.efilmcritic.com 27 August 1999.

Koszarski, Richard. 'Auteurism Revisited,' *Film History*, Vol.7, No.4, Winter 1995: 355-356.

Kroll, Jack. 'Chariots of Desire,' *Newsweek*, 99.6, 8 February 1982: 60.

Lane, Carrie. 'Screenwriter Talks of Difficulties of Breaking into Hollywood,' *Daily Free Press*, http://www.dailyfreepress.com/global_user_elements. 15 February 2006.

Lawson, Mark. 'Credit Where it isn't Due,' *The Guardian*, 17 September 2005.

Leconte, P., E.Molinaro, A. Techiné, P. Kane, A. Issermann, C. Sautet. 'The Direction Makes or Breaks a Script + Filmmakers on Screenwriting,' *Cahiers du Cinéma* No. 371, 1985.

Lee, Marc. 'Filmmakers on Film : Robert Towne on Jean Renoir's *La Grande Illusion* (1937)', *The Daily Telegraph*, 27 May 2006 : 20.

Leff, Leonard J. 'Resources for the Screenwriting Teacher,' *Journal of Film and Video*, Vol. 36, No. 3, 1984: 6-14.

Lehman, Ernest. 'If I say so myself,' *American Film*, Vol. 6, No. 7; 1981.

Leigh, Danny. 'Don't Fence Me In,' *Sight & Sound*, Vol.13, No.5, May 2003: 12-15.

Lemire, Christy. '*Ask the Dust* is Shockingly Disappointing,' www.msnbc.com, 8 March 2006.

Lennon, Elaine. 'The Edge of Melancholy: *Shampoo*,' *Senses of Cinema*, Issue 37 October-December 2005, archived at www.sensesofcinema.com; 'The *Yakuza*:: A Question of Authorship,' *Senses of Cinema*, Issue 37, October-December 2005, archived at www.sensesofcinema.com; 'Riding the New Wave: The Case of *Bonnie and Clyde*,' *Senses of Cinema*, Issue 38, January-March 2006, archived at www.sensesofcinema.com; '*Tequila Sunrise*:: Play it Again,' *Offscreen*, Vol. 12, Issue 3, March 2008, archived at www.offscreen.com.

Linderman, Deborah. 'Oedipus in *Chinatown*,' *Enclitic*, Vol. 2, No. 5, 1981: 190-203.

Linfield, Susan. 'Where Credit is Due,' *American Film*, Vol. 13 No. 2 1987: 46.

Loughney, Patrick. 'From Rip Van Winkle to Jesus of Nazareth: Thoughts on the Origins of the American Screenplay,' *Film History*, Vol.9, 1997: 277-289.

Lyman, Rick. 'Villains and Heroes,' *The New York Times*, 26 May 2000: E26.

Macaulay, Sean. 'Something of the Knight,' *The Times*, Screen, 15 April 2004: 2-3.

MacDonald, Scott. 'The City as Motion Picture: Notes on Some California City Films,' *Wide Angle*, Vol. 19, No. 4, October 1997: 109-130.

McCarthy, Todd. Reviews, *Variety*, 12 July 1993: 52.

McGinnis, Wayne. '*Chinatown*: Roman Polanski's Contemporary Oedipus Story,' *Literature/Film Quarterly* Summer 1975: 249-251.

McGowan, John. 'Oedipus at the Movies,' Southern Humanities Review, Vol. 20 No. 1, 1986.

Mahler, R. 'Script Prescriptions and the Nature of Screenwriting Consultation and Screenplay Doctor," *American Film*, Vol. 16, No. 3, 1991.

Major, Wade. 'Back on Track,' accessed at Box Office Online.

Mamet, David. 'They Think It's All Over – The Secret of a Great Ending – and the movies that are lucky enough to have one,' *The Guardian*, Film & Music, 16 May 2003: 5.

Maslin, Janet. 'Tom Cruise and Cars, and a Lot of Them,' *New York Times*, online archive.

Maynard, John. '*The Last Detail*,' AFTRS Network Events website 2002.

Menand, Louis. *For Keeps* Review, *New York Review of Books*, Volume 42, No. 5, March 1995: www.nybooks.com/article/1959.

Millar, Miles. 'I Wrote That!' The Guide, *The Guardian*, 27 February 1999: 14-15.

Miller, William. 'Resources for the Screenwriter and Screenwriting Teacher,' *Journal of Film and Video*, Vol. 42, No. 3, 1990: 66-72.

Milne, Tom. *Chinatown* Review, *Sight & Sound*, Autumn 1974 Vol.43, No.4: 243-244.

Naremore, James. 'Authorship and the Cultural Politics of Film Criticism,' *Film Quarterly*, Vol. 44, No. 1, 1990: 14-22.

Nathan, Ian. *Mission: Impossible* Review *Empire*, No. 92 February 1997: 102.

National Film Theatre programme. 'Cut To: Robert Towne,' May 1988: 4.

Newman, Kim. 'Poe's Eternal Life,' *The Guardian*, Screen, 9 July 1999: 8-9.

Nystrom, Derek. 'Hard Hats and Movie Brats: Auteurism and the Class Politics of the New Hollywood,' *Cinema Journal* 43, No. 3, Spring 2004: 18-41.

Oliver, Bill. '*The Long Goodbye* and *Chinatown*: Debunking the Private Eye Tradition,' *Literature/Film Quarterly*, Summer 1975 Vol. 5 No. 2: 240.

Paris Review, The. Screenwriting special issue, 138, Spring 1996.

Patterson, John. 'Bruckheimer Goes to War,' *The Guardian*, Film and Music, 27 October 2000: 2-4; 'The Depths of Depravity,' *The Guardian*, Film and Music, 22 February 2002: 5; 'The Player,' *The Guardian*, Film and Music: 8-9; 'On Film,' *The Guardian*, Film and Music, 20 April 2007: 2.

Pearson, Demetrius W. 'The Depiction and Characterization of Women in Sport Films,' in *Women in Sport and Physical Activity Journal*, V.10; N.1, 31 March 2001. Accessed online.

Perkins, V.F. 'Film Authorship: The Premature Burial,' *CineAction*, No. 21/22, Summer/Fall 1990: 58.

Petit, Chris. Review of *POLANSKI* by Christopher Sandford. *The Guardian*. Review. 16 October 2007. Accessed online at: www.books.guardian.co.uk/reviews.

P.F.D. *The Tomb of Ligeia* Review, *Monthly Film Bulletin*, Vol.31, No. 371, December 1964: 173.

Pollock, Dale. 'Towne: Toughing it Out to the Finish Line,' January 29, 1982, *The Los Angeles Times*, Calendar: 1.

Powers, James. 'Dialogue on Film: Ernest Lehman,' *American Film* 2, October 1976: 33-48.

Rainer, Peter. '*Chinatown*'s Robert Towne,' *Mademoiselle*, November 1974: 166; 234.

Ravenhill, Mark. 'Arts Comment,' *The Guardian*, Film and Music, 25 June 2007: 32.

Rayns, Tony. *The Yakuza* Review, *Monthly Film Bulletin*, Vol.42,No.49, 08 July 1975: 163.

Rich, B. Ruby. 'Dumb Lugs and Femmes Fatales,' *Sight & Sound*, Vol.5,No.11, November 1995: 6-10.

Rich, Frank. 'The Details are all right – and almost completely cold,' *New Times* 08 March 1974: 61-2.

Rosen, Marc Rodney. *WRITING FOR THE SCREEN*, Northwestern University, PhD, 1982.

Rosen, Marjorie. 'Francis Ford Coppola,' *Film Comment*, July 1974: 43-49.

Rothman, Cliff. 'Roth files vs. PSO in $2.3 million suit,' *The Los Angeles Times*, 27 March 1986.

Sanders, Lamar. '*CHINATOWN* – The Rewriting Process,' Lecture at the University College Dublin/New York University Scriptwriting Summer School, Dublin, 19 July 1993.

Sarris, Andrew. 'Notes on the Auteur Theory in 1962,' *Film Culture*, No. 27, Winter 1962-3. Reprinted in Caughie (ed.), op.cit.; and Mast, Cohen and Braudy, op.cit; 'The American Cinema,' *Film Culture*, No. 28, Spring 1963; 'The Auteur Theory and the Perils of Pauline,' *Film Quarterly*, Vol.16, No.4, Summer 1963: 26-32; 'Auteurism is Alive and Well and Living in Argentina,' *Film Comment* Vol. 26 No. 4 1990: 19-22; 'Notes of an Accidental Auteurist,' *Film History*, Vol. 7, 1995: 358-361.

Schickel, Richard. 'Not Fancy, Not Free,' *Time*, 18 February 1974

Schiff, Stephen. 'Talk of the Towne,' *Vanity Fair*, January 1989: 39-42.

Schrader, Paul. 'Notes on Film Noir,' *Film Comment*, Vol.8, No.1, Spring 1972; '*Yakuza-Eiga* A Primer,' *Film Comment* January 1974: 8-17.

Schruers, Fred. 'The Two Jacks,' *Premiere*, September 1990: 58-68.

Schulberg, Budd. 'The Hollywood Novel - The Love-Hate Relationship Between Writers and Hollywood', *American Film*, Vol/No. unknown

'Screenwriters Symposium,' *Film Comment*, Winter 1970-71: 86-100.

Seger, Linda and Carolyn Miller. 'The Storyteller's Art in a Changing World: Old Tools, New Forms,' *Creative Screenwriting*, Vol.8, No.2: 61-67.

Sellors, C. Paul. 'Collective Authorship in Film,' *Journal of Aesthetics and Art Criticism*, 65, 3, Summer 2007: 263-271.

Shadoian, Jack. 'Writing for the Screen… Some Thoughts on Dialogue,' *Literature/Film Quarterly*, Vol. 9, 1981: 85-91.

Shiller, Marc Daniel. 'Triangle of Mistrust in *Tequila Sunrise*,' *American Cinematographer*, January 1989: 48-53.

Simon, Alex. 'Mr Pre Comes to Towne,' *Venice*, September 1998: 32-35.

Siskel, Gene. 'Movies: Robert Towne – script, scalpel, action. Oscar,' *Chicago Tribune*, 9 May 1976, Section 6: 6; 'Hollywood's Mr. Fix-it,' *Sunday News*, 13 June 1976: 9.

Smith, Liz. 'Making His Mission Possible,' *Los Angeles Times*, 07 May 1996.

Spadoni, Robert. 'Geniuses of the Systems: Authorship and Evidence in Classical Hollywood Cinema,' *Film History*, Vol.7, 1995: 362-385.

Sragow, Michael. 'Ghostwriters: Unraveling the Enigma of Movie Authorship,' *Film Comment* 19, March-April 1983: 9-18; 'Return of the Native,' *New Times Los Angeles*, 3-9 September 1998: 13-14; 16-18; 'How *Chinatown* Screenwriter Robert Towne hooked up with Tom Cruise and John Woo to Script *M:i-2*.' www.salon.com 25 May 2000.

Staiger, Janet. 'Mass-Produced Photoplays: Economic and Signifying Practices in the First Years of Hollywood,' *Wide Angle*, Vol.4, No.3: 12-27.

Stewart, Garrett. '*The Long Goodbye* from *Chinatown*,' *Film Quarterly*, Vol. XXVIII, No. 2, Winter 1974-75: 25-32.

Straayer, Chris. '*Personal Best*: Lesbian/Feminist Audience,' *Jump Cut*, No. 29: 40-44

Strick, Philip. '*Mission: Impossible*,' *Sight & Sound*, Vol. 6, No.7, July 1996: 48.

'Superb and Raucous: Jack Nicholson in *The Last Detail*,' *Glamour*, April 1974.

Sweet, Matthew. 'Our Greatest Lost Film Critic,' *The Guardian*, Film & Music, 09 May 2008: 4.

Swires, Steve. 'Grab What You Can Get: The Screenwriter as Journeyman Plumber: A Conversation with Leigh Brackett,' *Films in Review*, September 1976: 413-421.

Taylor, Ella. 'Washed Up,' *LA Weekly*, 1-7 September 2000: 45.

Thompson, Anne. 'Towne Crier,' *LA Weekly*, 16 December 1988.

Thomson, David. 'Trouble in *Chinatown*,' *Vanity Fair*, November 1985: 59-61; 125-129.

Towne, Robert. 'Growing Up in a City of Senses,' *Los Angeles*, May 1975: 49-50; 'Dialogue on Film: Robert Towne,' *American Film*, Vol.1, No.3 December 1975: 33-48; 'I Wanna Make it like Real Life,' *Sight and Sound*, Vol.9, No.2, February 1999: 58-9; 'Why I Write Movies,' *Esquire*, July 1991: 86-87; 'A Lot of What Has Gone Wrong Was the Result of Choices I Made,' *The Guardian*, The Guide, 29 May 1999: 6; '*Chinatown* – A Screenwriter's Eulogy for Los Angeles,' *Architectural Digest*, April 2000; 'Robert Towne: Gauguin, Van Gogh, James Agee and Me,' *Los Angeles Times*, 03 November 2002.

Trainor, Richard. 'L.A. Graft: Robert Towne and the Stalled *Chinatown* Sequel,' *Sight and Sound* 55, 1986: 223-224; 'Blacklist,' *Sight and Sound*, Summer 1988: 188-9.

Turan, Kenneth. 'Robert Towne's Hollywood Without Heroes,' *New York Times*, 27 November 1988.

Velvet Light Trap, The. Special Issue on Authorship, Spring 2006. University of Austin, Texas.

Warga, Wayne. 'Writer Towne: Under the Smog, A Feel for the City,' *Los Angeles Times*, 18 August 1974.

Weinraub, Bernard. 'Giving Screenplays a Sense of Reality,' *The New York Times*, 08 September 1998: 1;5.

Weiss, Marion Wolberg. 'A Film By...,' *The Independent*, March 1998: 30-31; 60.

Whitman, Mark. *Chinatown* Review, *Films Illustrated*, August 1974: 472.

'Whose Picture Is It Anyway? A Debate on Possessory Credit and the Auteur Theory,' *Written By (The Journal of the Writers' Guild of America, West)*, October 1997, Vol.1, No.10: 46-52.

Wide Angle. Authorship issue, Vol.6 No. 1, 1984.

Wilder, Matthew. 'Your Guide to the Stars: Robert Towne Maps the Psychology of the American Bad-Ass,' www.citypages.com, Vol.27, No. 1315, 15 February 2006.

Wood, Nancy. 'An Outline of the Structure of the American Film Industry to 1950,' British Film Institute monograph, June 1985, reprinted May 1989.

Wood, Robin. 'To Have (Written) and Have Not (Directed),' reprinted in Nichols, (ed.), 1982, 297-305.

Wyver, John. 'The Great Authorship Mystery,' *The Listener*, 14 April 1983: 36.

The Yakuza Review. *Films and Filming*, Vol.21, No.12, September 1975: 36-38.

The Yakuza Review. *Films Illustrated*, Vol.4, No. 47, July 1975: 405-406.

'Your Write to Win,' *The Times*, 14 April 2003: 14.

Zehme, Bill. 'Private Dick,' *Sunday Times Magazine*, 1 July 1990: 41-50.

Websites:

www.afi.com

http://www.allmovie.com/cg/avg.dll?p=avg&sql=23:55

www.americanfilmfoundation.com/order/robert_towne.shtml

www.boxoffice.com

www.calendarlive.com

www.citypages.com

http://encarta.msn.com

www.findarticles.com

www.books.guardian.co.uk/reviews

www.hollywoodfilmfestival.com

www.lib.niu.edu/ipo/ii991034.html.

www.managing-creativity.com

www.mtv.com

www.network.aftrs.edu.au/events

www.nybooks.com/article/1959

www.nytimes.com

www.onthemedia.org/transcripts

www.palisadespost.com

www.premiere.com

www.salon.com

www.sensesofcinema.com

www.variety.com

www.writersstore.com/article.php?articles_id=14.

Made in the USA
Middletown, DE
01 May 2023